Lecture Notes in Computer Science

Lecture Notes in Artificial Intelligence 16074
Founding Editor

Jörg Siekmann

Series Editors

Randy Goebel, *University of Alberta, Edmonton, Canada*
Wolfgang Wahlster, *DFKI, Berlin, Germany*
Zhi-Hua Zhou, *Nanjing University, Nanjing, China*

The series Lecture Notes in Artificial Intelligence (LNAI) was established in 1988 as a topical subseries of LNCS devoted to artificial intelligence.

The series publishes state-of-the-art research results at a high level. As with the LNCS mother series, the mission of the series is to serve the international R & D community by providing an invaluable service, mainly focused on the publication of conference and workshop proceedings and postproceedings.

Takayuki Matsuno · Honghai Liu · Lianqing Liu ·
Zhouping Yin · Xiangyang Zhu · Weihong Ren ·
Zhiyong Wang · Yixuan Sheng
Editors

Intelligent Robotics and Applications

18th International Conference, ICIRA 2025
Okayama, Japan, August 6–9, 2025
Proceedings, Part I

Editors
Takayuki Matsuno
Okayama University
Okayama, Japan

Lianqing Liu
Shenyang Institute of Automation
Shenyang, China

Xiangyang Zhu
Shanghai Jiao Tong University
Shanghai, China

Zhiyong Wang
Harbin Institute of Technology
Shenzhen, China

Honghai Liu
Harbin Institute of Technology
Shenzhen, China

Zhouping Yin
Huazhong University of Science
and Technology
Wuhan, China

Weihong Ren
Harbin Institute of Technology
Shenzhen, China

Yixuan Sheng
Harbin Institute of Technology
Shenzhen, China

ISSN 0302-9743   ISSN 1611-3349 (electronic)
Lecture Notes in Artificial Intelligence
ISBN 978-981-95-2094-7   ISBN 978-981-95-2095-4 (eBook)
https://doi.org/10.1007/978-981-95-2095-4

LNCS Sublibrary: SL7 – Artificial Intelligence

© The Editor(s) (if applicable) and The Author(s), under exclusive license
to Springer Nature Singapore Pte Ltd. 2026

This work is subject to copyright. All rights are solely and exclusively licensed by the Publisher, whether the whole or part of the material is concerned, specifically the rights of translation, reprinting, reuse of illustrations, recitation, broadcasting, reproduction on microfilms or in any other physical way, and transmission or information storage and retrieval, electronic adaptation, computer software, or by similar or dissimilar methodology now known or hereafter developed.
The use of general descriptive names, registered names, trademarks, service marks, etc. in this publication does not imply, even in the absence of a specific statement, that such names are exempt from the relevant protective laws and regulations and therefore free for general use.
The publisher, the authors and the editors are safe to assume that the advice and information in this book are believed to be true and accurate at the date of publication. Neither the publisher nor the authors or the editors give a warranty, expressed or implied, with respect to the material contained herein or for any errors or omissions that may have been made. The publisher remains neutral with regard to jurisdictional claims in published maps and institutional affiliations.

This Springer imprint is published by the registered company Springer Nature Singapore Pte Ltd.
The registered company address is: 152 Beach Road, #21-01/04 Gateway East, Singapore 189721, Singapore

If disposing of this product, please recycle the paper.

Preface

With the theme "AI & Robotics for Smart Society", the 18th International Conference on Intelligent Robotics and Applications (ICIRA 2025) was held in Okayama, Japan, from August 6 to 9, 2025. The conference aimed to promote high-level academic exchange and innovation in robotics and artificial intelligence, providing a global platform for researchers, engineers, and practitioners to present their latest achievements and explore emerging trends in intelligent robotics and its applications to society.

ICIRA 2025 was organized by Okayama University, and co-organized by Harbin Institute of Technology. It was technically co-sponsored by Springer. The conference received a total of 329 paper submissions from around the world. Each submitted paper underwent a rigorous peer-review process, with at least three independent reviewers per paper. Based on the reviewers' evaluations and the discussions by the Program Committee, 165 high-quality papers were accepted for publication in *Springer's Lecture Notes in Artificial Intelligence (LNAI)* series. Among these, 107 papers were presented orally and 58 papers were presented as posters.

ICIRA 2025 featured 2 plenary speeches and 8 keynote speeches, delivered by internationally renowned scholars in the field. The technical sessions covered a wide range of topics, including intelligent perception and control, human–robot interaction, robotic manipulation, biomedical and rehabilitation robotics, soft robotics, and machine learning for robotics. The conference provided a vibrant and inspiring environment for academic exchange and collaboration.

We would like to extend our heartfelt appreciation to all the authors for their valuable contributions, and to the plenary and keynote speakers for sharing their insights. We also thank the reviewers for their professional and constructive evaluations. Special thanks are due to all members of the Organizing Committee, the Technical Program Committee, and the local volunteers for their dedication and efforts that ensured the success of ICIRA 2025.

August 2025

Takayuki Matsuno
Honghai Liu
Lianqing Liu
Zhouping Yin
Xiangyang Zhu
Weihong Ren
Zhiyong Wang
Yixuan Sheng

Organization

Honorary Chair

Youlun Xiong — Huazhong University of Science and Technology, China

General Chairs

Takayuki Matsuno — Okayama University, Japan
Honghai Liu — Harbin Institute of Technology, Shenzhen, China
Lianqing Liu — Shenyang Institute of Automation, Chinese Academy of Sciences, China
Zhouping Yin — Huazhong University of Science and Technology, China
Xiangyang Zhu — Shanghai Jiao Tong University, China

Program Chairs

Guoying Gu — Shanghai Jiao Tong University, China
Duanling Li — Beijing University of Posts and Telecommunications, China
Yuichiro Toda — Okayama University, Japan
Xinyu Wu — Shenzhen Institutes of Advanced Technology, Chinese Academy of Sciences, China
Hui Zhang — Hunan University, China

Publication Chairs

Weihong Ren — Harbin Institute of Technology, Shenzhen, China
Zhiyong Wang — Harbin Institute of Technology, Shenzhen, China
Yixuan Sheng — Harbin Institute of Technology, Shenzhen, China

Award Committee Chair

Limin Zhu — Shanghai Jiao Tong University, China

International Chairs

Zhiyong Chen	University of Newcastle, Australia
Naoyuki Kubota	Tokyo Metropolitan University, Japan
Zhaojie Ju	University of Portsmouth, UK
Eric Perreault	Northwestern University, USA
Hesheng Wang	Shanghai Jiao Tong University, China
Peter Xu	University of Auckland, New Zealand
Simon Yang	University of Guelph, Canada
Xingchen Yang	Imperial College London, UK
Houxiang Zhang	Norwegian University of Science and Technology, Norway

Advisory Committee

Jorge Angeles	McGill University, Canada
Tamio Arai	University of Tokyo, Japan
Hegao Cai	Harbin Institute of Technology, China
Tianyou Chai	Northeastern University, China
Jie Chen	Tongji University, China
Jiansheng Dai	King's College London, UK
Zongquan Deng	Harbin Institute of Technology, China
Han Ding	Huazhong University of Science and Technology, China
Xilun Ding	Beihang University, China
Baoyan Duan	Xidian University, China
Xisheng Feng	Shenyang Institute of Automation, Chinese Academy of Sciences, China
Toshio Fukuda	Nagoya University, Japan
Jianda Han	Shenyang Institute of Automation, Chinese Academy of Sciences, China
Qiang Huang	Beijing Institute of Technology, China
Oussama Khatib	Stanford University, USA
Yinan Lai	National Natural Science Foundation of China, China
Jangmyung Lee	Pusan National University, South Korea

Zhongqin Lin	Shanghai Jiao Tong University, China
Hong Liu	Harbin Institute of Technology, China
Honghai Liu	University of Portsmouth, UK
Shugen Ma	Ritsumeikan University, Japan
Daokui Qu	SIASUN, China
Min Tan	Institute of Automation, Chinese Academy of Sciences, China
Kevin Warwick	Coventry University, UK
Guobiao Wang	National Natural Science Foundation of China, China
Tianmiao Wang	Beihang University, China
Tianran Wang	Shenyang Institute of Automation, Chinese Academy of Sciences, China
Yuechao Wang	Shenyang Institute of Automation, Chinese Academy of Sciences, China
Bogdan M. Wilamowski	Auburn University, USA
Ming Xie	Nanyang Technological University, Singapore
Yangsheng Xu	Chinese University of Hong Kong, China
Huayong Yang	Zhejiang University, China
Jie Zhaoc	Harbin Institute of Technology, China
Nanning Zheng	Xi'an Jiaotong University, China
Xiangyang Zhu	Shanghai Jiao Tong University, China

Contents – Part I

Robotic Dexterous Manipulation and Intelligent Control

A Physics-Informed Neural Network-Based Momentum Observer Considering Velocity Effects for Contact Force Estimation in Industrial Robots 3
    Hongbo Hu, Zhongkai Zhang, Pengxin Zha, and Chungang Zhuang

A High-Precision and Compliant Interaction Method for Robot Based on Model Predictive Impedance Control 15
    Yuhao Zhang, Zhenwei Zhang, Licheng Hou, Yang Xiang, Qingmiao Zhu, Xingwei Zhao, and Bo Tao

Dynamics Modeling and Vibration Suppression of Industrial Robots Handling Flexible Payloads 27
    Wenyu Hu, Hongbo Hu, Zhongkai Zhang, and Chungang Zhuang

Dual-Channel Adaptive Impedance Algorithm with Leveling Module in Dual-Arm Collaborative Robots 39
    Yuhan Lu, Zhongkai Zhang, Pengxin Zha, Hongbo Hu, and Chungang Zhuang

RL-Force: Reinforcement Learning with Force Estimation for Humanoid Locomotion Subject to Continuous External Disturbances 52
    Weixian Lin, Letian Qian, Shuhan Wang, Junjie Qiang, Peng Sun, and Xin Luo

Intrinsic Vision-Based Learning for Proprioceptive Sensing of Soft Pneumatic Actuators 65
    Taoyuan Huang, Jieji Ren, Xinyu Yang, Longyan Wu, Jinnuo Zhang, Ningbin Zhang, and Guoying Gu

Visual-Guided Diffusion Policy and Mesh-DMP Integration for Robotic Freeform Surface Polishing 77
    Shuai Ke, Jiexin Zhang, Huan Zhao, Yikun Guo, Zhiao Wei, Jie Pan, and Han Ding

Boosting Industrial Changeover Efficiency: A Large-Model-Based Explore-Then-Reproduce Framework for Changeover Tasks 91
    Cheng Ding, Shunchong Li, and Hui Wang

Learning Human-Like Finger Gaiting on an Anthropomorphic Hand 103
  Kairui Yang, Dongjie Jiang, Lecheng Ruan, and Qining Wang

Learning Stable Nonlinear Dynamical Systems with Symmetric Negative
Definite Matrix Generation Network 115
  Tianxiang Jiang, Pingyun Nie, Jiexin Zhang, Erxuan Xie, Huaiwu Zou,
  and Bo Zhang

Object's CoM-Aware Pose Optimization of Humanoid Upperlimbs
for Dual-Arm Collaborative Carrying 127
  Tiancheng Ma, Chuanlin Zhao, and Xin Luo

Contact Driven Functional Grasp Synthesis via Hand-Object Interaction
State Representation 140
  Jian Liu, Zeyuan Yang, Lu Tang, Sijie Yan, and Han Ding

Intelligent Perception and Control Technologies for Marine Robotic Systems

Co-simulation of Trajectory Tracking Control for Underwater Vehicles:
A Case Study on RexROV Using Simulink and UUV Simulator 153
  Mingzhi Chen, Zexin Lu, Daqi Zhu, and Wen Pang

An Elastodynamic Modeling Approach on Component Mode Synthesis
for Hybrid Machining Cell 166
  Wei Ma, Haitao Liu, Guofeng Wang, Juliang Xiao, Qingpo Xu,
  Tianren Zhao, and Wei Han

Safety-Critical Flocking Control of Multiple Unmanned Surface Vehicles
Based on Exponential Control Barrier Functions 177
  Jiaxing Zhou, Lu Liu, Yanping Xu, and Zhouhua Peng

Research on Hybrid Buoy Inclined Landing Motion Control 189
  Dingze Wu, Qingchao Xia, Puzhe Zhou, and Canjun Yang

Fast and Automatic Dock for Precise UAV Landing on a USV in Marine
Environment 201
  Chongfeng Liu, Zhongzhong Cao, Zisui Guo, Ruoyu Xu, Cheng Liang,
  and Huihuan Qian

Positioning and Orientation for Single LiDAR of USVs Obstructed By
Offshore Operation Platform 215
  Wenhui Dong, Yanzheng Zhu, Jichao Yang, Jianping Xing,
  Shengli Wang, and Ranshuo Zhao

A Fault Diagnosis Scheme for Underwater Thrusters Considering Sensor
Faults 227
   *Ruiheng Liu, Yanhu Chen, Xinyu Fei, Shipang Qian, Lu Wang,
and Canjun Yang*

Bio-Inspired Soft Robotic Arms Capable of Object Grasping and Bipedal
Locomotion in Amphibious Environments 239
   *Lin Hong, Junjie Wang, Gan Zhang, Yixuan Sheng, Fumin Zhang,
and Lei Guo*

Position Compensation Method for Cable-Pulling Robot in Generator
Maintenance Without Rotor Removal 252
   Shentao Ma, Yan Zhou, Jiantao Wang, Jianhua Wu, and Zhenhua Xiong

Intelligent Technology in Neural Decoding, Modulation, and Interfacing

Research on Pose Control Dataset Augmentation Method Based
on Generative Adversarial Networks 267
   Zhe Sun, Han Xiao, and Peng Sun

Optimal Electrode Configuration for Wrist sEMG-Based Gesture
Recognition: A Systematic Evaluation of Number and Placement 279
   *Hai Wang, Ashirbad Pradhan, Xin Xia, Birong Dong, Ning Jiang,
and Jiayuan He*

Robotic Grinding of Thin-Walled Parts: Reinforcement Learning-Based
Chatter Suppression Method 294
   *Fuyong Zhang, Zhihao Xu, Yuming Li, Haifei Zhu, Zhaoyang Liao,
Hongmin Wu, Xubin Lin, and Xuefeng Zhou*

Electrode Shift-Robust Decomposition of Surface EMG Signals via Deep
Learning: A Simulation Study 306
   Zeyu Zhou, Yang Yu, and Xinjun Sheng

Enhancing Softness Discrimination in Vision-Based Tactile Sensors
via Modeling and Optimization of Gradient-Stiffness Elastomers 316
   Lunwei Zhang, Zihao Wang, Yao Jiang, and Tiemin Li

Filtering Selection for High-Density sEMG in Motor Unit Decomposition 328
   Zeming Zhao, Zeyu Zhou, Weichao Guo, and Xinjun Sheng

Sensory Input Shapes Motor Output: Decoding Corticomuscular
Coherence Under Vibration-Induced Modulation 340
   Xuefei Zhou, Huan Wen, Yueming Wang, Lin Yao, and Kedi Xu

Adaptive Network Design for SSVEP/SSMVEP Classification via SE
and Configurable Convolutions 350
    Yichen Lin, Xiuyuan Wu, Xinyang Du, Haoran Zhang, Wenke Lu,
    Yu Zhu, Zengle Ren, Pengjie Qin, Jinke Li, and Yue Ma

Multimodal Assessment of Visual-Motor Integration in Attention
Deficit/Hyperactivity Disorder 363
    Huan Wen, Mengyi Bao, Yucun Zhong, Haifeng Li, Lin Yao,
    and Yueming Wang

Comparison of Propagation and Activation Characteristics of Motor Units
Decomposed from Wrist and Forearm Surface Electromyography Signals 373
    Lingyan Tian and Chen Chen

High-Discrimination Multi-level Electrotactile Feedback via Compound
Perception Descriptors and Efficient Calibration 385
    Chen Yang, Naixing Gao, Xiaoxin Wang, Qiming Zeng, Bangquan Xie,
    Hongwei Zhang, and Yixuan Sheng

Cross-Task EEG Mental Workload Detection in Aviation: An LSTM
Framework Leveraging Task-Invariant Neural Signatures 397
    Huanpeng Ye, Yumeng Li, Bo Lv, Peiru An, and Yang Xu

Wearable Robots for Assistance, Augmentation and Rehabilitation of Human Movements

A Physiology-Informed Training Protocol for Cross-Paradigm Transfer
Learning in ErrP-Based Brain-Computer Interface 411
    Ruijie Luo, Yuxuan Wei, Ximing Mai, Guangye Li, and Jianjun Meng

Design and Implementation of Thermoplastic Composite Robotic Winding
System 423
    Huangchao Chen, Tianming Li, Dailin Zhang, Xingwei Zhao, and Bo Tao

A Stretchable Resistive Electronic Skin for Shape Sensing of End
Continua of Flexible Surgical Instruments 434
    Lizhi Pan, Tianze Zhang, Jianmin Li, and Jinhua Li

An Intelligent Process Decision-Making Method for Robotic Grinding
Random Defects via Incremental Learning and Database 446
    Tao Ding, Hao Wu, Guibin Xu, Zebin Hu, and Dahu Zhu

Knee Prosthesis Stair Ascending with Adaptive Clearance and Foot
Placement 459
    *Wenduo Zhu, Mengchen Cai, Haofei Hou, Shunyi Zhao, Lecheng Ruan,
    and Qining Wang*

A Hybrid FES-Soft Exosuit System to Improve Interlimb Symmetry
in Post-stroke Patients 472
    *Xingyu Lu, Yanwei Zhao, Zhengbo Wang, Yu Xia, Shuxiao Jin,
    Chunfang Wang, Gang Liu, Jianda Han, Ying Zhang, and Weiguang Huo*

Digital Twin Modeling and Performance Evaluation of a Gimbal Servo
System 484
    Yulong Xia, Mubang Xiao, Zhijie Wen, Lianfeng Liu, and Huimin Cai

Kinematics and Calibration of a Continuum Manipulator Considering
Nonconstant Elasticity 496
    Mubang Xiao, Xinrui Zhan, Huimin Cai, Zhijie Wen, and Shixun Fan

Predictive Modeling of Robot Deformation Errors via Incremental Learning ... 509
    *Ze-Sheng Guo, Zhao-Yang Liao, Zi-Wei Lu, Zhi-Hao Xu, Hong-Min Wu,
    and Xue-Feng Zhou*

Soft Robotics

Design and Analysis of a Morphing Wing Based
on Corrugated-Honeycomb Structure for UAV 525
    Guang Yang, Chunlong Wang, Yuqi Li, Hong Xiao, and Hongwei Guo

Design and Analysis of a Novel Metamaterial with Tunable Coefficient
of Thermal Expansion 536
    *Chunfeng Li, Hong Xiao, Guang Yang, Hongwei Guo, Yan Xia,
    Runchao Zhao, Jianguo Tao, and Rongqiang Liu*

Neural Implicit Embedded PWM Control Approach for Dielectric
Elastomer Actuators with Rate-Dependent Viscoelasticity 547
    Xuning Gou, Xingyu Chen, Guoying Gu, and Jiang Zou

Design of a Rigid–Elastic–Soft Coupled DELTA Mechanism with Variable
Cartesian Stiffness 559
    Xingyue Zhu, Zhenkun Liang, Hao Yuan, Hao Wang, and Genliang Chen

Pneumatic Kirigami Actuators with Programmable Motion for Versatile
Robotic Functionalities 571
    Yang Yu, Yanqi Yin, Ruiyu Bai, and Bo Li

Stress Monitoring and Adaptive Grasping for Robotic Grippers Using
Distributed Optical Fiber Sensing 583
  Baijin Mao, Xulong Shi, Yuyaocen Xiang, Yedong Huang, and Juntian Qu

Radial Basis Function Neural Network-Based Adaptive Trajectory
Tracking Control for Continuum Robots 595
  *Fuxin Du, Zhongtao Liu, Weikai He, Changwei Yin, Yang Zhang,
  and Rui Song*

Author Index 607

Contents – Part II

Hand-Centric Human-Robot Collaboration Advances in Perception, Control, and Interaction

Electrotactile Artifact Denoising via Function Interpolation for Integrated sEMG-Based Prosthetic Control 3
   Lina Guo, Yalong Tong, Yazhou Li, Peiyao Wang, Yi Wang, and Kairu Li

Admittance-Controlled Compliant Remote Center-of-Motion for Tele-Operated Transurethral Resection 16
   Chunheng Lu, Siqin Yang, Zhihong Song, Yu Shen, and Junchen Wang

Bioinspired Prosthetic Hand System with Multimodal Sensory Fusion for Naturalistic Grasping Behaviors 27
   Yue Zheng, Xiangxin Li, Lin Wang, Lan Tian, Xugang Jiang, Haoshi Zhang, and Guanglin Li

RoboImagine: A Robotic Video Generation Model, for Autoregressive Long-Term Task Video Generation with Geometric and Dynamic Consistency Augmentation 37
   Conglin Wang, Hongkun Yang, Chuanjiang Li, Siqi Wen, Yiming Gan, and Shuai Liang

A Soft-Skin Facial Robot Capable of Real-Time Emotion-Driven Actuation Through Visual Perception 54
   Xuanhe Fan, Huijuan Zhao, Shuangjiang He, Li Li, and Li Yu

Enhancing Robustness of Hand Gesture Recognition Against Sensor Data Loss by Fusing High-Density sEMG and Kinematics 67
   Yushuai Yan, Chengyu Lin, Chenglong Fu, and Yuquan Leng

Simulation-Driven Learning for Vision-Based Tactile Force Reconstruction in Surgical Master Manipulators Using Random Marker Particles 79
   Hui Chu, Xizhe Zang, Peng Wang, and Xu Wang

A Low-Cost Multisensor IMU-VIO Framework for Real-Time Full-Body Human Pose Estimation 91
   Lele Li, Zedong Liu, Dawei Liang, Chuanyu Si, Haotian Ju, Shouyi Zhang, Haoxiang Zhang, Hongwei Jing, Jian Qi, Tianjiao Zheng, and Yanhe Zhu

Shape Matching Method Based on Growing Neural Gas 103
  Jiaqi Zhang, Yuichiro Toda, and Takayuki Matsuno

Enhancing 4D ViT-Driven Gesture Recognition with Decomposed
HD-sEMG 114
  Yaolun Jin and Yinfeng Fang

Intelligent Technology in Healthcare

Mamdani Fuzzy Assessment System for Oral Motor Exercise Tasks 129
  Chyan Zheng Siow, Qingwei Song, Yuqi Zhang, Zongying Liu,
  Adnan Rachmat Anom Besari, and Naoyuki Kubota

Motion Planning of Self-balancing Exoskeleton Robot Based
on Spring-Loaded Inverted Pendulum 143
  Chenhao Wu, Jinke Li, Zengle Ren, Shisheng Zhang, Xueyan Shen,
  and Xinyu Wu

Doctor-Centered Mixed Reality Tele-Guidance Training System Design 155
  Yanzhuo Wang, Keyi Wang, Lan Wang, Haochu Chen, and Jinghang Li

A Novel Deep Learning Enhanced Particle Swarm Optimization
for Puncture Path Planning 166
  Jianfeng Yao, Zhuang Fu, Canhui Wu, Zi Fang, Bang Liu, and Fei Jing

Driving Logic Optimization and Fine Control of a Peripheral Electrical
Stimulator Based on FPGA 175
  Kening Gong, Li Jiang, Xiaoran Tang, and Hong Liu

Design and Implementation of a 4-DOF Wearable Assisted Puncture Robot 184
  Canhui Wu, Zhuang Fu, Jianfeng Yao, Zi Fang, Bang Liu, and Fei Jing

Towards Early Intervention of Knee Osteoarthritis: A Wearable System
for Gait Analysis and Functional Evaluation 197
  Haolan Xian, Changjiang Lei, Jinglin Zhou, Changquan Liu, Wei Sun,
  Zhiyong Wang, Chenglong Fu, and Yuquan Leng

A Flexible Fruit Wearable System for Real-Time and Long-Term Tomato
Growth Monitoring 210
  Xin Zhao, Qin Jiang, Yihui Fan, Han Ding, and Zhigang Wu

LLM-Based Structured Information Extraction for Urinary Incontinence
from Multi-modal Clinical Data 222
  Tianyu Wu, Mingxiang Luo, Xueyan Shen, Shengxiang Liang,
  Xinyu Wu, and Wujing Cao

A Tactile-Driven Multiple Instance Learning Framework for Automated
Industrial Detection 234
    Jingnan Wang, Pengjie Qin, Chuwen Huang, Yaling Wang, Yue Ma,
    Meng Yin, Wujing Cao, and Xinyu Wu

Hip Joint Angle Prediction for Lower Limb Continuous Movement
in Multitasking Scenarios 244
    Zixiang Yang, Hao Lu, Xin Shi, Pengjie Qin, Yujie Chen, and Wujing Cao

Design of a Soft Pneumatic Exosuit for Stroke-Induced Knee Rehabilitation ... 255
    Jinglin Zhou, Changjiang Lei, Haolan Xian, Yuanwen Zhang,
    Chenglong Fu, and Yuquan Leng

Dynamic Collision Avoidance for Slave Instruments in Robotic Cardiac
Surgery 266
    Xizhe Zang, Peng Wang, Xu Wang, and Hui Chu

Benchmarking State-of-the-Art Lower Limb Joint Moment Estimator
Against Advanced Time Series Models 275
    Hamza Azam, Wenzhu Xu, Haoyu Wang, Luying Feng, Ahmad Irshad,
    Canjun Yang, Mitja Gerževič, and Wei Yang

A Mixed Reality-Based SSMVEP Brain-Computer Interface
for Exoskeletons 285
    Xiuyuan Wu, Yichen Lin, Xinyang Du, Zengle Ren, Wujing Cao,
    Meng Yin, and Yue Ma

Outward Electrical Impedance Tomography for Atherosclerotic Arterial
Wall Detection 297
    Yanbo Hu, Zhenyu Cheng, Yichen Lin, and Xiaojing Long

A CNN–LSTM-Based Prediction Method of Lower-Limb Parameters
Across Multiple Locomotion Modes 309
    Wenke Lu, Yue Ma, Haoran Zhang, Yichen Lin, Xinyu Wu, Wujing Cao,
    Meng Yin, and Jianquan Sun

Binocular Vision-Based Spatiotemporal Feature Fusion Model for Elderly
Fall Risk Prediction 322
    Guangyu Liang, Chen Wang, Rui Zou, Jiatong Cui, Ziyun Ge,
    and Zeng-Guang Hou

Advanced Localization, Navigation and Control Technologies in Intelligent Robotic Systems

Lie Group Variational Integrators For Hybrid Flexible-Rigid Multibody
System Dynamics Based on Projective Geometric Algebra 337
   Guangzhen Sun and Ye Ding

High-Order Adaptive Integration of Contact Dynamics in MuJoCo 349
   Hongchen Li and Ye Ding

Path Planning in the Anode Block Area for Underwater Cleaning Robots 361
   Ang Gao, Bocong Li, Hang Su, and Canjun Yang

Experimental Optimization of Clap-and-Fling Wing Stroke Kinematics
and Geometry Configuration 373
   Wenjie Dai, Yuhan Liu, and Xuan Wang

Agile and Versatile Bipedal Robot Tracking Control Through
Reinforcement Learning 385
   Han Zheng, Jiayi Li, Linqi Ye, Houde Liu, and Bin Liang

Multi-robot Path Planning Based on IPPO Reinforcement Learning
and Imitation Learning 397
   Wen Ma, Gedong Jiang, Liming Wang, Zhipeng Li, Guo Li, and Feng Li

Design and Control of a Multi-UAV Cabin System 409
   Weilun Guo, Xinxing Mu, Weimin Li, Runze Liu, and Ningning Song

M2PT Dataset: A Multi-motion Pattern Dataset for SLAM Evaluation
on Diverse Terrains 421
   Yan Dong, Junru Chen, Enci Xu, and Bin Han

Design and Evaluation of a Generic Safe Control Transition System
for Human-Machine Cooperative Driving 433
   Yaowei Sun and Dachuan Li

Research on Robotic Visual Inspection Path and Pose Planning
for Automotive Paint Defects Considering Curvature Weights 446
   Minghui Yang, Yun Cheng, Chaoqun Wu, Huayi Cai, and Ruoyuan Jiang

Multi-agent Active Exploration Framework Based on Topological Map
Fusion for Indoor Environments 459
   Chenyu Bao, Junjie Hu, Shaobin Ling, Guoquan Ye, and Tin Lun Lam

An Attention-Based Diffusion Policy with Hybrid Farthest Point Sampling
for Robotic Intelligent Manipulation 471
   Yifei Dong, Yi An, Tiantian Xu, and Sheng Xu

Relative Pose Estimation of Substation Equipment for UAV Inspection
via Deep Point Cloud Registration 483
   *Jianming Liu, Duanjiao Li, Ying Zhang, Yun Chen, Shengbo Liu,
Chao Yang, Ning Ding, Xufang Pang, and Jianguo Zhang*

Wearable Robotics for Gait Analysis, Training, and Rehabilitation

Humanoid Locomotion with Roller Screw-Driven Knee Joints: Design,
Control, and Deployment 497
   *Yuchen Lin, Tian Xia, Mengdi Wang, Zhenwei Zhang, Honglei Lu,
Tao Ding, Yuhao Zhang, Xingwei Zhao, and Bo Tao*

Design and Implementation of a Multifunctional Desktop Pet Robot Dog
Based on Arduino Nano and ESP32-S3 509
   Di Li, Junkai Lin, Siqi Hou, and Yanyan Ji

From Sim-to-Real to Learn-in-Real: Real-World Online Learning
for Humanoid Robots 521
   Rankun Li, Yuhang Xie, Linqing Zhu, Linqi Ye, Qingdu Li, and Yan Peng

Smart Shoe System for Accurate Gait Phase Recognition 534
   Jiachen Wang, Jiakang Wang, Tian Liang, and Huanghe Zhang

Wearable AI-Driven Smart Insole for Long-Term Monitoring
of Lower-Limb Joint Mobility: A Pilot Study 545
   *Dinghuang Zhang, Yuxiang Huang, Ying Liu, Zhe Ding, Liucheng Guo,
and Dalin Zhou*

Tri Plane Rhythmic Signal Generation and Adaptive Oscillator Tracking:
A Novel Framework for Motion Analysis 557
   *Haoran Zhang, Yichen Lin, Xiuyuan Wu, Yu Zhu, Xinyang Du,
Xiangyang Wang, Jianquan Sun, and Yue Ma*

A Marker-Free Motion Capture System Built on Unsynchronized Cameras 567
   *Haofei Hou, Shunyi Zhao, Zuxin Fan, Wei Jin, Jintao Zhu,
Lecheng Ruan, and Qining Wang*

Embodied Intelligence in Biomimetic Robotics, Humanoid Robotics

Fluid Dynamics Around a Whisker 581
    Md.Mahbub Alam and Xiaoyu Shi

Interaction-Friendly Trajectories via Torque-and-Jerk-Constrained
Optimization 589
    Shize Zhao, Tianjiao Zheng, Chengzhi Wang, Sikai Zhao, Yanhe Zhu,
    and Jie Zhao

Tactile Servo Control Based on Reinforcement Learning Applied
to Flexible Wires Manipulation 601
    Yihan Shan, Changle Li, Zhe Gao, Gangfeng Liu, Xuehe Zhang,
    Chong Yao, Zhantao Xu, and Jie Zhao

An In-Situ Excitation Trajectory Optimizer for Industrial Robots
in Constrained Space with Human Collaboration 613
    Chengzhi Wang, Haotian Ju, Zhiyuan Yang, Tianjiao Zheng,
    Shize Zhao, Sikai Zhao, Dawei Liang, Hegao Cai, Jie Zhao,
    and Yanhe Zhu

Terrain-Adaptive Bipedal Locomotion via Reinforcement Learning
with Human-Inspired Stepping Strategy 624
    Yunpeng Liang, Yanzheng Zhao, and Weixin Yan

Research on Autonomously Exterior Wall Spraying Technology
for Tethered Unmanned Aerial Vehicles 637
    Liang Gao, Xu'an Zhao, Xu'ning Zhao, Tianjiao Zheng, Liyi Li,
    and Jie Zhao

A Study of the Effectiveness of Various Combined Control Schemes
Based on MPC and WBC in Humanoid Control 650
    Yinhui Chen, Dachuan Liu, Shilong Sun, Wenfu Xu, and Qingbin Gao

Development and Autonomous Tracking of Miniature Continuum
Endscope for Intraocular Microsurgery 662
    Chunbo Wang, Taixian Jin, Yunfei Wang, Zhuowen Zhang,
    Haoyan Zhang, Jiaqi Zhang, Jian Liang, Lei Zhong, He Zhang,
    and Jie Zhao

Air-Ground-Wall Robot with Multimodal Morphological Adaptation 675
    Juanxia Zhou, Jiajun Xu, Mengcheng Zhao, Peixin Wang, and Youfu Li

Design and Human-Robot Collaborative Control of Reconfigurable
Supernumerary Robotic Limb for Overhead Work 686
 *Peixin Wang, Jiajun Xu, Mengcheng Zhao, Juanxia Zhou, Xingyu Liu,
 and Youfu Li*

Learning Whole-Body Motion Control Through Instruction Learning
and Human Motion Data 698
 Zhipeng Xu, Kaixuan Chen, Linqi Ye, and Boyang Xing

Author Index 711

Contents – Part III

Magnetic Actuated Microrobots for Biomedical Engineering: Design, Control, and Application

Dynamic Parameter Identification in Haptic Robotic Systems via Artificial Bee Colony 3
   Jiachen Wang, Saeid Piri, and Huanghe Zhang

Template-Free Magnetic Programming Strategy for 3D-Transformable Soft Robots 15
   Junliang Chen, Dongdong Jin, and Xing Ma

Physics-Based Simulation of Magnetic Nanorobots Swarm 26
   Yihan Chen, Xiang Ji, Jialin Jiang, and Li Zhang

Dynamic Path Planning and Automatic Navigation for Microswarms 38
   Jialin Jiang and Li Zhang

Reinforcement Learning-Based Magnetic Levitation Control of a Capsule Endoscope for Path Tracking Using a Single Permanent Magnet 49
   Yongfeng Huang, Mingxue Cai, Guoyao Ma, Zhiqiang Chen, Chenyang Huang, Yang Yang, Hongwei Wang, and Tiantian Xu

Simulator for Identifying Contact-Prone Robot Parts to Accelerate Contact Judgment Between Needle Puncture Robot and Patient 60
   Takayuki Matsuno, Nanako Sakai, Yuichiro Toda, Tetsushi Kamegawa, Yusuke Matsui, and Takao Hirai

Innovative Design and Performance Evaluation of Robot Mechanisms

Autonomous Bolt Assembly Composite Robotic System Guided by Binocular Vision 75
   Tao Wang, Lei Zheng, Zhiran Zhang, Dailin Zhang, and Xingwei Zhao

Design and Simulation of a Bipedal Robot for Explosive Jumping Based on a Hybrid Linkage-Cam Mechanism 88
   Qiang Fu, Ke Li, Zhanchuan Qi, and Yunjiang Lou

Topological Analysis and Perception of Physical Vibration in Distributed Optical Fiber Vibration Sensing 101
   Zibin Liang, Song Wang, and Duanling Li

Design and Optimization of a Heavy-Duty Parallel Ship Motion
Simulation Platform 112
En Yang, Yan Hu, Chenbo Lang, Feng Gao, and Hao Zheng

Design and Analysis of a New Multiparameter Reconfigurable Morphing
Wing 124
Duanling Li, Ruixuan Dai, Junwei Zhang, Fengkun Xu, and Yizhu Guo

Experimental Study and Analysis of Wheel-Terrain Interaction for Crewed
Lunar Vehicle Based on Single-Wheel Testbed 136
*Xinrui Wu, Huaiguang Yang, Liang Ding, Lintao Yang, Jianguo Tao,
Haibo Gao, Zhehao Qiao, Ruyi Zhou, and Zongquan Deng*

Research on the Dynamics Modeling and Control Method of Vector
Quadrotor UAV with Variable Posture 150
Yunfan Pang, Zhonghai Zhang, Jiahui Cai, and Duanling Li

A Probability Theory-Based Method for Calculating the Cyclical Degree
of Freedom of Mechanisms 162
Fengyi Li, Hao Chen, Weizhong Guo, and Hang Fu

Design and Analysis of Variable Geometry Truss Robot 174
Kaijie Dong, Xiang Huai, Zhouyi Ren, Jingyao Li, and Duanling Li

AMM: An Aerial Modular Manipulator Based on Standardized Modules 185
*Yuelei Fang, Ye Li, Yijian Zhang, Ziqi Wang, Daming Liu,
Shouyi Zhang, Nanlin Zhou, Sikai Zhao, Jie Zhao, and Yanhe Zhu*

Structural Design and Simulation of Space Sleeve-Type Extension Arm ... 197
*Duanling Li, Qixiang Guo, Junwei Zhang, Junfeng huang, Shiqin Xie,
and Yizhu Guo*

Balloon Robot: Movement Recognition and Design of Robot 209
*Weihao Wang, Chyan Zheng Siow, Naoyuki Kubota,
Azhar Aulia Saputra, Qingwei Song, and Takenori Obo*

Time-Optimal Trajectory Planning for Hybrid Redundant Robotic Arm
Based on Prescribed Waypoints 222
*Peng Sun, Hanqi Zhang, Zongyuan Liu, Chentao Wu, Zhe Sun,
Yuan Wang, Liu Zhengqing, and Yanbiao Li*

Conceptual Design and Kinematic Analysis of a Biomimetic Robot Joint
(BRJ) Based on a Higher Pair Mechanism 235
Gaohan Zhu, Shixuan Chu, Yinghui Li, and Weizhong Guo

Sensation-Perception-Actuation-Rehabilitation Oriented Technologies for Wearable Exoskeletons

Muscle Synergy-Enabled Multimodal Swimming Motion Recognition 249
  Yuchao Liu, Jiajie Guo, Yibin Chen, Weipeng Li, Kamilo Melo, and Xuan Wu

Estimation of Human Lower Limb Kinematic Parameters Based on A-Mode Ultrasound Sensing 263
  Donghan Liu, Haoran Zheng, Han Wu, Guochao Xu, and Honghai Liu

Human Lower Limb Motor Ability Estimation Based on Human-Machine Coupling Interactive Contact Model 275
  Chao Gao, Jianhua Zhang, and Hui Li

Integrated Analysis of Cortico-Muscular Coupling and Muscle Synergy for Functional Assessment in Exoskeleton-Assisted Stroke Rehabilitation 287
  Siyu Feng, Qi Kuang, Ruikai Cao, Zhuoqun Wang, and Yixuan Sheng

Multidimensional Kinematic Analysis of Walking and Turning in Older Adults Using IMUs 298
  Luobin Zhang, Yongjie Weng, Peng Chen, Wei Wei, Mingyu Du, and Shibo Cai

Development of a Functional Electrical Stimulation Device Combined with Multi-modal Muscle Status Monitoring 310
  Longjie Yu, Xiangyu Cheng, Xin Chen, Kewen Zhang, Shibo Cai, and Mingyu Du

BioKFusion-Net: Simultaneous Estimation of Ground Reaction Forces/Moments and Joint Angles from IMU Data 323
  Zhujin Chen, Yao Liu, Hui Chen, Xinyu Wu, and Chunjie Chen

Effects of Rhythmic Auditory Cues on Brain Network Characterization During Human Gait Initiation 336
  Huilin Zhou, Zefeng Shou, Tao Meng, Xuelian Wang, Tao Liu, Wenan Zhang, Guokun Zuo, and Changcheng Shi

Effects of Exoskeleton-Assisted Sit-to-Stand Training Based on Cortical-Muscular Coherence 348
  Xiaoke Peng, Shiyu Han, Guoshun Zhao, and Anqin Dong

Pattern Analysis and Machine Intelligence: Vision, Language, Multimodal Learning, and Applications

TGP: Two-Modal Occupancy Prediction with 3D Gaussian and Sparse
Points for 3D Environment Awareness 361
   *Mu Chen, Wenyu Chen, Mingchuan Yang, Yuan Zhang, Tao Han,
Xinchi Li, Guilong Zhang, and Huaici Zhao*

YOLO-HG: A Hierarchical Global Perception Method for Heavy-Duty
Truck Parking Space Detection 373
   Zeyang Wang, Feng Zhao, and Dan Yang

An Accurate 3D Reconstruction Method for Large Workpieces Based
on 3D Vision 386
   Shenglun Zhang, Shibo Hu, Xingwei Zhao, Dailin Zhang, and Bo Tao

Insulator and Its Defect Detection Framework Based on Feature
Enhancement CenterNet 398
   *Xiaoming Mai, Zehui Zhang, Shutong Yao, Shuaibing Mi, Na Dong,
and Kuansheng Zou*

Adaptive 3D Scene Analysis Through Multi-modal Feature Integration
and Geometric Pattern Recognition 411
   Shijun Zhou, Xing Xie, and Jiandong Tian

Global to Local Mamba Low Light Image Restoration 422
   Xinhao Wu, Huijie Fan, Sen Lin, Qiang Wang, and Peng Wu

A Comparative Study of First and Second-Order Gradient Acceleration
in ICP 434
   Qing Tang, Ziwei Wang, Xiaojian Zhang, Mingxu Pan, and Sijie Yan

Visual-Tactile Fusion-Driven Diffusion Policy for Robotic Excavation
of Semi-buried Object in Granular Media 447
   *Linan Deng, Xing Liu, Yunlong Dong, Guijun Ma, Feng Hua,
Cheng Cheng, and Zuogong Yue*

RCTAMP: Enhancing Rule-Constrained TAMP via Multi-agent
Closed-Loop Collaboration Integrating Consensus Planning 460
   *Zhongxing Wei, Xiaodong Ye, Huachen Tan, Junhong Zhao,
Meiling Wang, and Yucheng Wang*

Efficient Skeleton-Based Action Segmentation via Multi-granularity
Perception 473
   *Zhihao Yang, Haoyu Ji, Wenze Huang, Bowen Chen, Zimo Jiang,
Weihong Ren, Zhiyong Wang, and Honghai Liu*

Tri-Axial Plantar Load Sensing for Identity Authentication with 1D-CNN
Classifier 484
   Zijie Liu, Yi Zhang, Hao Huang, Shabei Xu, Xiang Luo, and Jiajie Guo

Exploring the Mechanism Underlying Lower Limb Motor Dysfunction
in Ischemic Stroke Based on Multimodal Signals 494
   Jiaqi Shi, Hongyu Wang, Yulan Zhu, and Yanmei Zhu

FuPaD: Scalable Pose Estimation by Fusing Patch-Wise VGGT with Dense
Bundle Adjustment 508
   Dexin Qi, Tao Tao, Zhihong Zhang, and Xuesong Mei

ScaffoldOcc: Sparse Points Anchored Scaffold 3D Gaussian
for Hierarchical Semantic Occupancy Prediction 521
   Zhihong Zhang, Wenjun Wang, Dexin Qi, and Xuesong Mei

Dynamic Memory Reconciliation for Online Action Detection 534
   *Wenze Huang, Haoyu Ji, Zhihao Yang, Bowen Chen, Zimo Jiang,
Zhiyong Wang, Weihong Ren, and Honghai Liu*

Enhance Polyp Segmentation via Supervised Contrastive Learning ... 548
   Jiejie Yan and Yizhang Ruan

Online Prediction of Surface Roughness in Robotic Grinding System
for TC4 Workpieces Using PSO-XGBoost Algorithm 560
   Xiangye Zhu, Yusen Li, Xiaohu Xu, Yao Chu, and Sijie Yan

Cross-Subject Respiratory State Recognition Based on Ultrasonic
and IMU Signals 573
   Shuo Feng, Zhiyong Wang, and Jiaole Wang

Bio-mechatronic Integration and Rehabilitation Robots

Hybrid Pole Placement and Interval Type-2 Fuzzy Control for Bio-Inspired
Tendon-Driven Robotic Leg Stabilization 587
   *Rui Tian, Shuchen Ding, Chengyu Su, Liren Zhu, Shiyu Ma,
Wensong Zhao, and Zhe Lu*

Continuous Estimation Algorithm of Elbow Joint Angle Based on Mamba
Model 599
 Yangfan Zhou, Jiawei Liang, Yu Lu, Liang Zhang, Bi Zhang,
 and Xingang Zhao

A Bone Grinding Depth Prediction Method Based on Multimodal Sensing
Information 611
 Yiren Huang, Xu Liang, Guotao Li, Tingting Su, Hui Li, Kangkang Sun,
 Zihe Feng, Xinuo Zhang, and Yong Hai

Research on Parameter Adaptive Electrical Stimulation System Based
on WBAN 622
 Jingyu Wu, Tairen Sun, and Jiantao Yang

MBGADNet: Multi-Branch Generative Adversarial Denoising Network
with Semantic Preservation for EEG Artifact Removal 631
 Da Liao, Fengjun Mu, Kecheng Shi, Jun Wang, Zhe Li, Rui Huang,
 Zhinan Peng, and Hong Cheng

Design Optimization of Frameless Drive Motor in Robot Integrated
Modular Actuator Considering Duty Cycle Suitability 650
 Zimeng Guan, Fan Yang, Songtao Cai, Wenkai Xie, Yuanbo Liu,
 and Tenghui Dong

Cluster-Guided State Initialization Strategy for Flexible Humanoid
Locomotion 662
 Wenhao Tan, Zhiheng Li, Xing Fang, Yanyun Chen, Qian Zhang,
 Ran Song, and Wei Zhang

Design and Modeling of a Modular Cable-Driven Lower-Limb
Exoskeleton with Compact Torque Sensors 673
 Jia Yao, Zhijun Fu, Xiao Yang, Shuowen Yi, Siyu Liu, and Zhao Guo

Author Index 687

Robotic Dexterous Manipulation and Intelligent Control

A Physics-Informed Neural Network-Based Momentum Observer Considering Velocity Effects for Contact Force Estimation in Industrial Robots

Hongbo Hu[ID], Zhongkai Zhang[ID], Pengxin Zha[ID], and Chungang Zhuang[✉][ID]

School of Mechanical Engineering, Shanghai Jiao Tong University, Shanghai 200240, China
cgzhuang@sjtu.edu.cn

Abstract. End-effector contact force estimation is a critical technology for high-precision force control tasks in industrial robots, and its accuracy directly impacts the safety and compliance of operations. Traditional generalized momentum observers (GMOs) have shown limitations in dynamics model accuracy and adaptability to varying operational conditions. This paper introduces an enhanced GMO approach utilizing a physics-informed neural network (PINN) dynamics model to overcome these challenges. First, the PINN method is employed to establish a precise robot dynamics model, enabling efficient inference of the inertia matrix derivatives. Second, an adaptive gain adjustment mechanism is designed to dynamically optimize observer performance based on robot joint velocities, significantly enhancing the robustness and adaptability of the observer under disturbances across different frequencies. Finally, the effectiveness of the proposed method is validated through simulation experiments. The results demonstrate that the proposed method achieves effective contact force estimation under disturbances of varying frequencies and outperforms other GMO-based methods.

Keywords: Industrial Robot · Contact Force Estimation · Generalized Momentum Observer · Physics-informed Neural Network

1 Introduction

With the rapid development of industrial automation and intelligent manufacturing, the applications of industrial robots in tasks such as assembly [1], grinding [2] and human-robot collaboration [3] are becoming increasingly widespread. In these tasks, controlling the contact force between the robot's end-effector and the environment is one of the key factors ensuring task precision and safety. Accurate contact force estimation not only enhances the compliance and adaptability of robot operations but also prevents workpiece or robot damage caused by inaccurate force control [4]. However, due to the high cost and complex installation of end-effector force sensors, direct measurement of contact forces is often impractical in many real-world applications. Therefore, estimating the end-effector contact force indirectly through the robot's current signals and dynamics model has become a significant research direction in the field of robot control.

The core of contact force estimation lies in utilizing the robot dynamics model and observer algorithms to derive external forces from information such as joint driving torques, positions, and velocities. This technology not only reduces system costs but also enhances the intelligence and autonomy of robots. However, the accuracy of contact force estimation is influenced by various factors, including the precision of the dynamics model, the robustness of the observer algorithms, and the complexity of the robot's motion states.

Currently, methods for estimating end-effector contact forces in robots are primarily based on observer algorithms, among which the generalized momentum observer (GMO) and the extended state observer (ESO) are two classical approaches. The GMO-based method estimates external contact forces by observing changes in the generalized momentum of the robot system, exhibiting a certain degree of robustness to model uncertainties [5, 6]. The ESO-based method treats external contact forces as extended states of the system and estimates them in real-time using an observer, making it suitable for force estimation tasks in nonlinear systems [7, 8].

However, the performance of both GMO and ESO heavily relies on the accuracy of the robot dynamics model. In practical applications, errors in the dynamics model often arise due to model simplifications, parameter uncertainties, and nonlinear effects such as joint friction and elastic deformation [9]. These errors directly impact the estimation accuracy of the observer, particularly in scenarios involving high-speed motion or complex contact interactions.

To improve the accuracy of the dynamics model, numerous studies have focused on dynamics parameter identification methods. Traditional identification methods typically rely on least squares or optimization algorithms to fit dynamics parameters using excitation experiment data [10]. However, these methods exhibit limitations when dealing with nonlinear dynamics, especially in high-dimensional, nonlinear, and complex boundary conditions, where the computational complexity and identification accuracy of traditional approaches struggle to meet practical requirements.

In recent years, physics-informed neural networks (PINNs) have emerged as a novel machine learning approach, demonstrating advantages in dynamics modeling and parameter identification [11]. By embedding physical laws (e.g., dynamics equations) into the training process of neural networks, PINNs can leverage both experimental data and physical models, significantly enhancing the generalization ability and accuracy of the model. Compared to traditional identification methods, PINNs are better equipped to handle nonlinear dynamics and perform well even in scenarios with limited or noisy data [12]. Therefore, PINN-based dynamics modeling offers a new perspective for improving the performance of contact force estimation.

Additionally, the performance of observers across different frequency ranges is a critical issue in contact force estimation research. In the low-frequency range, the dynamics of the robot are relatively simple, and the impact of model errors and noise is minor; however, accurately modeling joint friction behavior at low frequencies is often challenging. On the other hand, in the high-frequency range, the nonlinear effects of the robot system become significantly more pronounced, and dynamics model errors increase, leading to a decline in observer estimation accuracy. Therefore, improving observer gain to achieve effective estimation under disturbances across different frequencies has become a challenging research focus.

To address the above issues, this paper proposes a physics-informed generalized momentum observer (PIGMO), which considers the joint velocity effects on observation performance and adaptively adjusts the observer gain to achieve effective estimation of disturbances across different frequencies. The main contributions include:

1) An improved GMO based on PINN robot dynamics model is proposed, enabling efficient inference of the inertia matrix derivatives.
2) The influence of robot joint velocities on observation performance is considered, and an adaptive observer gain adjustment mechanism is introduced. This mechanism reduces the gain at low velocities to minimize noise interference while increasing the gain at high velocities to enhance the ability to capture high-frequency dynamics.
3) The effectiveness of the proposed method is verified through simulations, demonstrating that this approach improves the robot's contact force observation performance under disturbances across different frequencies compared to GMO methods.

2 PINN-Based Momentum Observer

2.1 Dynamics Formulation of Robots

PINN represents a machine learning methodology that integrates physical laws into the neural network training process, effectively addressing nonlinear characteristics and enhancing model accuracy. In the domain of robot dynamics modeling, the deep Lagrangian networks (DeLaN) framework, which employs structured Lagrangian network layers for robot dynamics modeling, has demonstrated its superiority over traditional methods [13]. This paper aims to utilize the PINN approach for precise modeling of robot dynamics and subsequently reconstruct the GMO for external contact force estimation, thereby improving both the accuracy of robot dynamics modeling and the performance of contact force estimation.

In the analysis and modeling of robotic system dynamics, the generalized coordinates q are typically employed as the sole coordinates defining the system configuration. The Lagrangian can be defined as a function of these generalized coordinates, fully describing the dynamics of the given system. For a serial robotic system with n degrees of freedom (DOF), the second-order ordinary differential equation (ODE) form of the robotic dynamics model can be derived as:

$$\tau = M(q)\ddot{q} + \underbrace{\dot{M}(q)\dot{q} - \frac{1}{2}\left\{\frac{\partial}{\partial q}[\dot{q}^T M(q)\dot{q}]\right\}^T}_{:=C(q,\dot{q})\dot{q}} + G(q) \tag{1}$$

where $\tau \in \mathbb{R}^{n \times 1}$ represents the joint torque of the robot. $q \in \mathbb{R}^{n \times 1}$, $\dot{q} \in \mathbb{R}^{n \times 1}$, and $\ddot{q} \in \mathbb{R}^{n \times 1}$ represent the joint angles, angular velocities, and angular accelerations of the robot, respectively. $M(q)$ is the symmetric and positive definite inertia matrix, $C(q,\dot{q}) \in \mathbb{R}^{n \times n}$ denotes the Coriolis and centrifugal matrix, and $G(q) \in \mathbb{R}^{n \times 1}$ signifies the gravity vector.

Taking into account the joint friction and external contact forces, the robot dynamics model can be further refined as:

$$\tau = M(q)\ddot{q} + C(q,\dot{q})\dot{q} + G(q) + \tau_f + J^T F_{ext} \tag{2}$$

where $\tau_f \in \mathbb{R}^{n \times 1}$ represents the joint friction torque, $J \in \mathbb{R}^{6 \times n}$ is the velocity Jacobian of the robotic system, and $F_{ext} \in \mathbb{R}^{6 \times 1}$ denotes the external contact forces.

The joint friction in a robotic system is primarily associated with joint velocities and can generally be expressed using the Coulomb-viscous friction model as:

$$\tau_f(\dot{q}; f_c, f_v, f_b) = f_c \odot sign(\dot{q}) + f_v \odot \dot{q} + f_b \tag{3}$$

where $f_c \in \mathbb{R}^{n \times 1}, f_v \in \mathbb{R}^{n \times 1}$ and $f_b \in \mathbb{R}^{n \times 1}$ denote the Coulomb coefficient, the viscous coefficient and the friction offset of each joint of the robot, respectively. $sign(\cdot)$ is a sign function and $\odot$ represents the Hadamard product.

2.2 PINN-Based Structured Modeling of Robot Dynamics

To achieve structured modeling of robot dynamics based on PINNs, the inertia matrix M can be decomposed as:

$$M(q;\theta) = L(q;\theta)L^T(q;\theta) + \epsilon I \tag{4}$$

where $L(q;\theta) \in \mathbb{R}^{n \times n}$ is a lower triangular matrix, θ represents the training parameters of the PINN, ϵ is a positive regularization offset and I represents the identity matrix. This decomposition guarantees that the inertia matrix M maintains its positive definite property, adhering to the essential physical constraints.

Similarly, the gravitational term can also be expressed as $G(q;\psi)$, a function of ψ, which represents the network parameters. The lower triangular matrix $L(q;\theta)$ and the gravitational term $G(q;\psi)$ can be computed through a Lagrangian layer based on a ReLU network. Therefore, leveraging the PINN framework for robot dynamics modeling [12], the rigid body dynamics of the robot can be concisely formulated as:

$$\tau = \Theta(q,\dot{q},\ddot{q};\theta,\psi) + \tau_f(\dot{q};f_c,f_v,f_b) + J^T F_{ext} \tag{5}$$

where Θ represents the PINN-based structured robot inverse dynamics model.

During the training of the PINN for robot dynamics modeling, external forces can be neglected. By minimizing the error between the predicted joint torques $\hat{\tau}$ and the measured joint torques τ, the network parameters and friction coefficients of the dynamics model can be learned as follows:

$$\left(\theta^*, \psi^*, f_c^*, f_v^*, f_b^*\right) = \underset{\theta, \psi, f_c, f_v, f_b}{\arg\min} \ell\left(\widehat{\Theta} + \hat{\tau}_f, \tau\right) + \mu \Omega(\theta, \psi, f_c, f_v, f_b) \tag{6}$$

where $\Omega(\theta, \psi, f_c, f_v, f_b)$ represents the weight decay regularization, and μ is the decay coefficient, which can enhance the learning of a unique solution for the PINN.

Furthermore, to achieve contact force estimation, the Coriolis and centrifugal matrix needs to be computed, which can be expressed through structured calculations as:

$$C(q, \dot{q}) = \frac{d}{dt}(LL^T)\dot{q} - \frac{1}{2}\left\{\frac{\partial}{\partial q}[\dot{q}^T LL^T \dot{q}]\right\}^T \tag{7}$$

The computation of partial derivatives $d(LL^T)/dt$ and $\partial(\dot{q}^T LL^T \dot{q})/\partial q$ is essential for the application of robot inverse dynamics. However, since time t is not an input to the dynamics model, automatic differentiation techniques cannot be directly applied. Therefore, the following chain decomposition is adopted:

$$\frac{d}{dt}(LL^T) = L\frac{dL^T}{dt} + \frac{dL}{dt}L^T = L\frac{\partial L^T}{\partial q}\dot{q} + \frac{\partial L}{\partial q}\dot{q}L^T \tag{8}$$

The derivatives of $L(q; \theta)$ with respect to the network inputs can be computed through the recursive application of the chain rule, owing to the compositional structure and differentiability of the network:

$$\frac{\partial L}{\partial q} = \frac{\partial L}{\partial h_{N-1}}\frac{\partial h_{N-1}}{\partial h_{N-2}}\cdots\frac{\partial h_1}{\partial q} \tag{9}$$

where h_i denotes the output of the i-th network layer, which can be expanded as:

$$h_i = g_i(W_i^T h_{i-1} + b_i) \tag{10}$$

where W_i and b_i represent the network parameters of the i-th layer, and $g_i(\cdot)$ denotes a nonlinear activation function. Taking the derivative yields:

$$\frac{\partial h}{\partial h_{i-1}} = \text{diag}[g'(W_i^T h_{i-1} + b_i)_i]W_i \tag{11}$$

Substituting Eq. (11) into Eq. (9) enables the computation of $\partial L/\partial q$ through a chain calculation. Following this, $d(LL^T)/dt$ can be derived by Eq. (8). The derivation of $\partial(\dot{q}^T LL^T \dot{q})/\partial q$ follows an analogous approach:

$$\frac{\partial}{\partial q}(\dot{q}^T LL^T \dot{q}) = \dot{q}^T\left(\frac{\partial L}{\partial q}L^T + L\frac{\partial L^T}{\partial q}\right)\dot{q} \tag{12}$$

Thus, the joint torques of the robot can be predicted. Additionally, the structured PINN enables efficient computation of the robot's inertia matrix and its derivatives.

2.3 Physics Informed Generalized Momentum Observer

Building upon the structured modeling of robot dynamics based on PINNs, this paper proposes an enhanced GMO, termed the PIGMO, as shown in Fig. 1. This approach achieves efficient inference of the inertia matrix derivatives and high-precision estimation of the external contact forces during the observation process.

The fundamental idea of the GMO is to construct a disturbance observer based on the difference between the model-predicted generalized momentum $\hat{p}$ and the measured generalized momentum p:

$$\hat{\tau}_{ext} = K(p - \hat{p}) \tag{13}$$

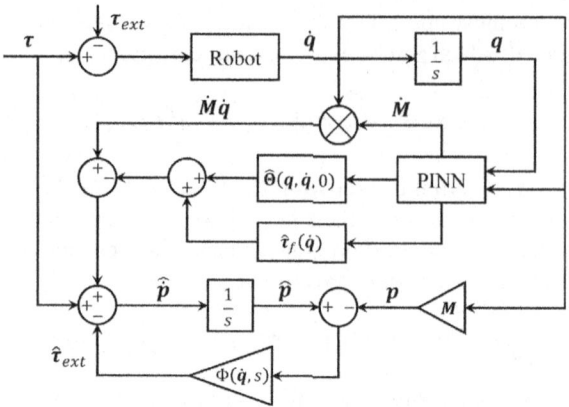

Fig. 1. Structure diagram of the proposed PIGMO.

where $\hat{\boldsymbol{\tau}}_{ext} \in \mathbb{R}^{n \times 1}$ represents the observed torque components of the external forces acting on each joint, and $\boldsymbol{K}$ is the observer gain matrix.

The generalized momentum is obtained by multiplying the robot system inertia matrix $\boldsymbol{M}$ with the joint velocity vector $\dot{\boldsymbol{q}}$, and its derivative can be expressed as:

$$\dot{p} = \dot{M}\dot{q} + M\ddot{q} \tag{14}$$

By substituting $M\ddot{q}$ using the dynamics equation and integrating, the model-predicted generalized momentum can be constructed as:

$$\hat{p} = \int \dot{\hat{p}} dt = \int [\dot{M}\dot{q} + \tau - \hat{\tau}_{ext} - \tau_f - C\dot{q} - G] dt$$
$$= \int [\dot{M}\dot{q} + \tau - \hat{\tau}_{ext} - \tau_f - \Theta(q, \dot{q}, 0)] dt \tag{15}$$

where $\Theta(q, \dot{q}, 0)$ represents the result of setting the acceleration terms in the robot inverse dynamics model to zero.

The computation of the derivative of the inertia matrix $\dot{M}$ constitutes the primary challenge in the inference of force observation. Existing robot contact force estimation methods based on GMOs typically employ the method described in [14]:

$$\dot{M} = C(q, \dot{q}) + C^T(q, \dot{q}) \tag{16}$$

Based on this transformation, C^T can be computed to avoid the calculation of $\dot{M}$. The specific method for computing C^T is detailed in [15], with an algorithmic complexity of $O(n^2)$. However, leveraging the structured modeling of robot dynamics based on PINNs, not only can the joint torque components be effectively predicted, but the derivative of the inertia matrix $\dot{M}$ can also be efficiently computed, as shown in Eq. (8). Therefore, the derivative of the generalized momentum can be modified as:

$$\dot{\hat{p}} = \frac{d}{dt}(LL^T)\dot{q} + M\ddot{q} = \left(L\frac{\partial L^T}{\partial q} + \frac{\partial L}{\partial q}L^T\right)\dot{q}^2 + M\ddot{q} = \left(L\frac{\partial L^T}{\partial q} + \frac{\partial L}{\partial q}L^T\right)\dot{q}^2 + \tau - \hat{\tau}_{ext} - \tau_f - \Theta(q, \dot{q}, 0) \tag{17}$$

Consequently, the generalized momentum can be revised from Eq. (15) as:

$$\hat{p} = \int \left[\left(L \frac{\partial L^T}{\partial q} + \frac{\partial L}{\partial q} L^T \right) \dot{q}^2 + \tau - \tau_{ext} - \tau_f - \Theta(q, \dot{q}, 0) \right] dt \tag{18}$$

Based on Eq. (13), the predicted values of the external torque components acting on each joint of the robot can be obtained as:

$$\hat{\tau}_{ext} = K \left(M\dot{q} - \int \left[\left(L \frac{\partial L^T}{\partial q} + \frac{\partial L}{\partial q} L^T \right) \dot{q}^2 + \tau - \tau_{ext} - \tau_f - \Theta(q, \dot{q}, 0) \right] dt \right) \tag{19}$$

Ultimately, the external contact force estimation is achieved:

$$\hat{F}_{ext} = \left(J^T \right)^+ \hat{\tau}_{ext} \tag{20}$$

where $\left(J^T \right)^+$ represents the pseudo-inverse of the robot Jacobian matrix transpose.

The advantage of the proposed PIGMO lies in its structured prediction of robot dynamics based on PINNs, enabling efficient computation of the inertia matrix derivatives. This approach avoids reliance on Eq. (16), which is only applicable to standard dynamics model parameters, i.e., the inertia matrix of the links being expressed at the center of mass rather than the origin of the link coordinate frame.

3 Adaptive Gain Adjustment Considering Velocity Effects

Differentiating the generalized momentum observer expression in Eq. (13) and applying the Laplace transform yields:

$$\hat{\tau}_{ext} = \frac{K}{sE + K} \tau_{ext} \tag{21}$$

where s is the Laplace operator and E is the n-dimensional identity matrix.

The above equation indicates that the external force observer constructed based on GMO essentially performs first-order filtering of the actual external force, which inherently introduces a delay in external force observation. The bandwidth of the observer is determined by the coefficient K and is independent of the robot motion. A larger gain results in faster response but increases susceptibility to noise and model uncertainties. Consequently, the methods based on GMOs must strike a balance between rapid response and obtaining accurate disturbance information.

To address the aforementioned issue, this paper incorporates the influence of joint velocities into the design of the GMO, proposing an adaptive gain adjustment mechanism. As shown in Fig. 1, the filter is a function of the joint velocities $\dot{q}$ and the frequency-domain variable s. The transfer function from the disturbance input to the observer output is rewritten as:

$$G(\dot{q}, s) = \frac{\hat{\tau}_{ext}}{\tau_{ext}} = \frac{\Phi(\dot{q}, s)}{sE + \Phi(\dot{q}, s)} \tag{22}$$

Equation (22) indicates that $\Phi(\dot{q}, s)$ should exhibit a high static gain to ensure that the observer output effectively tracks external disturbance information. Conversely, the uncertainty in the model at low speeds can introduce high-frequency disturbances to the observer, which requires $\Phi(\dot{q}, s)$ to have a low static gain at low speeds to reduce the impact of high-frequency disturbances. To meet those requirements, the following implementation function satisfying first-order low-pass filtering is proposed:

$$\Phi(\dot{q}, s) = \frac{\omega(\dot{q})}{s+\omega(\dot{q})} \tag{23}$$

Substituting into Eq. (22), the transfer function can be obtained as:

$$G(\dot{q}, s) = \frac{\omega(\dot{q})}{s^2+s\omega(\dot{q})+\omega(\dot{q})} \tag{24}$$

This design ensures that the poles are located in the left half-plane, guaranteeing the stability of the observer. Since $\omega(\dot{q})$ determines the observer bandwidth, an adaptive observer gain function based on joint velocity $\dot{q}$ is designed as follows:

$$\omega(\dot{q}) = \omega_h - (\omega_h - \omega_l)e^{-\gamma \dot{q}^2} \tag{25}$$

where ω_h and ω_l represent the upper and lower limits of the gain, respectively, representing the cutoff frequencies at high and low speeds, and γ is the attenuation factor.

Based on the aforementioned adaptive gain adjustment mechanism, the observer gain can be dynamically adjusted according to the joint velocities $\dot{q}$. This enables the reduction of gain at low velocities to minimize noise interference, while increasing the gain at high velocities to enhance the ability to capture high-frequency dynamics. In addition, the designed adaptive adjustment strategy does not affect the observation stability of GMOs.

4 Simulation Verification and Analysis

4.1 Dynamics Modeling Results Based on PINN

To validate the effectiveness of the proposed PIGMO for contact force estimation, this section implements the PINN dynamics modeling of the robot using Python Pytorch and conducts observer simulation verification in MATLAB Simscape.

A real 6-DOF serial SIASUN SN7B robot is used for excitation experiments. The robot and its simulation model are shown in Fig. 2, executing an excitation trajectory in the form of a fifth-order Fourier series. By collecting joint currents, angles, and velocities during the robot's motion, dynamics identification [9] is performed as a comparison to the proposed method. The motion data is divided into the same training and validation proportions for PINN-based dynamics modeling. A total of 120,000 samples are collected at a frequency of 1 kHz over a duration of 120 s. Among these, 100,000 samples are used for training, and 20,000 samples for validation. The designed PINN has three hidden layers, with the number of nodes set to [128, 128, 128]. The training batch size is set to 50, the learning rate is set to 5e − 4, and adaptive moment estimation (Adam) is chosen as the optimizer for the network.

Without loss of generality, the dynamics modeling results of the 2-th joint of the robot are compared between the identification-based and the PINN-based method, as shown

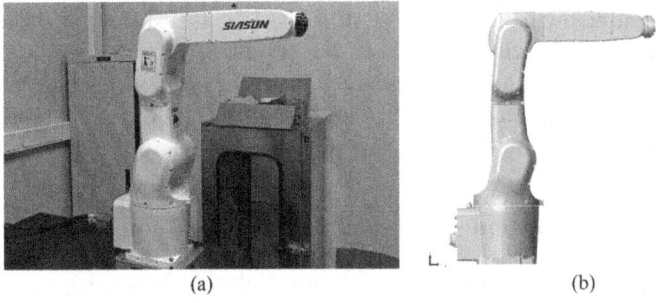

Fig. 2. SIASUN SN7B robot and its simulation model.

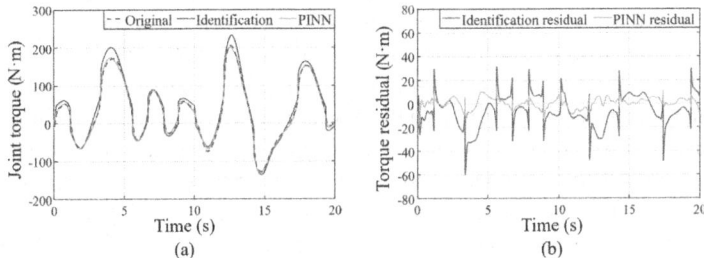

Fig. 3. Comparison of joint torque prediction results and torque residuals.

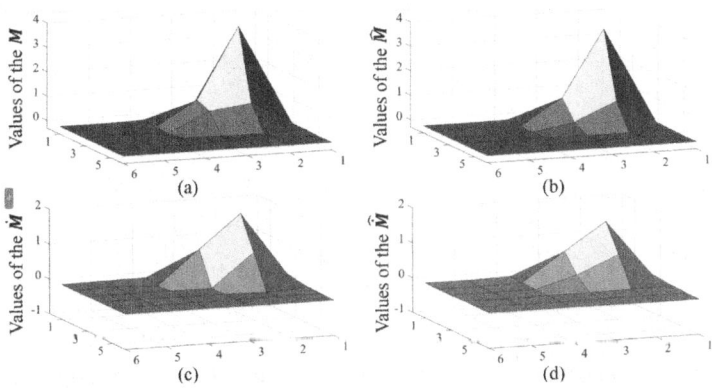

Fig. 4. Visualization and comparison of robot inertia matrix M and its derivatives $\dot{M}$.

in Fig. 3. Specifically, Fig. 3(a) presents the joint torque prediction results, and Fig. 3(b) shows the corresponding joint torque residuals. Benefiting from the effective learning of the nonlinear characteristics of the dynamics model, the PINN-based structured modeling approach achieves higher accuracy in robot dynamics modeling.

Additionally, since the robot contact force estimation relies on the robot inertial matrix, it is necessary to verify the accuracy of the predictions for the inertial matrix M and its derivatives $\dot{M}$. Figure 4 presents a visualization comparison, with Fig. 4(a) and

Fig. 4(c) representing the true values, Fig. 4(b) and Fig. 4(d) showing the predictions based on the PINN, as described in Eq. (8). The results indicate that, while achieving accurate prediction of robot joint torques, the PINN-based method can also effectively estimate the inertial matrix and its derivatives. This provides a theoretical foundation and feasibility support for the design of the proposed PIGMO.

4.2 Contact Force Estimation Results and Performance Comparison

After completing the dynamics modeling of the robot, the PINN-based dynamics model is imported into MATLAB Simscape, and the proposed PIGMO observer is constructed for the simulation of contact force estimation and performance validation. The GMO is used as a comparison group, with the observer gain for each joint set to 100. For the proposed PIGMO observer, the upper gain limit ω_h and lower gain limit ω_l are set to 150 and 80, respectively, and the attenuation factor γ is set to 0.05.

A step force signal of 50 N in the x-direction is applied to the robot's end-effector. The force estimation results of the proposed PIGMO are shown in Fig. 5(a), and the estimation residuals in Fig. 5(b). When responding to sudden forces, the PIGMO achieves faster and more stable contact force tracking compared to the GMO while maintaining the same response speed. The result stems from the proposed PIGMO observer's construction based on the PINN dynamics model, which incorporates more comprehensive nonlinear dynamics characteristics, mitigating model uncertainties.

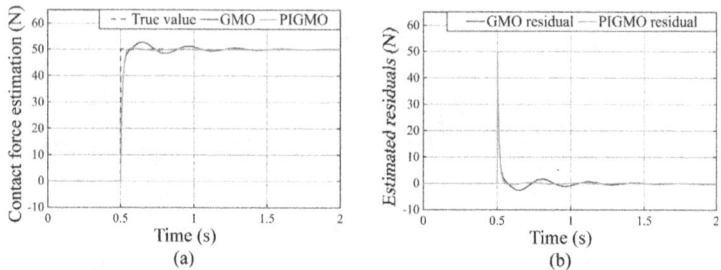

Fig. 5. Force estimation results and residuals under step force excitation.

To further validate the effectiveness of the proposed adaptive gain adjustment mechanism considering velocity effects, the contact force estimation performance is tested under a frequency-modulated sine wave in the x-direction. As shown in Fig. 6(a), when the force signal frequency is low, both the GMO and PIGMO achieve satisfactory force observation. As the frequency of the force signal increases, the variation frequency of the robot's joint velocities also gradually increases. This causes the GMO to struggle with maintaining accurate contact force tracking when the joint velocities are large, particularly when the contact force approaches its peak, resulting in significant force estimation residuals are shown in Fig. 6(b). However, with the adaptive gain adjustment mechanism, the gain of the PIGMO increases accordingly when the joint velocities increase, enabling superior force observation results.

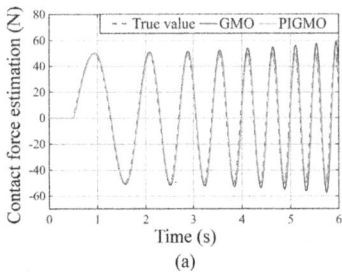 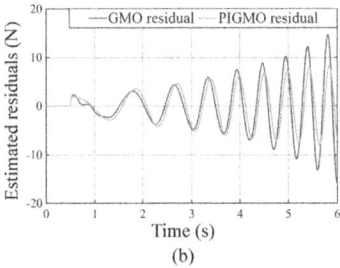

Fig. 6. Force estimation results and residuals under frequency-modulated sine excitation.

Table 1. Comparison of force estimation performance with other methods by MAE (N).

Method	Step force	Sinusoidal force
GMO	0.7289	3.7810
PIGMO	0.4211	3.1237

The simulation results demonstrate the effectiveness of the proposed PIGMO. Specifically, the external force estimation performance is evaluated using mean absolute error (MAE), as detailed in Table 1.

5 Conclusion

This paper addresses the issues of dynamics model accuracy and observer adaptability in robot end-effector contact force estimation by proposing a PIGMO observer based on the PINN dynamics model. An adaptive gain adjustment mechanism is designed to optimize the observer's performance during force interactions at different frequencies, enabling it to better adapt to complex contact force estimation tasks. Simulation results demonstrate that, compared to GMO methods, the proposed approach significantly improves estimation accuracy in high-speed motion and complex contact scenarios. Future research will further explore the application of this method in real-world industrial robot control scenarios and refine the observer gain adjustment mechanism to meet more complex force observation requirements.

Acknowledgement. This work was sponsored by The Explorers Program of Shanghai (Basic Research Funding) under Grant 24TS1414700 and the National Key Research and Development Program of China under Grant 2022YFB4700300. (Corresponding author: Chungang Zhuang).

References

1. Zhao, X., Zhao, H., Chen, P., Ding, H.: Model accelerated reinforcement learning for high precision robotic assembly. Int. J. Intell. Robot. 4(2), 202–216 (2020)

2. Li, J., Zou, L., Luo, G., Wang, W., Lv, C.: Enhancement and evaluation in path accuracy of industrial robot for complex surface grinding. Robot. Comput.-Integr. Manuf. **81**, 102521 (2023)
3. Aivaliotis, P., Aivaliotis, S., Gkournelos, C., Kokkalis, K., Michalos, G., Makris, S.: Power and force limiting on industrial robots for human-robot collaboration. Robot. Comput.-Integr. Manuf. **59**, 346–360 (2019)
4. Wu, P., Dong, H., Li, P., Bao, Y., Dong, W., Sun, L.: A new contact force estimation method for heavy robots without force sensors by combining CNN-GRU and force transformation. Technologies **13**(5), 192 (2025)
5. Long, S., Dang, X., Sun, S., Wang, Y., Gui, M.: A novel sliding mode momentum observer for collaborative robot collision detection. Machines **10**(9), 818 (2022)
6. Garofalo, G., Mansfeld, N., Jankowski, J., Ott, C.: Sliding mode momentum observers for estimation of external torques and joint acceleration. In: 36th IEEE International Conference on Robotics and Automation (ICRA), pp. 6117–6123. Montreal, QC, Canada (2019)
7. Han, L., Mao, J., Cao, P., Gan, Y., Li, S.: Toward sensorless interaction force estimation for industrial robots using high-order finite-time observers. IEEE Trans. Ind. Electron. **69**(7), 7275–7284 (2021)
8. Ren, T., Dong, Y., Wu, D., Chen, K.: Collision detection and identification for robot manipulators based on extended state observer. Control Eng. Practice **79**, 144–153 (2018)
9. Jubien, A., Gautier, M., Janot, A.: Dynamic identification of the Kuka LightWeight robot: comparison between actual and confidential Kuka's parameters. In: 2014 IEEE/ASME International Conference on Advanced Intelligent Mechatronics (AIM), pp. 483–488. Besancon, France (2014)
10. Sousa, C.D., Cortesão, R.: Inertia tensor properties in robot dynamics identification: a linear matrix inequality approach. IEEE/ASME Trans. Mechatron. **24**(1), 406–411 (2019)
11. Hu, H., Shen, Z., Zhuang, C.: A PINN-based friction-inclusive dynamics modeling method for industrial robots. IEEE Trans. Ind. Electron. **72**, 5136–5144 (2024)
12. Lahoud, M.G., Marchello, G., D'Imperio, M., Mueller, A., Cannella, F.: A deep learning framework for non-symmetrical coulomb friction identification of robotic manipulators. In: 41th IEEE International Conference on Robotics and Automation (ICRA), pp. 10510–10516. Yokohama, Japan (2024)
13. Lutter, M., Ritter, C., Peters, J.: Deep Lagrangian networks: using physics as model prior for deep learning. In: 7th International Conference on Learning Representations (ICLR), 149936. New Orleans, LA, USA (2019)
14. De Luca, A., Mattone, R.: Actuator failure detection and isolation using generalized momenta. In: 20th IEEE International Conference on Robotics and Automation (ICRA), pp 634–639. Taipei, Taiwan (2003)
15. De Luca, A., Ferrajoli, L.: A modified Newton-Euler method for dynamic computations in robot fault detection and control. In: 26th IEEE International Conference on Robotics and Automation (ICRA), pp. 3359–3364. Kobe, Japan (2009)

A High-Precision and Compliant Interaction Method for Robot Based on Model Predictive Impedance Control

Yuhao Zhang[✉], Zhenwei Zhang, Licheng Hou, Yang Xiang, Qingmiao Zhu, Xingwei Zhao, and Bo Tao

School of Mechanical Science and Engineering, Huazhong University of Science and Technology, Wuhan 430074, China
yuhao_zhang@hust.edu.cn

Abstract. Robots performing complex contact tasks (e.g., grinding) require a balance between compliance and motion precision. Model Predictive Control (MPC) achieves high-accuracy trajectory tracking by incorporating multi-objective constraints but suffers from high computational load and model sensitivity. In contrast, Impedance Control (IC) enables low-cost force interaction with tunable compliance but lacks inherent mechanisms for enforcing physical constraints, resulting in motion inaccuracies under force regulation. This paper proposes a nonlinear Model Predictive Impedance Control (MPIC) framework that synergizes MPC's predictive optimization with IC's compliance adaptability. MPIC solves a joint cost function to balance trajectory tracking and force regulation, enabling tasks like constant-force polishing and precise tangential velocity control. A hierarchical architecture that integrates end-effector impedance control with model predictive control converts Cartesian-space motion and force trajectories into joint-space torque commands for real-time implementation. The framework demonstrates effective coupling of compliance and precision in dynamically interacting scenarios.

Keywords: Robot-Environment Interaction · Model Predictive Control · Impedance Control · Hybrid Force/Position Control

1 Introduction

With the rapid advancement of smart manufacturing and precision machining technologies, robots performing complex contact tasks (e.g., grinding, polishing, and assembly) are increasingly required to achieve synergistic compliance and motion precision [1]. Model Predictive Control (MPC) and Impedance Control (IC) are two widely adopted strategies in robotic manipulation. For motion control tasks in robotics, MPC is commonly employed to achieve high computational accuracy [2, 3]. It allows the incorporation of multi-objective cost functions and physical constraints through iterative prediction processes. However, MPC typically involves high computational demand within each control cycle and is highly sensitive to model accuracy [4]. In contrast, IC features relatively low computational complexity and is extensively used in robotic tasks involving physical interactions [5–7]. Moreover, IC enables robots to exhibit compliance, and its control behavior can be easily tuned by adjusting impedance parameters, thus ensuring safe interaction with the environment while reducing the risk of damage to both the robot and the target object [8]. Despite these advantages, traditional IC lacks the ability to enforce physical constraints and may struggle to maintain precise motion control during force interactions [9].

For tasks that require both compliance and high precision, such as robotic grinding or polishing, they demand that the robot maintain a constant normal contact force while simultaneously ensuring a uniform tangential motion velocity. Relying solely on either MPC or IC is insufficient to meet these requirements, often resulting in suboptimal surface quality [10, 11]. While prior work [12] integrates MPC with IC, it assumes alignment between the force-compliant direction and trajectory tracking direction, which fails to address scenarios like robotic grinding that inherently require decoupling force and position regulation across orthogonal axes.

In this paper, we propose a nonlinear Model Predictive Impedance Controller (MPIC) for multi-directional force and position tracking in complex contact tasks such as grinding and polishing. MPIC not only adapts to variations in the external environment but also ensures accurate motion tracking, making it suitable for complex tasks that require both compliant interaction and high-precision trajectory control.

2 Problem Formulation

2.1 Robot Trajectory Tracking Problem

We consider the general dynamic model of a robot based on the Newton–Euler or Lagrangian formulation, expressed as:

$$M(q)\ddot{q} + C(q, \dot{q})\dot{q} + G(q) + d = \tau, \qquad (1)$$

where $q, \dot{q}, \ddot{q}$ represent the robot's joint angle, joint angular velocity, and joint angular acceleration respectively, $M(q)$ is the inertia matrix of the robot, $C(\ddot{q}, \dot{q})$ is the Coriolis/centrifugal force matrix of the robot, $G(q)$ is the robot's gravity matrix, d is the disturbance term of the robot's joint friction, and τ is the joint torque of the robot. The robot's joint angles and joint angular velocities are taken as state variables, which can be expressed as $x_1 = q, x_2 = \dot{q}$. The joint torque is the input variable and is expressed as $u = \tau$. In the form of $\dot{x} = f(x, u)$, the state space equation can be established in the robot joint space as follows:

$$\dot{x} = \begin{bmatrix} \dot{x}_1 \\ \dot{x}_2 \end{bmatrix} = \begin{bmatrix} x_2 \\ M(\dot{x}_1)^{-1}(u - C(x_1, x_2)x_2 - G(x_1) - d) \end{bmatrix}. \qquad (2)$$

To address trajectory tracking errors in the Cartesian space, the output variable y is defined as the robot's position in Cartesian space. Taking a two-link manipulator as an example, $y = \begin{bmatrix} y_1, y_2 \end{bmatrix}^T$, where y_1 and y_2 represent the X and Y coordinates of the robot in Cartesian space, respectively. The output variable $y = h(x)$ can thus be expressed as a function of joint states:

$$y = \begin{bmatrix} y_1 \\ y_2 \end{bmatrix} = \begin{bmatrix} l_1\cos(q_1) + l_2\cos(q_1 + q_2) \\ l_1\sin(q_1) + l_2\sin(q_1 + q_2) \end{bmatrix}, \quad (3)$$

where l_1 and l_2 denote the lengths of link 1 and link 2 respectively, q_1 and q_2 represent the joint angles of joint 1 and joint 2. As illustrated in Fig. 1, the trajectory tracking error of the robot consists of the deviation between the actual and desired positions, i.e., $e_1 = y - y_d$, and the deviation between the actual and desired velocities, i.e., $e_2 = \dot{y} - \dot{y}_d$. The goal of the trajectory tracking controller is to eliminate both the position and velocity errors, that is, to satisfy:

$$\lim_{t \to \infty} e_1 = \|h(x(t)) - y_d(t)\| = 0 \ \& \lim_{t \to \infty} e_2 = \|\dot{h}(x(t)) - \dot{y}_d(t)\| = 0. \quad (4)$$

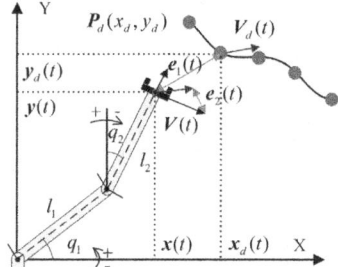

Fig. 1. Schematic of the robot trajectory tracking problem.

2.2 Robot Force Tracking Problem

In compliant force control problems, the robot is typically modeled as a mass-spring-damper system [Fig. 2]. Consider the impedance model of the robot in Cartesian space:

$$F = M\Delta\ddot{X} + D\Delta\dot{X} + K\Delta X, \quad (5)$$

where F represents the external force, $\Delta X = X - X_d$ is the displacement between the desired and current positions, M, D, and K are the mass, damping, and stiffness coefficients, respectively. However, to achieve force tracking functionality, compliance alone is insufficient. Therefore, the traditional impedance model is reformulated into a force tracking form as follows:

$$e_F = M\Delta\ddot{X} + D\Delta\dot{X} + K\Delta X, \quad (6)$$

in which, $e_F = F - F_d$, and F_d denotes the desired constant contact force. We assume that the robot maintains a constant external force, the deformation of the environment remains constant, then at the steady-state equilibrium point we have $\ddot{X}_d = \dot{X}_d = 0$. Substituting into Eq. (6) yields:

$$e_F = M\ddot{X} + D\dot{X} + K(X - X_d). \tag{7}$$

If the contact environment can be modeled as a linear stiffness system with stiffness $F_e = K_e(X_e - X)$, where K_e represents the stiffness of the environment and, X_e denotes the surface position of the environment when no external force is applied, and assuming that the stiffness remains constant during interaction, then the deformation X can be derived as:

$$X = X_e - F/X_e = X_e - (X_d + e_F)/K_e \tag{8}$$

Substituting Eq. (8) into Eq. (7), we obtain:

$$M(\ddot{e}_F + \ddot{F}_d) + D(\dot{e}_F + \dot{F}_d) + K(e_F + F_d) + K_e e_F = KK_e(X_e - X_d). \tag{9}$$

From Eq. (9), the steady-state force tracking error of the robot can be expressed as:

$$e_{F,ss} = \frac{KK_e}{K + K_e}((X_e - X_d) - F_d/K_e). \tag{10}$$

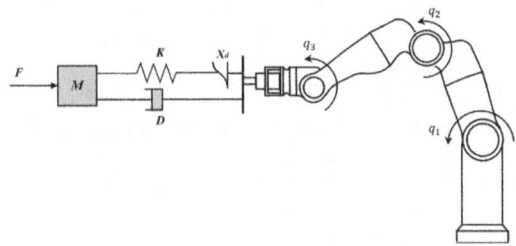

Fig. 2. Schematic diagram of the Cartesian space impedance control.

2.3 Robot Force/Position Hybrid Tracking Problem

When the robot performs a trajectory tracking task while also interacting with the environment through external contact forces, the entire process can be divided into three phases. Phase A: Before contact with the external object, the robot performs a pure trajectory tracking task. Phase B: At the moment of contact, a transition occurs from trajectory tracking to force compliance. Phase C: Once a stable contact with the external object is established, the robot faces a hybrid task involving both trajectory tracking and force control.

In this study, our objective is to design a robotic force controller that simultaneously ensures accurate force tracking and trajectory tracking. Specifically, in Phase A, the trajectory tracking error described in Eq. (4) is required to converge to zero. In Phase C, the force tracking error defined in Eq. (10) should also converge to zero, while maintaining trajectory accuracy. During the transition phase (Phase B), the controller is expected to ensure a stable and smooth dynamic response.

3 The Framework of Proposed Nonlinear Model Predictive Impedance Control

To further enhance the motion accuracy and force tracking performance of the robot under external forces, and to achieve high-precision force/position tracking characteristics, we consider the robot dynamics under external force based on Eq. (1). Since the robot's joint friction is relatively small compared to other variables, we ignore the influence of this item as:

$$M(q)\ddot{q} + C(q, \dot{q})\dot{q} + G(q) = \tau + \tau_e, \tag{11}$$

where, τ represents the joint torque of the robot, and τ_e denotes the torque due to external forces that can be expressed as:

$$\tau_e = J^T(q)F_e, \tag{12}$$

where $J^T(q)$ is the transpose of the robot's Jacobian matrix, and F_e is the external force applied to the robot.

Based on linear feedback techniques, the control torque applied to the robot τ can be written as:

$$\tau = M(q)v + C(q, \dot{q})\dot{q} + G(q) - J^T(q)F_e, \tag{13}$$

where v is the control input corresponding to the joint angular acceleration $v = \ddot{q}$. The relationship between joint angular acceleration $\ddot{q}$ and Cartesian acceleration $\ddot{x}$ can be described as:

$$\begin{cases} \dot{X} = J(q)\dot{q} \\ \ddot{X} = \dot{J}(q)\dot{q} + J(q)\ddot{q} \end{cases} \tag{14}$$

From Eq. (14), it can be solved as $v = J^{\dagger}(q)(\ddot{X} - \dot{J}(q)\dot{q})$, where $J^{\dagger}(q)$ denotes the pseudo-inverse of the Jacobian matrix. Letting $u = \ddot{X}$ be the Cartesian input, we then obtain the joint space input as: $v = J^{\dagger}(q)(u - \dot{J}(q)\dot{q})$.

By taking the robot's end-effector position, velocity, and external force as state variables, and adopting an environmental impedance model as the force prediction model, the end-effector force F_e can be expressed as $F_e = K_e(P_e - P) - D_e V$, where K_e is the environment stiffness, D_e is the environment damping, and P_e is the nominal surface position of the environment in the absence of external forces, we use the Cartesian acceleration u as the control input. The state-space model of the robot can then be formulated as follows:

$$\dot{x} = \begin{bmatrix} \dot{P} \\ \dot{V} \\ \dot{F} \end{bmatrix} = \begin{bmatrix} V \\ u \\ K_e(V^d - V) - D_e u \end{bmatrix} = f(x, u), \qquad (15)$$

where P denotes the displacement of the robot end-effector in Cartesian space, V and V^d denote its velocity and desired velocity in Cartesian space, respectively, and F denotes the force exerted by the robot end-effector.

By incorporating Eq. (15) as the iterative model within the MPIC framework, the rolling optimization problem can be formulated as follows:

$$\min_{u} J(x(t), u(t)) = \|x - x_d\|_{Q_N}^2 + \int_{t}^{t+T_p} (\|x - x_d\|_Q^2 + \|u\|_R^2) ds$$
$$\text{s.t.} \, \dot{x}(s) = f(x(s), u(s)), \, s \in [t, \, t + T_p]$$
$$F_e = M(\ddot{P} - \ddot{P}_d) + D(\dot{P} - \dot{P}_d) + K(P - P_d) \qquad (16)$$
$$c_1(x) \leq x \leq c_2(x)$$
$$u \in [u_{\min} \, u_{\max}]$$
$$x(t + T_p) \in X_f$$

where x_d represents the desired system state, N denotes the prediction horizon steps (corresponding to the prediction horizon T_p), and the cost function J quantifies the total cumulative cost over N future time steps, including the terminal cost term and the receding cost term. The matrices Q, Q_N, and R are the weighted quadratic norm coefficient matrices. The first constraint represents the robot dynamics (as defined in Eq. 11), the second constraint corresponds to the impedance control model, the third constraint enforces the robot's motion limits, the fourth constraint bounds the control inputs, and the fifth constraint specifies the terminal state condition.

Therefore, the general formulation of MPIC can be established to solve for the optimal control input u. The control input obtained from Eq. (16) serves as the input to the Cartesian system, which can be converted into joint space input v according to Eq. (14), and then further used in Eq. (13) to derive the corresponding joint torque input. As shown in Eq. (16), the objective function of the optimization problem incorporates the robot's position, velocity, and external force states, enabling the controller to perform multiple task modes. For instance, when the robot is not subject to external forces, high-precision trajectory tracking can be achieved. When external forces are present, the robot can exhibit compliance or execute force-tracking tasks, such as constant-force polishing. This MPIC framework provides a predictive strategy for both robot motion and force interaction, allowing for optimal control parameters to be iteratively computed by solving the optimization problem. The closed-loop control framework is illustrated in Fig. 3.

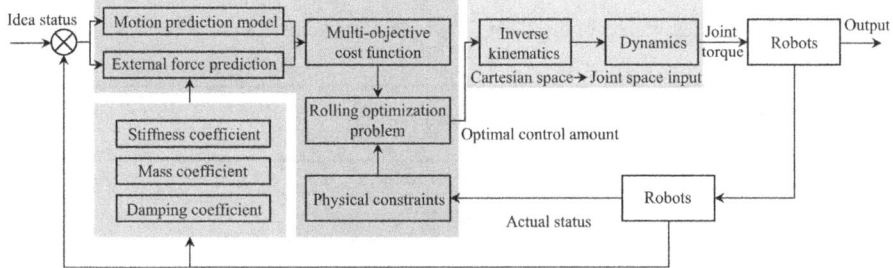

Fig. 3. Framework of the robot nonlinear model predictive impedance control.

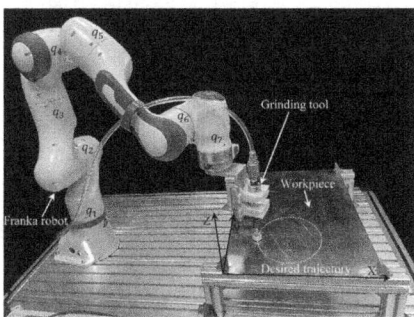

Fig. 4. Experimental setup for validating the MPIC framework. The robot end-effector is required to track a predefined trajectory while maintaining a specified contact force with the workpiece.

4 Experimental Validations

In this section, we apply the MPIC method to control the robot and conduct experiments using the Franka Panda robot (Franka Robotics GmbH.). The experimental setup is shown in Fig. 4. The MPIC algorithm was implemented in C++, leveraging the ACADO optimization library [13] to solve the model predictive optimization problem. The Franka ROS interface library and Libfranka driver library were utilized to interface with and control Franka robots, enabling real-time execution of impedance-based trajectory tracking and force regulation. The specific experimental parameters are listed in Table 1. The objective is to evaluate the motion performance and force response capability of the controller. Comparative experiments with the conventional Impedance Control (IC) method are also conducted to demonstrate the advantages of MPIC in terms of trajectory tracking accuracy, force tracking precision, and response time. The estimation of the environment stiffness and nominal surface position follows the approach in [11].

Table 1. Parameters of the MPIC controller during accuracy verifications.

Trajectory tracking accuracy verifications	Circular trajectory:	$\begin{cases} x(t) = 0.08 \cdot (1 - cos(0.625t)) \\ y(t) = 0.08 \cdot \sin(0.625t) \end{cases}$
External force tracking accuracy verification experiment	1) Constant-force target: $F_z^d = 5$ N, $z = p_e - F_z^d / K_e$ 2) Composite trajectory: $x = \begin{cases} 0.07+0.005 \cdot t^2, & t\in[0,2] \\ 0.09+0.04/\pi \cdot \sin(\pi(t-2)/2), & t\in[2,3] \\ 0.09+0.04/\pi, & t\in[3,5] \\ 0.09+0.04/\pi \cdot \cos(\pi(t-5)/2), & t\in[5,6] \\ 0.09-0.02 \cdot (t-6), & t\in[6,8] \\ 0.05-0.04/\pi \cdot \sin(\pi(t-8)/2), & t\in[8,9] \\ 0.05-0.04/\pi, & t\in[9,11] \\ 0.05-0.04/\pi \cdot \cos(\pi(t-11)/2), & t\in[11,12] \\ 0.05+0.02 \cdot (t-12)-0.005 \cdot (t-12)^2, & t\in[12,14] \end{cases}$ $\quad y = \begin{cases} 0.05-0.04/\pi, & t\in[0,2] \\ 0.05-0.04/\pi \cdot \cos(\pi(t-2)/2), & t\in[2,3] \\ 0.05+0.02 \cdot (t-3), & t\in[3,5] \\ 0.09+0.04/\pi \cdot \sin(\pi(t-5)/2), & t\in[5,6] \\ 0.09+0.04/\pi, & t\in[6,8] \\ 0.09+0.04/\pi \cdot \cos(\pi(t-8)/2), & t\in[8,9] \\ 0.09-0.02 \cdot (t-9), & t\in[9,11] \\ 0.05-0.04/\pi \cdot \sin(\pi(t-11)/2), & t\in[11,12] \\ 0.05-0.04/\pi, & t\in[12,14] \end{cases}$	
Franka Panda Robot	1) Control cycle: 1 ms 2) Control mode: joint torque control	
IC controller parameters	1) Robot stiffness coefficient: $K = 2000$ N/m 2) Robot damping coefficient: $D = 90$ N·m/s 3) Contact workpiece stiffness coefficient: $K_e = 3000$ N/m	
MPIC controller parameters	1) Prediction time domain $T_E = 20$ ms 2) $Q = \text{diag}(10^4, 10^4, 10^2, 10^2, 10^4, 10^2)$ $Q_N = 10\ Q, R = (10, 10, 10)$ 3) $V_x \in [-0.02, 0.02]$ m/s, $P_y \leq 0.09$ m	

In the trajectory tracking experiments, a two-dimensional circular reference trajectory is provided to the Franka robot. The tracking performance is evaluated based on trajectory and velocity tracking errors under different control schemes. In the force tracking experiments, a compound three-dimensional trajectory is assigned to the robot while it tracks a constant external force target. The tracking error and response time under MPIC are analyzed and compared with those under the IC controller using identical control parameters to further highlight the advantages of MPIC.

To evaluate the controller's performance in two-dimensional motion, the robot is tasked with tracking a circular trajectory with a diameter of 0.16 m at an angular velocity of 0.625 rad/s. In this scenario, the robot moves in both the X and Y directions simultaneously. The circular trajectory tracking curve under the MPIC controller is illustrated in Fig. 5(a), and the corresponding velocity tracking curve is shown in Fig. 5(b). The experimental results demonstrate that the MPIC method enables the robot to follow the circular trajectory with high precision at the specified velocity.

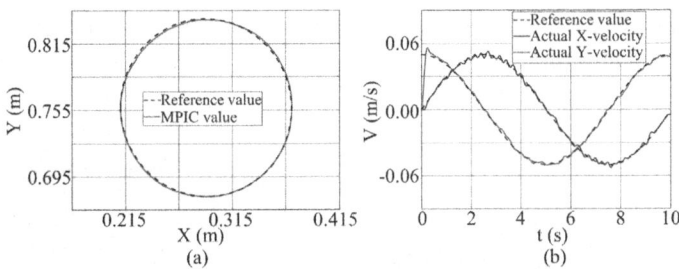

Fig. 5. Experimental results of a robot tracking a circular trajectory at a constant speed under an MPIC controller. (a) Robot trajectory tracking curve. (b) Robot speed tracking curve.

The magnified trajectory tracking errors under the IC and MPIC controllers for circular motion are shown in Fig. 6(a). The results once again demonstrate that the MPIC method yields significantly lower trajectory tracking errors compared to the traditional IC approach. Figure 6(b) presents the comparison of the mean absolute error in trajectory tracking under the circular trajectory task. In the Y direction, the IC controller results in an average trajectory error of 0.95 mm, while the MPIC controller, with the same impedance parameters, achieves an error of only 0.40 mm. In the X direction, the average trajectory error under IC is 0.80 mm, whereas MPIC reduces this error to just 0.25 mm. These results indicate that MPIC improves trajectory tracking accuracy by approximately 2–3 times in two-dimensional motion. Overall, the motion accuracy validation experiments confirm that the MPIC approach outperforms the conventional IC method in terms of trajectory tracking precision.

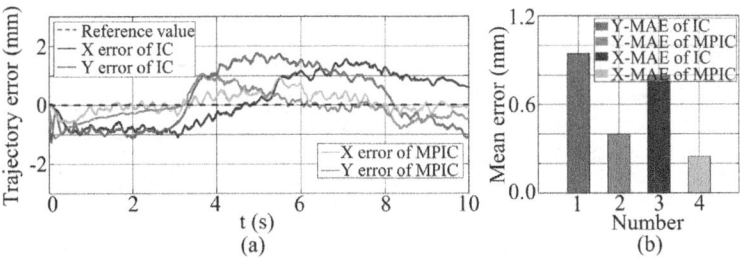

Fig. 6. Comparison results of uniform circular motion accuracy of robots under different controllers. (a) Comparison of robot trajectory tracking errors. (b) Comparison of average trajectory tracking error.

When the robot contacts the environment, it will be affected by external forces. By setting the composite trajectory in Table 1 for the robot, the robot moves along the three-dimensional composite trajectory under the MPIC method and maintains a constant contact force of 5 N in the Z direction. The result of the robot moving along the composite trajectory is shown in Fig. 7. From the experimental results, it can be seen that the trajectory of MPIC is closer to the reference trajectory, and the trajectory tracking accuracy is higher than that of the IC controller. In addition, the MPIC control framework can set constraints on the state variables of the robot. When the constraint of

Y-axis position P_y is set to be less than or equal to 0.08m, the robot trajectory will move along the constraint edge.

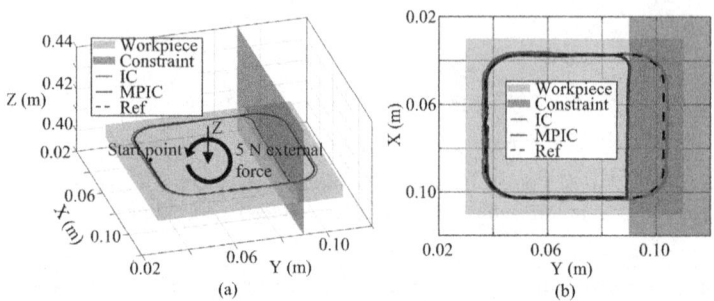

Fig. 7. Experimental results of a robot tracking a compound trajectory under external force contact. (a) Trajectory tracking under external force contact. (b) Track tracking top view.

As shown in Fig. 8, when the speed constraint $V_x \in [-0.02, 0.02]$ m/s is set, the robot speed under MPIC control will be constrained, while the robot speed under the IC control framework cannot be directly constrained, and the speed tracking curve will overshoot, and the speed tracking accuracy is significantly lower than that of the MPIC controller. The constraint property of MPIC is an additional attribute given to impedance control by the model prediction framework. This property can be used to construct the robot's motion constraints, impedance constraints, and external force constraints to adjust the robot's response characteristics.

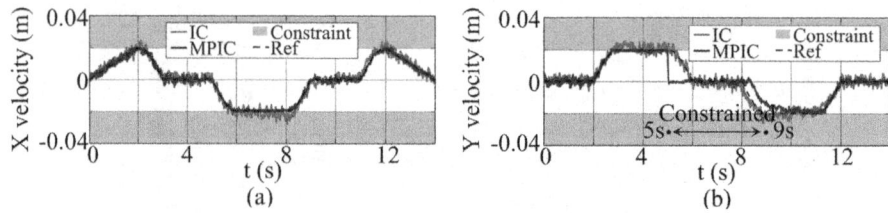

Fig. 8. Experimental results of robot velocity tracking under state constraints. (a) Comparison results of robot speed tracking in the X direction. (b) The robot's speed tracking comparison results in the Y direction.

The result in Fig. 9(a) compares the external force tracking performance of the MPIC and IC controllers. The experimental results show that the force convergence time under the IC controller is 0.205 s, whereas the MPIC controller, using the same impedance parameters, achieves force error convergence in only 0.052 s. This indicates that the MPIC controller improves the robot's force response time by a factor of four within the model predictive framework. In terms of force tracking accuracy, both controllers maintain the external force error within 1 N. Figure 9(b) presents the mean absolute error of the force tracking performance. The IC controller yields an average force error of 0.21 N, while the MPIC controller reduces the average error to 0.13 N, representing a 40% improvement in force tracking precision. These results demonstrate that MPIC enhances both trajectory and force tracking accuracy, while also supporting multi-objective constraints. Thus, MPIC serves effectively as both a motion and a force controller, making it particularly suitable for tasks involving force/position hybrid control.

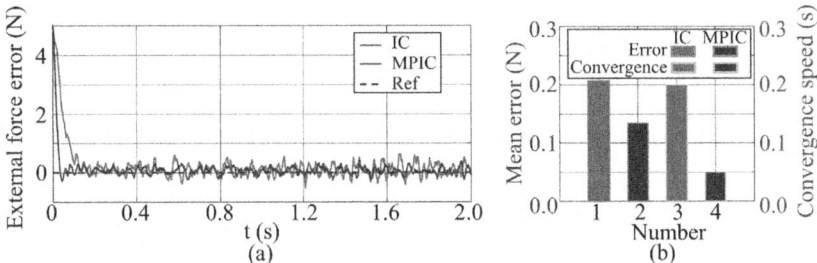

Fig. 9. Constant force tracking of a robot in model-predictive impedance control. (a) Comparison of robot external force tracking errors. (b) Comparison of external force accuracy and convergence speed.

5 Conclusion

In this paper, a Model Predictive Impedance Controller (MPIC) for robotic operations is developed, integrating Model Predictive Control (MPC) with Impedance Control (IC). The processes of iterative prediction, receding horizon optimization, and feedback correction are introduced, and the advantages of MPIC in robotic motion control are analyzed. Motion and force tracking experiments demonstrate that, compared with traditional impedance control under the same parameters, the MPIC method achieves significantly higher trajectory accuracy, force tracking precision, and response speed.

Acknowledgments. The authors would like to express their gratitude to the Key Laboratory of Advanced Manufacturing Technology for High Performance Parts, Ministry of Education for providing the research facilities throughout this work.

This work was supported in part by the Key Research & Development Program of Wuhan under Grant Number 2024060702030144, in part by the China Postdoctoral Science Foundation under Grant Number 2024M760998, and in part by the Postdoctor Project of Hubei Province under Grant Number 2024HBBHJD014.

References

1. Verl, A., Valente, A., Melkote, S., Brecher, C., Ozturk, E., Tunc, L.T.: Robots in machining. CIRP Ann. **68**(2), 799–822 (2019)
2. Shi, Y., Zhang, K.: Advanced model predictive control framework for autonomous intelligent mechatronic systems: a tutorial overview and perspectives. Annu. Rev. Control. **52**, 170–196 (2021)
3. Liang, J., Tian, Q., Feng, J., Pi, D., Yin, G.: A polytopic model-based robust predictive control scheme for path tracking of autonomous vehicles. IEEE T. Intell. Veh. **9**(2), 3928–3939 (2024)

4. Dai, L., Yu, Y., Zhai, D.-H., Huang, T., Xia, Y.: Robust model predictive tracking control for robot manipulators with disturbances. IEEE Trans. Ind. Electron. **68**(5), 4288–4297 (2021)
5. Fu, J., Burzo, I., Iovene, E., Zhao, J., Ferrigno, G., De Momi, E.: Optimization-based variable impedance control of robotic manipulator for medical contact tasks. IEEE Trans. Instrum. Meas. **73**, 1–8 (2024)
6. Shahriari, S.H.: Unified force-impedance control. Int. J. Robot. Res. **43**(13), 2112–2141 (2024)
7. Gong, C., Zhao, F., Liao, Z., Tao, T., Wang, X., Mei, X.: Simple rotation angle/axis representations based second-order impedance control. IEEE Robot. Autom. Lett. **9**(6), 5831–5838 (2024)
8. Zhang, Z., Li, T., Figueroa, N.: Constrained passive interactioncontrol: leveraging passivity and safety for robot manipulators. In: Proc. IEEE Int. Conf. Rob. Autom. (ICRA), pp. 418–424 (2024)
9. Zhang, Y., Zhao, X., Tao, B., Ding, H.: Multi-objective synchronization control for dual-robot interactive cooperation using nonlinear model predictive policy. IEEE Trans. Ind. Electron. **70**(1), 582–593 (2023)
10. Mu, Y., Zou, L., Wang, Z., Li, H., Yan, S., Wang, W.: A novel dynamic observer-based contact force control strategy in robotic grinding to improve blade profile accuracy. Robot. Comput.-Integr. Manuf. **94**, 102966 (2025)
11. Zhang, Y., Zhao, X., Chen, Y., Tao, B., Ding, H.: Observer-based variable impedance control using moving horizon estimation for robot machining thin-walled workpieces. IEEE Trans. Ind. Electron. **71**(6), 5972–5982 (2024)
12. Bednarczyk, M., Omran, H., Bayle, B.: Model predictive impedancecontrol. In: Proc. IEEE Int. Conf. Rob. Autom. (ICRA), pp. 4702–4708 (2020)
13. Houska, B., Ferreau, H.J., Diehl, M.: ACADO toolkit—an open-sourceframework for automatic control and dynamic optimization. Optimal Control Appl. Methods **32**(3), 298–312 (2011)

Dynamics Modeling and Vibration Suppression of Industrial Robots Handling Flexible Payloads

Wenyu Hu, Hongbo Hu, Zhongkai Zhang, and Chungang Zhuang(✉)

School of Mechanical Engineering, Shanghai Jiao Tong University, Shanghai 200240, China
cgzhuang@sjtu.edu.cn

Abstract. During high-speed handling of large-sized thin-walled structural components by industrial robots, flexible payloads undergo significant vibrations due to the flexibility. To describe and address the vibration issues in multi-degree-of-freedom industrial robots carrying flexible payloads, this paper established a dynamics model and developed an online modal parameters identification method with multi-mode vibration suppression methods. First, through the assumed modes method and Lagrange equation in modal coordinates, we establish the dynamics model for robot-payload systems where robot motions serve as excitation and modal coordinates describe response. Then, an online identification method is designed using the Levenberg-Marquardt algorithm to identify natural frequencies and damping ratios of multiple payload modes. Finally, based on the identified parameters, a joint-space multi-mode input shaper is developed and its capability to achieve approximate zero vibration during dynamic robot-load handling processes is theoretically demonstrated. Experiments confirmed that the proposed method effectively suppressed the vibration of regular and irregular payloads handled by a six degree-of-freedom industrial robot.

Keywords: Dynamics Modeling · Flexible Payloads · Industrial Robots · Input Shaping · Vibration suppression

1 Introduction

Industrial robot systems have been widely adopted in manufacturing across various industry fields. However, when performing tasks such as material handling and processing, industrial robots with flexible joints [1, 2], links [3] or payloads [4, 5] suffer from vibrations induced by those flexible components, leading to reduced control precision, degraded operational quality and even workpiece damage. Therefore, the vibration suppression of industrial robot systems with flexibility have attracted considerable attention. This study mainly focuses on vibration suppression for robots handling thin-plate flexible payloads, which is a common task in manufacturing.

Consider the dynamics modeling methods of robot moving flexible payloads, most scholars employ linear second-order system's transfer functions to describe the dynamic characteristics of the dynamics system [6, 7]. While this approach offers advantages such as concise formulation and computational convenience, it fails to adequately describe the vibration response of flexible payloads under motion-induced excitation in complex nonlinear dynamic systems involving multiple degree-of-freedom (DOF) industrial robots. Some scholars have employed finite element analysis (FEA) method to simulate the dynamic characteristics of complicated robot payloads handling tasks [3, 8]. However, the FEA approach needs precise CAD model and is difficult to handle unknown payloads in engineering applications [5].

Some studies have proposed combining the assumed modes method with Lagrange's modeling method to construct the dynamics model. By solving the Euler-Bernoulli equations of sheet-like payloads, the kinetic and potential energy can be calculated and then substituted into the Lagrange equation to establish the dynamics model for the robot-payload system. The approach has been extensively studied in single-link [9] and two-link flexible robots [10, 11]. To extend these approaches to six-axis robots moving flexible payloads, Mamedov et al. simplify long straight thin-plate payloads into a mass-spring-damper model [5]. However, the model proposed by [5] fails to capture the higher-order modal characteristics of the payload, thereby limiting the applications in vibration prediction and control performance.

On the other hand, for the vibration suppression tasks for robotic system, current approaches predominantly contain closed-loop control (e.g., PID control [4] and singular perturbation technique [12]) and open-loop control (e.g., trajectory optimization [13], notch filtering [2, 14] and input shaping [8, 15]). Among these, input shaping has been widely adopted due to its ease of implementation and effective vibration suppression performance.

The core of input shaping lies in determining shaper parameters based on the natural frequency and damping ratio of the target system. While nominal modal parameters (frequencies and damping ratios) of payloads can theoretically be calculated using manufacturer-provided nominal material parameters and geometric specifications, discrepancies between nominal and actual parameters result in the limited precision of such method. To obtain accurate shaper parameters, some studies apply the FEA approach [3, 8] or adaptive strategies [13, 16]. However, FEA approach, while effective, is computationally intensive and impractical for industrial applications and adaptive shaping method exhibit limited effectiveness in non-structural tasks with varying payloads. These inherent limitations in current parameter selection approaches compromise vibration suppression performance for flexible payloads.

This study primarily addresses the modeling, identification and vibration suppression tasks for industrial robots handling thin-plate flexible payloads. We integrate the assumed modes method with Lagrange's modeling method to construct a dynamics model for an n-DOF robot moving flexible payloads. Subsequently, by using end-effector force sensor data, we achieve online identification of multiple modal parameters based on the Levenberg-Marquardt (LM) algorithm. A multi-mode input shaper is then designed using the identified parameters, and the effectiveness of payloads vibration suppression through input shaping in robot joint trajectory is proved based on the proposed dynamics model. The effectiveness of the proposed vibration suppression technique for regular and irregular payloads is demonstrated through experiments.

This paper is organized as follows: Sect. 2 establishes the dynamics model of the robot handling flexible payloads, Sect. 3 discusses the proposed online modal parameters identification method and vibration suppression method, Sect. 4 presents experiment results and Sect. 5 summarizes the full study.

2 Payloads Dynamics Modeling

In this section, we establish the dynamics for an n-DOF robot handling a thin-plate flexible payload. Under the assumptions of continuity, small deformation and negligible shear deformation, the payload is idealized as a Euler-Bernoulli beam. Utilizing the assumed modes method, the shape functions for each vibration mode of the payload can be solved and superimposed. This enables the calculation of the position of any arbitrary point $P\prime$, resulting from lateral deflection of a point P' inside the payload, within the object frame:

$$y_b(x_p, t) = \sum_{i=1}^{k} \varphi_i(x_p) a_i(t), \quad x_p \in [0, L] \\ r_P^S = \begin{bmatrix} x_p & y_p + y_b(x_p, t) & z_p \end{bmatrix}^T \quad (1)$$

where $y_b(x_p, t)$ is the lateral deflection of point P', $\varphi_i(x_p)$ is the i-*th* mode shape function, $a_i(t)$ is the i-*th* generalized modal coordinate, r_P^S is defined as the coordinates of point $P\prime$ in the object frame $\{S\}$. Throughout the subsequent text, r_P^X denotes the coordinates of point $P\prime$ in an arbitrary frame $\{X\}$, L is the length of the payload and k is the considered number of finite order modes (Fig. 1).

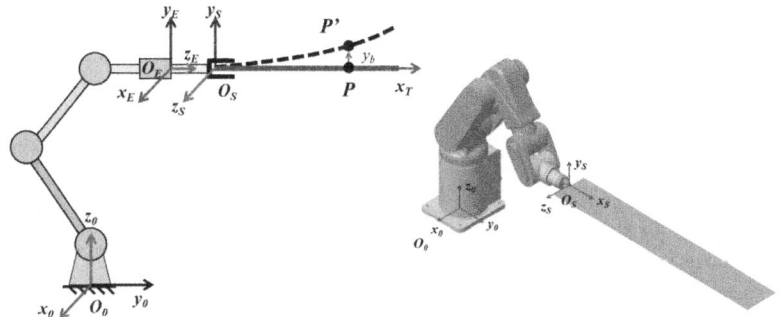

Fig. 1. Diagram of an n-DOF robot handling a flexible payload.

Consider the global position and velocity of point $P\prime$ in Cartesian space:

$$r_P^0 = R_E^0(r_P^E) + = r_{0,E}^0 = R_E^0(r_{E,S}^E + R_S^E r_P^S) + r_{0,E}^0 \\ \dot{r}_P^0 = \dot{R}_E^0(r_{E,S}^E + R_S^E r_P^S) + R_E^0 R_S^E \dot{r}_P^S) + \dot{r}_{0,E}^0 \\ = \underbrace{\dot{r}_{0,E}^0}_{term\ 1} + \underbrace{S(\omega_{0,E}^0) R_E^0(r_{E,S}^E + R_S^E r_P^S)}_{term\ 2} + \underbrace{R_E^0 R_S^E \dot{r}_P^S}_{term\ 3} \quad (2)$$

where $\{0\}$ is the global frame, $\{E\}$ is the robot end-effector frame, $\boldsymbol{R}_Y^X$ denotes the rotation matrix from any frame $\{Y\}$ to $\{X\}$, $\boldsymbol{r}_{Y,Z}^X$ represents the coordinates of the vector pointing from the origin of $\{Y\}$ (O_Y) to the origin of $\{Z\}$ (O_z) in frame $\{X\}$, $\dot{f} = \partial f/\partial t$ denotes the first-order time derivative of function f, $S(v)$ is the cross-product matrix for any vector v.

Equation (2) shows that due to the three velocity terms, the kinetic energy dT of the mass element $dm = \rho dx_p dy_p dz_p$ (ρ represents the payload density) at point P' can be calculated and expanded to six components as:

$$dT_P = \frac{1}{2}\left\|\dot{\boldsymbol{r}}_P^0\right\|_2^2 \cdot \rho dx_p dy_p dz_p$$
$$= dT_{BT} + dT_{BR} + dT_{BV} + dT_{C1} + dT_{C1} + dT_{C3} \tag{3}$$

where $\|\cdot\|_2$ is the 2-norm of the vector, $dT_{BT}, dT_{BR}, dT_{BV}$ are three major kinetic components: dT_{BT} corresponds to the kinetic energy generated by the payload's translational motion, dT_{BR} represents the kinetic energy generated by its rotational motion, and dT_{BV} accounts for the kinetic energy induced by transverse vibration of the payload. These three kinetic energy components are expressed as:

$$dT_{BT} = \frac{1}{2}\left\|\dot{\boldsymbol{r}}_{0,E}^0\right\|_2^2 \rho dx_p dy_p dz_p$$

$$dT_{BR} = \frac{1}{2}\left\|S\left(\boldsymbol{\omega}_{0,E}^0\right)\boldsymbol{R}_E^0\left(\boldsymbol{r}_{E,S}^E + \boldsymbol{R}_S^E \boldsymbol{r}_P^S\right)\right\|_2^2 \rho dx_p dy_p dz_p$$

$$dT_{BV} = \frac{1}{2}\left\|\boldsymbol{R}_E^0 \boldsymbol{R}_S^E \dot{\boldsymbol{r}}_P^S\right\|_2^2 \rho dx_p dy_p dz_p \tag{4}$$

Besides, there exists three cross-coupling kinetic energy terms $dT_{C1}, dT_{C1}, dT_{C3}$ represent, with their explicit expressions formulated as:

$$dT_{C1} = \frac{1}{2}\left[2(\dot{\boldsymbol{r}}_{0,E}^0)^T S\left(\boldsymbol{\omega}_{0,E}^0\right)\boldsymbol{R}_E^0\left(\boldsymbol{r}_{E,S}^E + \boldsymbol{R}_S^E \boldsymbol{r}_P^S\right)\right] \cdot \rho dx_p dy_p dz_p$$

$$dT_{C2} = \frac{1}{2}\left[2(\dot{\boldsymbol{r}}_{0,E}^0)^T \boldsymbol{R}_E^0 \boldsymbol{R}_S^E \dot{\boldsymbol{r}}_P^S\right] \cdot \rho dx_p dy_p dz_p$$

$$dT_{C3} = \frac{1}{2}\left[2\left(\boldsymbol{R}_E^0 \boldsymbol{R}_S^E \dot{\boldsymbol{r}}_P^S\right) S\left(\boldsymbol{\omega}_{0,E}^0\right)\boldsymbol{R}_E^0\left(\boldsymbol{r}_{E,S}^E + \boldsymbol{R}_S^E \boldsymbol{r}_P^S\right)\right]^T \cdot \rho dx_p dy_p dz_p \tag{5}$$

The potential energy U of a flexible payload primarily comprises two components: gravitational potential energy U_{BG} and the bending strain energy U_{BK}. By using Eq. (2), the gravitational potential energy of a mass element dm at point P' is expressed as:

$$dU_{BG} = -\boldsymbol{g}_0^T \left(\boldsymbol{R}_E^0\left(\boldsymbol{r}_{E,T}^E + \boldsymbol{R}_S^E \boldsymbol{r}_P^S\right) + \boldsymbol{r}_{0,E}^0\right) \cdot \rho dx_p dy_p dz_p \tag{6}$$

where $\boldsymbol{g}_0^T$ represents the gravity vector in frame $\{0\}$.

Under the linear elastic assumption, the bending strain energy is expressed as:

$$U_{BK} = \frac{1}{2}\int_0^L EI(y_b''(x))^2 dx \tag{7}$$

where E denotes the elastic modulus, I represents the second moment of area, $f' = \partial f/\partial x$ and $f'' = \partial^2 f/\partial x^2$ for any function f, and so forth. While the total kinetic energy T and potential energy $U = U_{BG} + U_{BK}$ of the payload can theoretically be calculated by integrating the aforementioned energy terms, the highly complex expressions make subsequent formulation of the Lagrange equation computationally intractable. However, in practical applications, the flexibility of the payload is much greater than that of the industrial robot links and joints. Thus, by assuming that the industrial robot possesses high rigidity of links and joints and superior control performance, the dynamics modeling process can be significantly simplified. Using this assumption and considering the mechanical damping, we apply the Lagrange equation to the modal coordinate $a = [a_1(t)a_2(t)\ldots a_n(t)]^T$:

$$-C\dot{a} = \frac{\partial}{\partial t}\left(\frac{\partial \mathcal{L}}{\partial \dot{a}}\right) - \frac{\partial \mathcal{L}}{\partial a} \quad (8)$$

where $\mathcal{L} = T - U$ is the system's Lagrangian and C is the modal damping matrix. It's observed that the expression for T_{BT} do not contain the modal coordinate components, thus no contributions into Eq. (8). Furthermore, $T_{C1}, T_{C2}, T_{C3}, T_{BR}$ (by neglecting the higher-order term of small deformation $y_b^2(x)$) and U_{BG} retain only first-order terms involving the modal coordinate a or its time derivative $\dot{a}$ since they are linear with respect to r_P^E and $\dot{r}_P^E$. Substituting these energy terms into Eq. (8) ultimately leaves expressions related to the motion of the robot itself. Consequently, the dynamic equations of the industrial robot moving a flexible payload can be formulated as:

$$M\ddot{a} + C\dot{a} + Ka = f(t) = f([q(t)\dot{q}(t)\ddot{q}(t)]) \quad (9)$$

where M is the modal mass matrix derived from dT_{BV}, K is the modal stiffness matrix derived from U_{BK} and $f([q(t)\dot{q}(t)\ddot{q}(t)])$ is the robot-motion-dependent generalized force vector.

It's worth noticed that the proposed dynamics modeling approach does not impose constraints on the payload's geometric regularity or material parameter uniformity (e.g., material density ρ and elastic modulus E). Consequently, the dynamics equation of irregular thin-plate payloads is consistent with Eq. (9).

Besides, Eq. (9) proves that payload vibration is excited by the generalized modal force f. Therefore, vibration suppression can be achieved by designing the robot's motion $q(t)$, $\dot{q}(t)$ and $\ddot{q}(t)$ to regulate f. Although f exhibits a complex formulation, the input shaping method does not require an explicit analytical expression of f in some conditions. A detailed discussion is provided in Sect. 3.2.

3 Payloads Identification and Vibration Suppression

In this section, we propose an online identification-based vibration suppression method for flexible payloads. Specifically, multiple modal parameters of the payload are first identified using end-effector force sensor data. Then a multi-mode input shaper is designed using the identified parameters. The proposed method is concluded in Fig. 2.

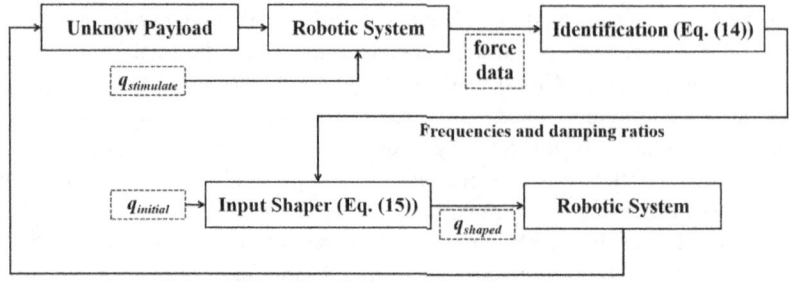

Fig. 2. The vibration suppression process of the proposed method.

3.1 Modal Parameters Identification

Consider the bending moment of the payload at any position x:

$$M_S(x,t) = -EI\frac{\partial^2 y_b(x,t)}{\partial x^2} = -EI\sum_{i=1}^{k}\varphi_i''(x)a_i(t) \tag{10}$$

The clamping torque in the vibration direction of the payload are equal to the bending moment at $x = 0$. Therefore, during the residual vibration phase, the moment can be expressed as the superposition of vibrations from different modes:

$$M_0(t) = \sum_{i=1}^{k}\frac{A_i\omega_i}{\sqrt{1-\xi^2}}e^{-\xi\omega_i t}\sin\left(\sqrt{1-\xi^2}\omega_i t + \theta_i\right) \tag{11}$$

where $M_0(t)$ represents the torque derived from the force sensor at the end effector, ω_i, A_i and θ_i are the natural frequency, the amplitude and the phase of the i-*th* mode, respectively; ξ is the damping ratio.

While the FFT enables rapid identification of modal frequencies in torque data, its identification accuracy is constrained by industrial efficiency requirements. Thus, we propose an identification method based on the LM algorithm to improve the identification accuracy. Let the optimization variable be defined as:

$$\boldsymbol{\Phi} = [A_1 \;\; \omega_1 \;\; \xi_1 \;\; \theta_1 \;\; A_2 \;\; \omega_2 \;\; \xi_2 \;\; \theta_2 \;\ldots\; \theta_k] \in \mathbb{R}^{4k} \tag{12}$$

The identification can be expressed as a nonlinear least-squares problem:

$$\begin{aligned}\min\; G(\boldsymbol{\Phi}) &= \tfrac{1}{2}\|\mathbf{r}(\boldsymbol{\Phi})\|_2^2 = \tfrac{1}{2}\sum_{i=1}^{N}\left|\tilde{M}_0(t_i;\boldsymbol{\Phi}) - M_{0i}\right|^2\\ \text{subject to}&: \;\forall j = 1,2,\ldots,k, \omega_j \geq 0,\;\; 0 < \xi_j < 1,\;\; \theta_j \in [0,\pi]\end{aligned} \tag{13}$$

where $G(\boldsymbol{\Phi})$ is the loss function, $\mathbf{r}(\boldsymbol{\Phi})$ is the residual error, $\tilde{M}_0(t_i;\boldsymbol{\Phi})$ is an estimation by substituting the i-*th* discrete time t_i and current $\boldsymbol{\Phi}$ into Eq. (11), M_{0i} is the actual force data at t_i.

The iterative formula of the LM algorithm is given by:

$$\boldsymbol{\Phi}_{u+1} = \boldsymbol{\Phi}_u - \left(\boldsymbol{J}(\boldsymbol{\Phi}_u)^\mathrm{T}\boldsymbol{J}(\boldsymbol{\Phi}_u) + \mu_u \boldsymbol{I}\right)^{-1}\boldsymbol{J}(\boldsymbol{\Phi}_u)^\mathrm{T}r(\boldsymbol{\Phi}_u) \tag{14}$$

where $\boldsymbol{\Phi}_u$ is the parameter at iteration u, $\boldsymbol{J}(\boldsymbol{\Phi}_u)$ is the Jacobian matrix, $\boldsymbol{J}(\boldsymbol{\Phi}_u)^\mathrm{T}\boldsymbol{J}(\boldsymbol{\Phi}_u)$ denotes an approximation of Hessian matrix, μ_u is the adaptive damp parameter.

By utilizing the first k-order frequencies and the damping ratio obtained via FFT and logarithmic decrement method as an initial guess for Eq. (13), rapid and precise identification of multiple modal parameters can be achieved.

3.2 Multi-mode Vibration Suppression

This part designs a multi-mode input shaper utilizing the identified modal parameters. The input shaping technique suppresses payload vibrations by convolving the input signal with a specifically designed impulse sequence. The principle of input shaping is illustrated in Fig. 3, where $f * g$ represents convoluting f and g in time domain.

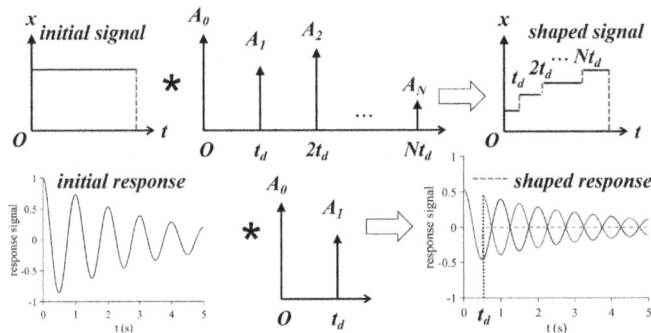

Fig. 3. The principle of input shaping.

Figure 3 also illustrates the simplest class of input shapers—the Zero Vibration (ZV) shaper, consisting of two impulses and is highly sensitive to the estimation of frequency and damping ratio. Therefore, we employ the Zero Vibration Derivative (ZVD) shaper to design a multi-mode shaper. $\forall i = 1, 2, \ldots, k$, we have:

$$I_i(t) = A_{i0}\delta(t) + A_{i1}\delta(t - t_{d,i}) + A_{i2}\delta(t - 2t_{d,i}) \\ I(t) = I_1(t) * I_2(t) * \ldots * I_k(t) \tag{15}$$

where $\delta(t)$ is the unit impulse function, A_{i0}, A_{i1} and A_{i2} is the amplitudes of the i-th mode shaper $I_i(t)$, $t_{d,i}$ is the time delay designed by zero vibration condition (ZVC):

$$\begin{bmatrix} A_{i0} & A_{i1} & A_{i2} \end{bmatrix} = \begin{bmatrix} \frac{1}{(1+h_i)^2} & \frac{2h_i}{(1+h_i)^2} & \frac{h_i^2}{(1+h_i)^2} \end{bmatrix}, t_{d,i} = \frac{\pi}{\omega_{d,i}} \tag{16}$$

where $h_i = e^{-\frac{\xi_i \pi}{\sqrt{1-\xi_i^2}}}, \omega_{d,i} = \sqrt{1-\xi_i^2}\omega_i$.

Lemma 1: By shaping the joint space trajectory $q(t)$, $\dot{q}(t)$ and $\ddot{q}(t)$ with $I_i(t)$, the i-th mode of the payload can achieve an approximate ZVC.

Proof: Consider the i-th row of the robot-payload dynamics in Eq. (9):

$$m_i \ddot{a}_i + c_i \dot{a}_i + k_i a_i = f_i(t) = f_i([q(t) \ \dot{q}(t) \ \ddot{q}(t)])$$

Given that $q(t)$, $\dot{q}(t)$ and $\ddot{q}(t)$ are continuous and differentiable while the time delay $t_{d,i}$ is sufficiently small for common flexible payloads, then f_i can be linearly approximated in the neighborhood of t:

$$f_i(I_i(t) * [q(t)\ \dot{q}(t)\ \ddot{q}(t)])$$
$$= f_i\left(\sum_{j=0}^{2} A_{ij}[q(t - jt_{d,i})\ \dot{q}(t - jt_{d,i})\ \ddot{q}(t - jt_{d,i})]\right)$$
$$\approx A_{i0}f_i(t) + A_{i1}f_i(t - t_{d,i}) + A_{i2}f_i(t - 2t_{d,i})$$
$$= I_i(t) * f_i(t)$$

which satisfy the ZVC.

Lemma 2: Using $I(t)$ to shape joint space trajectory can achieve the flexible payload multi-mode vibrations suppression.

Proof: Consider that

$$I_1(t) * I_2(t) * x(t)$$
$$= I_1(t) * (A_{20}x(t) + A_{21}x(t - t_{d2}) + A_{22}x(t - 2t_{d2}))$$
$$= A_{10}A_{20}x(t) + A_{10}A_{21}x(t - t_{d2}) + A_{10}A_{22}x(t - 2t_{d2}) +$$
$$A_{11}A_{20}x(t - t_{d1}) + A_{11}A_{21}x(t - t_{d2} - t_{d1}) +$$
$$A_{11}A_{22}x(t - 2t_{d2} - t_{d1}) + A_{12}A_{20}x(t - 2t_{d1}) +$$
$$A_{12}A_{21}x(t - t_{d2} - 2t_{d1}) + A_{12}A_{22}x(t - 2t_{d2} - 2t_{d1})$$
$$= I_2(t) * I_1(t) * x(t)$$

Then, $\forall i = 1, 2, \ldots, k$:

$$I_S(t) * x(t) = I_{S1} * \ldots * I_{S(i-1)} * I_{S(i+1)} * \ldots * I_{Sk} * (I_{Si} * x(t))$$
$$= I_{S1} * \ldots * I_{S(i-1)} * I_{S(i+1)} * \ldots * I_{Sk} *$$
$$= 0$$

which satisfy the ZVC.

4 Experiments

In this section, we present experiment results to validate the effectiveness of the proposed modal parameters identification method and vibration suppression method. The experiments were constructed using an SRE4–600 6-DOF industrial robot and an SRI-M4313M4C 6-axis force/torque sensor. To verify the vibration suppression effect of the proposed method on both regular and irregular payloads, four distinct payloads were selected for experimentation, including two regular rectangular thin-plate payloads with different materials and size (named as Al6061–01 and PMMA-02) and two payloads with irregular shape (named as PMMA-KNIFE and PMMA-ME), which are rigidly connected to the robot via a clamp at one end while the other end remains free. Additionally, two handling trajectories were implemented: a simple vertical motion (named as Trajectory 1) and a complex arc-shaped motion (named as Trajectory 2). The details of experiment platform are illustrated in Fig. 4.

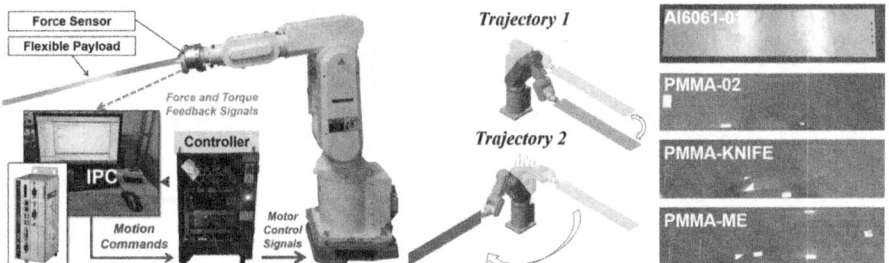

Fig. 4. The 6-DOF industrial experiment.

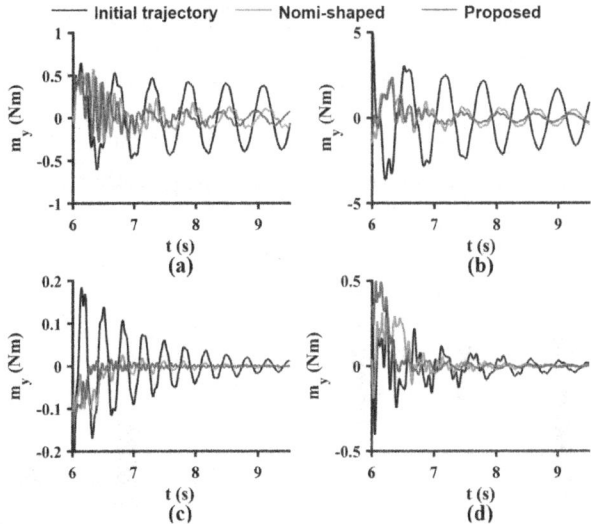

Fig. 5. Vibration data of regular payloads.

For the regular payloads, the robot executes three distinct trajectories: the original trajectory, the trajectory shaped with nominal modal parameters (named as nomi-shaped) and the trajectory shaped by the proposed identified parameters and multi-mode input shaper. The y-axis torque of the end-effector force sensor is recorded during each motion tasks, as illustrated in Fig. 5, where Fig. 5(a) shows the torque data of Al6061–01 under the initial and shaped trajectory 1, Fig. 5(b) shows the torque data of Al6061–01 under the trajectory 2. Figure 5(c) and (d) show the data of PMMA-02 in trajectory 1 and 2, respectively.

For the irregularly payloads, due to the intractability of deriving analytical solutions for their mode shape functions, the proposed identification-based parameter shaping method is applied for vibration suppression, as illustrated in Fig. 6, where Fig. 6(a) and (b) show the data of PMMA-KNIFE in trajectory 1 and 2, respectively; Fig. 6(c) and (d) show the data of PMMA-ME in trajectory 1 and 2, respectively.

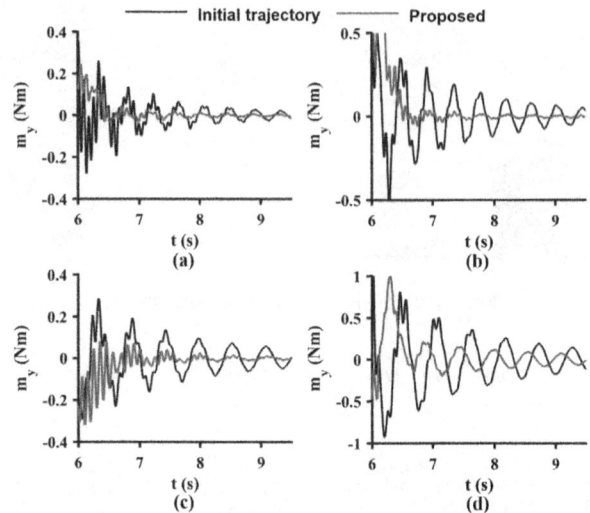

Fig. 6. Vibration data of irregular payloads

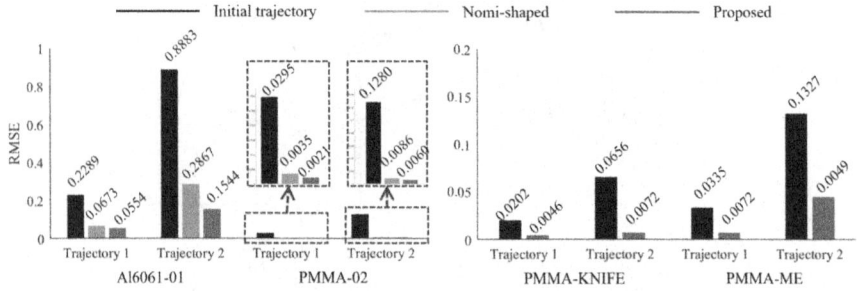

Fig. 7. The residual vibration RMSE of the flexible payloads under trajectory 1 and 2

The residual vibration root mean square error (RMSE) of torque data was statistically analyzed across all four payloads under different handling trajectories. For regular payloads, the proposed method achieved an 86.65% reduction for RMSE in average compared to the unshaped trajectories and a 33.25% reduction in average relative to nomi-shaped trajectories. For irregular payloads, the proposed method achieved an 85.27% reduction in RMSE versus the unshaped trajectories. The RMSE results of all payloads is shown in Fig. 7. These results collectively demonstrate that the proposed method achieves robust vibration suppression across diverse payloads and handling trajectories, thereby validating its generalization capability.

5 Conclusion

This paper proposes dynamics modeling method, modal parameters identification method and multi-mode input shaping method for industrial robots handling flexible payloads, aimed at suppressing vibrations during high-speed transportation of large-sized thin-plate structural components. Firstly, the dynamics model is constructed using assumed modes method and Lagrange equation in modal coordinates. Then, an identification method of natural frequencies and damping ratios of various orders of mode using the LM algorithm is proposed. Subsequently, the identified parameters are utilized to design a multi-mode input shaper. Experiments conducted on a 6-DOF industrial robot and different flexible payloads validate the effectiveness and robustness of the proposed approach. Future work will investigate the stability and versatility of the proposed method under industrial production environments with high-speed operations demand and external disturbances. Besides, the practical application of the proposed method in industrial robot payload-handling operations and extending the proposed methodology to complex scenarios such as flexible-body assembly and machining tasks can be further studied.

Acknowledgement. This work was sponsored by The Explorers Program of Shanghai (Basic Research Funding) under Grant 24TS1414700 and the National Key Research and Development Program of China under Grant 2022YFB4700300.

References

1. Moyrón, J., Moreno-Valenzuela, J.: Nonlinear PI "D"-type control of flexible joint robots by using motor position measurements is globally asymptotically stable. IEEE Trans. Autom. Control **68**(6), 3648–3655 (2023)
2. Zhu, Z., et al.: Improved notch filter method for vibration suppression of flexible joint robots with harmonic reducers. In: 16th International Conference on Intelligent Robotics and Applications (ICIRA), Singapore, Singapore, pp. 497–508 (2023)
3. Shi, M., Cheng, Y., Rong, B., Zhao, W., Yao, Z.: Research on vibration suppression and trajectory tracking control strategy of a flexible link manipulator. Appl. Math. Model. **110**, 78–98 (2022)
4. Kapsalas, C.N., Sakellariou, J.S., Koustoumpardis, P.N., Aspragathos, N.A.: An ARX-based method for the vibration control of flexible beams manipulated by industrial robots. Robot. Comput.-Integr. Manuf. **52**, 76–91 (2018)
5. Mamedov, S., Astudillo, A., Ronzani, D., Decré, W., Noël, J., Swevers, J.: An optimal open-loop strategy for handling a flexible beam with a robot manipulator. In: 40th IEEE International Conference on Robotics and Automation (ICRA), London, UK, pp. 3168–3174 (2023)
6. Md Zain, M.Z., Tokhi, M.O., Mohamed, Z.: Hybrid learning control schemes with input shaping of a flexible manipulator system. Mechatronics **16**, 209–219 (2006)
7. Pereira, E., Trapero, J.R., Díaz, I.M., Feliu, V.: Adaptive input shaping for single-link flexible manipulators using an algebraic identification. Control Eng. Pract. **20**, 138–147 (2012)
8. Zhou, T., Zu, J. Goldenberg, A. A.: Vibration controllability of flexible robot-payload systems. In: 17th IEEE International Conference on Robotics and Automation (ICRA), San Francisco, CA, USA, pp. 1484–1489 (2000)

9. He, W., Ouyang, Y., Hong, J.: Vibration control of a flexible robotic manipulator in the presence of input deadzone. IEEE Trans. Ind. Inform. **13**(1), 48–58 (2017)
10. Gao, H., He, W., Zhou, C., Sun, C.: Neural network control of a two-link flexible robotic manipulator using assumed mode method. IEEE Trans. Ind. Inform. **15**(2), 755–764 (2019)
11. Meng, Q., Lai, X., Yan, Z., Wu, M.: Tip position control and vibration suppression of a planar two-link rigid-flexible underactuated manipulator. IEEE T. Cybern. **52**(7), 6771–6783 (2022)
12. Esakki, B., Bhat, R.B., Su, C.: Trajectory tracking and vibration control of two planar rigid manipulators moving a flexible object. In: 4th International Conference on Intelligent Robotics and Applications (ICIRA), Aachen, Germany, pp. 376–387 (2011)
13. Ronzani, D., Mamedove, S., Swevers, J.: Vibration free flexible object handling with a robot manipulator using learning control. IFAC-PapersOnLine **56–2**, 9360–9365 (2023)
14. Xu, S., Wu, Z., Liu, P.: Reversible position domain notch filter for suppressing vibrations caused by kinematic errors in flexible joint robots. IEEE Trans. Ind. Electron. **72**(2), 1723–1731 (2025)
15. Newman, M., Lu, K., Khoshdarregi, M.: Suppression of robot vibrations using input shaping and learning-based structural models. J. Intell. Mater. Syst. Struct. **32**(9), 1001–1012 (2021)
16. Thomsen, D.K., Søe-Knudsen, R., Balling, O., Zhang, X.: Vibration control of industrial robot arms by multi-mode time-varying input shaping. Mech. Mach. Theory **155**, 104072 (2021)

Dual-Channel Adaptive Impedance Algorithm with Leveling Module in Dual-Arm Collaborative Robots

Yuhan Lu, Zhongkai Zhang, Pengxin Zha, Hongbo Hu, and Chungang Zhuang$^{(\boxtimes)}$

Robotics Institute, School of Mechanical Engineering, Shanghai Jiao Tong University, Shanghai 200240, China
cgzhuang@sjtu.edu.cn

Abstract. Dual-arm collaborative manipulation requires precise force control to ensure both task accuracy and workpiece safety. Traditional single-channel impedance controllers struggle to decouple internal and external force behaviors and cannot adapt their interaction dynamics online when workpiece compliance or contact conditions vary. This paper introduces a dual-channel adaptive impedance control algorithm with a leveling module to overcome these limitations. First, a dual-channel architecture is proposed that independently adapts virtual stiffness and damping gains based on measured internal force errors, protecting the workpiece from over-compression. Second, an external-force leveling module is designed to monitor residual force imbalances and apply corrective adjustments to maintain stable, balanced operation of the workpiece. Finally, the effectiveness of the proposed method is validated through simulation studies. The results demonstrate that our approach achieves faster convergence, lower steady-state force-tracking errors, and enhanced robustness under varying disturbance and complex contact scenarios compared to conventional single-channel and normal impedance controllers.

Keywords: Dual-arm Collaborative Robot · Dual-channel Adaptive Impedance Control · Leveling Algorithm · Force Decoupling

1 Introduction

With the rapid advancement of dual-arm robotic systems in industrial assembly [1], collaborative manipulation [2] and precision surface finishing [3], effective control of interaction forces at each end-effector has become essential for both task accuracy and workpiece integrity. In cooperative dual-arm tasks, internal forces, those transmitted through the workpiece between the two arms, must be carefully managed alongside external forces exchanged with the environment to prevent part deformation and maintain a stable grip [4].

Existing force-tracking schemes face two fundamental challenges. The first is that traditional impedance or admittance controllers depend on precise knowledge of environmental parameters such as workpiece stiffness and mass, which are often unknown in real-world tasks [5]. The second is that fixed-gain controllers cannot adapt online to rapid disturbances or variations in contact conditions, risking over-compression of delicate workpieces or loss of tracking under dynamic loads [6].

Early compliant control strategies for dual-arm robots employed constant impedance laws or hybrid position/force schemes to separate motion and force tasks [7]. While these methods achieve basic compliance, they cannot adjust interaction dynamics during execution and require manual retuning when workpiece properties change [8]. Subsequent approaches introduced adaptive stiffness adaptation, tuning virtual stiffness online based on internal force error to better accommodate unknown workpiece compliance, and symmetrical adaptive admittance strategies that modify virtual damping for dual-arm coordination under trajectory deviations [9].

Despite these advances, fixed-parameter impedance controllers still struggle with large or rapid variations in workpiece stiffness without manual intervention, often resulting in force overshoots or sluggish response when contact dynamics shift unexpectedly. Hybrid and admittance-based schemes can secure force tracking only by sacrificing position accuracy or tolerating residual inter-arm force imbalances, particularly under unmodeled dynamic disturbances or calibration uncertainties [10].

Recent reviews have highlighted the benefits of architectures that adapt stiffness and damping gains separately, mirroring human-like force modulation by shaping static and dynamic interaction responses independently [11]. Dual-channel impedance control frameworks, one channel for stiffness adaptation and another for damping adaptation, offer finer control over both internal and external force behaviors and hold promise for robust dual-arm manipulation [12].

Building on these insights, we partition the overall control algorithm into two coordinated subsystems. The internal-force protection subsystem applies a dual-channel adaptive impedance law that adjusts both virtual stiffness and damping gains online in response to measured internal force errors, ensuring the workpiece is not overcompressed or damaged. The external-force leveling subsystem employs a leveling module to monitor residual external force imbalances and issue corrective adjustments, maintaining stable, balanced workpiece motion. The main contributions of this paper are:

1. Proposed a dual-channel adaptive impedance architecture that integrates online stiffness and damping adaptation for robust internal-force protection under unknown contact dynamics.
2. An external-force leveling module that monitors unbalanced forces and applies corrective actions is considered to ensure stable workpiece operation.
3. Comprehensive validation is carried out through simulations, demonstrating faster convergence, lower steady-state force-tracking errors and enhanced robustness compared to conventional single-channel impedance and hybrid/admittance controllers.

2 Motion Control and Force Decoupling of Collaborative Task

2.1 Dual-Arm Motion Control with Closed-Chain Constraints

Coordinated load handling with dual arms is a typical task for dual-arm closely coordinated operations, which refers to a dual-arm robot lifting and moving a target workpiece through gripping. It is assumed that both the robotic arm and the workpiece being manipulated are rigid bodies. To better describe the relationship of the dual-arm system, it is necessary to model the entire robotic dual-arm and the gripped workpiece, as shown in Fig. 1.

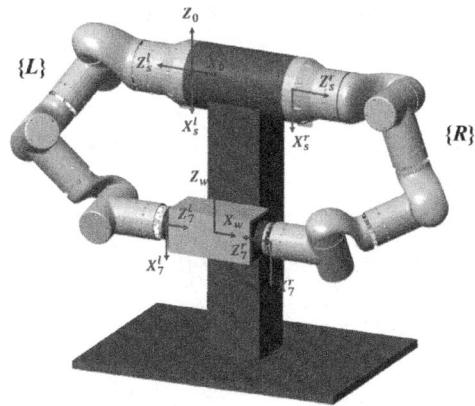

Fig. 1. Dual-arm robot kinematic closed chain configuration

The relevant coordinates are:

- The arm base coordinate relative to the world coordinate $\{0\}$, $_s^0 T$;
- The right arm base coordinate relative to the left arm base coordinate, $_r^l T$;
- The left/right arm end effectors coordinates relative to their base coordinate, $_7^s T_i$;
- The workpiece coordinate relative to the world coordinate $\{0\}$, $_w^0 T$;
- The workpiece coordinate relative to the end effectors coordinate, $_w^7 T_i$;

$i \in \{L, R\}$ represents the left and the right arm.

In dual-arm gripping control, for better simulating the environment of most dual-arm gripping tasks, both position control and force control methods are applied. A 6 degrees of freedom pose is utilized to set the motion trajectory of the center of mass of the gripped workpiece in the Cartesian space, which can be described as:

$$(\underbrace{x, y, z}_{\text{Position}}, \underbrace{\alpha, \beta, \gamma}_{\text{Orientation}}) \tag{1}$$

where α is the roll angle of the workpiece coordinate $\{w\}$ relative to the world coordinate $\{0\}$ (rotation around the x-axis), and β is the pitch angle rotating around the y-axis, then γ is the yaw angle rotating around the z-axis.

So that the rotation matrix of the workpiece coordinate {w} relative to the world coordinate {0} can be defined as:

$$^0_w R_{XYZ}(\alpha, \beta, \gamma) = R_Z(\gamma) R_Y(\beta) R_X(\alpha) \quad (2)$$

and then the homogeneous transformation matrix can be obtained:

$$^0_w T = \begin{bmatrix} & & & x \\ & ^0_w R_{XYZ}(\alpha, \beta, \gamma) & & y \\ & & & z \\ 0 & 0 & 0 & 1 \end{bmatrix} \quad (3)$$

Assuming that the dual arm robot is gripping stably, there is no gap between the robot end effectors and the workpiece, and the gripped workpiece has a relatively large rigidity with no deformation. Setting the distance between the center of the mass of the workpiece and the end effectors of dual arm previously, the homogeneous transformation matrix of the left and the right link7 coordinate {7} relative to the base-link coordinate {s}:

$$\begin{aligned} ^s_7 T_L &= (^0_s T)^{-1} {}^0_w T (^7_w T_L)^{-1}, \\ ^s_7 T_R &= (^0_s T'_r T)^{-1} {}^0_w T (^7_w T_R)^{-1} \end{aligned} \quad (4)$$

where l represents the distance between the center of the mass of the workpiece and the end effectors of dual arm.

Thus, the joint position is given by the single arm inverse kinematic:

$$q_i = IK(^s_7 T_i) \quad (5)$$

where q is the vector of system-input joint angles, and $i \in \{L, R\}$ represents the left and the right arm.

2.2 Dual-Arm Gripping Force Decoupling Model

Building on previous work [13], when multiple manipulators jointly grip a single workpiece, the total applied force can be rigorously split into an external component F_{ext} which governs the workpiece's rigid-body motion by balancing its dynamics and counteracting environmental contact forces, and an internal component T_{int}, which, while not affecting the workpiece's movement, is essential for securing a firm, stable, and safe grip. In this section, we therefore focus on carrying out this decomposition of total applied force into its external and internal constituents.

As Fig. 2, the origin O_w of the workpiece's coordinate frame is defined at its center of mass. The resultant external force acting on the workpiece is denoted as F_{env}. For each manipulator, a local coordinate frame O_i is defined at the contact point between the manipulator's end-effector and the workpiece. The contact force exerted by the i-th manipulator on the workpiece is represented as F_i.

The dynamics of dual-arm robot can be written as:

$$M(q)\ddot{q} + C(q, \dot{q}) + G(q) + f(q, \dot{q}) = \tau_m - J^T F \quad (6)$$

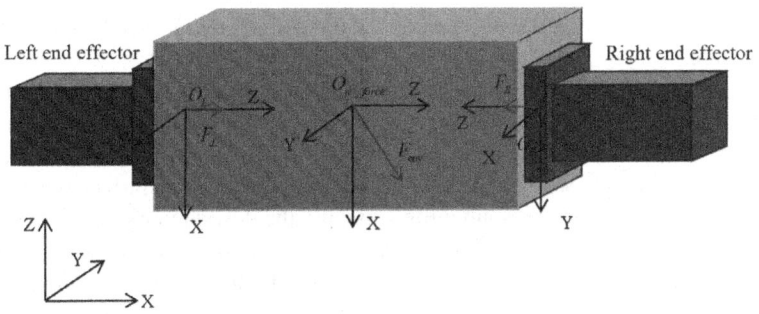

Fig. 2. Dual-arm robot end effectors and workpiece gripping model

where M represents the inertia matrix of the dual-arm robot. The matrix is a positive definite symmetric matrix given by $M = [M_L, M_R]$, and J is the Jacobian matrix which is given by $J = [J_L, J_R]$, and q is the joint angle vector, which can be obtained as $q = [q_L, q_R]^T$. $\dot{q}, \ddot{q}$ represent the joint angular velocity vector and the joint angular acceleration vector, respectively. C represents the Coriolis force and centrifugal force vector, f represents the internal force generated by friction in the joint, G is the gravitational force, τ_m represents the driving torque output by the built-in motor of the joint, and F represents the contact force vector between the robotic arm and the workpiece contact.

Similar to the dual-arm robot dynamics, the dynamics of the target workpiece can be constructed as:

$$M_w \ddot{y} + C_w \dot{y} + G_w = F_w + F_{env} \tag{7}$$

where $y, \dot{y}, \ddot{y}$ are the position, velocity, and acceleration vectors of the workpiece, respectively. F_w refers to the contact force exerted by the robotic arm on the workpiece, F_{env} is the contact force between the external environment and the workpiece. The contact approach and relative pose of the robotic arm with the workpiece directly determine the relationship between the force at the contact point and the force at the execution point:

$$F_w = J_w^T F \quad J_w = \begin{bmatrix} J_{wL}^T & J_{wR}^T \end{bmatrix}^T \tag{8}$$

where J_{wL}, J_{wR} represent the grasp matrix of the left and the right arm. According to previous work [14], the grasp matrix can be written as:

$$J_{wi} = \begin{bmatrix} I_{3\times 3} & S(r_i) \\ O_{3\times 3} & I_{3\times 3} \end{bmatrix} \tag{9}$$

in which $I_{3\times 3}, O_{3\times 3}$ denote the identity matrix and the zero matrix respectively, and r_i represents the vector of the i-th arm end effector coordinate system origin to the workpiece centroid coordinate system origin. $S(\bullet)$ represents the anti-symmetric matrix operator.

The dual-arm robot and the target workpiece it grips together form a closed dynamic system, which we consider as an integrated whole in our analysis. The contact forces between the robot arms and the workpiece can be partially defined as the internal forces of the system.

These internal forces arise from the interaction caused by the relative motion tendency between the workpiece and the robot arms, and they do not affect the position, velocity, or acceleration of the workpiece. The other part is referred to as the external force, which enables the workpiece to overcome environmental disturbances and initiate motion, serving as the driving source for achieving the desired workpiece trajectory.

According to this definition, it is clear that the external forces acting on the workpiece have no influence on the internal forces, regardless of whether they are applied or not. This separation allows the internal and external forces of the robot arms to be analyzed independently from the environment. The decomposition of internal and external forces is as follows:

$$\begin{aligned} F_{ext} &= J_w^{T-} J_w^T F \\ F_{int} &= \left(I_{2n \times 2n} - J_w^{T-} J_w^T \right) F \end{aligned} \quad (10)$$

where n denotes the degrees of freedom of single arm, and J_w^{T-} represents the generalized inverse matrix of J_w^T.

In this manner, once the contact force and the vector of end effector to the workpiece centroid is known, the internal force and external force can be calculated by Eq. (10), then they can be applied into the proposed algorithm afterwards.

3 Dual-Channel Adaptive Impedance Algorithm with the Leveling Module

The presence of accumulated nonlinearities in the dual robotic arm system, such as joint friction and kinematic inaccuracies at the end effectors, makes it challenging to maintain smooth and stable dual-arm cooperative manipulation. It is essential to dynamically regulate the balance of the gripped workpiece during manipulation and ensure that the internal forces applied remain within a safe range.

The contact force F can be measured using a six-axis force/torque sensor mounted at the end effector of the robotic arm. By performing internal-external force decomposition, the measured force can be separated into the internal force component F_{int} and the external force component F_{ext}, which are then used as inputs to the workpiece impedance and manipulator impedance models, respectively, therefore, the algorithm flowchart is shown in Fig. 3.

3.1 Dual-Channel Adaptive Impedance Control Algorithm Design

After decomposing the contact force between the manipulator and the workpiece into internal and external components, the internal force F_{int} is fed directly as the input to the Cartesian space impedance controller, thereby shaping the system's compliance to maintain a stable, damage-free grip. The impedance control law can be derived as:

$$M_i \ddot{x}_e + D_i \dot{x}_e + K_i x_e = F_e \quad (11)$$

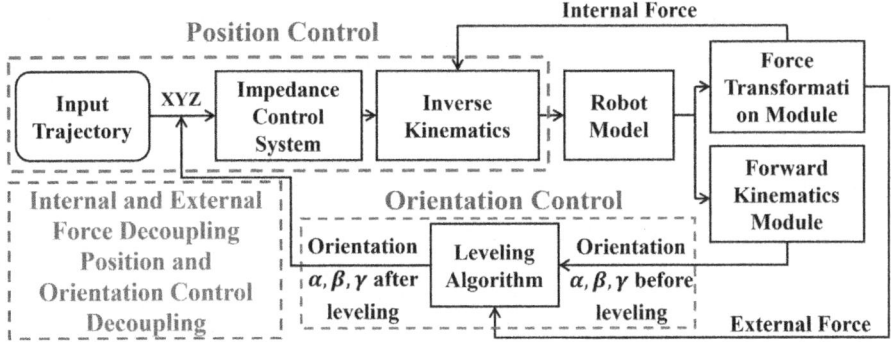

Fig. 3. The block diagram of the adaptive impedance control algorithm with internal-external force decoupling

where M_i, D_i, K_i are the inertia matrix, damping matrix, stiffness matrix, respectively, which are positive definite. F_e is the error of internal force.

Where the tracking error is:

$$x_e = x - x^*, \quad \dot{x}_e = \dot{x} - \dot{x}^*, \quad \ddot{x}_e = \ddot{x} - \ddot{x}^* \tag{12}$$

where $x_e, \dot{x}_e, \ddot{x}_e$ are the position, velocity, acceleration error, respectively.

However, when gripping an uncertain workpiece with a dual-arm collaborative robot, the system may face unknown changes in stiffness and damping. Traditional fixed-parameter impedance control is difficult to adapt to such dynamic changes. Therefore, It is necessary to make real-time adjustments for stiffness and damping, respectively. The dual-channel adaptive variable impedance law is proposed as:

$$M_i \ddot{x}_e + D_i(t) \dot{x}_e + K_i(t) x_e = F_e \tag{13}$$

where $K_i(t) = \lambda(t)/b \cdot x_e$. $\lambda(t)$ is the cumulative error gain of stiffness, which can be calculate as $\lambda(t) = \lambda(t - T) + \frac{\sigma}{b} F_e$. σ is the update rate and b is the normalization factor. T is the sampling period. In the same way, $D_i(t) = \varepsilon(t)/b \cdot \dot{x}_e$. $\varepsilon(t)$ is the cumulative error gain of damping, which can be calculate as $\varepsilon(t) = \varepsilon(t - T) + \frac{\gamma}{b} F_e$, γ is the update rate of $\varepsilon(t)$.

Thus, the end effectors position after compensating can be denoted as:

$$x_r = x_d + \frac{1}{K_i(t)} F_e - \frac{D_i(t)}{K_i(t)} \dot{x}_e - \frac{M_i}{K_i(t)} \ddot{x}_e \tag{14}$$

3.2 Stability and Convergence of Dual-Channel Adaptive Impedance Control

In this section, global asymptotic stability of the proposed dual-channel adaptive impedance controller is established. Following the Lyapunov-based methodology, a Lyapunov function is proposed:

$$V(t) = \frac{1}{2} \dot{\mathbf{e}}^T M \dot{\mathbf{e}} + \frac{1}{2} \mathbf{e}^T K_i(t) \mathbf{e} + \frac{b}{2\sigma} \|\lambda(t) - \lambda_0\|^2 + \left\|\frac{b}{2\sigma}\right\|^2 + \|\varepsilon(t) - \varepsilon_0\|^2 \tag{15}$$

where $K_i(t) = \lambda(t)/b \cdot e$, $D_i(t) = \varepsilon(t)/b \cdot \dot{e}$, and λ_0, ε_0 are the initial estimates. Clearly $V(t) \geq 0$ and $V(t) = 0$ only if $e = \dot{e} = 0$ and $\lambda = \lambda_0$, $\varepsilon = \varepsilon_0$.

The derivative form of the Lyapunov function is obtained:

$$\dot{V} = \dot{e}^T M \ddot{e} + \frac{1}{2}\dot{K}_i e^T e + e^T K_i \dot{e} + \frac{b}{\sigma}(\lambda - \lambda_0)^T \dot{\lambda} + \frac{b}{\sigma}(\varepsilon - \varepsilon_0)^T \dot{\varepsilon}. \tag{16}$$

substituting closed-loop dynamics:

$$M\ddot{e} = -D_i \dot{e} - K_i e + \Delta f \tag{17}$$

then Lyapunov function can be described as:

$$\dot{V} = -\dot{e}^T D_i \dot{e} + \dot{e}^T \Delta f + \frac{1}{2}\dot{K}_i e^T e^T + \frac{b}{\sigma}(\lambda - \lambda_0)^T \dot{\lambda} + \frac{b}{\sigma}(\varepsilon - \varepsilon_0)^T \dot{\varepsilon} \tag{18}$$

substituting $\dot{K}_i = \frac{\dot{\lambda}}{b}e + \frac{\lambda}{b}\dot{e}$, $\dot{\lambda} = \frac{\sigma}{b}\Delta f$, leads to exact cancellation of all cross-terms involving $\dot{e}^T \Delta f$ and the adaptive updates, leaving

$$\dot{V} = -\dot{e}^T D_i \dot{e} \leq 0 \tag{19}$$

since D_i is positive definite the derivative form of the Lyapunov function $\dot{V} \leq 0$, which in turn implies that e and $\dot{e}$ remain bounded. To show that $\dot{V}$ is uniformly continuous, computing its second derivative along system trajectories:

$$\ddot{V}(t) = \frac{d}{dt}\left(-\dot{e}^T D_i \dot{e}\right) = -2\dot{e}^T D_i(t)\ddot{e} - \dot{e}^T \dot{D}_i(t)\dot{e} \tag{20}$$

Because $\ddot{e}$ and $\dot{D}_i$ are both bounded under the control law, $\ddot{V}(t)$ is bounded. It follows that $\lim_{t\to\infty} \dot{V} = 0$, which forces $\dot{e} \to 0$. Restricting attention to the invariant set where $\dot{e} = 0$ in the closed-loop error dynamics shows that e must also converge to zero. Therefore, the equilibrium $(e, \dot{e}) = (0,0)$ is uniformly asymptotically stable. Finally, since $V(t)$ is radially unbounded in e and $\dot{e}$, this stability holds globally.

3.3 The Leveling Module of Orientation Regulation

To ensure stable dual-arm gripping, the desired internal force is prescribed as a fixed magnitude, which is large enough to prevent workpiece slippage yet below the deformation threshold, and the end effector position of both manipulators are adjusted so that the actual internal force tracks this set value.

The leveling module is responsible for adjusting the end effectors attitude so that the workpiece remains level under asymmetric contact forces. Starting from the previous homogeneous transform $T_{w,last}$, which contains the last known end effector orientation. Firstly, extracting the last known Euler angles α_{last}, β_{last}, γ_{last} about the sensor frame via

$$\beta_{last} = \arcsin(-T_{w,last}(3,1))$$
$$\alpha_{last} = \arcsin\left(\frac{T_{w,last}(3,2)}{\cos\beta_{last}}\right) \tag{21}$$
$$\gamma_{last} = \arcsin\left(\frac{T_{w,last}(2,1)}{\cos\beta_{last}}\right)$$

Next, let the left and right end-effector force readings in the horizontal plane be f_x^L, f_y^L, f_x^R, f_y^R, and define their discrete-time derivatives by

$$\dot{f}_x^L = \frac{f_x^L - f_{x,\text{last}}^L}{\Delta t}, \quad \dot{f}_y^L = \frac{f_y^L - f_{y,\text{last}}^L}{\Delta t} \tag{22}$$

and similar for $\dot{f}_x^R, \dot{f}_y^R$, where Δt is the controller sampling period.

Then the incremental corrections $\Delta\alpha$, $\Delta\beta$, $\Delta\gamma$ can be computed using the proportional-derivative law:

$$\Delta\alpha = K_p\left(f_x^L - f_x^R\right) + K_v\left(\dot{f}_x^L - \dot{f}_x^R\right),$$
$$\Delta\beta = K_p\left(-f_y^L + f_y^R\right) + K_v\left(-\dot{f}_y^L + \dot{f}_y^R\right), \tag{23}$$
$$\Delta\gamma = -K_p \gamma_{\text{last}}$$

where K_p sets the stiffness of the force-difference feedback correcting roll and pitch by sensing left-right and front-back imbalances, and K_v damps rapid force changes to suppress oscillation. The yaw correction $\Delta\gamma$ is a simple proportional term driving γ back toward zero.

Finally, the updated attitude can be given by:

$$\begin{bmatrix} \alpha \\ \beta \\ \gamma \end{bmatrix} = \begin{bmatrix} \alpha_{\text{last}} \\ \beta_{\text{last}} \\ \gamma_{\text{last}} \end{bmatrix} + \begin{bmatrix} \Delta\alpha \\ \Delta\beta \\ \Delta\gamma \end{bmatrix} \tag{24}$$

the updated attitude is passed to the inverse-kinematics module. In this way, the balance module continually levels the gripped workpiece by using force-difference feedback to generate smooth, stable attitude adjustments.

4 Simulation Validation

To verify the proposed algorithm and analysis, a series of simulation has been conducted. This paper employs MATLAB Simulink module to test dual-channel adaptive impedance control and the leveling module. All the simulation below is conducted during a slowly lift process.

1) Leveling module

To simulate the inclined gripping situation, a constant angle is configured to the orientation of the workpiece, and for simplifying the description, the roll angle α is taken for analyzing. Set the initial roll angle $\alpha = 0.1$ rad, and the $K_p=1.0e-02$ and $K_v=1.0e-07$ in Eq. (23).

Figure 4 shows us the adjustment of leveling module when the workpiece is inclined with the preset K_p and K_v parameters. The inclined angle is compensated rapidly and reaches 0 rad, which means the leveling module can effectively maintain the balance of workpiece and make sure it is gripped smoothly.

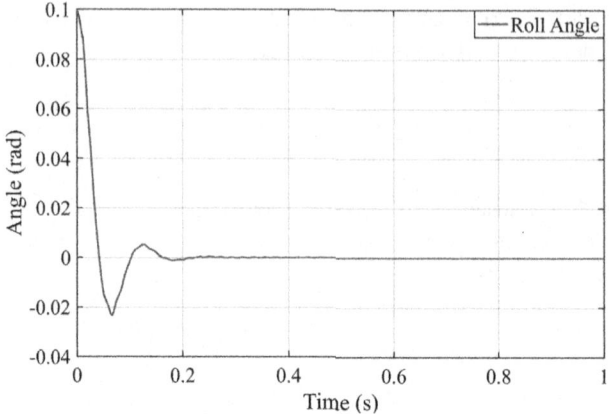

Fig. 4. The roll angle regulation by leveling module

2) Dual-channel adaptive impedance control

To keep the workpiece gripped, the internal force is set as 20 N, and to simulate the effect of the Dual-channel adaptive impedance control in the real situation, the kinematic error and the external disturbance are employed respectively and simultaneously. And we reproduce the damping-adaptive only impedance control for comparison. The initial kinematic error e_x is given on x-axis direction, and for simplicity is set equal to 0.01 m. To simplify the variation, the internal force shown in Fig. 5 is compensated from 20 N to 0 N.

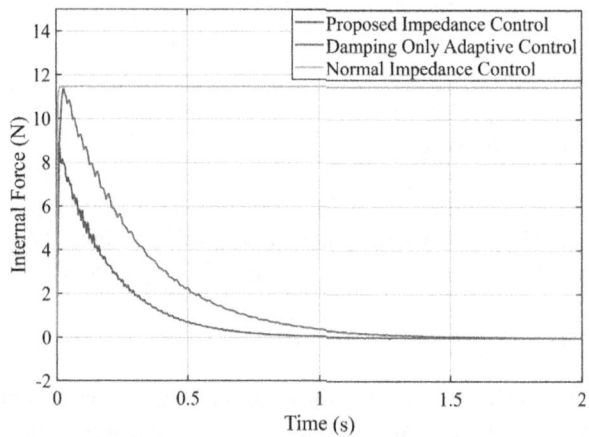

Fig. 5. The internal force regulation of kinematic error-applied situation

From Fig. 5 it can be observed that the normal impedance control has the biggest amplitude and internal force eventually converges to 11.5 N. The damping-adaptive only method has the smaller amplitude and internal force converges to 0 N at 1.8 s.

The proposed method has the smallest amplitude and the internal force converges to 0N at 1 s. Because the stiffness is adaptive, the proposed control law can better and faster adjust when the kinematic error is employed.

During the dual-arm gripping process, it is necessary to maintain stable when the external disturbance is applied. To simulate the situation, an external disturbance is applied to the end effector of one arm. The compensated internal force is the factor for evaluating the quality of algorithm. External disturbances are applied equally to all three XYZ axes, with identical variations being described as:

$$F(t) = \begin{cases} 0, & 0 \leq t < 0.5, \\ 150t - 75, & 0.5 \leq t < 1, \\ 75, & 1 \leq t < 2.5, \\ 450 - 150t, & 2.5 \leq t < 3, \\ 0, & 3 \leq t \leq 4. \end{cases} \quad (25)$$

To simplify the display of internal force, the force on x-axis is selected to present in Fig. 6.

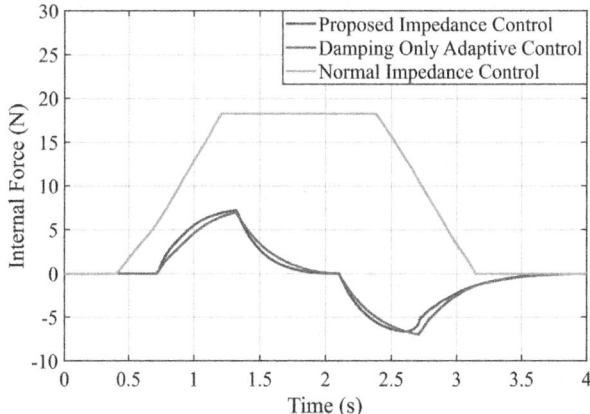

Fig. 6. The internal force regulation of external disturbance-applied situation

The compensated internal force of normal impedance control eventually converges to 19 N. The compensated force of damping-adaptive only method converges to 0 N, so as the proposed method. But the proposed method has faster response. This because the stiffness of proposed method is adaptive, which can automatically adjust to the most suitable stiffness when applying a time-varying external disturbance. The other two axes are similar to x-axis.

5 Conclusion

This paper addresses the challenges of accurate force decoupling and impedance adaptation in dual-arm collaborative robot gripping by proposing a dual-channel adaptive impedance algorithm with a leveling module. The dual-channel architecture independently regulates internal and external forces, and an adaptive gain update law tunes stiffness and damping online to ensure stability across varying contact scenarios; the leveling module further balances force distribution between arms. Simulation results indicate that, compared to standard impedance controllers and single-channel impedance controllers, the proposed method delivers faster convergence, lower force-tracking error, and improved grip stability under complex interactions. Future work will validate the approach on industrial robot platforms, generalize the leveling module to dynamic payloads, and enhance adaptive laws for unstructured environments.

Acknowledgement. This work was sponsored by The Explorers Program of Shanghai (Basic Research Funding) under Grant 24TS1414700 and the National Key Research and Development Program of China under Grant 2022YFB4700300. (Corresponding author: Chungang Zhuang).

References

1. Cui, Y., Xu, Z., Zhong, L., Xu, P., Shen, Y., Tang, Q.: A task-adaptive deep reinforcement learning framework for dual-arm robot manipulation. IEEE Trans. Autom. Sci. Eng. **22**, 466–479 (2024)
2. Kim, H., Ohmura, Y., Kuniyoshi, Y.: Goal-conditioned dual-action imitation learning for dexterous dual-arm robot manipulation. IEEE Trans. Robot. **40**, 2287–2305 (2024)
3. Huang, S., Yang, J., Hu, P., Wu, H., Ning, X., Gao, S.: High stiffness 6-DOF dual-arm cooperative robot and its application in blade polishing. IEEE Trans. Autom. Sci. Eng. **21**, 5929–5941 (2023)
4. Abbas, M., Narayan, J., Dwivedy, S.: A systematic review on cooperative dual-arm manipulators: modeling, planning, control, and vision strategies. Int. J. Intell. Robot. **7**(4), 683–707 (2023)
5. An, Q., Zhang, Y., Huang, X., Li, H., Xia, X.: Impedance control in serial-parallel hybrid space robots for assembly operations. Acta Astronaut. **232**, 316–329 (2025)
6. Jiao, C., Yu, L., Su, X., Wen, Y., Dai, X.: Adaptive hybrid impedance control for dual-arm cooperative manipulation with object uncertainties. Automatica **140**, 110232 (2022)
7. Iskandar, M., Ott, C., Albu-Schäffer, A., Siciliano, B., Dietrich, A.: Hybrid force-impedance control for fast end-effector motions. IEEE Robot. Autom. Lett. **8**(7), 3931–3938 (2023)
8. Duan, J., Gan, Y., Chen, M., Dai, X.: Adaptive variable impedance control for dynamic contact force tracking in uncertain environment. Robot. Auton. Syst. **102**, 54–65 (2018)
9. Duan, J., Gan, Y., Chen, M., Dai, X.: Symmetrical adaptive variable admittance control for position/force tracking of dual-arm cooperative manipulators with unknown trajectory deviations. Robot. Comput.-Integr. Manuf. **57**, 357–369 (2019)
10. Babarahmati, K., Kasaei, M., Tiseo, C., Mistry, M., Vijayakumar, S.: Robust and dexterous dual-arm tele-cooperation using adaptable impedance control. In: 41th IEEE International Conference on Robotics and Automation (ICRA), Yokohama, Japan, pp. 17337–17343 (2024)

11. Ghonasgi, K., Mirsky, R., Haith, A., Stone, P., Deshpande, A.: A novel control law for multi-joint human-robot interaction tasks while maintaining postural coordination. In: 36thIEEE/RSJ International Conference on Intelligent Robots and Systems (IROS), Detroit, USA, pp. 6110–6116 (2023)
12. Liang, X., et al.: An adaptive time-varying impedance controller for manipulators. Front. Neurorobotics **16**, 789842 (2022)
13. Siciliano, B., Khatib, O., Kröger, T.: Springer Handbook of Robotics. 2nd edn. Springer. Berlin (2008)
14. Caccavale, F., Chiacchio, P., Marino, A., Villani, L.: Six-DOF impedance control of dual-arm cooperative manipulators. IEEE-ASME Trans. Mechatron. **13**(5), 576–586 (2008)

RL-Force: Reinforcement Learning with Force Estimation for Humanoid Locomotion Subject to Continuous External Disturbances

Weixian Lin, Letian Qian, Shuhan Wang, Junjie Qiang, Peng Sun, and Xin Luo[(✉)]

School of Mechanical Science and Engineering of Huazhong University of Science and Technology, Wuhan 430074, China
mexinluo@hust.edu.cn

Abstract. Continuous external disturbances impose a significant influence on humanoid robot locomotion, causing command execution failures. Limited by the absence of force information, these controllers are limited to passive recovery rather than active adjustment. To address this issue, this study proposes RL-Force, an asymmetric reinforcement learning framework that integrates curriculum learning with a co-trained external force estimator using only proprioceptive sensors. The estimator infers a force vector and a point of application, thereby assisting the policy in adapting to external forces. Simulated experiments with a self-built humanoid robot demonstrate superior velocity tracking and adaptive posture adjustment compared to baseline methods. The saliency analysis underscores the critical role of force information in policy inference, improving recovery from disturbances.

Keywords: Humanoid Robot · Reinforcement Learning · Force Estimation

1 Introduction

Recent advancements in learning-based control have significantly enhanced the locomotion capabilities of humanoid robots, enabling agile maneuvers such as walking, parkour, and dancing [1–3]. However, in practical applications, merely relying on locomotion is often insufficient to accomplish task objectives. Humanoid robots must physically interact with the environment, manipulating tools or moving obstacles, which introduce complex dynamic loads. These loads can be categorized as attached loads and external disturbances. Attached loads are rigidly connected objects, such as tools or equipment, that alter the robot's inertial properties. External disturbances are forces from the external environment, such as pushing or pulling, that influence dynamic behavior without modifying inertial properties.

Prior research has addressed attached loads effectively through techniques like domain randomization and mass identification, enabling robust task execution under varying loads [4, 5]. For external disturbances, a robot must dynamically adjust its motion strategy to maintain balance while responding to varying force directions and magnitudes. Existing learning frameworks fail to enable robots to learn to proactively adjust their postures like humans to effectively counteract a large continuous force. For instance, when subjected to a large and horizontal force for a period of time, robots tend to fall or passively drift along the direction of the applied force, even though their desired velocity is zero [6]. This is because they only simulate instantaneous external force disturbances in simulation environments and have not been trained on scenarios involving continuous external forces. This highlights the limitations of current controllers in handling continuous and high-magnitude external forces.

Furthermore, external forces are usually treated as disturbance terms, which only allows the control policy to passively adapt to disturbances and adopt more conservative behaviors. When known external forces are fed as inputs to the policy to be trained, the policy has the potential to learn an active adjustment policy. However, external forces are applied to arbitrary points on a robot's body, making them difficult to measure directly by sensors. Therefore, it is necessary to estimate external forces as the policy input using proprioceptive sensors.

In this work, we proposed an asymmetric reinforcement learning framework named RL-Force for humanoid locomotion that integrates curriculum learning and an explicit force estimator, enabling robots to effectively handle continuous external forces without relying on external force sensors. Experiments in a simulated environment demonstrate that the proposed method significantly improves the robot's ability to maintain stable walking and adapt its posture under sudden and continuous external forces. A saliency analysis of the external force input was performed to quantify its influence on the control policy, which proves the role of external force input.

2 Related Works

2.1 Reinforcement Learning for Humanoid Locomotion

Model-free reinforcement learning (RL) has advanced motion control for bipedal and humanoid robots, enabling robust locomotion policies. Using simulated unflattened terrains and domain randomization, researchers have trained robots to walk on stairs and slopes without vision sensors [4, 7, 8]. To boost policy performance, studies have incorporated hard-to-measure state variables, such as the base linear velocity and foot contact states, via co-trained estimators [9]. However, the locomotion of humanoid robots under sustained external disturbances (e.g., continuous pushing) remains underexplored, which presents a critical challenge to maintaining robot stability.

2.2 Locomotion with External Disturbances

Humanoid robots require stable locomotion under external disturbances and load in the real world. Traditional methods use simplified models and additional sensors like foot force sensors for force estimation [10, 11]. Data-driven approaches train policies in simulation without external sensors, showing adaptability to unknown disturbances [12]. Some research used privileged learning on quadruped robots to handle transient forces [13]. While these approaches represent promising progress in handling external disturbances, it is unclear whether explicitly incorporating external force information can significantly enhance the adaptability of learning-based controllers, and whether external force estimation can be achieved using only proprioceptive sensors.

3 Method

3.1 Overview of RL-Force Framework

In this work, we propose a learning-based framework that enables a humanoid robot to adapt to sustained external disturbances while standing and walking, as illustrated in Fig. 1 the framework incorporates an explicit external force estimator that is jointly trained with the policy and value networks. The estimated force is provided as an additional input to the policy network, allowing the robot to adapt its motions based on inferred external disturbances.

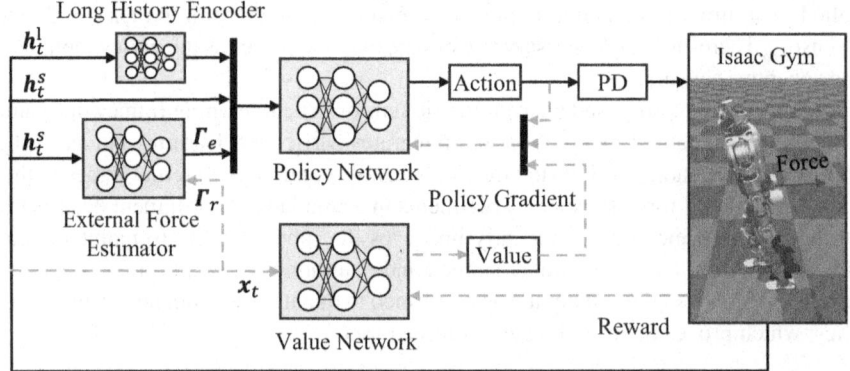

Fig. 1. RL-Force Framework for Humanoid Robot Adaptive Control under External Disturbances. We propose an asymmetric actor-critic architecture where an external force estimator infers external disturbances $\Gamma_e(F, p)$ including the point of application p and force vector F based on proprioceptive sensing. The estimated external disturbance is provided as an input to the policy network. Dashed lines indicate active processes only during training. The policy network outputs desired joint targets, which are converted by a PD controller into actual joint torques applied to the simulation environment. Meanwhile, the value network evaluates the state value and guides the update of both policy networks through policy gradients.

3.2 Reinforcement Learning for Robot Control

The locomotion control problem for humanoid robots can be formulated as a discrete-time Markov Decision Process (MDP), defined by the tuple (S, A, P, R, γ). Here, S is the state space, A is the action space, $P : S \times A \times S \to [0, 1]$ is the function of transition probability function, $R : S \times A \to \mathbb{R}$ is the reward function, $\gamma \in [0, 1]$ is the discount factor. The policy π accepts the current state and outputs a distribution over the action space to determine the robot's behavior. At each time step t, the policy selects an action a_t, based on the current state s_t. The environment transitions to the next state s_{t+1} and returns a scalar reward r_t. The goal of reinforcement learning is to find an optimal policy π^* that maximizes the expected cumulative return:

$$\pi^* = \mathop{\mathrm{argmax}}_{\pi} \mathbb{E}_\pi \left[\sum_{t=0}^{\infty} \gamma^t r_t \right] \tag{1}$$

Action Space. The action a_t represents the offset of each joint relative to the desired joint position among the 12 degrees of freedom of the robot's legs. These offsets are used to calculate the motor torque τ_t, with the calculation formula given by:

$$\tau_t = K_p(a_t + q_{init} - q_t) + K_d(0 - \dot{q}_t) \tag{2}$$

where, K_p and K_d are the proportional gain vector and derivative gain vector, q_{init} represents the default joint angle configuration of the corresponding robot.

State Space. The robot's state s_t is composed of (x_t, o_t), where x_t is a privileged vector that is typically unobtainable directly in real robots. It includes the body linear velocity, foot contact state, friction coefficient, and the external force vector and point of application. o_t is the observable vector that the real robot can acquire, including the commanded linear and angular velocity, body angular velocity, body Euler angles, joint velocities, and joint angles. Additionally, it includes representations of leg phases ($\sin\theta$, $\cos\theta$), with the phase set to (0, 0) when the robot is in a standing state. The phase input is correlated with the robot's contact sequence, desired joint positions, and foot-lifting height rewards.

Reward. The reward function is shown in Table 1, which is built upon the humanoid gym [14] and incorporates the standing state term. Additionally, we use 5th-order polynomials to calculate both the target joint pos q_{target} and the target foot height $p_{feet,target,z}$, aiming to slow down the velocity at touchdown and reduce touchdown noise. We employ the following 5th-order polynomial function $s(t)$ to generate the foot reference trajectory and joint reference trajectory:

$$s(t) = \sum_{i=0}^{5} a_i t^i \tag{3}$$

In this equation, t represents the phase time. By setting the initial conditions for position, velocity, and acceleration to zero, and the terminal conditions for position to h with zero velocity and acceleration, substitution into the equation yields:

$$a_0, a_1, a_2 = 0, a_3 = \frac{10h}{T^3}, a_4 = -\frac{15h}{T^4}, a_5 = \frac{6h}{T^5} \tag{4}$$

where T is the duration.

We generate a complete z-direction swing leg trajectory by splicing two fifth-order polynomial segments: during the first half of the swing phase, a fifth-order polynomial is used for lifting the leg; during the second half, a symmetric polynomial is employed for lowering the leg, thereby achieving a smooth, symmetric trajectory for both elevation and descent:

$$S(t) = \begin{cases} s(t), & 0 \leq t < T, \\ s(2T - t), & T \leq t \leq 2T. \end{cases} \tag{5}$$

Table 1. Reward Function Components. We use $\varphi(e, w) = exp\left(-w \cdot |e|^2\right)$ to simplify the notation, where c denotes the command, c_s is the standing command, ϕ is the Euler angles, and ω is the angular velocity. $\Delta d_{min/max}$ Represents the distance that is either smaller than the minimum set value or larger than the maximum set value. b_{acc} Denotes the base link acceleration vector, q the joint positions, and $\dot{q}$ the joint velocities. $1_{d(t)}$ And $1_{f(t)}$ denote the desired and actual contact states, respectively, and $F_{L,R}$ represents the feet contact forces.

Name	Equation	Scale
Lin. velocity tracking	$\varphi(v_{xy} - c_{xy}, 5)$	1.5
Ang. velocity tracking	$\varphi(\omega_z - c_z, 5)$	1.2
Orientation tracking	$\varphi(\phi_{rp}, 10)$	0.5
Base height tracking	$\varphi(p_z - 1.034, 100)$	0.2
Feet contact tracking	$\varphi(1_{f(t)} - 1_{d(t)}, \infty)$	1.2
Joint Position Tracking	$\varphi(q - q_{target}(t), 2)$	1.
Feet Clearance Tracking	$|p_{feet,z} - p_{feet,target,z}(t)| \cdot (1 - 1_{f(t)})$	1.5
Vel Mismatch	$\varphi(v_z^2, 10) + \varphi(|w_{xy}|, 5)$	0.5
Base Acc	$\varphi(b_{acc}, 3)$	0.2
Feet Slip	$\|v_{feet,xy}\|_2 \cdot 1_{f(t)}$	-0.05
Feet Distance	$0.5[\varphi(\Delta d_{feet,min}, 100) + \varphi(\Delta d_{feet,max}, 100)]$	0.2
Knee Distance	$0.5[\varphi(\Delta d_{knee,min}, 100) + \varphi(\Delta d_{knee,max}, 100)]$	0.2
DOF Velocity	$\dot{q}_i^2$	-0.0005
Stand Still	$\varphi(q - q_{init}, 1) \; c_s = 1$ $0 \quad c_s = 0$	2.5
Default Joint	$\varphi(q - q_{init}, 100)$	0.5
Energy Cost	τ^2	-0.00001
Action Smoothness	$\|a_t - 2a_{t-1} + a_{t-2}\|_2$	-0.002
Feet Contact	$clip(F_{L,R} - 1200, 0, 400)$	-0.01

3.3 External Force Curriculum

To simulate scenarios such as a robot pulling a cart or being pushed, external forces are applied to specific points on the robot's base using randomized points of application and force vectors. Even as the robot's pitch or roll angles change, the orientation of force typically remains fixed in the world coordinate frame. Therefore, we apply external forces in the world coordinate frame to ensure that the force direction remains constant relative to the global coordinate system, independent of the robot's pitch or roll angles. Additionally, in our preliminary tests, we found that the robot's ability to withstand external forces in the x-direction is higher than that in the y-direction. To enable the robot to withstand larger forces in the x-direction. We couple the direction of the external force with the robot's yaw angle, allowing it to rotate with the robot's heading. The ranges of force magnitudes and points of application are first defined, as detailed in Table 2, and then transformed appropriately for application in the world coordinate frame.

Table 2. The ranges of random forces and points

Random Forces/ Points	x	y	z
F_i	[−200, 200]	[−100, 100]	[−100, 100]
p_i	[−0.1, 0.1]	[−0.1, 0.1]	[−0.1, 0.4]

For each sample in the environment index set ε, we first independently sample a force vector $\boldsymbol{F} = (F_x, F_y, F_z)$ and a point $\boldsymbol{p} = (p_x, p_y, p_z)$ within the intervals specified in the robot's local coordinate system at every 5 s. The process of mapping to the world coordinate system can be expressed as:

$$\boldsymbol{p}_{world} = \boldsymbol{P}_{base} + \boldsymbol{R}_z(\psi)\boldsymbol{p} \tag{6}$$

$$\boldsymbol{F}_{world} = \boldsymbol{R}_z(\psi)\boldsymbol{F} \tag{7}$$

$$\boldsymbol{R}_z(\psi) = \begin{bmatrix} \cos\psi & -\sin\psi & 0 \\ \sin\psi & \cos\psi & 0 \\ 0 & 0 & 1 \end{bmatrix} \tag{8}$$

where the position of the base in the world coordinate system is $\boldsymbol{P}_{base}$, and the yaw angle is ψ. The external force rotates only with the yaw of the base in the world coordinate system and does not rotate with the pitch or roll of the robot.

Curriculum learning increases the random force range $[-F_i, F_i]$ based on the currently obtained velocity reward until reaching the maximum range. Let the average linear velocity tracking reward over the environment index set ε be:

$$\bar{R}_v = \frac{1}{|\mathcal{E}|} \sum_{i \in \mathcal{E}} \frac{r_{v,i}}{L_{\max}} \tag{9}$$

where $r_{v,i}$ is the total linear velocity reward for the i th environment, and $L_{\max}$ is the maximum simulation duration. Define the velocity reward scaling factor as s_v. When $\bar{R}_v > 0.7 s_v$, update the random external force range as follows:

$$F_i \leftarrow \text{clip}(F_i + 10, 0, F_i^{\max}) \tag{10}$$

3.4 Training Setup

External Force Estimator. The external force estimator consists of a multi-layer perceptron (MLP) with three hidden layers containing 256, 256, and 128 units respectively, using the ELU activation function. The estimator takes as input a short-term history $h_t^s = [o_{t-H_s+1}, \ldots o_t]$ and outputs the force vector and point of application. The loss function is MSE, and it is updated synchronously with the PPO algorithm.

Policy Training. The policy is trained using the Proximal Policy Optimization (PPO) algorithm. Both the policy and value networks are structured as MLP with three hidden layers containing 512, 256, and 128 units respectively, using the ELU activation function. The policy network inputs consist of three components: the output from a long-term history network, short-term history information h_t^s, and estimated force information Γ. The long history network inputs $h_t^l = [o_{t-H_l+1}, \ldots o_t]$, , through a temporal convolutional network (CNN) with two 1D convolutional layers. These layers have 32 and 16 output channels, kernel sizes of 6 and 4, strides of 3 and 2, and use the RELU activation function. Following a flattened layer, a fully connected layer with 128 units and ELU activation maps to an output layer with 64 dimensions. All policies are further trained based on a pre-trained policy without external disturbances.

3.5 Saliency Analysis

To investigate the impact of the external force term as an input to the policy, we adopted the integrated gradients method [15]. For the i-th term of the feedback state $x \in \mathbb{R}^n$ at time step t, the normalized saliency value $S(x_{i,t})$ is computed as follows:

$$G(x_{i,t}) = \sum_{j=1}^{m} \left| \frac{x_{i,t}}{p} \sum_{k=1}^{p} \frac{\partial F_j\left(\frac{kx_t}{p}\right)}{\partial x_{i,t}} \right| \tag{11}$$

$$\epsilon = \frac{1}{nN} \sum_{t=1}^{N} \sum_{i=1}^{n} G(x_{i,t}) \tag{12}$$

$$S_d(x_{i,t}) = \begin{cases} G(x_{i,t}) - \epsilon, & G(x_{i,t}) > \epsilon \\ 0, & \text{else} \end{cases} \tag{13}$$

$$S(x_{i,t}) = \frac{S_d(x_{i,t})}{\max\limits_{i \in \{1,\ldots,n\}, t \in \{1,\ldots,N\}} S_d(x_{i,t})} \tag{14}$$

where $F(x_t) \in \mathbb{R}^m$ denotes the action generated at time step t, $p = 25$ is the number of steps for Riemann approximation in the integration, and N is the total number of time steps in the entire motion process.

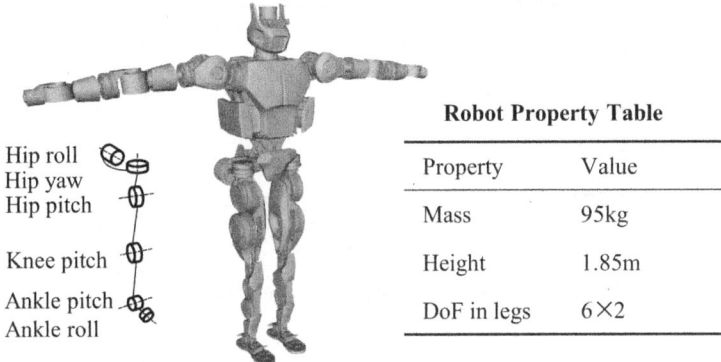

Fig. 2. The Dazhuang Humanoid Robot

4 Experience and Analysis

4.1 Implementation and Simulation Setup

We used the Isaac Gym simulator for training. The simulated robot is the Dazhuang humanoid, as shown in Fig. 2. The network processes historical observation parameters were set to $H_s=3$, $H_l=100$, and the gait cycle period was set to 1s. Training was performed at a control frequency of 100 Hz on an NVIDIA RTX 4090D GPU.

Comparison Group Setup. To evaluate the impact of curriculum learning and explicit force estimation on a model's ability to resist external disturbances, we designed a set of experimental groups as summarized in Table 3.

Table 3. Experimental Group Configuration

Group	Force Load	Curriculum	Estimation of force	Real force
Baseline	×	×	×	×
F	✓	×	×	×
FE	✓	×	✓	×
FC	✓	✓	×	×
FCE	✓	✓	✓	×
FCR	✓	✓	×	✓

Curriculum Progression. Figure 3 shows the curriculum progression curves during training. The FCR group exhibits the fastest curriculum advancement, significantly outperforming both FCE and FC, indicating that access to ground-truth external forces is highly beneficial for learning under external disturbances. The FCE group progresses slightly faster than FC, suggesting that explicit force estimation can partially assist the policy learning process.

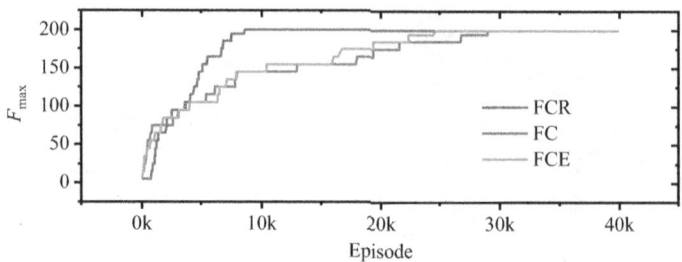

Fig. 3. Curriculum Learning Curve for External Forces

Velocity Tracking Test. To test the velocity tracking performance of different policies under continuous external forces, we applied external forces of -200 N in the x-direction and -100 N in the y-direction respectively, and controlled the robot to walk in the direction opposite to the forces. Figure 4 shows the process of the FCE group recovering to a standing position after being subjected to external forces. The performance in the velocity tracking task is summarized in Table 4. The actual velocity trajectories in the x direction are shown in Fig. 5. The baseline model fails to maintain balance under the applied force and falls, resulting in the highest tracking errors. The F and FE groups exhibit continuous backward motion under the force, indicating weak resistance and poor tracking performance. In contrast, models trained with curriculum learning (FC and FCE) can stably track the commanded velocity. The maximum velocity error typically occurs immediately after the external force is applied. The FCE group slightly outperforms FC, due to the assistance of explicit force estimation. However, there remains a notable performance gap compared to FCR, which has ground-truth force input.

These results suggest that curriculum learning plays a critical role in enabling the policy to resist external disturbances. While explicit force estimation provides modest improvements over models without estimation, it still falls short of the performance achievable with ground-truth supervision.

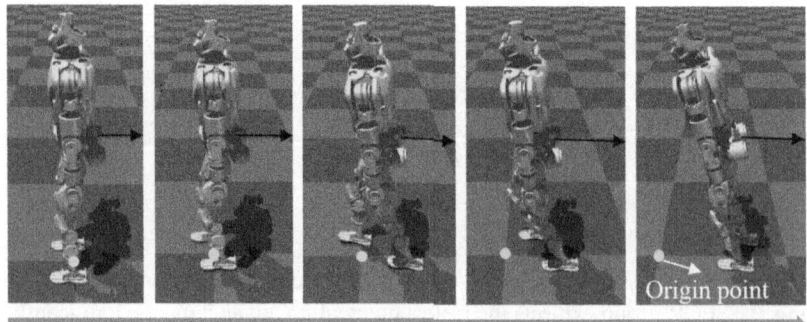

Fig. 4. Adaptive Standing Recovery of Robots under Continuous External Perturbations

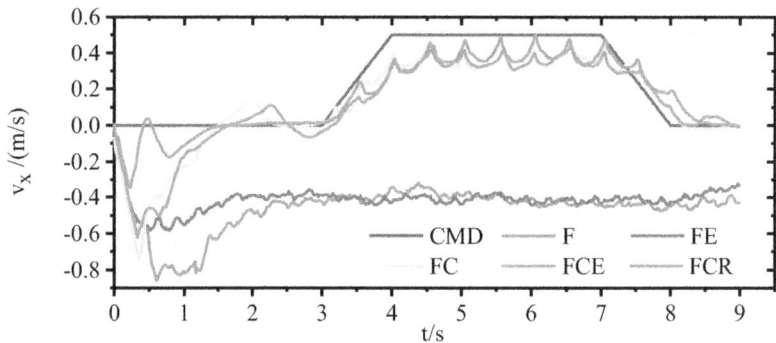

Fig. 5. Velocity tracking plots of experimental policies. At the initial time, a sustained external force of − 200 N in the x-direction is applied to the robot. After 3 s, a command of forward velocity (CMD) is sent.

Table 4. Velocity Tracking Error Comparison Table. We evaluate performance using maximum tracking error (ME) and root mean square error (RMSE).

Direction		Baseline	F	FE	FC	FCE	FCR
X (−200 N)	ME	5.418	0.952	0.942	0.748	0.622	**0.343**
	RMSE	2.549	0.711	0.676	0.179	0.171	**0.107**
Y (−100 N)	ME	2.091	0.600	0.681	0.532	0.506	**0.431**
	RMSE	0.851	0.224	0.269	0.194	0.181	**0.166**

Force Estimator Accuracy Analysis. To further understand the performance gap between the FCE and FCR groups, we conducted a comparative analysis of the outputs from their respective force estimators. During the training of the FCR policy, we also trained a supervised force estimator in parallel, which we used for subsequent evaluation. Figure 6 shows the estimated x-direction external force during the first 4 s of the velocity tracking test.

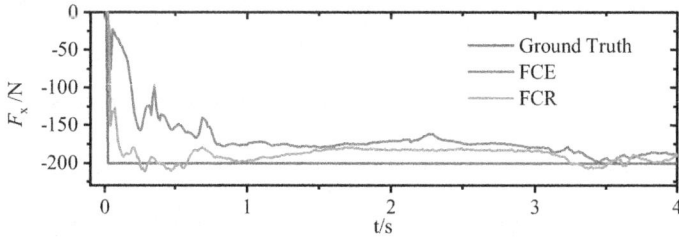

Fig. 6. External force Estimation plots of Estimator of FCE and FCR

It is evident that the estimator trained in the FCE group exhibits higher latency and larger errors compared to the one trained alongside the FCR policy. The FCR policy also demonstrates faster recovery after the external force is applied, suggesting that faster policy convergence facilitates more accurate and stable estimator training. This also highlights the limitation of the estimator's ability to track dynamic processes.

In an additional experiment, we replaced the ground-truth force input of the FCR policy with the estimator trained jointly with ground-truth supervision. This led to unstable behavior in both the policy and the estimator. The policy instability can be attributed to the mismatch between the ground-truth inputs used during training and the noisy estimates during inference. The estimator produced abnormal outputs, indicating that it had not learned a generalizable mapping from proprioceptive inputs to external force, but rather overfit to the specific dynamics of the policy it was co-trained with.

We further computed the Pearson correlation coefficient between the estimated x-direction force and the torso pitch angle, which yielded a value of -0.81. This strong negative correlation suggests that the estimator relies on pitch motion to infer external force, Confirming the conclusion that it lacks robustness across different policies.

Saliency Analysis. To investigate the influence of ground-truth external force input on policy behavior under disturbance, we conducted a saliency analysis on the policies from the FCR and FCE groups. As shown in Fig. 7, the FCR policy exhibits strong sensitivity to the x-direction force input, indicating a high degree of reliance on accurate external force information during disturbance recovery.

In comparison, the FCE policy also relies on the output of its learned force estimator, but to a lesser extent. This reduced reliance can be attributed to the noise and bias in the estimated forces, which decreases the policy's trust in the estimator and results in slower recovery to a stable walking state. These findings highlight the importance of accurate force inputs for effective disturbance compensation.

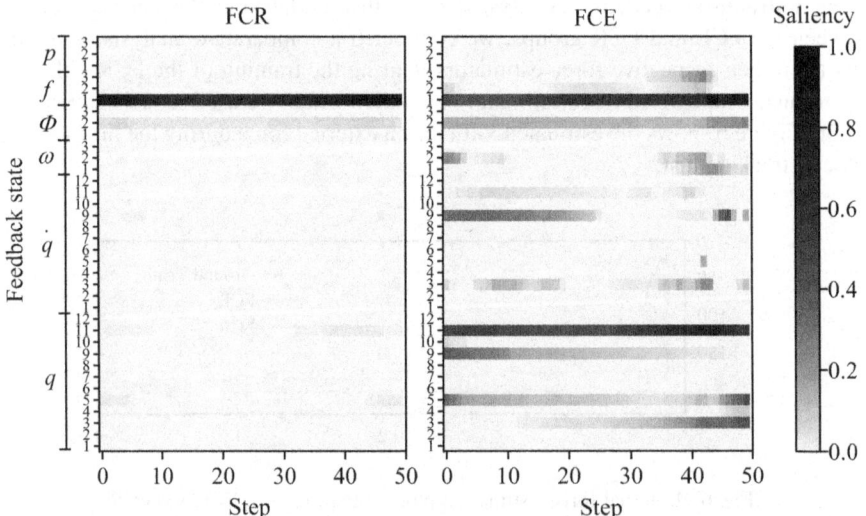

Fig. 7. Saliency map of feedback states

5 Conclusion and Future Work

This study demonstrates the efficacy of the RL-Force framework in enabling humanoid robots to robustly adapt to continuous external force disturbances during locomotion. The integration of curriculum learning and an explicit external force estimator, trained jointly with the policy and value networks, facilitates stable walking and dynamic posture adjustments without external sensors. Experimental results highlight the critical role of curriculum learning in enhancing disturbance resistance. Compared to real force input, the external force estimator plays a limited auxiliary role in enabling the robot to regain stability. Analysis of the force estimator shows limitations in tracking dynamic forces, such as latency and dependence on torso pitch, indicating that the estimator is overfitting to the dynamics of specific policies. Saliency analysis underscores the policy's reliance on force inputs for effective recovery under continuous disturbance and emphasizes the need for better estimators.

Future research will integrate model-based approaches with additional sensors, such as accelerometers and foot force sensors, to enhance the accuracy of force estimation and improve its generalizability. The ultimate objective is to enable the control policy to approach the performance achievable with known external force inputs.

Acknowledgments. This work was supported by the National Natural Science Foundation of China (Grant No. 52375014) and the Wuhan Major Science and Technology Project "Generative Artificial Intelligence-Driven Humanoid Robot Research and Application for Special Environment Operations" (Grant No. 2024060902020442).

References

1. Li, Z., Peng, X.B., Abbeel, P., Levine, S., Berseth, G., Sreenath, K.: Reinforcement learning for versatile, dynamic, and robust bipedal locomotion control. Int. J. Rob. Res. **44**, 840–888 (2025)
2. Zhuang, Z., Yao, S., Zhao, H.: Humanoid parkour learning. In: Presented at the 8th Annual Conference on Robot Learning (2024)
3. Ji, M., et al.: ExBody2: advanced expressive humanoid whole-body control. arXiv:2412.13196 (2024)
4. Gu, X., et al.: Advancing humanoid locomotion: mastering challenging terrains with denoising world model learning. arXiv:2408.14472 (2024)
5. Wang, H., et al.: BeamDojo: learning agile humanoid locomotion on sparse footholds. arXiv:2502.10363 (2025)
6. Marum, B. van, Shrestha, A., Duan, H., Dugar, P., Dao, J., Fern, A.: Revisiting reward design and evaluation for robust humanoid standing and walking. In: 2024 IEEE/RSJ International Conference on Intelligent Robots and Systems (IROS), pp. 11256–11263 (2024)
7. Siekmann, J., Green, K., Warila, J., Fern, A., Hurst, J.: Blind bipedal stair traversal via sim-to-real reinforcement learning. arXiv:2105.08328 (2021)
8. Liao, Q., Zhang, B., Huang, X., Huang, X., Li, Z., Sreenath, K.: Berkeley Humanoid: a research platform for learning-based control. arXiv:2407.21781 (2024)
9. Wang, Z., Wei, W., Yu, R., Wu, J., Zhu, Q.: Toward understanding key estimation in learning robust humanoid locomotion. In: 2024 IEEE/RSJ International Conference on Intelligent Robots and Systems (IROS), pp. 11232–11239 (2024)

10. Li, J., Yuan, Z., Dong, S., Zhang, J., Sang, X.: External force observer aided push recovery for torque-controlled biped robots. Auton. Robots **46**, 553–568 (2022)
11. Hawley, L., Suleiman, W.: External force observer for medium-sized humanoid robots. In: 2016 IEEE-RAS 16th International Conference on Humanoid Robots (Humanoids), pp. 366–371 (2016)
12. Dao, J., Green, K., Duan, H., Fern, A., Hurst, J.: Sim-to-real learning for bipedal locomotion under unsensed dynamic loads. arXiv:2204.04340 (2022)
13. Xiao, Z., Zhang, X., Zhou, X., Zhang, Q.: PA-LOCO: learning perturbation-adaptive locomotion for quadruped robots. arXiv:2407.04224 (2024)
14. Gu, X., Wang, Y.J., Chen, J.: Humanoid-Gym: reinforcement learning for humanoid robot with zero-shot sim2real transfer. arXiv:2404.05695 (2024)
15. Yu, W., et al.: Identifying important sensory feedback for learning locomotion skills. Nat. Mach. Intell. **5**, 919–932 (2023)

Intrinsic Vision-Based Learning for Proprioceptive Sensing of Soft Pneumatic Actuators

Taoyuan Huang[1], Jieji Ren[1(✉)], Xinyu Yang[1], Longyan Wu[2], Jinnuo Zhang[1], Ningbin Zhang[1(✉)], and Guoying Gu[1]

[1] Robotics Institute and State Key Laboratory of Mechanical System and Vibration, School of Mechanical Engineering, Shanghai Jiao Tong University, Shanghai 200240, China
{jiejiren,zhangnb,zhangnb,guguoying}@sjtu.edu.cn
[2] Shanghai Innovation Institute, Shanghai 200231, China

Abstract. Soft pneumatic actuators offer numerous advantages, including dexterity in confined spaces and compliance when handling irregularly shaped objects. However, their inherent lack of proprioception remains a major challenge. In this study, we propose a vision-based approach using an internal camera to capture visual features such as stripe patterns and brightness variations within the actuator cavity. For calibration, an external tracking system provides ground truth pose data for each configuration. A neural network is trained to establish the mapping between the internal visual features and the corresponding actuator poses. Finally, we validate the effectiveness of our method through peg-in-hole experiments.

1 Introduction

In recent years, soft robots [13] have developed rapidly due to their inherent compliance and structural flexibility, making them particularly suitable for applications such as adaptive grasping [5], wearable systems [19], and bio-inspired locomotion [9,17]. By leveraging soft materials [23] and continuum structures [25], these robots achieve high environmental adaptability, allowing them to perform tasks that are difficult for traditional rigid robots.

Soft pneumatic actuators [3,12,20] are the most prevailing for soft robots. These actuators have the advantages of being lightweight [6,22], achieving large strokes [15], resilience to impacts [10], distributing force evenly [24], and operating without relying on high electric/magnetic fields [4] or high temperatures [27]. However, one of the major challenges in controlling soft robots lies in the lack of proprioception due to their continuous deformable nature.

Proprioceptive sensing is essential for achieving closed-loop control and adaptive behaviors in soft pneumatic actuators. Previous works have explored various sensing strategies to enable proprioceptive capabilities in soft pneumatic actuators. These include embedded resistive strain sensors [11,16], optical waveguide-based strain sensors [28], and stretchable distributed fiber-optic sensors [29]. While these methods have shown promise, they often suffer from challenges such as complex integration of embedded hardware [1], signal degradation over time due to material fatigue or drift in the light path [21], and limited scalability [26], especially in high-degree-of-freedom soft robotic systems.

To address these limitations, we propose a vision-based proprioception framework for soft pneumatic actuators that uses an internal camera to observe brightness and stripe deformation patterns within the actuator's inner cavity (Fig. 1). By synchronizing this internal visual data with ground-truth poses captured by an external motion tracking system, we construct a supervised dataset for training. A neural network is then employed to establish the non-linear mapping between internal visual features and the actuator's pose. This approach provides a low-cost, easy-to-integrate, and robust solution for proprioception in soft pneumatic actuators.

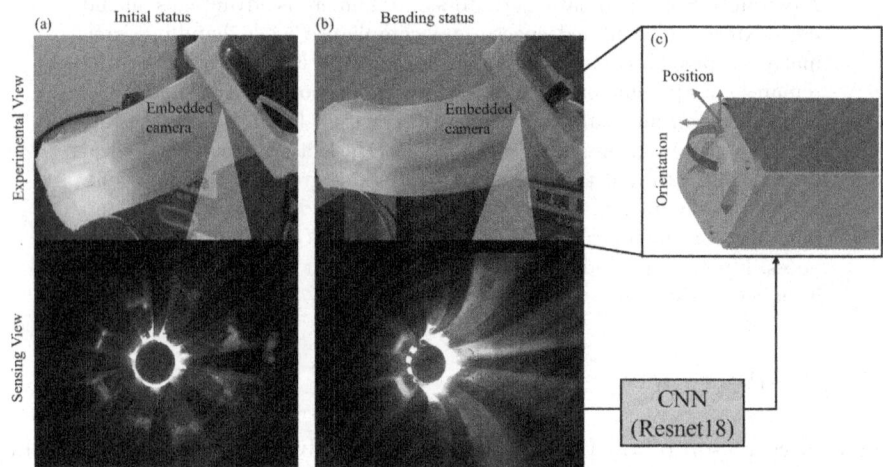

Fig. 1. Overview of design concept. (a) Experimental view and sensing view of the actuator in the initial status. (b) Experimental view and sensing view of the actuator in the bending status. (c) Predicted actuator's pose via machine learning.

2   Hardware Design and Fabrication

The soft actuator used in this study adopts a fiber-reinforced pneumatic structure (Fig. 2). The actuator consists of an inner and outer chamber. The inner cavity has a circular cross-section with a diameter of 30 mm and an internal square air chamber measuring 35 mm × 35 mm × 100 mm. The outer chamber measures 40 mm × 40 mm × 104 mm.

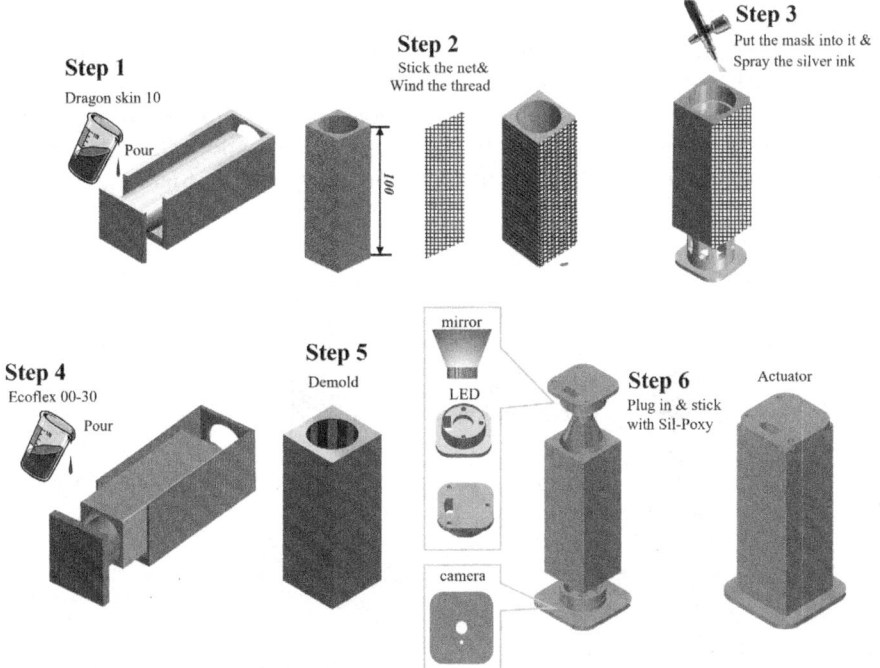

Fig. 2. Fabrication of the proprioceptive soft pneumatic actuator

To fabricate the actuator, custom molds were first designed according to these dimensions. The inner cavity mold was treated with a release agent and fixed with hot glue. Dragon Skin 10 silicone was poured into the mold and left to cure at room temperature. After curing, the actuator was demolded, and the outer surface was treated with a silicone bonding agent (e.g., primer 770). A fishbone-like constraint layer made of white gauze (Young's modulus, 2 GPa) was bonded to the actuator surface using cyanoacrylate adhesive. The braided fibers were then evenly wound around the air chambers with a 1 mm spacing to enhance the axial constraint. Following this, the outer chamber was cast using Ecoflex 00–30 silicone, completing the fabrication of the unsealed actuator body.

To enable internal optical sensing, a striped reflective coating was applied to the inner cavity surface. A cylindrical mask with a diameter of 31 mm and height of 116 mm, featuring a 1:1 stripe duty cycle, was inserted into the actuator. We choose this characteristic because of its simple design. The snug fit ensured stable positioning during spraying. A high-reflectance silver ink was evenly sprayed using an airbrush to form the reflective pattern. This design ensures effective light reflection even under actuator bending, preventing occlusion of the internal camera field of view.

The bottom cap houses a camera (OV5640) and an air inlet, while the top cap integrates a programmable LED ring arranged in a 3Red-3Green-2Blue configuration. Additionally, three reflective markers are placed on the distal end to facilitate pose tracking using external motion capture systems. The base cap is designed with mechanical mounting features (e.g., 50 mm × 50 mm footprint, 9 mm × 9 mm × 2 mm recess, Ø9 mm cable hole, and Ø3 mm air inlet). The top cap includes a reflective shield to prevent direct light exposure to the camera and to ensure uniform light distribution inside the actuator (Fig. 3).

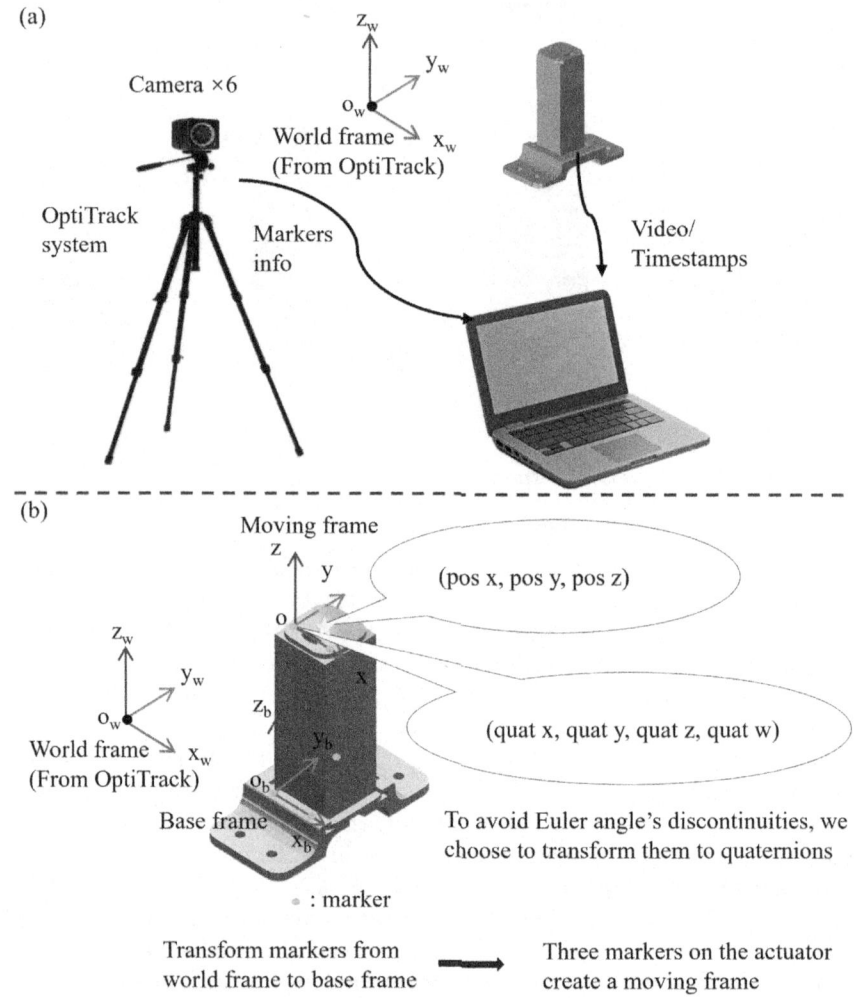

Fig. 3. Experimental setup for the actuator calibration. (a) Setup of the propriocetive equipment. (b) The procedure of data processing.

To acquire ground-truth pose data, we utilized an OptiTrack motion capture system. A total of six reflective markers were attached: three on the actuator base to define the reference coordinate frame, and three on the distal end cap to establish the end-effector coordinate system. This configuration enables accurate estimation of the actuator's spatial orientation and end-effector pose in Euler angles during post-processing.

Marker data, including marker identifications (IDs), 3 dimension (3D) positions, and timestamps, were extracted from the Motive software using a custom script and saved in .txt format. Simultaneously, a bottom-mounted internal camera recorded the actuator's deformation process at 30 frames per second with a resolution of 640×480. The video was saved in .mp4 format, and the corresponding frame timestamps were stored separately in a .txt file to enable precise synchronization with the motion capture data during preprocessing.

Before model training, all raw video and motion capture data must undergo a unified screening and processing pipeline. Each valid data sample must consist of three files: a .mp4 video file, a corresponding video timestamp file (.txt), and a marker data file (.txt) containing 3D positions and timestamps of six markers. Any missing file renders the sample invalid and it is discarded.

Because valid 3D coordinates are only available when each marker is simultaneously detected by at least two cameras, occasional marker loss can occur during actuator motion. To ensure data integrity, marker data is grouped by six IDs per frame, and any sample that does not contain all six markers is excluded from further processing.

For valid data samples, we extract all marker positions and corresponding timestamps and align them with the timestamp sequence of the video frames. Only the frames with successfully matched timestamps are retained for further processing. The matched position and timestamp data are stored in structured tables for use in subsequent stages.

To standardize the coordinate system, we first rotate the default world coordinate system of OptiTrack so that the Z-axis points upward and the X-axis points forward, generating a reference transformation matrix. We define standard unit vectors for each axis and project the original 3D coordinates into this temporary coordinate system.

Next, we identify the three markers fixed on the actuator's mounting base to construct the global reference frame. These markers are selected based on their positional stability across frames. One marker is chosen as the origin, the X-axis is defined by the direction to the second marker, and the Z-axis is obtained by taking the cross product of the X-axis and the vector from the origin to the third marker. The Y-axis is then determined by the right-hand rule, thereby completing the base coordinate system.

All marker coordinates are then transformed into this base frame. Among them, the three markers on the actuator's end cap are used to define a local coordinate frame. The marker with the highest X value is selected to define the X axis, and the Z axis is obtained by taking the cross product between the X axis and the vector to the remaining marker. The Y-axis is again derived by using the right-hand rule.

With both coordinate systems established, we compute the relative transformation between the end-effector frame and the base frame to determine the actuator's orientation. Additionally, we calculate the geometric center of the three end-effector markers in the base coordinate system. This center point provides a robust and smooth representation of the actuator tip's position, which is less sensitive to individual marker jitter or loss and is used as the translational component of the actuator pose.

To avoid discontinuities and singularities associated with Euler angles, such as gimbal lock and angle flipping near ±180°, the orientation is further converted into quaternions. For frames with discontinuous rotations, interpolation is applied to smooth out abrupt transitions.

Finally, for each valid data sample, a .csv file is generated containing the aligned timestamps, Euler angles, quaternion representations, and the position of the actuator's geometric center. This file serves as the training label for the convolutional neural network model used in subsequent prediction tasks.

3 Proprioception Algorithm

We choose ResNet-18 as the primary network architecture because it has demonstrated strong performance in image recognition tasks while maintaining high computational efficiency. This network employs a residual learning structure that effectively alleviates the common gradient vanishing problem in deep networks during training [7], and it has a relatively small parameter size (approximately 11.7 million), making it easy to train and deploy. It should be emphasized that ResNet-18 is widely used as a standard baseline model in image processing tasks [2,14], achieving a good balance between model complexity and performance. Therefore, it is well-suited for medium-scale datasets, limited computational resources, and scenarios requiring rapid iteration.

The goal of this study is to build an image regression model that can directly predict the end-effector's pose from input images. The model outputs a four-dimensional unit quaternion representing the spatial orientation of the end-effector, which is then converts into Euler angles during application for subsequent control and analysis [18]. To achieve this, we use videos along with their corresponding pose annotation tables as input data. The videos are segmented into image frames based on timestamps and matched one-to-one with pose data from the tables, thus constructing a dataset of image-pose pairs.

In visualization and validation analysis, we observe ambiguity in the sign of the quaternion-to-Euler angle conversion, which can cause the same pose to be represented by different numerical values and affect loss convergence during validation [8]. To avoid this issue, we preprocess Euler angles during training and validation to ensure consistent sign alignment, thereby improving model stability and accuracy.

Regarding loss function design, mean squared error (MSE) is used for position regression, while geodesic loss, which is designed to better capture rotational differences, is applied to pose estimation. This approach more accurately reflects the rotational error between quaternions [30], enhancing the robustness of pose estimation.

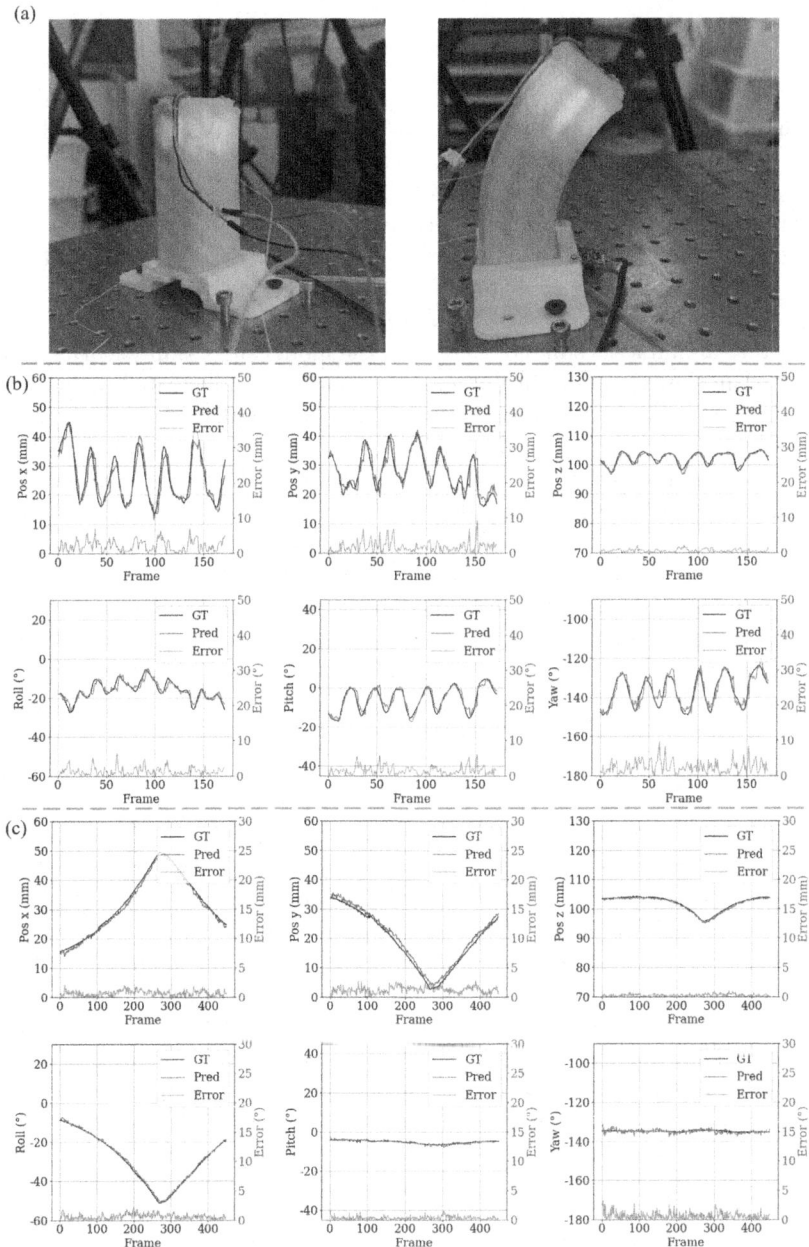

Fig. 4. Evaluation of the proprioceptive sensing. (a) Experimental setups for the actuator in the initial status (left panel) and bending status (right panel). (b) Pose prediction versus ground truth under random external force. (c) Pose prediction versus ground truth under pneumatic actuation.

4 Experiments

4.1 Prediction Accuracy Evaluation

To verify the reliability of the proposed approach, we conducted a systematic comparison between the predicted results and the ground truth (Fig 4). In addition to the active degrees of freedom, we introduced passive degrees of freedom to the soft actuator. This design ensures that the system can still accurately infer the end-effector pose under external forces.

Figure 4(b) shows the model's performance under random external force. It can be observed that the predicted 3D positions and quaternions closely match the ground truth. The average position error remains below 2 mm, and the Euler angle errors are all less than 3.5°. Notably, the model successfully learns to track the entire motion sequence during active actuation, as illustrated in the figure.

Furthermore, we evaluated the model on a complete test sequence that involves only active actuation in Fig. 4(c). The results show that even though passive deformation data was included in training, the model maintains high prediction accuracy for purely active movements, position error is around 1 mm and Euler angle error is below 0.8°. This indicates that the inclusion of passive motion during training does not significantly degrade performance in active cases. It is worth noting that the Euler angles shown in the figure are derived from the predicted quaternions for visualization purposes. Unlike Euler angles, quaternions provide a singularity-free representation of rotation, making them more suitable for learning-based pose estimation.

4.2 Peg-in-Hole Task

To intuitively validate the effectiveness of our proprioceptive method and demonstrate the adaptive capabilities of the soft pneumatic actuator, we design an insertion experiment (Fig. 5). The goal is to show how pose awareness of the actuator supports precise and flexible task execution.

In the experiment, a soft pneumatic actuator and its mounting frame are installed on the end-effector of a robotic arm, with a cylindrical peg fixed to the actuator tip. Successful insertion requires two key pieces of information: the position and orientation of the insertion hole, and the pose of the actuator tip, estimated through proprioceptive sensing. A custom-designed insertion target with through-holes is mounted on a platform. The robotic arm starts from a horizontal orientation and pitches downward by approximately 60°. During this motion, we apply pneumatic pressure to bend the actuator toward a desired pose. Once the actuator reaches the target pitch of 30°, pneumatic input stops based on proprioceptive feedback, allowing the actuator to passively maintain its bent shape.

While maintaining this posture, the robotic arm moves forward toward the holes. The peg measures 3.5 mm in diameter, and the hole 5 mm. To further explore the actuator's adaptive behavior, an additional hole of the same diameter is placed adjacent to the first, tilted at a 5° angle. During insertion, the

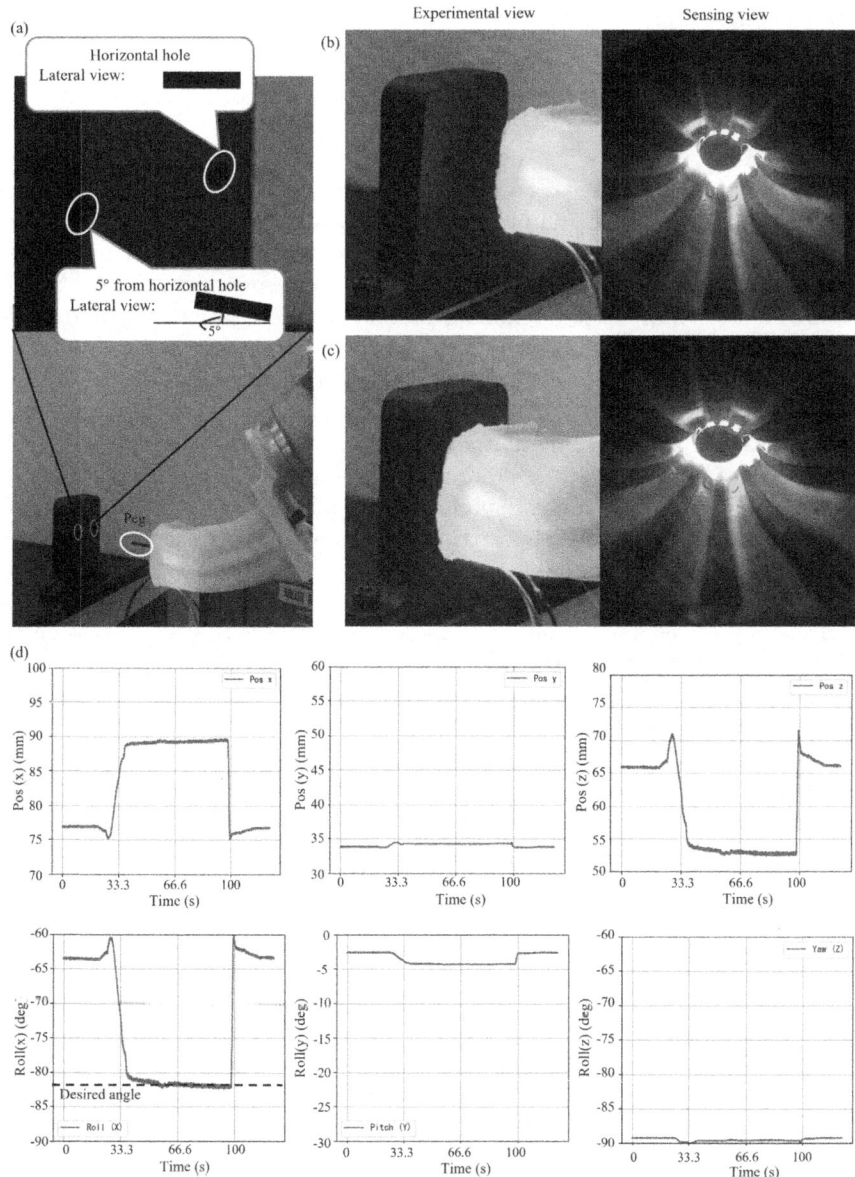

Fig. 5. Peg-in-hole experiment. (a) Experimental setups. (b) Experimental and sensing views during the horizontal hole insertion. (c) Experimental and sensing views during insertion into a hole tilted 5° from the horizontal direction. (d) Predicted pose of the actuator during operation.

actuator bends toward the tilted hole and completes the task without external sensing or re-planning. This result highlights the actuator's ability to accommodate positional and angular variations, supporting flexible and robust performance in contact-rich tasks.

5 Conclusion

In this study, we introduce an optical approach to enable proprioception in soft pneumatic actuators. The complete workflow encompasses both hardware and software development. On the hardware side, we design end caps, molds, and masks, and apply striped visual features through a spraying process. On the software side, we develop a pipeline for data acquisition, processing, and model training. Quantitative evaluations show that the proposed method achieves high accuracy under both active bending and passive twisting conditions. Additionally, the system remains low-cost due to the accessibility and affordability of the materials used. Finally, a functional application experiment demonstrates the effectiveness of the method in a practical insertion task.

Although the current dataset is relatively small and cannot yet eliminate all actuator-related errors, we believe there is substantial room for improvement. Future work will proceed along several directions. On the hardware side, we aim to reduce the actuator's size and explore alternative reflective patterns to identify the most effective configuration. We will also address the issue of the actuator disappearing from the camera's view under large bending angles. On the data side, we plan to expand the dataset and further refine the model to enhance performance and generalizability.

Acknowledgement. This work was partly supported in part by the National Natural Science Foundation of China (Grant Nos. 52305029 and 52025057), the National Key R&D Program of China (Grant No. 2024YFB4707504), and the Science and Technology Commission of Shanghai Municipality (Grant No. 24511103400).

References

1. Bai, H., Li, S., Barreiros, J., Tu, Y., Pollock, C.R., Shepherd, R.F.: Stretchable distributed fiber-optic sensors. Science **370**(6518), 848–852 (2020)
2. Deng, J., Dong, W., Socher, R., Li, L.J., Li, K., Fei-Fei, L.: Imagenet: a large-scale hierarchical image database. In: 2009 IEEE Conference on Computer Vision and Pattern Recognition, pp. 248–255. IEEE (2009)
3. Ge, L., Wang, T., Zhang, N., Gu, G.: Fabrication of soft pneumatic network actuators with oblique chambers. J. Visualized Exp. JoVE (138), 58277 (2018)
4. Gu, G.Y., Zhu, J., Zhu, L.M., Zhu, X.: A survey on dielectric elastomer actuators for soft robots. Bioinspiration biomimetics **12**(1), 011003 (2017)
5. Gu, G., Zhang, N., Chen, C., Xu, H., Zhu, X.: Soft robotics enables neuroprosthetic hand design. ACS Nano **17**(11), 9661–9672 (2023)
6. Gu, G., et al.: A soft neuroprosthetic hand providing simultaneous myoelectric control and tactile feedback. Nat. Biomed. Eng. **7**(4), 589–598 (2023)

7. He, K., Zhang, X., Ren, S., Sun, J.: Deep residual learning for image recognition. In: Proceedings of the IEEE Conference on Computer Vision and Pattern Recognition, pp. 770–778 (2016)
8. Huynh, D.Q.: Metrics for 3D rotations: comparison and analysis. J. Math. Imaging Vision **35**(2), 155–164 (2009)
9. Kim, S., Laschi, C., Trimmer, B.: Soft robotics: a bioinspired evolution in robotics. Trends Biotechnol. **31**(5), 287–294 (2013)
10. Liu, K., et al.: Biomimetic impact protective supramolecular polymeric materials enabled by quadruple h-bonding. J. Am. Chem. Soc. **143**(2), 1162–1170 (2020)
11. Park, Y.L., Chen, B.R., Wood, R.J.: Design and fabrication of soft artificial skin using embedded microchannels and liquid conductors. IEEE Sens. J. **12**(8), 2711–2718 (2012)
12. Polygerinos, P., Galloway, K.C., Savage, E., Herman, M., O'Donnell, K., Walsh, C.J.: Soft robotic glove for hand rehabilitation and task specific training. In: 2015 IEEE International Conference on Robotics and Automation (ICRA), pp. 2913–2919. IEEE (2015)
13. Rus, D., Tolley, M.T.: Design, fabrication and control of soft robots. Nature **521**(7553), 467–475 (2015)
14. Russakovsky, O., et al.: Imagenet large scale visual recognition challenge. Int. J. Comput. Vision **115**(3), 211–252 (2015)
15. Shao, Q., Zhang, N., Shen, Z., Gu, G.: A pneumatic soft gripper with configurable workspace and self-sensing. In: 2020 17th International Conference on Ubiquitous Robots (UR), pp. 36–43. IEEE (2020)
16. Shen, Z., et al.: High-stretchability, ultralow-hysteresis conductingpolymer hydrogel strain sensors for soft machines. Adv. Mater. **34**(32), 2203650 (2022)
17. Sheng, X., Xu, H., Zhang, N., Ding, N., Zhu, X., Gu, G.: Multi-material 3D printing of caterpillar-inspired soft crawling robots with the pneumatically bellow-type body and anisotropic friction feet. Sens. Actuators, A **316**, 112398 (2020)
18. Sola, J.: Quaternion kinematics for the error-state kalman filter (2017)
19. Yang, D., Feng, M., Gu, G.: High-stroke, high-output-force, fabric-lattice artificial muscles for soft robots. Adv. Mater. **36**(2), 2306928 (2024)
20. Yang, X., et al.: Multidirectional bending soft pneumatic actuator with fishbone-like strain-limiting layer for dexterous manipulation. IEEE Rob. Autom. Lett. (2024)
21. Zhang, A., Truby, R.L., Chin, L., Li, S., Rus, D.: Vision-based sensing for electrically-driven soft actuators. IEEE Rob. Autom. Lett. **7**(4), 11509–11516 (2022)
22. Zhang, N., Ge, L., Xu, H., Zhu, X., Gu, G.: 3D printed, modularized rigid-flexible integrated soft finger actuators for anthropomorphic hands. Sens. Actuators, A **312**, 112090 (2020)
23. Zhang, N., et al.: Soft robotic hand with tactile palm-finger coordination. Nat. Commun. **16**(1), 2395 (2025)
24. Zhang, N., Zhao, Y., Gu, G., Zhu, X.: Synergistic control of soft robotic hands for human-like grasp postures. Sci. China Technol. Sci. **65**(3), 553–568 (2022)
25. Zhang, N., et al.: Biomimetic rigid-soft finger design for highly dexterous and adaptive robotic hands. Science Advances **11**(17) (2025)
26. Zhang, S., Shan, J., Fang, B., Sun, F.: Soft robotic finger embedded with visual sensor for bending perception. Robotica **39**(3), 378–390 (2021)
27. Zhang, Y.F., et al.: Fast-response, stiffness-tunable soft actuator by hybrid multi-material 3D printing. Adv. Func. Mater. **29**(15), 1806698 (2019)

28. Zhao, H., O'Brien, K., Li, S., Shepherd, R.F.: Optoelectronically innervated soft prosthetic hand via stretchable optical waveguides. Sci. Rob. **1**(1), eaai7529 (2016)
29. Zhao, X., Wang, Z., Li, Z., Liu, H., Yang, Y.: Stretchable distributed fiber-optic sensors. Science **371**(6527), 948–952 (2021)
30. Zhou, Y., Barnes, C., Lu, J., Yang, J., Li, H.: On the continuity of rotation representations in neural networks. In: Proceedings of the IEEE/CVF Conference on Computer Vision and Pattern Recognition, pp. 5745–5753 (2019)

Visual-Guided Diffusion Policy and Mesh-DMP Integration for Robotic Freeform Surface Polishing

Shuai Ke, Jiexin Zhang[✉], Huan Zhao, Yikun Guo, Zhiao Wei, Jie Pan, and Han Ding

State Key Laboratory of Intelligent Manufacturing Equipment and Technology, Department of Mechanical Science and Engineering, Huazhong University of Science and Technology, Wuhan 430074, China
zhangjiexin@hust.edu.cn

Abstract. Learning processing skills from human demonstrations has become a growing research focus, particularly in robotic polishing. Current studies mainly emphasize trajectory reproduction, lacking task-level planning and the ability to generate precise position and orientation actions on freeform surfaces from visual input. To address this, we propose an action generation strategy tailored for robotic polishing on freeform surfaces. This method leverages RGB-D images to generate surface-aware actions. First, the 3D geometry of the workpiece is captured using an RGB-D camera and reconstructed into a structured triangular mesh. Then, a diffusion model infers continuous polishing actions from image observations. These actions are embedded onto the freeform surface using Mesh-DMP to ensure geometric consistency. The proposed framework integrates vision-driven policy generation with surface-constrained motion modeling, enhancing generalization and control in unstructured tasks. Experimental results demonstrate the effectiveness of our approach in generating high-quality polishing trajectories on complex surfaces.

Keywords: imitation learning · diffusion model · visual-guided policy · robotic manufacturing

1 Introduction

As manufacturing moves toward greater variety, smaller batch sizes, and higher flexibility, robotic technology—due to its structural versatility and diverse tool interfaces—is becoming a powerful complement to traditional CNC machines [1]. Compared to machine tools, robots exhibit significant advantages in complex part machining and irregular surface processing. They enable rapid switching of fixtures and end-effectors and support a wide range of tools such as grinding heads, polishing pads, and laser nozzles [2,3]. However, traditional offline programming methods typically rely on manually defining processing paths in 3D models or point-by-point teaching through teach pendants [4]. These approaches are time-consuming, labor-intensive, and ill-suited to meet the efficient production needs of industries like aerospace and rail transportation, which involve low-volume, structurally complex parts. To address this challenge, imitation learningbased trajectory generation methods have emerged as a research hotspot, as they integrate expert demonstrations into robotic programming, significantly improving programming efficiency and reducing labor costs [5].

To reduce the difficulty of programming for complex surface parts, Learning from Demonstration (LfD) has become a key strategy for robotic trajectory generation. One of the earliest approaches is Behavior Cloning (BC) [6], which uses supervised learning to directly fit expert demonstration trajectories point-by-point, allowing the robot to reproduce similar behaviors. However, BC is highly sensitive to noise, lacks generalization, and performs poorly when there is a mismatch between demonstration and execution conditions. To overcome these limitations, statistical imitation learning methods have been introduced. For instance, Gaussian Mixture Models (GMM) and Gaussian Mixture Regression (GMR) have been employed to probabilistically model multiple demonstrations [7], capturing motion redundancy and enabling smooth trajectory reconstruction under temporal misalignment. Hidden Markov Models (HMM) further capture temporal structures through latent state sequences. These statistical models exhibit stronger robustness to variations in demonstration speeds and external disturbances [8]. However, they typically rely on careful feature selection and time alignment, and their generalization capability remains limited when faced with novel tasks.

In recent years, Dynamic Movement Primitives (DMPs) have emerged as a mainstream method in imitation learning due to their ability to embed demonstration trajectories into stable nonlinear dynamical systems [9]. By constructing a damped spring system and incorporating external forcing terms, DMPs encode trajectories parametrically, maintaining both stability and convergence while allowing flexible modulation and generalization. Owing to their simplicity, clear dynamical interpretation, and compatibility with data-driven learning, DMPs have been widely applied in robotic manipulation tasks such as grasping [10], assembly [11], and welding [12]. They effectively reduce the complexity of robotic programming and deployment while ensuring trajectory reusability and task adaptability.

Nevertheless, despite the effectiveness of DMPs in encoding and modulating Euclidean-space trajectories, their limitations become apparent in high-dimensional policy modeling required for complex task planning and execution [9]. First, they lack high-level policy planning capabilities, making them insufficient for modeling long-horizon, multi-stage tasks. Additionally, generalization still requires explicitly defined start and goal positions. Second, in tasks involving geometrically constrained freeform surface trajectories, DMPs lack geometric adaptability and fail to ensure high-precision surface adherence [13]. Traditional DMP frameworks can only generate trajectories similar in shape to the demonstrated ones and are unable to synthesize new actions from visual inputs, limiting their applicability to autonomous robotic machining of freeform parts.

To address these challenges, we propose MP-Diffusion, an imitation learning-based trajectory generation framework optimized for robotic processing of complex freeform surfaces. The method first reconstructs the surface geometry using a depth camera and triangular mesh modeling. It then incorporates Mesh-DMP [14] to ensure that the generated motion sequences not only conform to surface geometry constraints but also exhibit favorable dynamic adaptability. Additionally, a diffusion model is employed to process RGB image observations and plan robot actions at the task level. This framework significantly improves data efficiency and enables the generation of motion sequences that satisfy both complex geometric constraints and dynamic response requirements. MP-Diffusion is particularly well-suited for fine manipulation tasks involving flexible parts in robotic polishing, cleaning, and other high-precision applications.

2 Related Work

In industrial automation, surface processing tasks such as grinding and polishing of complex-shaped workpieces require robots to perform contact operations on freeform surfaces. However, traditional offline programming methods struggle to adapt to the constantly changing geometry of workpieces and are typically implemented in an open-loop manner [15], lacking the capability for rapid closed-loop adaptation to dynamic conditions. On one hand, there is a lack of stable and convergent dynamic adjustment mechanisms during trajectory execution, making it difficult to cope with rapid changes in surface curvature. On the other hand, existing methods often lack fast closed-loop adaptation based on RGB images [16]. Moreover, strategies purely based on visual and motion modeling tend to ignore rich contact information, thus lacking robustness when surface or contact conditions change. Although recent advances in force-feedback-based adaptive control methods—such as impedance control or adaptive gain strategies—have improved the adaptability to surface variations by dynamically adjusting the contact orientation and normal force of the tool, these approaches are still susceptible to processing vibrations and measurement noise, which limits their stability and reliability in industrial applications.

While Dynamic Movement Primitives (DMPs) have demonstrated strong capabilities in robot trajectory learning and generalization—particularly in encoding and generalizing point-to-point or periodic motions through stable dynamical systems—their application to freeform surface processing remains challenging [9]. Traditional DMPs primarily focus on the kinematic description of trajectories and lack modeling of physical interaction between the robot and the environment, making it difficult to meet the high-precision requirements of simultaneous control over position, orientation, and contact force in surface processing [17]. The recently proposed Mesh-DMP method extends DMPs to discrete surface domains by defining differential operators on triangular meshes and projecting external forces onto the surface to reproduce trajectories with geometric consistency [14]. However, it still overlooks the feedback and modeling mechanisms involved in the actual processing tasks, limiting its robustness and adaptability in complex real-world applications. Other studies have explored improvements to DMPs from the perspectives of time-scale separation and curvature parameterization, such as introducing arc-length parametrization to improve trajectory reproduction accuracy [18], or using Gaussian Mixture Models to jointly encode trajectories and contact forces. Nevertheless, challenges remain in terms of synchronized orientation representation and numerical precision degradation. Furthermore, due to the inherent structure of DMPs, their generalization ability remains limited, as new trajectories require explicitly defined start and end points—an approach that falls short in diverse and variable processing scenarios.

To enhance the generalization capability of DMPs in dynamic processing contexts, recent research has focused on deeply integrating DMPs with various machine learning techniques to overcome limitations in generalization and perception-driven control. On one hand, deep neural networks have been introduced to learn DMP parameters [19,20], enabling trajectory encoding to be generated directly from raw perceptual data such as images, thereby facilitating perception-driven motion generation. For instance, convolutional neural networks can extract task-relevant visual features and serve as conditional inputs to modulate the initial state and external force terms of DMPs, enabling the generation of new trajectories under visual guidance. On the other hand, integrating reinforcement learning strategies further improves the adaptability of DMPs in dynamic environments [21], allowing rapid policy updates and generalization with minimal interactions under frequently changing task requirements and processing conditions. In addition, generative models such as Variational Autoencoders (VAEs) [22] and Generative Adversarial Networks (GANs) [23] have been incorporated into DMP frameworks to extract trajectory priors from visual information, maintaining high performance even in low-data scenarios. Notably, diffusion models have recently achieved remarkable success in image generation and understanding, effectively modeling complex data distributions via iterative denoising mechanisms. These capabilities have been extended to robotic tasks such as assembly and manipulation, demonstrating strong motion diversity and task generalization. However, such approaches often lack low-level motion control mechanisms, limiting their practical performance in real-world operations [24] (Fig. 1).

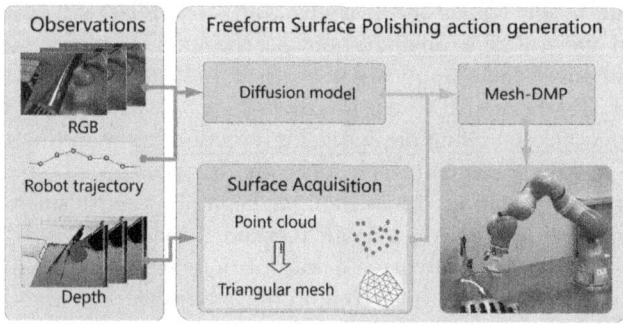

Fig. 1. Framework of the Visual-Guided Diffusion Policy and Mesh-DMP Integration method.

In summary, the deep integration of DMPs with visual perception and learning mechanisms represents a key pathway for evolving from traditional trajectory reproduction tools to intelligent motion generation systems. This integration provides new technical support for efficient adaptation and generalization in robotic freeform surface processing tasks.

3 Method

3.1 Problem Formulation

This paper aims to generate action sequences for robotic polishing tasks on freeform surfaces. We focus on predicting a sequence of surface actions $\mathcal{A} = \{a_t\}_{t=1}^T$, where each action $a_t \in \mathbb{R}^k$ represents the target state of the robot end-effector at time t, including task-relevant control dimensions such as position and contact direction. The dimension k of the task space depends on the application scenario.

The action generation process is conditioned on perception of the surface geometry. Specifically, an RGB-D camera captures an RGB image $I \in \mathbb{R}^{H \times W \times 3}$ and a depth image $D \in \mathbb{R}^{H \times W}$, from which a dense point cloud $P \in \mathbb{R}^{N \times 3}$ is reconstructed. Using this point cloud, a triangular mesh $\mathcal{M} = (\mathcal{V}, \mathcal{F})$ is constructed to model the surface geometry, where $\mathcal{V}$ is the set of mesh vertices and $\mathcal{F}$ the set of faces.

We adopt an imitation learning (IL) framework to train a diffusion model that generates surface action sequences from visual observations. Each training sample consists of an observation sequence $\mathcal{O} = \{o_{t-m+1}, \ldots, o_t\}$ and a corresponding action sequence $\mathcal{A} = \{a_{t+1}, \ldots, a_{t+n}\}$, where o_t is the visual observation at time t, and n, m denote the lengths of the prediction and observation windows, respectively. The training dataset $\mathcal{D} = \{d_i\}_{i=1}^N$ consists of human demonstrations, each being a full sequence of image-action pairs $(o_t, a_t)_{t=1}^{T_i}$. Demonstrations are segmented into multiple short sequences for training to enhance robustness and generalization.

At inference time, the diffusion model generates an intended surface trajectory $\hat{\mathcal{A}} = \{\hat{a}_{t+1}, \ldots, \hat{a}_{t+n}\}$ conditioned on the current visual input. This trajectory is then encoded and executed on the triangular mesh surface $\mathcal{M}$ via the Mesh-DMP module. Mesh-DMP learns the surface dynamics of the action sequence during training, and utilizes logarithmic/exponential maps and parallel transport on the discrete mesh to enable projection and reproduction of the trajectory along the surface, ensuring smooth and accurate execution.

Formally, our goal is to generate a surface-aligned action sequence $\hat{\mathcal{A}}$ conditioned on the current image I_t and corresponding mesh $\mathcal{M}$, and to execute it on the surface using Mesh-DMP, enabling dynamic and precise trajectory following for robotic manipulation on freeform surfaces. The framework of the Visual-Guided Diffusion Policy and Mesh-DMP Integration method is illustrated in Fig. 2.

3.2 Surface Acquisition and Encoding

To enable trajectory modeling on free-form surfaces, we first acquire geometric information of the workpiece using an RGB-D camera, and encode it into a discrete surface structure suitable for Mesh-DMP. The overall process includes generating a point cloud from the depth image, constructing a triangular mesh, and embedding the mesh as the domain for trajectory generation.

Given a depth image $D \in \mathbb{R}^{H \times W}$, where each pixel (u, v) corresponds to a depth value $D(u, v)$, and an intrinsic matrix $K \in \mathbb{R}^{3 \times 3}$, the 3D coordinate $\mathbf{p} \in \mathbb{R}^3$ of the pixel is recovered via:

$$\mathbf{p} = D(u, v) \cdot K^{-1} \begin{bmatrix} u \\ v \\ 1 \end{bmatrix} \tag{1}$$

Applying this transformation to all pixels yields a point set:

$$\mathcal{P} = \{\mathbf{p}_i\}_{i=1}^{N}, \quad N = H \times W \tag{2}$$

which forms a dense point cloud of the free-form surface.

We then reconstruct a triangular mesh $\mathcal{M} = (\mathcal{V}, \mathcal{F})$, where the vertex set $\mathcal{V} = \{\mathbf{v}_i\} \subset \mathbb{R}^3$ and face set $\mathcal{F} = \{\mathcal{T}_j\}$, with each face defined as:

$$\mathcal{T}_j = (i_1, i_2, i_3), \quad i_k \in \mathcal{V} \tag{3}$$

To ensure mesh consistency, we perform Delaunay triangulation under the following constraints:

Constraint 1. Each edge appears in at most two faces:

$$\forall e \in \mathcal{E}, \quad |\{\mathcal{T}_k \in \mathcal{F} \mid e \in \mathcal{T}_k\}| \leq 2 \tag{4}$$

where the symbol $\mathcal{E}$ denotes the set of edges.

Constraint 2. Normals of adjacent faces are aligned:

$$\mathbf{n}_{T_i} \cdot \mathbf{n}_{T_j} > 0, \quad \forall \, T_i, T_j \text{ sharing an edge} \tag{5}$$

The tangent space of each triangle $\mathcal{T}_k \in \mathcal{F}$ is given by:

$$\mathcal{T}_k = \text{span} \{\mathbf{v}_j - \mathbf{v}_i, \, \mathbf{v}_k - \mathbf{v}_i\} \tag{6}$$

This mesh is then used as the trajectory embedding manifold in Mesh-DMP, supporting geometrically constrained trajectory generation for the robot end-effector. Mesh-DMP generalizes classical DMPs from Euclidean space to discrete surface manifolds, introducing differential operators:

$$\log_{\mathbf{v}_i}(\mathbf{v}_j), \quad \exp_{\mathbf{v}_i}(\mathbf{v}), \quad \Gamma_{\mathbf{v}_i \to \mathbf{v}_j}(\cdot) \tag{7}$$

These operators compute tangent vectors between points, map tangent vectors back to mesh vertices, and transport tangent vectors across the mesh, respectively. They enable encoding continuous relative spatial relations over surface trajectories. Ultimately, the triangular mesh offers a discrete representation of the free-form surface geometry for motion modeling. The procedural flow of the Surface Acquisition and Encoding method is illustrated in Fig. 2.

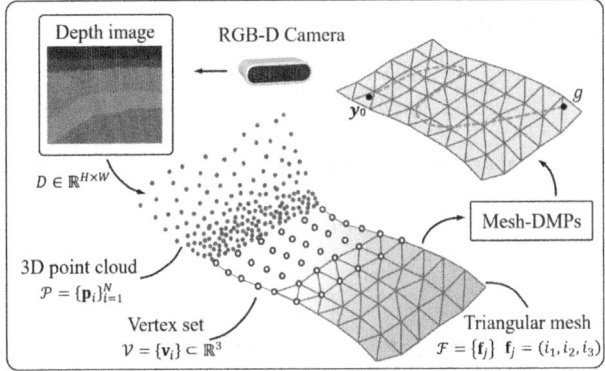

Fig. 2. The procedural flow of the Surface Acquisition and Encoding method.

3.3 Mesh-DMP Method Analysis

Dynamic Movement Primitives (DMPs) provide a simple and parametric formulation to represent complex motor skills. However, classical DMPs are defined in Euclidean space and thus lack intrinsic consistency when generalized to tasks constrained by curved surfaces. Mesh-DMP addresses this limitation by extending DMP trajectory modeling onto a discrete surface manifold [14]. By embedding trajectory dynamics into a triangular mesh structure, Mesh-DMP enables geometrically consistent trajectory reproduction on arbitrary surfaces. Unlike methods that require explicit surface parameterization or ad hoc projection, Mesh-DMP leverages differential geometric tools—such as geodesics, logarithmic and exponential maps, and parallel transport—to enable surface-consistent motion modeling.

To model motion on a discrete mesh $\mathcal{M} = (\mathcal{V}, \mathcal{F})$, Mesh-DMP introduces discrete geodesics, logarithmic maps, exponential maps, and parallel transport. Given two points $m_1, m_2 \in \mathcal{M}$, the geodesic path is defined as:

$$\gamma = \{p_1 p_2, \ldots, p_{n_\gamma - 1} p_{n_\gamma}\} \tag{8}$$

with endpoints $p_1 = m_1$ and $p_{n_\gamma} = m_2$, where all $p_i \in \mathcal{M}$.

The logarithmic map projects m_2 to a tangent vector at m_1:

$$\log_{m_1}(m_2) = \frac{p_1 p_2}{\|p_1 p_2\|} \sum_{i=1}^{n_\gamma - 1} \|p_i p_{i+1}\| \tag{9}$$

The exponential map is the inverse operation:

$$\exp_{m_1}(v) = m_2 \quad \text{such that} \quad \log_{m_1}(m_2) = v \tag{10}$$

Parallel transport of a tangent vector $v \in T_{m_1}\mathcal{M}$ to $T_{m_2}\mathcal{M}$ is given by:

$$\Gamma_{m_1 \to m_2}(v) := Rv \tag{11}$$

where $R \in \mathbb{R}^{3\times 3}$ is the unique rotation aligning

$$w_1 = \frac{p_1 p_2}{\|p_1 p_2\|}, \quad w_2 = \frac{p_{n_\gamma - 1} p_{n_\gamma}}{\|p_{n_\gamma - 1} p_{n_\gamma}\|} \qquad (12)$$

The DMP formulation in Euclidean space is [14]:

$$\begin{aligned}\dot{z} &= \Omega\left(\alpha(\beta(g-y)-z)+f(\phi)\right) \\ \dot{y} &= \Omega z \\ \dot{\phi} &= \frac{1}{\Omega}\end{aligned} \qquad (13)$$

Mesh-DMP extends this system to the mesh manifold as:

$$\begin{aligned}\nabla_z z &= \Omega\left[\alpha(\beta\log_y(g)-z)+T(y,z)f(\phi)\right] \\ \dot{y} &= \Omega z\end{aligned} \qquad (14)$$

Here, $\nabla_z z$ denotes the covariant derivative on the manifold, $T(y,z) \in \mathbb{R}^{3\times 3}$ transforms vectors from the local tangent space to the global coordinate frame, and $f : \mathbb{R} \to T_y \mathcal{M}$ is a learned forcing term defined in the tangent space. This formulation enables trajectory generalization and stability under complex surface constraints.

3.4 Diffusion-Based Policy Generation via Visual Guidance

To accomplish high-precision polishing on freeform surfaces, we introduce a visual-guided diffusion-based policy generation mechanism. The core idea is to train a trajectory-level diffusion probabilistic model [24] under an imitation learning framework. Given a sequence of image observations $\mathcal{O} = \{o_{t-m+1}, \ldots, o_t\}$, the model predicts the surface action sequence

$$\hat{\mathcal{A}} = \{\hat{a}_{t+1}, \ldots, \hat{a}_{t+n}\} \qquad (15)$$

where each $\hat{a}_i \in \mathbb{R}^k$ denotes the target state of the robot end-effector at timestep t_s, and k is the task-space dimensionality.

The forward diffusion process progressively corrupts the clean trajectory τ^0 by adding Gaussian noise:

$$q(\tau^{(i)}|\tau^{(i-1)}) = \mathcal{N}(\tau^{(i)}; \sqrt{1-\beta_i}\tau^{(i-1)}, \beta_i \mathbf{I}) \qquad (16)$$

for $i = 1, \ldots, N$, where β_i denotes the noise variance at step i.

The reverse denoising process is parameterized as

$$p_\theta(\tau^{(i-1)}|\tau^{(i)}) = \mathcal{N}(\tau^{(i-1)}; \mu_\theta(\tau^{(i)}, i), \Sigma_i) \qquad (17)$$

and the model is trained by minimizing the simplified denoising objective:

$$\mathcal{L}(\theta) = \mathbb{E}_{i,\epsilon,\tau^0}\left[\left\|\epsilon - \epsilon_\theta(\tau^{(i)}, i)\right\|^2\right] \qquad (18)$$

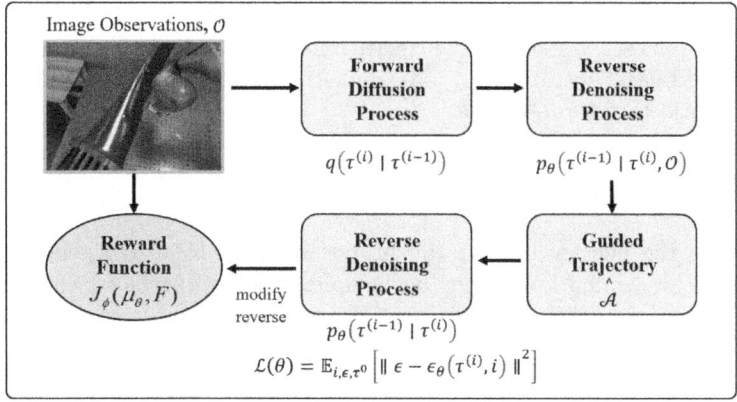

Fig. 3. Visual-guided diffusion-based action generation.

where $\epsilon \sim \mathcal{N}(0, \mathbf{I})$ is Gaussian noise, and ϵ_θ predicts the noise added at step i (Fig. 3).

To guide trajectory generation using visual intent, we define a reward function $J_\phi(\mu_\theta, \mathcal{O})$ derived from the image observation sequence. During sampling, we modify the reverse process as:

$$p_\theta(\tau^{(i-1)}|\tau^{(i)}, \mathcal{O}) \approx \mathcal{N}\left(\tau^{(i-1)}; \mu_\theta + \alpha \Sigma_i \nabla_\tau J_\phi(\mu_\theta, \mathcal{O}), \Sigma_i\right) \tag{19}$$

where α is a positive scalar controlling the guidance strength.

To further enhance the execution stability and physical consistency of the model in contact-based manipulation tasks, we extend the guidance function $J_\phi(\mu_\theta, O)$ to support multi-modal perception, where the observation O includes contact feedback signals $F = \{f_1, f_2, \ldots, f_T\}$ from force sensors. Each f_t denotes the contact force measurement at time step t.

We design a contact-force-based guidance function as follows:

$$J_\phi(\mu_\theta, F) = -\sum_{t=1}^{T} \left\| \hat{f}_t(\mu_{\theta,t}) - f_t^*(\mu_{\theta,t}) \right\|^2$$

With this design, the guidance term effectively leverages contact perception to optimize the diffusion model's trajectory generation, making the results more consistent with the desired contact behavior characteristics (e.g., sufficient normal force, stable contact, and consistent contact region). This approach provides a unified and differentiable contact-aware sampling guidance mechanism applicable to various contact-rich robotic manipulation tasks.

At inference time, given current observation $\mathcal{O}$ and the triangle mesh representation of the surface $\mathcal{M} = (\mathcal{V}, \mathcal{F})$, the model outputs the guided trajectory

$$\hat{\mathcal{A}} = \{\hat{a}_{t+1}, \ldots, \hat{a}_{t+n}\} \tag{20}$$

which is passed to the Mesh-DMP module for execution on $\mathcal{M}$ using discrete differential operators such as the logarithmic map $\log_{\mathcal{M}}(\cdot)$, exponential map $\exp_{\mathcal{M}}(\cdot)$, and parallel transport $\mathcal{P}_{\mathcal{M}}(\cdot)$, ensuring accurate surface adherence and dynamic trajectory reproduction.

4 Experiment

To validate the effectiveness of the proposed method, we designed a robotic experiment for wiping operations on complex freeform surfaces, covering both task execution capability and comparative evaluation against a baseline method.

4.1 Experimental Setup for Freeform Surface Wiping

We constructed an experimental system to simulate robotic polishing on the freeform surface of an impeller blade. A soft cleaning sponge is mounted at the robot's end-effector to emulate a compliant contact polishing tool. To simulate surface contamination such as rust or residue, cleaning foam is sprayed at random positions on the blade surface. The success of the polishing action is determined by whether the robot can effectively remove the foam (Fig. 4).

The robotic platform employs a KUKA LBR iiwa14 R820 collaborative robot operating in impedance control mode, with a position control frequency of 200 Hz and an impedance controller frequency of 1 kHz. In addition to the cleaning sponge, an Intel RealSense D435i RGB-D camera is mounted near the robot wrist to provide local image observations. A second camera, Intel RealSense L515, is fixed on a tripod and used to capture global RGB images as well as depth images from a top-down view. These visual data streams are used as inputs to the diffusion model. In particular, the depth map from the L515 is used to reconstruct a triangular mesh model of the blade's freeform surface.

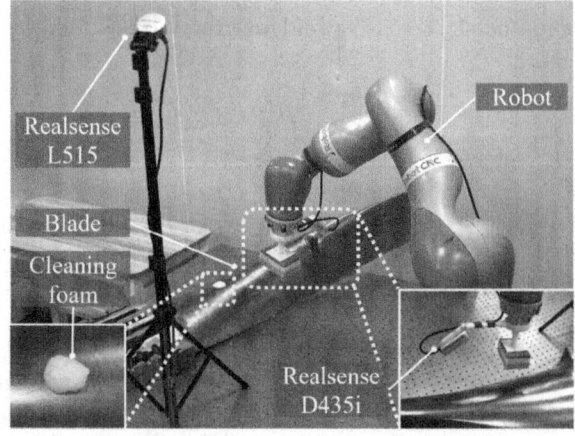

Fig. 4. Experimental setup for freeform surface wiping.

During the data collection phase, an operator performs demonstrations via teleoperation, wiping away foam sprayed randomly on the blade surface. The demonstrations are recorded in the form of synchronized RGB video streams from both cameras and the robot's joint trajectory. After temporal alignment and preprocessing, these data are used to train the diffusion model. In the policy inference stage, a new polishing action is generated by first reconstructing a triangular mesh of the blade surface using the L515 depth image. The diffusion model then takes the synchronized RGB image sequences from both cameras and the robot end-effector pose history as input to produce a new sequence of polishing motions.

The diffusion-based trajectory generation model employed in this work is implemented using an 8-layer Transformer decoder with 256-dimensional embeddings and 4-head causal attention. The input consists of multi-view image features extracted by a ResNet-18 encoder, combined with the current state and timestep embeddings as conditional vectors. Trajectory sampling is performed using a DDIM scheduler with 100 diffusion steps, and the model is trained to predict Gaussian noise. During training, the AdamW optimizer with cosine learning rate scheduling is utilized, and an exponential moving average (EMA) is applied to enhance training stability.

4.2 Comparative Experiment

To evaluate the effectiveness of the proposed method in freeform surface polishing tasks, we selected a baseline approach that directly generates robot actions using a diffusion model [24], without surface-aware constraints. Both methods were tested under identical experimental setups and task conditions. During each wiping trial, a failure was recorded if any cleaning foam remained after execution; otherwise, the attempt was considered successful. The models were trained using 200 demonstration sequences. In the evaluation phase, we conducted 20 test trials for each method. Representative snapshots of the wiping process are shown below (Fig. 5).

Each trial in the figure illustrates the robot's state transitions before wiping (Before), during wiping (Wiping action), and after wiping (After). In all successful cases, the proposed method consistently maintained stable contact between the cleaning sponge and the freeform surface of the workpiece, effectively removing the foam and demonstrating strong trajectory adherence and task reliability. In contrast, the baseline method showed partial wiping behavior in some trials, but often failed to maintain stable contact with the surface, resulting in deviation from the target region or complete loss of contact. Across all 20 comparative trials, the success rates are summarized in Table 1.

The baseline method generates action sequences directly in Euclidean space using a diffusion model, without explicitly modeling the geometric constraints of the surface. As a result, the generated trajectories tend to drift or deviate when attempting to follow complex surfaces, making it difficult for the robot end-effector to maintain consistent contact. In contrast, our proposed method incorporates a Mesh-DMP module after trajectory generation, embedding the

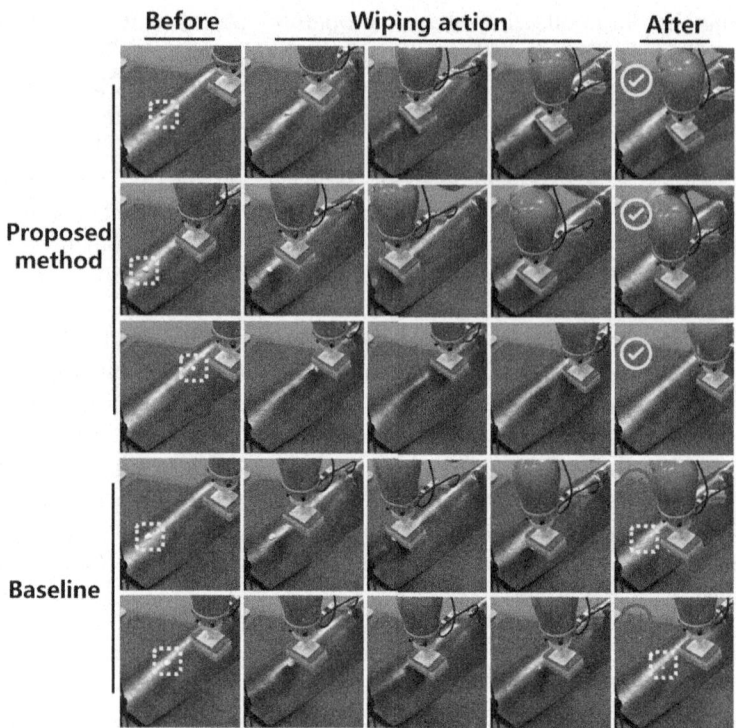

Fig. 5. Comparative experiment.

Table 1. Success Rates of Different Methods in Freeform Surface Wiping

Method	Success Rates
Proposed method	20/20
Baseline	9/20

action sequence into a discrete surface manifold. By leveraging differential geometric operations such as logarithmic maps, exponential maps, and parallel transport, the trajectory is continuously propagated across the surface. This leads to smoother, surface-adherent motions, enhancing both the robustness of the wiping action and the overall task success rate.

5 Conclusion

In response to the limitations of current imitation learning methods for robotic polishing—particularly their weak task-level planning capability and inability to generate accurate position and orientation actions on freeform surfaces from visual information—this paper proposes a novel strategy generation framework that integrates a visually guided diffusion model with Mesh-DMP for robotic freeform surface polishing. The proposed method enables visually conditioned action generation on complex surfaces. Specifically, RGB-D observations are used to reconstruct a triangle mesh representation of the target workpiece, and a diffusion model is trained to directly generate action sequences from visual inputs. These actions are then embedded onto the surface manifold via Mesh-DMP, ensuring geometrically consistent trajectory reproduction. Polishing simulation experiments were conducted on the freeform surface of a turbine blade. Compared with conventional vision-only planning methods, the proposed approach produces trajectories that adhere more closely to the target surface and improves the task completion success rate by 55 %. The results demonstrate the effectiveness of our method in practical scenarios and highlight its potential for applications in flexible manufacturing and surface finishing.

Acknowledgments. This work was supported by the National Natural Science Foundation of China under Grant Nos. 52505016, U24A20130, 52090054, and in part by the Postdoctoral Fellowship Program of CPSF under Grant Number GZC20240539, and in part by China Postdoctoral Science Foundation under Grant Number 2024M760999.

References

1. Li, X.F., Huang, T., Zhao, H., et al.: A review of recent advances in machining techniques of complex surfaces. Sci. China Technol. Sci. **65**(9), 1915–1939 (2022)
2. Zhu, D., Feng, X., Xu, X., et al.: Robotic grinding of complex components: a step towards efficient and intelligent machining–challenges, solutions, and applications. Rob. Comput. Integr. Manuf. **65**, 101908 (2020)
3. Guo, Q., Yang, Z., Xu, J., et al.: Progress, challenges and trends on vision sensing technologies in automatic/intelligent robotic welding: State-of-the-art review. Rob. Comput. Integr. Manuf. **89**, 102767 (2024)
4. Li, W., Wang, Y., Liang, Y., et al.: Learning from demonstration for autonomous generation of robotic trajectory: status quo and forward-looking overview. Adv. Eng. Inform. **62**, 102625 (2024)
5. Jaquier, N., Welle, M.C., Gams, A., et al.: Transfer learning in robotics: an upcoming breakthrough? A review of promises and challenges. Int. J. Rob. Res. **44**(3), 465–485 (2025)
6. Jia B, Manocha D. Sim-to-real robotic sketching using behavior cloning and reinforcement learning. 2024 IEEE International Conference on Robotics and Automation (ICRA). IEEE, 2024: 18272–18278
7. Ti B, Gao Y, Li Q, et al. Dynamic movement primitives for movement generation using GMM-GMR analytical method. 2019 IEEE 2nd International Conference on Information and Computer Technologies (ICICT). IEEE, 2019: 250–254
8. Wang Z, Peer A, Buss M. An HMM approach to realistic haptic human-robot interaction. World Haptics 2009-Third Joint EuroHaptics conference and Symposium on Haptic Interfaces for Virtual Environment and Teleoperator Systems. IEEE, 2009: 374-379
9. Saveriano, M., Abu-Dakka, F.J., Kramberger, A., et al.: Dynamic movement primitives in robotics: a tutorial survey. Int. J. Rob. Res. **42**(13), 1133–1184 (2023)

10. Li, Z., Zhao, T., Chen, F., et al.: Reinforcement learning of manipulation and grasping using dynamical movement primitives for a humanoidlike mobile manipulator. IEEE/ASME Trans. Mechatron. **23**(1), 121–131 (2017)
11. Zhao, H., Chen, Y., Li, X., et al.: Robotic peg-in-hole assembly based on reversible dynamic movement primitives and trajectory optimization. Mechatronics **95**, 103054 (2023)
12. Zappa I, Fracassi G, Zanchettin A M, et al. Parameterization of robotic welding trajectories from demonstration. 2023 11th International Conference on Control, Mechatronics and Automation (ICCMA). IEEE, 2023: 146-151
13. Han, L., Yuan, H., Xu, W., et al.: Modified dynamic movement primitives: robot trajectory planning and force control under curved surface constraints. IEEE Trans. Cybern. **53**(7), 4245–4258 (2022)
14. Vedove, M.D., Abu-Dakka, F.J., Palopoli, L., et al.: MeshDMP: motion planning on discrete manifolds using dynamic movement primitives. arXiv preprint arXiv:2410.15123, 2024
15. Zhou, P., Zhao, X., Tao, B., et al.: Combination of dynamical movement primitives with trajectory segmentation and node mapping for robot machining motion learning. IEEE/ASME Trans. Mechatron. **28**(1), 175–185 (2022)
16. Gao, X., Ling, J., Xiao, X., et al.: Learning Force-Relevant Skills from Human Demonstration. Complexity **2019**(1), 5262859 (2019)
17. Ke S, Zhao H, Li X, et al. Robotic grinding skills learning based on geodesic length dynamic motion primitives. IEEE/ASME Trans. Mech. (2025)
18. Gašpar, T., Nemec, B., Morimoto, J., et al.: Skill learning and action recognition by arc-length dynamic movement primitives. Robot. Auton. Syst. **100**, 225–235 (2018)
19. Zhang, Y., Li, M., Yang, C.: Robot learning system based on dynamic movement primitives and neural network. Neurocomputing **451**, 205–214 (2021)
20. Ridge, B., Gams, A., Morimoto, J., et al.: Training of deep neural networks for the generation of dynamic movement primitives. Neural Netw. **127**, 121–131 (2020)
21. Yuan, Y., Li, Z., Zhao, T., et al.: DMP-based motion generation for a walking exoskeleton robot using reinforcement learning. IEEE Trans. Industr. Electron. **67**(5), 3830–3839 (2019)
22. Xu, B., Ud Din, M., Hussain, I.: Conditional variational auto encoder based dynamic motion for multitask imitation learning. Sci. Rep. **15**(1), 9196 (2025)
23. Xu, X., You, M., Zhou, H., et al.: GAN-based editable movement primitive from high-variance demonstrations. IEEE Rob. Autom. Lett. **8**(8), 4593–4600 (2023)
24. Janner, M., Du, Y., Tenenbaum, J.B., et al.: Planning with diffusion for flexible behavior synthesis. arXiv preprint arXiv:2205.09991, 2022

Boosting Industrial Changeover Efficiency: A Large-Model-Based Explore-Then-Reproduce Framework for Changeover Tasks

Cheng Ding[✉], Shunchong Li, and Hui Wang

Jaka Robotics Co., LTD., No. 18, Nangu Road, Minhang District, Shanghai, China
{cheng.ding,shunchong.li,hui.wang}@jaka.com

Abstract. Current industrial changeover tasks heavily rely on manual programming, leading to significant time consumption and demanding specialized operator skills. This paper proposes a novel framework that leverages multimodal large language models (MLLMs) for initial scene understanding and decision-making, followed by a VLA model for task exploration and trajectory generation to enhance the programming intelligence of cobots. The core mechanism involves an "explore-then-reproduce" strategy: the VLA model autonomously explores and records successful task trajectories during initial setup, which are then rapidly reproduced for subsequent identical changeover batches. Preliminary experiments demonstrate a significant reduction in changeover time by approximately 30% and reduce the programming skill requirements for operators. This work represents the first successful application of large models' exploration and reproduction mechanisms to enhance the intelligence and versatility of cobots in addressing industrial changeover challenges, offering a new paradigm for flexible manufacturing.

Keywords: Intelligent Cobot Programming · Flexible Manufacturing · Vision-Language-Action Models · Self-directed Learning and Programming

1 Introduction

Traditional industrial manufacturing has historically relied on a deployment-then-production paradigm, characterized by long deployment cycles (often ranging from **several months to over a year** for complex systems) followed by years of sustained mass production of a single product type [9]. For instance, the automotive industry traditionally maintained a vehicle model for approximately **5-7 years** before a significant redesign or new platform introduction [16]. However, this established model is undergoing a profound transformation [12,20]. In recent years, diverse and personalized end-user demands have driven a paradigm shift towards **multi-variety, small-batch production** and a heightened need for **flexible manufacturing** [3,18]. This shift dramatically shortens product life cycles and, consequently, deployment and production durations. The electric vehicle (EV) industry, for example, often sees major model updates or new generations every **2-4 years** [4,19]. In high-tech sectors like 3C (Consumer Electronics, Communications, Computer) industries, particularly for Printed Circuit Boards (PCBs) of display panels, product cycles can be as short as **a few weeks to a few months** [5,11]. The deployment cycle and production cycle of the production line are rapidly shortening as shown in Fig. 1.

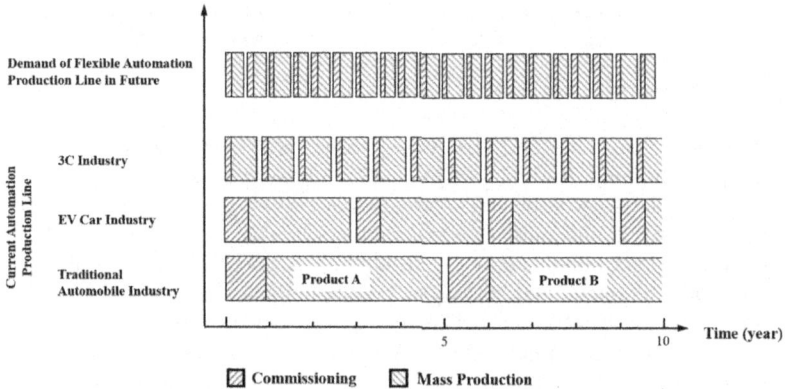

Fig. 1. Trends in product deployment and production cycle.

This accelerating pace of product evolution renders traditional industrial robot programming methods increasingly inadequate for rapid changeover requirements. Conventional approaches such as **Teach Pendant Programming** [14], **Offline Programming (OLP)** [6], and the use of **High-Level Programming Languages** [10] often demand specialized programming skills and significant manual effort for each new product configuration. While leading robot manufacturers like ABB, FANUC, KUKA, and JAKA have introduced graphical programming interfaces as shown in Fig. 2 to lower the entry barrier and reduce deployment time, these still necessitate dedicated training for operators and impose considerable changeover periods. Moreover, the efficiency and production rhythm of the production line remain highly dependent on the individual programmer's skill.

In the academic community, considerable effort has been dedicated to addressing these challenges. Early work on **Learning from Demonstration (LfD)** [1,7,15,23] aimed to simplify robot programming by enabling robots to learn from human demonstrations. While LfD significantly reduced the programming burden, it often struggled with generalization to novel product variations or environmental conditions, making each changeover still complex and preventing substantial reductions in deployment time.

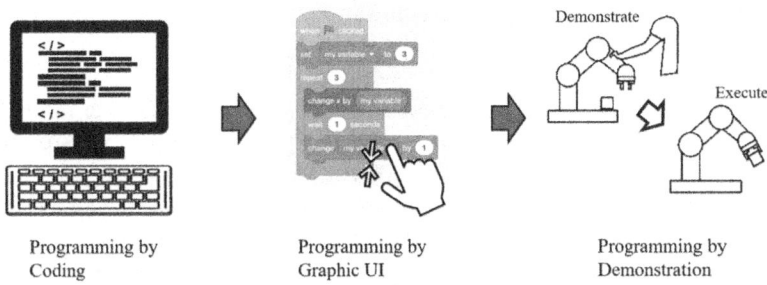

Fig. 2. Schematic diagrams of different programming techniques.

More recently, **Vision-Language-Action (VLA) models** have emerged as a rapidly developing field, endowing robots with unprecedented task generalization capabilities [8,13,22]. These models integrate multimodal information, allowing robots to interpret high-level language instructions and visual observations to generate corresponding actions. However, despite their promise, current VLA models face challenges in terms of success rate, reliability, and inference speed, particularly in the stringent and safety-critical environments of industrial applications [17]. Most existing research on VLA models is confined to laboratory settings or daily life scenarios, with successful large-scale industrial deployment remaining elusive. We have made a four-layer division of the evolution path of manipulation intelligence as shown in Fig. 3. Currently, the industrial sector is generally still at stage One, while laboratories and living scenarios are at stage two or three. Our key insight stems from recognizing that even in multi-variety, small-batch industrial production, tasks typically follow an "initial deployment, then production for a defined period" pattern. This implies that continuous, real-time perception for every single operation is often not a prerequisite that

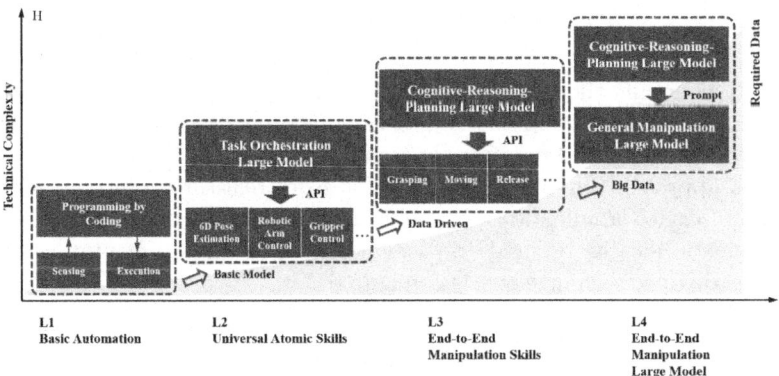

Fig. 3. The evolution path of manipulation intelligence.

presents a unique opportunity to circumvent the current real-time inference limitations of large models.

This paper proposes an innovative solution that leverages the characteristics of industrial changeover tasks to unlock the vast potential of large models. Our core idea revolves around an **explore-then-reproduce mechanism**. Specifically, the VLA model autonomously explores and records successful operational trajectories during the initial execution of a new changeover task. Once validated, these successful trajectories are then rapidly reproduced and accelerated for all subsequent instances of the same task, effectively replacing time-consuming manual programming. This approach not only dramatically reduces changeover time but also significantly lowers the skill threshold for operators, freeing them from tedious programming work.

The main contributions of this paper are summarized as follows:

- This paper is the first to apply the explore-reproduce mechanism of VLA to industrial changeover scenarios, validating its feasibility in addressing industrial changeover efficiency problems.
- We significantly reduce the reliance of industrial changeover tasks on manual skills, thereby enhancing the flexibility and efficiency of automated production lines and bringing significant economic benefits and competitive advantages to enterprises.

The remainder of this paper is structured as follows: Sect. 2 details the proposed methodology, including the specific implementation of the large models for scene understanding, object matching, exploration and trajectory reproduction. Section 3 describes the experimental platform, setup, and presents detailed experimental results, comparing them with baseline methods. Section 4 discusses the experimental results in depth, including the advantages, limitations, and potential industrial implications of the method. Finally, Sect. 5 summarizes the whole paper.

2 Methodology

This section details the proposed methodology for leveraging large models in industrial changeover commissioning tasks. Our objective is to enhance product changeover efficiency and minimize human intervention in automatic production line. This approach fundamentally deviates from real-time inference for robot control in service applications by adopting an **"explore-then-reproduce" strategy**, specifically tailored for scenarios where environmental conditions remain static once a changeover is configured.

2.1 System Overview and Architecture

The overall system architecture comprises two primary modules: a Perception and Scene Understanding Module powered by Multimodal Large Language Models (MLLMs), and a VLA-based Exploration and Trajectory Generation Module

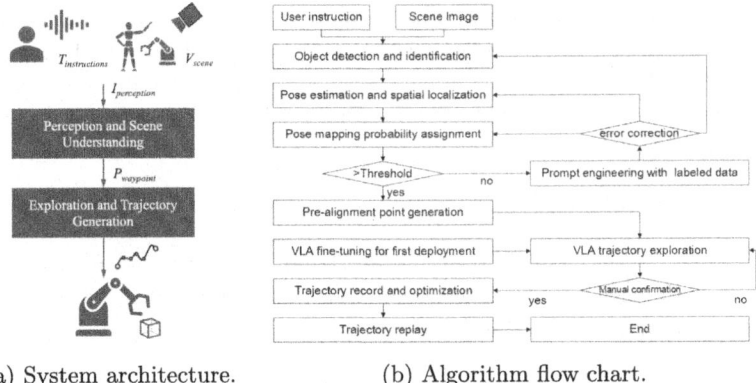

(a) System architecture.   (b) Algorithm flow chart.

Fig. 4. System architecture and algorithm flow chart for the proposed framework.

as depicted in Fig. 4 a. The workflow initiates with an MLLM-driven perception phase, which interprets high-level textual instructions from operators and analyzes visual input. This module is responsible for identifying specific components, their approximate locations, and the target manipulation areas. The input to this module can be represented as:

$$I_{\text{perception}} = \{T_{\text{instruction}}, V_{\text{scene}}\} \qquad (1)$$

where $T_{\text{instruction}}$ denotes the textual instruction and V_{scene} represents the visual scene data.

Subsequently, this rich, semantically grounded information is fed into the VLA-based module. During the initial setup for a new product changeover, the VLA model which is pre-trained for the corresponding tasks enters an **exploration phase**, where it autonomously attempts and learns successful trajectories for the given task. Crucially, successful execution trajectories are meticulously recorded. For all subsequent instances of the same task, the system transitions to a **trajectory reproduction and acceleration phase**, where previously learned and optimized trajectories are executed at high speed. This effectively eliminates the need for human programming efforts or extensive recomputation. This two-stage approach capitalizes on the strengths of MLLMs for robust understanding and VLA models for flexible action generation, while specifically addressing the time-consuming changeover challenges in nowadays traditional industrial automation.

2.2 Perception and Scene Understanding Module

This Module translates instructions and raw visual data into high-level robot programs.

Object Detection and Identification. Upon initiating a new changeover task, the system captures images of the workspace and target objects. A pre-trained MLLM, takes the raw image V_{raw} as input and, guided by an initial textual prompt $P_{\text{detection}}$, outputs bounding boxes B and semantic labels L for each identified object:

$$\text{MLLM}(V_{\text{raw}}, P_{\text{detection}}) \to \{(B_1, L_1), (B_2, L_2), \dots\} \tag{2}$$

This approach is more robust than traditional computer vision methods as it inherently leverages a vast semantic understanding of objects and contexts, crucial for generating subsequent robot programs.

Pose Estimation and Spatial Localization. For many industrial applications in production line, the complex 6D pose estimation problem can be dimensionally reduced to a 3-DoF problem, requiring only x, y, and R_z (rotation about the z-axis). Utilizing a top-view RGB-D camera, the approximate centroid position (x_p, y_p) of objects within bounding boxes and their rotation angles R_z in the horizontal plane are easily obtained by the MLLM. Given that RGB and depth images from the RGB-D camera are already aligned, the spatial coordinates of an object's centroid (X_c, Y_c, Z_c) relative to the camera can be directly calculated from the depth map $D(x, y)$ at the detected centroid pixel (x_p, y_p):

$$Z_c = D(x_p, y_p) \tag{3}$$

$$X_c = (x_p - c_x) \cdot Z_c / f_x \tag{4}$$

$$Y_c = (y_p - c_y) \cdot Z_c / f_y \tag{5}$$

where (c_x, c_y) are the camera's principal points and (f_x, f_y) are the focal lengths. These camera coordinates are then transformed into the robot's coordinate system (X_R, Y_R, Z_R) using the hand-eye calibration matrix $T_{\text{camera}}^{\text{robot}}$:

$$(X_R, Y_R, Z_R, 1)^T = T_{\text{camera}}^{\text{robot}} (X_c, Y_c, Z_c, 1)^T \tag{6}$$

This transformation enables the robot to perform precise key points tracking.

Given the identified and localized objects, the MLLM is tasked with determining the optimal placement strategy. This matching process can be framed as a probabilistic assignment problem. The MLLM, equipped with its multimodal understanding, interprets visual cues (e.g., shape similarity between boards and slots, labels on grids) and textual instructions (e.g., "PCB_001 goes to slot_A"). It generates a probability distribution $P(A_{ij})$ over possible board-to-grid assignments A_{ij}, where i is a board and j is a slot:

$$P(A_{ij}) = \text{MLLM}(V_{\text{cues}}, T_{\text{rules}}) \tag{7}$$

If the highest probability for a match, $\max(P(A_{ij}))$, does not exceed 60%, the system prompts for manual assistance. Through prompt engineering, a photo of labeled bounding boxes of the matched objects is sent to the MLLM's knowledge base. Crucially, the MLLM also generates critical pre-alignment points for the robot's motion. While the VLA model could theoretically accomplish the matching problem and generate way points, the combinatorial complexity would necessitate an impractical amount of operational demonstration data. By providing MLLM-recommended pre-alignment and way points, the VLA model requires significantly fewer demonstration data, thus streamlining the process.

2.3 VLA-Based Exploration and Trajectory Generation Module

This module is responsible for converting the high-level robot programs from the MLLM module into executable robot motions. It operates in two distinct phases: an initial exploration phase for new changeover tasks and a rapid reproduction phase for subsequent, identical tasks.

Initial Exploration Phase for New Changeover Configurations. Based on the MLLM's matching results and recommended pre-alignment points $P_{\text{pre-align}}$, the VLA model's primary task is to generate a fine trajectory from these pre-defined points to the accurate manipulation points P_{mani}. This involves learning the subtle manipulations required for successful grasping and precise insertion. The VLA model aims to learn a policy $\pi(a_t|s_t)$ that maps current state s_t to action a_t:

$$\pi : \mathcal{S} \to \mathcal{A} \tag{8}$$

where $\mathcal{S}$ is the state space (visual observations, robot joint states) and $\mathcal{A}$ is the action space (robot joint commands or end-effector poses).

Although the VLA model has been pre-trained on numerous manipulation tasks, when the VLA model is first introduced to a production line, a fine tuning process is required for the model to be familiar with the products to get a higher success rate to save the exploration time later. This is crucial because industrial scenarios often exhibit subtle differences from pre-trained environments. The set of initial demonstrations $D = \{(s_1, a_1), \ldots, (s_N, a_N)\}$ informs the VLA model's initial policy learning. After this initial training, the model can execute tasks with a typical success rate $\eta \subset [60\%, 100\%]$. To make the exploration process more robust and easier, an admittance control strategy is adopted during execution, allowing for compliant interaction with the environment. The operator then selects a successful execution as the **template trajectory**, which can be further refined offline to generate a robust and optimized master trajectory.

Once a successful trajectory T_{master} for a specific task has been recorded and refined during the initial exploration phase, the system switches to the **reproduction phase** for all subsequent, identical tasks. This constitutes the core mechanism for achieving high efficiency in industrial changeover problems.

The pre-recorded joint-space or task-space trajectories are directly played back by the robot controller. Unlike the exploration phase, which might involve slower, more cautious movements, the reproduction phase prioritizes speed. **Trajectory optimization algorithms** are applied offline to smooth the recorded path and identify maximum achievable velocities and accelerations while respecting robot kinematic and dynamic constraints. This effectively "accelerates" the learned trajectory to industrial production speeds. The optimized trajectory $T_{\text{optimized}}$ is obtained by minimizing a cost function $C(T)$ subject to robot constraints:

$$T_{\text{optimized}} = \arg\min_{T} C(T) \quad \text{s.t.} \quad \dot{q}_{\max}, \ddot{q}_{\max} \tag{9}$$

where $\dot{q}_{\max}$ and $\ddot{q}_{\max}$ are the maximum joint velocities and accelerations, respectively.

3 Case Study

3.1 Experimental Platform Setup

Our experimental platform is designed to simulate a typical industrial pick-and-place changeover scenario, specifically focusing on the packaging of circuit boards into material trays. We place several cut circuit boards in a fixed material tray to simulate the circuit boards on the fixed fixture after cutting. Then, we pick up the small circuit boards from the fixed fixture and transfer them to the empty material tray by the robot.

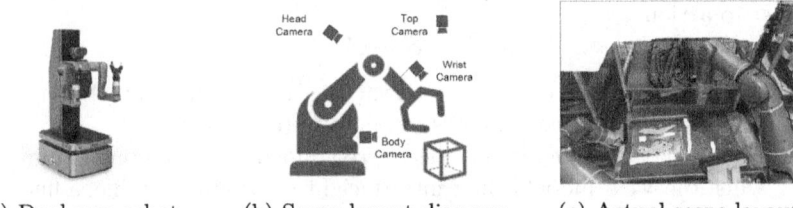

(a) Dual-arm robot (b) Scene layout diagram (c) Actual scene layout

Fig. 5. The experimental setup.

In our case, we adopted a dual-arm robot as shown in Fig. 5 a. Each arm has seven joints and is equipped with an RGBD camera. The Configuration of the work cell is shown in Fig. 5 c. One arm controlled the position so that the camera could take a top view. We used it to detect the entire environmental state and provide input information for the MLLM, specifically Qwen2.5-VL-72B [21]. The other arm simulated the robot responsible for material handling on the production line. Apart from the camera installed on the wrist, the camera on the head and the camera on the body provide different views, enabling the VLA model, specifically OpenPi [2], to output reliable results.

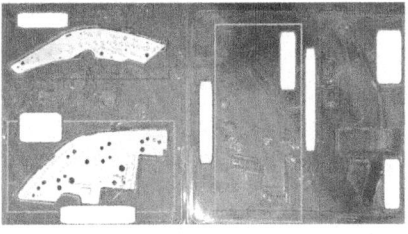 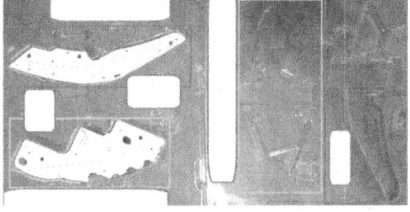

(a) Material tray A (b) Material tray B

Fig. 6. Object detection and matching before and after product changeover.

3.2 Case Study Description

In this case study, two PCBs needed to be placed onto a material tray. The task requires an accuracy of about 1 mm. We simulated the role of an integrator, providing the client with an initial configuration. For the manual programming method, we utilized JAKA's graphical programming interface to develop the program framework and debugged the precise points. The provided manual program architecture included four accurate pick-and-place points, four rough pre-pick-and-place points, and two path transition points. For the VLA method, we collected 50 sets of data for the pick-and-place processes of each of the two existing PCB types. Subsequently, an OpenPI model was trained for 6 h on 4 GeForce RTX 4090 Graphics Cards and deployed according to the methodology described in the previous chapter. A comprehensive user manual was provided to the client for both methods. Subsequently, we simulated a product changeover process, involving the replacement of a material tray as shown in Fig. 6. This new tray also contained two PCB slots, with one PCB type remaining consistent and the other being replaced by a new category. We recruited five volunteers within the company: Intern A (newly joined), Employee B (less than one year of experience), Employee C (approximately two years of experience), Employee D (approximately three years of experience), and Employee E (over five years of experience). The primary comparative metrics included the time required for changeover and the cycle time for the robot to execute a single task after programming and debugging were completed.

3.3 Results and Analysis

The results are shown in Fig. 7.

In the manual reprogramming test results, Volunteer A expended more time, primarily due to the sole reliance on the teach pendant for debugging. Although Volunteer B utilized robot dragging for auxiliary positioning, debugging was conducted sequentially point by point according to the program order. In practice, efficiency could be enhanced by first debugging the precise pick-and-place points and subsequently determining the pre-pick-and-place points. The performance of the other volunteers was comparable, with differences primarily attributed to

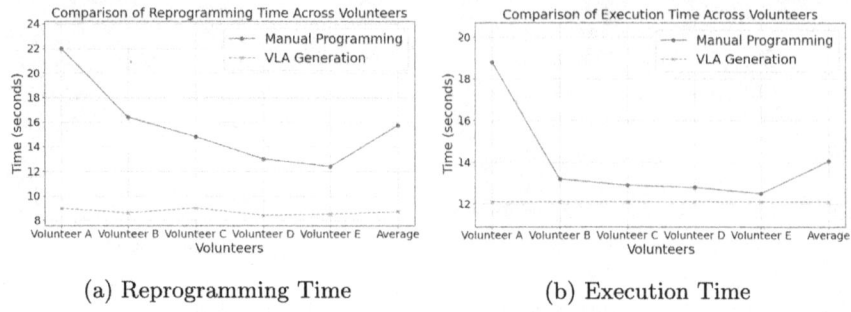

(a) Reprogramming Time (b) Execution Time

Fig. 7. Comparison of Reprogramming and Execution Times Across Volunteers.

variations in proficiency. In the VLA reprogramming tests, the time spent by all volunteers was similar, with data fluctuations stemming from random variations in VLA exploration attempts.

Regarding execution efficiency, the transition points set by Volunteer A were suboptimal, and the robot exhibited a stop-start motion at each point before accelerating to the next, resulting in lower efficiency. The performance of the other volunteers was generally consistent, with slight efficiency differences primarily arising from the rationality of their point settings. Conversely, the execution times of the strategies generated by VLA were entirely consistent and superior to those achieved by experienced engineers.

The average time required for our method is 8.7 min, which is 29.8% less than the 12.4 min required for manual programming by the professional engineer. The experimental results validate the efficacy of our VLA-based approach for industrial changeover tasks. We have demonstrated a substantial reduction in changeover time by leveraging automated exploration and rapid reproduction.

4 Discussion

The experimental results presented in Sect. 3 robustly validate the efficacy of our proposed large-model-based methodology. The most compelling advantage of our method is the substantial reduction in product changeover time. This efficiency gain is critical in modern manufacturing, where small-batch, high-mix production demands rapid adaptation and minimal downtime. Our approach effectively transforms a traditionally time-consuming, manual programming process into an automated and swift operation.

A key strength of our system is its learning capability over time. As the system performs more changeovers for various product configurations, it accumulates a larger library of manipulation data. This means that for frequently recurring changeover tasks, the time spent in the initial "explore" phase diminishes, leading to even greater time savings in the long run. This continuous improvement mechanism makes the system increasingly efficient and robust with extended use, mirroring the benefits of experience in human operators but at an accelerated and scalable rate.

Furthermore, our research demonstrates a strategic and effective way to integrate VLA models into a factory setting. This approach not only optimizes current changeover processes but also serves as a crucial mechanism for collecting valuable, real-world robotic interaction data. This data can be instrumental for future research, enabling the development of even more generalized and robust VLA models, ultimately accelerating the advancement of AI in manufacturing.

The main limitation of this study is that it cannot cope with all the product changeover scenarios. For example, when the shape and color of the object are very different each time, the experience accumulated by the model is no longer effective. More pre-training data is needed to improve the model performance and reduce the exploration time, which is a burden for users.

5 Conclusion

This paper introduced a novel large-model-based framework for automating product changeover tasks in industrial scenarios. Our experimental results conclusively show an average 29.8% reduction in changeover time compared to traditional manual programming. This significant improvement is achieved by strategically leveraging Multimodal Large Language Models for robust scene understanding, coupled with a unique "explore-then-reproduce" mechanism for robot action generation with VLA model. Crucially, our approach dramatically reduces the reliance on specialized human programming skills, making robot operation more accessible in factory settings. This work demonstrates the immense potential of MLLMs and VLA models in industrial automation by effectively utilizing the generalization ability of the models.

Acknowledgments. This research was supported by JAKA Robotics Co., LTD.

References

1. Argall, B.D., Chernova, S., Veloso, M., Browning, B.: A survey of robot learning from demonstration. Robot. Autonomous Syst. **57**(5), 469–483 (2009)
2. Black, K., et al.: π0: a vision-language-action flow model for general robot control (2024). https://arxiv.org/abs/2410.24164
3. Bortolini, M., Galizia, F.G., Mora, C.: Reconfigurable manufacturing systems: literature review and research trend. J. Manufact. Syst. **49**, 93–106 (2018)
4. Brown, S., Pyke, D., Steenhof, P.: Electric vehicles: the role and importance of standards in an emerging market. Energy Policy **38**(7), 3797–3806 (2010)
5. Calmon, A.P., Graves, S.C.: Inventory management in a consumer electronics closed-loop supply chain. Manufact. Serv. Opera. Manage. **19**(4), 568–585 (2017)
6. Craig, J.J.: Introduction to robotics: mechanics and control, 3/E. Pearson Educ, India (2009)

7. Ding, C., Du, W., Wu, J., Xiong, Z.: Template-based imitation learning for manipulating symmetric objects. Mechatronics **78**, 102609 (2021)
8. Driess, D., et al.: Palm-e: an embodied multimodal language model. In: Proceedings of the 40th International Conference on Machine Learning, pp. 8469–8488 (2023)
9. Grau, A., Indri, M., Bello, L.L., Sauter, T.: Robots in industry: the past, present, and future of a growing collaboration with humans. IEEE Industr. Electron. Magazine **15**(1), 50–61 (2020)
10. Koolen, T., Deits, R.: Julia for robotics: simulation and real-time control in a high-level programming language. In: 2019 International Conference on Robotics and Automation (ICRA), pp. 604–611. IEEE (2019)
11. Lee, S.M., Trimi, S.: Innovation for creating a smart future. J. Innov. Knowl. **3**(1), 1–8 (2018)
12. Löfving, M., Almström, P., Jarebrant, C., Wadman, B., Widfeldt, M.: Evaluation of flexible automation for small batch production. Procedia Manufact. **25**, 177–184 (2018)
13. Ma, Y., Song, Z., Zhuang, Y., Hao, J., King, I.: A survey on vision-language-action models for embodied ai. arXiv preprint arXiv:2405.14093 (2024)
14. Morley, E.C., Syan, C.S.: Teach pendants: how are they for you? Industr. Robot Int. J. **22**(4), 18–22 (1995)
15. Ravichandar, H., Polydoros, A.S., Chernova, S., Billard, A.: Recent advances in robot learning from demonstration. Ann. Rev. Control, Robot. Autonom. Syst. **3**(1), 297–330 (2020)
16. Sabadka, D., Molnár, V., Fedorko, G.: Shortening of life cycle and complexity impact on the automotive industry. TEM J. **8**(4) (2019)
17. Sapkota, R., Cao, Y., Roumeliotis, K.I., Karkee, M.: Vision-language-action models: Concepts, progress, applications and challenges. arXiv preprint arXiv:2505.04769 (2025)
18. Srivastava, S.K., Bag, S.: Recent developments on flexible manufacturing in the digital era: a review and future research directions. Global J. Flexible Syst. Manage. **24**(4), 483–516 (2023)
19. Verma, M., Verma, A., Khan, M.: Factors influencing the adoption of electric vehicles in Bangaluru. Transp. Develop. Econom. **6**(2), 17 (2020)
20. Wang, M., Huang, H., Li, J.: Transients in flexible manufacturing systems with setups and batch operations: modeling, analysis, and design. IISE Trans. **53**(5), 523–540 (2021)
21. Wang, P., et al.: Qwen2-vl: enhancing vision-language model's perception of the world at any resolution. arXiv preprint arXiv:2409.12191 (2024)
22. Zhou, H., et al.: Language-conditioned learning for robotic manipulation: a survey. arXiv preprint arXiv:2312.10807 (2023)
23. Zhu, Z., Hu, H.: Robot learning from demonstration in robotic assembly: a survey. Robotics **7**(2), 17 (2018)

Learning Human-Like Finger Gaiting on an Anthropomorphic Hand

Kairui Yang, Dongjie Jiang, Lecheng Ruan[✉], and Qining Wang[✉]

School of Advanced Manufacturing and Robotics, Peking University,
Beijing 100871, China
ruanlecheng@ucla.edu, qiningwang@pku.edu.cn

Abstract. A key challenge in dexterous non-prehensile manipulation lies in dynamic finger gaiting—the sequential repositioning of fingers to achieve continuous object motion. The pen-spinning task, requiring precise, sequential multi-finger coordination without a stable grasp, serves as an ideal testbed for investigating such gaiting. Prior work, often limited by hand morphology, has typically yielded simpler policies reliant on fingertip balancing rather than dynamic finger gaiting. In this work, we investigate learning finger gaiting on an anthropomorphic hand in simulation. However, achieving this skill through reinforcement learning (RL) introduces significant challenges, particularly in policy exploration and the processing of complex observations. To address these, our framework employs waypoint-guided initialization and utilizes normalized contact forces as a form of privileged information during training. Our simulation results demonstrate the emergence of dynamic finger gaiting, enabling the efficient execution of the pen-spinning task. This work thereby establishes a viable methodology for acquiring complex coordination skills on high-degree-of-freedom (DoF) anthropomorphic hands.

Keywords: Finger Gaiting · Dexterous Manipulation · Non-prehensile Manipulation · Reinforcement Learning

1 Introduction

The pursuit of human-level dexterity is a primary driver of advancements in robotic manipulation. While robots excel in prehensile tasks involving firm grasps [1–3], they are often challenged by non-prehensile manipulation. These tasks, such as reorienting, rolling, or spinning objects, demand dynamic control without a secure grasp [4,5]. Finger gaiting, a central focus of this paper, is a key strategy for such non-prehensile scenarios. This bio-inspired approach involves coordinated, sequential finger contacts to maintain continuous object control through alternating support and propulsion phases [6]. This technique enables object manipulation beyond a fixed grasp, which is fundamental for expanding robotic dexterity beyond static paradigms and for achieving versatile interaction in unstructured environments.

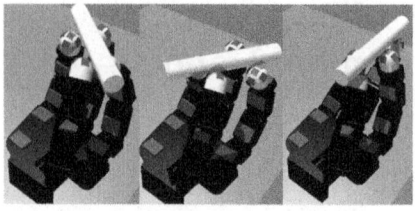 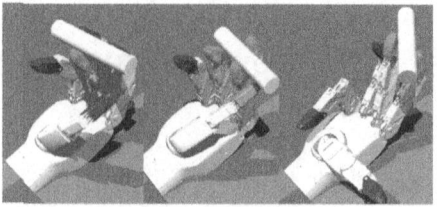

(a) Fingertip Balancing Strategy (b) Dynamic Finger Gaiting Strategy

Fig. 1. Influence of hand morphology on pen-spinning. (a) A hand with limited DoF and broad fingertips defaults to a simpler fingertip balancing strategy. (b) In contrast, a high-DoF anthropomorphic hand enables a more complex and human-like dynamic finger gaiting strategy.

We investigate the complexities of finger gaiting using pen-spinning as a representative task [7]. This task is particularly suitable because it demands precise temporal coordination of multiple fingers and continuous, nuanced force modulation—core challenges in dynamic non-prehensile manipulation.

The ability to execute such intricate maneuvers is highly dependent on hand morphology. Prior work using less anthropomorphic hands (Fig. 1 (a)) often yielded simpler policies restricted to fingertip balancing [7]. In this work, we employ a high-DoF anthropomorphic hand (Fig. 1 (b)), observing that its superior dexterity and versatile contact surfaces (e.g., finger pads and tips) are essential for enabling the development of more sophisticated, human-like manipulation strategies.

However, this morphological complexity also introduces significant algorithmic challenges for learning. The vast action space of a high-DoF system complicates policy learning, a difficulty exacerbated in non-prehensile tasks that lack the inherent stability of a firm grasp. Although RL is emerging as a powerful paradigm for managing high-dimensional action spaces in dexterous manipulation [8,9], learning sophisticated finger gaiting on anthropomorphic hands remains hindered by the following critical challenges:

1. **Ineffective Exploration in High-Dimensional Spaces:** The vast action space of a high-DoF hand renders standard exploration methods, such as random joint sampling, ineffective. For a task like finger gaiting, which requires specific initial contacts to begin, the probability of discovering a viable starting state through random exploration is exceedingly low. This necessitates a more guided approach to steer exploration toward productive regions of the state-action space.
2. **Difficulty Interpreting Complex Sensorimotor Information:** An anthropomorphic hand generates high-dimensional streams of proprioceptive and contact data. For dynamic control, the policy must learn to interpret this complex information and discern subtle yet critical differences—such as the force vectors required for stable support versus active propulsion. Process-

ing this noisy, high-dimensional data to produce precise motor commands in real-time poses a substantial learning challenge.

To address these challenges, our framework integrates targeted solutions. We address the exploration challenge with a reference waypoint-guided initialization strategy, which leverages human demonstrations to bootstrap the learning process from viable initial states. To manage the complexity of sensorimotor control, we utilize privileged 3D net contact force information. This data is carefully processed and normalized to provide a clean, informative signal for the policy.

Our primary contributions are as follows:

1. **A Novel Learning Framework for Dynamic Finger Gaiting:** We present a complete RL-based framework that successfully combines waypoint-guided initialization and the strategic use of privileged contact information, enabling a high-DoF anthropomorphic hand to learn sophisticated finger gaiting.
2. **A Reference Waypoint-Guided Initialization Strategy:** We propose and validate an initialization strategy that uses reference waypoints derived from human demonstration. These waypoints represent critical contact transitions in the pen-spinning cycle, effectively bootstrapping the learning process for complex finger gaiting.
3. **Empirical Demonstration of Emergent Finger Gaiting:** We empirically demonstrate that our framework enables an anthropomorphic hand to learn sophisticated pen-spinning through emergent dynamic finger gaiting, achieved in just 1.5 h of training. This result validates our approach and showcases its effectiveness in acquiring complex, human-like manipulation skills.

The remainder of this paper is structured as follows. Section 2 reviews related work on dexterous manipulation and finger gaiting. Section 3 details our proposed methodology, including the learning framework and reward design. Section 4 presents our experimental setup and results, followed by Sect. 5, which discusses the findings and outlines future research directions.

2 Related Work

2.1 Reinforcement Learning for In-Hand Manipulation

Reinforcement learning has emerged as a foundational approach for unlocking complex skills in high-degree-of-freedom (DoF) dexterous hands [1]. Seminal research demonstrated that RL could achieve in-hand object reorientation in simulation with successful transfer to the real world, establishing a powerful paradigm for the field [2]. Building on this work, the research community has extended the complexity by tackling challenges such as bimanual manipulation [8], long-horizon tasks [10], and generalized reorientation skills [11]. This trend toward leveraging higher-DoF systems and addressing more intricate tasks underscores the ambition to replicate human-level dexterity.

However, this ambition has revealed persistent challenges. As the dimensionality of robotic hands increases, so does the complexity of exploration and control, making skill acquisition significantly more difficult [12]. Moreover, while these studies have achieved impressive functional outcomes, the learned behaviors do not typically exhibit the dynamic and nuanced strategies characteristic of human manipulation, such as finger gaiting. Much of the existing work on in-hand manipulation [13] [11,14] has focused on achieving stable control rather than eliciting the sophisticated, sequential finger movements that are central to our work.

2.2 Finger Gaiting as a Benchmark for Human-Like Manipulation

Finger gaiting—the sequential repositioning of fingers to maintain continuous control of an object—is a hallmark of human dexterity, enabling manipulation beyond a static grasp [6]. This non-prehensile skill is fundamental for advanced interaction, and pen-spinning serves as an ideal benchmark task due to its stringent requirements for precise timing and dynamic force modulation [7].

Critically, the ability to develop such sophisticated strategies is deeply intertwined with the hand's physical morphology. As observed in prior work [7], hand designs with limited DoF or broad, homogeneous fingertips often lead to simpler policies, such as fingertip balancing, which prioritize stability over agility (Fig. 1 (a)). In contrast, dynamic finger gaiting involves a complex interplay of supporting and propulsive actions from different finger segments. This more dynamic, human-like behavior is hypothesized to emerge more readily on highly anthropomorphic hands that feature slender digits and the high DoF necessary for fine-grained, independent control (Fig. 1 (b)). While the field is trending toward more capable hardware, learning to exploit these anthropomorphic features for dynamic gaiting remains a significant, unaddressed challenge. This paper specifically focuses on bridging this gap by investigating whether targeted RL strategies can elicit emergent finger gaiting on a high-DoF anthropomorphic hand.

3 Methodology

Our methodology builds upon foundational work that achieved pen-spinning on a robotic hand with fewer degrees of freedom [7]. We adapt and extend this approach to a high-DoF anthropomorphic hand, which presents a greater challenge in learning dynamic finger gaiting. Our approach centers on an RL framework enhanced by two key strategies designed to make this complex skill tractable: a waypoint-guided initialization strategy to bootstrap learning and the strategic use of privileged 3D net force information to master nuanced physical interactions.

3.1 Reinforcement Learning Framework

Settings and Notations. We formulate the pen-spinning task as a standard reinforcement learning problem. The goal is to train a policy $\pi(a_t|o_t)$ that maps

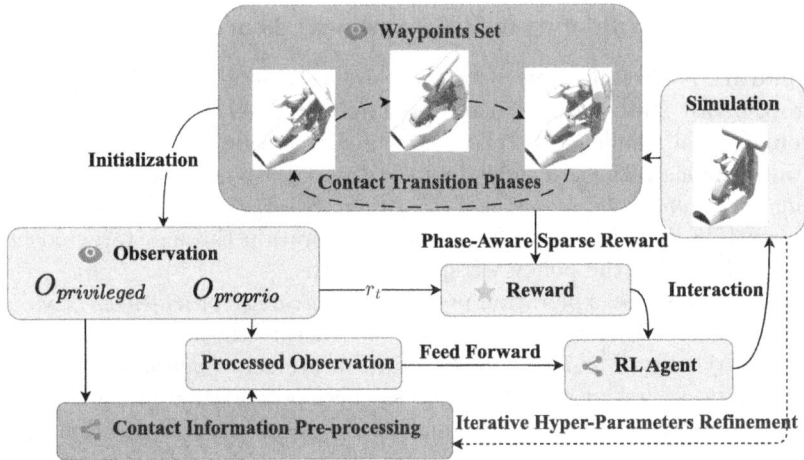

Fig. 2. The training pipeline for learning finger gaiting. The process begins with waypoint-guided initialization derived from a human demonstration. An RL agent then learns by interacting with the simulation, guided by proprioceptive and privileged observations. A key feature is the feedback loop that iteratively refines contact force normalization parameters based on interaction data to improve policy performance.

observations to actions to maximize a cumulative reward. We employ Proximal Policy Optimization (PPO) [15] as the core learning algorithm. The agent controls an anthropomorphic hand with N_{DoF} degrees of freedom.

The key notations are defined as follows:

- **Observation (o_t):** The observation for the policy is composed of proprioceptive information O_{pro} (joint angles q, velocities $\dot{q}$, and previous target joint angles) and privileged information O_{pri} (fingertip positions, 3D net contact forces, object pose and velocities, and an object point cloud).
- **Action (a_t):** The action space $a_t = \Delta q_{\text{tgt}} \in \mathbb{R}^{N_{\text{DoF}}}$ defines the incremental adjustments to the target joint angles. These adjustments are converted into joint torques τ using a Proportional-Derivative (PD) controller, which then drive the simulation.

Reward Function. The total reward is calculated using the following formula with empirically determined weights:

$$R_{tot} = w_{rot}r_{rot} + w_{sta}r_{sta} + w_{smo}r_{smo} + w_{vel}r_{vel} + w_{way}r_{way}$$

where r_{rot} encourages continuous rotation, r_{sta} penalizes deviations from the target height and orientation, r_{smo} promotes smooth movements, r_{vel} discourages excessive speed, and r_{way} is a sparse reward for reaching key manipulation stages. The terms w_{rot}, w_{sta}, w_{smo}, w_{vel}, and w_{way} represent the corresponding weights for each reward component (Fig. 2).

3.2 Waypoint Guidance in Reinforcement Learning

Standard RL is often ineffective for complex, sequential tasks like finger gaiting due to the vast state-action space, which makes meaningful exploration highly improbable. This challenge is well-documented, and solutions often involve incorporating demonstrations or guided exploration [9]. To address this, we propose a *Waypoint-Guided Reinforcement Learning* strategy, which leverages human demonstration data in two ways: guiding exploration through targeted initialization and shaping the policy via sparse rewards.

First, to solve the exploration problem, the strategy provides effective initial states. We define reference waypoints by extracting them from a human pen-spinning trajectory. These waypoints represent crucial *transitional states* within the gaiting cycle, not merely static poses. These potential waypoints are refined by applying perturbations and evaluating the resulting configurations against criteria such as contact stability and robustness. Configurations scoring above a threshold are selected as initial waypoints for training episodes, which begin from states sampled from Gaussian distributions centered around them. This significantly biases exploration towards dynamically relevant regions of the state space.

Second, these same waypoints are used to provide a sparse *waypoint achievement reward* (r_{way}). This reward signal acts as an intermediate target, explicitly encouraging the policy to progress through the key transitional stages of the manipulation. By combining targeted initialization with reward-based guidance, this strategy accelerates learning and facilitates credit assignment. Such guidance is particularly critical for a high-DoF hand with slender fingertips, as it steers learning towards intricate finger gaiting rather than simpler balancing behaviors that might otherwise emerge [7].

3.3 Privileged Contact Information Pre-processing

Finger gaiting requires the precise modulation of contact forces to differentiate between supportive, propulsive, and guiding touches—a distinction critical for manipulating an object through sequential contacts. Binary contact information alone is inadequate for learning these nuanced interactions, as success depends on both the magnitude and direction of applied forces. Consequently, a hand model with heterogeneous fingertips capable of rich surface interactions benefits significantly from detailed net force data to master complex finger gaiting. In contrast, for hands with wider, more homogeneous fingertips that favor stable balancing over fine propulsion, simpler strategies reliant on fingertip balancing can emerge [7]. For these balancing approaches, binary contact data (indicating only the presence or absence of contact) can suffice, as they do not require the detailed force vector information essential for the propulsive and re-grasping actions of finger gaiting.

We incorporate detailed 3D net contact force vectors as part of the privileged information O_{pri}. For each of the five fingertips, we consider the 3D net force vector $\boldsymbol{f}_{\text{tip},i} = (F_x, F_y, F_z)_i \in \mathbb{R}^3$. These vectors are directly available in the simulation environment, resulting in a net contact force component within $\boldsymbol{O}_{\text{pri}}$.

Net Force Vector Normalization: Raw 3D net force values can vary widely in scale, potentially destabilizing the learning process. We apply a normalization scheme to each force component F_c (where $c \in \{x, y, z\}$ for each fingertip):

$$F'_c = \frac{\text{clip}(F_c, F_{\min}, F_{\max}) - F_{\min}}{F_{\max} - F_{\min}} \quad (1)$$

This scales the clipped force component to the range $[0, 1]$, where $F_{\min}$ and $F_{\max}$ are pre-set limits based on expected force ranges. An alternative mapping to the range $[-1, 1]$ using hyperbolic tangent normalization can also be employed:

$$F_{\text{norm},i} = \tanh(k \cdot F_i) \quad (2)$$

where the scaling factor k is empirically selected. Both techniques ensure that net force inputs are consistently scaled, helping the policy network interpret these critical signals for effective finger gaiting.

4 Experiments and Results

All experiments were performed within the Isaac Gym simulation environment on an NVIDIA RTX 4090 GPU. The simulation operated with a physics timestep of 5 ms and a control frequency of 20 Hz. The dexterous hand used in these experiments is the Linker Hand, a five-fingered hand with 21 DoF (Fig. 1 (b)). Its design is notably anthropomorphic, featuring slender fingertips and human-like pulp surfaces. The manipulated object was a cylindrical pen with a radius of 12 mm, a length of 120 mm, and a mass of 60 g.

We assessed multiple training configurations by varying initialization strategies and the method of processing contact information. As illustrated in Fig. 3, we defined two primary initialization approaches: one using three waypoints from a human demonstration to guide dynamic learning, and another using six static balancing poses. For each initialization, we compared three methods for processing contact information: a baseline without force normalization, a method with a single, fixed normalization, and a strategy that iteratively refines the contact force normalization based on performance during training. We also tuned various learning hyperparameters, such as reward weights, and selected the optimal set for our final training strategy. The performance of these key configurations is detailed in Fig. 3 (c).

4.1 Validation of Reference Waypoint-Guided Initialization

Strategic initialization using reference waypoints derived from human demonstration proved critical to successful policy learning.

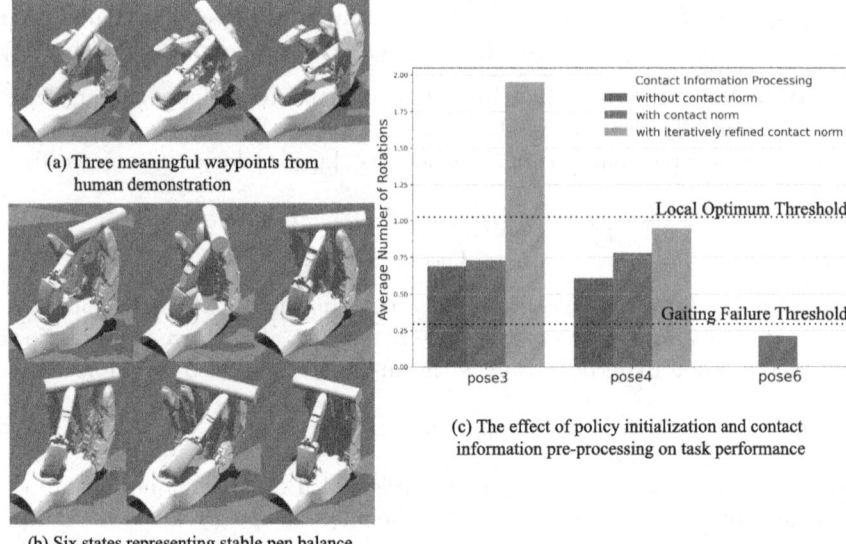

Fig. 3. Comparison of initialization strategies and their impact on performance. (a) Dynamic waypoints derived from a human trajectory. (b) Static states representing stable balancing poses. (c) Performance results show that trajectory-derived initialization (pose3) combined with iteratively refined contact normalization is crucial for success, significantly outperforming initialization from stable static states (pose6).

Comparison with Random Initialization: Ablation studies confirmed that policies trained with random initialization, i.e., without reference waypoints, consistently failed to produce any successful finger gaiting behaviors. This outcome highlights the critical role of guided initialization in mastering this complex task with a high-DoF hand and aligns with prior research demonstrating the benefits of demonstrations in RL [7].

Impact of Reference Waypoint Set: The choice of reference waypoints had a marked effect on performance, as detailed in Fig. 3. The initialization strategy using three waypoints from a human trajectory (Fig. 3 (a)), when combined with iteratively refined normalization, yielded the highest average of 1.95 rotations. In contrast, the strategy of initializing from six stable balancing poses (Fig. 3 (b)) proved significantly less effective for learning the gaiting motion, achieving a maximum of only 0.21 average rotations. While these static poses can be suitable for simpler balancing tasks on other hand morphologies, they were less effective here.

These results indicate that a concise set of waypoints depicting critical transitional stages of the desired motion is more effective for guiding exploration than a larger set of waypoints or a set of static poses. As shown in Fig. 4, this superior guidance enables the discovery of policies that can sustain the motion, leading to significantly longer episode lengths and higher cumulative rewards.

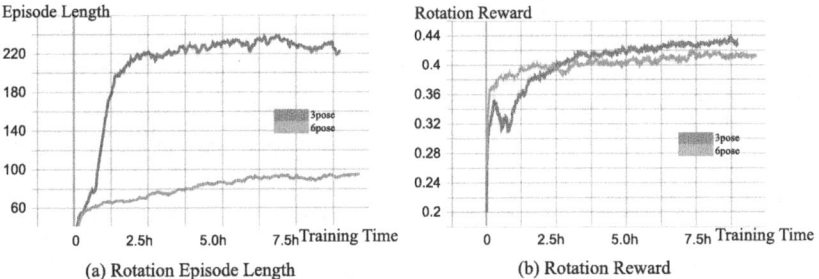

Fig. 4. Effect of initialization strategy on learning. (a) Policies initialized with dynamic waypoints (3-pose) achieve significantly longer episode durations than those initialized with static poses (6-pose). (b) Although both configurations learn the basic rotation task, as indicated by their comparable rotation rewards, only the 3-pose policy acquires a sustainable finger-gaiting strategy, enabling continuous motion and higher cumulative rewards.

4.2 Validation of Contact Force Processing

The use of detailed 3D net force vectors as privileged information, coupled with an effective normalization strategy, was crucial for learning the task. An ablation study in which these force vectors were replaced with binary contact data resulted in a significant performance decrease, underscoring that continuous net force data are more informative than simple binary signals for this complex, contact-rich manipulation task.

Furthermore, we systematically evaluated three contact force normalization methods, with results shown in Fig. 3 (c). For the best-performing 3-pose initialization, the baseline without normalization achieved an average of 0.69 rotations. Applying a single, fixed normalization improved performance slightly to 0.73 rotations. However, the strategy of iteratively refining the contact norm during training yielded a substantial improvement, reaching an average of 1.95 rotations. This demonstrates that adapting the normalization scheme to the policy's evolving force-application behavior provides a more stable and effective learning signal.

4.3 Comprehensive Performance in Pen-Spinning

The optimal configuration, which paired three human-derived reference waypoints with an iteratively refined contact norm, successfully learned a stable pen-spinning policy that averaged 1.95 rotations (Fig. 3 (c)). This consistent, periodic motion was a direct result of the acquired finger gaiting capabilities. As depicted in Fig. 5, the learned policies demonstrated emergent and complex finger gaiting, characterized by:

1. **Multi-Contact Coordination:** The hand utilized finger pads, sides, and proximal segments, a clear departure from simpler fingertip-balancing strategies.

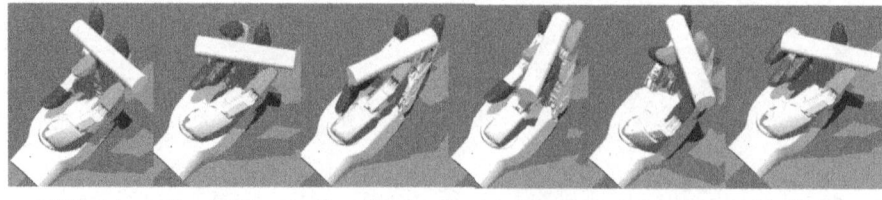

Initial Contact   Finger Transition   Support Transfer   Finger Re-engagement   Thumb Disengagement   Cycle Completion

Fig. 5. The emergent finger gaiting cycle from the learned policy. The sequence shows a full rotation, featuring sophisticated, human-like coordination, such as alternating support, smooth handoffs, and anticipatory repositioning of the fingers. The states of the contact forces at the five observed fingertips are indicated by the color of their respective links. Green links correspond to forces exceeding current threshold, whereas red links represent forces below it. (Color figure online)

2. **Anticipatory Movements:** Fingers predictively repositioned themselves to prepare for subsequent contacts in the gaiting sequence.
3. **Dynamic Force Modulation:** The policy demonstrated smooth and contextually appropriate adjustments in contact forces to support, propel, and guide the pen.
4. **Adaptive Stability:** The hand maintained robust control, making real-time corrections to counteract minor disturbances.

These sophisticated behaviors starkly contrast with the static balancing common on less anthropomorphic hands [7], confirming that a suitable hand morphology paired with targeted learning strategies can foster human-like manipulation skills.

5 Discussion

5.1 Summary of Key Findings and Advantages

This research demonstrates that a high-DoF anthropomorphic hand can learn dynamic, human-like finger gaiting through a tailored RL framework. Our primary contributions include a waypoint-guided initialization strategy to overcome high-dimensional exploration challenges and the use of privileged 3D net force information to master nuanced contact dynamics. The resulting emergent gaiting, achieved with high training efficiency within 1.5 h, validates that combining appropriate hardware morphology with targeted learning techniques can produce complex skills that surpass simpler balancing strategies. This work opens avenues for other challenging non-prehensile tasks and suggests that acquiring such skills is feasible without prohibitive computational costs.

Furthermore, transferring learned behaviors from low-DoF to high-DoF systems is a significant challenge in robotics. This paper offers a practical case study in this domain. We show that a reward structure from a less complex hand can be successfully migrated to a high-DoF hand by adapting physically-grounded

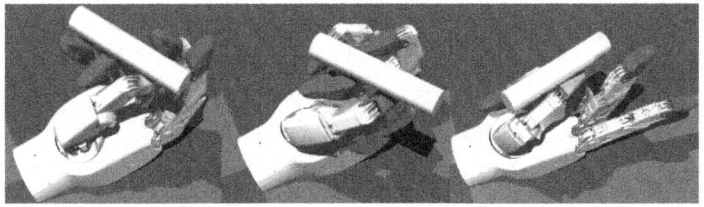

Fig. 6. An example of a policy failure state. The hand becomes trapped in a local optimum, from which it cannot continue the rotation.

penalties, such as joint torques, to the new embodiment. This highlights a viable method for leveraging findings from simpler systems to unlock sophisticated skills on more capable hardware, ensuring stable and efficient learning across different platforms.

5.2 Future Work

Future research will pursue several key directions. A primary goal is to avoid local optima, as illustrated in Fig. 6, by developing more robust, task-agnostic reward functions and integrating richer tactile sensing modalities.

The ultimate validation of our approach hinges on transferring the learned policies to the physical world, which is the most critical future direction for this research. Achieving a successful transfer will require significant enhancements to the gaiting skill's robustness, including enabling higher speeds, recovery from perturbations, and generalization to diverse objects. To manage the immense complexity of this task on a physical high-DoF hand, it will also be crucial to explore advanced hierarchical or bio-inspired control architectures. While the efficient demonstration of learned finger gaiting in simulation already underscores the potential for developing robots with human-like dexterity, dedicated research into this sim-to-real transfer is essential for fully realizing that potential.

Acknowledgements. This work was supported by the National Natural Science Foundation of China under Grant 52475001. The authors gratefully acknowledge the Beijing Super Cloud Computing Center for providing computational resources and Linkerbot Co., Ltd. for supplying the URDF model of the dexterous hand.

References

1. Tang, C., Abbatematteo, B., Hu, J., Chandra, R., Martín-Martín, R., Stone, P.: Deep reinforcement learning for robotics: a survey of real-world successes. In: Proceedings of the AAAI Conference on Artificial Intelligence, vol. 39, pp. 28694–28698 (2025)
2. OpenAI: Andrychowicz, M., et al. Learning dexterous in-hand manipulation. Int. J. Robot. Res. **39**(1), 3–20 (2020)

3. Zhang, J., et al.: Dexgraspnet 2.0: learning generative dexterous grasping in large-scale synthetic cluttered scenes. In: 8th Annual Conference on Robot Learning (2024)
4. Wang, D., Liu, C., Chang, F., Huan, H., Cheng, K.: Multi-stage reinforcement learning for non-prehensile manipulation. IEEE Robot. Autom. Lett. (2024)
5. Cheng, X., Patil, S., Temel, Z., Kroemer, O., Mason, M.T.: Enhancing dexterity in robotic manipulation via hierarchical contact exploration. IEEE Robot. Autom. Lett. **9**(1), 390–397 (2023)
6. Bicchi, A.: Hands for dexterous manipulation and robust grasping: a difficult road toward simplicity. IEEE Trans. Robot. Autom. **16**(6), 652–662 (2000)
7. Wang, J., et al.: Lessons from learning to spin " pens". arXiv preprint arXiv:2407.18902 (2024)
8. Chen, Y., et al.: Towards human-level bimanual dexterous manipulation with reinforcement learning (2022)
9. Nair, A., McGrew, B., Andrychowicz, M., Zaremba, W., Abbeel, P.: Overcoming exploration in reinforcement learning with demonstrations (2018)
10. Cheng, S., Danfei, X.: League: guided skill learning and abstraction for long-horizon manipulation. IEEE Robot. Autom. Lett. **8**(10), 6451–6458 (2023)
11. Qi, H., et al.: General in-hand object rotation with vision and touch. In: Conference on Robot Learning, pp. 2549–2564. PMLR (2023)
12. Nasiriany, S., Liu, H., Zhu, Y.: Augmenting reinforcement learning with behavior primitives for diverse manipulation tasks. In: 2022 International Conference on Robotics and Automation (ICRA), pp. 7477–7484. IEEE (2022)
13. Chen, T., Xu, J., Agrawal, P.: A system for general in-hand object re-orientation. In: Conference on Robot Learning, pp. 297–307. PMLR (2022)
14. Chen, T., Tippur, M., Wu, S., Kumar, V., Adelson, E., Agrawal, P.: Visual dexterity: in-hand reorientation of novel and complex object shapes. Sci. Robot. **8**(84), eadc9244 (2023)
15. Schulman, J., Wolski, F., Dhariwal, P., Radford, A., Klimov, O.: Proximal policy optimization algorithms. arXiv preprint arXiv:1707.06347 (2017)

Learning Stable Nonlinear Dynamical Systems with Symmetric Negative Definite Matrix Generation Network

Tianxiang Jiang[1], Pingyun Nie[1], Jiexin Zhang[2], Erxuan Xie[1,2], Huaiwu Zou[3], and Bo Zhang[1(✉)]

[1] State Key Laboratory of Mechanical System and Vibration, School of Mechanical Engineering, Shanghai Jiao Tong University, Shanghai 200240, China
{jtianxiang,niepingyun,b_zhang}@sjtu.edu.cn
[2] State Key Laboratory of Intelligent Manufacturing Equipment and Technology, School of Mechanical Science and Engineering, Huazhong University of Science and Technology, Wuhan 430074, Hubei, China
{zhangjiexin,u202110854}@hust.edu.cn
[3] Shanghai Aerospace System Engineering Institute, Shanghai 201108, China

Abstract. When encoding robotic tasks through autonomous dynamical systems (DSs) represented as velocity fields, neural networks serve as ideal modeling tools due to their powerful nonlinear approximation capabilities. However, existing neural network-based methods guarantee only local asymptotic stability. To overcome this limitation, we propose a global asymptotic stability DSs constructed around a symmetric negative definite matrix generation network (SNDM-GenNet). This neural architecture leverages inverse Cholesky Decomposition to enforce symmetric negative definiteness on its output matrix. Through Lyapunov stability theory, we rigorously prove the global convergence of all system trajectories to the target equilibrium. Validation on the LASA handwriting dataset and experiments on a 6-DOF collaborative robot (Chinrobo CRB-7) confirm the method's efficacy.

Keywords: Autonomous Dynamic System · SNDM-GenNet · Global Asymptotic Stabllity

1 Introduction

The conventional development paradigm for robotic automation tasks is heavily reliant on programmers' coding expertise and domain-specific knowledge, resulting in critical bottlenecks such as high technical barriers and prolonged development cycles. In recent years, the programming paradigm based on Learning from Demonstration (LFD) has emerged as a promising solution to overcome these challenges [1–3]. By leveraging intuitive motion task demonstrations and implicit constraint extraction, this approach enables non-professionals to efficiently program robots for complex tasks [4–7]. Of particular significance is DS learning approach in LFD technology, which formulates robotic motion as a system of differential equations. This formulation ensures solution existence throughout the operational space while enabling the robot to respond to sudden disturbances in dynamic environments without requiring trajectory replanning [8,9]. Trajectory learning methods based on DS have emerged as a research hotspot in the field of LFD, with their core challenge focusing on establishing nonlinear DSs possessing stable and convergent properties [10].

Gaussian Mixture Models represent a well-established technique for learning nonlinear DS. Khansari-Zadeh proposed the Binarized Merging algorithm constructs GMMs via iterative optimization and derives local asymptotic stability conditions [11]. However, its stability region determination relies on numerical methods with limited generalizability. Stable Estimator of DS (SEDS) [12,13] encodes dynamic motions as Gaussian mixture autonomous nonlinear ordinary differential equations, achieving guaranteed global asymptotic stability through a optimization framework. This provides theoretical guarantees for trajectory tracking in perturbed environments. Nevertheless, SEDS's stringent Lyapunov stability constraints hinder effective trajectory learning when encountering stability critical points. The Control Lyapunov Function Dynamic Movement method advances this paradigm by integrating Weighted Skewed Asymmetric Quadratic Functions with real-time convex optimization strategies [14], successfully decoupling the coupling between stability constraints and regression method selection. Ravichandar's team achieved kinematic singularity avoidance and error control in joint-space trajectory learning through quaternion-based pose representation and contraction theory constraints [15]. Concurrently, Shavit's asymptotically stable joint-space DS resolves the long-standing challenge of simultaneous convergence between task-space attractors and pose synchronization [16]. Neumann established the relationship between the original space and the transformed space using diffeomorphism. By learning a stable DS in the transformed space, a complex DS in the original space can be obtained [17,18]. With increasing dimensionality, the computational complexity of GMMs exhibits exponential growth, whereas neural networks demonstrate a much more gradual rise in computational cost.

Neural networks provide significant advantages for learning DS due to their powerful nonlinear fitting capabilities. Kuroe and Kawakami introduced a neural network-based approach to reconstruct vector fields, where prior knowledge of inherent vector field properties is leveraged to enhance accuracy, but stability considerations were not incorporated [19]. Lemme's vector field neural network enforces point-wise Lyapunov stability constraints during the learning process to achieve local asymptotic stability within operational regions, yet it lacks sufficient guarantees for global stability [20].

In this paper, we propose a neural network architecture termed as SNDM-GenNet, constructing a globally asymptotically stable Dynamical System (DS) with this network. Through Lyapunov stability theory, we rigorously prove the stability guarantees of the proposed DS. Validation on the LASA dataset demonstrates the method's effectiveness. Furthermore, we demonstrate the practical viability of the proposed through experiments on a 6-DOF cooperative robot (Chinrobo CRB-7).

2 Problem Statement

When learning robot actions, our learning data consists of one or more sets of robot demonstration trajectories $D = \{T_n\}_{n=1}^{N}$ (such as joint angles and end effector poses), where $T_n = \{x_{n,k}, \dot{x}_{n,k}\}_{k=1}^{K}$. The DS is an important tool for learning robot demonstration trajectories and can be expressed as $\dot{x} = f(x; \theta)$, where θ is the parameter to be learned by the DS. In essence, it is a set of differential equations. Our ultimate goal is for this DS to learn the optimal θ^* according to $\min \sum_{n=1}^{N} \sum_{k=1}^{K} \|\dot{x}_{n,k} - f(x_{n,k})\|_2^2$ and Validate the feasibility of the learned DS through robot experimentation. Robot demonstration trajectories typically exhibit a high degree of complexity and diversity. To endow the DS with the capacity to effectively learn an array of intricate trajectories, the adoption of a nonlinear DS becomes imperative.

Ensuring global asymptotical stability in nonlinear DS, particularly those synthesized by neural networks,has long remained a formidable challenge.Currently, DS generated via Gaussian Mixture Models can achieve global asymptotic stabilitysubject to specific constraints.In contrast, research on neural network-generated DS has achieved only local asymptotic stability, severely constraining their real-world applicability.This limitation constitutes the primary focus of our study. In the subsequent section,we present a methodological framework for synthesizing globally asymptotically stable DS using neural networks.

3 Learning Globally Asymptotically Stable DS with Neural Network

In this section, we present a globally asymptotically stable DS architecture along with the construction methodology of its core component SNDM-GenNet. Experimental validation is subsequently conducted on the LASA dataset to verify the proposed method. The diagram of our proposed method is shown below in Fig. 1. We construct the output of the fully connected neural network into a lower triangular positive definite matrix $\mathbf{L}$. Based on the principle of inverse Cholesky decomposition, we can obtain a negative definite matrix $\mathbf{A}$. Assuming the equilibrium point is x^*, we can then construct a globally stable DS $\dot{x} = \mathbf{A}(x - x^*)$ that converges to x^*. To learn the trajectory, we also need to use the backpropagation algorithm of the neural network to perform gradient descent and update the weight parameters ω and bias parameters b of neural network. After multiple iterations, we can obtain a globally stable DS that not only converges to x^* but also learns the characteristics of the demonstrated trajectory.

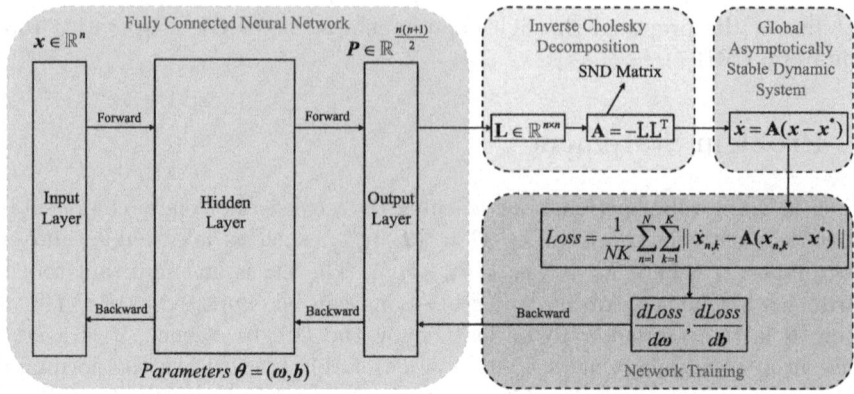

Fig. 1. Neural network-based framework for globally asymptotically stable DS.

3.1 Mathematical Structures for Guaranteeing Stability in DS

We aim to achieve end-to-end synthesis of DS via neural networks, where the network directly maps positional state x as input and outputs velocity $\dot{x}$ via the mapping $\dot{x} = Net(x; \theta)$, trained by gradient descent with custom loss functions [21]. However, the direct application of this architecture fails to guarantee global asymptotic stability of the resulting DS. To resolve the stability limitations, we introduce the following architecture:

$$\dot{x} = \mathbf{A}(x; \theta)(x - x^*) \tag{1}$$

where $\mathbf{A}(x; \theta) \prec 0$, $\forall x \in \mathbb{R}^d$, $\prec 0$ indicates that $\mathbf{A}(x; \theta)$ is a symmetric negative definite matrix generated by SNDM-GenNet, θ represents the parameters of the neural network, x^* is the unique equilibrium point of the DS.

Let us now review the Lyapunov stability theory for demonstrating the global asymptotic stability of DS.

Theorem 1 (Lyapunov Stability Theorem). *A DS $\dot{x}$ is globally asymptotically stable at the point x^* if there exists a continuous and continuously differentiable Lyapunov function $V(x) : \mathbb{R}^d \to \mathbb{R}$ satisfying the following conditions:*

$$V(x) > 0 \quad \forall x \neq x^* \tag{2}$$

$$\|x\| \to \infty \Rightarrow V(x) = \infty \tag{3}$$

$$\dot{V}(x) < 0 \quad \forall x \neq x^* \tag{4}$$

$$V(x^*) = 0 \quad \dot{V}(x) = 0 \tag{5}$$

Proof. Consider a Lyapunov function $V(x)$ of the form:

$$V(x) = \frac{1}{2}(x - x^*)^{\mathrm{T}}(x - x^*) \tag{6}$$

Since $V(\boldsymbol{x})$ is a quadratic function, it inherently satisfies conditions (2) and (3). We now examine whether condition (4) holds, where $\dot{V}(\boldsymbol{x})$ (the time derivative of $V(\boldsymbol{x})$) can be derived as follows:

$$\begin{aligned}\dot{V}(\boldsymbol{x}) &= \frac{dV}{dt} = \frac{dV}{d\boldsymbol{x}}\frac{d\boldsymbol{x}}{dt} \\ &= \frac{1}{2}\frac{d}{d\boldsymbol{x}}((\boldsymbol{x}-\boldsymbol{x}^*)^T(\boldsymbol{x}-\boldsymbol{x}^*))\dot{\boldsymbol{x}} \\ &= (\boldsymbol{x}-\boldsymbol{x}^*)^T\dot{\boldsymbol{x}} = (\boldsymbol{x}-\boldsymbol{x}^*)f(\boldsymbol{x}) \\ &= (\boldsymbol{x}-\boldsymbol{x}^*)^T\mathbf{A}(\boldsymbol{x};\boldsymbol{\theta})(\boldsymbol{x}-\boldsymbol{x}^*)\end{aligned} \quad (7)$$

Since matrix $\mathbf{A}(\boldsymbol{x};\boldsymbol{\theta})$ is negative definite, according to the definition of a negative definite matrix, the quadratic form satisfies:

$$(\boldsymbol{x}-\boldsymbol{x}^*)^T\mathbf{A}(\boldsymbol{x};\boldsymbol{\theta})(\boldsymbol{x}-\boldsymbol{x}^*) < 0, \forall \boldsymbol{x} \neq \boldsymbol{x}^* \quad (8)$$

which satisfies condition (4). Substituting $\boldsymbol{x} = \boldsymbol{x}^*$ into $V(\boldsymbol{x})$ and $\dot{V}(\boldsymbol{x})$, we obtain:

$$V(\boldsymbol{x}^*) = \frac{1}{2}(\boldsymbol{x}-\boldsymbol{x}^*)^T(\boldsymbol{x}-\boldsymbol{x}^*)|_{\boldsymbol{x}=\boldsymbol{x}^*} = 0 \quad (9)$$

$$\dot{V}(\boldsymbol{x}^*) = (\boldsymbol{x}-\boldsymbol{x}^*)^T\mathbf{A}(\boldsymbol{x};\boldsymbol{\theta})(\boldsymbol{x}-\boldsymbol{x}^*)|_{\boldsymbol{x}=\boldsymbol{x}^*} = 0 \quad (10)$$

Therefore, the DS described by Equation (1) satisfies global asymptotic stability.

3.2 Constructing SND Matrices Using Neural Networks

In the stability analysis of DS, when the coefficient matrix $\mathbf{A}(\boldsymbol{x};\boldsymbol{\theta})$ in Eq. (1) is negative definite, it ensures that the system $\dot{\boldsymbol{x}} = \mathbf{A}(\boldsymbol{x};\boldsymbol{\theta})(\boldsymbol{x}-\boldsymbol{x}^*)$ exhibits globally asymptotically stable characteristics. The negative definite matrix requires all its eigenvalues to be strictly distributed in the left half-open region of the complex plane. Although matrices satisfying this condition theoretically possess infinite possibilities in the mathematical space, traditional analytical methods face significant limitations in constructing such matrices: First, it is challenging to establish a unified mathematical framework covering all forms of negative definite matrices; second, there lacks an adaptive construction mechanism applicable to complex nonlinear systems.

The Cholesky Decomposition theorem not only provides a standard decomposition form $\mathbf{M} = \mathbf{L}\mathbf{L}^T$ for every symmetric positive definite matrix $\mathbf{M}$ (where $\mathbf{L}$ is a lower triangular matrix with strictly positive diagonal elements), but more notably, its inverse process also maintains the strict positive definiteness of the structure.

Proposition 1 (Inverse Cholesky Decomposition). *Given a lower triangular matrix $\mathbf{L} \in \mathbb{R}^{n \times n}$ with strictly positive diagonal entries, the matrix $\mathbf{M} = \mathbf{L}\mathbf{L}^T$ is symmetric positive definite (i.e., all its eigenvalues are strictly greater than zero).*

Proof. By properties of matrix transposition:

$$\mathbf{M}^{\mathrm{T}} = (\mathbf{L}\mathbf{L}^{\mathrm{T}})^{\mathrm{T}} = (\mathbf{L}^{\mathrm{T}})^{\mathrm{T}}\mathbf{L}^{\mathrm{T}} = \mathbf{L}\mathbf{L}^{\mathrm{T}} = \mathbf{M} \tag{11}$$

Hence, $\mathbf{M} = \mathbf{M}^{\mathrm{T}}$ holds.

For any nonzero vector $x \in \mathbb{R}^n$:

$$\begin{aligned} x^{\mathrm{T}}\mathbf{M}x &= x^{\mathrm{T}}\mathbf{L}(\mathbf{L}^{\mathrm{T}}x) \\ &= (\mathbf{L}^{\mathrm{T}}x)^{\mathrm{T}}(\mathbf{L}^{\mathrm{T}}x) \\ &= \|\mathbf{L}^{\mathrm{T}}x\|_2^2 \geq 0 \end{aligned} \tag{12}$$

Since $\mathbf{L}$ has strictly positive diagonal entries, its determinant $\det(\mathbf{L}) = \prod_{i=1}^{n} l_{ii} > 0$, implying $\mathbf{L}^{\mathrm{T}}$ is invertible. For $x \neq \mathbf{0}$:

$$\mathbf{L}^{\mathrm{T}}x \neq \mathbf{0} \implies \|\mathbf{L}^{\mathrm{T}}x\|_2^2 > 0 \tag{13}$$

Thus $x^{\mathrm{T}}\mathbf{M}x > 0$, establishing positive definiteness.

For an n-dimensional lower triangular matrix $\mathbf{L}$, the neural network requires $\dfrac{n(n+1)}{2}$ outputs. Taking the 2-dimensional case as an example, the following explains how to construct a negative definite symmetric matrix $\mathbf{A}$. Neural network generates raw parameters $[p_1, p_2, p_3]$. To ensure the positive definiteness of matrix $\mathbf{L}$ and enhance numerical stability, the parameters must be adjusted as follow:

$$\tilde{p}_1 = |p_1| + \epsilon,\ \tilde{p}_2 = |p_2| + \epsilon,\ \tilde{p}_3 = p_3 \tag{14}$$

where ϵ is a small positive constant($e.g., \epsilon = 10^{-1}$). By substituting the parameters $\tilde{p}_1, \tilde{p}_2, \tilde{p}_3$ into the predefined structure, we construct a lower triangular matrix $\mathbf{L}$, and subsequently compute the negative definite symmetric matrix $\mathbf{A}$ through the transformation $\mathbf{A} = -\mathbf{L}\mathbf{L}^{\mathrm{T}}$.

$$\mathbf{L} = \begin{pmatrix} \tilde{p}_1 & 0 \\ \tilde{p}_3 & \tilde{p}_2 \end{pmatrix} \Rightarrow \mathbf{A} = -\mathbf{L}\mathbf{L}^{\mathrm{T}} = -\begin{pmatrix} \tilde{p}_1^{\,2} & \tilde{p}_3\tilde{p}_1 \\ \tilde{p}_3\tilde{p}_1 & \tilde{p}_2^{\,2} + \tilde{p}_3^{\,2} \end{pmatrix} \tag{15}$$

We call this network that generates symmetric negative definite matrices SNDM-GenNet.

3.3 Learning Stable DS on the LASA Dataset

In the preceding sections, we have rigorously proven that the DS represented by Eq. 1 is globally asymptotically stable and proposed a systematic methodology for constructing such systems. To empirically validate the efficacy of our approach, we will employ the LASA Handwriting Dataset [22]—a dataset curated by the École Polytechnique Fédérale de Lausanne (EPFL) and widely adopted for evaluating performance in DS learning methodologies. Prior to presenting the experimental results, we delineate the configurations of each component within our framework as follows.

Construct a fully connected feedforward neural network $N_\theta : \mathbb{R}^2 \to \mathbb{R}^3$ with the structure $2 \times 10 \times 10 \times 3$, where:

1) Input Layer: 2 neurons receive the system state vector $x = [x_1, x_2]^T \in \mathbb{R}^2$ whose dimensionality aligns with the 2D motion space of the LASA handwriting dataset (commonly used for kinesthetic demonstration trajectory modeling).
2) Hidden Layers: Dual 10-neuron hidden layers employ adaptive parameter sharing to dynamically adjust nonlinear mapping capabilities based on trajectory complexity:

$$h_k = \sigma(W_k h_{k-1} + b_k), \quad k \in \{1, 2\} \tag{16}$$

where $\sigma(.)$ denotes the sigmoid activation function $\frac{1}{1+e^{-z}}$, ensuring bounded gradients critical for Lyapunov-stable parameter updates.
3) Output Layer: 3 neurons generate elements of the lower-triangular matrix $L \in \mathbb{R}^{2 \times 2}$

$$L = \begin{pmatrix} \tilde{p}_1 & 0 \\ \tilde{p}_3 & \tilde{p}_2 \end{pmatrix} \tag{17}$$

By applying the inverse Cholesky Decomposition, we derive the matrix $A = -LL^T$ thereby enforcing global asymptotic stability through its negative definiteness. Then, we further interpret the dynamical mapping from x to $A(x - x^*)$ as an extended neural network, whose loss function is formulated as follows:

$$Loss = \frac{1}{NK} \sum_{n=1}^{N} \sum_{k=1}^{K} \|\dot{x}_{n,k} - A(x_{n,k}; \theta)(x_{n,k} - x^*)\|_2^2 \tag{18}$$

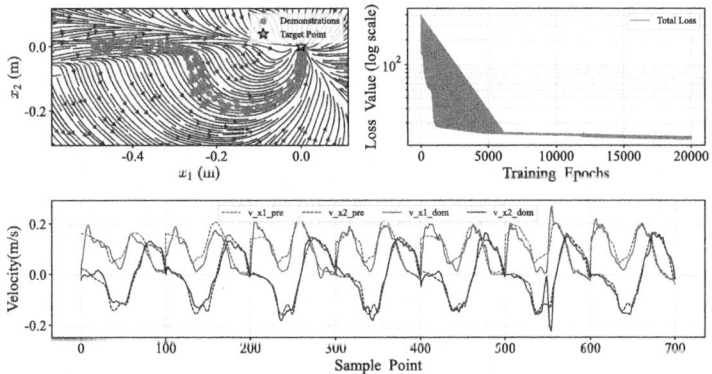

Fig. 2. Neural network learning results for trajectory Spoon.

Figure. 2 illustrates the training performance of one of the nine demonstration trajectories-the Spoon trajectory. The training was conducted for a total of

20,000 epochs, taking approximately 1 min, and resulted in a final loss value of 0.00139 m²/s². The velocities generated by the DS at various points along the demonstration trajectory basically match the velocities of the demonstration itself.

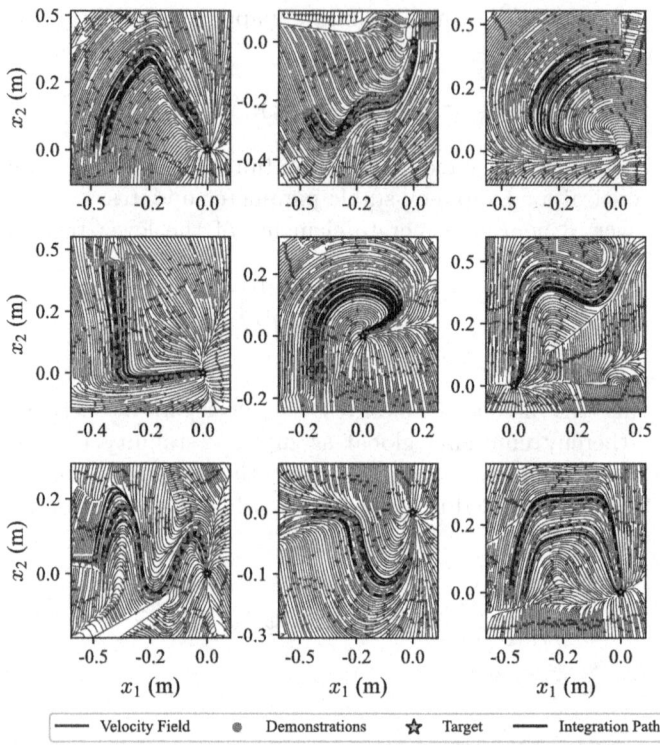

Fig. 3. Performance evaluation on the library of 9 human handwriting motions.

We validated the proposed method using 9 trajectories from the LASA dataset. As illustrated in Fig. 3, despite training only on demonstration trajectories, all velocity fields in the diagram converge asymptotically to the equilibrium point along their respective directions, demonstrating the global asymptotic stability of our DS. Furthermore, the black integral curves faithfully track the red demonstration trajectories, while neighboring trajectories asymptotically converge toward them. This phenomenon clearly demonstrates the system's ability to accurately replicate complex trajectories and its robust generalization capabilities.

4 Experiments

For some trajectories, if there is insufficient smoothness (such as discontinuities in velocity) or poor continuity, the robotic manipulator may experience oscillation or motion instability during execution. In this section, we experimentally verify whether the generated velocity field can be effectively executed within the robotic manipulator, while also detailing our experimental setup.

4.1 Experimental Setup

The experimental validation is performed on the CRB-7 robot from Chinrobo, a 6-DOF cooperative robot. The CRB7 robot is controlled via the Beckhoff CX2030 instead of its original host computer. All joints of the CRB-7 robotare configured in the current control mode. The CX2030 sends control commands and receives feedback, such as motor currents, joint positions, joint velocities, and joint torques, through EtherCAT communication, with a communication frequency set at 4 kHz [23].

4.2 Feasibility Experiment of Dynamic Systems

In the experiment, a black marker is fixed at the end of the robotic arm to draw a trajectory on the whiteboard below. The end-effector of the robotic arm is always kept perpendicular to the whiteboard. The experiment adopts the classical impedance control method. A trajectory is integrated based on the initial position of the end-effector, and the impedance controller is used to track this trajectory. The stiffness of the impedance control is set as $\mathbf{K} = [1000\ 1000\ 1000\ 10000\ 10000\ 1100]$ (Units: Nm/rad for elements 1–3, N/m for elements 4–6).

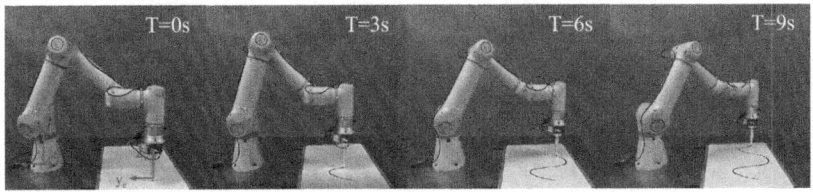

Fig. 4. Sine shape trajectory execution experiment in DS

Figure 4 and Fig. 5 shows the entire process of the collaborative robot drawing the Sine-shape trajectory and the speed tracking during the drawing. As can be seen from the desired velocity curve in the figure, it has a relatively smooth trend without any oscillations or sudden changes. After comparing it with the actual velocity curve, it is found that overall, the speed tracking performance of the robotic arm is good. However, since the velocity corresponding to the initial point of the collaborative robot in the velocity field is non-zero, an overshoot phenomenon occurs in the y-direction during the initial stage of the robot, but this phenomenon did not compromise end-effector trajectory tracking stability.

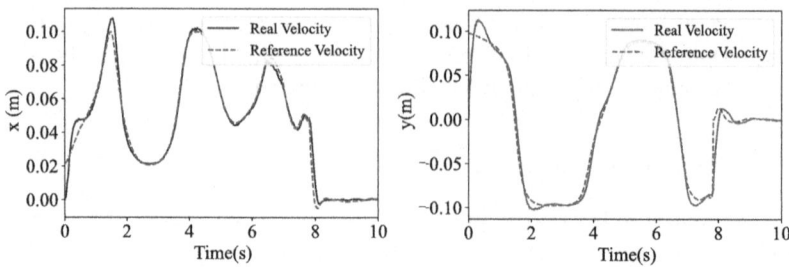

Fig. 5. Velocity tracking performance in Sine shape trajectory execution experiment.

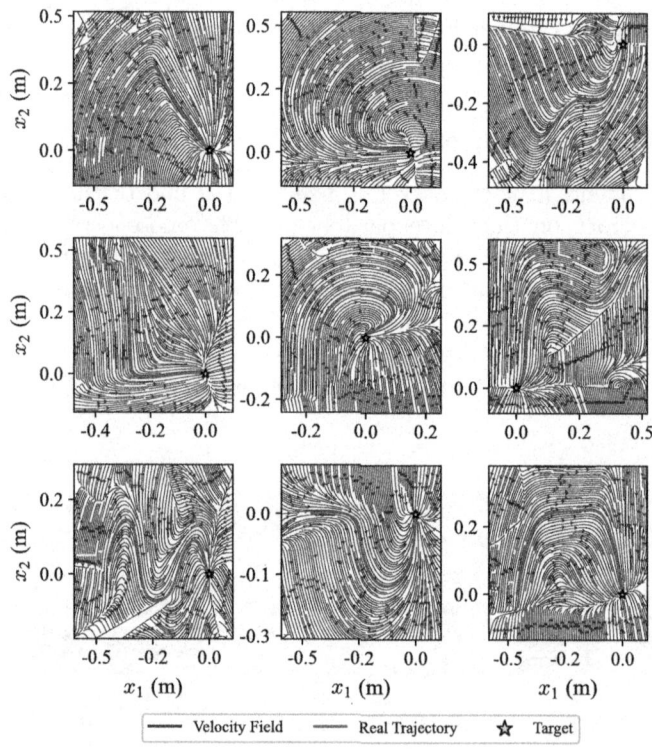

Fig. 6. Experimental verification of trajectory execution effect in DS.

As shown in the Fig. 6, the end-position trajectory data collected from the collaborative robot is plotted into the corresponding velocity fields. The trajectory executed by the collaborative robot is basically consistent with the velocity directions of the velocity fields. The demonstration trajectory is successfully executed on the robot without any oscillations or instability. Therefore, the DS learned by the method proposed in this paper can be applied to robots.

5 Conclusion

This paper introduces SNDM-GenNet, a novel neural network architecture designed to guarantee that its output, under any input, forms a symmetric negative definite matrix. This property is achieved through the integration of inverse Cholesky decomposition within the network structure. By replacing the system matrix of a dynamic system with SNDM-GenNet, we establish a globally asymptotically stable dynamic system. The global asymptotic stability of the resulting DS is rigorously proven using Lyapunov stability theory. Experimental validation on the LASA dataset demonstrates the efficacy of the proposed approach. Furthermore, successful execution of learned demonstration trajectories on a collaborative robot confirms the practical feasibility of the generated DS in robotic applications.

Acknowledgements. This work was supported by the National Natural Science Foundation of China (Grant Nos. 52375506, U21B6002), the Postdoctoral Fellowship Program of the China Postdoctoral Science Foundation (No. GZC20240539) and USCAST2023-18.

References

1. Ravichandar, H., Polydoros, A.S., Chernova, S., Billard, A.: Recent advances in robot learning from demonstration. Ann. Rev. Control, Robot. Auton. Syst. **3**(1), 297–330 (2020)
2. Billard, A., Calinon, S., Dillmann, R., Schaal, S.: Survey: Robot Programming by Demonstration. Springer Handbook of Robotics, pp. 1371–1394 (2008)
3. Chernova, S., Thomaz, A.L.: Robot Learning from Human Teachers. Springer, Heidelberg (2022)
4. Zhang, J., et al.: Dexterous hand towards intelligent manufacturing: a review of technologies, trends, and potential applications. Robot. Comput. Integr. Manuf. **95**, 103021 (2025)
5. Hou, T., Ding, Y., Zhu, X.: A geometric framework for stiffness mappings of compliant robotic systems on the special Euclidean group. IEEE Trans. Rob. **40**, 2181–2200 (2024)
6. Zhang, J.X., Nie, P.Y., Zhang, B.: A variable structure passivity control method for elastic joint robots based on cascaded high-order state estimation. Science China Technol. Sci. **67**(2), 395–407 (2024)
7. Zhang, J., Hou, T., Ding, Y., Zhang, B., Liu, H.: On the passive virtual viscous element injection method for elastic joint robots. IEEE Trans. Robot. (2025)
8. Bai, H., Nie, P., Hou, T., Zou, H., Zhang, J., Zhang, B.: A dynamical systems-based peg-in-hole assembly method using temporal logic task planner. In: Lan, X., Mei, X., Jiang, C., Zhao, F., Tian, Z., (eds.) Intelligent Robotics and Applications, pp. 132–147. Springer, Singapore (2025). https://doi.org/10.1007/978-981-96-0789-1_10
9. Zhang, J., Nie, P., Chen, Y., Zhang, B.: A joint acceleration estimation method based on a high-order disturbance observer. IEEE Robot. Autom. Lett. **7**(4), 12615–12622 (2022)

10. Hou, T., Bai, H., Ding, Y., Ding, H.: Generation of conservative dynamical systems based on stiffness encoding. arXiv preprintarXiv:2411.01120 (2024)
11. Mohammad Khansari-Zadeh, S., Billard, A.: BM: an iterative algorithm to learn stable non-linear dynamical systems with Gaussian mixture models. In: 2010 IEEE International Conference on Robotics and Automation, pp. 2381–2388. IEEE. Anchorage (2010)
12. Mohammad Khansari-Zadeh, S., Billard, A.: Learning stable nonlinear dynamical systems with Gaussian mixture models. IEEE Trans. Robot. **27**(5), 943–957 (2011)
13. Figueroa, N., Billard, A.: A Physically-Consistent Bayesian Non-Parametric Mixture Model for Dynamical System Learning
14. Mohammad Khansari-Zadeh, S., Billard, A.: Learning control Lyapunov function to ensure stability of dynamical system-based robot reaching motions. Robot. Auton. Syst. **62**(6), 752–765 (2014)
15. Harish Chaandar Ravichandar and Ashwin Dani: Learning position and orientation dynamics from demonstrations via contraction analysis. Auton. Robot. **43**(4), 897–912 (2019)
16. Shavit, Y., Figueroa, N., Salehian, S.S.M., Billard, A.: Learning augmented joint-space task-oriented dynamical systems: a linear parameter varying and synergetic control approach. IEEE Robot. Autom. Lett. **3**(3), 2718–2725 (2018)
17. Neumann, K., Steil, J.J.: Learning robot motions with stable dynamical systems under diffeomorphic transformations. Robot. Auton. Syst. **70**, 1–15 (2015)
18. Perrin, N., Schlehuber-Caissier, P.: Fast diffeomorphic matching to learn globally asymptotically stable nonlinear dynamical systems. Syst. Control Lett. **96**, 51–59 (2016)
19. Kuroe, Y., Kawakami, H.: Vector field approximation by model inclusive learning of neural networks. In: de Sá, J.M., Alexandre, L.A., Duch, W., Mandic, D. (eds.) ICANN 2007. LNCS, vol. 4668, pp. 717–726. Springer, Heidelberg (2007). https://doi.org/10.1007/978-3-540-74690-4_73
20. Lemme, A., Neumann, K., Reinhart, R.F., Steil, J.J.: Neural learning of vector fields for encoding stable dynamical systems. Neurocomputing **141**, 3–14 (2014)
21. Zhang, H., Cheng, L., Zhang, Y., Wang, Y.: Neural Liénard system: learning periodic manipulation skills through dynamical systems. Sci. China Inf. Sci. **67**(12), 222207 (2024)
22. S. M. Khansari-Zadeh and A. Billard. LASA Handwriting Dataset. GitHub repository, 2021. Accessed: 2025/10/04 22:57:39
23. Nie, P., Zou, H., Zhang, J., Bai, H., Jiang, T., Zhang, B.: A robust identification method for robot drive gains using a payload. In: International Conference on Intelligent Robotics and Applications, pp. 162–175. Springer, Cham (2024)

Object's CoM-Aware Pose Optimization of Humanoid Upperlimbs for Dual-Arm Collaborative Carrying

Tiancheng Ma, Chuanlin Zhao, and Xin Luo[✉]

School of Mechanical Science and Engineering of Huazhong University of Science and Technology, Wuhan 430074, China
mexinluo@hust.edu.cn

Abstract. Humanoid robots are increasingly deployed to perform tasks involving dexterous manipulation and heavy-load carrying. However, when handling objects with an offset center of mass, uneven force distribution between the arms and reduced dynamic stability can arise, leading to higher energy consumption, motor overheating, or degraded control performance. A promising solution is to use coordinated dual-arm manipulation to adjust the object's pose, thereby reducing the negative effects of load imbalance. Achieving this requires precise coordination of motion and force between both arms. To this end, we propose a collaborative pose optimization strategy for dual-arm systems that explicitly incorporates object inertial properties into the planning process. The pose adjustment is formulated as a constrained optimization problem considering kinematic feasibility, grasp equilibrium, torque limits, and collision avoidance. The resulting optimal terminal pose serves as a reference for trajectory planning. We further employ an MPC-based planner to generate joint-space motions that track the adjustment trajectory while satisfying task constraints. Simulation results show that the proposed method reduces joint torque under various eccentric loading conditions while ensuring stable, constraint-compliant execution through active object pose adjustment. The resulting motions satisfy joint limits, torque constraints, and collision avoidance, achieving a balanced and robust manipulation configuration.

Keywords: Center of mass awareness · Dual-arm manipulation · Pose optimization

1 Introduction

In recent years, humanoid robots have become a prominent focus in robotics research and are increasingly being adopted in real-world applications such as domestic service, logistics, healthcare, and disaster response [1, 2]. As a key enabler of physical interaction in these tasks, dual-arm systems play a pivotal role in object manipulation—particularly when handling large, heavy, or irregularly shaped objects.

Nevertheless, when carrying heavy objects—especially those with an eccentric center of mass—these systems often encounter significant challenges. During dual-arm manipulation of such objects, two primary issues may arise: (a) Asymmetric force and torque distribution – the offset center of mass leads to unbalanced load sharing between the two arms, causing uneven joint torques and subjecting certain joints to sustained high stress [3, 4]; (b) Reduced whole-body stability – the external load may cause a shift in the robot's overall center of mass, making it more difficult to maintain balance and increasing the likelihood of instability during task execution. To mitigate the challenges introduced by load asymmetry, a promising strategy is to regulate the object's pose through dual-arm coordination, thereby improving balance and stability during manipulation, as well as reducing the overall joint torque exerted by the arms.

In the context of dual-arm manipulation planning, most existing studies focus on symmetrical objects with a centralized center of mass [5–7], which typically result in balanced force distributions during execution. Relatively little attention has been paid to scenarios involving asymmetric or irregular objects, where load imbalance poses significant challenges to coordination and stability. Actually, when dealing with irregular-shaped objects or those with significantly offset CoM, the system requires superior coordination capabilities and force control strategies to maintain grip stability and prevent overload on individual arms.

Although the existing trajectory planning methods of dual-arm systems have made significant progress in gripping posture, collision avoidance, and time optimization [8], they generally focus on kinematic objectives and pay limited attention to joint torque allocation [9] and object posture adjustment strategies during the operation process. As a result, when manipulating objects with complex geometry or significant CoM offset, problems such as uneven load distribution and unstable gripping often occur. Duan et al. [10] proposed a stable grasping control method based on contact parameterization to ensure reasonable torque distribution of the dual arms, but when modeling, it was assumed that the object's CoM coincides with its geometric center. Di Leva et al. [11] investigated time-optimal and internal force-optimized trajectories for cooperative grasping of eccentric objects, but only considered small CoM offsets relative to the box's geometric center. In the study of Shu et al. [12], although the CoM information of the gripped object was considered, it was used to keep the object horizontally stable. Dio et al. [13] employed a hierarchical quadratic programming (HQP) framework to explicitly incorporate dynamic constraints (such as joint torque limits and internal force limits) into the optimization problem, achieving physically feasible and near-limit performance in heavy object manipulation. Nevertheless, they also assumed that the CoM of the object was centered, without considering richer object information.

To address the load imbalance caused by object CoM offset, we propose a collaborative pose optimization strategy that explicitly incorporates inertial properties—such as mass and center-of-mass location—into the planning process. First, a quasi-static optimization problem is formulated to compute the optimal manipulation pose along with a corresponding joint configuration. Based on this reference pose, an object adjustment trajectory is designed, and the required end-effector forces are optimized accordingly. Finally, a Cartesian-space adjustment motion is generated using a model predictive control (MPC) framework, enabling the robot arms to perform smooth and coordinated compensation motions. This approach results in a more balanced torque distribution and enhanced manipulation efficiency.

The rest of this paper is organized as follows. Section 2 presents the modeling of the system's kinematics and the dynamic model of the object motion. Section 3 formulates a quasi-static optimization for manipulation pose and introduces a trajectory planning scheme for object adjustment, incorporating force optimization and control execution. Section 4 demonstrates the effectiveness of the proposed method through numerical simulations. Section 5 concludes the paper and discusses future work.

2 System Model

2.1 Kinematic and Contact Modeling

Once the object is firmly gripped by both arms, a closed-chain constraint is formed among the manipulators, the body, and the object. Consider a system composed of two arms rigidly gripping a common rigid body, as illustrated in Fig. 1. Two arms hold a box containing mass blocks using a clamping plate.

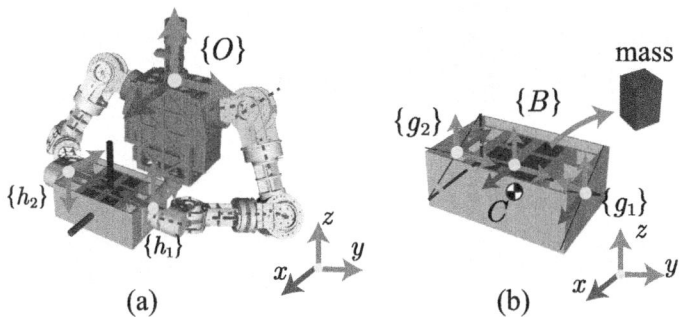

Fig. 1. Kinematic model of the dual-arm system: (a) manipulator and base frames, with left arm joint axes; (b) object frames and masses.

Each arm has n_i degrees of freedom, where $i = \{1, 2\}$ denotes the left and right arms, respectively. As illustrated in Fig. 1(a), $\{O\}$ is defined as the frame fixed to the robot's body. $\{h_i\}$ represent the centers of the end-effector surface for the respective arms. In Fig. 1(b), $\{B\}$ is defined at the geometric center of the object. It is assumed that the object's geometric center lies on the line connecting the origins of the $\{h_1\}$ and $\{h_2\}$. $\{g_i\}$ denote the centers of the contact surfaces between the grippers and the object, presumed to be located at the geometric center of the object's lateral surfaces. During the stable gripping phase, it is further assumed that the origins of $\{h_i\}$ and $\{g_i\}$ coincide. The point C represents the object's center of mass.

The pose of a coordinate frame is represented as $T = (R, p) \in SE(3)$. The relationships between $\{h_i\}$ and $\{O\}$, $\{h_i\}$ and $\{g_i\}$, $\{g_i\}$ and $\{B\}$ are governed by the following transformations:

$$^O T_{h_1} = {^O T_{h_2}}\,{^{h_2}T_{h_1}}, \quad \begin{cases} ^O T_{h_1} = {^O T_{g_1}}\,{^{g_1}T_{h_1}} \\ ^O T_{h_2} = {^O T_{g_2}}\,{^{g_2}T_{h_2}} \end{cases}, \quad \begin{cases} ^O T_{g_1} = {^O T_B}\,{^B T_{g_1}} \\ ^O T_{g_2} = {^O T_B}\,{^B T_{g_2}} \end{cases} \tag{1}$$

where ^bT_a denotes the pose of $\{a\}$ relative to $\{b\}$. Let $\boldsymbol{q}_i = [q_i^1, \ldots, q_i^{n_i}]^T \in \mathbb{R}^{n_i}$ represents the joint angles of the i-th arm, then $^OT_{e_i} = fkine(\boldsymbol{q}_i)$, where *fkine* denotes the forward kinematic function.

We use $\boldsymbol{P}_B = [x_B, y_B, z_B]^T \in \mathbb{R}^3$ represent the object's position and ZYX Euler angles $\boldsymbol{\Theta}_B = [\alpha, \beta, \gamma]^T \in \mathbb{R}^3$ represent its orientation. It is assumed that the initial pose of the object is known. Once the arms establish a closed kinematic chain, $^{g_i}T_{h_i}, i = \{1,2\}$ is determined and remains constant even as the object's pose changes.

The contact model describes interactions between each gripper and the object surface. Two assumptions are made: (a) the object is rigid; (b) the contact model is unilateral planar contact, with no relative sliding between the gripper and the object during operation. According to [14], contact models can be categorized into frictionless point contact, point contact, soft contact, and unilateral planar contact. This paper adopts the unilateral planar contact model, as depicted in Fig. 2.

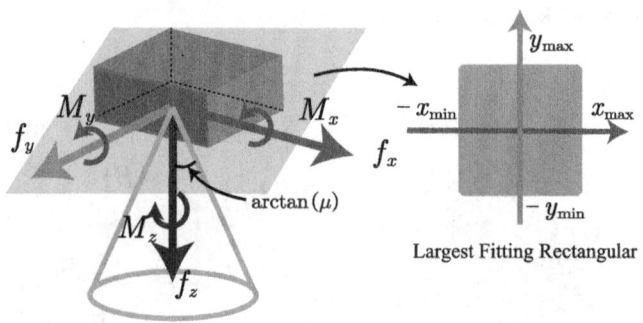

Fig. 2. Unilateral planar contact and the largest fitting rectangular

The contact force is denoted as $\boldsymbol{f} = [f_x, f_y, f_z, M_x, M_y, M_z]^T \in \mathbb{R}^6$. The contact stability constraints can be expressed as follows:

$$f_z > 0 \tag{2}$$

$$\sqrt{f_x^2 + f_y^2} \leq \mu f_z \tag{3}$$

$$-y_{min} \leq -\frac{M_x}{f_z} \leq y_{max} \tag{4}$$

$$-x_{min} \leq \frac{M_y}{f_z} \leq x_{max} \tag{5}$$

$$|M_z| \leq \mu_z f_z \tag{6}$$

where $x_{min}, x_{max}, y_{min}, y_{max}$ is the size of the largest fitting rectangle in the contact surface. μ denotes the static friction coefficient between the gripper and the object surface; μ_z denotes the torsional friction coefficient.

2.2 Dynamic Modeling of Object Motion

Strict mechanical constraints are a prerequisite for the manipulation of objects by robotic arms. This paper employs friction constraints on the contact surface and the dynamic model of the object's motion to ensure contact stability. To facilitate planning under these constraints, the object's path and orientation are parameterized by $s \in [0,1]$, with $\mathbf{r}(s) = [x(s), y(s), z(s)]^T$ and $\boldsymbol{\theta}(s) = [\theta_x(s), \theta_y(s), \theta_z(s)]^T$, respectively, as depicted in Fig. 3. The motion law of the path parameter $s(t)$ allows the trajectory to be defined as

$$\begin{cases} \dot{\mathbf{r}}(s) = \mathbf{r}'(s)\dot{s} \\ \ddot{\mathbf{r}}(s) = \mathbf{r}''(s)\dot{s}^2 + \mathbf{r}'(s)\ddot{s} \\ \dot{\boldsymbol{\theta}}(s) = \boldsymbol{\theta}'(s)\dot{s} \\ \ddot{\boldsymbol{\theta}}(s) = \boldsymbol{\theta}''(s)\dot{s}^2 + \boldsymbol{\theta}'(s)\ddot{s} \end{cases} \quad (7)$$

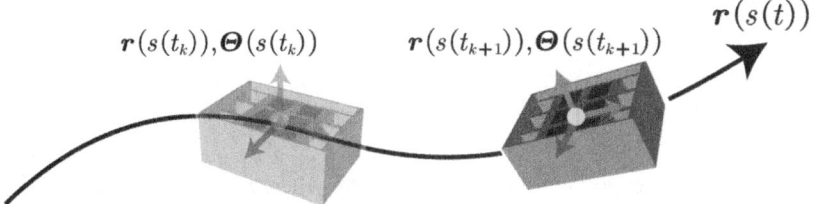

Fig. 3. Parametric formulation of the object's motion

The dynamic model of the object can be expressed as follows:

$$\mathbf{F}_c = \begin{bmatrix} \mathbf{f}_c \\ \boldsymbol{\tau}_c \end{bmatrix} = \begin{bmatrix} m(\dot{\mathbf{v}}_c - \mathbf{g}) \\ \bar{\mathbf{I}}_c \dot{\boldsymbol{\omega}}_c + [\boldsymbol{\omega}_c]\bar{\mathbf{I}}_c \boldsymbol{\omega}_c \end{bmatrix} \quad (8)$$

where $\mathbf{F}_c \in \mathbb{R}^6$ represents the resultant external force acting on the object. $\bar{\mathbf{I}}_c \in \mathbb{R}^{3\times 3}$ denotes the rotational inertia at the center of mass; m is the mass of the object; $\dot{\mathbf{v}}_c$ is the acceleration of the CoM under external forces; $\mathbf{g}$ is the gravitational acceleration vector; $\boldsymbol{\omega}_c$ is the angular velocity at the CoM. $[*]$ indicates the skew-symmetric matrix. The relationship between $\dot{\mathbf{v}}_c, \boldsymbol{\omega}_c, \dot{\boldsymbol{\omega}}_c$ and the parameter s is given by

$$\begin{cases} \dot{\mathbf{v}}_c(t) = \ddot{\mathbf{r}}(s(t), \dot{s}(t), \ddot{s}(t)) \\ \boldsymbol{\omega}_c(t) = \mathbf{A}\dot{\boldsymbol{\theta}}(s(t), \dot{s}(t)) \\ \dot{\boldsymbol{\omega}}_c(t) = \dot{\mathbf{A}}\dot{\boldsymbol{\theta}}(s(t), \dot{s}(t)) + \mathbf{A}\ddot{\boldsymbol{\theta}}(s(t), \dot{s}(t), \ddot{s}(t)) \end{cases} \quad (9)$$

with

$$\mathbf{A} = \begin{bmatrix} 0 & -\sin\alpha & \cos\alpha\cos\beta \\ 0 & \cos\alpha & \cos\beta\sin\alpha \\ 1 & 0 & -\sin\beta \end{bmatrix}$$

The dynamic model of a single robotic arm can be expressed as

$$M_i(q_i)\ddot{q}_i + C_i(q_i, \dot{q}_i)\dot{q}_i + g_i(q_i) = \tau_i - J_i^T F_{ext,i} \tag{10}$$

where $M_i \in \mathbb{R}^{n_i \times n_i}$ is the mass matrices; $C_i \in \mathbb{R}^{n_i \times n_i}$ is the Coriolis matrices; $g_i \in \mathbb{R}^{n_i}$ represents the gravity term; $\tau_i \in \mathbb{R}^{n_i}$ is the joint driving torque; The force exerted by the i-th arm on the external environment is $F_{ext,i} = [f_{ext,i}^T, \tau_{ext,i}^T]^T \in \mathbb{R}^6$. When solving a quasi-static optimization problem, it's assumed that $\dot{v}_c = \dot{\omega}_c = \omega_c = 0, \dot{q}_i = \ddot{q}_i = 0$. Consequently, the static equation for the dual-arm system can be written as

$$\begin{bmatrix} \tau_1 \\ \tau_2 \end{bmatrix} = \begin{bmatrix} g_1 \\ g_2 \end{bmatrix} + \begin{bmatrix} J_1^T F_{ext,1} \\ J_2^T F_{ext,2} \end{bmatrix} \in \mathbb{R}^{2n_i \times 1} \tag{11}$$

Taking the object as the subject of analysis, its static equilibrium condition can be expressed as

$$\begin{cases} \sum_{i=1}^{2} f_{g_i} + f_c = 0 \\ \sum_{i=1}^{2} r_{cg_i} \times f_{g_i} + \sum_{i=1}^{2} \tau_{g_i} + \tau_c = 0 \end{cases} \tag{12}$$

Equation (12) is expressed at the object's CoM, where $r_{cg_i} \in \mathbb{R}^3$ is a vector pointing from C to $\{g_i\}.f_{g_i}, \tau_{g_i} \in \mathbb{R}^3$ denotes the force exerted by the arm on the object's lateral surface, which is related to the end-effector force of the arm by the expression

$$F_{h_i} = [Ad_{T_{g_ih_i}}]^T F_{g_i} = \begin{bmatrix} R_{g_ih_i}^T & R_{g_ih_i}^T[r_{g_ih_i}]^T \\ 0_{3 \times 3} & R_{g_ih_i}^T \end{bmatrix} \begin{bmatrix} \tau_{g_i} \\ f_{g_i} \end{bmatrix} = \begin{bmatrix} \tau_{h_i} \\ f_{h_i} \end{bmatrix} \tag{13}$$

where $[Ad_T]$ denotes the adjoint transformation matrix. In the following discussion, the resultant force at the object's CoM is expressed in the object's coordinate frame $\{B\}$.

3 Pose Optimization

To alleviate the end-effector load imbalance caused by uneven mass distribution within the object, we propose a collaborative pose optimization strategy. This strategy enables the manipulators to actively adjust the position and orientation of the object while satisfying joint position and torque limits, as well as collision constraints, to achieve a optimized manipulation posture. The overall procedure consists of two stages. First, an optimal manipulation pose is computed through quasi-static optimization and employed as a terminal constraint for subsequent planning. Second, based on the initial and terminal poses, a Cartesian adjustment trajectory is generated, during which the intermediate end-effector forces are optimized. This trajectory then serves as the reference for an MPC-based planner, which computes joint-space trajectories that satisfy multiple constraints.

3.1 Terminal Pose Optimization

Select the optimization variable $X = [q_1^T, q_2^T, P_B^T, \Theta_B^T, F_{g1}^T, F_{g2}^T]^T \in \mathbb{R}^{2n_i+6+2\times 6}$ and construct the following optimization problem

$$X^* = \underset{X}{\operatorname{argmin}} f(X) = \underset{X}{\operatorname{argmin}} \sum_{i=1}^{2} \sum_{j=1}^{n_i} (\tau_{i,j}(X))^2 \quad (14)$$

$$\text{s.t.} \quad \Gamma(q_1, q_2, P_B, \Theta_B) = 0 \quad (15)$$

$$\Psi(q_1, q_2, P_B, \Theta_B, F_{g1}, F_{g2}) = 0 \quad (16)$$

$$\Phi(F_{g1}, F_{g2}) \leq 0 \quad (17)$$

$$\underline{q}_i \leq q_i \leq \bar{q}_i, |\tau_i| \leq \tau_{max}, i = \{1, 2\} \quad (18)$$

$$P_{Bmin} \leq P_B \leq P_{Bmax}, \Theta_{Bmin} \leq \Theta_B \leq \Theta_{Bmax} \quad (19)$$

$$d_{min}^{(m,k)}(q_1, q_2) - \epsilon \geq 0, \forall (m, k) \in \mathbb{C} \quad (20)$$

Equation (14) represents the sum of the squared power across all joints, where $\tau_{i,j}$ denotes the torque of the j-th motor on the i-th arm, which is dependent on the X. Equation (15) incorporates the kinematic relationship defined in Eq. (1). Equation (16) includes the static equilibrium constraints from Eq. (8)–(12). Equation (17) represents the contact stability defined by Eq. (2)–(6). Equation (20) imposes the collision distance constraint, where $d_{min}^{(m,k)}$ is the minimum distance between collision pair (m, k), ϵ is the collision threshold, and $\mathbb{C}$ denotes the set of collision pairs.

3.2 Generation of the Adjustment Trajectory

After obtaining the optimal manipulation pose, it is necessary to design an adjustment trajectory and compute physically feasible end-effector forces for both manipulators. The adjustment trajectory of the object is first generated using linear interpolation for position and spherical linear interpolation for orientation in quaternion space. Based on the interpolated object trajectory, the corresponding end-effector trajectories in Cartesian space are derived through geometric relationships, ensuring that the manipulators can cooperatively track the object's motion.

To compute the joint-space reference trajectories, we adopt a model predictive control (MPC) framework. This approach allows for fast and iterative solving of the joint angles over a short prediction horizon, while considering multiple constraints such as joint limits, joint velocity limits, and collision avoidance. The resulting joint trajectories enable the manipulators to perform smooth and feasible motion along the planned object adjustment path. The MPC problem is formulated as follows:

$$\min_{\{x_k, u_k\}} = \sum_{k=0}^{N-1} R\|u_k\|^2 + \sum_{k=0}^{N}(Q_1\|e_1(x_k)\|^2 + Q_2\|e_2(x_k)\|^2) + Q_q\|q_N - q_{des,end}\|^2 \tag{21}$$

$$\text{s.t.} \quad x_{k+1} = f(x_k, u_k), \forall k = 0, \ldots, N-1 \tag{22}$$

$$q_k \in [q_{min}, q_{max}], \dot{q}_k \in [\dot{q}_{min}, \dot{q}_{max}] \tag{23}$$

$$d_{min}^{(m,j)}(q_k) - \epsilon \geq 0, \forall (m,j) \in \mathbb{C} \tag{24}$$

Let $x_k = [q_{1,k}; q_{2,k}] \in \mathbb{R}^{2n_i}$ denote the system state, and $u_k = [\dot{q}_{1,k}; \dot{q}_{2,k}] \in \mathbb{R}^{2n_i}$ the control input. The matrices R, Q_1, Q_2, Q_q represent the weighting matrices for input effort, left end-effector pose error, right end-effector pose error, and terminal joint configuration deviation, respectively. The end-effector pose error for each arm is denoted as $e_i(x_k)$, which includes both position and orientation errors. The position error is defineded as $e_{pos}(x_k) = p_k - p_k^{des}$ and the orientation error is expressed using quaternion representation as $e_{ori} = q_w \vec{q}_{ref} - q_{w,ref} \vec{q} + \vec{q} \times \vec{q}_{ref}$. The state evolution is described by the following discrete-time equation: $x_{k+1} = x_k + u_k$. The desired terminal joint configuration $q_{des,end}$ is obtained from the quasi-static pose optimization.

In addition, it is also required to compute the end-effector forces during the adjustment motion. To this end, a small-scale optimization problem is formulated and solved at each interpolated trajectory point to determine the corresponding end-effector forces. The optimization problem is defined as follows:

$$\operatorname*{argmin}_{\{F_{g1}, F_{g2}\}} \|F_{g1}\|^2 + \|F_{g2}\|^2 \tag{25}$$

$$\text{s.t.} \mathbf{H}(F_{g1}, F_{g2}, F_C) = 0 \tag{26}$$

$$\Phi(F_{g1}, F_{g2}) \leq 0 \tag{27}$$

$$F_{gi} \in [F_{gi,min}, F_{gi,max}], i = 1,2 \tag{28}$$

Equation (25) represents the same equality constraint as defined in Eq. (12), while Eq. (27) is equivalent to Eq. (17).

4 Simulation

4.1 Experimental Setup

The simulated dual-arm model corresponds to our dual-arm robotic system, as depicted in Fig. 1. Each arm is configured with 7 DoFs and adopts an anthropomorphic structure. The rated torque and joint angle ranges for each joint motor are specified in Table 1.

The manipulated object consists of a box with uniformly spaced storage compartments and several rectangular mass blocks placed within, as shown in Fig. 1(b). Six mass blocks are selected, each weighing 2 kg. By varying the placement of these blocks within the box, different eccentric loading conditions are simulated. In computing the object's total mass and inertia, the mass of the box itself is neglected. Three representative loading configurations are selected for analysis, as illustrated in Fig. 4, where $^B p_c$ denotes the center-of-mass position expressed in the body frame $\{B\}$.

Table 1. The rated torque and joint angle ranges for each joint motor.

Joint	Rated Torque(Nm)	Joint Angle(rad)
L1_joint, R1_joint	120	[−0.2618, 1.5707]
L2_joint, R2_joint	80	[−0.1745, 1.5707]
L3_joint, R3_joint	80	[−3.1400, 3.1400]
L4_joint, R4_joint	120	[0, 2.0944]
L5_joint, R5_joint	30	[−3.1400, 3.1400]
L6_joint, R6_joint	30	[−1.5707, 1.2000]
L7_joint, R7_joint	10	[−3.1400, 3.1400]

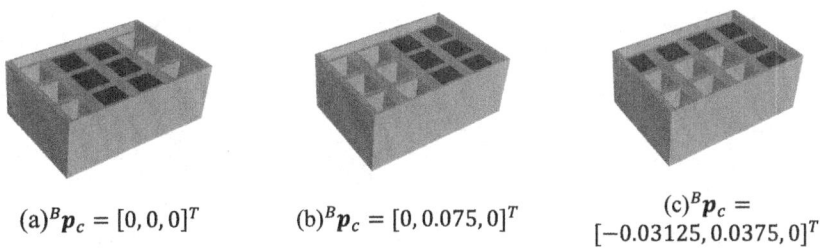

(a) $^B p_c = [0, 0, 0]^T$ (b) $^B p_c = [0, 0.075, 0]^T$ (c) $^B p_c = [-0.03125, 0.0375, 0]^T$

Fig. 4. Three different load types

To validate the effectiveness of the proposed pose adjustment strategy, numerical simulations were conducted using the IPOPT solver integrated with CppAD. For a given object, the adjustment strategies are classified into two cases based on the adjustable degrees of freedom: Case 1: no adjustment; Case 2: adjustment of both Θ_B and P_B. The initial values of the terminal pose optimization variables are set as follows:

$$X_{init} = \left[q_1^T, q_2^T, P_B^T, \Theta_B^T, F_{g1}^T, F_{g2}^T \right]^T$$
$$= [0.3269, 0.4726, -0.6877, 1.7972, -1.1454, -0.7956, 0.212, \qquad (29)$$
$$0.3269, 0.4726, -0.6877, 1.7972, -1.1454, -0.7956, 0.212,$$
$$0, 0, 0, 0.4, 0, -0.25, 0, -125, 58.8, 0, 0, 0, 0, 125, 58.8, 0, 0, 0]^T$$

The remaining parameters are set as follows

$$\begin{cases} \mu = 0.5, \mu_c = 0.1, \epsilon = 0.025\,m \\ \boldsymbol{P}_{Bmin} = [0.25, -0.15, -0.5]^T, \boldsymbol{P}_{Bmin} = [0.55, 0.15, 0]^T \\ -\boldsymbol{\Theta}_{Bmin} = \boldsymbol{\Theta}_{Bmax} = [3.1415, 3.1415, 3.1415]^T \\ R = diag[10, \ldots, 10] \\ \boldsymbol{Q}_i = diag[1000, \ldots, 1000] \\ \boldsymbol{Q}_q = diag[50, \ldots, 50] \end{cases} \quad (30)$$

4.2 Results

Three loading configurations, labeled A, B, and C, are tested. Individual experiments within each configuration are denoted as A-Case1, A-Case2, etc. The schematic of the simulation results is presented in Fig. 5, with the optimized final pose, contact forces on both sides, and the objective function values summarized in Table 2. The data in the table indicate that all optimized variables satisfy the imposed constraints.

The experimental results indicate that, under symmetric manipulation configurations, load eccentricity can lead to an overall increase in joint torque demands, as observed in A-Case1 and B-Case2. After applying the quasi-static optimal manipulation pose computed from the first optimization problem, the torque requirements are significantly reduced across all three load conditions.

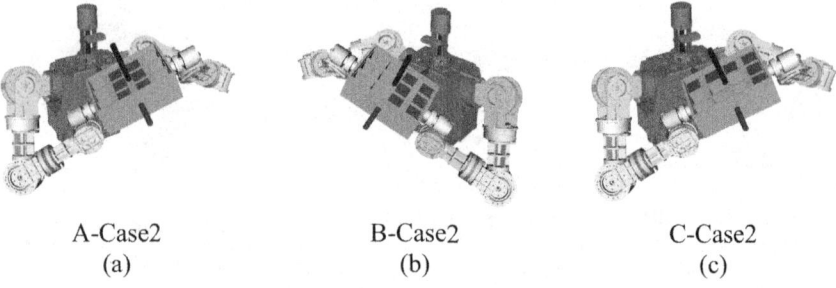

| A-Case2 | B-Case2 | C-Case2 |
| (a) | (b) | (c) |

Fig. 5. The terminal pose optimization of three categories with case2

During the adjustment phase, joint trajectories are generated by solving the MPC problem. The actual end-effector poses, computed via forward kinematics, are illustrated in Fig. 6. Within the prescribed time horizon, the MPC solver successfully computes joint-space trajectories that satisfy all imposed constraints. The final attitude errors of the three cases are (radians): 0.00389, 0.001453, 0.00417.

Object's CoM-Aware Pose Optimization   137

Table 2. Optimization results

Case	$[P_B^T, \Theta_B^T]^T$	$[F_{g1}^T, F_{g2}^T]^T$	$f(X)$
A-Case1	[0.4, 0, −0.25, 0, 0, 0]	[0, −117.6, 58.8, 5.88, 0, 5.88, 0, 117.6, 58.8, −5.88, 0, −5.88]	4738.5
A-Case2	[−0.281, 0.003, 0, −0.294, −0.143, 0.439]	[−8.76, −82.01, 40.06, 4.10, 4.65, 4.10, −7.99, 131.54, 65.28, −0.32, −4.65, −4.22]	2060.78
B-Case1	[0.4, 0, −0.25, 0, 0, 0]	[0, −117.6, 58.8, 5.88, 0.02, 5.88, 0, 117.6, 58.8, 2.94, −0.02, −5.88]	5171.22
B-Case2	[0.279, −0.022, 0, 0.269, 0.145, −0.482]	[−8.53, −131.57, 65.23, 6.58, −4.01, 5.14, −8.41, 77.67, 37.91, −2.94, 4.01, −3.88]	1806.59
C-Case1	[0.4, 0, −0.25, 0, 0, 0]	[0, −117.6, 58.8, 5.88, 1.84, 5.88, 0, 117.6, 58.8, −1.47, 1.84, −5.88]	4709.21
C-Case2	[0.282, 0.039, 0, −0.303, 0.141, 0.423]	[−8.98, −83.70, 40.88, 4.19, 6.47, 4.19, −7.59, 131.48, 65.30, 3.46, −3.16, −5.27]	2084.34

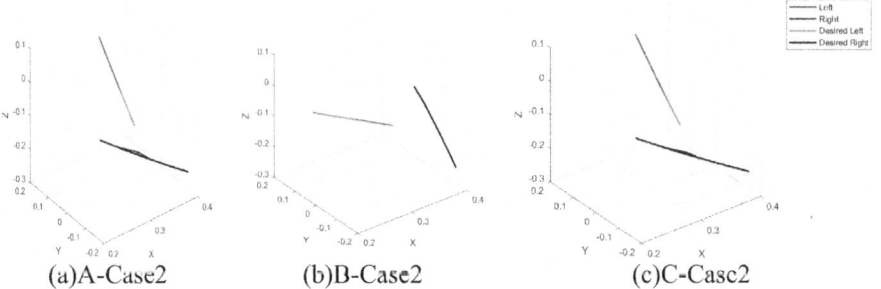

(a) A-Case2   (b) B-Case2   (c) C-Case2

Fig. 6. The actual end position is within the expected value.

5 Conclusion

This paper proposes a collaborative pose optimization strategy to mitigate load imbalance arising from uneven mass distribution during dual-arm manipulation. The approach consists of three stages: (a) computing an optimal manipulation pose via quasi-static optimization to serve as a terminal reference; (b) generating a Cartesian adjustment path along which intermediate contact forces are optimized; and (c) solving a model predictive control (MPC) problem to produce joint-space trajectories that satisfy all constraints. The proposed method enables the manipulators to actively adjust the object's pose while satisfying joint limits, torque constraints, and collision avoidance, thereby achieving a balanced and stable manipulation configuration. Simulation results show that the optimized pose effectively reduces joint torque demands across various eccentric loading scenarios. The MPC solver successfully computes joint-space trajectories that remain feasible within the prescribed time horizon and satisfy all imposed constraints. Future work will involve replacing the end-effector gripper with a dexterous hand to achieve more anthropomorphic and rational manipulation when handling objects with offset centers of mass or complex geometries.

Acknowledgments. This work was supported by the National Natural Science Foundation of China (Grant No. 52375014) and the Wuhan Major Science and Technology Project "Generative Artificial Intelligence-Driven Humanoid Robot Research and Application for Special Environment Operations" (Grant No. 2024060902020442).

References

1. Gu, Z., et al.: Humanoid locomotion and manipulation: current progress and challenges in control, planning, and learning. arXiv preprint arXiv:2501.02116 (2025)
2. Zhao, Z., Yue, X., Xie, J., Fang, C., Shao, Z., Guo, S.: A dual-agent collaboration framework based on LLMs for nursing robots to perform bimanual coordination tasks. IEEE Robot. Autom. Lett. **10**(3), 2942–2949 (2025)
3. Cruciani, S., Almeida, D., Kragic, D., Karayiannidis, Y.: Discrete bimanual manipulation for wrench balancing. In: IEEE International Conference on Robotics and Automation (ICRA), pp. 2631–2637. IEEE, Paris (2020)
4. Costanzo, M., De Maria, G., Natale, C.: Tactile feedback enabling in-hand pivoting and internal force control for dual-arm cooperative object carrying. IEEE Robot. Autom. Lett. **7**(4), 11466–11473 (2022)
5. Zhao, X., Zhang, Y., Ding, W., Han, T., Ding, B.: A dual-arm robot cooperation framework based on a nonlinear model predictive cooperative control. IEEE/ASME Trans. Mechatron. **29**(5), 3993–4005 (2024)
6. Dehio, N., Wang, Y., Kheddar, A.: Dual-arm box grabbing with impact-aware MPC utilizing soft deformable end-effector pads. IEEE Robot. Autom. Lett. **7**(2), 5647–5654 (2022)
7. Jiao, C., Yu, L., Su, X., Wen, Y., Dai, X.: Adaptive hybrid impedance control for dual-arm cooperative manipulation with object uncertainties. Automatica **140**, 110232 (2022)
8. Abbas, M., Narayan, J., Dwivedy, S.K.: A systematic review on cooperative dual-arm manipulators: modeling, planning, control, and vision strategies. Int. J. Intell. Robot. Appl. **7**, 683–707 (2023)

9. Hu, Y.-R., Goldenberg, A.A.: Dynamic control of multiple coordinated redundant manipulators with torque optimization. In: IEEE International Conference on Robotics and Automation (ICRA), pp. 1000–1005. IEEE, Cincinnati (1990)
10. Duan, A., et al.: Robust grasping by bimanual robots with stable parameterization-based contact servoing. IEEE/ASME Trans. Mechatron. **29**(5), 3924–3935 (2024)
11. Di Leva, R., Gattringer, H., Müller, A., Carricato, M.: Force and time-optimal trajectory planning for dual-arm unilateral cooperative grasping. Mech. Mach. Theory **201**, 105729 (2024)
12. Shu, X., Ni, F., Min, K., Liu, Y., Liu, H.: A novel dual-arm adaptive cooperative control framework for carrying variable loads and active anti-overturning. ISA Trans. **148**, 477–489 (2024)
13. Dio, M., Völz, A., Graichen, K.: Cooperative dual-arm control for heavy object manipulation based on hierarchical quadratic programming. In: IEEE/RSJ International Conference on Intelligent Robots and Systems (IROS), pp. 643–648. IEEE, Detroit (2023)
14. Murray, R.M., Li, Z., Sastry, S.S.: A Mathematical Introduction to Robotic Manipulation, 1st edn. CRC Press, Boca Raton (2017)

Contact Driven Functional Grasp Synthesis via Hand-Object Interaction State Representation

Jian Liu, Zeyuan Yang(✉), Lu Tang, Sijie Yan, and Han Ding

State Key Lab of Intelligent Manufacturing Equipment and Technology,
Huazhong University of Science and Technology, Wuhan 430074, China
yangzeyuan@hust.edu.cn

Abstract. Grasping operations that fulfill object functional requirements endow robotic manipulation with practical significance. This work proposes a novel strategy framework for guiding dexterous hands to approach target states collision-free, via contact point-driven manipulation and hand-object interaction characterization. First, we semantically parameterizes finger links of the dexterous hand, to generate human-like grasp configurations capable of grasping and manipulating objects, based on functional requirement-oriented contact point set. Second, an Interaction Bisector Surface based hand-object spatial representation is adopted, to facilitate inverse motion planning from known contact states to non-contact configurations. Through reinforcement learning, we achieve inverse grasp trajectory planning to guide the generation of forward grasping motions. Finally, a high-DoF arm-dexterous hand simulation system is implemented, validating the method's efficacy across diverse objects. Experimental results demonstrate that our strategy effectively generates grasp configurations, conforming to common functional intuitions while producing high-quality dexterous trajectories.

Keywords: Dexterous Hand · Functional Grasp · Grasping Process Planning

1 Introduction

Functional grasp states are defined as hand configurations, that align with the intended functional use of the object, serving as a crucial guarantee for achieving manipulability goals of real-world objects [1]. This concept can be refined into two aspects: physical credibility and functional accessibility [2,3]. The physical credibility level can be traced to analytical methods related to grasp quality metrics, including quantifying relevant metrics in the grasp wrench space [4], achieving higher stiffness performance by adjusting joint angles [5], or generating grasp poses via gradient-based optimization [6,7]. However, achieving mere stability

Supported by the National Key R&D Program of China (No. 2024YFB4711200).

is insufficient to meet subsequent manipulation requirements [8]. Consequently, recent research has proposed numerous methods addressing functional accessibility [9]. These approaches, originating from either the object or the hand itself, aim to obtain the desired grasp state [10,11]. This includes using object-centric contact graph representations to generate grasp states through object surface topography and contact points [12]. To overcome the generalization difficulties inherent in single hand-object mapping relationships, works like [13] proposed hand-agnostic intermediate representations. These enable efficient generation of diverse grasp poses and facilitate grasp state transfer across multiple dexterous hands and grasped objects. Furthermore, reinforcement learning (RL) strategies have also demonstrated effectiveness in this domain. [14] addressed dexterous tool-use scenarios with chopsticks by first acquiring a suitable grasp model, and then employing deep RL to train a physically-based hand controller adaptable to diverse hand morphologies.

Grasp process planning ensures collision-free finger movements, guiding high-DOF dexterous hands to designated contact states [15,16]. Optimization-based methods formulate the grasping process as a constrained planning problem, utilizing obstacle penalty functions to guarantee collision-free motion [17]. While some studies guide finger movements via constructed potential fields, others embed the inverse kinematics of dexterous hands into the grasp planning process, integrating them into a unified optimization framework [18]. To address the potential mismatch between initial planning and execution, a framework combining pre-execution planning, online perception and re-planning, enabling the generation of dexterous hand approach trajectories [19]. Recent research has shown that characterizing the hand-object contact state during grasping provides effective guidance for achieving collision-free and target-aligned grasp motions [20].

To address the aforementioned limitation, functional areas of objects are defined based on everyday usage experience. Subsequently, constrained by the semantic encoding of the object's functional areas, a set of finger contact points $\mathcal{P}$ is utilized to generate dexterous hand configurations $\{t_b, R_b, \theta\}$ that align with task intent. Specifically, the key points of finger links of the dexterous hand are semantically encoded, with emphasis placed on the critical role during grasping. Guided by this, a deep learning model is trained by matching specified link points of the dexterous hand to functionally constrained contact point set specified on the object surface. This approach successfully yields human-like grasping strategies.

Second, this work proposes an inverse trajectory planning approach based on the Interaction Bisector Surface (IBS). Defined as the Voronoi diagram between two approaching 3D geometries of objects, the IBS is widely used in biology, graphics, and related fields due to its effectiveness in characterizing spatial relationships between objects. Starting from the target grasp state α_{end}, we leverage the IBS to model hand-object spatial relations and introduce a novel objective function. Combined with reinforcement learning, this framework enables the search for an inverse collision-free trajectory $\tau = \{\alpha_{\text{end}}, \cdots, \alpha_0\}$.

Finally, an arm-dexterous hand robotic system was constructed, and simulation experiments for grasping diverse objects were conducted across multiple objects. To ensure grasp credibility, the stability of acquired grasps was verified by maintaining grasp configurations for 60 simulation timesteps, while the feasibility of collision-free trajectories was validated by varying joint configurations of the robotic system.

Experimental results validate the effectiveness of our proposed approach. Our contact point-driven grasp state generation method effectively produces the base pose and joint angles of the dexterous hand, based on the object's surface characteristics or functional requirements, ensuring grasp stability and facilitating subsequent manipulation. Starting from specified contact states, our IBS-guided trajectory planning generates collision-free grasping trajectories, addressing the limitation of traditional methods in aligning trajectories with target contact states.

In summary, our main contributions are:

- A contact points driven regional alignment method is proposed to incorporate object functional requirements.
- An IBS-based inverse grasping trajectory planning framework is used, to generate collision-free grasping motions backward from specified contact states.
- Validation on an arm-dexterous hand robotic system demonstrates our strategy's efficacy, in generating both functionally compliant grasping trajectories and final configurations.

2 Methodology

2.1 Functional Grasp

Functional grasping is a critical task in robotic manipulation. It guides finger link positions of a dexterous hand to align with specified regions on an object. This alignment establishes the foundation for subsequent object usage and functional operations. For example, in door-opening actions (e.g., pushing/pulling a handle), finger links should contact opposite sides of the handle. Further rotation leverages friction to move the handle relative to the door. In other scenarios (e.g., twisting bottle caps or operating power tools), specific finger links reach designated areas to enable rotation or pressing operations. Hence, suitable base pose and corresponding joints configuration of the dexterous hand must be determined.

This work formulates the dexterous hand configuration task for functional grasping objectives as, given object surface point cloud $\mathcal{S}$ and contact point set $\mathcal{P}$, compute the palm base position t_b, the palm base orientation R_b and the finger joint angles θ. The overall framework is shown as Fig. 1. This is formally expressed as:

$$\{\mathcal{P}, \mathcal{S}\} \Rightarrow \{t_b, R_b, \theta\}, \tag{1}$$

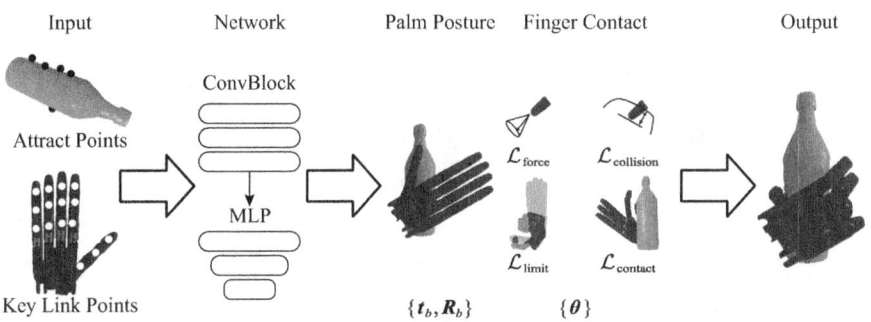

Fig. 1. The overall architecture of grasp states generation framework.

where the contact point set $\mathcal{P} = \{\boldsymbol{p}_i, \boldsymbol{n}_i \in \mathbb{R}^3 \mid i = 1, \cdots, m\}$ contains m contact points, and the $\boldsymbol{n}_i$ represents the contact normal vector at each point, also, $\mathbb{R}$ denotes the set of real numbers. The finger links position $\boldsymbol{p}_j^{\text{link}}$ of the dexterous hand is determined jointly by the base posture and the joint angles $\boldsymbol{\theta}_j$ in the corresponding kinematic chain:

$$\boldsymbol{p}_j^{\text{link}} = \boldsymbol{R}_b \text{fk}(\boldsymbol{\theta}_j) + \boldsymbol{t}_b, \tag{2}$$

where, $\text{fk}(\boldsymbol{\theta}_j)$ denotes the forward kinematics function. To ensure the generation of suitable grasping states, we need to design appropriate loss functions.

The force closure constrained $\mathcal{L}_{\text{force}}$ ensures friction distribution within the friction cone:

$$\mathcal{L}_{\text{force}} = \sum_i \max(0, \boldsymbol{f}_{i,t} - \mu \boldsymbol{f}_{i,n}), \tag{3}$$

where μ is the coefficient of friction, and $\boldsymbol{f}_{i,t}, \boldsymbol{f}_{i,n}$ denote the magnitudes of the tangential and normal components of the contact force at the i-th point, respectively.

The collision constraint penalizes finger links penetration into the object surface. Sole reliance on contact points alone may not adequately capture penetration states. This work therefore establishes a coordinate system origin at the object's centroid. This allows determining whether finger links positions penetrate inwardly beyond the surface point cloud $\mathcal{S}$. An exponential penalty function is applied to this signed distance, ensuring significant penalty escalation during penetration:

$$\mathcal{L}_{\text{collision}} = \sum_{j,k} \exp(-\beta_k \cdot \inf\{\text{dist}(\boldsymbol{p}_j^{\text{link}}, \mathcal{S})\}), \tag{4}$$

where β_k acts as weighting term to prioritize finger importance. This distribution is critical for grasp tasks requiring only specific fingers, ensuring non-task fingers minimally influence the loss evaluation.

The joint limit constraint imposes a linear penalty on joint angles $\boldsymbol{\theta}$ to ensure that they remain within operational bounds:

$$\mathcal{L}_{\text{limit}} = \sum_j \max(0, |\theta_j| - \theta_{\max}), \tag{5}$$

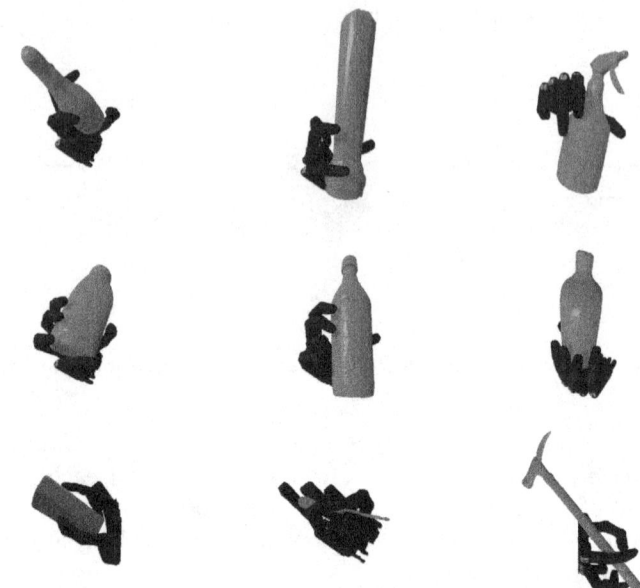

Fig. 2. Functional grasp results on diverse objects achieved through contact point-finger links alignment strategy.

The contact traction constraint aligns finger links with target contact points. It is defined as a weighted sum of distances between corresponding point pairs. Constraining this term to approach zero ensures each finger link reaches its intended region:

$$\mathcal{L}_{\text{contact}} = \sum_{j} \|\boldsymbol{p}_j^{\text{link}} - \boldsymbol{p}_j\|, \tag{6}$$

where $\|\cdot\|$ denotes the 2-norm.

The overall loss function is defined as the weighted sum of the aforementioned individual loss functions:

$$L = \lambda_1 \mathcal{L}_{\text{force}} + \lambda_2 \mathcal{L}_{\text{collision}} + \lambda_3 \mathcal{L}_{\text{limit}} + \lambda_4 \mathcal{L}_{\text{contact}}. \tag{7}$$

2.2 Grasping Process Planning

The IBS comprises points equidistant to both object point clouds. For any point P_{IBS} on the surface:

$$P_{\text{IBS}} = \{p \mid \inf\{\text{dist}(p, a) \mid a \in A\} = \inf\{\text{dist}(p, b) \mid b \in B\}\} \tag{8}$$

where A and B represent the point clouds of the two objects respectively, and dist denotes the distance function. Starting from key link points of the dexterous hand, we determine the closest distance from each point to both object point clouds. These equidistant points collectively form the interaction bisector surface.

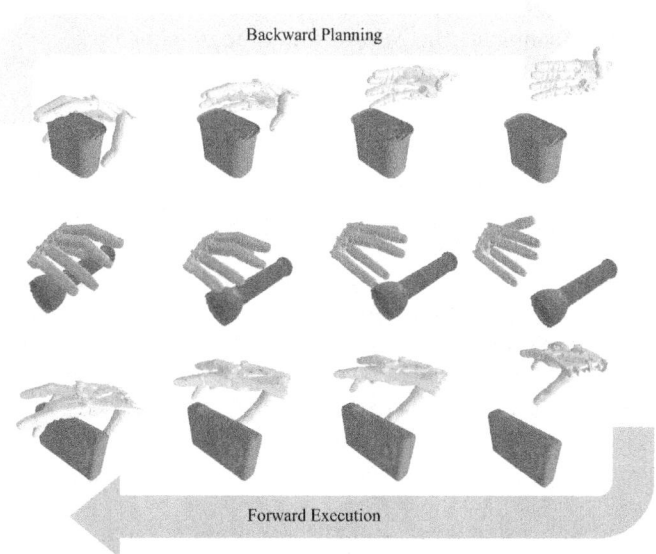

Fig. 3. Forward grasping process execution guided by Interaction Bisector Surface based backward planning.

Dexterous hand grasp planning typically begins from an initial pose α_0, seeking a pose sequence that terminates at the desired grasp configuration α_{end}. When functional object manipulation requires specific final grasp states, we employ an inverse process: starting from the target grasp configuration, a collision-free trajectory $\tau = \{\alpha_{\text{end}}, \cdots, \alpha_2, \alpha_1\}$ is generated backwards to the initial pose:

$$\max_{\tau} Q(\tau), C(\alpha_i) \geq 0, \forall \alpha_i \in \tau, \tag{9}$$

where Q evaluates trajectory quality, and $C(\cdot)$ indicates collision status. For each hand link center $\boldsymbol{p}_j^{\text{Link}}$, compute the minimum Euclidean distance d_o^j to object point cloud $\mathcal{S}$ and direction vector v_o^j:

$$d_o^j = \min_{s \in \mathcal{S}} \|\boldsymbol{p}_j^{\text{Link}} - s\|, \tag{10}$$

$$v_o^j = \frac{\arg\min_{s \in \mathcal{S}} \|\boldsymbol{p}_j^{\text{Link}} - s\| - \boldsymbol{p}_j^{\text{Link}}}{d_o^j}, \tag{11}$$

The IBS guidance point is then the midpoint along this direction:

$$\boldsymbol{p}_{\text{IBS}} = \boldsymbol{p}^{\text{Link}} + \frac{1}{2} d_o^j v_o^j, \tag{12}$$

The action space encompasses configuration changes of the dexterous hand, comprising the position increment of the palm base position Δt_b, the Euler angle increment Δe_b and the joint angles increment $\Delta \theta$. Considering constraints during contact detachment, the reward function is defined as:

$$r_t = \omega_{\text{away}} \text{clip}(\Delta d, -0.1, 0.1) + \omega_{\text{coll}} \mathbb{I}_{\delta<0} + \\ \omega_{\text{smoo}} \|a_t\|^2 + \omega_{\text{end}} \mathbb{I}_{\theta \in \Theta_{\text{open}}} \quad (13)$$

where $\Delta d = \|p_{\text{IBS}}(t) - p_{\text{IBS}}(t-1)\|$ quantifies the inter-frame displacement of the interaction bisector surface point. The indicator $\mathbb{I}_{\delta<0}$ evaluates link penetration into the object, where $\delta = \min_j d_o^j(t) - d_{\text{safe}}$. The term a_t denotes the action increment at step t, penalizing abrupt motions via the smoothness reward $\|a_t\|^2$. Terminal reward $\mathbb{I}_{\theta \in \Theta_{\text{open}}}$ activates upon reaching non-contact target states, signaling episode completion.

The PPO-CLIP reinforcement learning strategy restrains excessive policy updates. Its objective function is defined as:

$$\mathcal{L}^{\text{CLIP}} = \mathbb{E}_t \left[\min \left(r_t(\theta) \hat{A}_t, \text{clip}(r_t(\theta), 1-\epsilon, 1+\epsilon) \right) \right] \quad (14)$$

where the importance sampling ratio $r_t(\theta) = \frac{\pi_\theta(a_t|s_t)}{\pi_{\theta_{\text{old}}}(a_t|s_t)}$ quantifies policy deviation. The truncation function constrains $r_t(\theta)$ within bounded limits. The generalized advantage estimation (GAE) is computed as:

$$\hat{A}_t = \sum_{k=0}^{\infty} (\gamma \lambda)^k \delta_{t+k} \quad (15)$$

where γ denotes the discount factor for future rewards, while λ represents the trace decay parameter in GAE. The temporal difference error δ_{t+k} is:

$$\delta_t = r_t + \gamma V_\phi(s_{t+1}) - V_\phi(s_t) \quad (16)$$

with $V_\phi(s_t)$ being the state value function.

3 Experimental Setup and Verification

Our object dataset comprises YCB [21] and GD [22] datasets. Initial contact point set for functional regions are designated as attractors to guide the dexterous hand toward target contact states. These contact points are primarily derived from the annotated dataset published in [1], where we refine the contact regions into discrete contact points. For certain objects, size constraints prevent larger multi-fingered hands from contacting specified regions (e.g., small bottle caps). Alternatively, scenarios requiring fewer contact points allow redundant fingers to be treated independently. Such cases exclude non-essential fingers from consideration. Contact point set cardinality determines this configuration, prioritizing grasp feasibility and functional realizability.

Figure 2 demonstrates the effects of loss functions in generating functional grasps. The joint limit constraint ensures generated joint angles satisfy the dexterous hand's physical limits. Specifying upper/lower bounds for position and orientation enhances convergence speed during initial training stages. The contact

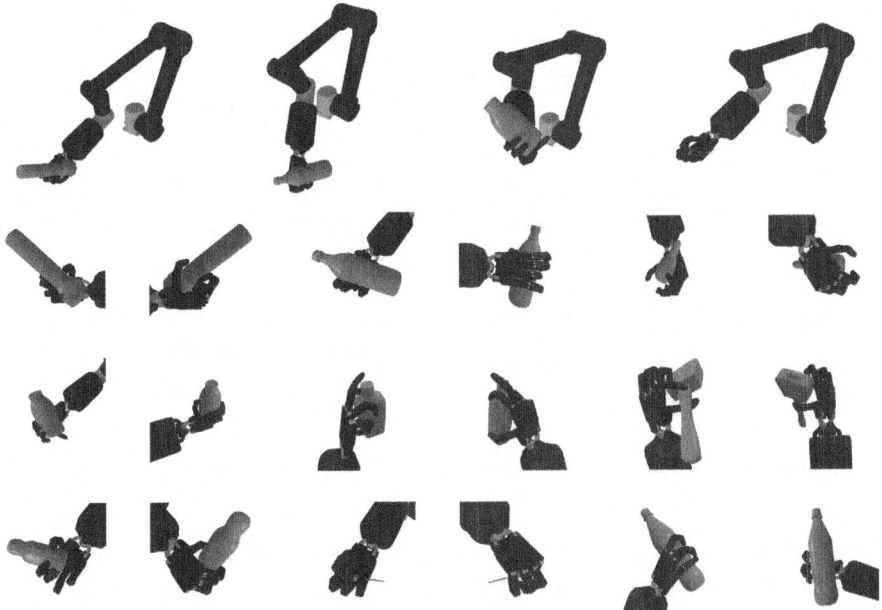

Fig. 4. Simulation grasping experiments on an arm-dexterous hand robotic system.

traction constraint significantly reduces finger links to target distances. However, position-based constraints alone cannot guarantee optimal contact states. Thus, the friction cone constraint aligns contact forces properly with the object surface, preventing slippage caused by excessive tangential forces. Pure traction constraints permit finger links penetration beyond contact points. Such configurations risk damaging objects or the hand itself through excessive compression when deployed in real-world scenarios. The collision constraint strongly penalizes this penetration behavior.

Figure 3 illustrates the transition from grasp to separation states guided by the contact bisector surface. The pre-defined grasp states satisfy functional requirements for object manipulation. From these states, base frame pose in Θ_{open} aligns with the direction from the palm base frame origin to the interaction bisector point. Safe separation is achieved when the dexterous hand's workspace envelope no longer intersects the object point cloud.

Finally, we evaluated the dexterous robotic system as shown as Fig. 4, comprising an industrial robotic arm and dexterous hand, executing grasps using our methodology. Crucially, prior work considered the dexterous hand component in isolation, directly generating its base frame pose. However, when integrated with the robotic arm, certain poses induce arm-environment collisions, particularly downward-tilted wrist-arm configurations. To mitigate this, we simplified the validation protocol: a) objects with poor grasp reachability were initialized at elevated heights above the base plane; b) the dexterous robotic system grasped

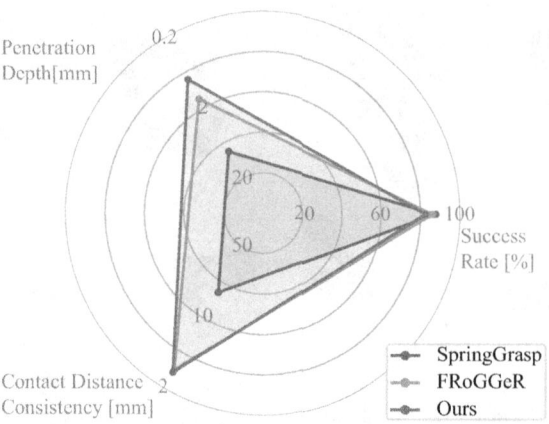

Fig. 5. Comparison with different dexterous grasp synthesis baselines.

these objects; c) grasp validity was assessed by maintaining the grasp for fixed timesteps followed by vertical lifting.

Additionally, we compare the comprehensive performance of the proposed method against several baselines [6,7] as shown in Fig. 5. Beyond the aforementioned simulation success rate, two metrics are evaluated: penetration depth and contact distance consistency. Here, penetration depth denotes the maximum interpenetration distance between objects and the hand, indicating finger intrusion into objects. Contact distance consistency represents the maximum deviation of signed distances among active contact points, quantifying contact distribution uniformity to prevent single-finger overload or contact imbalance. Comparative experiment results demonstrated that the proposed method maintained a high success rate while exhibiting lower penetration depth and superior contact distance consistency, indicating enhanced contact effectiveness.

4 Conclusion

This work proposes a grasping strategy framework that generates dexterous hand grasp configurations, and plans grasping trajectories based on functional requirements of objects. Grasp state generation experiments demonstrate that by matching contact points on the target object with key posture of the hand's finger links, the proposed method effectively produces desired grasps with generalization across diverse scenarios. Trajectory planning experiments validate the efficacy of the IBS in characterizing hand-object contact states. Through an inverse planning strategy, the framework achieves tight coupling between grasping processes and outcomes.

Future work should focus on advanced contact point generation and evaluation methods to obtain high-quality contact point set for guiding grasp synthesis. Additionally, in-hand object relocation and practical operational requirements warrant further investigation.

References

1. Zhu, T., Wu, R., Lin, X., Sun, Y.: Toward human-like grasp: Dexterous grasping via semantic representation of object-hand. In: International Conference on Computer Vision, pp. 15721–15731 (2021)
2. Bohg, J., Morales, A., Asfour, T., Kragic, D.: Data-driven grasp synthesis - a survey. IEEE Trans. Rob. **30**(2), 289–309 (2014)
3. Babin, V., Gosselin, C.: Mechanisms for robotic grasping and manipulation. Ann. Rev. Control, Robot. Auton. Syst. **4**(1), 573–593 (2021)
4. Ferrari, C., Canny, J.: Planning optimal grasps. In: IEEE International Conference on Robotics and Automation, vol. 3, pp. 2290–2295 (1992)
5. Garate, V.R., Pozzi, M., Prattichizzo, D., Tsagarakis, N., Ajoudani, A.: Grasp stiffness control in robotic hands through coordinated optimization of pose and joint stiffness. IEEE Robot. Autom. Lett. **3**(4), 3952–3959 (2018)
6. Li, A.H., Culbertson, P., Burdick, J.W., Ames, A.D.: Frogger: Fast robust grasp generation via the min-weight metric (2023)
7. Chen, S., Bohg, J., Liu, C.K.: Springgrasp: synthesizing compliant, dexterous grasps under shape uncertainty (2024)
8. Gupta, A., Eppner, C., Levine, S., Abbeel, P.: Learning dexterous manipulation for a soft robotic hand from human demonstrations. In: 2016 IEEE/RSJ International Conference on Intelligent Robots and Systems (IROS), pp. 3786–3793. IEEE Press, Daejeon (2016)
9. Hampali, S., Rad, M., Oberweger, M., Lepetit, V.: Honnotate: a method for 3d annotation of hand and object poses. In: 2020 IEEE/CVF Conference on Computer Vision and Pattern Recognition (CVPR), pp. 3193–3203 (2020)
10. Jain, D., Li, A., Singhal, S., Rajeswaran, A., Kumar, V., Todorov, E.: Learning deep visuomotor policies for dexterous hand manipulation. In: 2019 International Conference on Robotics and Automation (ICRA), pp. 3636–3643 (2019)
11. Qin, Y., et al.: Dexmv: imitation learning for dexterous manipulation from human videos. In: Avidan, S., Brostow, G., Cissé, M., Farinella, G.M., Hassner, T. (eds.) European Conference on Computer Vision (ECCV), pp. 570–587. Springer, Cham (2022)
12. Brahmbhatt, S., Handa, A., Hays, J., Fox, D.: Contactgrasp: functional multi-finger grasp synthesis from contact. In: 2019 IEEE/RSJ International Conference on Intelligent Robots and Systems (IROS), pp. 2386–2393 (2019)
13. Li, P., et al.: Gendexgrasp: generalizable dexterous grasping. In: IEEE International Conference on Robotics and Automation, pp. 8068–8074 (2023)
14. Yang, L., et al.: Oakink: a large-scale knowledge repository for understanding hand-object interaction. In: IEEE Conference on Computer Vision and Pattern Recognition, pp. 20953–20962 (2022)
15. Hang, K., Stork, J.A., Pollard, N.S., Kragic, D.: A framework for optimal grasp contact planning. IEEE Robot. Autom. Lett. **2**(2), 704–711 (2017)
16. Kalashnikov, D., et al.: Scalable deep reinforcement learning for vision based robotic manipulation. In: Proceedings of the 2nd Conference on Robot Learning, pp. 651–673. PMLR (2018)
17. Pan, Z., Zhang, D., Tu, C., Gao, X.: Planning of power grasps using infinite program under complementary constraints. IEEE Robot. Autom. Lett. **7**(1), 650–657 (2022)
18. Fan, Y., Tomizuka, M.: Efficient grasp planning and execution with multifingered hands by surface fitting. IEEE Robot. Autom. Lett. **4**(4), 3995–4002 (2019)

19. Farias, C., Marturi, N., Stolkin, R., Bekiroglu, Y.: Simultaneous tactile exploration and grasp refinement for unknown objects. IEEE Robot. Autom. Lett. **6**(2), 3349–3356 (2021)
20. She, Q., Hu, R., Xu, J., Liu, M., Xu, K., Huang, H.: Learning high-dof reaching-and-grasping via dynamic representation of gripper-object interaction. ACM Trans. Graph. **41**(4) (2022)
21. Calli, B., Singh, A., Walsman, A., Srinivasa, S., Abbeel, P., Dollar, A.M.: The YCB object and model set: Towards common benchmarks for manipulation research. In: International Conference on Advanced Robotics, pp. 510–517 (2015)
22. Kappler, D., Bohg, J., Schaal, S.: Leveraging big data for grasp planning. In: 2015 IEEE International Conference on Robotics and Automation (ICRA), pp. 4304–4311 (2015)

Intelligent Perception and Control Technologies for Marine Robotic Systems

Co-simulation of Trajectory Tracking Control for Underwater Vehicles: A Case Study on RexROV Using Simulink and UUV Simulator

Mingzhi Chen, Zexin Lu, Daqi Zhu$^{(\boxtimes)}$, and Wen Pang

University of Shanghai for Science and Technology, Shanghai 200093, China
zdq367@aliyun.com

Abstract. This study presents a co-simulation framework that integrates MATLAB/Simulink with the UUV Simulator to enhance the validation of trajectory tracking control strategies for underwater vehicles. Centered on the RexROV platform, the framework synchronizes high-fidelity hydrodynamic modeling with real-time control logic implementation. A cascaded PID architecture employing dual-loop position and velocity regulation is systematically compared with a conventional single-loop position controller across various operational scenarios, including station-keeping, linear trajectory tracking, and spiral path following. Results indicate that the cascaded controller offers superior handling of nonlinear dynamics and coupled motions, yielding significantly improved steady-state performance. The core innovation of this framework lies in its physics-informed simulation environment, which rigorously incorporates hydrodynamic effects. By bridging theoretical control design with practical implementation, the proposed methodology offers a credible and synchronized validation platform. While not aiming to replace modern nonlinear or adaptive techniques, this framework emphasizes practical advantages such as ease of tuning, low computational cost, and compatibility with industrial deployment. It enhances environmental realism beyond that of traditional single-tool simulations while remaining compatible with rapid prototyping workflows, thereby providing researchers with a standardized yet flexible testbed for evaluating underwater control systems in ecologically representative conditions.

Keywords: Simulink · RexROV · UUV Simulator · Trajectory Tracking · PID

1 Introduction

Underwater Remotely Operated Vehicles (ROVs) are essential in marine exploration, defense, and scientific research, performing tasks such as salvage, pipeline inspection, intelligence gathering, and anti-submarine warfare. Consequently, ROVs have become a key research focus among leading maritime nations [1]. Trajectory tracking control is central to ROV operations, especially in complex underwater environments with strong nonlinearities, dynamic coupling, and external disturbances. Ensuring control algorithm robustness and adaptability under these conditions is critical.

Initial studies largely relied on proportional-integral-derivative (PID) control. Jiang [2] improved PID tuning using ant colony and enhanced particle swarm optimization algorithms, achieving faster responses and reduced overshoot. Subsequent research moved toward model-based approaches. Qin [3] developed an adaptive terminal sliding mode controller with radial basis function neural networks, improving tracking accuracy. Wei et al. [4] further enhanced this using a nonlinear disturbance observer and adaptive sliding mode control, reducing chattering and minimizing dependency on prior system knowledge.

More recent advances focus on hierarchical and hybrid control methods. Wang et al. [5] introduced a cascaded PID controller with angle and angular velocity regulation, improving pitch tracking by 35% over single-loop designs. Sun [6] proposed a fuzzy adaptive sliding mode controller for Autonomous Underwater Vehicles (AUVs) to counteract environmental disturbances and eliminate chattering. Wang [7] adopted a model predictive control (MPC)-based approach to enhance stability in dynamic conditions, while Xie et al. [8] extended this with a cascaded linear MPC framework for ROV trajectory tracking. Liu et al. [9] demonstrated the feasibility of a Simulink-based hovering control system using an active disturbance rejection controller (ADRC).

However, these approaches often involve high computational costs and complex tuning procedures, limiting their use in real-time and field applications. To address the gap between theoretical control design and practical deployment, this study employs a high-fidelity co-simulation framework that integrates Simulink with the UUV Simulator. Using the RexROV platform, we compare cascaded and single-loop PID controllers in three scenarios: station-keeping, linear trajectory tracking, and spiral trajectory tracking. Results demonstrate that the cascaded PID design, through velocity-loop saturation and hierarchical decoupling, effectively suppresses nonlinear coupling and improves tracking accuracy. Our work highlights the continued relevance of classical control methods like PID, emphasizing their ease of implementation, robustness, and suitability for rapid engineering iteration.

The remainder of this paper is structured as follows: Sect. 2 presents the trajectory tracking problem and the modeling of underwater vehicles. Section 3 details the Simulink controller design and ROS communication interface. Section 4 presents simulation results for station-keeping, straight-line tracking, and spiral trajectory tracking. Section 5 concludes the study and discusses future directions.

2 Trajectory Tracking and Modeling of Underwater Vehicles

Trajectory tracking for Underwater Remotely Operated Vehicles (ROVs) involves controlling the vehicle's thrusters to follow a predefined path in a complex underwater environment. Due to the vehicle's six-degree-of-freedom nonlinear motion and the dynamic nature of the underwater domain, achieving accurate and robust control is essential for mission success.

2.1 Coordinate System Definition

Two coordinate systems are established: the fixed coordinate system $E\text{-}XYZ$ and the body-fixed coordinate system $o\text{-}xyz$, as shown in Fig. 1. The fixed coordinate system, also referred to as the inertial frame, is denoted with origin E. The positive direction of the Ex-axis points north, Ey points west, and Ez is perpendicular to the water surface, pointing upward. This coordinate system follows the right-hand rule. The body-fixed coordinate system is attached to the underwater vehicle, with its origin O located at the vehicle's center of gravity and moving with the vehicle. Conventionally, Ox points in the forward direction of the vehicle, Oy points to the port (left) side, and Oz is perpendicular to the vehicle, pointing upward.

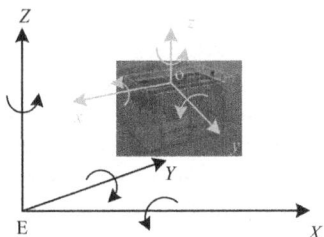

Fig. 1. Coordinate System Definition.

2.2 Simulation Model of the Underwater Vehicle

The notations are defined as follows. The position of the vehicle in the fixed coordinate system can be represented as $\eta_1 = [x,y,z]^T$, and the orientation is described by $\eta_2 = [\varphi, \theta, \psi]^T$. The velocities in the body-fixed coordinated system is defined as $v = [u, v, w, p, q, r]^T$, includes the vehicle's surge velocity u, sway velocity v, heave velocity w, roll rate p, pitch rate q, and yaw rate r.

In this study, the simulation is conducted using the RexROV model from the UUV Simulator [11], which is equipped with four horizontal and four vertical thrusters and can be controlled via ROS commands. The RexROV model represents orientation using quaternions instead of Euler angles, providing numerical stability and avoiding singularities that may occur at pitch angles near $\pm\pi/2$. The UUV Simulator applies the Gazebo platform to integrate three core functionalities. It incorporates various UUV sensors including DVL, SINS, cameras, magnetometers, and pressure-based depth sensors. It also Simulates propulsion systems such as thrusters and control fins. In addition, it replicates underwater conditions including hydrodynamic effects and current flows.

3 Controller Implementation in Simulink

Simulink, as a graphical modeling and simulation environment within MATLAB, provides a block-diagram-based approach for system development. Its drag-and-drop interface enables efficient construction of dynamic system models, supporting the complete workflow from modeling and simulation to controller design, automatic code generation, and hardware deployment. The co-simulation between Simulink and RexROV significantly streamlines the development and validation of control algorithms.

This study implements two trajectory tracking controllers for the RexROV: Cascaded PID: A dual-loop structure with position and velocity control loops; Single-loop PID: A basic position-only control structure.

Figure 2 shows the overall architecture of the RexROV trajectory tracking controller in Simulink, which connects to the ROS system in an Ubuntu virtual machine via the ROS Toolbox. The ROS Toolbox, a MATLAB package specialized for ROS/ROS 2 communication and development, enables cross-platform topic communication. For RexROV trajectory simulation, the system subscribes to the /rexrov/pose_gt topic, which contains two message types: Pose: Position in the fixed frame and orientation represented by quaternions; Twist: Linear and angular velocities in the fixed frame. The "Change" module converts quaternions to Euler angles, while the "Position" and "angles" modules record the actual pose in MATLAB's workspace via "To Workspace" blocks.

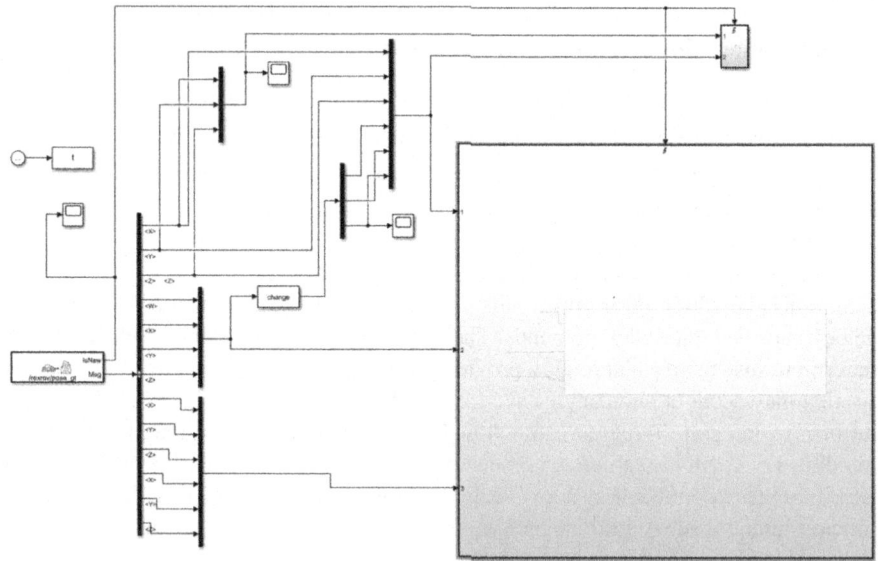

Fig. 2. Overall Architecture of RexROV Trajectory Tracking Controller in Simulink.

3.1 Cascaded PID Controller

Figure 3 illustrates the cascaded PID controller implemented using S-functions. The controller architecture includes the following components:

Waypoint Generator (wayz): Input: None; Output: 6D desired pose $\eta_d = [x_d, y_d, z_d, \varphi_d, \theta_d, \psi_d]^T$; this module generates the reference trajectory and outputs the desired pose.

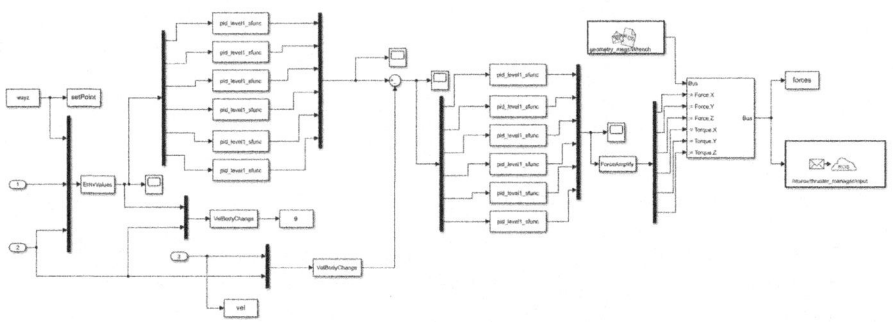

Fig. 3. Cascaded PID Controller.

Error Calculator (ErrorValues): Inputs: Desired pose, actual pose (position and quaternions), and velocities; Output: Body-frame transformed error between actual and desired states.

Velocity Transformer (VelBodyChange): Inputs: Orientation quaternions and velocities in fixed frame; Output: Transformed velocities in body frame.

PID Core (pid_level1_sfunc): A configurable S-function PID with tunable P/I/D gains, output saturation limits, and anti-windup mechanism (integrator reset when saturated). The system implements dual-loop control across all six degrees of freedom (DoFs).

Force Amplifier: Scales controller output by RexROV's inertia matrix, so it converts generalized forces to thruster-specific command.

3.2 Single-Loop PID Controller

The single-loop PID controller, illustrated in Fig. 4, retains the same overall structure but omits the velocity control layer, relying solely on position-loop PID control to generate thruster force outputs.

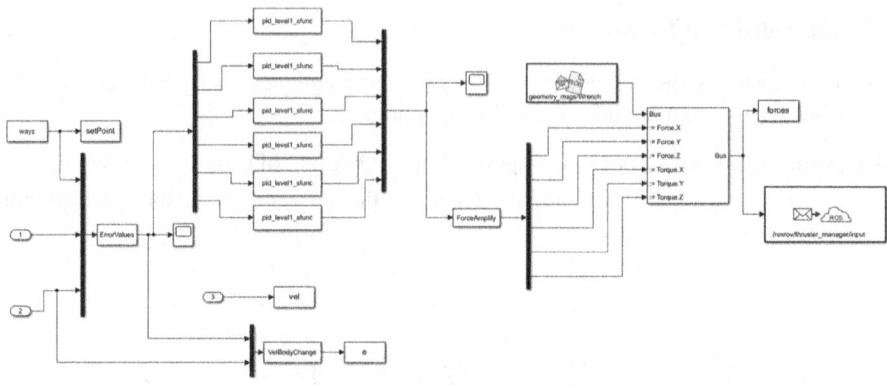

Fig. 4. Single-loop PID Controller.

3.3 PID Parameter Tuning Methodology

The PID parameters used in both the cascaded and single-loop control structures were obtained through a hybrid tuning approach combining empirical methods and iterative simulation refinement. All parameters were tuned and validated under the station-keeping task and subsequently reused across the linear and spiral trajectory tracking scenarios to ensure a fair and consistent basis for comparison. This consistent tuning strategy allowed us to isolate the effects of controller structure rather than parameter-specific optimizations. A summary of the final parameter sets is provided in Tables 1 and 2.

Table 1. Cascaded PID Controller Parameters.

Control Loop	Proportional (P)	Integral (I)	Derivative (D)	Saturation Limit
Position Loop	0.8	0.0005	0.0005	1
Velocity Loop	10	2	0	1.611
Attitude Loop	0.3	0.001	0.001	2
Angular Velocity Loop	10	2	1	5

Table 2. Single-Loop PID Controller Parameters.

Control Loop	Proportional (P)	Integral (I)	Derivative (D)	Saturation Limit
Position Control	0.8	0.0005	0.0005	1.611
Attitude Control	0.3	0.001	0.001	5

4 Integrated Simulation Practice

The UUV model simulation, based on a ROS environment and using the RexROV platform, comprises the following key components: Marine Environment Simulation: Utilizes the ocean_wave module to simulate wave-induced effects. Vehicle Model: Implements a full 6-DOF dynamic model of the RexROV, including integrated onboard sensors. Thrust Allocation System: The thruster_manager node distributes thrust across eight thrusters.

In all control scenarios, the UUV starts from an initial pose of $\eta = [20,0, 0,0, 0,0]^T$, with zero initial velocity.

4.1 Station-Keeping Control

In the station-keeping control experiment, the target pose is set as $\eta_d = [100, -100, -30, 0, 0, 2.9671]^T$. A comparative study is conducted to evaluate the performance of the cascaded PID and single-loop PID controllers. Figure 5 shows the motion trajectories under both control strategies, while Fig. 6 presents the time-domain error characteristics across all six degrees of freedom.

As shown in Fig. 5, both controllers are able to guide the RexROV to the target pose. However, they exhibit distinct dynamic behaviors: the single-loop PID shows noticeable oscillations during the final convergence phase, while the cascaded PID achieves smoother convergence due to the velocity loop's saturation mechanism.

The error evolution curves in Fig. 6 further highlight the difference: the cascaded PID exhibits smooth convergence in all degrees of freedom, whereas the single-loop PID suffers from overshoot and oscillation. The average and final errors are listed in Table 3.

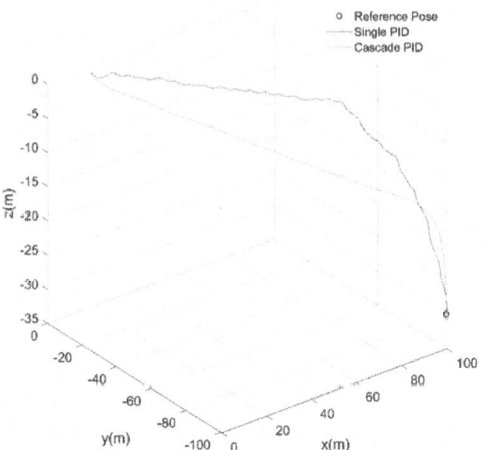

Fig. 5. Station-Keeping Simulation Result.

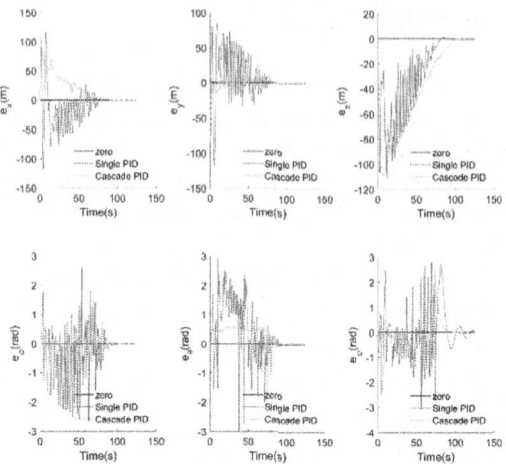

Fig. 6. Time-Domain Error Curves.

The cascaded PID controller stabilizes by 100 s, with final errors in all degrees of freedom under 0.05 m/rad. In contrast, the single-loop PID takes approximately 25 s longer to converge. The single-loop PID lacks explicit velocity control, limiting only the thruster output range. This leads to a more aggressive control style, which compromises attitude stability compared to the cascaded PID. These results demonstrate that the cascaded PID controller, through velocity-loop saturation and hierarchical tuning, effectively suppresses coupling-induced oscillations in the ROV's attitude control.

Table 3. Average and Final Errors in Station Keeping Control.

Metric	x (m)	y (m)	z (m)	φ (rad)	θ (rad)	ψ (rad)
Single-loop PID Avg. Error	17.60	19.51	26.42	0.550	0.690	0.754
Cascaded PID Avg. Error	19.12	3.79	40.08	0.076	0.354	0.234
Single-loop PID Final Error	0.242	0.151	0.307	0.004	0.008	0.125
Cascaded PID Final Error	0.004	0.012	0.009	0.012	0.042	0.023

Note: Average error is the mean of absolute errors over the full simulation period (0–125 s). Final error is the mean error after 100 s.

4.2 Station-Keeping Control

This experiment is designed to evaluate the performance of the controllers in tracking a 3D linear trajectory, defined by the following parametric equations:

$$\begin{cases} x_d(t) = 0.5 \cdot \min(t, 100) \\ y_d(t) = 0.5 \cdot \min(t, 100) \\ z_d(t) = -0.5 \cdot \min(t, 100) \\ \psi_d(t) = \pi/4 \end{cases} \tag{1}$$

Co-simulation of Trajectory Tracking Control   161

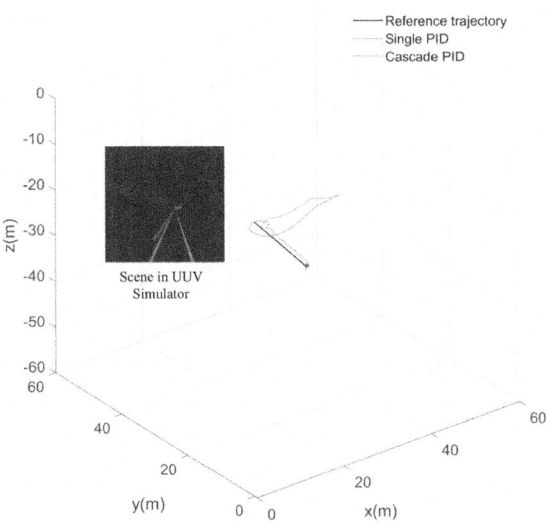

Fig. 7. 3D Linear Trajectory Tracking.

The desired roll and pitch angles are set to zero. The control simulation runs for 150 s, during which the reference pose remains constant after 100 s. At the 100-s mark, the RexROV under cascaded PID control has already stabilized at the target pose, whereas the single-loop PID controller remains in a phase of oscillatory convergence. The tracking result is shown in Fig. 7, while its error curves are shown in Fig. 8. The average and final errors in 6 DOF are listed in Table 4.

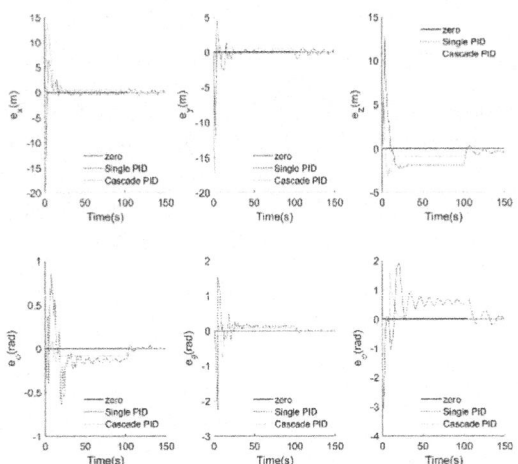

Fig. 8. Error Evolution Over Time in Linear Tracking.

Table 4. Average and Final Errors in Linear Trajectory Tracking.

Metric	x (m)	y (m)	z (m)	φ (rad)	θ (rad)	ψ (rad)
Single-loop PID Avg. Error	0.76	0.51	1.56	0.133	0.151	0.532
Cascaded PID Avg. Error	0.88	0.61	0.76	0.057	0.082	0.105
Single-loop PID Final Error	0.29	0.32	0.40	0.018	0.018	0.209
Cascaded PID Final Error	0.02	0.02	0.05	0.003	0.004	0.004

Note: Average error is calculated over the full duration 0–150 s. Final error is the mean error during the steady-state phase 100–150 s.

During the tracking phase (T < 100 s), the cascaded PID controller demonstrates superior trajectory tracking performance, with significantly smoother convergence. The single-loop PID suffers from notable overshoot. In the steady-state phase, the cascaded PID achieves average errors significantly lower than those of the single-loop PID—up to 10 times smaller in some DOFs. These results validate the dual benefits of the cascaded PID controller: it effectively suppresses attitude oscillations induced by the nonlinear coupling of the ROV via velocity loop saturation (1.0 m/s), leading to faster and more stable convergence.

4.3 Spiral Trajectory Tracking Control

This experiment evaluates the controllers in tracking a 3D spiral trajectory, defined by the following parametric equations:

$$\begin{cases} x_d(t) = 5 \cdot \sin[0.2 \cdot \min(t, 100)] \\ y_d(t) = 5 - 5 \cdot \cos[0.2 \cdot \min(t, 100)] \\ z_d(t) = -0.5 \cdot \min(t, 100) \end{cases} \quad (2)$$

The desired yaw angle is aligned with the tangent direction of the trajectory, while the desired roll and pitch angles are set to zero. The control simulation runs for 145 s, during which the reference pose remains fixed after 100 s. As in previous experiments, the RexROV under cascaded PID control reaches the target pose smoothly by 100 s, whereas the single-loop PID controller continues to oscillate.

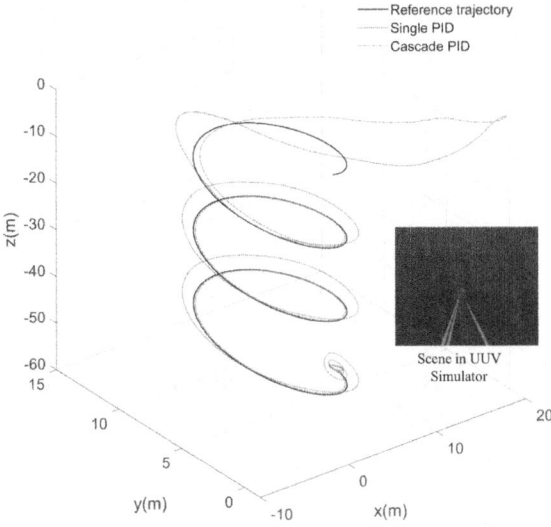

Fig. 9. Spiral Trajectory Tracking.

The result is shown in Fig. 9. The error cures are shown in Fig. 10 accordingly, and the exact values are listed in Table 5. Once again, the cascaded PID controller exhibits closer adherence to the reference trajectory during the tracking phase, with smaller errors and significantly higher final accuracy than the single-loop PID. These results further confirm the advantages of the cascaded PID design in complex dynamic environments. Note: the average errors are the errors in the whole simulation periods, while the final errors are those in the periods after 100 s.

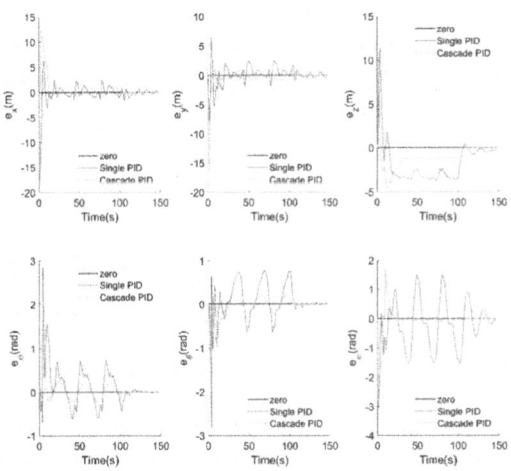

Fig. 10. Error Evolution Over Time in Spiral Tracking.

Table 5. Spiral Trajectory Tracking Error Comparison.

Metric	x (m)	y (m)	z (m)	φ (rad)	θ (rad)	ψ (rad)
Single-loop PID Avg. Error	1.02	0.88	2.2886	0.2910	0.283	0.682
Cascaded PID Avg. Error	0.93	0.62	1.1565	0.0909	0.130	0.101
Single-loop PID Final Error	0.24	0.28	0.3200	0.008	0.008	0.141
Cascaded PID Final Error	1.38×10^{-5}	3.55×10^{-7}	0.0174	$1.03 \times 10^{--5}$	$3.96 \times 10^{--4}$	7.35×10^{-6}

5 Conclusion

In this study, a cross-platform co-simulation framework integrating Simulink and the UUV Simulator was employed to systematically compare the performance of cascaded and single-loop PID controllers in ROV trajectory tracking tasks. The results highlight several key findings: (1) the cascaded PID architecture, with its hierarchical design and velocity loop constraints, effectively decouples kinematics and dynamics, offering faster and more stable convergence compared to the oscillatory behavior observed in single-loop PID under strongly coupled dynamics; (2) the ROS Toolbox-based communication framework enabled seamless integration between the controller and simulation environment, providing a reusable and efficient solution for rapid underwater vehicle prototyping. Future enhancements may combine these classical foundations with modern adaptive mechanisms, but the core framework presented here offers a robust baseline for practical system development.

References

1. Li, S., Wu, Y., Li, C., Zhao, H., Li, Y.: Application and prospect of unmanned underwater vehicle. Bull. Chin. Acad. Sci. **37**(7), 910–920 (2022)
2. Chanjuan, J.: Research on the optimization of PID control of remotely operated underwater vehicle. Harbin Eng. Univ. (2010)
3. Yaochang, Q.: Research on motion control for underwater manipulator based on terminal sliding mode. Harbin Engineering University (2012)
4. Wei, Y.H., Zhou, W.X., Chen, W., Hu, J.X., Li, G.C.: Design of adaptive terminal sliding mode controller based on nonlinear disturbance observer for ROV depth changing. Control Decis. **31**(2), 373–377 (2016)
5. Wang, J., Song, Y., Wei, G., Yuan, B.: Application of cascade PID control in the pitch control system of a remotely operated vehicle. J. Univ. Shanghai Sci. Technol. **39**(3), 229–235 (2017)

6. Sun, Q., Chen, J., Wan, Y.: Trajectory-tracking control of autonomous underwater vehicles based on fuzzy adaptive sliding mode method. Ship Sci. Technol. **39**(23), 53–58 (2017)
7. Wang, J., Song, Y., Zhang, S., Liu, Y.: Modeling, parameters identification and sliding mode control for the pitch control system of a remotely operated vehicle. In: Proceedings of the 35th Chinese Control Conference, pp. 2146–2150. Chengdu, China (2016)
8. Xie, J., Chen, M., Zhu, D.: A cascaded model predictive control based trajectory tracking controller for an autonomous and remotely operated vehicle with LOS guidance. Ships Offshore Struct. **19**(10), 1635–1649 (2024)
9. Yuan, L., Mingzhi, C., Daqi, Z.: Design and development of ROV for ship hull inspection using ADRC. In: Intelligent Robotics and Applications - 16th International Conference, pp. 287–296. Hangzhou, China (2023)
10. Fossen, T.I.: Handbook of Marine Craft Hydrodynamics and Motion Control. Wiley, Chichester (2011)
11. Manhães, M.M.M., Scherer, S.A., Voss, M., Douat, L.R., Rauschenbach, T.: UUV simulator: a Gazebo-based package for underwater intervention and multi-robot simulation. In: OCEANS 2016 MTS/IEEE Monterey, pp. 1–8. Monterey, CA, USA, (2016)

An Elastodynamic Modeling Approach on Component Mode Synthesis for Hybrid Machining Cell

Wei Ma, Haitao Liu(✉), Guofeng Wang, Juliang Xiao, Qingpo Xu, Tianren Zhao, and Wei Han

Tianjin University, Tianjin 300072, China
liuht@tju.edu.cn

Abstract. This paper proposes an efficient semi-analytical elastodynamic modeling approach for predicting the low-order dynamic of a hybrid machining cell. The system is composed of two subsystems: a hybrid robot and a machine frame. First, the elastic dynamic models of motion of limbs within the hybrid robot are developed using the Matrix Structure Analysis, and super-element models are constructed via the Component Mode Synthesis (CMS) approach. Subsequently, the dynamic model of entire system is established by assembling the super-element models of the hybrid robot and the machine frame. To further improve computational efficiency, mode synthesis approach is applied again to reduce the degrees of freedom of the assembled system. Experimental modal testing is conducted on a physical prototype to validate the proposed model. The results show that the predicted natural frequencies and frequency response functions at the spindle end face center point exhibit strong agreement with experimental measurements, thereby confirming the accuracy and effectiveness of the proposed modeling approach.

Keywords: Dynamics · Hybrid Machining Cell · Component Mode Synthesis

1 Introduction

The hybrid machining cell refers to a robotic system consisting of a hybrid robot as the primary mechanism, integrated with machine frame. This type of robot has advantages such as large workspace, high mobility, and strong on-site operational capabilities, making it especially suitable for in-situ machining of large and complex components [1, 2]. Dynamic behaviors are important technical indicators for evaluating the machining performance of robots, reflecting the robot system's ability to resist vibration under dynamic cutting forces. Developing a dynamic model that can rapidly and accurately predict the low-frequency dynamic of such systems is a key issue for dynamic optimization design and cutting stability analysis of these robots [3, 4].

Available methods for robotic elastic dynamics modeling can be classified into Finite Element Analysis (FEA) method [5, 6], lumped parameter method [7, 8], and semi-analytical method [9–13], depending on the discretization approach of the system's mass, damping, and stiffness distributions. The FEA method relies entirely on commercial software and can accurately describe the deformation field of complex systems. However, for robots with different configurations, it requires repeated remeshing and model rebuilding, which leads to low modeling efficiency and high computational cost. The lumped parameter method uses the Rayleigh-Ritz basis to discretize the entire structure into a multi-degree-of-freedom system composed of a series of lumped inertial, elastic, and damping elements. Although it significantly improves computational efficiency, the accuracy is relatively low, making it suitable only for dynamic systems where inertial and elastic parameters can be distinctly separated, such as the Stewart platform.

The semi-analytical method constructs the dynamic model of individual components using substructure and dynamic condensation techniques. Subsequently, Lagrange's equation or substructure synthesis is applied to assemble the dynamic equations of the entire system. This approach enables rapid and accurate evaluation of the system's dynamic behavior over the entire workspace. Dong [9] using the Tricept robot as an example, combined screw theory and structural dynamics with static condensation techniques [14] to establish a semi-analytical elastic dynamics model with 9 degrees of freedom (DOF). Ma [10] employed the rigid multipoint constraint method to represent interface nodes using condensed nodes, and combined it with Component Mode Synthesis [15] (CMS) to establish an improved reduced dynamic model for the 3-PRS parallel mechanism. It is worth noting that, despite extensive research in the field of robotic kinematic modeling, most studies have not fully considered the impact of the frame's dynamic behavior on the overall system.

This paper presents a dynamic modeling method that accurately captures the low-order dynamic of a hybrid machining cell. After briefly reviewing existing dynamic modeling methods, the remaining sections of the paper are organized as follows. Section 2 combines the matrix structural analysis (MSA) method with CMS to establish the dynamics of the hybrid robot and the machine frame. Through the rotational joint between the two subsystems, the models are assembled, and the elastodynamics model of the hybrid machining cell is obtained using modal synthesis. In Sect. 3, the computational results of the proposed model are compared with experimental data obtained from modal testing on a physical prototype to validate the model's accuracy. Finally, the conclusions are presented in Sect. 4.

2 Dynamic Modeling of the Hybrid Machining Cell

By locking all the actuated joints, the system can be regarded as an instantaneous structure at a given configuration. This section presents a semi-analytical dynamic model, developed using CMS and screw theory, which accurately predicts the low-order dynamic behavior of the hybrid machining cell.

2.1 System Description

The hybrid machining cell consists of two subsystems: the TriMule hybrid robot and the machine frame, as shown in the CAD model in Fig. 1. The former is composed of a 1T2R (3 DOF) parallel mechanism with and a 2 DOF A/C wrist connected in series. The latter is connected at one end to the 1T2R parallel mechanism via a rotational joint, while the other end is fixed to the ground. The reference frame, denoted as $\mathcal{K}$, is established on the frame with the origin at the midpoint $A_{1,0}$ of $\overline{A_{2,0}A_{3,0}}$. The x-axis coincides with the axis of the rotating bracket, the z-axis normal to the triangular plane $\Delta A_{1,1}A_{2,0}A_{3,0}$, and the y-axis follows the right-hand rule. The body-fixed frame $\mathcal{K}_C$ is established at the endpoint C of the end effector. The w-axis coincides with the axis vector of the tool, and the u-axis is parallel to the A-axis of the wrist.

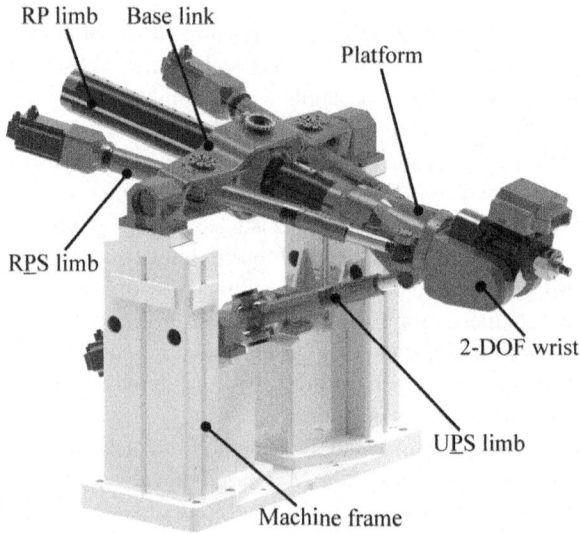

Fig. 1. 3D model of hybrid machining cell. The TriMule hybrid robot is composed of 2-DOF wrist, platform, UPS limb, RP limb, RPS limb and Base link.

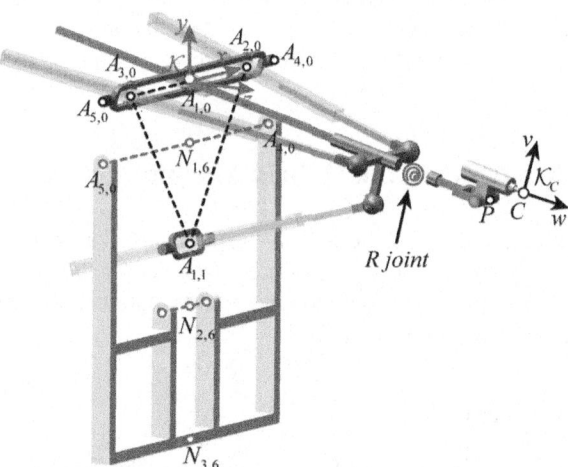

Fig. 2. Schematic diagram of hybrid machining cell showing the interconnections between substructures in the dynamic modeling.

2.2 Dynamic Modeling

The schematic diagram of the hybrid machining cell is shown in Fig. 2. Firstly, the 1T2R mechanism is divided into a total of five substructures for the base link, the three actuated limb-body and the passive limb-body. Then, the 1T2R mechanism is divided into five subsystems: the base link, three actuated limb-body, and the passive limb-body. Next, the MSA method is used to model the limb-body as equivalent spatial beam models, while the base link and platform are treated as rigid body. In order to use as few generalized coordinates as possible to characterize the low-order modes of the limb, the CMS method is then applied to establish the super-element models of the subsystems. Finally, the passive joints are represented as a multi-degree-of-freedom spring model, and deformation compatibility conditions are formulated between the interface nodes of adjacent subsystems. Based on this, the super-element models of all subsystems are assembled using the stiffness model of the passive joints, resulting in the elastodynamics model of the 1T2R mechanism is as

$$\begin{bmatrix} M_{\xi_P\xi_P} & M_{\xi_Pq} & M_{\xi_P\eta} & M_{\xi_Px_1} \\ & M_{qq} & M_{q\eta} & M_{qx_1} \\ & & M_{\eta\eta} & M_{\eta x_1} \\ \text{sym} & & & M_{x_1x_1} \end{bmatrix} \begin{pmatrix} \ddot{\xi}_P \\ \ddot{q} \\ \ddot{\eta} \\ \ddot{x}_1 \end{pmatrix} + \begin{bmatrix} K_{\xi_P\xi_P} & K_{\xi_Pq} & K_{\xi_P\eta} & K_{\xi_Px_1} \\ & K_{qq} & K_{q\eta} & K_{qx_1} \\ & & K_{\eta\eta} & K_{\eta x_1} \\ \text{sym} & & & K_{x_1x_1} \end{bmatrix} \begin{pmatrix} \xi_P \\ q \\ \eta \\ x_1 \end{pmatrix} = \begin{pmatrix} f_P \\ 0 \\ 0 \\ f_{x_1} \end{pmatrix} \tag{1}$$

$$\boldsymbol{q} = \begin{pmatrix} \boldsymbol{q}_1^T & \boldsymbol{q}_2^T & \boldsymbol{q}_3^T \end{pmatrix}^T \boldsymbol{x}_1 = \begin{pmatrix} \boldsymbol{\xi}_{1,0} \\ \boldsymbol{\xi}_{1,1} \end{pmatrix} \boldsymbol{q}_1 = \begin{pmatrix} q_{1,i} & q_{2,i} \end{pmatrix}^T i = 1, 2, 3$$

where $K_{\xi_P\xi_P}, K_{\xi_Pq}, K_{\xi_P\eta}, K_{\xi_Px}, K_{qq}, K_{q\eta}, K_{qx}, K_{\eta\eta}, K_{\eta x}$ and K_{xx} ($M_{\xi_P\xi_P}, M_{\xi_Pq}, M_{\xi_P\eta}, M_{\xi_Px}, M_{qq}, M_{q\eta}, M_{qx}, M_{\eta\eta}, M_{\eta x}$ and M_{xx}) denote the partitioned stiffness (mass) matrix associated with the generalized coordinates $\left(\boldsymbol{\xi}_P^T \ \boldsymbol{q}^T \ \boldsymbol{\eta}^T \ \boldsymbol{x}_1^T \right)^T$; f_P and $\boldsymbol{\xi}_P$ denote the nodal force and deflection vectors at P; $\boldsymbol{q}$ is the internal modal coordinate of each limb-body obtained through the CMS method; f_{x_1} and x_1 represent the nodal force and deflection vectors at nodes $A_{1,0}$ and $A_{1,1}$; $\boldsymbol{\eta}$ represents the deflection vectors of the remaining interface nodes except for $\boldsymbol{\xi}_P, \boldsymbol{q}$ and $\boldsymbol{x}_1$.

Considering that the low-order dynamic of the A/C wrist mainly depend on the torsional stiffness of the transmission system and the inertia of the rotating components, the structural parts are treated as rigid body, with the transmission system stiffness equivalent to a torsional spring. This allows the derivation of the expressions for the kinetic and elastic potential energy of the A/C wrist, as

$$T_{WT} = \frac{1}{2}\begin{pmatrix} \dot{\xi}_4 \\ \dot{\xi}_5 \end{pmatrix}^T \begin{bmatrix} M_4 & \\ & M_5 \end{bmatrix} \begin{pmatrix} \dot{\xi}_4 \\ \dot{\xi}_5 \end{pmatrix} V_{WT} = \frac{1}{2}\boldsymbol{\rho}^T \boldsymbol{K}_\rho \boldsymbol{\rho} \tag{2}$$

$$\boldsymbol{\rho} = \begin{pmatrix} \rho_4 \\ \rho_5 \end{pmatrix} \boldsymbol{K}_\rho = \begin{bmatrix} k_4 & \\ & k_5 \end{bmatrix}$$

where ξ_j ($j = 4$ for the C axis and $j = 5$ for the A axis) is the deflection twist with respect to part j; M_j denotes the mass matrix of the part j with respect to P; ρ_j and k_j, denote the deformation and stiffness coefficient of the j-th virtual joint.

Considering that the A/C wrist is connected to the 1T2R mechanism via a torsional spring, and based on the addition theorem of instantaneous motions, the absolute deflection vector of component j can be expressed as

$$\xi_4 = \xi_P + \rho_4 \hat{\xi}_4 \tag{3}$$

$$\xi_5 = \xi_P + \rho_4 \hat{\xi}_4 + \rho_5 \hat{\xi}_5 \tag{4}$$

$$\xi_5 = T^{-1} \xi_C \tag{5}$$

$$\hat{\xi}_4 = \begin{pmatrix} 0 \\ s_4 \end{pmatrix} \hat{\xi}_5 = \begin{pmatrix} 0 \\ s_5 \end{pmatrix} T = \begin{bmatrix} R & [r \times] R \\ 0 & R \end{bmatrix} r = l_v v + l_w w$$

where $\hat{\xi}_j$ is and unit twist of the j-th axis with S_j being its unit vector. ξ_C is the deflection vector evaluated in $\mathcal{K}_C$; R denotes the orientation matrix of $\mathcal{K}_C$ with respect to $\mathcal{K}$, and $r = \overrightarrow{AP}$.

Substituting Eq. (3)–(5) into Eq. (1) and (2), we can obtain the elastodynamics model of the TriMule hybrid robot as

$$\begin{bmatrix} M_{x_H x_H} & M_{x_H \xi_{1,0}} & M_{x_H \xi_{1,1}} & M_{x_H \xi_C} \\ & M_{\xi_{1,0} \xi_{1,0}} & M_{\xi_{1,0} \xi_{1,1}} & M_{\xi_{1,0} \xi_C} \\ & & M_{\xi_{1,1} \xi_{1,1}} & M_{\xi_{1,1} \xi_C} \\ \text{sym} & & & M_{\xi_C \xi_C} \end{bmatrix} \begin{pmatrix} \ddot{x}_H \\ \ddot{\xi}_{1,0} \\ \ddot{\xi}_{1,1} \\ \ddot{\xi}_C \end{pmatrix}$$
$$+ \begin{bmatrix} K_{x_H x_H} & K_{x_H \xi_{1,0}} & K_{x_H \xi_{1,1}} & K_{x_H \xi_C} \\ & K_{\xi_{1,0} \xi_{1,0}} & K_{\xi_{1,0} \xi_{1,1}} & K_{\xi_{1,0} \xi_C} \\ & & K_{\xi_{1,1} \xi_{1,1}} & K_{\xi_{1,1} \xi_C} \\ \text{sym} & & & K_{\xi_C \xi_C} \end{bmatrix} \begin{pmatrix} x_H \\ \xi_{1,0} \\ \xi_{1,1} \\ \xi_C \end{pmatrix} = \begin{pmatrix} 0 \\ f_{1,0} \\ f_{1,1} \\ f_C \end{pmatrix} \tag{6}$$

$$x_H = \begin{pmatrix} \rho^T & q^T & \eta^T \end{pmatrix}^T$$

where f_C is the external wrench evaluated at C in $\mathcal{K}_C$. For further details on the dynamic modeling process of the TriMule hybrid robot, please refer to [9].

As shown in Fig. 2, three interface nodes $N_{1,6}$, $N_{2,6}$, and $I(N_{3,6})$ of the machine frame are considered. Node $N_{1,6}$ is the center point of the universal joint of the UP limb. Node $N_{2,6}$ represents the center point of the universal joint of the UPS limb, coinciding with node $A_{1,1}$. Node $N_{3,6}$ is the center point of the bottom surface of the machine frame and is fixedly connected to the ground. The mass and stiffness matrix of the machine frame are obtained by analyzing the SuperElement module in the commercial finite element software SAMCEF. The elastodynamics model of the machine frame can be established as

$$\begin{bmatrix} M_{\xi_{1,6} \xi_{1,6}} & M_{\xi_{1,6} \xi_{2,6}} & M_{\xi_{1,6} \xi_{3,6}} \\ & M_{\xi_{2,6} \xi_{2,6}} & M_{\xi_{2,6} \xi_{3,6}} \\ \text{sym} & & M_{\xi_{3,6} \xi_{3,6}} \end{bmatrix} \begin{pmatrix} \ddot{\xi}_{1,6} \\ \ddot{\xi}_{2,6} \\ \ddot{\xi}_{3,6} \end{pmatrix} + \begin{bmatrix} K_{\xi_{1,6} \xi_{1,6}} & K_{\xi_{1,6} \xi_{2,6}} & K_{\xi_{1,6} \xi_{3,6}} \\ & K_{\xi_{2,6} \xi_{2,6}} & K_{\xi_{2,6} \xi_{3,6}} \\ \text{sym} & & K_{\xi_{3,6} \xi_{3,6}} \end{bmatrix} \begin{pmatrix} \xi_{1,6} \\ \xi_{2,6} \\ \xi_{3,6} \end{pmatrix} = \begin{pmatrix} f_{\xi_{1,6}} \\ f_{\xi_{2,6}} \\ f_{\xi_{3,6}} \end{pmatrix} \tag{7}$$

where $f_{i,6}$ and $\xi_{i,6}$ ($i = 1 \sim 3$) represent the nodal force and deflection vectors at $N_{1,6}$, $N_{2,6}$ and $N_{3,6}$.

Only the elastic potential energy of the revolute joints and universal joints connecting the TriMule hybrid robot and the machine frame is taken into account, that is

$$V_R = \frac{1}{2}\begin{pmatrix}\xi_{1,0}\\ \xi_{1,6}\end{pmatrix}^T \begin{bmatrix} K_R & -K_R \\ -K_R & K_R \end{bmatrix}\begin{pmatrix}\xi_{1,0}\\ \xi_{1,6}\end{pmatrix}$$
$$V_U = \frac{1}{2}\begin{pmatrix}\xi_{1,1}\\ \xi_{2,6}\end{pmatrix}^T \begin{bmatrix} K_U & -K_U \\ -K_U & K_U \end{bmatrix}\begin{pmatrix}\xi_{1,1}\\ \xi_{2,6}\end{pmatrix}$$
(8)

where K_R denotes the stiffness matrix of the revolute joint at the connection between the base link and the machine frame; K_U denotes the stiffness matrix of the universal joint of the UPS limb, as shown in Fig. 2.

Taking into account the kinetic energy and elastic potential energy of the TriMule hybrid robot and the machine frame, that is, assembling Eq. (6) and (7) using Eq. (8), the kinetic energy and elastic potential energy of the entire system measured in the reference frame $\mathcal{K}$ are obtained

$$T = \frac{1}{2}\dot{x}_{TF}^T M_{TF} \dot{x}_{TF} \quad V = \frac{1}{2}x_{TF}^T K_{TF} x_{TF} \qquad (9)$$

$$x_{TF} = \left(x_H^T\ \xi_{1,0}^T\ \xi_{1,1}^T\ \xi_{1,6}^T\ \xi_{2,6}^T\ \xi_C^T\ \xi_{3,6}^T\right)^T$$

The CMS method is used again to reduce the internal node DOF of the hybrid machining cell, and the elastodynamics model of the hybrid machining cell is obtained as

$$M\begin{pmatrix}\ddot{p}\\ \ddot{x}\end{pmatrix} + K\begin{pmatrix}p\\ x\end{pmatrix} = \begin{pmatrix}0\\ f\end{pmatrix} \qquad (10)$$

$$\begin{pmatrix}\eta_{TF}\\ x\end{pmatrix} = \begin{bmatrix}\Phi_{IN} & \Psi_{IJ}\\ 0 & 1\end{bmatrix}\begin{pmatrix}p\\ x\end{pmatrix} x = \begin{pmatrix}\xi_C\\ \xi_{3,6}\end{pmatrix} f = \begin{pmatrix}f_C\\ f_{3,6}\end{pmatrix}$$

$$\eta_{TF} = \left(x_H^T\ \xi_{1,0}^T\ \xi_{1,1}^T\ \xi_{1,6}^T\ \xi_{2,6}^T\right)^T$$

$$\Psi_{IJ} = K_{II}^{-1} K_{IJ} \Phi_{IN} = [\phi_1 \cdots \phi_{11}] p = [p_1 \quad p_{11}]$$

where f and x represent the nodal force and deflection vector at interface node C and interface node $N_{3,6}$, respectively. η_{TF} represents the collection of the nodal deflections of the remaining internal nodes. Φ_{IN} is the preserved first 11 fixed-interface dominant modes. The interface modes can be obtained by solving the eigenvalue problem $(K_{II} - \lambda M_{II})\phi = 0$. p represents the modal coordinate corresponding to the CMS method used again.

By constructing the eigenvalue problem of Eq. (10), the modal parameters of the hybrid machining cell can be obtained. According to the modal analysis theory [16], the frequency response function (FRF) matrix of the end point C is

$$H_{C_i C_i}(\omega) = \sum_{k=1}^{N} \frac{\Phi_{C_i,k} \Phi_{C_i,k}^T}{(\omega_k^2 - \omega^2 + j2\xi_k \omega_k \omega)} i = x, y, z \qquad (11)$$

where ω_k and ξ_k represent the k-th mode circular frequency and damping ratio of the entire system, respectively. $\boldsymbol{\Phi}_{C_i,k}$ and $\boldsymbol{\Phi}_{C_j,k}$ represent the k-th mode shape vectors at point C.

3 Verification

In this section, experimental modal test is carried out using a full-size hybrid machining cell as an example to verify the effectiveness of the proposed approach.

3.1 Experimental Setup

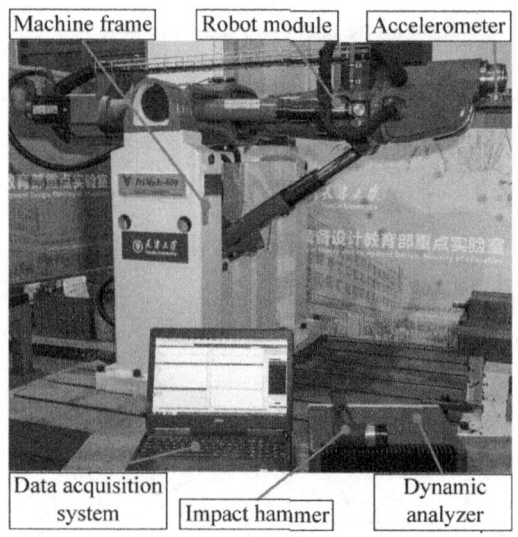

Fig. 3. Experimental setup for the FRF test. Modal experiments were conducted on the engineering prototype developed at Tianjin University.

The experimental modal test setup is shown in Fig. 3. The single-input and multi-output (SIMO) modal test is carried out on the physical prototype of the hybrid machining cell using the hammer impact method. The impact hammer (PCB 086D20) hits the spindle end face point C, and the excitation direction is consistent with the direction of the coordinate axes of the body-fixed frame $\mathcal{K}_c$. At the same time, the accelerometer (PCB LW306141) is arranged at point C to measure acceleration signals in three directions. As shown in Fig. 4, considering that the dynamic behaviors of the entire system vary with the configuration, four typical specific configurations are selected in the whole range for modal test. P1 is the reference configuration, located at the center of the reference plane within the task workspace. P4 represents the X-direction limit configuration, positioned at the edge of the task workspace. P2 and P3 correspond to the Y-direction limit configurations; they are the furthest reachable positions for applying excitation during the experiment, although they do not represent the robot's actual motion limits. The Least

Squares Complex Exponential (LSCE) method is used to identify the natural frequencies, damping ratios, and mode shapes of the entire system, and the FRF function is reconstructed based on the identification results [17].

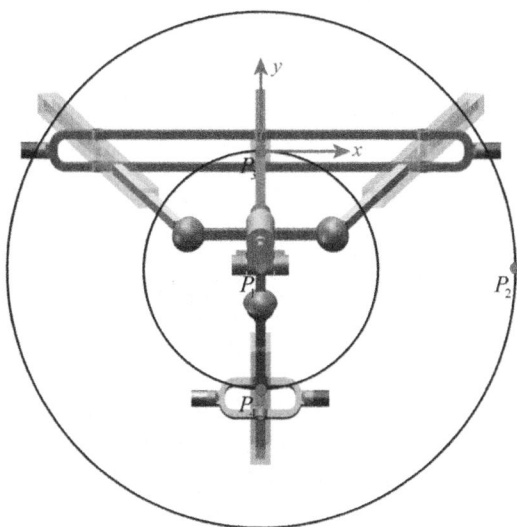

Fig. 4. Four representative robot configurations selected for modal experiments to investigate the variation of dynamic behaviors with configuration.

The relative error of the frequencies is used to quantitatively assess the differences between the natural frequencies of each model and the experimental measurements [18].

$$Error = \left| \frac{\omega_{re}^A - \omega_{re}^E}{\omega_{re}^E} \right| \times 100\% \qquad (12)$$

where subscript e represents the excitation locations and r represents the response locations. ω_{re}^E is the measured natural frequency; ω_{re}^A is the natural frequencies of semi-analytical models.

3.2 Results and Discussion

In order to verify the effectiveness of the proposed approach, this section conducts comparative analysis on the full-size TriMule-600 hybrid robot as the research object. First, the low-order natural frequencies obtained from the proposed model, the model presented in reference 9, and modal testing are compared at four representative configurations, in order to evaluate the predictive accuracy of each model with respect to dynamic behaviors and to investigate the influence of the machine frame structure on the overall dynamic performance of the system. Subsequently, the FRFs calculated by the proposed model are compared with experimental measurements at the reference configuration P_1, further verifying the accuracy of the proposed modeling approach. Table 1 shows the comparison results of the theoretical value and experimental measurement value of the natural frequency of the entire system calculated at four different configurations.

Table 1. Natural frequencies calculated by the semi-analytical model and measured data at different configurations.

Configuration\Mode order		1st	2nd	3rd	4th	5th
P_1	MT	28.288	35.250	41.245	55.409	58.717
	SA 1	31.558	35.840	47.062	52.178	54.015
	Error	11.6%	1.7%	14.1%	5.8%	8.0%
	SA 2	33.255	36.386	48.319	53.094	53.575
	Error	17.6%	3.2%	17.2%	4.2%	8.8%
P_2	MT	27.818	33.063	40.652	53.866	58.584
	SA 1	28.753	32.411	46.449	51.758	54.175
	Error	3.4%	2.0%	14.3%	3.9%	7.5%
	SA 2	30.738	33.744	47.557	51.734	53.382
	Error	10.5%	2.1%	17.0%	4.0%	8.9%
P_3	MT	27.754	34.785	40.219	53.147	56.497
	SA 1	30.052	36.361	47.049	52.216	53.692
	Error	8.3%	4.5%	17.0%	1.8%	5.0%
	SA 2	31.804	36.904	48.288	52.758	53.657
	Error	14.6%	6.1%	20.1%	7.3%	5.0%
P_4	MT	27.780	35.298	41.219	54.951	58.242
	SA 1	31.904	34.430	46.974	51.782	54.236
	Error	14.9%	2.5%	14.0%	5.8%	6.9%
	SA 2	33.502	34.973	48.222	52.929	53.121
	Error	20.6%	0.9%	17.0%	3.7%	8.8%

SA 1: Semi-analytical model of hybrid machining cell (this paper)
SA 2: Semi-analytical model of TriMule hybrid robot[9]
MT: Data measured by modal test

As shown in Table 1, the maximum deviation between the results obtained by the proposed approach and the experimental measurements occurs at the third mode at configuration P_3, with a frequency difference of 6.83 Hz and a relative error of 17%. For the remaining modes, the frequency differences are all within 5 Hz, with relative errors below 15%. In contrast, the semi-analytical model that neglects the machine frame structure exhibits a maximum error of 8.069 Hz and a relative error of 20.1% for the third mode at configuration P_3. Additionally, at configuration P_4, its first mode shows a relative error of 20.6%. These results demonstrate that the proposed modeling approach provides significantly improved accuracy in predicting the dynamic behaviors of the hybrid robot across multiple configurations, highlighting its effectiveness and reliability.

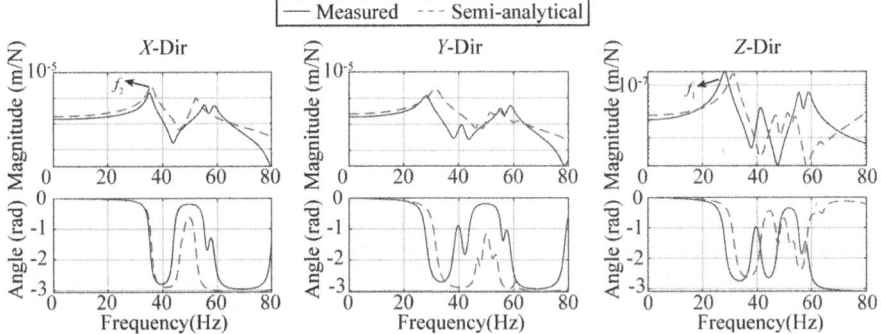

Fig. 5. FRFs of the end effector at P_1 configuration

The FRF characterizes the dynamic behavior of a system under excitations of varying frequencies. The measured FRF matrix of the entire machine is reconstructed using a modal parameter identification technique. The reconstructed results are then compared with the FRFs computed by the proposed modeling approach, in order to assess the accuracy and applicability of the method in predicting frequency-domain responses. Figure 5 shows the measured FRF and the FRF of the semi-analytical model of the end effector at the P_1 configuration. The two curves exhibit good consistency within the range of 0 to 60 range, which includes the first several dominant modes of the system. This frequency range is defined as the low-frequency band based on the modal distribution characteristics and its relevance to the robot's elastic dynamic behavior. Beyond 60 Hz, discrepancies increase due to the influence of higher-order modes and modeling simplifications, but this range is not the focus of the current study. The reasons for this phenomenon may be twofold: first, the semi-analytic model oversimplifies the structure; second, issues such as noise in the measured FRF, inaccurate sensor positioning, modal truncation errors, and the violation of linearity and reciprocity in the actual structure contribute to the discrepancy between the measured FRF and the theoretical values. Overall, the proposed modeling approach demonstrates high accuracy in characterizing the frequency response behavior of the hybrid machining cell.

4 Conclusions

This paper presents an elastodynamic modeling approach based on component mode synthesis for the hybrid machining cell. In the modeling process, first, the influence of the frame on the dynamic behavior of the entire system is considered. Second, the modal synthesis method is employed to characterize the low-order modes of the entire system using a minimal set of generalized coordinates. Using the full-size TriMule robot as the experimental subject, the effectiveness of the proposed method is demonstrated through a comparison with the measured natural frequencies. Most of the errors are within 10%. The results of eigenvalue and frequency response function analysis show that the proposed dynamic model can predict the full set of low-order dynamics with sufficient computational accuracy.

Acknowledgements. This work was partially supported by National Natural Science Foundation of China (Grant No. 52325501).

References

1. Dong, C.L., Liu, H.T., Xiao, J.L., Huang, T.: Dynamic modeling and design of a 5-DOF hybrid robot for machining. Mech. Mach. Theory **165**, 104438 (2021)
2. Han, J.L., Shan, X.L., Liu, H.T., Xiao, J.L., Huang, T.: Fuzzy gain scheduling PID control of a hybrid robot based on dynamic characteristics. Mech. Mach. Theory **184**, 105283 (2023)
3. Altintas, Y., Brecher, C., Weck, M., Witt, S.: Virtual machine tool. CIRP Ann. **54**, 115–138 (2005)
4. Fallaha, C.J., Saad, M., Kanaan, H.Y., Al-Haddad, K.: SlidingMode robot control with exponential reaching law. IEEE Trans. Ind. Electron. **58**(2), 600–610 (2011)
5. Ma, Y., Niu, W.T., Luo, Z.J., Yin, F.W., Huang, T.: Static and dynamic performance evaluation of a 3-DOF spindle head using CAD–CAE integration methodology. Robot. Comput.-Integr. Manuf. **41**, 1–12 (2016)
6. Son, H.S., Choi, H.J., Park, H.W.: Design and dynamic analysis of an arch-type desktop reconfigurable machine. Int. J. Mach. Tools Manuf **50**, 575–584 (2010)
7. Hong, D., Kim, S., Choi, W.C., Song, J.B.: Analysis of machining stability for a parallel machine tool. Mech. Based Des. Struct. Mech. **31**, 509–528 (2006)
8. Tyapin, I., Hovland, G.: The Gantry-Tau parallel kinematic machine-kinematic and elastodynamic design optimization. Meccanica **46**, 113–129 (2011)
9. Dong, C., Liu, H., Huang, T., Chetwynd, D.G.: A screw theory-based semi-analytical approach for elastodynamics of the tricept robot. J. Mech. Robot. **11**(3), 031005 (2019)
10. Ma, Y.W., Tian, Y.L., Liu, X.P., Lu, C.H.: Dynamic modeling and analysis of the 3-PRS power head based on the screw theory and rigid multipoint constraints. Sci. China-Technol. Sci. **66**, 1869–1882 (2023)
11. Wu, L., Dong, C., Wang, G., Liu, H., Huang, T.: An approach to predict lower-order dynamic behaviors of a 5-DOF hybrid robot using a minimum set of generalized coordinates. Robot. Comput. Integr. Manuf. **67**, 102024 (2021)
12. Zhang, H., Xu, Z., Han, H., Han, C., Yu, Y., Xia, M.: A virtual joint method of analytical form for parallel manipulators. Proc. Inst. Mech. Eng. Part C: J. Mech. Eng. Sci. **235**(23), 6893–6907 (2021)
13. Piras, G., Cleghorn, W.L., Mills, J.K.: Dynamic finite-element analysis of a planar high-speed, high-precision parallel manipulator with flexible links. Mech. Mach. Theory **40**, 849–862 (2005)
14. Guyan, R.J.: Reduction of stiffness and mass matrices. AIAA J. **3**, 380 (1964)
15. Craig, R.R., Jr., Bampton, M.C.: Coupling of substructures for dynamic analyses. AIAA J. **6**(7), 1313–1319 (1968)
16. Ewins, D.J.: Modal Testing: Theory, Practice and Application. Wiley, Hoboken (2009)
17. Modak, S.V.: Analytical and Experimental Modal Analysis. CRC Press, Boca Raton (2023)
18. van der Valk, P.L.C., Voormeeren, S.N., de Valk, P.C., Rixen, D.J.: Dynamic models for load calculation procedures of offshore wind turbine support structures: overview, assessment, and outlook. ASME. J. Comput. Nonlinear Dyn. **10**, 041013 (2015)

Safety-Critical Flocking Control of Multiple Unmanned Surface Vehicles Based on Exponential Control Barrier Functions

Jiaxing Zhou, Lu Liu$^{(\boxtimes)}$, Yanping Xu, and Zhouhua Peng

Dalian Maritime University, Dalian 116026, China
{zhoujx1334,luliu,xuyanping_e,zhpeng}@dlmu.edu.cn

Abstract. This paper addresses the flocking control problem for a group of unmanned surface vehicles (USVs) to follow a leader USV guided by a parameterized path in an environment with obstacles. The locations and shapes of the obstacles are unknown, and only the closest collision points and collision vectors can be locally measured. A safety-critical flocking control method is proposed for achieving collision avoidance and establishing a flocking behavior for USVs. Specifically, control inputs of virtual reference points are designed based on an artificial potential function. For the leader USV, a nominal path following guidance law is designed to follow a predefined parameterized path. For the follower USVs, a flocking guidance law is designed to follow the virtual reference points. An exponential control barrier function is designed based on the closest collision points. A constrained quadratic programming problem incorporating exponential control barrier function is established to calculate optimal yaw rate guidance signals. The effectiveness of the proposed control method for safety-critical flocking control of USVs is validated through simulation results.

Keywords: unmanned surface vehicles (USVs) · flocking · collision avoidance · exponential control barrier function

1 Introduction

In recent years, unmanned surface vehicles (USVs) have become crucial for performing a wide range of marine tasks in both civilian and military fields [1-3]. Cooperative systems involving multiple USVs can greatly improve the efficiency

---

This work was supported in part by the National Natural Science Foundation of China under Grant 52271304, 52471372, and in part by the Natural Science Foundation of Liaoning Province under Grant 2024-MS-009, and in part by the Liaoning Revitalization Talents Program under Grant XLYC2403051, XLYC2402054, and in part by the Key Basic Research of Dalian under Grant 2023JJ11CG008, and in part by the Fundamental Research Funds for the Central Universities 3132023508.

of accomplishing complex or dangerous missions [4–6]. A key research focus in the field of multiple USVs systems is the development of distributed control strategies that rely on local interactions to achieve various collective behaviors, such as rendezvous [7], formation [8], containment [9], and flocking [10–12]. Specifically, the flocking control aims to synchronize the speeds of all controlled objects and maintain a stable, desired distance between them.

In the process of establishing flocking behavior for USVs, ensuring the safety of USVs has emerged as a critical issue. Various collision avoidance methods have been proposed, such as artificial potential functions, model predictive control, deep reinforcement learning, and control barrier functions (CBFs). Among these, the CBFs combined with quadratic programming (QP) method are a novel controller synthesis method that solves an optimization problem online with safety as a hard constraint. In [13], a backup strategy-based CBF is executed to guarantee obstacle avoidance for multiple agents. In [14], an input-to-state safe CBF for a heavy-duty truck is proposed. In [15], a formation control method based on neurodynamic optimization is proposed, and safety-critical containment maneuvering is achieved within input constraints. Although several collision avoidance methods based on CBFs have been implemented for the safety control, most of these approaches require a clear understanding of obstacle boundaries, which is difficult to obtain in practical application scenarios.

Motivated by the above observations, this paper presents a safety-critical flocking control method for multiple USVs in the presence of obstacles. Firstly, the control inputs of the virtual reference points are designed based on the artificial potential functions, and the nominal guidance laws are designed for the leader USV and the follower USVs to follow a given parameterized path and the virtual reference points. Then, the exponential control barrier functions (ECBFs) based on local measurements are proposed. Meanwhile, a QP is formulated to compute the optimal guidance signals for yaw rate inputs under the ECBFs to avoid obstacles and neighboring USVs. Simulation results prove the effectiveness of the proposed control method for multiple USVs. The main contributions of this paper are as follows:

1. In contrast to the flocking control methods proposed in [10–12], which can not avoid obstacles, the proposed method based on ECBFs can effectively avoid collisions with obstacles, as well as neighboring USVs.
2. In contrast to the collision avoidance control methods proposed in [13–15], which rely on knowing the locations and shapes of obstacles in advance, the proposed safety-critical flocking control method for USVs can achieve collision avoidance using only local measurements of the closest collision points.
3. In contrast to the control methods based on the CBFs proposed in [13–15], which necessitate simultaneous modulation of both forward velocity and yaw rate for collision avoidance, the proposed method based on the ECBFs is able to avoid collisions by optimizing the desired yaw rate only, and the forward velocity can be flexible.

The remainder of this paper is organized as follows: Sect. 2 covers preliminaries and problem formulation. Section 3 presents the design and analysis of the proposed control method. Section 4 provides the simulation results. Finally, Sect. 5 concludes the paper.

2 Preliminaries and Problem Formulation

2.1 Graph Theory

A graph $\mathcal{G} = \{\mathcal{V}, \mathcal{E}\}$ is composed of a node set $\mathcal{V} = \{n_1, ..., n_N\}$ and a edge set $\mathcal{E} = \{(n_i, n_j) \in \mathcal{E} \times \mathcal{E}\}$. Each edge (n_i, n_j) represents the communication from node i to node j. The adjacency matrix $\mathcal{A} = [a_{ij}] \in \Re^{N \times N}$ is used to describe the connectivity of the graph, where $a_{ij} = 1$ if $(n_j, n_i) \in \mathcal{E}$ and $a_{ij} = 0$ otherwise.

2.2 Problem Formulation

Consider a complex marine environment comprising several obstacles and a swarm of USVs numbered from 0 to N. The 0th USV is the leader USV, and the USV from 1 to N are the follower USV. Each USV is equipped with a sensor that can detect obstacles within a circular range extending a distance r_d from the USV's center. The kinematics of the ith USV can be expressed as

$$\begin{cases} \dot{x}_i = u_i \cos \psi_i - v_i \sin \psi_i, \\ \dot{y}_i = u_i \sin \psi_i + v_i \cos \psi_i, \\ \dot{\psi}_i = r_i, \end{cases} \quad (1)$$

where $\boldsymbol{p}_i = [x_i, y_i]^T$ denotes the position vector in the earth-fixed frame, and ψ_i is the heading angle; u_i, v_i, r_i are the surge velocity, sway velocity, and yaw rate in the body-fixed frame.

Define $U_i = \sqrt{u_i^2 + v_i^2}$ as the total velocity, $\psi_{i\omega} = \psi_i + \beta_i$ as the course angle, and $\beta_i = \arctan(v_i/u_i)$ as the sideslip angle. The kinematics of the ith USV can be rewritten as

$$\begin{cases} \dot{x}_i = U_i \cos \psi_{i\omega}, \\ \dot{y}_i = U_i \sin \psi_{i\omega}, \\ \dot{\psi}_{i\omega} = r_i + \beta_{id}. \end{cases} \quad (2)$$

where $\beta_{id} = \dot{\beta}_i$.

Let $[x_{id}(\theta_i), y_{id}(\theta_i)]$ be the path for the ith USV, where θ_i represent the path variable, and the tangential angle on the path is defined as $\psi_{id} = \arctan 2(\dot{y}_{id}, \dot{x}_{id})$. The along-track error x_{ie} and the cross-track error y_{ie} can be expressed as follows:

$$\begin{bmatrix} x_{ie} \\ y_{ie} \end{bmatrix} = \begin{bmatrix} \cos \psi_{id} & -\sin \psi_{id} \\ \sin \psi_{id} & \cos \psi_{id} \end{bmatrix}^T \begin{bmatrix} x_i - x_{id} \\ y_i - y_{id} \end{bmatrix}, \quad (3)$$

Taking the time derivative of (3) along (2), the dynamics of x_{ie} and y_{ie} become

$$\begin{cases} \dot{x}_{ie} = U_i \cos(\psi_{i\omega} - \psi_{id}) + \dot{\psi}_{id} y_{ie} - u_{id}^* \dot{\theta}_i, \\ \dot{y}_{ie} = U_i \sin(\psi_{i\omega} - \psi_{id}) - \dot{\psi}_{id} x_{ie}, \end{cases} \quad (4)$$

where $u_{id}^* = \sqrt{(\dot{x}_{id})^2 + (\dot{y}_{id})^2}$.

Let $[x_{0d}, y_{0d}]$ be the given parameterized path for the ith USV. Let $[x_{id}, y_{id}]$ be the virtual reference points for the follower USVs, where $i = 1, ..., N$. The virtual reference points have Double Integrator (DI) dynamics with a linear drag term

$$\begin{cases} \dot{x}_{id} = \eta_{ix}, \\ \dot{y}_{id} = \eta_{iy}, \\ \dot{\eta}_{ix} = \zeta_{ix} - c_1 * \eta_{ix}, \\ \dot{\eta}_{iy} = \zeta_{iy} - c_2 * \eta_{iy}, \end{cases} \quad (5)$$

where c_1 and c_2 are drag coefficients, η_{ix} and η_{iy} are velocity, and ζ_{ix} and ζ_{iy} are control input.

Consider L_s static obstacles $\mathcal{O}_s$, $s \in 1, ..., L_s$. Define $\boldsymbol{p}_{io} = [x_{io}, y_{io}]^T$ as the closest collision point corresponding to the ith USV and the oth obstacle. The closest collision point is the nearest point on the obstacle boundary to the current position of the USV. Define $\boldsymbol{d}_{io} = \boldsymbol{p}_i - \boldsymbol{p}_{io}$ as the collision vector, which is directed from the closest collision point toward the position of USV.

The control method design in this paper is based on the following assumptions.

Assumption 1. At any given moment, the USV can determine the distance from its center to the boundary of each obstacle within its sensing range, such as through the use of infrared sensors or LIDAR.

Assumption 2. The minimum distance between the boundaries of any two obstacles is greater than the diameter of the USV.

The control objective of this paper is to develop a safety-critical flocking control method for a group of N USVs. Specifically, the control objective is outlined as follows:

1) Path following task:

$$\lim_{t \to \infty} x_{0e} \leq \iota_1, \lim_{t \to \infty} y_{0e} \leq \iota_2, \quad (6)$$

where ι_1 and ι_2 are minor positive constants.

2) Virtual reference point tracking task:

$$\lim_{t \to \infty} x_{ie} \leq \iota_{i3}, \lim_{t \to \infty} y_{ie} \leq \iota_{i4}, \quad (7)$$

where ι_{i3} and ι_{i4} are minor positive constants.

3) Heading alignment task:

$$\lim_{t \to \infty} \psi_i - \psi_0 \leq \iota_{i5}, \tag{8}$$

where ι_{i5} is minor positive constants.

4) Velocity consensus task:

$$\lim_{t \to \infty} U_i - U_0 \leq \iota_{i6}, \lim_{t \to \infty} r_i - r_0 \leq \iota_{i7}, \tag{9}$$

where ι_{i6} and ι_{i7} are minor positive constants.

5) Connectivity preservation task:

$$\|\boldsymbol{p}_i(t) - \boldsymbol{p}_j(t)\| < \bar{R}, \tag{10}$$

where $\|\boldsymbol{p}_i(t_0) - \boldsymbol{p}_j(t_0)\| < \bar{R}$.

6) Collision avoidance task:

$$\|\boldsymbol{d}_{is}\| \geq d_s, i = 0, ..., N, s = 1, ..., L_s, \tag{11}$$
$$\|\boldsymbol{d}_{ij}\| \geq d_n, i = 0, ..., N, j = 0, ..., N, \tag{12}$$

where d_s and d_n are the set safe distances between the USV and the static obstacle and another USV, respectively.

3 Design and Analysis

3.1 Nominal Guidance Laws Design

Define $\psi_{ie} = \psi_{iw} - \alpha_{i\psi}$, $\dot{\theta}_i = v_s - \omega_i$, and the error dynamics in (4) can be put into

$$\begin{cases} \dot{x}_{ie} = U_i - 2U_i \sin^2\left(\frac{\psi_{iw} - \psi_{id}}{2}\right) + \dot{\psi}_{id} y_{ie} - u_{id}^*(v_s - \omega_i), \\ \dot{y}_{ie} = U_i \sin(\alpha_{i\psi} - \psi_{id}) + \varrho_i - \dot{\psi}_{id} x_{ie}, \\ \dot{\psi}_{ie} = r_i + \beta_{id} - \dot{\alpha}_{i\psi}, \end{cases} \tag{13}$$

where $\varrho_i = U_i \sin(\psi_{iw} - \psi_{id}) - U_i \sin(\alpha_{i\psi} - \psi_{id})$.

Nominal guidance laws are designed for leader USV as follows:

$$\begin{cases} \bar{\alpha}_{0u} = -k_{01} x_{0e}/\Pi_{0u} + u_{0d}^* v_s + 2U_0 \sin^2\left(\frac{\psi_{0w} - \psi_{0d}}{2}\right), \\ \bar{\alpha}_{0r} = -k_{02} \psi_{0e}/\Pi_{0u} - \beta_{0d} + \dot{\psi}_{0r} - y_{0e} \varrho_0/\psi_{0e}, \\ \alpha_{0\psi} = \psi_{0d} + \arctan\left(-\frac{y_{0e}}{\Delta_0}\right), \end{cases} \tag{14}$$

where k_{01} and k_{02} are positive control gains, $\Pi_{0u} = \sqrt{(x_{0e})^2 + (\Delta_{0x})^2}$, $\Pi_{0r} = \sqrt{(\psi_{0e})^2 + (\Delta_{0\psi})^2}$, Δ_{0x} and $\Delta_{0\psi}$ are positive constants, Δ_0 is a look-ahead distance, v_s is reference speed.

To ensure stable flocking behavior, the following potential functions have been introduced

$$V_{ij}^p = \begin{cases} \frac{L^2-(N_1)^2}{(N_1)^2} + \frac{(N_1)^2}{L^2-(N_1)^2} - 2, & \underline{R} < \|\boldsymbol{p}_{ij}\| < \bar{R} \\ 0, & \|\boldsymbol{p}_{ij}\| \geq \bar{R} \text{ or } \|\boldsymbol{p}_{ij}\| \leq \underline{R} \end{cases}, \quad (15)$$

and

$$\frac{\partial V_{ij}^p}{\partial \boldsymbol{p}_{ij}} = \begin{cases} \frac{-2\boldsymbol{p}_{ij} L^2}{\|\boldsymbol{p}_{ij}\|(N_1)^3} + \frac{2\boldsymbol{p}_{ij} L^2 N_1}{\|\boldsymbol{p}_{ij}\|(L^2-(N_1)^2)^2}, & \underline{R} < \|\boldsymbol{p}_{ij}\| < \bar{R} \\ 0_2, & \|\boldsymbol{p}_{ij}\| \geq \bar{R} \text{ or } \|\boldsymbol{p}_{ij}\| \leq \underline{R} \end{cases}, \quad (16)$$

where $N_1 = \|\boldsymbol{p}_{ij}\| - \underline{R}$, $\boldsymbol{p}_{ij} = \boldsymbol{p}_i - \boldsymbol{p}_j$, $\boldsymbol{p}_i$ and $\boldsymbol{p}_j$ are positions on a 2-D plane, $\underline{R}$ is the smallest safe distance between $\boldsymbol{p}_i$ and $\boldsymbol{p}_j$, $\bar{R}$ is the maximal communication range, and $L = \bar{R} - \underline{R}$. Note that if $\underline{R} < \|\boldsymbol{p}_{ij}\| < L/2 + \underline{R}$, then $\partial V_{ij}^p / \partial \boldsymbol{p}_{ij} < 0$; and if $L/2 + \underline{R} < \|\boldsymbol{p}_{ij}\| < \bar{R}$, then $\partial V_{ij}^p / \partial \boldsymbol{p}_{ij} > 0$. Thus, V_{ij}^p reaches at its unique minimum at $\sqrt{2}L/2 + \underline{R}$ for $\underline{R} < \|\boldsymbol{p}_{ij}\| < \bar{R}$.

Consider a Lyapunov function as

$$V_i = \frac{1}{2} \sum_{j=1}^{N} a_{ij} V_{ij}^p + a_{i0} V_{i0}^p \quad (17)$$

The gradient of V_i is determined as follows:

$$\nabla_{\boldsymbol{p}_i} V = \sum_{j=0}^{N} a_{ij} \frac{\partial^T V_{ij}^p}{\partial \boldsymbol{p}_i} \quad (18)$$

The control inputs of the virtual reference points are designed as follows:

$$\begin{bmatrix} \zeta_{ix} \\ \zeta_{iy} \end{bmatrix} = -\nabla_{\boldsymbol{p}_i} V - \begin{bmatrix} \frac{k_{iu}(\dot{x}_{id}-\dot{x}_0)}{\sqrt{(\|(\dot{x}_{id}-\dot{x}_0)\|^2)+\delta_{iu}^2}} \\ \frac{k_{iv}(\dot{y}_{id}-\dot{y}_0)}{\sqrt{(\|(\dot{y}_{id}-\dot{y}_0)\|^2)+\delta_{iv}^2}} \end{bmatrix}, \quad (19)$$

where k_{iu} and k_{iv} are positive control gains, δ_{iu} and δ_{iv} are positive constants.

According to (5) and (19), the virtual reference points $[x_{id}, y_{id}]$ can be obtained. subsequently, the nominal guidance laws for the follower USVs are designed as

$$\begin{cases} \bar{\alpha}_{iu} = -k_{i1} x_{ie}/\Pi_{iu} + u_{id}^* v_s + 2U_0 \sin^2\left(\frac{\psi_{iw}-\psi_{id}}{2}\right), \\ \bar{\alpha}_{ir} = -k_{i2} \psi_{ie}/\Pi_{iu} - \beta_{id} + \dot{\psi}_{ir} - y_{ie}\varrho_i/\psi_{ie}, \\ \alpha_{i\psi} = \psi_{id} + \arctan\left(-\frac{y_{ie}}{\Delta_i}\right), \end{cases} \quad (20)$$

where k_{i1} and k_{i2} are positive control gains, $\Pi_{iu} = \sqrt{(x_{ie})^2 + (\Delta_{ix})^2}$, $\Pi_{ir} = \sqrt{(\psi_{ie})^2 + (\Delta_{i\psi})^2}$, Δ_{ix} and $\Delta_{i\psi}$ are positive constants, Δ_i is a look-ahead distance, v_s is reference speed.

3.2 Optimal Guidance Laws Design

The ECBF for static obstacles is defined as follows:

$$h_{is} = D_{is} + (x_{is} - x_i)^2 d_{2s} + (y_{is} - y_i)^2 d_{3s}, \tag{21}$$

where the distance functions D_{is} are defined as

$$D_{is} = \text{dist}(\boldsymbol{p}_i, \boldsymbol{p}_{is}) - (d_{1s} + \max\{d_{2s}, d_{3s}\}), \tag{22}$$

where $\boldsymbol{p}_{is}$ is the closest collision point for static obstacles, the parameter d_{1s} represents the minimum safe distance, and the variables d_{2s}, d_{3s} be chosen sufficiently small such that $d_{2d} \neq d_{3d}$ and $d_{2s}, d_{3s} < d_{1s}$. d_{2s} and d_{3s} are introduced to ensure that $L_g L_f h_{is} \neq 0$ so that h_{is} can always be used to steer the USV away from the obstacle. Following [16–18], given the ECBF h_{is}, the forward invariance of $\mathcal{S}$ is ensured if the locally Lipschitz continuous controller r_i satisfies

$$L_f^2 h_{is} + L_g L_f h_{is} r_i + \alpha_1 h_{is} + \alpha_2 \dot{h}_{is} \geq 0, \tag{23}$$

where α_1 and α_2 is a function of class $\mathcal{K}$.

The ECBF for neighboring USVs is defined as follows:

$$h_{ij} = D_{ij} + (x_{ij} - x_i)^2 d_{2n} + (y_{ij} - y_i)^2 d_{3n}, \tag{24}$$

where the distance functions D_{ij} are defined as

$$D_{ij} = \text{dist}(\boldsymbol{p}_i, \boldsymbol{p}_{ij}) - (d_{1n} + \max\{d_{2n}, d_{3n}\}), \tag{25}$$

where $\boldsymbol{p}_{ij}$ is the closest collision point for neighboring USVs, the parameter d_{1n} represents the minimum safe distance, and the variables d_{2n}, d_{3n} be chosen sufficiently small such that $d_{2n} \neq d_{3n}$ and $d_{2n}, d_{3n} < d_{1n}$. d_{2n} and d_{3n} are introduced to ensure that $L_g L_f h_{ij} \neq 0$ so that h_{ij} can always be used to steer the USV away from the neighboring USVs. Following [16–18], given the ECBF h_{ij}, the forward invariance of $\mathcal{S}$ is ensured if the locally Lipschitz continuous controller r_i satisfies

$$L_f^2 h_{ij} + L_g L_f h_{ij} r_i + \alpha_3 h_{ij} + \alpha_4 \dot{h}_{ij} \geq 0, \tag{26}$$

where α_3 and α_4 is a function of class $\mathcal{K}$.

The optimal safe guidance signal generation is formulated as a convex quadratic programming problem, referred to as

$$r_i^* = \underset{r_i}{\operatorname{argmin}} \frac{1}{2} \|r_i - \bar{\alpha}_{ir}\|^2,$$

$$\text{s.t.} \begin{cases} L_f^2 h_{is} + L_g L_f h_{is} r_i + \alpha_1 h_{is} + \alpha_2 \dot{h}_{is} \geq 0, \\ L_f^2 h_{ij} + L_g L_f h_{ij} r_i + \alpha_3 h_{ij} + \alpha_4 \dot{h}_{ij} > 0, \\ r_{\min} \leq r_i \leq r_{\max}. \end{cases} \tag{27}$$

The constraint ensures that the solution r_i^* will be close to the nominal guidance law $\bar{\alpha}_{ir}$. Therefore, the optimal guidance laws are expressed as

$$\begin{cases} \alpha_{iu} = \bar{\alpha}_{iu}, \\ \alpha_{ir} = r_i^*. \end{cases} \tag{28}$$

4 Simulation Results

In this section, simulation results are provided to illustrate the effectiveness of the proposed safety-critical flocking control method. Consider a motion scenario where seven USVs form a flocking formation pattern with three static obstacles in the environment. The initial and target positions of the USVs are provided in Table 1. The obstacles satisfy Assumption 1. The circular obstacles are set at $[120, -13]^T$ and $[180, 54]^T$, with radii $r_{z1} = 10$ and $r_{z2} = 10$, respectively. The five vertices of the polygonal obstacle are located at $[175, 50]^T$, $[195, 50]^T$, $[195, 60]^T$, $[185, 65]^T$, and $[175, 60]^T$. The communication graph among the leader and follower USVs is plotted in Fig. 1. The control parameters employed in the simulation are given as $k_{i1} = 0.5$, $k_{i2} = 0.5$, $v_s = 0.7$, $\Delta_{ix} = 1$, $\Delta_{i\psi} = 1$, $\Delta_i = 5$, $k_{iu} = 0.8$, $k_{iv} = 0.8$, $\delta_{iu} = 1$, $\delta_{iv} = 1$, $c_1 = 1$, $c_2 = 1$, $\bar{R} = 30$, $\underline{R} = 1$, $d_{1s} = 5$, $d_{2s} = 0.2$, $d_{3s} = 0.1$, $d_{1n} = 1$, $d_{2n} = 0.1$, $d_{3n} = 0.05$, $\alpha_1 = 0.8$, $\alpha_2 = 0.6$, $\alpha_3 = 0.8$, $\alpha_4 = 0.6$.

Table 1. The Initial State of the USVs in the Simulation

Name	Initial position	Initial heading	Initial velocity
USV0	$[0, 20]^T$	0	$(0, 0)$
USV1	$[-10, 25]^T$	0	$(0, 0)$
USV2	$[-10, 15]^T$	0	$(0, 0)$
USV3	$[-20, 25]^T$	0	$(0, 0)$
USV4	$[-22, 15]^T$	0	$(0, 0)$
USV5	$[-20, 35]^T$	0	$(0, 0)$
USV6	$[-20, 5]^T$	0	$(0, 0)$

Figures 2, 3, 4 and 5 present the simulation results. Figure 2 illustrates that a flocking formation pattern is formed by 7 USVs guided by the given parameterized path and the virtual reference points. It can also be observed that the distance between neighboring connected USVs is preserved and USVs successfully avoiding the static obstacles. Figure 3 shows that the headings of USVs are synchronized, and their total velocities and yaw rates reach consensus. It can be observed that the heading alignment task and the velocity synchronization task are achieved. Figure 4 illustrates the magnitude of the d_{is}, $i = 0, \ldots, 6$, and the safe distance d_s. It can be observed that these distances consistently exceed the predefined safety threshold, providing numerical evidence that no collisions occur between the USVs and the static obstacles. Figure 5 illustrates the minimum magnitude of d_{ij}, $i = 0, \ldots, 6$, and the safe distance d_n. It can be observed that these distances consistently exceed the predefined safety threshold, providing numerical evidence that no collisions occur between the USVs and connectivity preservation are achieved.

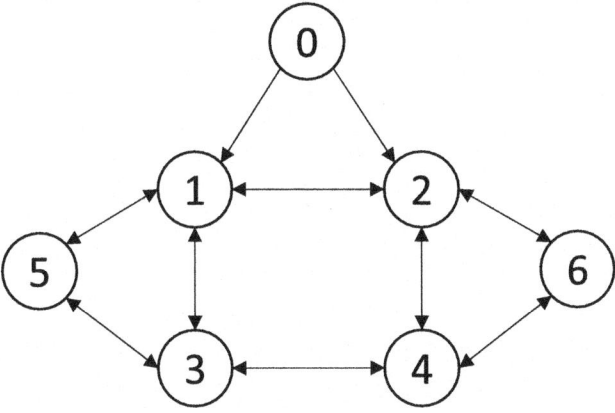

Fig. 1. Communication graph in the simulation.

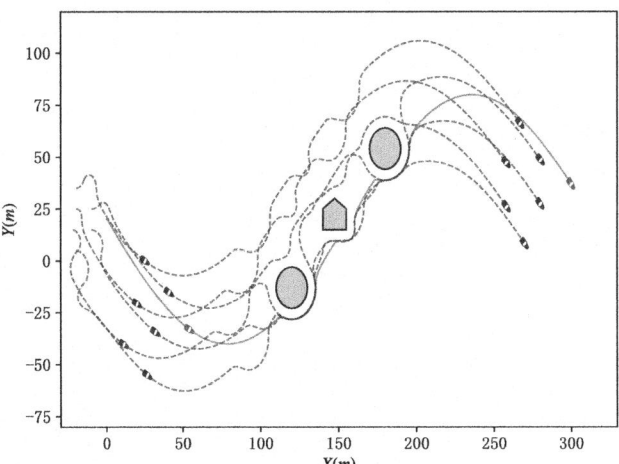

Fig. 2. Flocking pattern of USVs in the simulation.

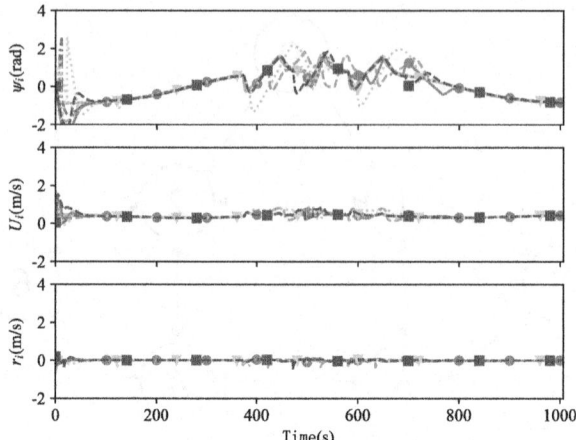

Fig. 3. The headings, total velocities and yaw rates of USVs in the simulation.

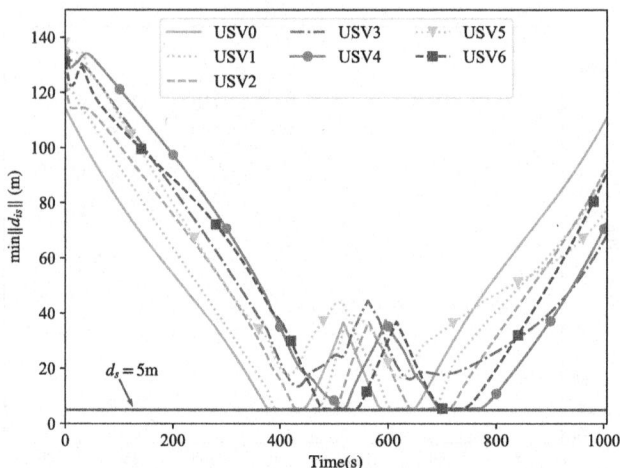

Fig. 4. The minimal magnitude of the collision vector between the USVs and the three static obstacles in the simulation.

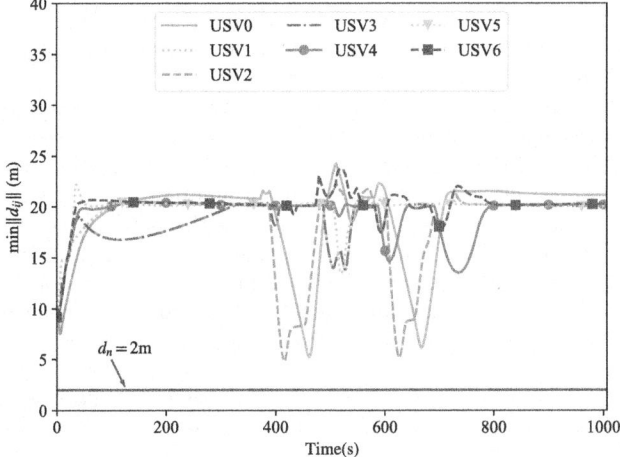

Fig. 5. The minimal magnitude of the collision vector between the USVs in the simulation.

5 Conclusion

In this paper, an guidance design method for flocking control of a fleet of USVs is proposed in the presence of obstacles. First, the control inputs of the virtual reference points are designed based on the artificial potential function, and the nominal guidance laws are designed for the leader USV and the follower USVs. Next, ECBFs are developed based on the closest collision point. Finally, a constrained QP problem incorporating the ECBFs is formulated to compute the optimal guidance laws. The simulation results validate the feasibility and effectiveness of the proposed safety-critical flocking control method.

References

1. Peng, Z., Wang, J., Wang, D., Han, Q.-L.: An overview of recent advances in coordinated control of multiple autonomous surface vehicles. IEEE Trans. Industr. Inf. **17**(2), 732–745 (2021)
2. Gu, N., Wang, D., Peng, Z., Wang, J., Han, Q.-L.: Advances in line-of-sight guidance for path following of autonomous marine vehicles: an overview. IEEE Trans. Syst. Man, Cybern. Syst. **53**(1), 12–28 (2023)
3. Xiang, X., Yu, C., Lapierre, L., Zhang, J., Zhang, Q.: Survey on fuzzy-logic-based guidance and control of marine surface vehicles and underwater vehicles. Int. J. Fuzzy Syst. **20**(2), 572–586 (2018)
4. Zhao, Y., Ma, Y., Hu, S.: USV formation and path following control via deep reinforcement learning with random braking. IEEE Trans. Neural Netw. Learn. Syst. **32**(12), 5468–5478 (2021)
5. Qin, H., Chen, H., Sun, Y., Wu, Z.: The distributed adaptive finite-time chattering reduction containment control for multiple ocean bottom flying nodes. Int. J. Fuzzy Syst. **21**(2), 607–619 (2018)

6. Cui, R., Yang, C., Li, Y., Sharma, S.: Adaptive neural network control of AUVs with control input nonlinearities using reinforcement learning. IEEE Trans. Syst. Man, Cybern. Syst. **47**(6), 1019–1029 (2017)
7. Peng, Z.H., Wang, D., Liu, H.T.H., Sun, G., Wang, H.: Distributed robust state and output feedback controller designs for rendezvous of networked autonomous surface vehicles using neural networks. Neurocomputing **115**(4), 130–141 (2013)
8. Peng, Z., Wang, D., Li, T., Han, M.: Output-feedback cooperative formation maneuvering of autonomous surface vehicles with connectivity preservation and collision avoidance. IEEE Trans. Cybern. **50**(6), 2527–2535 (2019)
9. Gu, N., Wang, D., Peng, Z.: Observer-based finite-time control for distributed path maneuvering of underactuated unmanned surface vehicles with collision avoidance and connectivity preservation. IEEE Trans. Syst. Man, Cybern. Syst. **51**(8), 5105–5115 (2021)
10. Ghapani, S., Mei, J., Ren, W., Song, Y.: Fully distributed flocking with a moving leader for Lagrange networks with parametric uncertainties. Automatica **67**, 67–76 (2016)
11. Feng, Z., Hu, G.: Connectivity-preserving flocking for networked Lagrange systems with time-varying actuator faults. Automatica **109**, 108509 (2019)
12. Peng, Z., Jiang, Y., Liu, L., Shi, Y.: Path-guided model-free flocking control of unmanned surface vehicles based on concurrent learning extended state observers. IEEE Trans. Syst. Man, Cybern. Syst. **53**(8), 4729–4739 (2023)
13. Chen, Y., Singletary, A., Ames, A.D.: Guaranteed obstacle avoidance for multi-robot operations with limited actuation: a control barrier function approach. IEEE Control Syst. Lett. **5**(1), 127–132 (2021)
14. Alan, A., Taylor, A.J., He, C.R., Orosz, G., Ames, A.D.: Safe controller synthesis with tunable input-to-state safe control barrier functions. IEEE Control Syst. Lett. **6**, 908–913 (2022)
15. Gu, N., Wang, D., Peng, Z., Wang, J.: Safety-critical containment maneuvering of underactuated autonomous surface vehicles based on neurodynamic optimization with control barrier functions. IEEE Trans. Neural Netw. Learn. Syst. **34**(6), 2882–2895 (2023)
16. Kolathaya, S., Ames, A.D.: Input-to-state safety with control barrier functions. IEEE Control Syst. Lett. **3**(1), 108–113 (2019)
17. Ames, A.D., Xu, X., Grizzle, J.W., Tabuada, P.: Control barrier function based quadratic programs for safety critical systems. IEEE Trans. Autom. Control **62**(8), 3861–3876 (2017)
18. Taylor, A.J., Singletary, A., Yue, Y., Ames, A.D.: A control barrier perspective on episodic learning via projection-to-state safety. IEEE Control Syst. Lett. **5**(3), 1019–1024 (2021)

Research on Hybrid Buoy Inclined Landing Motion Control

Dingze Wu[1,4], Qingchao Xia[1,2(✉)], Puzhe Zhou[3], and Canjun Yang[4]

[1] Ningbo Innovation Center, Zhejiang University, Ningbo 315100, China
mynameisxia@zju.edu.cn
[2] Hanjiang National Laboratory, Wuhan 430000, China
[3] Hangzhou Applied Acoustics Research Institute, Hangzhou 310023, China
[4] The State Key Laboratory of Fluid Power and Mechatronic Systems, Zhejiang University, Hangzhou 310027, China

Abstract. Bottom-sitting silent observation is a critical technique for acquiring ambient ocean noise and an effective approach to extending the operational time of virtual mooring. The pitch angle at which a hybrid buoy contacts the seabed is a key determinant of its post-landing stability, while the contact velocity determines whether the collision will damage the buoy. Premature adjustment of pitch angle or buoyancy will reduce the gliding distance during descent. To address this, an extreme landing strategy with an inclined bottom contact (maintaining a certain pitch angle and velocity upon bottom contact) is proposed. The minimum seabed height at which each adjustment mechanism begins to regulate was determined by analyzing the stability conditions for the inclined landing of the hybrid buoy. A sliding mode controller for the inclined landing motion and a dynamic model of the hybrid buoy were established. Preliminary validation through dynamic simulation demonstrates the feasibility and effectiveness of the proposed landing approach, providing a foundation for further experimental studies.

Keywords: inclined landing · underwater buoy · sliding mode control · dynamics simulation

1 Introduction

As one of the most widely used ocean observation platforms, Argo buoys are unable to conduct long-term continuous observation operations in designated sea areas due to the lack of lateral movement freedom. After the concept of underwater gliders was proposed, a technology called "virtual mooring" was attempted for long-term observation of designated sea areas [1]. During the virtual mooring operation, bottom-sitting silent observation is an effective means to extend the operational duration of the vehicle and

---

This work was supported by the National Natural Science Foundation of China (No. 52205074), the National Key Research and Development Program of China (No. 2021YFC2800202, No. 2021YFC2800X00), and the Open Fund Project of Hanjiang National Laboratory (No. KF2024005).

collect background noise data from specific marine areas. Ensuring a smooth and safe landing of the vehicle on the seabed has become a crucial step for long-term virtual mooring [2].

In recent years, various strategies have been proposed to enhance underwater vehicle landing performance. Wang et al. [3] introduced an active cushioning strategy that combines impedance parameter tuning with a spring-loaded inverted pendulum model, facilitating the free-dive deployment of an underwater hexapod robot. This method effectively alleviated issues related to excessive joint torque and toe impact forces during landing. Zhang et al. [4] optimized the landing gear configuration of a large-wingspan underwater glider, mitigating the influence of seabed currents and improving landing stability. Zhu et al. [5] investigated the effects of the AUV's water entry position and mass on its landing performance, establishing force models for the variable buoyancy system and vertical thrusters. They subsequently proposed two landing strategies: free-fall descent and vertical thrust control. Zhou et al. [2] proposed an adaptive robust sliding mode control based on a nonlinear disturbance observer to address the impact of system parameter uncertainty and external time-varying disturbances on vehicle landing, for vertical plane motion tracking control of the vehicle. In follow-up work, Zhou et al. [6] employed Lyapunov derivatives to derive the homogenized motion equations for pitch angle and vertical velocity tracking. Additionally, anti-windup compensators and disturbance observers were incorporated to enhance the robustness of the adaptive control system.

The aforementioned research has made significant contributions to the advancement of landing control strategies for underwater vehicles. However, a notable limitation remains: vehicles typically transition into either vertical or horizontal attitude well above the seabed, thereby reducing the effective glide distance during descent. During the landing process, collision is an unavoidable phenomenon. The utilization of seabed interaction within acceptable limits can effectively extend the gliding distance during descent. Furthermore, the reaction force exerted by the seabed can facilitate a more rapid adjustment of the attitude, promoting the vehicle to a stable landing configuration. This paper proposes an inclined landing strategy, wherein the hybrid buoy maintains a specified pitch angle and descent velocity at the moment of seabed contact. This approach is designed to maximize the gliding distance while ensuring post-contact attitude stability.

The main contributions of this paper are as follows: The stability conditions for the hybrid buoy during inclined landing are analyzed, determining the minimum seabed height required to trigger the buoyancy and center of gravity (CG) adjustment mechanisms; Based on sliding mode control, a controller for the inclined landing motion of the hybrid buoy was designed, achieving smooth switching control of pitch angle and depth during the landing process; A dynamic model of the hybrid buoy is constructed, and the effectiveness of the inclined landing control method is validated through dynamic simulation.

2 Hybrid Buoy Inclined Landing Process Analysis

To address the limitation of Argo buoys, which lack degrees of freedom for lateral motion, this study proposes a CG adjustment system based on an omnidirectional merged double-block mechanism. This system enables full-range CG adjustments within a specified axial range and allows for 360° circumferential rotation. The multiple degrees of freedom and wide range of adjustment of the CG give the hybrid buoy the ability to perform a range of functions, including in-situ steering, inclined landing motion, and vertical bottom-sitting silent observation. The CG adjustment mechanism comprises an axially movable platform and two weight blocks capable of full circumferential rotation. Assuming two weight blocks rotate around the $+y$ and $-y$ axes by angles δ_1 and δ_2, respectively, with weights m_{d1} and m_{d2}, and the distances from the mass centers of the two blocks to the central axis are r. The initial axial position of the movable platform is r_{d0}, the axial moving distance is r_d, and the weight is m_{d3}. For model simplification, the circumferential mass distribution of the movable platform is assumed to be uniform. When the buoy is in a vertical position, the double blocks are symmetrically distributed, so the static mass can also be considered to be uniformly distributed in the circumferential direction of the hybrid buoy. The position of the static mass can be represented as $(r_{sx}, 0, 0)$ and the weight can be expressed as m_s. The position of the hybrid buoy in the inertial coordinate system is denoted as $b_i = [x_i, y_i, z_i]$, and its attitude is represented by $\Omega_i = [\phi, \theta, \psi]$. The velocity in the body coordinate system is denoted as $v_b = [u, v, w]$, and the angular velocity is represented by $\dot{\Omega}_b = [p, q, r]$. In addition to the CG adjustment mechanism, the hybrid buoy incorporates a buoyancy regulation system, a phase-change chamber, a power generation module, side wings, tail wings, and a bottom-seating ring. The hybrid buoy prototype and the corresponding coordinate axes are illustrated in Fig. 1.

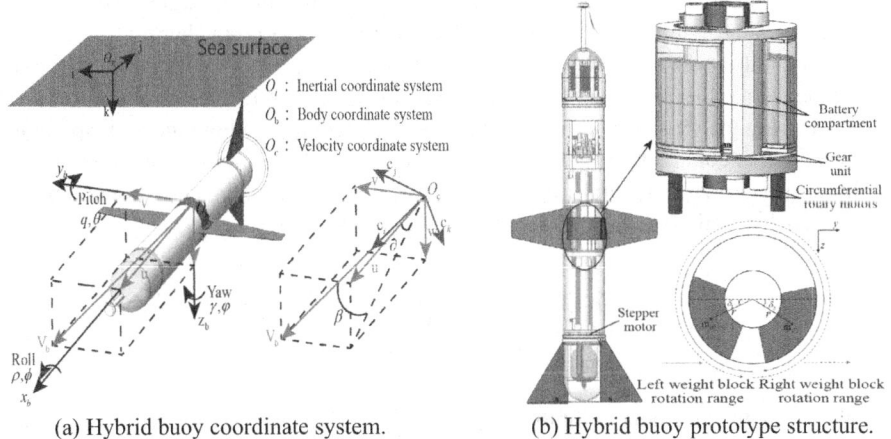

(a) Hybrid buoy coordinate system. (b) Hybrid buoy prototype structure.

Fig. 1. Hybrid buoy schematic.

During the process of the hybrid buoy landing, to prevent overturning upon seabed contact, it is crucial to not only adjust the CG to a position below the center of buoyancy

(CB), but also to ensure that the vertical projection of the CG lies within the region defined by the CB and the support surface at the point of contact [7]. Consequently, the adjustment time and the pitch angle at the moment of bottom contact must satisfy the following equation:

$$t_s \geq \frac{r_{bx} - r_{cx}}{v_d}$$
$$\theta_{d1} \geq \arctan(\frac{r_{cx}}{R_{bt} - r_{cy}}) \quad (1)$$

where v_d denotes the axial displacement velocity of the CG adjustment platform, R_{bt} represents the maximum contact radius when the buoy contacts the seabed, and r_{bx} denotes the relative displacement of the buoyancy adjustment mechanism. r_{cy} And r_{cx} represent the relative position of the CG, which can be expressed as:

$$r_{cx} = \frac{m_s r_{sx} + (m_{d1} + m_{d2} + m_{d3})(r_{d0} + r_d)}{m_s + m_{d1} + m_{d2} + m_{d3}}$$
$$r_{cy} = \frac{m_{d1} r \cos\delta_1 - m_{d2} r \cos\delta_2}{m_{d1} + m_{d2}} \quad (2)$$

In addition to the bottom-seating ring, the hybrid buoy is equipped with tail wings located at the rear. However, since the tail wings contribute only marginally to the overall contact area compared to the bottom-seating ring, their influence on the stability during seabed contact can be considered negligible. The axial movement of the CG adjustment mechanism consumes much more time than the circumferential rotation time of the weight blocks. The limiting bottom contact situation is when the CG and the CB are located on the same cross-section. The radius of the bottom-seating ring is 200 mm ($R_{bt} = 200$ mm). According to Eq. (1), the limiting bottom contact angle θ_{d1} ranges between 78° and 84°, depending on the circumferential rotation angle of the weight blocks. Given the symmetric distribution of the weight blocks on the hybrid buoy during the bottom-sitting observation, the subsequent analysis focuses solely on the scenario where the weight blocks are separated, corresponding to a limiting bottom contact angle of 78°. During the virtual mooring operation, the glider angles along the corresponding paths can be calculated by spatial trigonometric relations, as both the target and initial positions are known. The pitch angle of steady-state motion can be determined through its relationship with the angle of attack and the glide angle [8]:

$$\alpha_s = \frac{K_L}{2K_D}\tan(\gamma_s)(-1 + \sqrt{1 - 4\frac{K_D}{K_L^2}\cot(\gamma_s)(K_{D0}\cot(\gamma_s) + K_{L0})})$$
$$\theta_s = \gamma_s + \alpha_s \quad (3)$$

The axial displacement r_{ds} of the weight blocks during the steady-state gliding phase and the axial displacement r_{dl} of the weight blocks during the landing process can be determined using the following equation:

$$r_d = \frac{-m_b r_b - m_s r_s - \tan(\theta_s)(m_{d1} r \sin(\delta_1) + m_{d2} r \sin(\delta_2))}{m_{d1} + m_{d2} + m_{d3}}$$
$$+ \frac{((m_{f3} - m_{f1})uw + (K_{M_0} + K_M \alpha_d)\|v_b\|^2)}{(m_{d1} + m_{d2} + m_{d3})g\cos(\theta_s)} - r_{d0} \quad (4)$$

A high bottom contact velocity can lead to irreversible structural damage to the buoy and may also result in excessive penetration into the seabed sediment. Therefore, it is essential to ensure that the bottom contact velocity of the hybrid buoy remains within an acceptable range [9]. To evaluate the maximum contact stress experienced during seabed impact, a finite element analysis was performed using LS-DYNA. The simulations were conducted for impact velocities of 50 mm/s, 100 mm/s, 200 mm/s, and 300 mm/s, assuming a bottom contact angle of 78°. The corresponding simulation results are presented in Fig. 2.

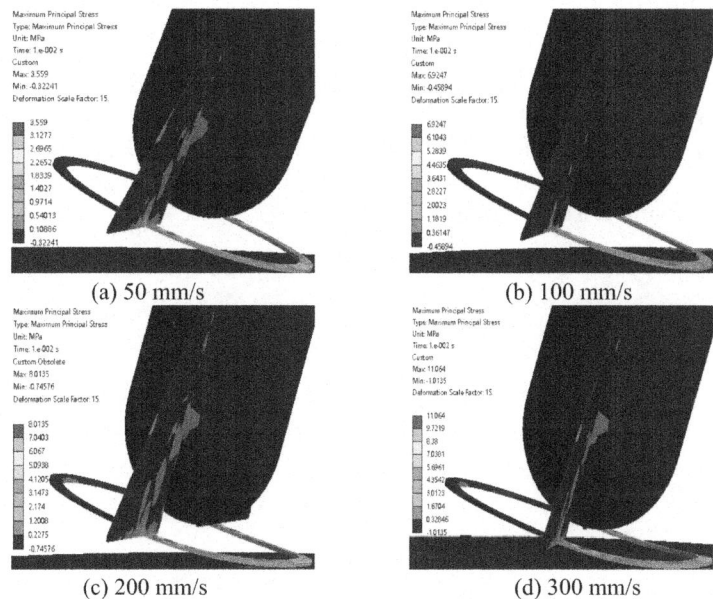

Fig. 2. Instantaneous maximum stress simulation for hybrid buoy bottom contact.

According to the seabed subsidence model proposed by Bekker [10], the relationship between the normal stress and the sinkage depth can be expressed as:

$$\sigma_z = \left(\frac{K_c}{w} + K_\varphi\right) Z^n \tag{5}$$

where σ_z represents the normal stress, w denotes the width of the indentation plate, and Z is the sinkage depth. K_c and K_φ correspond to the cohesive deformation modulus and frictional deformation modulus, respectively, while n is the subsidence index. These parameters are taken as 1620 N/m, 77100 N/m, and 0.7, respectively, as referenced in [10]. The normal stress calculated in the finite element simulation for each of the bottom contact velocities is 2.33 MPa, 4.73 MPa, 6.81 MPa, and 8.48 MPa. According to Eq. (5), the calculated seabed sinkage depths corresponding to these stress values are 1.22 mm, 3.36 mm, 5.66 mm, and 7.74 mm. Following seabed contact, the hybrid buoy is subjected to a reaction force, which imparts a transient angular velocity. To prevent the buoy from overturning due to the impact, it is essential to determine both the angular velocity acquired during the collision and the corresponding rotational angle until stabilization. To facilitate analysis, the landing motion is simplified to a two-dimensional plane, wherein the hybrid buoy is modeled as a rigid rectangular body of length a and width b, and the sideslip angle is assumed to be zero. Based on the generalized impulse-momentum theorem, the following governing equations can be derived:

$$m(\dot{x}_{c2} - \dot{x}_{c1}) = 0$$
$$m(\dot{z}_{c2} - \dot{z}_{c1}) = I \qquad (6)$$
$$J_c(\dot{\theta}_2 - \dot{\theta}_1) = -I \cdot \frac{a}{2}\cos(\theta)$$

To simplify the landing model, the seabed is assumed to be a smooth surface. The hybrid buoy is subjected only to a collision impulse along the z-axis, denoted as I, with $I_x = 0$. This leads to the following velocity conditions: $\dot{x}_{c2} = \dot{x}_{c1} = u\cos\theta$, $\dot{z}_{c1} = u\sin\theta$. Furthermore, the impact of the hybrid buoy upon the seabed is modeled as a perfectly elastic collision with a restitution coefficient $e = -1$.

$$m\dot{z}_{c2} - mu\sin\theta = I$$
$$\frac{1}{12}m(a+b)^2\dot{\theta}_2 = I\frac{a}{2}\cos(\theta) \qquad (7)$$
$$e = \frac{\dot{z}_{a2}}{\dot{z}_{a1}} = \frac{\dot{z}_{a2}}{u\sin(\theta)} = -1$$

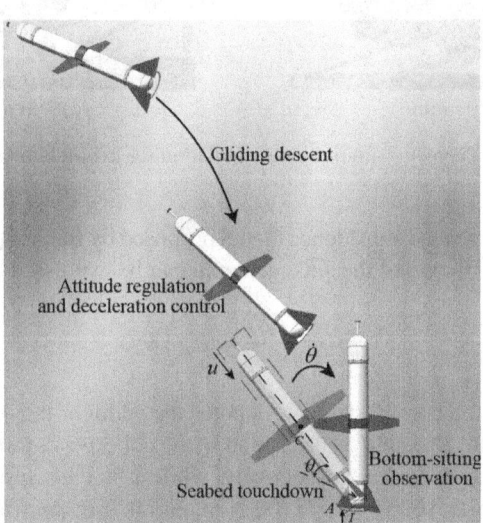

Fig. 3. Schematic diagram of the hybrid buoy landing process.

The landing process of the hybrid buoy is illustrated in Fig. 3, where the point of contact with the seafloor is defined as point A. According to Eq. (6), (7) and $v'_A =$

$v'_C + v'_{AC}$, the relationship between the z-axis velocity and angular velocity can be expressed as:

$$\dot{z}_{a2} = \frac{(a+b)^2 \dot{\theta}_2}{6a\cos(\theta)} + u\sin(\theta) + \frac{a}{2}\dot{\theta}_2 \cos(\theta) \tag{8}$$

The correlation among the pitch angular velocity at the moment of contact, the bottom contact angle, and the impact velocity is given by:

$$\dot{\theta}_2 = \frac{-6au\sin(2\theta)}{(a+b)^2 + 3a^2\cos^2(\theta)} \tag{9}$$

After the hybrid buoy tilts upon contacting the seabed and acquires a pitch angular velocity, it continues to experience a viscous hydrodynamic moment, which gradually decelerates the motion until the angular velocity reaches zero. The relationship between the pitch moment and the pitch angular acceleration can be expressed as:

$$\ddot{\theta}_2 = \frac{T_{DL2}}{J_c} = \frac{(K_{M0} + K_M\alpha + K_q q)(u^2 + w^2)}{J_c} \tag{10}$$

The time required for the angular velocity to decelerate to zero can be determined based on the relationship between angular velocity and time:

$$t_f = \frac{\dot{\theta}_2 J_c}{T_{DL2}} \tag{11}$$

The pitch angle rotated during this deceleration period is:

$$\Delta\theta_d = \int_0^{t_f} (\dot{\theta}_2 - \frac{T_{DL2}}{J_c} t) dt = -\frac{\dot{\theta}_2^2 J_c}{2 T_{DL2}} \tag{12}$$

To ensure that the hybrid buoy remains stable and does not tip over after deceleration, the following condition for θ_{d2} must be satisfied:

$$\theta_{d2} = \theta_{d1} + \Delta\theta_d < \pi - \arctan(\frac{r_{cx}}{R_{bt} - r_{cy}}) \tag{13}$$

The constraint on the bottom contact velocity required to prevent reverse tilting can be derived from Eq. (13) and (12). Considering the impact stresses, the depth of seafloor sediment sinking, and the non-tipping condition upon impact, the bottom contact velocity of the hybrid buoy is set at 0.1 m/s. The relationship between vertical velocity and buoyancy during the cushioning deceleration phase can be expressed as:

$$\dot{z}_i = -\sqrt{\frac{B\sin(\gamma)}{L\tan(\gamma) - D}} = -\sqrt{\frac{B\sin(\gamma)}{(K_{L0} + K_L\alpha)\tan(\gamma) - (K_{D0} + K_D\alpha^2)}} \tag{14}$$

From the above equation, the steady-state velocity u_{bs} can be determined when the hybrid buoy is in steady-state gliding motion with a buoyancy of B_s. Given a target speed of 0.1 m/s, the corresponding buoyancy to the extreme bottom contact angle is denoted as

B_t. The time required for buoyancy adjustment, transitioning from steady-state gliding to inclined landing motion, can be calculated based on the oil pump flow rate:

$$t_B = \frac{B_s - B_t}{\rho g q} \tag{15}$$

The distance traveled by the hybrid buoy during buoyancy regulation can be expressed as:

$$D_a = \int_0^{t_B} \dot{z}_i + \frac{-L(t)\cos(\gamma(t)) + D(t)\sin(\gamma(t)) + B_s + \rho g Q t}{m_s + m_{d1} + m_{d2} + m_{d3} + m_b} t dt \tag{16}$$

By incorporating the above equation with the time required for each mechanism to adjust, the minimum height from the seabed at which the CG and buoyancy adjustment mechanisms begin to adjust can be determined. This enables the computation of the corresponding landing trajectory of the hybrid buoy.

3 Hybrid Buoy Inclined Landing Controller Design

The inclined landing control of the hybrid buoy is composed of two primary components: buoyancy control and pitch angle control. The control variables for buoyancy and pitch angle adjustment are the axial displacement velocity of the weight blocks and the displacement of the hydraulic motor. The relationship among buoyancy, pitch angle, and motor velocity can be expressed as:

$$\dot{B} = kq$$
$$\ddot{\theta} = \frac{1}{J_2}((m_{f3} - m_{f1})uw - (r_{d1}P_{d1} + r_{d3}P_{d3})\dot{\theta}$$
$$- m_d g(r_{d1}\cos(\theta) + r_{d3}\sin(\theta)) + T_{DL2}) \tag{17}$$
$$\dot{r}_{d1} = v_d$$

where k denotes the conversion factor that maps hydraulic motor displacement to effective buoyancy. m_{f1} and m_{f3} represent the additional mass of the hybrid buoy. Sliding mode control (SMC) can effectively achieve control of nonlinear systems, while also having advantages such as fast response speed and fewer tuning parameters [11, 12]. Therefore, in this paper, SMC is selected for regulating both the buoyancy and CG adjustment mechanisms. The error and corresponding sliding surfaces for both control subsystems are defined as:

$$e_B = B - B_t$$
$$e_\theta = \theta - \theta_t$$
$$S_B = e_B + \lambda_B \int_0^t e_B(\tau)d\tau \tag{18}$$
$$S_\theta = \dot{e}_\theta + \lambda_\theta e_\theta$$

The control objective is to ensure that the control input u converges to zero in finite time, thereby driving the system state to the desired equilibrium. To achieve this, the following reaching law is employed:

$$\dot{s} = -\eta \tanh(s) - \eta s \tag{19}$$

The Lyapunov function is constructed for the sliding surface as follows:

$$V(s) = \frac{1}{2}s^2 \tag{20}$$

According to Eq. (19), (20), $\dot{V}(s)$ can be expressed as:

$$\dot{V}(s) = s\dot{s} = -\eta(\tanh(s)s + s^2) \tag{21}$$

According to the Lyapunov stability theorem, the condition that $\dot{V}(s)$ is negative definite ensures the convergence of the sliding surface s to zero. Therefore, the effectiveness of the SMC in achieving the reaching motion is guaranteed by maintaining $\eta > 0$. By combining Eq. (17) and Eq. (19), the resulting control inputs u_q and u_{v_c} for the buoyancy and pitch angle control systems can be expressed as:

$$\begin{aligned}
u_q &= \frac{1}{k}(-\eta_B \tanh(s_B) - \eta_B s_B - \lambda_B e_B) \\
r_{d1} &= \frac{1}{P_{d1}\dot{\theta} + m_d g \cos(\theta)}((m_{f3} - m_{f1})uw - r_{d3}P_{d3}\dot{\theta} \\
&\quad - m_d g r_{d3}\sin(\theta) + T_{DL2} + J_2(\eta_\theta \tanh(s_\theta) + \eta_\theta s_\theta + \lambda_\theta \dot{\theta})) \\
u_{v_c} &= \varepsilon_\theta \tanh(r_{d1}{'} - r_{d1})
\end{aligned} \tag{22}$$

where r'_{d1} denotes the actual position of the weight blocks. λ, η, ε represent the sliding surface gain, the convergence gain, and the output gain, respectively.

4 Dynamic Simulation Verification

Since the circumferential rotation of the weight blocks primarily affects the roll and yaw angles, with minimal impact on the pitch angle. Consequently, the movable mass is treated as a whole with a total mass m_d and a center of mass position defined as $r_d = [r_{dx}, r_{dy}, r_{dz}]$. For model simplification, both r_{sx} and r_{d0} are assumed to be zero. To simulate the landing motion of the hybrid buoy, dynamic equations based on the Newton-Euler method are established [13]:

$$\begin{pmatrix} \dot{b}_i \\ \dot{\Omega}_i \\ \ddot{\Omega}_b \\ \dot{v}_b \\ \dot{r}_d \\ \dot{m}_b \end{pmatrix} = \begin{pmatrix} R_b^i v_b \\ R_b^i \hat{\Omega}_b \\ J^{-1}\overline{T} \\ M^{-1}\overline{F} \\ v_d \\ u_{mass} \end{pmatrix} \tag{23}$$

$$\begin{aligned}
\overline{T} &= (J\dot{\Omega}_b + \hat{r}_d P_d + \hat{r}_b P_b) \times \dot{\Omega}_b + (Mv_b \times v_b) + (\dot{\Omega}_b \times r_d) \times P_d \\
&\quad + (\dot{\Omega}_b \times r_b) \times P_b + (m_d \hat{r}_d + m_b \hat{r}_b) g R_i^b k + R_c^b T_{ext} \\
\overline{F} &= (Mv_b + P_d + P_b) \times \dot{\Omega}_b + m_n g R_i^b k + R_c^b F_{ext} \\
F_{ext} &= [-D, 0, -L] \\
T_{ext} &= [0, T_{DL2}, 0] \\
M &= m_s E + M_f
\end{aligned} \qquad (24)$$

An inclined landing motion dynamics simulation of the hybrid buoy is conducted using MATLAB, in which the seabed with an inclination angle of 6° is set to be located at a water depth of 30 m. The hybrid buoy initially descends at a pitch angle of $-135°$ and then adjusts to $-102°$ as it approaches the seabed. The bottom contact velocity is set to 0.1 m/s. After contacting the seabed, the buoy will perform 90 s of bottom-setting silent observation, and then ascend by gliding at a pitch angle of $-45°$. The buoyancy regulation range is defined as ± 0.3 kg. Simulations were conducted using the MATLAB ode45 solver. As the hybrid buoy is designed for long-term observation missions, its energy capacity is limited. Therefore, the control strategy must minimize energy consumption and avoid energy consumption caused by frequent control. To this end, the control system operates at 5-s intervals.

The motion attitude of the hybrid buoy during simulation is illustrated in Fig. 4, while operational parameters and control signals are provided in Fig. 5. In these figures, the red line denotes the desired trajectory, the blue line represents the actual system response, and the green line indicates the command trajectory. As shown in Fig. 4, the inclined landing controller effectively guides the hybrid buoy through all mission phases: gliding descent, inclined landing, bottom-sitting observation, and gliding ascent.

The operational parameters in Fig. 5(a) further confirm the effective regulation of the buoyancy and CG adjustment systems using SMC. The buoyancy system control performed as anticipated, exhibiting negligible oscillation or overshoot. The maximum steady-state error of pitch angle control is 1.3% without overshooting. This discrepancy arises primarily from the differences in control mechanisms: the buoyancy adjustment is directly governed by the displacement of a hydraulic motor linked to an external oil bladder, which behaves linearly, while pitch angle regulation is achieved via the axial displacement of the weight blocks, introducing nonlinearity into the system. The velocity of the hybrid buoy decreases rapidly to zero after impacting, while gaining a large angular velocity for a brief period, which is consistent with a normal bottom contact scenario. As seen in Fig. 5(b), the controller exhibited no frequent oscillations and converged to zero within a short duration, thereby minimizing energy consumption throughout the control process. These results collectively demonstrate the effectiveness of the proposed inclined landing motion control, which not only maximizes the descent gliding distance under limited energy constraints but also ensures the safety and post-landing stability of the hybrid buoy.

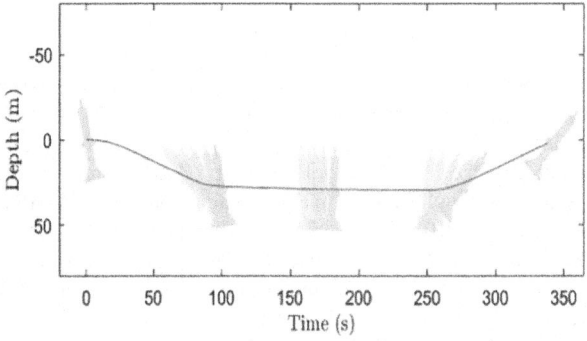

Fig. 4. Hybrid buoy operational attitude simulation results

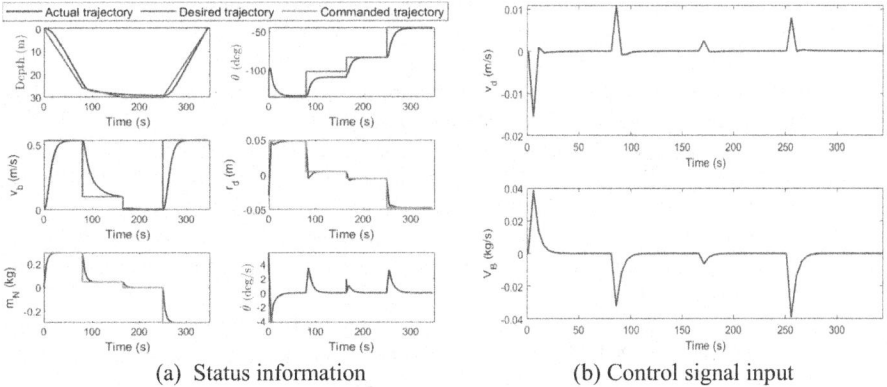

(a) Status information   (b) Control signal input

Fig. 5. Hybrid buoy operation parameter simulation results

5 Conclusion

This study presents a control strategy for the inclined landing motion of a hybrid buoy, aimed at maximizing gliding distance during descent. By analyzing the stability conditions of the hybrid buoy after bottom contact, the maximum bottom contact speed and bottom contact angle within the safety range are determined. The relationship among the minimum seabed height required for the center of gravity adjustment mechanism and buoyancy adjustment mechanism begins to regulate, the velocity, and pitch angle during steady-state gliding was established. Meanwhile, a sliding mode controller for inclined landing motion and a dynamic model of the hybrid buoy were established, and the feasibility of inclined landing motion control was initially verified through dynamic simulation. However, these simulations were conducted under idealized environmental conditions. Future research will focus on the inclined landing motion of hybrid buoys under varied seabed conditions. The realism of the collision model will be enhanced by incorporating a contact model for seabed sediments. Additionally, lake trials are planned to assess the robustness and practical applicability of the proposed method.

References

1. Yang, C., et al.: Research on ocean-current-prediction-based virtual mooring strategy for the portable underwater profilers. Appl. Ocean Res. **142**, 103810 (2024). https://doi.org/10.1016/j.apor.2023.103810
2. Zhou, H., Wei, Z., Zeng, Z., Yu, C., Yao, B., Lian, L.: Adaptive robust sliding mode control of autonomous underwater glider with input constraints for persistent virtual mooring. Appl. Ocean Res. **95**, 102027 (2020). https://doi.org/10.1016/j.apor.2019.102027
3. Wang, L., Lu, Y., Zhang, Y., Chen, W., Zhao, X., Gao, F.: Design and soft-landing control of underwater legged robot for active buffer landing on seabed. Ocean Eng. **266**, 112764 (2022). https://doi.org/10.1016/j.oceaneng.2022.112764
4. Zhang, B., Song, B., Mao, Z., Li, B.: Layout optimization of landing gears for an underwater glider based on particle swarm algorithm. Appl. Ocean Res. **70**, 22–31 (2018). https://doi.org/10.1016/j.apor.2017.11.008
5. Zhu, X., Song, B., Zhang, D., Wang, S.: Analysis of landing strategies and influencing factors of an autonomous underwater vehicle. Ocean Eng. **237**, 109448 (2021). https://doi.org/10.1016/j.oceaneng.2021.109448
6. Zhou, H., et al.: Robust adaptive control of underwater glider for bottom sitting-oriented soft landing. Ocean Eng. **293**, 116725 (2024). https://doi.org/10.1016/j.oceaneng.2024.116725
7. De Viragh, Y., Bjelonic, M., Bellicoso, C.D., Jenelten, F., Hutter, M.: Trajectory optimization for wheeled-legged quadrupedal robots using linearized ZMP constraints. IEEE Robot. Autom. Lett. **4**, 1633–1640 (2019). https://doi.org/10.1109/LRA.2019.2896721
8. Wu, D., et al.: Research on the dynamical behavior of air-dropped underwater profiler and virtual mooring strategy for variable pitch angle. Ocean Eng. **328**, 121053 (2025). https://doi.org/10.1016/j.oceaneng.2025.121053
9. Zhu, Y., Xu, X., Wang, J., Yang, C., Li, Q., Cai, M.: A hybrid underwater profiler used for persistent monitoring. In: OCEANS 2015 - MTS/IEEE Washington, pp. 1–5. IEEE, Washington (2015). https://doi.org/10.23919/OCEANS.2015.7401913
10. Xiong, H., Chen, Y., Li, Y., Zhu, H., Yu, C., Zhang, J.: Dynamic model-based back-stepping control design for-trajectory tracking of seabed tracked vehicles. J. Mech. Sci. Technol. **36**, 4221–4232 (2022). https://doi.org/10.1007/s12206-022-0740-3
11. Mat-Noh, M., Arshad, M.R., Mohd-Mokhtar, R., Khan, Q.: Back-stepping sliding mode control strategy for autonomous underwater glider. In: 2017 13th International Conference on Emerging Technologies (ICET), pp. 1–6. IEEE, Islamabad (2017). https://doi.org/10.1109/ICET.2017.8281729
12. Zhang, X., Yao, B., Lian, L., Mao, Z.: Adaptive neural network sliding mode tracking control with prescribed performance for an underwater glider under input saturation. Ocean Eng. **307**, 118150 (2024). https://doi.org/10.1016/j.oceaneng.2024.118150
13. Zhang, S., Yu, J., Zhang, A., Zhang, F.: Spiraling motion of underwater gliders: modeling, analysis, and experimental results. Ocean Eng. **60**, 1–13 (2013). https://doi.org/10.1016/j.oceaneng.2012.12.023

Fast and Automatic Dock for Precise UAV Landing on a USV in Marine Environment

Chongfeng Liu[1], Zhongzhong Cao[1], Zisui Guo[1], Ruoyu Xu[2], Cheng Liang[3], and Huihuan Qian[1(✉)]

[1] The Chinese University of Hong Kong, Shenzhen, Shenzhen, China
hhqian@cuhk.edu.cn
[2] The Chinese University of Hong Kong, Sha Tin, Hong Kong
[3] Shenzhen Institute of Artificial Intelligence and Robotics for Society, Shenzhen, China

Abstract. The cooperative system of Unmanned Aerial Vehicles (UAVs) and Unmanned Surface Vessels (USVs) have been widely applied in the marine field and show great potential. However, limited by the endurance of UAVs, achieving the safe recovery and landing of UAVs in the disturbed marine environment has become an urgent problem to be solved. This paper proposes a solution that enables UAVs to land precisely and safely on a USV and be locked in the disturbed marine environment. The proposed solution is elaborately demonstrated and verified through docking design, landing simulation, and field experiments. Specifically, using the visual information from ArUco markers, UAVs can automatically identify the landing platform and dock with it, establishing a tethered-UAV system for subsequent landing. This study simulates the automatic identification process of the landing platform by UAVs in a simulated marine environment are driven by actual disturbance data and further conduct multiple sets of outdoor landing experiments. The experimental results show that the proposed system can effectively achieve the precise landing and positioning of UAVs. Notably, the proposed solution achieves the autonomous landing of UAVs under Sea State II conditions for the first time. Moreover, this method can lock UAVs within a limited space, enabling multiple UAVs to land on one USV. It also provides possibilities for post-landing operations such as energy replenishment.

Keywords: UAV landing · UAV-USV · docking · mechanical design

1 Introduction

In the past few decades, Unmanned Aerial Vehicle (UAV) technology has witnessed extensive applications in various domains, including photography [1,2], logistics and delivery [3], inspection [4,5] and so on. Remarkably, integrating UAVs with Unmanned Surface Vessels (USVs) has opened up new possibilities in marine applications. The UAV-USV cooperative system combines the aerial perspective of UAVs and the long-range mobility and good payload ability of USVs [6]. However, the recovery or landing of UAVs in the UAV-USV system poses a significant challenge. Unlike landing on stationary or land-based moving platforms, landing on a USV's platform under the disturbed sea surface is far more complex. The constantly changing sea disturbance, including winds, waves, and currents, introduces uncertainties that make precise landing and positioning difficult for UAVs. This study addresses the issues of accurate UAV landing and positioning on USV landing platforms in such challenging environments.

In fact, the problem of UAV landing on stationary platforms has been well-solved [8,9]. Researchers are still working on achieving precise UAV landings on moving objects, which is affected by factors such as vehicle speed, road surface flatness, lighting conditions, and wind speed [7]. References [10–12,14,15], and [16] discuss various UAV landing methods. In these methods, researchers have applied, RTK GPS, vision and image processing technologies, anti-interference algorithms [13], state estimation [15], trajectory planning and tracking techniques [14]. Some of the researchers have enabled UAVs to land on moving land vehicles with centimeter-level precision [28]. However, these methods can't guarantee that every landing attempt of the UAV is at the same landing point, which means that the landing platforms for UAVs still need to be relatively large. Moreover, these studies do not address or consider the positioning of UAVs after touchdown. As a result, UAVs are prone to displacement or falling on moving or bumpy vehicle surfaces. Researchers tend to focus only on a single technique and fail to consider the overall issues of UAV landing and afterward positioning.

In disturbed water environments, the landing platform can exhibit up to six Degrees of Freedom (DoFs), while mobile targets on the ground typically have only three DoFs. The landing problem in such an environment faces greater challenges compared to that on land. Many researchers have used large USVs [16] or large landing platforms [17], and have predominantly been conducted in calm inland lakes. In [18], despite using a relatively large landing surface, the UAV nealy slid off the platform into the water because there was no immediate positioning of the UAV after landing. On the other hand, many previous studies have only focused on the UAV's positioning mechanism design while neglecting comprehensive real-world validation [29].

Tethered UAV landing is considered a promising method for solving the problem in water environments with significant disturbances [19,20]. In our previous work [31], we proposed a solution of establishing a tethered UAV system to guide its landing, enabling multiple UAVs to land and park on a limited platform, proving the system's effectiveness and feasibility. At the same time, we solved the problem that the flight distance of a traditional tethered UAV is restricted by the rope [21]. However, this work is very unstable in successfully achieving a tethered UAV state since the UAV is manually remote controlled and it is difficult to make a payload to a floating platform for docking. Moreover, the experiments were conducted on an inland lake where external interference was very limited. Subsequently, we further proposed using a collaborative manipulator with 7 DoFs to grab the UAV to assist it in quickly achieving a tethered state, leveraging the flexibility of the manipulator to speed up the establishing tethered-state process [22]. Among them, a Motion Capture (MoCap) system was used to solve the mutual positioning problem between the end effector of the manipulator and the UAV. However, the cost of this solution has increased significantly due to the introduction of the manipulator and the MoCap system, and it also occupies a lot of space on the USV's deck. Shanghai University designed a docking device. Through this docking device, another tethered UAV can dock with the flying and be recovered UAV, thereby achieving recovery [23]. This method ingeniously combines the tethered UAV method. However, they only demonstrated the docking process, and the effectiveness of this solution is unpredictable under significant interference.

Summarizing all the limitations mentioned above, this paper proposes an solution to achieve highly autonomous and precise landing, and positioning of the UAV in disturbed marine environments. The work presented in this paper is actually an upgrade based on our previous works. By achieving the goal of fast and automatic docking, we have overcome the limitations of the previous works. From simulations to real-world experiments, we have for the first time achieved accurate and safe landing as well as stable and reliable positioning of UAVs under Sea State II, fully verifying the advantages of the proposed solution. Here is a video link summarizing the content of the paper: https://github.com/chongfengliu/ICIRA2025-Paper-Demo. The main contributions of this paper are as follows:

1. This work presents a fully autonomous method for safe and accurate UAV landing under Sea State II, demonstrated for the first time. The whole solution pave the way for the UAV energy replenishment after landing.
2. The docking system we proposed can establish a fast and automatic docking in a disturbed environment with reliable performance.

The paper is organized as follows. Section 2 presents the overall system. Section 3 covers the analysis of establishing a stable docking, including error estimation and alignment validation. Section 4 conducts the simulation of UAV landing, and Sect. 5 elaborates on the process of real experiments outdoors and at sea. Followed by the conclusion and future work.

2 Overall Systems Description

The left parts of Fig. 1 shows that the main components of the overall system includes a UAV onboard release mechanism and a ground station (working as the landing platform) on the USV.

2.1 Components

The release mechanism, as shown in Fig. 1(c) is an onboard subsystem of the UAV. Its primary function is to release or retract a circular metal block (dashed

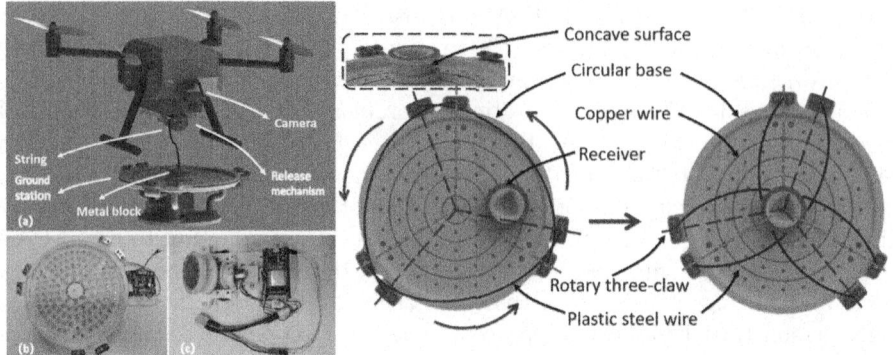

Fig. 1. Left: overall system. Right: the principle of alignment driven by the motor. The plastic steel wires form an open state initially and change to a closed state after the alignment. The metal block is locked tightly with a concave surface.

red circle in Fig. 1(c)). This metal block is connected to one end of the rope in the release system, and the other end of the rope is fixed to a reel, which is attached to the output shaft of the motor. When the block is released, it becomes a suspended load of the UAV. The motor can wind and unwind the string to control the lowering and retracting of the metal block.

As shown in Fig. 1, our proposed ground station (landing platform) contains a motor, and a specially designed circular base with magnets embedded inside. The main feature of the station is the stable align and lock function. The green dashed area in Fig. 1(b) is the contact area for the metal block in release subsystem, and the red dashed area is the lock position. The size of the station is larger than the mentioned metal block, which allows the block to touch down at random locations on the station base, providing a certain degree of error tolerance. The right part of Fig. 1 shows the principle of aligning for position correction. Three plastic steel ropes with a certain degree of elasticity are employed here. Their two ends are respectively connected to the circular base (the red dashed lines) and a rotary three-claw (the blue dashed lines). This rotary three-claw can rotate clockwise or counterclockwise with a certain angle under the drive of the motor to achieve an opening or closing action. The receiver has a concave surface design, which fits the plastic steel wire. During the closing action, the receiver will move to the center of the circular base (the lock area in Fig. 1(c)).

As mentioned, the system proposed in this paper is an upgrade of our previous works. Similarly, the UAV tries to establish a tethered state first, then the UAV is guided to descent driven by a motor until the UAV touches down. The specific landing process is as follows:

1. Visual Positioning: The unmanned aerial vehicle (UAV) flies above the landing platform and continuously acquires its relative position to the landing platform by identifying the markers.

2. Docking: When the UAV is in a proper position, the release system will rapidly release the metal block. The iron block comes into contact with the ground station and is quickly aligned to the center position and is locked.
3. Descent: The UAV slowly descends via the string-retracting system and finally lands at the center of the ground station.
4. Re-takeoff: The ground station can be opened. With the metal block unrestrained, the UAV takes off again.

2.2 Electronics

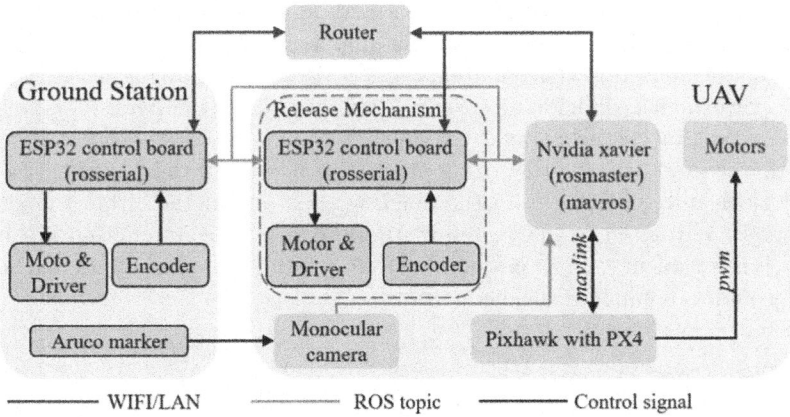

Fig. 2. The electronics.

Our entire system operates within the Robot Operating System (ROS) architecture, as shown in the right sub-figure of Fig. 2. The UAV uses the PIXHAWK [24] and the open-sourced Flight Control Unit (FCU) of PX4 [25]. The upper-level component employs the NVIDIA Jetson Xavier, and we use a monocular camera to detect Aruco markers. The onboard release mechanism and the ground station are independent subsystems, but they need to establish wireless communication during operation. We adopted the ESP32 chip, a powerful microprocessor with flexible self-networking capabilities, enabling the two to automatically establish wireless communication. Both subsystems use Direct Current (DC) motors and a motor driver for automatic control. Among them, the gray boxes represent the modules we designed, and the blue boxes represent off-the-shelf components. The clutch (mentioned in Section III) is controlled via a solid-state relay triggered by a GPIO pin on the ESP32. This was accounted for in the ESP32 PCB design, which also features a built-in motor driver interface. Through the *rosserial* package, the control board can be transformed into a ROS node. Mavros is a ROS package that based on mavlink protocol offers the communication interface between the high level processor and the Pixhawk. With the Mavros, the user can control the UAV under ROS framework. As for the relative position estimation, ArUco marker that includes a set of QR codes is applied to feed back depth information [26].

3 Fast and Automatic Docking

Due to the significant disturbances inherent in the marine environment, two critical issues must be addressed in the docking system: how to ensure that the metal block can be quickly connected to the ground station during rapid release and how to achieve reliable locking after connection. One solution involves fully lowering the metal block, treating it as a suspended payload of the UAV, so that contact can be established through landing pad localization and UAV trajectory planning. However, this approach imposes stringent requirements on the UAV's disturbance rejection capability and trajectory tracking accuracy, making stable performance difficult to ensure. Moreover, given the persistent presence of environmental disturbances, once contact occurs, the system must detect it immediately and activate the locking mechanism without delay. Otherwise, the metal block may separate from the magnetic field and detach from the ground station. To address these challenges, we propose a docking system that integrates a clutch mechanism with a contact detection module, enabling rapid and secure locking under dynamic marine conditions.

3.1 Fast Dock Design

In the proposed release mechanism, the clutch is employed to decouple the motor and the reducer from the reel, enabling rapid deployment of the metal block. The clutch remains engaged during retraction or when the block is required to stay in its stowed position, allowing the motor via a predefined reduction ratio to directly drive the reel and regulate the retraction speed. As illustrated in the left part of Fig. 3, the half-sectional view presents both the engaged and disengaged states of the clutch. In the disengaged state, the reel (green module) is mechanically isolated from the motor and reducer, permitting rapid descent of the metal block. In contrast, when the clutch is engaged, the reel is actively driven by the motor to execute the retraction.

3.2 Contact Detection Design

As mentioned, when the block contacts the ground station, the ground station needs to align and lock as soon as possible; otherwise, the UAV may escape from the base. Thus, we have considered adding a contact detection function to detect the contact immediately. As the right part of Fig. 3 shows, the idea of contact detection is based on what we call equivalent key circuitry, similar to identifying a key presses. Here, copper wires are embedded into the base's surface, arranged in concentric circles, and the distance between two adjacent wires is less than the diameter of the metal block. Therefore, the adjacent copper wires will be

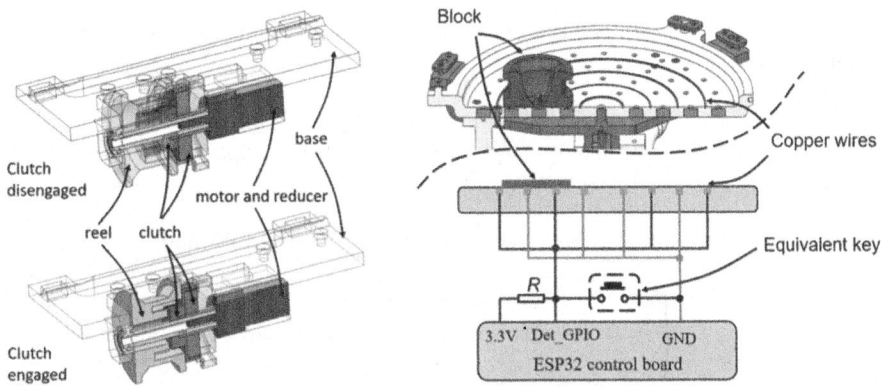

Fig. 3. Left: Illustration of the clutch's two operational states. In the disengaged state, the reel is mechanically decoupled from the motor, allowing the metal block to descend freely. When engaged, the motor directly drives the reel, enabling controlled retraction. Right: Schematic of the contact detection mechanism. Electrical conduction between adjacent copper wires connects the blue and green wires, functioning similarly to a keypress trigger.

conductive when the block contacts the surface of the ground station, like a key pressed down.

One of the adjacent wires is connected to the digital ground (GND) and the other is connected to one GPIO of the controller ESP32, as the green and blue lines imply. The GPIO is also connected to the 3.3V power source through a pull-up resistor of R. Before the contact occurs, the GPIO voltage is high, and it changes to a low voltage when the receiver contacts the ground station.

4 Simulation

Validating our system in the real sea requires a great deal of preparatory work, in this section, we conducted landing experiments in simulation in advance.

4.1 UAV Dynamics

The UAV position dynamics can be obtained based on the Newton's ruler.

$$\begin{bmatrix} \dot{v}_x \\ \dot{v}_y \\ \dot{v}_z \end{bmatrix} = g \begin{bmatrix} 0 \\ 0 \\ 1 \end{bmatrix} - \frac{f_T}{m} \boldsymbol{R}_b^e \begin{bmatrix} 0 \\ 0 \\ 1 \end{bmatrix} \quad (1)$$

where f_T is the total thrust from the propellers, m is the mass of the UAV, and element $\dot{v}_x$, $\dot{v}_y$, $\dot{v}_z$ represent the acceleration the UAV along each axis. The $\boldsymbol{R}_b^e$ is the transfer matrix from the UAV body coordinate system to the earth coordinate system (inertial coordinate system), which can be expressed as equation shows.

$$R_b^e = \begin{bmatrix} c_\theta c_\psi & -c_\varphi s_\psi + s_\varphi s_\theta c_\psi & s_\varphi c_\psi + c_\varphi s_\theta c_\psi \\ c_\theta s_\psi & c_\varphi c_\psi + s_\varphi s_\theta c_\psi & -s_\varphi c_\psi + c_\varphi s_\theta s_\psi \\ -s_\theta & c_\theta s_\varphi & c_\theta c_\varphi \end{bmatrix} \quad (2)$$

Thus, the position dynamics of UAV can be further obtained.

$$\begin{cases} \dot{v}_x = -\frac{f_T}{m}(\cos\psi \sin\theta \cos\phi + \sin\psi \sin\phi) \\ \dot{v}_y = -\frac{f_T}{m}(\sin\psi \sin\theta \cos\phi + \cos\psi \sin\phi) \\ \dot{v}_z = g - \frac{f_T}{m}\cos\phi \cos\theta \end{cases} \quad (3)$$

where θ, ψ, ϕ are the eluer angles. The UAV dynamics implies how to control the UAV for basic motions.

4.2 Simulation Results

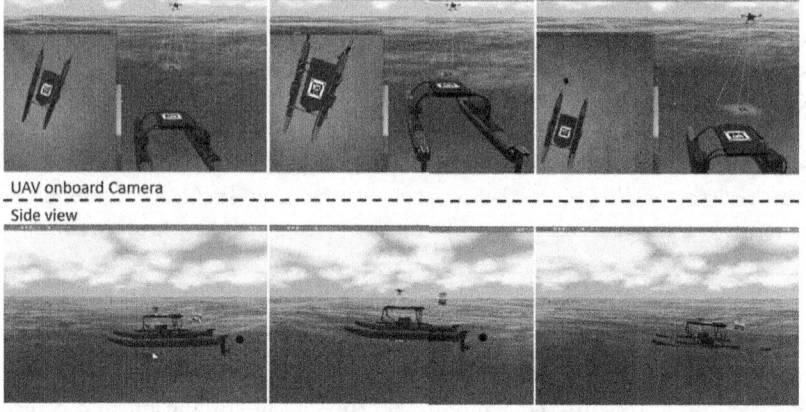

Fig. 4. UAV landing in simulation.

We utilized the Virtual RobotX (VRX) simulation system, which is a general-purpose open-source testing tool [27]. As a plugin for Gazebo, it can simulate the operational behavior of USVs in complex marine environments. We employed the simulation model of a common USV, the Wave Adaptive Modular Vessel (WAM-V). In this experiment, we placed a set of multi-scale ArUco markers on the landing platform of the USV [30]. We collected over 100 h of disturbance data. Part of this data was collected in the real marine environment from the sea areas of Qixing Bay in Shenzhen and Eastern Bay in Huizhou, China. The simulation framework is driven by real-world ocean disturbance data, encompassing wave elevation and pose information obtained from RTK GPS and IMU sensors (available at: https://github.com/chongfengliu/Ocean-Disturbance-Data). Using this dataset, realistic ocean wave conditions were reconstructed to emulate a representative marine environment. This setup facilitated the development of a real-time operable UAV landing system with practical fidelity. The simulation environment serves as a valuable tool for informing and guiding the design of autonomous UAV landing strategies under disturbed sea conditions. Figure 4 shows the simulation results. The top row of the figures mainly presents the perspective of the airborne camera. From the sub-figures in the bottom row, it can be seen that although the USV is heaving up and down, the drone can eventually land on the deck.

5 Experiments

5.1 Block Release Strategy

The UAV identifies the ArUco marker using its onboard monocular camera and determines its relative position to the ground station via coordinate transformation. Upon arriving at a location approximately 1 meter above the ground station, the UAV transitions into a stable hovering state, initiating the landing sequence. The UAV will determine the distance from the QR code on the platform by recognizing it, and then calculate the offset in the horizontal direction to determine when to throw the string. Assume that d_x and d_y respectively represent the relative position difference between the two. When d_x and d_y are both less than a preset value, the release mechanism release the metal block. Then the metal block will come into contact with the ground station, and then be quickly aligned and locked. Although the UAV did not successfully dock at once during some tests, that is, the UAV enabled the clutch and released the metal block, but it missed the docking, based on our control logic, the wincher system will change the state of the clutch and immediately retract the string. Once the release conditions are met again, a second drop will be performed, as shown in the left sub-figure of Fig. 6.

5.2 Experiment A: Precise Landing on an Undulating Platform

Before the sea trials, a comprehensive series of landing experiments was conducted on land at the campus of the Chinese University of Hong Kong, Shenzhen. To replicate wave-induced motion, an oscillating platform was constructed using a lever-based mechanism. The entire process was documented on video for analysis. As illustrated in Fig. 5, the UAV proceeded through the phases of approach, docking, descent, and final touchdown. The top sub-figures display footage captured from an external viewpoint, while the bottom sub-figures show the UAV's onboard camera perspective, annotated with ArUco marker detection results.

The right sub-figure of Fig. 6 visualizes the detection status of ArUco markers during the UAV's descent after establishing the tethered-UAV system, where

Fig. 5. UAV landing in an artificial heave platform. Upper row figure: the testing scenarios; Lower row figures are the collected sequences from the onboard camera of UAV. Also, the tracking of Aruco marker are highlighted.

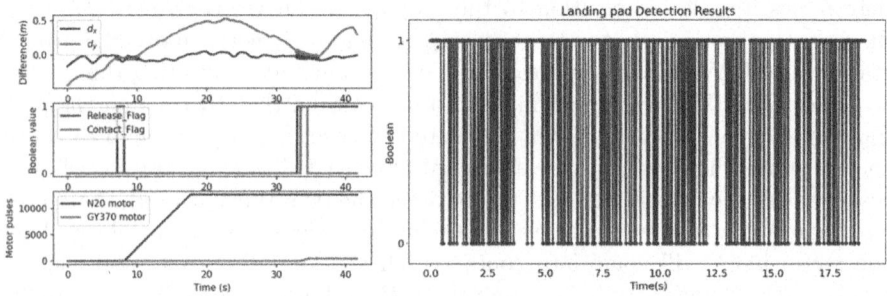

Fig. 6. Experimental results. Left: the logic of releasing the metal block for establishing docking. Right: The Aruco markers detection results during UAV descent.

a value of 1 indicates successful detection and 0 indicates a loss. The overall detection rate during descent reached 70%, demonstrating the robustness of the tethered-UAV system. Despite intermittent marker loss, the system provided sufficient visual feedback to ensure accurate landing.

5.3 Experiment B: Precise Landing on Maritime Environments

The set of experiments was conducted in the real-world marine environment in Eastern Bay, Huizhou, China. The results demonstrated that even under Sea State II, the UAV could land safely, stably with high precision. It is noteworthy that in over 20 landing experiments, despite significant environmental disturbances such as wind and waves, the UAV was able to land accurately without falling into the water. In fact, after verifying the docking and position correction, once the docking was successful, the safety of the UAV was ensured. Figure 7 and Fig. 8 respectively show the landing scenario of the unmanned aerial vehicle

Fig. 7. Sequences of UAV landing in real world maritime environment. The blue circle represents the UAV and the red circle indicates the metal block. (Color figure online)

(UAV) under Sea State II and the attitude data of the IMU. Among them, the two main pitch and roll angles of the IMU reached 10.2 degrees and 9.6 degrees respectively. Such amplitudes can only be obtained under Sea State II. Figure 9 shows some other disturbance data, such as the drift distance of the ship per second, the average wind speed, and the undulation data.

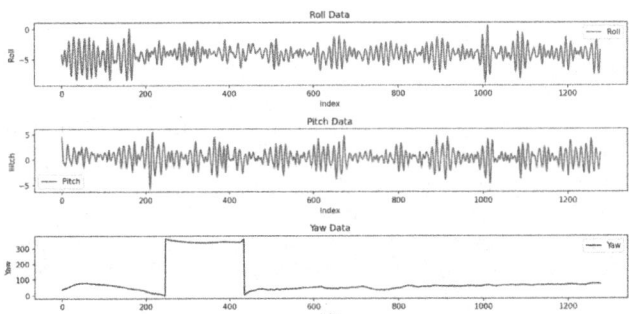

Fig. 8. The IMU data visualizations.

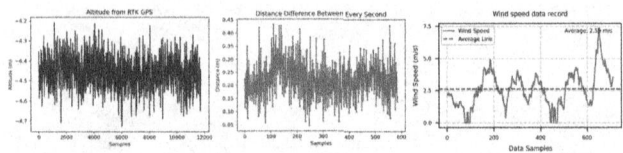

Fig. 9. The disturbance data visualization including the boat undulation, drifting and wind speed.

6 Conclusion and Future Work

In this paper, we demonstrated the precise UAV landing in the real-world maritime environment of Sea State II for the first time. The specific idea is to establish a tethered-UAV for precise landing based on the proposed fast and automatic docking system. The UAV landing scheme proposed in this paper has a very high landing accuracy, and also finishes the positioning of the UAV after touchdown. The high accuracy also means the landing space is much smaller than others' works.

In future work, we aim to incorporate automated charging and battery-swapping capabilities, along with conducting extended validation in real-world marine environments. An integrated collaborative platform will be developed to exploit the synergistic capabilities of heterogeneous robotic systems, allowing for efficient coordination between multiple UAVs and a single USV.

Funding. This work was supported in part by the NSFC under Grant 62473324, in part by the Guangdong Basic and Applied Basic Research Foundation, and University Stability Support Program from Shenzhen Science and Technology Innovation Commission under Grant 2022A1515240063.

References

1. Sieberth, T., Wackrow, R., Chandler, J.H.: Automatic detection of blurred images in UAV image sets. ISPRS J. Photogramm. Remote. Sens. **122**, 1–16 (2016). https://doi.org/10.1016/j.isprsjprs.2016.09.010
2. Li, X., Yang, L.: Design and implementation of UAV intelligent aerial photography system. In: Proceedings of the 4th International Conference on Intelligent Human-Machine Systems and Cybernetics (IHMSC), pp. 26–27. IEEE, Nanchang (2012). https://doi.org/10.1109/IHMSC.2012.144
3. Kuru, K., Ansell, D., Khan, W., Yetgin, H.: Analysis and optimization of unmanned aerial vehicle swarms in logistics: an intelligent delivery platform. IEEE Access **7**, 15804–15831 (2019). https://doi.org/10.1109/ACCESS.2019.2892716
4. Nikolic, J., Burri, M., Rehder, J., Leutenegger, S., Huerzeler, C., Siegwart, R.: A UAV system for inspection of industrial facilities. In: Proceedings of the 2013 IEEE Aerospace Conference, Big Sky (2013). https://doi.org/10.1109/AERO.2013.6496959

5. Liu, Y., Dong, J., Li, Y., Gong, X., Wang, J.: A UAV-based aircraft surface defect inspection system via external constraints and deep learning. IEEE Trans. Instrum. Meas. **71** (2022). https://doi.org/10.1109/TIM.2022.3198713
6. Novák, F., Báča, T., Saska, M.: Collaborative object manipulation on the water surface by a UAV-USV team using tethers. In: Proceedings of the 2024 IEEE/RSJ International Conference on Intelligent Robots and Systems (IROS), Abu Dhabi (2024). https://doi.org/10.1109/IROS58592.2024.10802469
7. Paris, A., Lopez, B.T., How, J.P.: Dynamic landing of an autonomous quadrotor on a moving platform in turbulent wind conditions. In: Proceedings of the 2020 IEEE International Conference on Robotics and Automation (ICRA), Paris (2020). https://doi.org/10.1109/ICRA40945.2020.9197081
8. Sudevan, V., Shukla, A., Karki, H.: Vision based autonomous landing of an Unmanned Aerial Vehicle on a stationary target. In: Proceedings of the 2017 17th International Conference on Control, Automation and Systems (ICCAS), Jeju, South Korea (2017). https://doi.org/10.23919/ICCAS.2017.8204466
9. Wang, C.: Customer satisfaction evaluation of food delivery platforms – taking meituan as an example. In: Proceedings of the 2020 International Conference on Big Data Economy and Information Management (BDEIM), Zhengzhou, China (2020). https://doi.org/10.1109/BDEIM52318.2020.00037
10. Chen, K., Sun, Q., Sun, H., Liu, Q., Chen, Z.: Tightly coupled lidar-inertial-GPS environment detection and landing area selection based on powered parafoil UAV. IEEE Trans. Instrum. Meas. **74** (2024). https://doi.org/10.1109/TIM.2024.3480211
11. Baca, T., et al.: Autonomous landing on a moving vehicle with an unmanned aerial vehicle. J. Field Robot. (2019). https://doi.org/10.1002/rob.21858
12. Kong, W., Zhou, D., Zhang, D., Zhang, J.: Vision-based autonomous landing system for unmanned aerial vehicle: a survey. In: Proceedings of the 2014 International Conference on Multisensor Fusion and Information Integration for Intelligent Systems (MFI), Beijing, China (2014). https://doi.org/10.1109/MFI.2014.6997750
13. Li, D., Zhou, J., Huang, J., Zhang, D., Li, P., Law, R.: State prediction and anti-interference-based flight path-following for UAVs. IEEE Trans. Intell. Transp. Syst. **24**(12), 15236–15247 (2023). https://doi.org/10.1109/TITS.2023.3308932
14. Gao, Y., Ji, J., Wang, Q., Jin, R., Lin, Y., Shang, Z.: Adaptive tracking and perching for quadrotor in dynamic scenarios. IEEE Trans. Robot. **40**, 499–519 (2023). https://doi.org/10.1109/TRO.2023.3335670
15. Zhou, X., Wang, M., Cui, C., Wang, Y., Xu, C., Gao, F.: Internal and external disturbances aware motion planning and control for quadrotors. IET Cyber Syst. Robot. (2024). https://doi.org/10.1049/csy2.12122
16. Shao, G., Ma, Y., Malekian, R., Yan, X., Li, Z.: A novel cooperative platform design for coupled USV-UAV systems. IEEE Trans. Ind. Inform. **15**(9), 4913–4922 (2019). https://doi.org/10.1109/TII.2019.2912024
17. Xu, Z.C., Hu, B.B., Liu, B., Wang, X.D., Zhang, H.T.: Vision-based autonomous landing of unmanned aerial vehicle on a motional unmanned surface vessel. In: Proceedings of the 2020 39th Chinese Control Conference (CCC), Shenyang, China (2020). https://doi.org/10.23919/CCC50068.2020.9188979
18. Gupta, P.M., Pairet, É., Nascimento, T., Saska, M.: Landing a UAV in harsh winds and turbulent open waters. IEEE Robot. Autom. Lett. **8**(2), 744–751 (2023). https://doi.org/10.1109/LRA.2022.3231831
19. Schuchardt, B.I., Dautermann, T., Donkels, A., Krause, S., Peinecke, N., Schwoch, G.: Maritime operation of an unmanned rotorcraft with tethered ship deck landing

system. CEAS Aeronaut. J. **12**, 3–11 (2021). https://doi.org/10.1007/s13272-020-00465-2
20. Talke, K.A., De Oliveira, M., Bewley, T.: Catenary tether shape analysis for a UAV–USV team. In: 2018 IEEE/RSJ International Conference on Intelligent Robots and Systems (IROS), Madrid, Spain (2018). IEEE. https://doi.org/10.1109/IROS.2018.8594280
21. Lima, R.R., Rocamora, B.M., Pereira, G.A.S.: Continuous vector fields for precise cable-guided landing of tethered UAVs. In: IEEE Robotics and Automation Letters, vol. 8, no. 7, pp. 4370–4377 (2023). IEEE https://doi.org/10.1109/LRA.2023.3281940
22. Xu, R., Liu, C., Cao, Z., Wang, Y., Qian, H.: A manipulator-assisted multiple UAV landing system for USV subject to disturbance. Ocean Eng. **299**, 117306 (2024). https://doi.org/10.1016/j.oceaneng.2024.117306
23. Zhou, J., Jiang, K., Chen, R., Yang, Y., Li, K.: A tethered aerial recovery system for UAV landing on USV. In: Proceedings of the 2024 9th International Conference on Automation, Control and Robotics Engineering (CACRE), Jeju Island, Republic of Korea, pp. 1–6 (2024). https://doi.org/10.1109/CACRE62362.2024.10635025
24. Meier, L., Tanskanen, P., Fraundorfer, F., Pollefeys, M.: PIXHAWK: a system for autonomous flight using onboard computer vision. In: Proceedings of the 2011 IEEE International Conference on Robotics and Automation (ICRA), Shanghai, China, 9–13 May 2011. IEEE. https://doi.org/10.1109/ICRA.2011.5980229
25. Meier, L., Honegger, D., Pollefeys, M.: PX4: A node-based multithreaded open source robotics framework for deeply embedded platforms. In: Proceedings of the 2015 IEEE International Conference on Robotics and Automation (ICRA), Seattle, WA, USA, 26–30 May 2015. IEEE. https://doi.org/10.1109/ICRA.2015.7140074
26. Khazetdinov, A., Zakiev, A., Tsoy, T., Svinin, M., Magid, E.: Embedded ArUco: a novel approach for high precision UAV landing. In: 2021 International Siberian Conference on Control and Communications (SIBCON), Kazan, Russia, 13–15 May 2021. IEEE. https://doi.org/10.1109/SIBCON50419.2021.9438855
27. Bingham, B., Agüero, C., McCarrin, M., Klamo, J., Malia, J., Allen, K.: Toward maritime robotic simulation in gazebo. In: OCEANS 2019 MTS/IEEE SEATTLE, Seattle, WA, USA, pp. 1–7. IEEE (2019). https://doi.org/10.23919/OCEANS40490.2019.8962724
28. Keipour, A., et al.: Visual servoing approach to autonomous UAV landing on a moving vehicle. Sensors **22**(17), 6549 (2022). https://doi.org/10.3390/s22176549
29. Lin, J., Wang, Y., Miao, Z., Zhong, H., Fierro, R.: Low-complexity control for vision-based landing of quadrotor UAV on unknown moving platform. IEEE Trans. Ind. Inform. **18**(8), 5348–5358 (2021). https://doi.org/10.1109/TII.2021.3129486
30. Chen, L., Liu, C., Guo, S., Qian, H.: Vision-guided UAV landing on a swaying ocean platform in simulation. In: Proceedings of the 2023 IEEE International Conference on Real-time Computing and Robotics (RCAR), Datong, China (2023). https://doi.org/10.1109/RCAR58764.2023.10249476
31. Liu, C., Jiang, Z., Xu, R., Ji, X., Zhang, L., Qian, H.: Design and optimization of a magnetic catcher for UAV landing on disturbed aquatic surface platforms. In: Proceedings of the 2022 IEEE International Conference on Robotics and Automation (ICRA), Philadelphia, USA (2022). https://doi.org/10.1109/ICRA46639.2022.9812270

Positioning and Orientation for Single LiDAR of USVs Obstructed By Offshore Operation Platform

Wenhui Dong[1], Yanzheng Zhu[2(✉)], Jichao Yang[2], Jianping Xing[1], Shengli Wang[2], and Ranshuo Zhao[1]

[1] Shandong University, Jinan 250101, China
202320383@mail.sdu.edu.cn
[2] Shandong University of Science and Technology, Qingdao 266590, China
yanzhengzhu@sdust.edu.cn

Abstract. This paper presents a new algorithm for real-time positioning and orientation of unmanned surface vessels (USVs) based on a single LiDAR. To address the perception challenges in environments where GNSS works not, this algorithm achieves online and efficient identification of point cloud clusters through dynamic area division, and prioritizes the selection of the point cloud clusters that are most valuable for continuous tracking of USV navigation. By adaptively determining the calculation area based on the real-time position information of the USV, the high-precision reference positions are obtained through point cloud cluster identification, and the position and heading angle of the USV are synchronously solved using geometric constraint. Both the performance and real-time capabilities of proposed algorithm are demonstrated through experiment results, providing an effective solution for the state measurement of USVs in GNSS-constrained environments.

Keywords: Offshore operation platform · Positioning and orientation of USVs · LiDAR

1 Introduction

In recent years, offshore operation platforms have become an important way to exploring the ocean. The pile foundations that form the basis of offshore operation platforms require regular erosion safety monitoring [1]. Unmanned surface vessels (USVs) have become the best choice for erosion monitoring. During the mission of USVs equipped with monitoring equipment, their positioning and orientation data come from the Global Navigation Satellite System (GNSS). However, offshore operation platforms will completely block GNSS signals, which will prevent USVs that rely on the GNSS from conducting autonomous navigation in areas where GNSS works not. It is well known that LiDAR is less affected by environmental factors and can be used as an ocean environment sensing equipment. This paper innovatively proposes a simple and effective positioning and orientation algorithm for USVs based on LiDAR, providing a new option for USVs to operate in areas where GNSS works not.

GNSS and INS (Inertial Navigation System) are usually combined together to achieve high-precision positioning and orientation of the vehicle [2–4]. However, the prolonged absence of GNSS information still causes significant deviations in the positioning and orientation data of the vehicle. Moreover, high-precision INS equipment is extremely expensive. The method of inferring the vehicle's own pose information by reverse inference using visual odometry has also become a new option for vehicle positioning and orientation [5]. However, the high complexity caused by the light reflection and diffraction phenomena in the marine environment leads to a decrease in the capturing ability of visual sensors. The processing method using visual data requires more computing power and is difficult to ensure high-frequency positioning and orientation data.

To overcome these shortcomings, this paper aims to solve the positioning and orientation problems of USVs in areas where GNSS works not under offshore platforms through LiDAR. LiDAR is used for optical distance measurement within a three-dimensional range and is less affected by lighting and marine environmental factors [6,7]. For USVs operating beneath offshore operation platforms, a positioning and orientation algorithm based on LiDAR is proposed. Considering that the generated point cloud data does not contain any identification information, an online point cloud identification method based on region division is proposed. Ultimately, in an environment where GNSS works not, the USVs are able to achieve real-time positioning and orientation through the use of LiDAR.

The rest of this paper is organized as follows: Sect. 2 introduces an online partitioned point cloud clustering identification method. Section 3 presents the established simulation experiment platform and analyzes the experimental trajectory. Section 4 discusses the positioning and orientation accuracies of the developed algorithm, and also analyzes the abnormal situations in the experiment. Section 5 summarizes this paper.

2 LiDAR Positioning and Orientation Algorithm

This paper selects the offshore operation platform with four foundations as the research environment. The planar coordinate positions of the four pile foundations are $[X_i, Y_i]$, where $i = A, B, C, D$ represent the numbers of the four pile foundations, respectively.

In this paper, a single LiDAR is chosen as the positioning and orientation sensor for the USVs. A new algorithm is proposed to implement the online real-time partitioned point cloud clustering and identification.

At first, an PCL (Point Cloud library) is applied to handle the LiDAR point cloud data [8]. The point cloud data outside the working area is filtered out by the pass through filter, the Statistical Outlier Removal filter is used to remove the sparse outlier clouds. Then, the KD-tree accelerated point cloud Euclidean clustering algorithm is used to cluster the point cloud data to obtain the pile foundation point cloud clustering. Finally, an PCA (Principal Components Analysis) algorithm is borrowed to obtain the position of each pile foundation point cloud fitting bounding box in the LiDAR coordinate system for the pile foundation point cloud cluster.

The point cloud cluster formed by the cylindrical pile foundation presents an arc-shaped state. Capturing the point closest to the USVs in the point cloud cluster is the planar distance between the vertex of the arc surface of the point cloud cluster and the USVs.

The distance can be calculated between each point in the three-dimensional point cluster and the shipborne LiDAR respectively, and the formed distance information can be sorted. At first, the 20 points with the smallest distances will be selected for average value calculation. The average value is taken and the correction radius is added as the distance from the center of the pile foundation to the shipborne LiDAR, as shown in (1).

$$\begin{cases} d_i = \sqrt{(Point_i.x)^2 + (Point_i.y)^2 + (Point_i.z)^2} \\ D = \frac{\sum_{n=1}^{20} \min[d]_n + R}{20} \end{cases} \quad (1)$$

where $\min[d]_n$ means that d_i is sorted from small to large, and the n points are selected. R is the radius of the pile foundation. D as the planar projection distance between the ship-borne LiDAR and the pile base point cloud cluster.

2.1 Online Real-Time Partition Point Cloud Cluster Identification Method

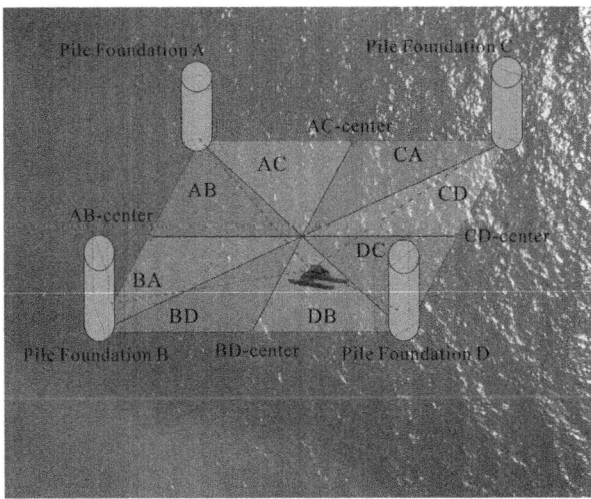

Fig. 1. Schematic diagram of blocked area partition for offshore operation platform.

The operation area of the offshore operation platform is determined by four pile foundations. As shown in Fig. 1, the operation area is divided into eight zones, and each zone is numbered. Based on the known pile foundation coordinates $[X_i, Y_i]$, the coordinate constraints of each partition can be calculated, and the constraint conditions are shown in Table 1.

Table 1. Partition constraint conditions, where x and y represent the position of the USV in the ENU coordinate system, and K and B represent the slope and intercept of the line in which the two pile foundations are located in the ENU coordinate system.

Partition code	Partition Constraints
AB	$y < K_{AD} * x + B_{AD}$ && $y > K_{BC} * x + B_{BC}$ && $y > K_{AB-center} * x + B_{AB-center}$
AC	$y > K_{AD} * x + B_{AD}$ && $y > K_{BC} * x + B_{BC}$ && $y < K_{AC-center} * x + B_{AC-center}$
BA	$y < K_{AD} * x + B_{AD}$ && $y > K_{BC} * x + B_{BC}$ && $y < K_{AB-center} * x + B_{AB-center}$
BD	$y < K_{AD} * x + B_{AD}$ && $y < K_{BC} * x + B_{BC}$ && $y < K_{AC-center} * x + B_{AC-center}$
CA	$y > K_{AD} * x + B_{AD}$ && $y > K_{BC} * x + B_{BC}$ && $y > K_{AC-center} * x + B_{AC-center}$
CD	$y > K_{AD} * x + B_{AD}$ && $y < K_{BC} * x + B_{BC}$ && $y > K_{AB-center} * x + B_{AB-center}$
DB	$y < K_{AD} * x + B_{AD}$ && $y < K_{BC} * x + B_{BC}$ && $y > K_{AC-center} * x + B_{AC-center}$
DC	$y > K_{AD} * x + B_{AD}$ && $y < K_{BC} * x + B_{BC}$ && $y < K_{AB-center} * x + B_{AB-center}$

Based on the planar position of USVs and pile foundation position, a three-level progressive zoning model is established. The basic zoning is constituted by the connecting lines (Fig. 1), and the positioning range is gradually narrowed layer by layer through geometric relationships. The specific process is provided as follows:

1. First level partition identification (coarse-grained localization):
   Using diagonal $AD(BC)$ as the first level partition baseline, calculate the planar position relationship between the current position (x, y) of the USV and diagonal $AD(BC)$, and determine the first level partition to which the USV belongs based on partition constraints;
2. Second level partition identification (medium granularity positioning):
   Based on the results of the first level partition, dynamically select the auxiliary reference line $BC(AD)$, further segment the first level partition results, calculate the plane position relationship between the current position (x, y) of the USV and the diagonal $AD(BC)$, determine the second level partition

to which the USV belongs according to the partition constraint conditions, and further refine the partition results of the USV;
3. Third level partition identification (fine-grained positioning):
Use the midpoints of the four edges to construct a baseline reference centerline $AB_{center} - AB_{center}$ or $AC_{center} - BD_{center}$, dynamically select the baseline reference centerline based on the results of the second level partition, calculate the plane position relationship between the current position (x, y) of the USV and the baseline reference centerline, determine the partition to which the USV belongs based on the partition constraints. And finally determine the partition where the USV is located.

Table 2. Distance between point cloud clusters and USV within the partition and their corresponding point cloud cluster ownership relationships.

Partition code	Partition condition	
AB	$min[Dis]_1 \rightarrow A_{cloud}$	$min[Dis]_2 \rightarrow B_{cloud}$
AC	$min[Dis]_1 \rightarrow A_{cloud}$	$min[Dis]_2 \rightarrow C_{cloud}$
BA	$min[Dis]_1 \rightarrow B_{cloud}$	$min[Dis]_2 \rightarrow A_{cloud}$
BD	$min[Dis]_1 \rightarrow B_{cloud}$	$min[Dis]_2 \rightarrow D_{cloud}$
CA	$min[Dis]_1 \rightarrow C_{cloud}$	$min[Dis]_2 \rightarrow A_{cloud}$
CD	$min[Dis]_1 \rightarrow C_{cloud}$	$min[Dis]_2 \rightarrow D_{cloud}$
DB	$min[Dis]_1 \rightarrow D_{cloud}$	$min[Dis]_2 \rightarrow B_{cloud}$
DC	$min[Dis]_1 \rightarrow D_{cloud}$	$min[Dis]_2 \rightarrow C_{cloud}$

After obtaining the partition information, the point cloud clusters are identified based on the distance between the USV and the pile foundation cloud clusters. The correspondence between the distances of point cloud clusters in each partition and the pile foundations to which the point cloud clusters belong is shown in Table 2.

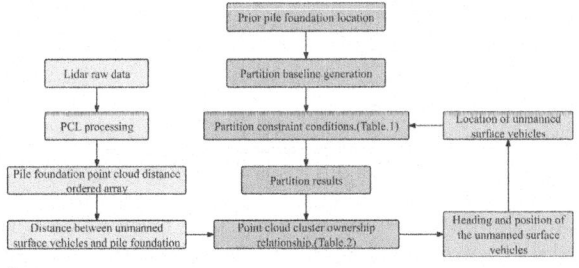

Fig. 2. Single LiDAR positioning and orientation algorithm.

As shown in the example in Fig. 1, according to the partition constraints in the Table.1, the first-level partition identification takes AD as the reference to determine that whether the USV is in the AB, BA, BD, DB partition. Selecting BC as the secondary partition identification baseline to determine whether the USV is in the BD, DB partition. The three-level partition identification takes $AC_{center} - BD_{center}$ as the benchmark, and finally determines that the USV is in the DB partition. Based on the relationship between the partitioned point cluster groups and the real-time distance calculation, the ownership information of point cluster can be marked. According to the introduction of the proposed algorithm, the algorithm flowchart of this paper is shown in Fig. 2.

The USV crossing the partition boundary causes the distance between the pile foundation and the USV to be very close to the minimum value in the array and there is a jump. Therefore, A quadrant-based point cloud identification method is proposed to cross the partition of the USV. Based on the point cloud identification information and quadrant features before crossing the boundary, the point cloud clusters at the current moment are identified. As the USV approaches the partition boundary, it will be switched to this method.

2.2 Calculation of the Plane Position and Heading of USVs

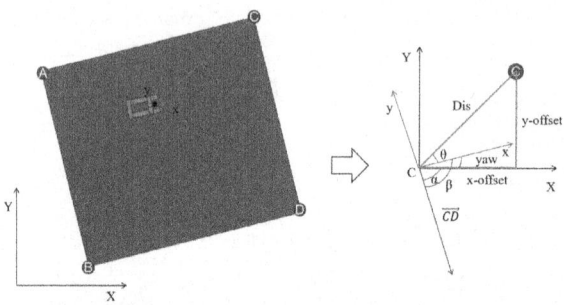

Fig. 3. Schematic diagram of the plane position and heading solution of USV.

As shown in Fig. 3, the direction angle α of the vector $\overrightarrow{CD}$ is calculated, which is formed by pile foundation C and pile foundation D in the geographic coordinate system:

$$\alpha = \arccos \frac{X_D - X_C}{\sqrt{(X_D - X_C)^2 + (Y_D - Y_C)^2}} \quad (2)$$

Then, the direction angle β of the vector $\overrightarrow{CD}$ is calculated, which is formed by pile foundation C and pile foundation D in the three-dimensional LiDAR coordinate system:

$$\beta = \arccos \frac{x_D - x_C}{\sqrt{(x_D - x_C)^2 + (y_D - y_C)^2}} \qquad (3)$$

Further, the angle θ is determined between the vector formed by the origin of the LiDAR and the pile foundation C and the x-axis of the LiDAR in the coordinate system:

$$\theta = \arccos \frac{x_C}{\sqrt{x_C^2 + y_C^2}} \qquad (4)$$

Based on the above calculations, the position and heading of the USV are constructed as:

$$\begin{cases} X_{ship} = X_C - D*\cos(\theta + yaw) - L*\cos(yaw) \\ Y_{ship} = Y_C - D*\sin(\theta + yaw) - L*\sin(yaw) \\ Yaw = \beta - \alpha \end{cases} \qquad (5)$$

where L represents the lever arm value between the LiDAR and the USV in the x-axis direction. The LiDAR is installed on the central axis of the USV.

3 Simulation

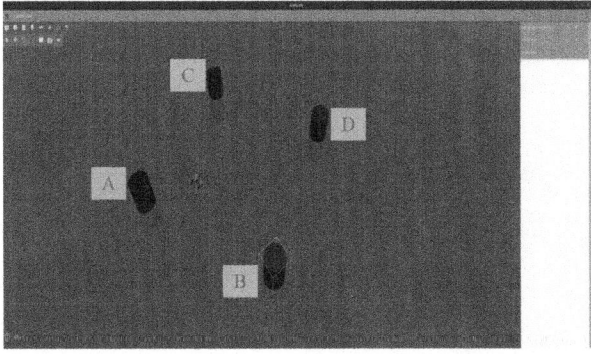

Fig. 4. VRX-USV and simulated pile foundations in Gazebo simulation environment.

The simulation experiment is based on the Ubuntu22.04+ROS2+Gazebo environment and adopts the open-source simulation USV model. Equipped with a LiDAR module, the vertical opening angle is $\pm 15°$, and a Gaussian noise with a standard deviation of $\sigma = 0.01$m is added. The lever arm value between the LiDAR and the USV center is $x = 0.7$m, and the USV maintains a speed of 3 knots (Fig. 4).

The simulated environmental wind direction is 240°, and the wind speed is generated by the Mersenne Twister algorithm based on random seed 10. The environmental wave is generated based on the PMS wave model. It is a sine wave with a period of 5 s, an average wave direction of 0, and the Angle between the average wave direction and the maximum and minimum component waves is 0.4.

Table 3. The position and heading solution results of three groups of experiments

Index	Experiment 1			Experiment 2			Experiment 3		
	Mean	Max	RMSE	Mean	Max	RMSE	Mean	Max	RMSE
East Error [m]	0.0672	0.2521	0.0848	0.0786	0.2138	0.0922	0.0740	0.2971	0.0926
North Error [m]	0.0668	0.2402	0.0887	0.0361	0.1897	0.0521	0.0687	0.2531	0.0865
Yaw Error [°]	0.5374	1.1802	0.0673	0.4921	1.1383	0.5465	0.7952	1.8417	0.9146
Distance Error [m]	0.1074	0.2642	0.1227	0.097	0.3184	0.1059	0.1128	0.2988	0.1268

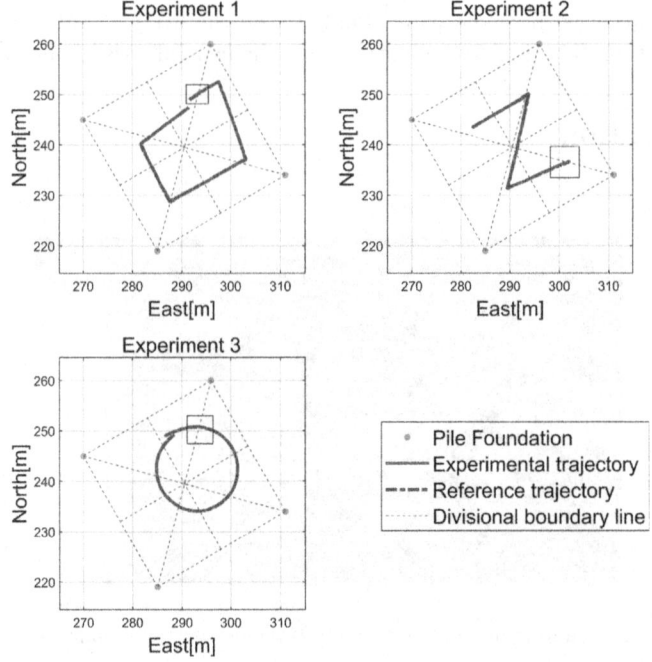

Fig. 5. Experimental trajectory of USV. The black box is at the position shown in Fig. 6.

A right-handed coordinate system is employed in the Gazebo simulation environment, while the world coordinate system makes use of a northeast-upward (ENU) coordinate system. The heading of USV is 0° towards the east, with range of $[-180°, 180°]$. Four cylindrical simulated pile foundations are placed in the rectangular area around the USV. The diameter of the pile foundation is set at 4 m.

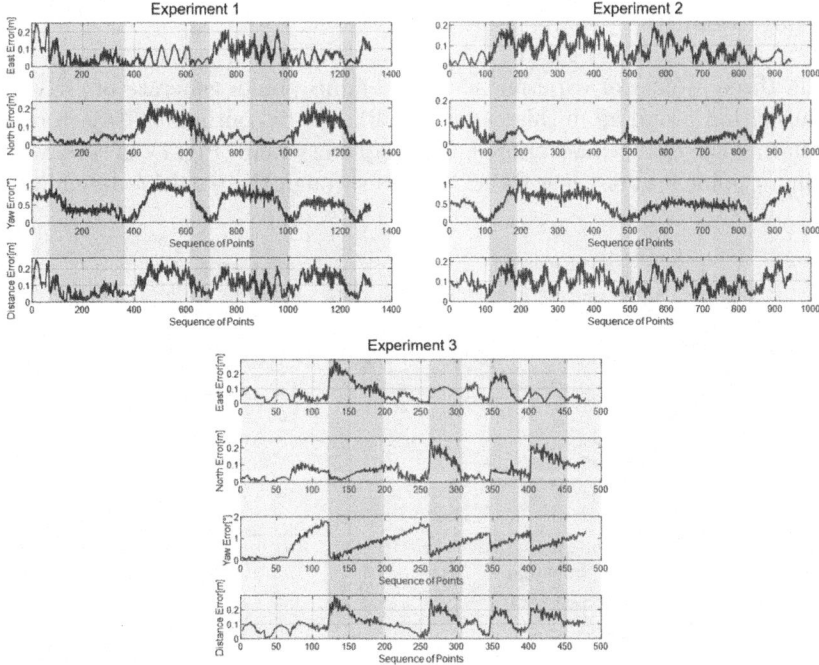

Fig. 6. The experimental errors of the trajectories of the USV in the three groups. The gray and green boxes represent the division of partition trajectories. (Color figure online)

At first, a LiDAR positioning solution node is developed based on ROS2, and the LiDAR sensor data is subscribed. The proposed algorithm is used to calculate the position and heading of the USV in real-time. Three types of common trajectories are designed in the experiments. The calculated position and heading of the proposed algorithm are recorded in real-time, and the real position and heading values of USV are recorded simultaneously as the comparison data.

In the simulation experiments of the three trajectories, the motion dynamics of USV are shown in Fig. 5. It is shown that the real-time trajectory calculated by this algorithm is basically consistent with the real trajectory in the simulation environment. The trajectory offset error, planar position error and heading angle error in the three groups of experiments are calculated respectively, all of which are plotted in Fig. 6. The specific values are given in Table 3.

Based on the experimental results of three trajectory navigation tests, we can find that the algorithm proposed in this paper has high accuracy and stability. Moreover, the accuracy of plane position calculation is in the decimeter level, and the accuracy of heading settlement is $\leq 1°$, which can meet the needs of USVs operating under offshore platforms. However, sudden changes are inevitable in all three experiments, which will be analyzed and discussed below.

4 Discussion

In the three groups of experiments, some jump points generate of USV using the algorithm proposed in this paper, resulting in discontinuous trajectories. By calculating the error and overlaying the trajectory map (Fig. 7), it is shown that the jump point occurs when the USV goes through the partition boundary.

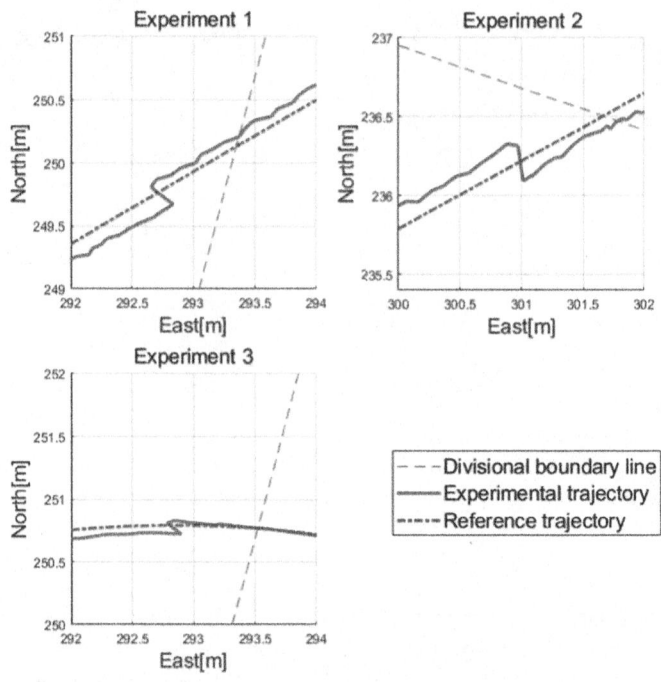

Fig. 7. Trajectory discontinuities caused by partition boundary crossings.

The behaviors of the USV are analyzed when crossing the boundary positions of the partitions during the three groups of experiments. At this time, the position and heading solutions are compared with the settlement results within the partitions. The comparison data are shown in Table 4.

When the USV goes through the partitions, due to the switching of the point cloud clusters used for calculating the position and heading, there might be discontinuity in the position and heading data. During the following period, the position and heading errors of the USV would first increase and then decrease. However, the planar position accuracy of the algorithm proposed in this study is 0.1 m, and the accuracy of the heading solution is 0.8°, which can meet the requirements for USV to conduct monitoring operations in the sea area blocked by the offshore platform.

Table 4. The algorithmic calculation errors across the constrained positions of the partitions and within the normal positions for each partition in the three groups of experiments.

Experimental	Index	Mean		Max		RMSE	
		Special	Normal	Special	Normal	Special	Normal
Experimental 1	East Error [m]	0.1288	0.0263	0.2481	0.0438	0.1502	0.0282
	North Error [m]	0.0441	0.065	0.0732	0.1191	0.0462	0.0691
	Yaw Error [°]	0.8088	0.4188	1.1802	0.594	0.8162	0.4314
	Distance Error [m]	0.1424	0.0714	0.2503	0.1238	0.1571	0.0746
Experimental 2	East Error [m]	0.034	0.0446	0.08	0.0856	0.0434	0.0489
	North Error [m]	0.118	0.0278	0.1897	0.0656	0.1224	0.0326
	Yaw Error [°]	0.8283	0.0843	1.0303	0.2315	0.8326	0.1055
	Distance Error [m]	0.1242	0.0544	0.2037	0.0929	0.1299	0.0588
Experimental 3	East Error [m]	0.1484	0.1767	0.2971	0.2633	0.1772	0.1813
	North Error [m]	0.0385	0.0350	0.0687	0.0624	0.0438	0.0386
	Yaw Error [°]	0.8137	0.4071	1.8417	0.6646	1.1156	0.4383
	Distance Error [m]	0.1636	0.1819	0.2988	0.2642	0.1825	0.1854

Note: "Special" represents the experimental value error during the stage of crossing the partition boundary line, while "Normal" represents the experimental value error within the partition.

5 Conclusions

For the positioning and orientation problem of USV in the GNSS signal blocked area beneath the offshore operation platform, this paper proposes a low-cost positioning and orientation method based on a single LiDAR. This method adopts a regional division strategy to achieve online real-time recognition and tracking of point cloud clusters, and selects the most optimal point cloud cluster as the basis for calculation. To verify the performance of the algorithm, simulation experiments with three typical motion trajectories (rectangular, Z-shaped, and circular) are conducted. The experimental results are shown in the following, i.e., i) The proposed point cloud cluster identification method can effectively identify point clouds and achieve adaptive switching of the calculation basis. ii) The positioning accuracy of the system reaches the decimeter level, and the heading estimation accuracy is better than 1°. Compared with the traditional multi-sensor scheme, this method only requires a single LiDAR to achieve precise navigation, significantly reducing the system complexity and hardware cost, and is suitable for the autonomous operation tasks of USV beneath the offshore operation platform.

References

1. Qin, B., Qu, R., Yang, W., Xie, Y.: A study on the scour surrounding the fixed foundation of an offshore wind turbine under complex waves, tidal currents, and pile vibration conditions. Energies **17**(7), 1561 (2024). https://doi.org/10.3390/en17071561
2. He, Y., Li, J., Liu, J.: Research on GNSS ins & GNSS/INS integrated navigation method for autonomous vehicles: a survey. IEEE Access **11**, 79033–79055 (2023). https://doi.org/10.1109/ACCESS.2023.3299290
3. El-Diasty, M.: Evaluation of KSACORS-based network GNSS-INS integrated system for Saudi coastal hydrographic surveys. Geomat. Nat. Hazards Risk **11**(1), 1426–1446 (2020). https://doi.org/10.1080/19475705.2020.1799081
4. Yuan, Y., et al.: An improved Kalman filter algorithm for tightly GNSS/INS integrated navigation system. Math. Biosci. Eng. **21**(mbe-21-01-040), 963–983 (2024). https://doi.org/10.3934/mbe.2024040
5. Cortes-Vega, D., Alazki, H., Rullan-Lara, J.L.: Visual odometry-based robust control for an unmanned surface vehicle under waves and currents in a urban waterway. J. Mar. Sci. Eng. **11**(3), 515 (2023). https://doi.org/10.3390/jmse11030515
6. Yao, Z., Chen, X., Xu, N., Gao, N., Ge, M.: Lidar-based simultaneous multi-object tracking and static mapping in nearshore scenario. Ocean Eng. **272**, 113939 (2023). https://doi.org/10.1016/j.oceaneng.2023.113939
7. Villa, J., Aaltonen, J., Koskinen, K.T.: Path-following with lidar-based obstacle avoidance of an unmanned surface vehicle in harbor conditions. IEEE-ASME Trans. Mechatron. **25**(4), 1812–1820 (2020). https://doi.org/10.1109/TMECH.2020.2997970
8. Rusu, R.B., Cousins, S.: 3D is here: point cloud library (PCL). In: 2011 IEEE International Conference on Robotics and Automation, pp. 1–4. Shanghai, China (2011). https://doi.org/10.1109/ICRA.2011.5980567

A Fault Diagnosis Scheme for Underwater Thrusters Considering Sensor Faults

Ruiheng Liu, Yanhu Chen, Xinyu Fei, Shipang Qian, Lu Wang, and Canjun Yang[✉]

State Key Laboratory of Fluid Power and Mechatronic Systems, Zhejiang University, Hangzhou 310027, China
ycj@zju.edu.cn

Abstract. As an important component of underwater vehicles, the fault diagnosis of underwater thrusters has been wildly studied. However, the overall diagnostic method for underwater thrusters considering sensor faults has largely remained unexplored. This paper proposes a new method, which first establishes the physical model of the underwater thruster and the load torque model. Based on this, simulating the initial deployment phase of the underwater vehicle, an adaptive Kalman filter (AKF) is used for thruster motor parameter identification to diagnose sensor faults. After confirming that the sensor's health status is good, the underwater operating state of the vehicle is simulated. A variable structure sliding mode observer (VS-SMO) is used to decouple the vehicle's speed and torque. At the same time, the load torque is observed online using the speed and current signals obtained from fault-free sensors. The recognition and classification of four fault modes are achieved through the variation of the load torque. Finally, the feasibility of the proposed aspects is verified through simulation experiments. The results show that the proposed method can effectively diagnose sensor bias faults, as well as the propeller entanglement, jamming, its breaking and falling off.

Keywords: Underwater Thruster · Sensor Fault Diagnosis · Propeller Fault Diagnosis · Torque Observation

1 Introduction

The underwater vehicle is an electromechanical system that performs tasks remotely or autonomously, capable of effectively expanding human activities in fields such as marine engineering construction, deep-sea resource exploration, underwater target search and rescue, and ocean farming [1]. It is a powerful tool for humanity's exploration of the ocean. The underwater thruster, as a key component of the underwater vehicle, presents a risk of mission failure, loss, or damage when it malfunctions [2]. Therefore, effective fault diagnosis methods are required to enable rapid detection and accurate identification of thruster faults [3], ensuring the safety of the underwater vehicle.

Fault diagnosis methods for underwater thrusters can generally be divided into three categories: qualitative analysis diagnosis methods, analytical model diagnosis methods, and signal processing diagnosis methods [4]. The main approach of qualitative methods is to infer based on the correlation between components and faults. Xu et al. proposed a fault tree model for underwater vehicle, this model maps the logical causal relationships between system failures and component failures, with thruster failure being one type of component failure [5]. Zhang et al. suggested a grey qualitative constraint filtering method based on higher-order derivative, probability grey number and persistence time for underwater vehicle fault diagnosis [6]. The analytical model-based methods are generally based on state observer methods. Chu et al. presented an innovative design scheme of terminal sliding mode observer, which use a fault reconstruction method based on an equivalent output error injection [7]. An active fault scheme was proposed by Baldini et al., the diagnosis is based on a sliding mode observer which generates three residuals and allows to evaluate the health condition of each actuator of the underwater vehicle [8]. Signal processing diagnosis methods generally involve providing the system's input and performing fault diagnosis by extracting feature information from the output signals. Gao et al. developed a multi-source signal common features extractor. This extractor obtains common features from measured and estimated currents, leveraging these variations to detect and assess faults accurately [9]. To solve the low decomposition accuracy of the sparse decomposition algorithm for signals in the time domain, a time-shift operator-based decomposition algorithm is proposed for decomposing the time-domain signals by Lv et al. [10].

Among the above thruster fault diagnosis methods, it is mostly assumed that the data obtained from sensor measurements is accurate, while overlooking sensor faults. For underwater vehicles engaged in prolonged missions, sensors are susceptible to degradation over time due to factors such as wear and tear [11]. A fault diagnosis framework with sensor self-diagnosis was proposed by Min, it uses a residual consistency checking algorithm based on sensor redundancy to detect and isolate failed sensors in sensor self-diagnosis [12]. However, sometimes due to the limitations in space and budget, redundant design is difficult to implement.

In this study, we considered both sensor bias faults and four specific fault modes of the thruster, including entanglement, jamming, breaking and falling off. For sensor faults, we use the AKF for parameter identification. For propeller faults, we adopt a both model and signal approach, utilizing the VS-SMO to observe the load torque signal, thus enabling fault diagnosis.

This work is now completed under the following assumptions:

(1) Sensor faults and internal thruster faults will not occur simultaneously.
(2) The entire system is fault-free in the initial stage of the deployment.

2 Model Building

2.1 Motor Mathematical Model

Regard as a PMSM-driven equipment, the underwater thruster can be generally modeled as [13]:

$$J\frac{dw_m}{dt} = T_e - T_L - Bw_m \qquad (1)$$

$$\begin{cases} \dfrac{d}{dt}i_q = -\dfrac{R}{L_d}i_q - \dfrac{1}{L_q}pw_m(L_d i_d + \Psi_f) + \dfrac{1}{L_q}u_q \\ \dfrac{d}{dt}i_d = -\dfrac{R}{L_d}i_d + w_e\dfrac{L_q}{L_d}i_d + \dfrac{1}{L_d}u_d \end{cases} \quad (2)$$

where w_m is the angular speed of the motor, J is the total inertia of the system. T_e is the electromagnetic torque, T_L is the load torque, B is the friction torque coefficient, i_q and i_d are the dq-axis stator currents, u_q and u_d are the dq-axis stator voltages, L_q and L_d are the dq-axis stator inductances, R is the stator resistance, Ψ_f is the rotor flux, p is the number of pole pairs.

The electromagnetic torque equation of PMSM is as follows:

$$T_e = \frac{3}{2}p(\Psi_f + (L_d - L_q)i_d)i_q \quad (3)$$

In this study, we use field-oriented control, so $i_d \approx 0$, T_e can be simplified as:

$$T_e = K_1 i_q (K_1 = \frac{3}{2}p\Psi_f) \quad (4)$$

2.2 Load Torque Model

For underwater thruster, the load torque consists of two main components. The first is the propeller torque, which is the thrust generated by the rotating propeller to overcome water resistance. The second is the viscous damping torque generated by the water in contact with the rotating propeller output shaft and the propeller surface. This torque is proportional to the rotational speed [14]. Therefore, the load torque of the thruster can be expressed as:

$$T_L = kw_m|w_m| + rw_m \quad (5)$$

where k represents the propeller coefficient of the propeller, and its value is related to the shape of the propeller blade, r represents the damping coefficient of the propeller, and its value is influenced by the contact area between the propeller and the water body.

2.3 Simulation Model

The schematic diagram of the underwater thruster system proposed in this study is depicted in Fig. 1. This system primarily consists of a Surface-mounted Permanent Magnet Synchronous Motor (SPMSM), which is designed to operate with high efficiency and precision. To achieve optimal performance, the system utilizes a dual closed-loop control strategy, one for regulating the current and the other for controlling the speed [15]. The given motor parameters are listed in Table 1. These parameters play a crucial role in the performance analysis and fault diagnosis of the underwater thruster system.

The overall fault diagnosis process of the underwater thruster proposed in this paper is shown in Fig. 2. A simulation model is established to simulate a real thruster, with the

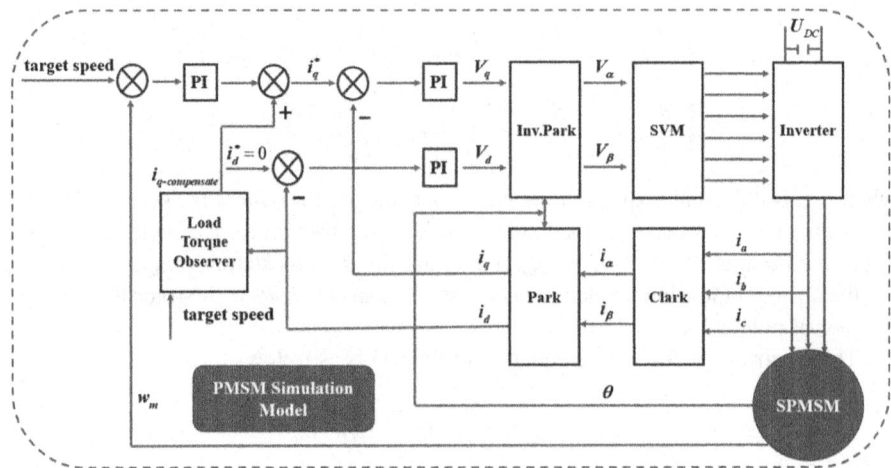

Fig. 1. PMSM structure

target rotational speed as the control signal. Initially, the load torque is set to zero, simulating the power-on self-checking state of the underwater vehicle before it is launched into the water. The rotational speed and current of the thruster are measured by sensors, which are used as input parameters for the AKF. The filter outputs the given parameter values for the thruster motor. By comparing the outputs and the given ones, the health status of the sensor can be known. After ensuring the sensor's health status is good, the underwater vehicle can be launched to perform the task. According to (5), the load torque will change in response to variations in speed.

Table 1. Parameters of the motor.

Parameter	Value	Unit
Pole-pair number p	4	–
Stator resistance r	0.268	Ω
Stator inductor $L_q = L_d$	2.2	mH
Rotor flux linkage Ψ_f	0.12258	wB
Rotational inertia J	0.0146	$kg \cdot m^2$
Friction torque coefficient f	0.0016655	N

However, torque measurement is often challenging. Therefore, an improved SMO is used to online monitor the changes in the load torque of the thruster. The degree of load torque variation serves as the basis for fault diagnosis, different faults in the thruster will lead to different variations in the load torque.

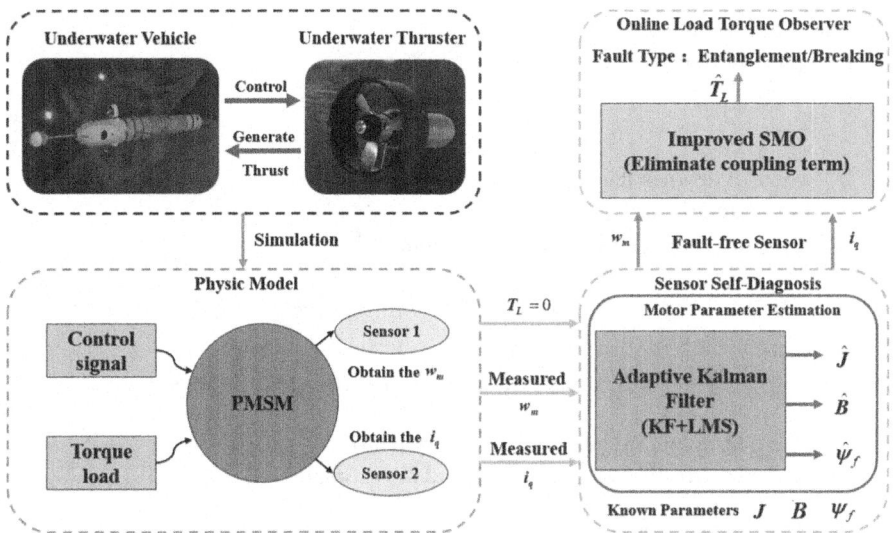

Fig. 2. Fault diagnosis process

3 Sensor Self-diagnosis Scheme

3.1 The Adaptive Kalman Filter

In the actual operation of the system, it is often accompanied by system noise and measurement noise. The Kalman filter is the optimal linear state estimator when the noise is zero-mean, uncorrelated, and Gaussian distributed [16]. In this section, the sensor self-diagnosis scheme based on the AKF is introduced in detail.

Generally, methods for estimating unknown parameters include converting the discrete-time model into the following structured form:

$$\begin{cases} x_{k+1} = x_k + b_k(x_k, u_k) + \Psi_k(y_k, u_k)\theta + h_k \\ y_k = x_k + v_k \end{cases} \quad (6)$$

where $x_k \in \mathbb{R}^n$ denotes the state of the system, which can be measured by sensors, $y_k \in \mathbb{R}^n$ denotes the discrete-time measurement of the state, $u_k \in \mathbb{R}^p$ denotes the control input, the parameter of the system is represented by $\theta \in \mathbb{R}^r$, $\Psi_k \in \mathbb{R}^{n \times r}$ denotes the coefficient matrix of the unknow variables, $h_k \in \mathbb{R}^p$ denotes the system noise, $v_k \in \mathbb{R}^p$ denotes the measurement noise. The distribution of the noise is as follows:

$$\begin{cases} h_k \sim N(0, Q_k) \\ v_k \sim N(0, R_k) \end{cases} \quad (7)$$

where $Q_k \in \mathbb{R}^{n \times p}$ denotes the system noise covariance matrix, $R_k \in \mathbb{R}^{n \times p}$ denotes the measurement noise covariance matrix.

In this form, the parameter estimation algorithm is as follows[17]:

(1) Define the functions $b_k(x_k, u_k)$ and $\Psi_k(y_k, u_k)$.

(2) Initialize $P_{0|0}, R_1, Q_1, \gamma_0$ and S_0.
(3) Compute the state estimation gain matrix K_k:

$$P_{k|k-1} = P_{k-1|k-1} + Q_k, \Sigma_k = P_{k|k-1} + R_k, K_k = P_{k|k-1}\Sigma_k^{-1}, P_{k|k} = (I - K_k)P_{k|k-1} \quad (8)$$

where P denotes the state estimate covariance matrix, Σ denotes the improved covariance matrix.

(4) Compute the parameter estimation gain matrix $\prod_k$:

$$\gamma_k = (I - K_k)\gamma_{k-1} + (I - K_k)\Psi_k(y_k, u_k), \Omega_k = \gamma_k + \Psi_k(y_k, u_k), \Lambda_k = (\Sigma_k + \Omega_k S_{k-1}\Omega_k^T)^{-1} \quad (9)$$

$$\prod_k = S_{k-1}\Omega_k^T \Lambda_k, S_k = S_{k-1} - S_{k-1}\Omega_k^T \Lambda_k \Omega_k S_{k-1} \quad (10)$$

where $\Omega, \Lambda, \gamma, S$ denotes the auxiliary matrix.

(5) Compute the error between the mode and the estimate:

$$\tilde{y}_k = y_k - (\hat{x}_{(k-1|k-1)} + b_k(y_k, u_k) + \Psi_k(y_k, u_k)\hat{\theta}_{k-1}) \quad (11)$$

(6) Estimate the $\hat{x}_{(k|k)}$ and $\hat{\theta}_k$:

$$\hat{x}_{(k|k)} = \hat{x}_{(k-1|k-1)} + b_k(y_k, u_k) + \Psi_k(y_k, u_k)\hat{\theta}_{k-1} + K_k\tilde{y}_k + \gamma_k(\hat{\theta}_k - \hat{\theta}_{k-1}) \quad (12)$$

$$\hat{\theta}_k = \hat{\theta}_{k-1} + \prod_k \tilde{y}_k \quad (13)$$

3.2 Sensor Fault Simulation and Diagnosis

A thruster with good control performance is the foundation for achieving sensor fault diagnosis and propeller fault diagnosis. To verify the control performance of the established thruster simulation model and simulate the real operating state of the underwater thruster, a set of speed signals is selected as the target speed control signal. This signal is the thruster speed percentage signal from the underwater vehicle developed by our team during the 0-10s of the docking mission in Qingjiang, Hubei, China. The maximum speed is 2369 rpm. In the actual process, the percentage signal is mapped to a speed signal ranging from -2369 rpm to 2369 rpm, the sampling time is $\Delta t = 0.0002$ s. Figure 3(a) shows the docking curve of the underwater vehicle when performing this docking task. Figure 3(b) shows the simulation results of the thruster under normal operating conditions.

In the actual operation of the thruster, we use current sensors and hall speed sensors to collect the three-phase current signals and speed signals of the motor. Since dq-axis current is commonly used in motor control, the sensor fault is reflected on the q-axis current during the simulation process. In this paper, only the sensor bias fault is considered, which means the sensor output shifts to a value higher than the normal value. In the simulation, this fault is implemented by adding a step signal to the normal reading of the sensor, defined as follows [18]:

$$S_{bias}^N = S_{healthy}^N + v \quad v = constant \quad (14)$$

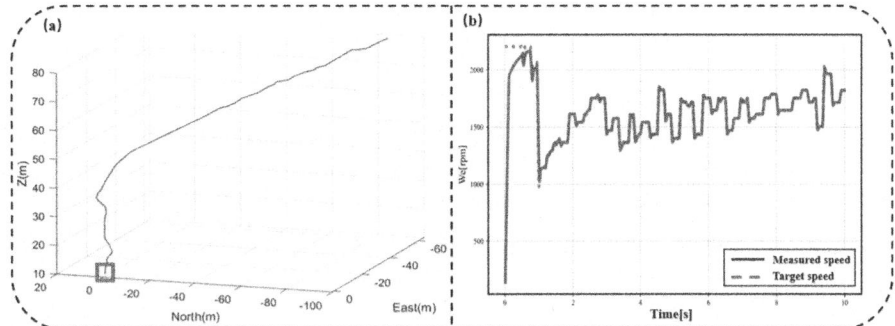

Fig. 3. (a) Docking trajectory of the underwater vehicle. (b) Thruster speed control with the reference signal

Sensor self-diagnosis is performed during the vehicle's initial deployment phase, before it's submerged in water. The target thruster speed is set, and the load torque is 0. Using sensors, the thruster's speed and current are measured, and discrete signals are used with the AKF to identify motor parameters. If a sensor bias fault occurs, the motor parameters identified by the AKF will differ from the actual values, thus diagnosing the fault occurrence time.

Consider the electrical equations and kinematic equations of the underwater thruster, and express them as state-space equations:

$$\begin{pmatrix} \dot{w}_m \\ \dot{i}_q \end{pmatrix} = \begin{pmatrix} -\frac{B}{J} & \frac{K_1}{J} \\ -\frac{4\Psi_f}{L_q} & 0 \end{pmatrix} \begin{pmatrix} w_m \\ i_q \end{pmatrix} + \begin{pmatrix} 0 \\ \frac{1}{L_q} \end{pmatrix} u_q \quad (15)$$

In order to implement sensor fault diagnosis, assume that the motor parameters are unknown and consider the impact of noise. The state-space equations are discretized as:

$$\begin{pmatrix} w_m(k+1) \\ i_q(k+1) \end{pmatrix} = \begin{pmatrix} w_m(k) \\ i_q(k) \end{pmatrix} + \begin{pmatrix} w_m(k) & 0 \\ i_q(k) & 0 \\ u_q & 0 \\ 0 & w_m(k) \\ 0 & i_q(k) \\ 0 & u_q \end{pmatrix}^T \begin{pmatrix} \theta_1 \\ \theta_2 \\ \theta_3 \\ \theta_4 \\ \theta_5 \\ \theta_6 \end{pmatrix} + \begin{pmatrix} h_1(k) \\ h_2(k) \end{pmatrix} \quad (16)$$

In this case:

$$\theta_1 = 0, \quad \theta_2 = -\frac{4\Psi_f \Delta t}{L_q}, \quad \theta_3 = \frac{\Delta t}{L_q}, \quad \theta_4 = \frac{K_1 \Delta t}{J}, \quad \theta_5 = -\frac{B \Delta t}{J}, \quad \theta_6 = 0 \quad (17)$$

The system (20) resemble (6) with:

$$\boldsymbol{b}_k(\boldsymbol{x}_k, \boldsymbol{u}_k) = \boldsymbol{0} \quad (18)$$

$$\boldsymbol{\Psi}_k(\boldsymbol{y}_k, \boldsymbol{u}_k) = \begin{pmatrix} w_m(k) & i_q(k) & u_q & 0 & 0 & 0 \\ 0 & 0 & 0 & w_m(k) & i_q(k) & u_q \end{pmatrix} \quad (19)$$

$$\boldsymbol{h}_k = \begin{pmatrix} h_1(k) \\ h_2(k) \end{pmatrix} \tag{20}$$

Due to the significant change in the inductance of the internal motor as the temperature increases during thruster operation, θ_4 and θ_5 are chosen as the parameters for identification. Four types of faults are introduced during the simulation time as follows:

(a) Fault 1: A velocity sensor faults occurring at $t = 5$, a current sensor error occurring at $t = 7$.
(b) Fault 2: A velocity sensor faults occurring at $t = 5$.
(c) Fault 3: A current sensor faults occurring at $t = 7$.
(d) Fault 4: A velocity sensor faults and a current sensor fault occurring at $t = 5$.

The outcomes of the sensor faults are visualized in Fig. 4. According to Table 1, the actual value of θ_4 is 0.01, and the actual value of θ_5 is 2.28×10^{-5}. Data shows that within the first 5 s, as both the current sensor and the velocity sensor are in a healthy state, the estimated values of θ_4 and θ_5 quickly converged to their actual values. After the faults occur, the estimated value of θ_4 deviates significantly from the actual value, correctly identifying the time when the fault happens. For θ_5, although the deviation is minor, especially after the sensor fault is occurred at $t = 7$, the fault time can still be identified, but the fault threshold setting needs to be smaller.

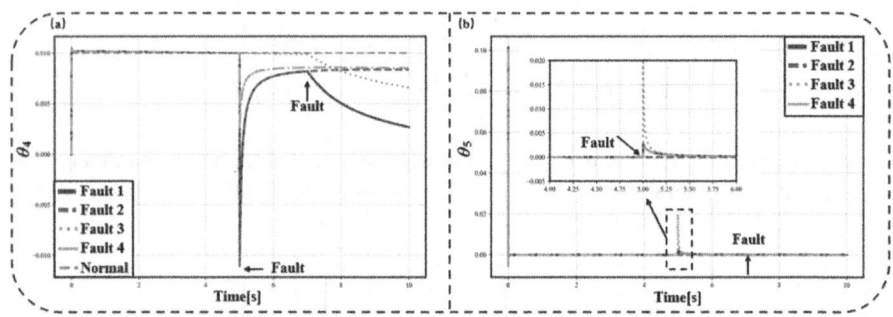

Fig. 4. (a) Identification of θ_4. (b) Identification of θ_5.

4 Thruster System Fault Diagnosis Scheme

4.1 The Variable Structure Sliding Mode Observer

When underwater vehicles perform tasks underwater, they often assign time-varying target speeds to the underwater thrusters to achieve the task objectives. However, the variation in speed causes issues with the load torque estimation of a conventional sliding mode observer (SMO). To eliminate the chattering signal in the load torque estimation of the conventional sliding mode controller, this paper adopts the VS-SMO algorithm [19]. A decoupling term is added to the load torque adaptive law, which eliminates the coupling error between load torque and speed.

It is assumed that the load torque is constant within a very short time, which means

$$\dot{T}_L = 0 \tag{21}$$

The design of the VS-SMO is as follows

$$\begin{cases} \hat{\dot{w}}_m = \frac{1}{J}(T_e - \hat{T}_L - Bw_m - Csgn(w_m)) + ks_m \\ \hat{\dot{T}}_L = gs_m - \frac{g}{k}\dot{e}_1 \end{cases} \tag{22}$$

where $\hat{w}_m$ and $\hat{T}_L$ denote the estimated value of w_m and T_L, k denotes the switching gain, g denotes the feedback gain, $s_m = sgn(\hat{w}_m - w_m)$, $-g\dot{e}_1/k$ denote the decoupling term. The stability of this observer has been proven, and in this simulation, $k = -1900$, $g = 200$. Figure 5 shows the observation results of the step change in the load torque using the designed VS-SMO. The data indicates that both the conventional SMO and the VS-SMO are able to observe the change in load torque, but the VS-SMO clearly eliminates the chattering signal.

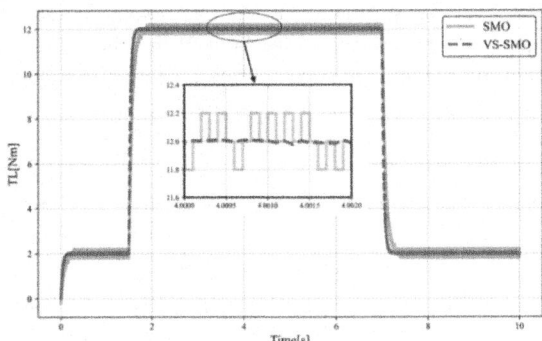

Fig. 5. Comparison of torque estimation between SMO and VS-SMO

4.2 Different Fault Types of Propellers

According to (5), the torque formula of the underwater thruster with failure can be expressed as

$$T_L = \mu k w_m |w_m| + \lambda r w_m \tag{23}$$

where λ denotes the propeller fault coefficient, μ denotes the damping fault coefficient. Different types of failure correspond to different failure coefficients. When $\lambda = \mu = 1$, it indicates that the thruster is in healthy state.

Four types of faults are defined in this paper. The entanglement of the propeller will mainly cause r to increase, the jamming of the propeller will mainly cause r to sharp increase, the breaking of the propeller will mainly cause k to decrease and the falling off of the propeller cause k to sharp decrease. The failure coefficient settings corresponding to different failures are shown in the Table 2.

Table 2. Fault characteristics parameters of the thrusters.

Fault type	μ	λ
Entanglement	1	3
Jamming	1	10
Breaking	0.1	1
Falling off	0	0

4.3 Propeller Fault Simulation and Diagnosis

Simulate the propeller of an underwater vehicle in a fault-free state, and apply load torque to the thruster according to (23). The proposed observer can online observe the load torque and the entanglement and jamming are occurred at $t = 5$. Figure 6a shows the observed load torque data over the simulation time while Fig. 6b shows the observed speed data over the simulation time. The results indicate that the observed torque variation represents the severity of the fault. When the entanglement fault occurs in the propeller, it can still maintain normal operation. However, when the jamming of the propeller occurs, the load torque increases sharply, and the thruster's normal operation is affected.

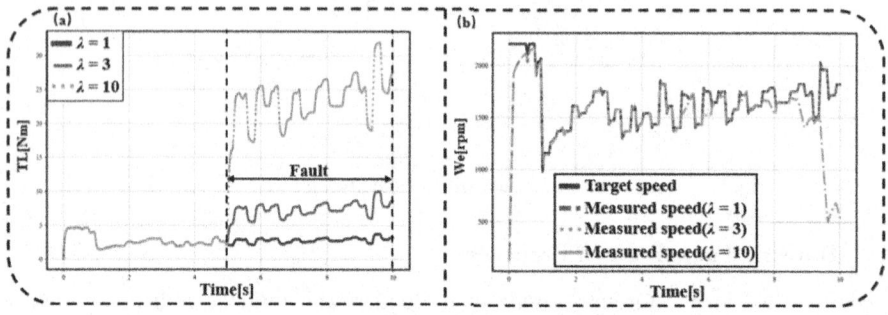

Fig. 6. (a) Load torque observation. (b) Thruster speed control with different faults.

Figure 7 shows the torque observation data when the breaking and falling off faults occur in the propeller. The result indicate that the VS-SMO can detect changes in load torque to classify the fault type. When the falling off occurs in the propeller, both the propeller coefficient r and the damping coefficient k sharply drop to zero, causing the observed load torque to be zero, which in turn affects the overall motion of the underwater vehicle.

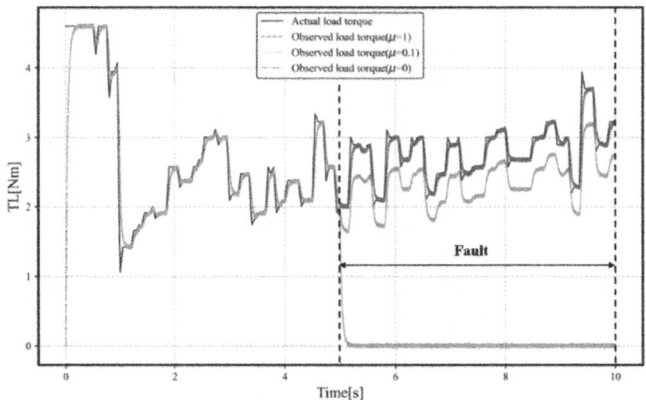

Fig. 7. Load torque observation with different faults.

5 Conclusion

This paper proposes a fault diagnosis method for underwater thrusters which considers sensor faults. By utilizing AKF to identify the motor parameters of the thruster before the deployment of the underwater vehicle, the identified parameters are compared with known motor parameters to diagnose sensor bias faults. Once the sensor's status is confirmed to be normal, the speed and current signals collected by the fault-free sensors are used to observe the load torque by VS-SMO during the operation of the underwater vehicle. The type of propeller faults is inferred based on the changes in load torque. The simulation employs a target signal, which is the speed signal of the underwater vehicle developed by our team during docking tasks. Simulation results demonstrate that the proposed method can effectively diagnose both sensor bias fault and four types of propeller faults. In the future, we will consider incorporating more fault types into the diagnosis scheme. Meanwhile, we will validate the feasibility of the proposed fault diagnosis scheme during actual docking operations of the underwater vehicle.

References

1. Liu, F., Tang, H., Qin, Y., Duan, C., Luo, J., Pu, H.: Review on fault diagnosis of unmanned underwater vehicles. Ocean Eng. **243**, 110290 (2022)
2. Zhu, D., Cheng, X., Yang, L., Chen, Y., Yang, S.X.: Information fusion fault diagnosis method for deep-sea human occupied vehicle thruster based on deep belief network. IEEE Trans. Cybern. **52**, 9414–9427 (2022)
3. Chu, Z., Gu, Z., Chen, Y., Zhu, D., Tang, J.: A fault diagnostic approach for underwater thrusters based on generative adversarial network. IEEE Trans. Instrum. Meas. **73**, 1–14 (2024)
4. Hu, Z.: Research progress on thruster fault diagnosis technology for deep-sea underwater vehicle. J. Propuls. Technol. **41**, 2465 (2020)
5. Xu, H., Li, G., Liu, J.: Reliability analysis of an autonomous underwater vehicle using fault tree. In: 2013 IEEE International Conference on Information and Automation (ICIA), pp. 1165–1170 (2013)

6. Thruster fault diagnosis in autonomous underwater vehicle based on grey qualitative simulation. Ocean Eng. **105**, 247–255 (2015)
7. Fault reconstruction using a terminal sliding mode observer for a class of second-order MIMO uncertain nonlinear systems. ISA Trans. **97**, 67–75 (2020)
8. A model-based active fault tolerant control scheme for a remotely operated vehicle. IFAC-Pap. **51**, 798–805 (2018)
9. Gao, S., Wang, Y., Zhang, Z., Wang, B., He, B., Zio, E.: Hybrid fault diagnosis method for underwater thrusters based on the common features of multi-source signals. Mech. Syst. Signal Process. **222**, 111740 (2025)
10. Fault feature extraction method based on optimized sparse decomposition algorithm for AUV with weak thruster fault. Ocean Eng. **233**, 109013 (2021)
11. Hasan, A., Salvo Rossi, P.: A unified sensor and actuator fault diagnosis in digital twins for remote operations. Mech. Syst. Signal Process. **222**, 111778 (2025)
12. Min, H., et al.: A fault diagnosis framework for autonomous vehicles with sensor self-diagnosis. Expert Syst. Appl. **224**, 120002 (2023)
13. Shi, T., Wang, Z., Xia, C.: Speed measurement error suppression for PMSM control system using self-adaption kalman observer. IEEE Trans. Ind. Electron. **62**, 2753–2763 (2015)
14. Gan, W., Dong, Q., Chu, Z.: Fault diagnosis method for an underwater thruster, based on load feature extraction. Electronics **11**, 3714 (2022)
15. Wang, L., Tang, Z., Zhang, P., Liu, X., Wang, D., Li, X.: Double extended sliding-mode observer-based synchronous estimation of total inertia and load torque for PMSM-driven spindle-tool systems. IEEE Trans. Ind. Inform. **19**, 8496–8507 (2023)
16. Hasan, A.: Online parameter estimation in digital twins for real-time condition monitoring. IEEE Access **13**, 14789–14800 (2025)
17. Adaptive kalman filter for actuator fault diagnosis. IFAC-Pap. **50**, 14272–14277 (2017)
18. Hasan, Md.N., Jan, S.U., Koo, I.: Wasserstein GAN-based digital twin-inspired model for early drift fault detection in wireless sensor networks. IEEE Sens. J. **23**, 13327–13339 (2023)
19. Tang, S., Shi, T., Cao, Y., Lin, Z., Wang, Z., Yan, Y.: Simultaneous identification of load torque and moment of inertia of PMSM based on variable structure extended sliding mode observer. IEEE Trans. Power Electron. **39**, 8585–8596 (2024)

Bio-inspired Multifunctional Soft Robotic Arm for Object Manipulation and Self-Locomotion

Lin Hong[1(✉)], Junjie Wang[2], Gan Zhang[2], Yixuan Sheng[3], Fumin Zhang[1], and Lei Guo[4]

[1] The Hong Kong University of Science and Technology, Kowloon, Hong Kong
eelinhong@ust.hk
[2] Southeast University, Nanjing 210096, China
[3] Harbin Institute of Technology (Shenzhen), Shenzhen 518055, China
[4] Beihang University, Beijing 100191, China

Abstract. Inspired by the remarkable grasping and locomotion capabilities of octopus arms, this paper presents the design, fabrication, and experimental evaluation of a bio-inspired soft robotic arm capable of object grasping and bipedal locomotion in both aquatic and terrestrial environments. By integrating soft materials, pneumatic actuation, and control systems, the soft robotic arm replicates key biological features and functions of octopus arms, enabling object grasping and bipedal locomotion in amphibious environments. Experimental results show that the soft robotic arm can grasp objects with diameters ranging from 52 mm to 76 mm, supporting a maximum payload of 185 g in air and 524.5 g underwater. In addition, a pair of robotic arms enables effective underwater bipedal locomotion at 1.51 cm/s. These findings validate the effectiveness of the proposed design and highlight its potential for practical applications in amphibious environments.

Keywords: Bio-inspired robot · Soft robotic arm · Object grasping · Bipedal locomotion

1 Introduction

Soft robots have emerged as a transformative approach in robotic design, enabling robots to exhibit flexibility, adaptability, and safe interaction with both humans and their environments [1]. Unlike traditional rigid-body robots, soft robots employ compliant structures to operate effectively in unstructured settings. Among various biological inspirations, the octopus stands out due to its remarkable intelligence, environmental adaptability, and multifunctional capabilities [2]. Octopus arms, composed entirely of soft muscle tissue and lacking any rigid skeletal structure, are capable of dexterous object grasping and agile locomotion [3]. These abilities arise from their intrinsic flexibility, distributed actuation, and intelligent control, enabling octopuses to grasp irregular objects, navigate confined spaces, and transition seamlessly between aquatic and terrestrial domains [4].

L. Hong and J. Wang—contribute equally to this work

© The Author(s), under exclusive license to Springer Nature Singapore Pte Ltd. 2026
T. Matsuno et al. (Eds.): ICIRA 2025, LNAI 16074, pp. 239–251, 2026.
https://doi.org/10.1007/978-981-95-2095-4_20

This unique combination of features makes the octopus arm an ideal biological model for the design of soft robotic arms. Inspired by the grasping capabilities of octopus arms, numerous studies have proposed bio-inspired soft grippers. Wu et al. [5] introduced a gripper modeled after the glowing sucker octopus, incorporating umbrella-shaped dorsal and ventral membranes between the arms. This design employed a 3D-printed linkage mechanism to actuate a modular soft suction disc through pneumatic deformation, enabling the gripper to lift objects via suction force. Xie et al. [6] developed an electronics-integrated soft octopus arm capable of reaching, sensing, grasping, and interacting within a wide spatial domain. In terms of locomotion, Ishida et al. [7] designed a soft underwater walking robot with a morphologically adaptable structure, achieving a stable locomotion speed of 15 mm/s in still water. To enhance environmental compatibility, [8] proposed a bipedal locomotion robot inspired by the coconut octopus, integrating a spring-loaded inverted pendulum model with cable-driven rolling arms. The system demonstrated stable movement over uneven underwater terrain, achieving an average walking speed of 6.48 cm/s and a peak speed of 8.14 cm/s. To advance multifunctional behavior, [9] presented a soft robotic gripper with six independently controlled arms. Capable of executing eight distinct grasping modes, the system also demonstrated omnidirectional crawling, swimming, grasping, and object retrieval in confined underwater environments. In [10], a bionic swimming platform was proposed, combining asymmetric passive morphing arms with an umbrella-like quick-return mechanism. Powered by only two constant-speed motors, the robot emulated octopus-like propulsion, reaching a peak speed of 314 mm/s during its second power stroke. Another octopus-inspired robot, featuring eight soft limbs, was developed to perform underwater bipedal locomotion, multi-arm swimming, and object manipulation [11]. Its cable-driven limbs enabled seabed interaction and three-dimensional navigation. Experimental validation demonstrated an average bipedal locomotion speed of 7.26 cm/s and a swimming speed of 8.6 cm/s. Yu et al. [12] introduced Hexapus, an underwater robot with multimodal locomotion capabilities. A hierarchical actuation system powered a high-torque central motor for general movement, while smaller motors controlled the shape of the appendages.

Despite significant advancements, most existing soft robotic arms remain task-specific designs and are typically restricted to operation within a single domain. Achieving multifunctionality across diverse environments remains a major challenge. In this paper, we address these limitations by presenting the design, fabrication, and evaluation of a soft robotic arm inspired by the biomechanics of octopus arms. The proposed system integrates soft silicone-based structures, pneumatic actuation, and control systems, enabling it to replicate the flexibility, compliance, and multifunctionality observed in its biological counterpart. Most notably, the soft robotic arm achieves both object grasping and locomotion in underwater and terrestrial environments, demonstrating genuine cross-domain adaptability without requiring structural reconfiguration. The remainder of this paper is organized as follows: Sect. 2 introduces the design of the soft robotic arm; Sect. 3 presents simulation analyses; Sect. 4 describes the prototype fabrication of the soft robotic arm; Sect. 5 validates the performance of the soft robotic arm through physical experiments; and Sect. 6 concludes the paper.

2 Structural Design

Unlike traditional single- or multi-segment integrated designs, our soft robotic arm consists of two modules: the main body and the end-effector, as shown in Fig. 1. The main body is responsible for initial positioning and posture adjustment during grasping and bipedal locomotion, while the end-effector is designed to perform object grasping and ground contact during bipedal locomotion. Both the main body and the end-effector have a length of 250 mm. Utilizing pneumatic actuation, the soft robotic arm achieves flexible deformation and enables coordinated control between the two modules through precise air-pressure regulation across a multi-channel system.

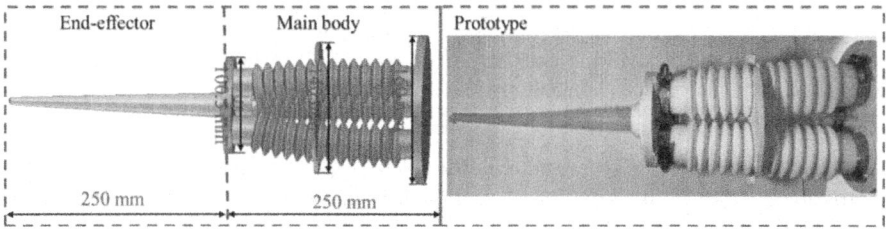

Fig. 1. 3D model of the soft robotic arm and the fabricated prototype.

2.1 Main Body Design

The main body of the proposed soft robotic arm is designed to achieve axial extension and contraction, as well as bending capabilities, inspired by the biological features of the octopus arm, as shown in Fig. 2A. To realize these motion capabilities, the arm integrates two actuation subsystems: one dedicated to producing bending and the other to regulating axial extension and contraction.

Specifically, to achieve the axial extension and contraction, three soft corrugated pneumatic actuators were arranged in a triangular, symmetrically parallel configuration and anchored by rigid end caps. Each actuator contained periodic pleats that undergo substantial axial deformation under pneumatic pressure, enabling the arm to extend, contract, or bend according to the applied pressure distribution. In addition, the arm employed disk-shaped end caps coupled with a constraint ring, which emulates the pressure-modulating function of circular muscles, as shown in Fig. 2B. This architecture enhances internal stability during actuation and facilitates coordinated motion control of the entire continuum structure. By modularly combining the corrugated actuators with the passive constraint elements, the soft robotic arm achieves smooth posture adjustment and compliant deformation in both terrestrial and underwater environments, thereby fulfilling the requirements of cross-domain, multimodal operations.

2.2 End-Effector Design

The end-effector is 250 mm in length and tapers at an angle of 4.5° from base to tip. In cross-section, the internal cavity forms an annular sector with an outer radius R_0,

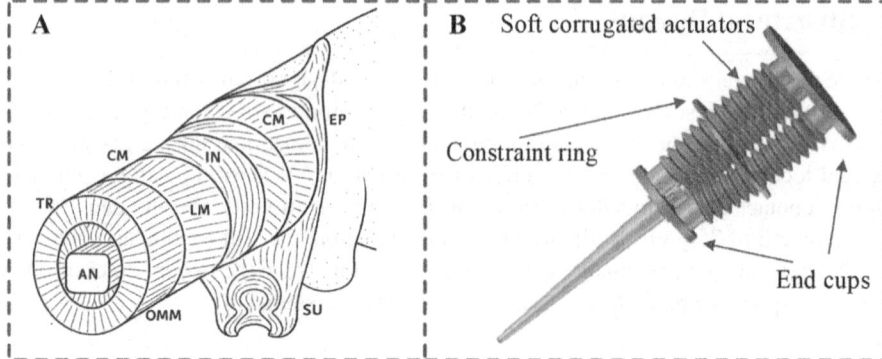

Fig. 2. Biological principles and robotic design. (A) Octopus vulgaris arm muscle system. LM: longitudinal muscle fibers; CM: circumferential muscle layer; OMM: median oblique muscle layer. (B) Components of the main body.

equal to half of the total cross-sectional radius. This sector spans 120° and occupies approximately 5% of the total cross-sectional area, as shown in Fig. 3. Bending is achieved by inflating the internal annular sector cavity. The tapered profile provides the end-effector with high flexibility. By regulating the internal pressure, the end-effector can grasp objects of varying sizes while reducing the risk of damaging delicate targets. Additionally, its ability to deform in confined spaces enhances its environmental adaptability.

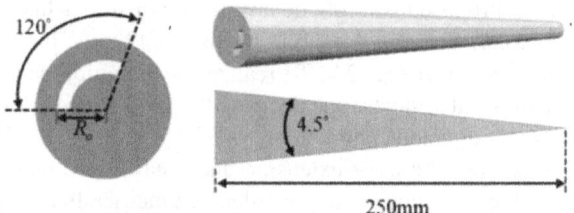

Fig. 3. Design of the end-effector.

3 Simulations and Analysis

3.1 Simulation Results of the Main Body and the End-Effector

For a single corrugated actuator, the length increases from 178 mm to 251 mm as the internal pressure rises from 0 kPa to 26 kPa, resulting in a maximum axial extension ratio of 41% (see Fig. 4A). The deformation is confined within the corrugated segment, while both end caps respond almost linearly, confirming good controllability and mechanical repeatability. For the end-effector, the internal pressure is gradually increased from 0 kPa to 180 kPa to induce directional bending. At 180 kPa, a minimum bending radius of 35 mm is achieved (see Fig. 4B). The data further reveal a positive correlation between the taper angle and the resulting bending radius, underscoring the effectiveness of the conical structural design.

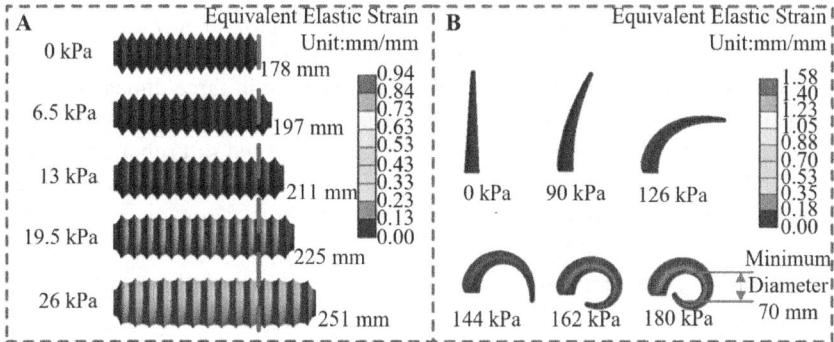

Fig. 4. (A) Extension of a single corrugated actuator. (B) Bending of the end-effector.

3.2 Simulation Results of the Soft Robotic Arm

For the soft robotic arm, differentiated pneumatic pressure applied to the three corrugated actuators enables the arm to achieve stable bending toward a specified direction.

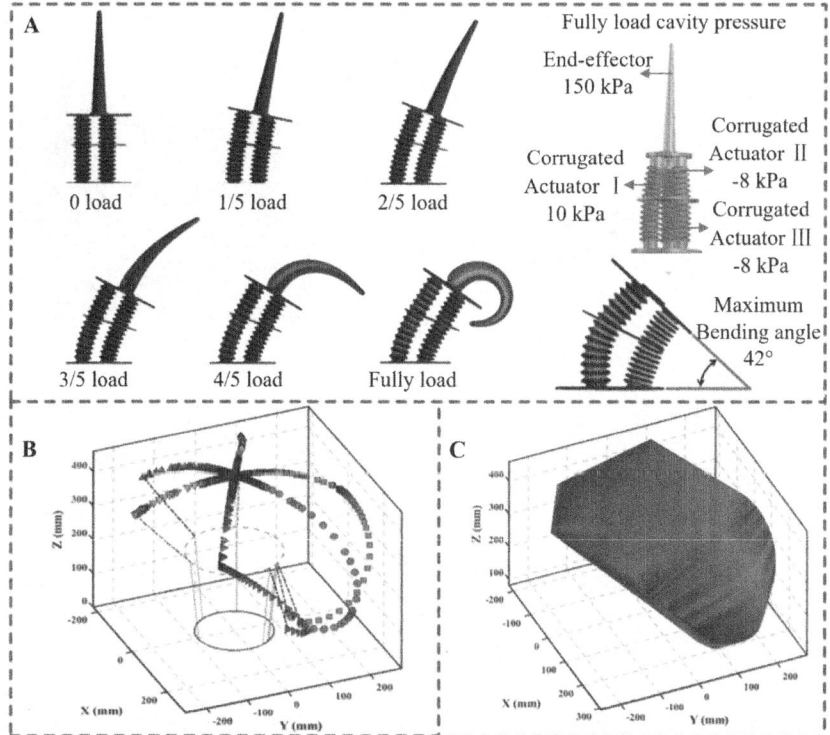

Fig. 5. (A) Deformation of the soft robotic arm. (B) Reachable position of the arm's tip. (C) Working space of the soft robotic arm.

244 L. Hong et al.

The maximum bending angle of the arm reaches approximately 42°, as shown in Fig. 5A. Together, the arm body and the end-effector form a two-stage actuation system that produces a continuous and smooth motion trajectory in three-dimensional space. The reachable position and workspace of the arm's tip are visualized in Fig. 5B and 5C, respectively. Simulation results demonstrate that the proposed soft robotic arm exhibits strong bending performance and a broad operational workspace, validating its potential for practical applications in unstructured environments.

4 Prototype Fabrication

A prototype of the soft robotic arm, integrated with an external pneumatic control system, was fabricated to verify the effectiveness of its structural design, actuation performance, and functional capabilities. Three corrugated actuators embedded in the arm body were manufactured via composite molding using nitrile rubber. The assembled arm body measures 250 mm in length and weighs 889 g. The end-effector was fabricated through mold casting, with a vacuum deaerator employed during the molding process to eliminate air bubbles. The end-effector weighs 91.3 g and was connected to the arm through direct insertion, followed by adhesive sealing. The pneumatic control system connects to the air tube via a quick-release connector, enabling efficient air delivery.

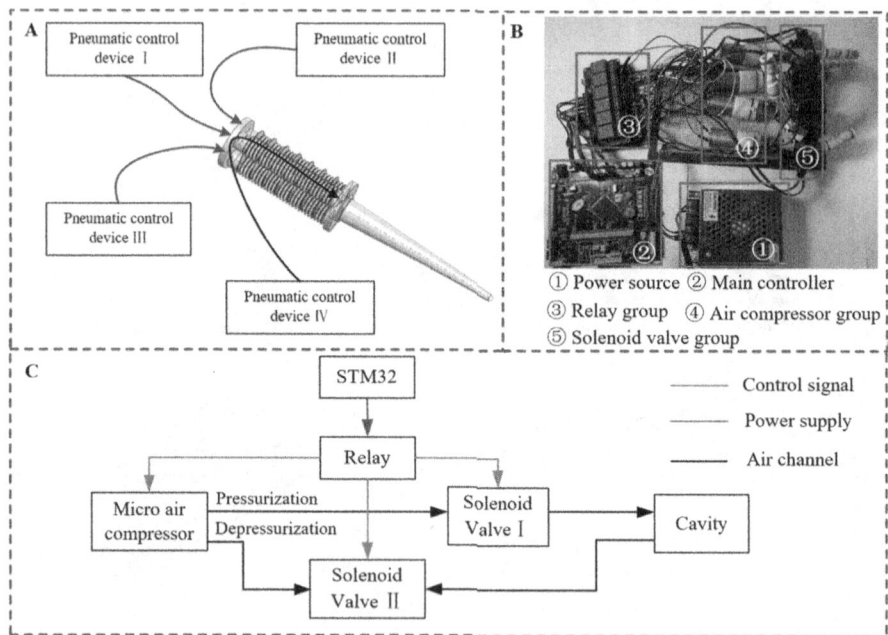

Fig. 6. Pneumatic control system. (A) Air channel schematic diagram. (B) Physical pneumatic control system and its components. (C) Diagram of single air channel pressure control.

An embedded control platform based on STM32 microcontroller is utilized in conjunction with four pneumatic control units (see Fig. 6A) to independently control the three corrugated actuators and the end-effector. An external micro air compressor is employed to supply pressurized air to the control units. As shown in Fig. 6B, the pneumatic control system consists of a power source, a main controller, a relay group, an air compressor group, and a solenoid valve group. Each pneumatic control unit regulates the pressure within an individual cavity. As shown in Fig. 6C, during pressurization, solenoid valve I connects the pressurization port of air compressor to the cavity. During depressurization, solenoid valve II connects the depressurization port to the cavity. The activation sequence of each air channel can be programmed or adjusted via remote control signals, enabling either predefined motion trajectories or manual operations.

5 Physical Experiments and Analysis

To evaluate the object grasping and bipedal locomotion performance of the soft robotic arm in amphibious environments, two experimental platforms were established: one for terrestrial testing and the other for underwater testing. For terrestrial experiments, the gantry was used to provide stable support and allowing for flexible mounting and positioning of the robotic arm, as shown in Fig. 7A. For underwater experiments, the robotic arm was placed in a transparent glass water tank measuring 900 × 500 × 500 mm, as shown in Fig. 7B. The suspension height of the robotic arm on both platforms could be flexibly adjusted by vertically repositioning screws and nuts on the support brackets.

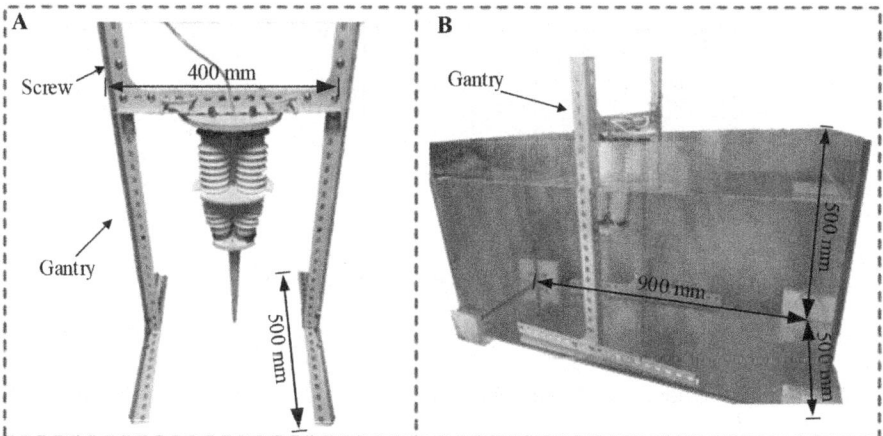

Fig. 7. Established experimental platform. (A) Experimental setup for terrestrial experiments. (B) Experimental setup for aquatic experiments.

5.1 Axial Extension, Contraction, and Bending Test

The performance of axial extension and contraction, as well as bending was evaluated under terrestrial conditions. The initial length of the soft robotic arm was measured to be 501 mm. In the axial extension and contraction test, the length of the main body could be precisely controlled within a range of 403 mm to 573 mm (see Fig. 8A). In the bending test, the arm exhibited stable performance across six preset directions spaced at 60° intervals. It achieved smooth bending motion from the initial position of 0° to a maximum bending angle of 85° within 6 s (see Fig. 8B). The results confirm arm's reliable capabilities for axial extension/contraction and directional bending.

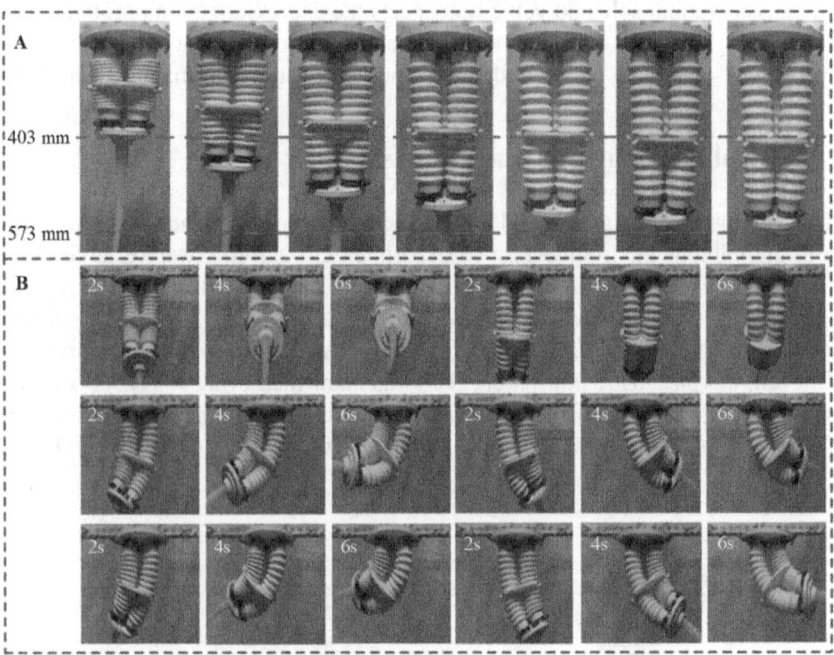

Fig. 8. Performance of axial extension, contraction, and bending. (A) Axial extension and contraction test results. (B) Multi-directional bending test results.

5.2 Object Grasping in Open Amphibious Environments

In the object grasping experiments, the soft robotic arm successfully grasped eight objects with diameters ranging from 52 mm to 76 mm and masses between 12 g and 185 g in air (See Fig. 9), demonstrating adaptability to a variety of object sizes and weights.

Fig. 9. Grasping various objects in the terrestrial environment using the soft robotic arm.

Furthermore, the soft robotic arm effectively grasped a water-filled bottle with a diameter of 75 mm and a total weight of 524.5 g underwater (See Fig. 10) confirming its capability for grasping heavier objects in aquatic environments.

Fig. 10. Comparison of grasping an object in air and underwater conditions.

5.3 Object Grasping in Confined Amphibious Environments

In experiments involving object retrieval through narrow openings, the end-effector successfully passed through a small trapezoidal gate (40 mm upper base, 80 mm lower base, and 100 mm in height) and grasped lightweight objects such as paper cups, as shown in Fig. 11.

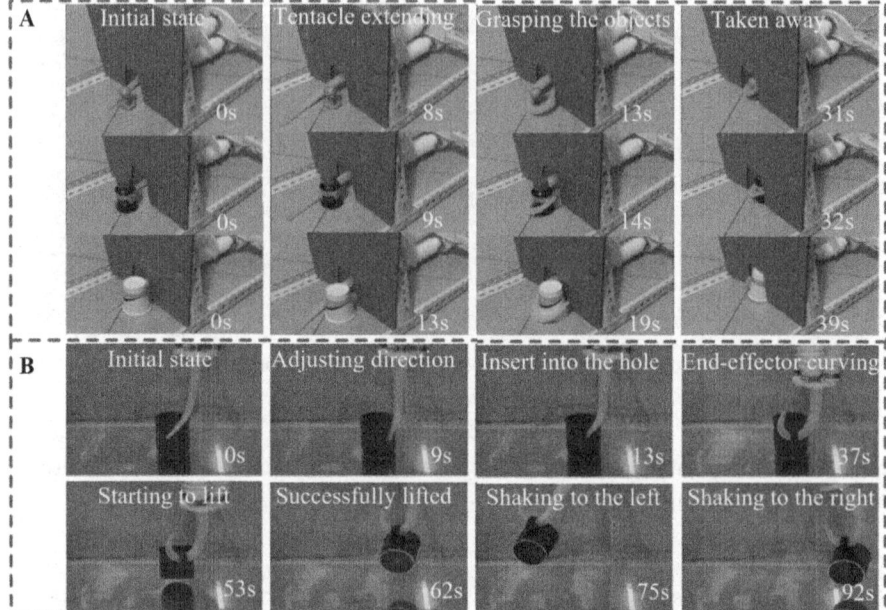

Fig. 11. Object grasping performance in open amphibious environments. (A) Grasping objects through a small trapezoidal gate in terrestrial environments. (B) Grasping and lifting a cup in underwater environments.

In underwater scenarios, the end-effector accurately navigated through the handle of a bottle with an inner diameter of 4.5 cm and successfully grasped the target object (see Fig. 11B) Coordinated with the bending and extension capabilities of the soft robotic arm, the complete grasp-and-lift operation was executed within 62 s. These results demonstrate the soft robotic arm's superior performance of object grasping in confined-space, as well as the effectiveness of coordinated control between the main body and end-effector in executing practical underwater tasks.

5.4 Underwater Bipedal Locomotion Test

The soft robotic arm was mounted on a metal bracket, which constrained its movement direction during the underwater bipedal locomotion test. The average speed was determined by recording the time required for the arm to push the bracket from one end of the tank to the other. In the single-arm locomotion experiment, the robotic arm successfully propelled the bracket forward, achieving an average speed of 11.6 mm/s, as shown in Fig. 12A. Building on asynchronous gait patterns observed in arthropods, an underwater bipedal locomotion test was conducted using two arms. Coordinated motion of the dual-arm system resulted in an increased average speed of 15.1 mm/s, as shown in Fig. 12B.

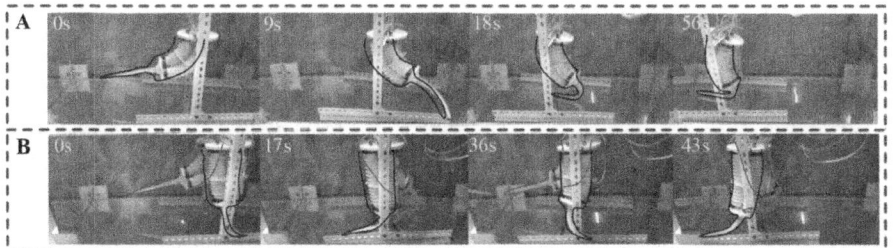

Fig. 12. Snapshots of underwater locomotion tests. (A) Single-arm locomotion experiment. (B) Dual-arm locomotion experiment.

5.5 Underwater Multifunction Experiments

To further demonstrate the multifunctional capabilities of the designed soft robotic arm, a dual-arm configuration was tested underwater. In this setup, one soft robotic arm was designated for locomotion and the other for grasping tasks. The locomotion arm generated propulsion to move the robotic system forward, while the other arm simultaneously performed object grasping. This coordinated operation highlights the system's ability to perform concurrent tasks in underwater environments. The experimental results are shown in Fig. 13, the robotic system successfully achieved forward movement while grasping a submerged target, validating the feasibility of cooperative control between locomotion and manipulation functions.

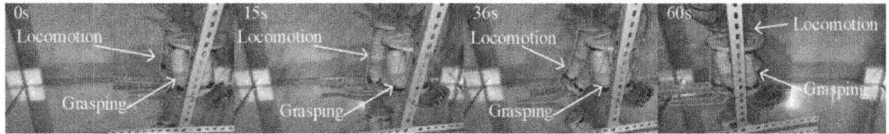

Fig. 13. Snapshots of the underwater multifunction experiment using a dual-arm configuration.

The experimental results of the soft robotic arm are summarized in Table 1. It can be observed that the system closely meets or exceeds the design specifications, particularly in terms of grasped target diameter, payload capacity, and underwater locomotion speed. These results validate the effectiveness of the proposed design and demonstrate that the arm was capable of performing both object grasping and bipedal locomotion in terrestrial and aquatic environments.

Table 1. Summary of experimental results for the soft robotic arm.

Function type	Metric	Environments	Design specifications	Experimental results	Ratio
Grasping	Target Diameter	Amphibious	>10 mm	52–76 mm	240%

(*continued*)

Table 1. (*continued*)

Function type	Metric	Environments	Design specifications	Experimental results	Ratio
	Load Capacity	Terrestrial	100 g	185 g	185%
		Aquatic	500 g	524.5 g	105%
Locomotion	Average Speed	Single-arm	10 mm/s	11.6 mm/s	116%
		Dual-arm	12 mm/s	15.1 mm/s	125%

6 Conclusion

Inspired by the biological features of octopus arms, a soft robotic arm capable of both object grasping and locomotion in amphibious environments was developed. The prototype features a lightweight, modular design that enables ease of assembly and adaptability. Simulation results validated the feasibility of the proposed design, while physical experiments confirmed that the prototype meets the intended performance criteria, successfully demonstrating object grasping and locomotion in both terrestrial and aquatic environments. However, the control system is constrained by the limited capacity of the external air compressor and closed-loop feedback control for individual arms and coordinated control strategies for multi-arm systems have not yet been implemented. Future work will focus on developing advanced sensors and control algorithms to enable real-time feedback control of multi-arm systems and support more complex task in amphibious environments.

References

1. Yasa, O., et al.: An overview of soft robotics. Annu. Rev. Control Robot. Auton. Syst. **6**(1), 1–29 (2023)
2. Yue, T., et al.: Embodying soft robots with octopus-inspired hierarchical suction intelligence. Sci. Robot. **10**(102), eadr4264 (2025)
3. Mather, J.A.: How do octopuses use their arms? J. Comp. Psychol. **112**(3), 306 (1998)
4. Laschi, C., Cianchetti, M., Mazzolai, B., Margheri, L., Follador, M., Dario, P.: Soft robot arm inspired by the octopus. Adv. Robot. **26**(7), 709–727 (2012)
5. Wu, M., et al.: Glowing sucker octopus (stauroteuthis syrtensis)-inspired soft robotic gripper for underwater self-adaptive grasping and sensing. Adv. Sci. **9**(17), 2104382 (2022)
6. Xie, Z., et al.: Octopus-inspired sensorized soft arm for environmental interaction. Sci. Robot. **8**(84), eadh7852 (2023)
7. Ishida, M., Drotman, D., Shih, B., Hermes, M., Luhar, M., Tolley, M.T.: Morphing structure for changing hydrodynamic characteristics of a soft underwater walking robot. IEEE Robot. Autom. Lett. **4**(4), 4163–4169 (2019)
8. Wu, Q., et al.: A novel underwater bipedal locomotion soft robot bio-inspired by the coconut octopus. Bioinspir. Biomim. **16**(4), 046007 (2021)
9. Wu, M., et al.: Octopus-inspired underwater soft robotic gripper with crawling and swimming capabilities. Research **7**, 0456 (2024)

10. Zhang, B., et al.: Octopus-swimming-like robot with soft asymmetric arms. arXiv preprint arXiv:2410.11764 (2024)
11. Wu, Q., et al.: An underwater biomimetic robot that can swim, bipedal walk and grasp. J. Bionic Eng. **21**(3), 1223–1237 (2024)
12. Yu, Q., Gravish, N.: Multimodal locomotion in a soft robot through hierarchical actuation. Soft Rob. **11**(1), 21–31 (2024)

Position Compensation Method for Cable-Pulling Robot in Generator Maintenance Without Rotor Removal

Shentao Ma[1], Yan Zhou[1], Jiantao Wang[2], Jianhua Wu[1], and Zhenhua Xiong[1](✉)

[1] State Key Laboratory of Mechanical System and Vibration, School of Mechanical Engineering, Shanghai Jiao Tong University, Shanghai 200240, China
mexiong@sjtu.edu.cn
[2] China Nuclear Power Operations Co., Ltd., Beijing, China

Abstract. For the maintenance of large generators, deploying robots within the narrow air gap between the stator and rotor significantly improves efficiency and cost-effectiveness compared to traditional methods requiring rotor removal. Among various actuation mechanisms, cable-pulling robots with non-contact inspection capabilities have shown strong potential in practical applications. However, cable sag caused by gravity can lead to path deviations, which result in positioning errors and undetectable areas. To address this problem, a position compensation method based on flexible cable simulation is proposed. By employing finite element modeling of the robot-cable system, the method can dynamically adjust cable anchor points to compensate for the robot's position deviations. Additionally, a Compensation Feasibility Map is introduced to visualize compensation difficulty across different regions inside the generator. Simulations of three generator models validate the method's effectiveness and generalizability. The impact of key parameters—such as inspection length, air gap width, and cable pretension—on compensation performance is also analyzed, which offers theoretical guidance for practical implementation.

Keywords: Cable-type inspection robot · position compensation · non-pumping rotor maintenance

1 Introduction

Regular maintenance is crucial to ensure the safe and stable operation of large-scale generators [1]. The stator and rotor, as the generator's core components, are separated by an extremely narrow gap [2], making direct manual inspection impractical, as shown in Fig. 1(a). Consequently, conventional methods typically require rotor removal to access the internal structure as shown in Fig. 1(b), which is both time-consuming and labor-intensive, and poses certain safety risks. Advances in robotics have led to the development of compact robots capable of navigating confined spaces [3–5]. These systems can enter the stator-rotor air gap and perform internal inspections without rotor extraction. Equipped with vision and other sensors, they enable targeted observation and data collection, offering significant improvements in efficiency, safety, and maintenance cycle, along with notable economic benefits. Nevertheless, the confined space and complex structure of the stator present great challenges for precise motion control of the robot. Specifically, when conducting internal inspections, the spatial and structural constraints increase the risk of substantial positioning errors. Accurate movement to designated inspection points is a prerequisite for effective operation. Therefore, research on motion planning for such robots is of considerable practical importance in enabling comprehensive inspection within the generator.

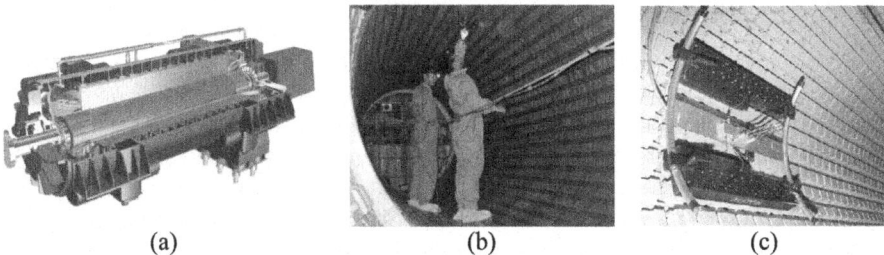

(a)   (b)   (c)

Fig. 1. Generator maintenance. (a) Generator. (b) Maintenance with rotor removal. (c) Contact-type robots.

Inspection robots can be classified into contact and non-contact types, depending on whether they physically interact with the internal structures of the generator [6, 7]. Contact-type robots adhere to the surface of the stator or rotor and rely on onboard actuators for movement. In contrast, non-contact robots are typically mounted on support structures like rails or cable systems that span the air gap between the stator and rotor. Their positioning and mobility are achieved through movement along these supporting elements. Due to the significant differences in drive mechanisms and mechanical configurations, the motion control strategies for the two types vary considerably.

Contact-type inspection robots primarily utilize magnetic adhesion to attach to the inner surfaces of generators and move along the stator or rotor via onboard drive mechanisms, as illustrated in Fig. 1(c). Significant research and industrial efforts have contributed to advancements in this field by institutions including Alstom, General Electric, Siemens, and IRIS Power [8–12], with further developments driven by academic research [13]. Despite significant advances in structural design and control, magnetically adhered robots still face several limitations. Magnetic adhesion is highly sensitive to surface conditions and electromagnetic interference, increasing the risk of unintentional detachment. Their mobility is limited in complex curved regions and during channel transitions. Furthermore, the climbing mechanism typically operates at low speed, reducing inspection efficiency. Space constraints on the robot body also hinder the integration of multiple functional modules (e.g., adhesion, drive, sensing), thereby limiting the diversity and depth of inspection capabilities.

Non-contact inspection robots can be categorized into two main types based on their support structures: rail-based and cable-pulling robots. Rail-based robots operate on rigid tracks, using adjustments of the track position to access different inspection points [14]. In contrast, cable-pulling robots employ flexible cables as their support system, relying on cable tension and retraction to achieve movement and positioning. This configuration offers advantages in structural lightness and deployment flexibility [15]. Within non-contact solutions, rail-based robots are well-suited for generators with relatively short axial lengths, allowing for precise motion control under stable support conditions. However, for large-scale generators with extended axial dimensions, rigid tracks are often impractical due to structural constraints, high deployment complexity, and limited adaptability, thereby restricting their applicability. By comparison, cable-pulling robots form a flexible support system through tensioned cables anchored at both ends, enabling effective coverage over long inspection paths. This makes them particularly suitable for large generators and highlights their greater potential.

Non-contact cable-pulling robots offer key advantages over contact-type robots, including fall prevention, improved stability, and enhanced safety. The stable support structure also facilitates better motion accuracy and faster inspection, increasing overall efficiency. However, the cables' inherent flexibility can cause sagging under gravity, leading to deviations between the robot's actual trajectory and the intended path, thereby affecting positioning accuracy. More critically, the cables may contact internal generator components, creating blind spots during inspection. This issue is influenced by various factors, such as robot and cable materials, structural design, and the geometric dimensions of the stator and rotor. Given its complexity, it requires advanced modeling and control strategies to effectively address positioning errors and obstacle avoidance in constrained environments.

To address positioning deviations and inspection failures caused by cable sag in cable-pulling robots, this paper proposes a position compensation method based on flexible cable deformation simulations. The method employs vertically adjustable support structures at both ends of the cable. When gravity-induced deviation occurs, the system can dynamically adjust the cable anchor points to correct the robot's position. Adjustment values are derived from simulations of the robot-cable system at various inspection locations. By incorporating the actual geometry of the stator and rotor, physical simulations estimate cable deformation at each point, enabling precise compensation parameter calculation. To evaluate the method's applicability across different generator types, a Compensation Feasibility Map is introduced, which can visually illustrate compensation difficulty throughout the generator, supporting the path planning, structural design, and on-site operation of the robot. Simulation studies further analyze the influence of key parameters on compensation performance, offering practical guidance for system configuration. This method improves positioning accuracy and operational efficiency in constrained environments and advances the practical deployment of non-contact inspection technologies of generators, thereby filling a gap in the relevant technological field.

2 The Proposed Method

2.1 Analysis of Cable-Pulling Maintenance Problems

The cable-pulling robotic inspection method for generators without rotor removal (hereafter referred to as the cable-pulling inspection method) offers significant potential in generator maintenance due to its non-contact operation and high efficiency. In this approach, the robot is deployed via working cables stretched across the air gap between the stator and rotor, enabling internal inspection and maintenance. However, as illustrated in Fig. 2(a), the working cables tend to sag vertically under the combined effects of the robot's weight and the cables' own mass. This sag results in a positional deviation between the actual working height h_{target} and the target height h_{target}, defined as $\Delta h = h_{target} - h_{actual}$. Such deviations may compromise inspection accuracy and, more critically, lead to potential collisions between the robot and generator components. Addressing this positioning error is a key challenge for the effective implementation of the cable-pulling inspection method.

In the implementation of position compensation for cable-pulling robots, it is essential to account not only for the local position deviation Δh at the inspection point but also for the geometric constraints of the stator-rotor air gap. As shown in Fig. 2(b), an imprecisely calculated compensation strategy may cause spatial interference between the working cables and the generator structure, rendering the correction ineffective. In this case, the required upward adjustment on the right cable end, H_{r-req}, exceeds the maximum permissible compensation height H_{max} at that position, making the compensation unfeasible. Notably, the value of H_{max} varies across different inspection points and must be determined by considering both the specific dimensions of the stator and rotor and the circumferential location of the target point. Therefore, accurately identifying potential position deviations and the corresponding geometric constraints at various inspection points is critical for developing feasible compensation strategies.

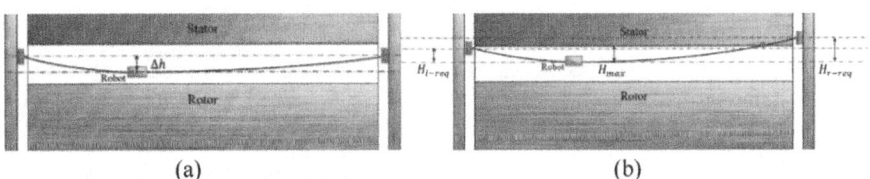

(a) (b)

Fig. 2. Cable-pulling maintenance model. (a) Model of Δh. (b) Compensation failure

2.2 Position Compensation Method

To address the aforementioned issues, this paper proposes a position compensation method based on vertical adjustment of the working cables. Given the known geometric parameters of the generator—such as stator and rotor lengths and the air gap width—the method employs finite element simulation and computation to estimate the position deviation Δh at each inspection point. It then calculates the required compensation displacements at the left and right cable ends, denoted as H_{l-req} and H_{r-req}, under different compensation plan, as illustrated in Fig. 2(b). By comparing these values with the corresponding maximum allowable compensation limits at each location, feasible compensation parameters can be identified and selected.

As shown in Fig. 3, the generator under inspection is modeled geometrically as a combination of a stator cylinder and a rotor cylinder. The location of each inspection point is defined by two parameters: the axial position x and the circumferential angle θ, where $x \in [0, L_{gen}]$, $\theta \in [0, 2\pi)$, and L_{gen} denotes the axial length of the inspection region within the generator.

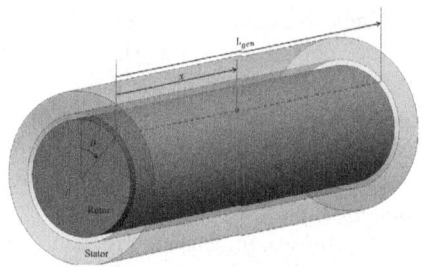

Fig. 3. Position definition of the generator awaiting maintenance.

The workflow of the proposed method is illustrated in Fig. 4 that comprises three primary steps. Firstly, finite element analysis is performed for each inspection point based on the geometric parameters of the generator to obtain candidate compensation parameters. Secondly, the actual compensable range for inspection points at different circumferential angles is calculated. Finally, the feasibility of each candidate compensation parameter is evaluated, and viable compensation parameters suitable for generator inspection are identified.

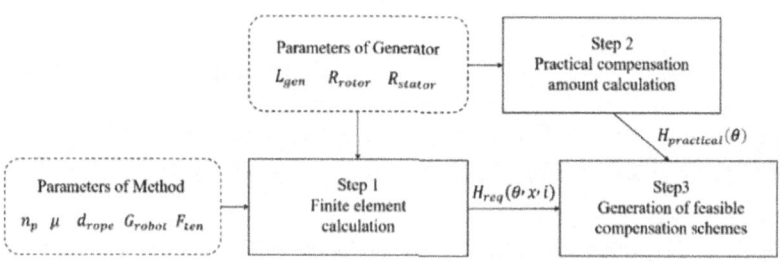

Fig. 4. Position compensation flowchart of cable-pulling robot.

Step 1: Finite Element Calculation. For each inspection point, the robot's position error $\Delta h(\theta, x)$ is computed using finite element analysis. Based on this, multiple lifting compensation plans $P(\theta, x, i)$ can be generated by adjusting the heights of both cable endpoints to offset the sag, and restore the robot to its target position, where $i = 1, 2, \ldots, n_p$, and n_p is the total number of compensation plan at each target inspection point. Each compensation plan corresponds to a pair of candidate lifting values at the left and right cable ends, denoted as $H_{l-req}(\theta, x, i)$ and $H_{r-req}(\theta, x, i)$. For example, when $n_p = 3$ and the step size is 10 mm, the difference between the two compensation values can be 0 mm, 10 mm, or −10 mm, generating 3 candidate plans at each point.

During the finite element analysis, appropriate simplifications and parameter settings were applied to ensure modeling efficiency without compromising accuracy. Key simulation parameters include the rope diameter d_{rope}, robot weight G_{robot}, and cable pretension F_{ten}. Based on previous investigations, generator lengths typically exceed 7 m, while the inspection robot is generally around 350 mm in length. Therefore, in the simulation, the robot is reasonably simplified as a point mass to improve computational efficiency without compromising accuracy. This simplification streamlines the modeling process while maintaining sufficient computational precision.

Step 2: Practical Compensation Amount Calculation. The calculation of the feasible compensation begins with determining the maximum allowable compensation amount H_{max}. Based on the simplified geometric model of the generator's stator and rotor, it is established that for inspection points located at the same radial angle θ, the corresponding $H_{max}(\theta)$ remains constant. The calculation is shown in Eq. (1). In this context, R_{stator} and R_{rotor} denote the inner radius of the stator and the outer radius of the rotor, respectively. R_{target} represents the radial position of the inspection point, which is usually set to the average of R_{stator} and R_{rotor} for balanced access to both stator and rotor. For points at different radial positions, H_{max} is constrained by potential interference between the cable and either the stator or rotor; near the generator's centerline, reduced contact allows a larger H_{max}.

$$H_{max}(\theta) = \begin{cases} H_1(\theta), \text{ if } \cos\theta \geq 0 \\ H_2(\theta), \text{ if } \cos\theta \leq 0 \text{ and } |R_{target}\sin\theta| \leq R_{rotor} \\ H_3(\theta), \text{ if } \cos\theta \leq 0 \text{ and } |R_{target}\sin\theta| > R_{rotor} \end{cases}$$

$$H_1(\theta) = \sqrt{R_{stator}^2 - R_{target}^2\sin^2\theta} - R_{target}\cos\theta \quad (1)$$

$$H_2(\theta) = -R_{target}\cos\theta - \sqrt{R_{rotor}^2 - R_{target}^2\sin^2\theta}$$

$$H_3(\theta) = -R_{target}\cos\theta + \sqrt{R_{stator}^2 - R_{target}^2\sin^2\theta}$$

In practical engineering applications, inspection robots tolerate a certain range of positioning errors that do not affect operational performance. Here, the allowable error is defined as a parameter related to the air gap width. As shown in Eq. (2), the practical compensable amount $H_{practical}(\theta)$ is determined jointly by the maximum allowable compensation and the permissible error:

$$H_{practical}(\theta) = H_{max}(\theta) + \mu * (R_{stator} - R_{rotor}) \quad (2)$$

where μ represents the error tolerance coefficient, typically set to 10%.

Step 3: Generation of Feasible Compensation Plan. By comparing the candidate compensation amounts at the left and right ends of the working cable with $H_{practical}(\theta)$ at each inspection point, feasible compensation plans $P_{pass}(\theta, x, i)$ can be identified. These plans must satisfy both conditions: $H_{l-req}(\theta, x, i) \leq H_{practical}(\theta)$ and $H_{r-req}(\theta, x, i) \leq H_{practical}(\theta)$. Such compensation plans form the feasible strategy set for different inspection points, providing guidance for the operation of cable-pulling generator inspection robots.

2.3 Indicators: Compensation Feasibility Map and Diversity Index

To clearly demonstrate the effectiveness of the proposed method across different types of generators, two evaluation metrics are introduced: the Compensation Feasibility Map (CF Map) and the Diversity Index. The details are as follows:

During the finite element simulations, the inspection positions are discretized based on the number of inspection channels and the spacing between points within each channel. Let n_θ denote the number of channels, and n_x the number of inspection points along the axial direction x within each channel. A total of $n_p \times n_\theta \times n_x$ finite element analyses are conducted to obtain the distribution of position errors and all candidate compensation plans for the entire inspection domain. As shown in Fig. 5, two maps are used to illustrate the accessibility of inspection points. Figure 5(a) presents the Detection Feasibility Map (DF Map), describing the feasibility of detection in each point. A point is considered detectable if the robot's sagging error satisfies $\Delta h \leq \mu * (R_{stator} - R_{rotor})$. CF Map shown in Fig. 4(b) represent the number of feasible compensation plans per point, indicating the effectiveness of the proposed method. Based on this number, each point is classified as Feasible (at least one plan exists at this point), Appropriate (feasible plans $\geq 1/3$ of total number n_p), or Optimal ($\geq 2/3$), reflecting different levels of detectability.

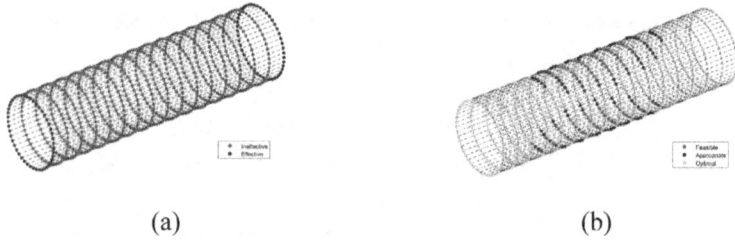

(a) (b)

Fig. 5. Examples of two detection maps. (a) DF Map. (b) CF Map

To evaluate the applicability of the proposed compensation method across different generator models, Diversity Index γ_{pass} is defined in Eq. (3), which measures the proportion of feasible plans relative to the total number of candidate plans. $\sum P_{pass}(\theta, x, i)$ denotes the total count of feasible plans across all inspection points.

$$\gamma_{pass} = \frac{\sum P_{pass}(\theta, x, i)}{n_p \cdot n_\theta \cdot n_x} \qquad (3)$$

3 Simulation Verification

3.1 Simulation Environments

According to equipment data from multiple thermal and nuclear power enterprises, the inspection region between the stator and rotor measuring approximately 7 to 13 m. To ensure the representativeness of the simulation, we select three representative generator types: the CAP1400 nuclear half-speed turbine generator, the AP1000 nuclear half-speed turbine generator produced by Harbin Electric Corporation, and the TA1100-78 brushless excitation generator provided by Dongfang Electric Corporation. These generators serve as the basis for constructing three representative simulation models, covering typical length and air gap configurations. The models and their key dimensional parameters are illustrated in Fig. 6.

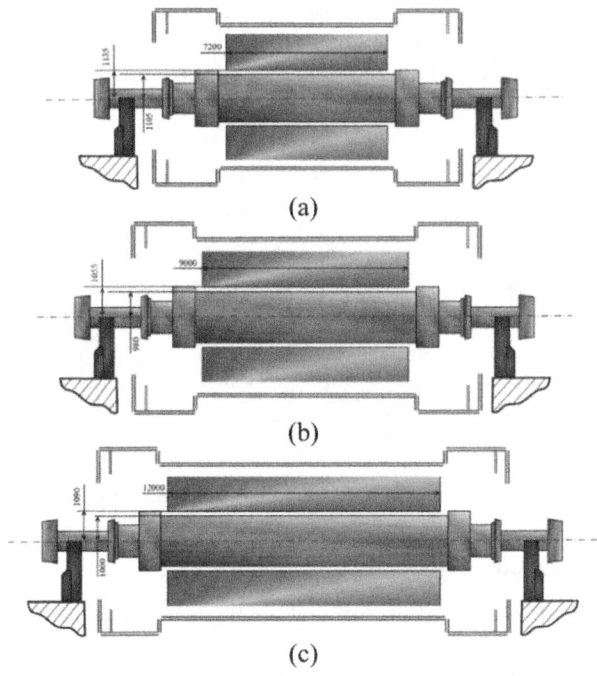

Fig. 6. Three generator simulation models. (a) CAP1400. (b) AP1000. (c) TA1100-78

Based on prior research on inspection robots and cable-pulling inspection, the simulation parameters are set as follows: a 3 kg robot is used as the inspection unit, suspended by two steel cables with a radius of 10 mm. Cable length is set according to the generator's inspection region and subjected to varying levels of pretension. 48 equally spaced inspection channels are arranged along the stator circumference, with inspection points placed every 500 mm along each channel, centered within the air gap. For each point, the adjustment step for the left-right anchor compensation difference is set to 10 mm, with the number of compensation plans n_p determined by the air gap width. All finite element modeling and simulation are conducted in Adams.

3.2 Simulation Results

3.2.1 Results of Original Method

Through finite element analysis, Δh of the robot across different inspection regions were obtained for the three simulation scenarios. Based on whether these errors fall within the acceptable range. The resulting DF Map is illustrated in Fig. 7. Simulation results show that without compensation, significant deviations occur between the robot's actual position and its intended targets. Positioning errors often exceed acceptable limits, restricting effective inspection to a small area near the outer edge of the generator. This leads to low coverage and limited task accessibility, greatly reducing the system's practical applicability.

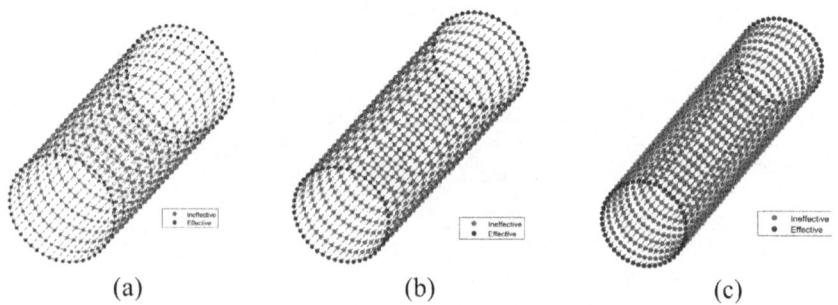

Fig. 7. Simulation without compensation method. (a) CAP1400. (b) AP1000. (c) TA1100-78

3.2.2 Results of Proposed Method

Subsequently, the proposed compensation method is applied. $H_{l-req}(\theta, x, i)$ and $H_{r-req}(\theta, x, i)$ are calculated for all inspection points, along with the $H_{practical}(\theta)$. Based on the number of feasible plans at each location, the CF Map are generated, and the Diversity Index γ_{pass} are computed, as illustrated in Fig. 8.

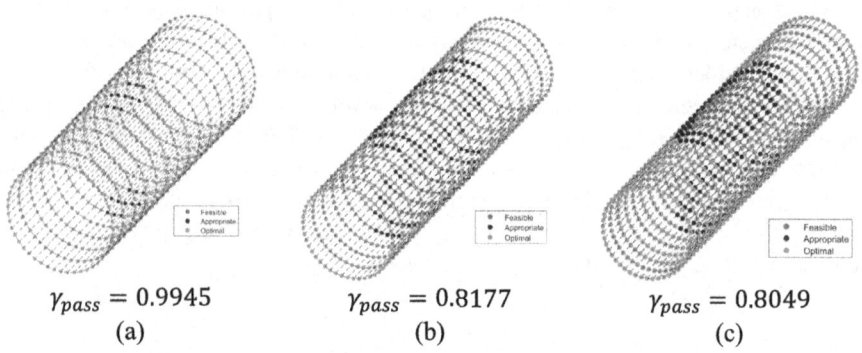

$\gamma_{pass} = 0.9945$ $\gamma_{pass} = 0.8177$ $\gamma_{pass} = 0.8049$
(a)   (b)   (c)

Fig. 8. Effect of the compensation method. (a) CAP1400. (b) AP1000. (c) TA1100-78

As shown by the CF Map, the proposed compensation method enables the robot to successfully reach all inspection points in all three simulation scenarios. Additionally, the results reveal several noteworthy phenomena. Firstly, feasible compensation plans are scarce in the upper and lower regions ($\theta \approx 0°, 180°$) near the generator's central axis. Gravity maximally sags the cable in these spots, demanding large anchor adjustments. Simultaneously, the stator/rotor geometry provides minimal clearance $H_{max}(\theta)$ for these adjustments, making compensation difficult. Secondly, the Diversity Index γ_{pass} decreased with longer generator spans. Longer cables sag more under gravity, requiring larger corrections. However, the generator's fixed radial dimensions limit the range of $H_{practical}(\theta)$, causing the required larger adjustments on longer spans to more frequently exceed feasible limits.

4 Parameter Analysis

To further evaluate the applicability and performance trends of the proposed compensation method across different generator types, this section analyzes the effects of three key parameters: inspection region length, air gap width, and cable pretension. Based on the AP1000 simulation model from the previous section as the reference, each parameter is varied independently for comparison. The compensation effectiveness is quantitatively assessed by defining the overall success rate as the proportion of inspection points with at least one feasible compensation plan.

4.1 Inspection Region Length

This subsection analyzes the impact of generator length on the performance of the proposed compensation method. R_{stator} and R_{rotor} are fixed at 980 mm and 1080 mm, respectively, with zero cable pretension. Based on this configuration, six simulations are constructed with inspection region lengths ranging from 9 m to 14 m with 1 m increments. The compensation method is applied to each case, and the corresponding compensation success rates are calculated to evaluate the effect of length variation. The simulation results are summarized in Table 1.

Table 1. The variation of success rate with length.

Length(m)	9	10	11	12	13	14
Success rate	100.00%	100.00%	100.00%	92.16%	84.07%	77.21%

Simulation results indicate that as the length of the inspection region increases, the effectiveness of the compensation method declines, reflected in a noticeable reduction in the compensation success rate. This trend suggests that with longer cable, the robot's positional deviation increases, leading to higher required compensation values that may exceed the system's feasible correction limits. To maintain compensation feasibility over extended inspection paths, it is necessary to either adjust other parameters or optimize boundary conditions to suppress the amplification of position errors.

4.2 Gap Width

This subsection analyzes the impact of air gap width on the effectiveness of the compensation method. The inspection region length is set to 9 m, with zero pretension applied to the cables. R_{rotor} is fixed at 980 mm, while the air gap width is varied from 100 mm to 50 mm. The corresponding simulation results are summarized in Table 2.

Table 2. The variation of success rate with gap width.

Gap width (mm)	100	90	80	70	60	50
Success rate	100.00%	100.00%	100.00%	96.08%	84.56%	75.25%

Under the above parameters, the required compensation at each inspection position remains constant. As the air gap width decreases, $H_{practical}$ across different inspection channels is significantly reduced, leading to a lower pass rate for compensation plans. Consistent with the previous analysis, the feasibility of the compensation method begins to decline from the upper and lower central regions of the generator.

4.3 Pretension

This subsection analyzes the effect of pretension on the performance of the compensation method. R_{stator} and R_{rotor} are set consistent with Fig. 6(b), with inspection region length fixed at 11 m. The pretension force applied to the cables is gradually increased from 0 N to 50 kN. Table 3 present the simulation results.

Table 3. The variation of success rate with pretension.

Pretension (kN)	0	10	20	30	40	50
Success rate	80.39%	84.56%	89.95%	95.59%	100.00%	100.00%

As the pretension force increases, the success rate of the compensation method improves. This is attributed to the effective shortening of the cable length under higher tension, which reduces sag caused by self-weight and alters the force distribution in the flexible elements, thereby decreasing the system's sensitivity to gravitational loading on the robot. However, in practical applications, increasing pretension also raises engineering risks; thus, any adjustment to this parameter must be carefully considered.

5 Conclusions

In generator maintenance without rotor removal, cable-pulling inspection robots that operate within the narrow stator-rotor air gap suffer from gravitational sag, leading to detection errors or collisions. This paper proposes a compensation method based on flexible cable simulation. Finite element analysis is used to compute robot position errors at each inspection point and generate corresponding upward compensation plans, which are evaluated against practical compensation limits to identify feasible solutions. Evaluation metrics are introduced to quantify the method's effectiveness and adaptability across different generator models.

Simulations on three representative generators demonstrate that the proposed method provides reliable compensation under varied conditions. The effects of inspection region length, air gap width, and cable pretension on compensation performance are also analyzed, offering guidance for parameter selection.

Future work will focus on optimizing the finite element analysis process and developing more efficient models for feasible plan computation to improve overall computational efficiency. Additionally, path planning based on the identified feasible compensation plans will be explored to support optimal inspection trajectory design for cable-pulling robots, offering both theoretical and engineering insights.

Acknowledgement. This work is supported in part by Shanghai Technology Innovation Action Plan (Grant No.24511103303).

References

1. Canali, C., Leggieri, S., Ludovico, D., et al.: Fully automated robotic inspection of power generators. In: 2024 20th IEEE/ASME International Conference on Mechatronic and Embedded Systems and Applications (MESA), pp. 1–6. IEEE (2024)
2. Lee, C.H.: Electric Power Principle: Sources, Conversion, Distribution and Use, 2nd edn. (2021)
3. Kwansud, P., Srinonchat, J.: Location identification of generator inspection robot (GIR) using image processing technique. In: 2017 56th Annual Conference of the Society of Instrument and Control Engineers of Japan (SICE), pp. 395–400. IEEE (2017)
4. Kuwahara, H., Hiraguri, K., Terai, F.: Development of pushing control mechanisms for generator inspection robot. In: 2020 IEEE 16th International Workshop on Advanced Motion Control (AMC), pp. 135–142. IEEE (2020)
5. Kostrykin, L., Rohr, C., Rohr, K.: Globally optimal and scalable video image stitching for robotic visual inspection of electric generators. In: 2021 21st International Conference on Control, Automation and Systems (ICCAS), pp. 1141–1145. IEEE (2021)
6. Kadota, N., Kota, Y.A.N.O., Mizuno, D., Morimoto, Y.: Endless-track traveling apparatus, and movable body of generator inspection robot including the same. U.S. Patent 11,319,003 (2022)
7. Xie, X., Li, C., Li, X., Chen, W.: A stator channel wedge loosening offline detection system based on an intelligent maintenance robot of a large hydro generator. Machines **10**(8), 655 (2022)
8. Moser, R., Mark, B.: Automated robotic inspection of large generator stators. In: 2007 IEEE/ASME International Conference on Advanced Intelligent Mechatronics, pp. 1–5. IEEE (2007)
9. Fischer, W., Caprari, G., Siegwart, R., Moser, R.: Robotic crawler for inspecting generators with very narrow air gaps. In: 2009 IEEE International Conference on Mechatronics, pp. 1–5. IEEE (2009)
10. Fischer, R., Fischer, W., Honold, S., Loosli, D.: The 'DIRIS' class of in-situ generator inspection systems. In: 2012 2nd International Conference on Applied Robotics for the Power Industry (CARPI), pp. 193–196. IEEE (2012)

11. Fischer, W., Caprari, G., Siegwart, R., Moser, R.: Compact climbing robot rolling on flexible magnetic rollers, for generator inspection with the rotor still installed. Industr. Rob.: Int. J. **39**(3), 236–241 (2012)
12. Zhang, G., et al.: A modular air-gap crawler for motor and generator in-situ inspection. In: 2015 IEEE International Conference on Industrial Technology (ICIT), pp. 3166–3171. IEEE (2015)
13. Ma, H., Zhai, C., Gao, Y., Xie, Q., Li, D., Fang, J.: Design and development of generator non-pumping rotor fault detection robot. In: 2023 Asia-Pacific Conference on Image Processing, Electronics and Computers (IPEC), pp. 187–192. IEEE (2023)
14. Nguyen, M.Q.: Generator retaining ring scanning robot. U.S. Patent Application 14/285,591 (2014)
15. Luigi, M., Vincenzo, S.: An apparatus and troubleshooting method for monitoring the operability of rotating electric generators such as turboalternators. Eur. Patent Appl. (1995)

Intelligent Technology in Neural Decoding, Modulation, and Interfacing

Research on Pose Control Dataset Augmentation Method Based on Generative Adversarial Networks

Zhe Sun[✉], Han Xiao, and Peng Sun

Zhejiang University of Technology, Hangzhou 310014, Zhejiang, China
sunzhe91@zjut.edu.cn

Abstract. With the advancement of deep learning technologies, significant progress has been made in deep learning-based robot pose control methods. However, these methods rely heavily on large-scale labeled datasets for model training, and the acquisition of labeled data is time-consuming and labor-intensive, significantly limiting the application of deep learning in pose control. Recent developments in generative models have made dataset augmentation using generative algorithms an effective approach to address this challenge. This paper proposes a method that leverages Generative Adversarial Networks (GANs) to learn the distribution of pose data and generate new robot pose samples. Analysis using the Maximum Mean Discrepancy (MMD) and 1-Nearest Neighbor (1-NN) metrics reveals that the distribution of generated data closely resembles that of real data, indicating that the GAN-generated samples are of high quality and can effectively mitigate the small-sample problem in training pose control models.

Keywords: Pose Control · GAN · Data Augmentation

1 Introduction

With the rapid advancement of robotic intelligence technologies, high-precision pose control has become increasingly critical in the fields of industrial automation and service robotics. Deep learning-driven pose control models require large volumes of labeled data for training. However, in practical applications, the acquisition of large-scale pose control datasets is constrained by the cost of hardware sensors and the complexity of dynamic environments, making it a key bottleneck that limits the deployment of these technologies.

Significant progress has been made in deep learning-based human pose recognition and control research. Zhou et al. [1] proposed a human pose recognition method based on deep attention mechanisms to enhance status assessment and control optimization during human-robot collaboration. By utilizing quaternion-based calibration and forward kinematic analysis methods, they improved the accuracy of pose reconstruction, achieving commendable results. Li et al. [2] proposed an AR-assisted, deep reinforcement learning-based pose-awareness technique to enhance safety performance in human–robot interaction. The approach incorporates worker visual augmentation, robot velocity control, Digital Twin-enabled motion preview and collision detection, as well as Deep Reinforcement Learning-based robot collision avoidance and motion planning, all integrated in an Augmented Reality-assisted framework. Zheng et al. [3] conducted a detailed review of deep learning-based pose recognition and control methods. Numerous advanced deep learning techniques have been employed to enhance the robustness and accuracy of pose recognition and control. However, these methods typically rely on precisely annotated pose sequence data, which includes multimodal information such as joint angles, end-effector poses, and inertial measurement unit (IMU) readings. In practical applications, robotic systems often face challenges such as long data acquisition cycles and noisy measurements caused by dynamic disturbances, making it difficult to meet the requirements of model training in terms of both data quantity and quality.

To address this issue, data augmentation using generative models has emerged as a promising research direction for overcoming the limitations imposed by small sample sizes. Among various generative models, Generative Adversarial Networks (GANs), as one of the most advanced frameworks, have demonstrated unique advantages in the field of robotics. By leveraging adversarial training mechanisms to learn the underlying data distribution, GANs have been successfully applied in multiple related domains. Gulakala et al. [4] utilized GANs to augment the Covid-19 dataset, thereby enhancing the diagnostic effectiveness of Covid-19. Naaz et al. [5] utilized GANs to augment the battery state dataset, thereby enhancing the intelligent assessment of battery states.

Although existing research has confirmed the potential of GANs in motion data generation, specific challenges remain in the context of robotic pose control. Unlike conventional motion data, pose control sequences exhibit strong spatiotemporal dependencies and physical constraints. Even minor generation errors may lead to control failure. For example, the positioning error tolerance for robotic manipulators is typically within millimeters, while the allowable center-of-mass deviation for bipedal robots is generally less than 2°. These high-precision requirements make traditional generative approaches prone to producing "pose drift" that violates dynamic constraints, significantly reducing the usability of the generated data.

To this end, this study explores the application of GANs for data augmentation in robotic pose control. We propose optimized learning strategies to enhance the quality of generated data and construct evaluation metrics for quantifying the distributional differences between synthesized and real-world data. The ultimate goal is to achieve high-fidelity pose control data augmentation, providing a novel solution for improving the performance of control models under limited data conditions.

2 Basic Theory

2.1 Generative Adversarial Networks

Generative adversarial networks (GANs), first introduced by Goodfellow et al. in 2014, have since garnered significant attention within the field. GANs train generative models through an adversarial process involving two neural networks: a discriminator and a generator. The training objective is for the generator network G to learn the probability distribution of real data.

Early GANs used fully connected neural networks to construct both the generator and discriminator models. A set of noise variables is defined $p_z(z)$ and mapped to the data space via a neural network $G(z; \theta_g)$. Another neural network $D(x; \theta_d)$ outputs a single scalar indicating the probability that x belongs to the real data. The discriminator model D is trained using gradient descent to maximize the probability of correctly distinguishing between real and generated data. Simultaneously, the generator model G is trained to minimize $\log(1 - D(G(z)))$. This process represents a binary minimax game between G and D, which can be expressed as Eq. 1:

$$\min_G \max_D V(D, G) = \mathbb{E}_{x \sim p_{data}(x)}[\log D(x)] + \mathbb{E}_{z \sim p_z(z)}[\log(1 - D(G(z)))] \quad (1)$$

where p_{data} is the distribution of real data and p_z is the distribution from the latent space.

The original GAN faced numerous issues, including training difficulties and instability. To enhance the usability of GANs, subsequent research proposed several new versions that significantly improved training stability, such as Wasserstein GAN (WGAN) and its improved variant WGAN-GP.

WGAN uses the Wasserstein distance as the loss function for training GANs [6], addressing the vanishing gradient problem when there is no overlap between real and generated distributions. The definition of the Wasserstein distance is shown in Eq. 2:

$$W(P_r, P_g) = \inf_{\gamma \in \prod(P_r, P_g)} \mathbb{E}_{(x,y) \sim \gamma}[\|x - y\|] \quad (2)$$

where $\prod(P_r, P_g)$ is the set of all joint distributions with marginals P_r and P_g. However, the exact solution for $\inf_{\gamma \sim \prod(P_r, P_g)}$ cannot be directly computed, so Eq. 2 is reformulated into Eq. 3:

$$W(P_r, P_\theta) = \sup_{\|f\|_L \leq 1} \mathbb{E}_{x \sim P_r}[f(x)] - \mathbb{E}_{x \sim P_\theta}[f(x)] \quad (3)$$

Here, the function f must satisfy the Lipschitz continuity condition, i.e., $\|f\| \leq 1$. To meet this condition, WGAN restricts the parameters of the discriminator network D to lie within $[-c, c]$.

Subsequent research found that WGAN could sometimes fail to converge due to forcing the parameter range to satisfy the Lipschitz condition. Therefore, a strategy using gradient penalty was proposed to replace the forced restriction, leading to the development of a new GAN variant called WGAN-GP [7]. This novel structure is stable during training, easy to converge, and has been widely adopted.

2.2 Evaluation of Data Distribution Consistency

Evaluating Generative Adversarial Network (GAN) models is a highly challenging task. For complex generated data, it is essential to assess not only the differences between the probability distributions of generated and real data but also the diversity of the generated data itself. Currently, there is no universally accepted standard evaluation method. Xu et al. [8] conducted a comprehensive comparative analysis of common GAN evaluation methods and concluded that the Kernel Maximum Mean Discrepancy (MMD) and 1-Nearest Neighbor (1-NN) metrics are two highly effective evaluation metrics. These metrics can distinguish between real and generated samples, identify issues such as mode dropping and mode collapsing, and detect overfitting.

The Kernel MMD metric can be defined as:

$$MMD^2(P_r, P_g) = \mathbb{E}_{\substack{x_r, x_r' \sim P_r \\ x_g, x_g' \sim P_g}} \left[k(x_r, x_r') - 2k(x_r, x_g) + k(x_g, x_g') \right] \quad (4)$$

Under a fixed kernel function K, the MMD metric quantifies the discrepancy between the real distribution P_r and the generated distribution P_g. A smaller MMD value indicates a smaller difference between the two distributions. The Parzen window estimation proposed by Gretton et al. [9] can be considered a special case of MMD.

The 1-NN metric is used for pairwise sample testing to evaluate the similarity between two distributions. Given two sets of samples $S_r \sim P_r^n$ and $S_g \sim P_g^n$, where $|S_r|=|S_g|$, the leave-one-out (LOO) accuracy of a 1-NN classifier trained on both distributions can be computed, with S_r labeled as positive samples and S_g as negative samples. Unlike other accuracy metrics, when $|S_r| = |S_g|$ is sufficiently large, the LOO accuracy is expected to be approximately 50% when the two distributions are identical. An LOO accuracy below 50% suggests that the generated distribution overfits the real distribution, while an LOO accuracy significantly above 50%, approaching 100%, indicates a substantial difference between the two distributions.

In this study, we employ the MMD and 1-NN metrics to evaluate the quality of generated data and assess the extent of divergence between the generated and real data distributions.

3 Data Augmentation Methods

3.1 Parameter Selection

The robot pose recognition system relies on the synergistic integration of multi-source sensor parameters, systematically categorized into three groups: trunk-related parameters, limb-related parameters, and head- and foot-related parameters. The following sections elucidate the scientific rationale for parameter selection from the perspectives of functional requirements and technical implementation [10].

The robot pose recognition system integrates key parameters: trunk IMU triaxial acceleration measures X, Y, Z motion to distinguish static and dynamic poses like walking or running; spinal curvature tracks bending angles for poses such as leaning; upper limb IMU angular velocity captures gestures like arm swinging; lower limb IMU Euler angles provide leg orientation for sitting or standing; knee/elbow joint angles quantify flexion for kneeling or manipulation; head IMU quaternion encodes head orientation for gaze detection; and bipedal pressure distribution assesses foot pressure for stability in standing or walking, enhancing pose recognition and dynamic stability.

Based on the above categorization, the selected sensor parameters include: trunk IMU triaxial acceleration, upper limb IMU angular velocity, lower limb IMU Euler angles, spinal curvature, bipedal pressure distribution, head IMU quaternion, knee joint angles, and elbow joint angles. This parameter set, through the synergistic analysis of multimodal sensor data, achieves comprehensive pose characterization from core dynamics to local details, laying a technical foundation for a high-precision, robust robot pose recognition system.

3.2 Algorithm Construction

Due to the advantages of the WGAN-GP model in terms of training stability, this paper is based on this model to construct the generator and discriminator using deep convolutional networks, and optimizes and improves the model and parameter settings according to the characteristics of the dataset, ultimately achieving high-quality data generation.

The algorithm mainly consists of two parts: 1. The generator network G, which adopts an up-sampling deep convolutional network; 2. The discriminator network D, which employs a down-sampling deep convolutional network.

The role of the generator network G is to receive input noise data and generate data samples through the forward propagation algorithm of the network. The data structure is in a two-dimensional matrix form. The training objective of the generator network G is to learn the mapping from the noise latent space to sample data x. The loss function of the generator network G is expressed as Eq. 5, representing the distribution of generated data. As can be seen from the loss function, its calculated value is related to the diagnostic result of the discriminator, which is also the inseparable part of the two processes of generative adversarial.

$$L_G = -\mathbb{E}_{x \sim p_g}[D(x)] \quad (5)$$

The role of the discriminator network D is to receive real data samples and generated data samples, and ultimately provide a binary probability value indicating whether the data belongs to real data through the forward propagation algorithm of the network. The label with the higher probability is taken as the final determination value. The discriminator network D and the generator network G are trained under a mutually adversarial state. The loss function of the discriminator network D is represented as Eq. 6, where represents the distribution of generated data, represents the distribution of real data, and represents the distribution of sampled data between real and fake data. The generator network and the discriminator network improve together in adversarial learning, ultimately enabling the generator network G to generate sample data whose probability distribution is very close to that of real data.

$$L = \mathbb{E}_{\tilde{x} \sim P_g}[D(\tilde{x})] - \mathbb{E}_{x \sim P_r}[D(x)] + \lambda \mathbb{E}_{\hat{x} \sim P_{\hat{\omega}}}\left[(\|\nabla_{\hat{x}} D(\hat{x})\|_2 - 1)^2\right] \quad (6)$$

The goal of the generator network is to produce high-quality data that closely matches the real data distribution to confuse the discriminator network. Conversely, the discriminator network continuously optimizes to accurately distinguish between generated and real data. In such an adversarial training process, both networks jointly optimize until the generator network can produce samples extremely close to real data. To enhance the quality of generated data, each GAN model only generates one type of fault data, and multiple GAN models collectively achieve the expansion of the fault dataset.

3.3 Model Optimization

The GAN model is known for its training difficulties. Building on the basic structure of existing models, training convergence is achieved by adjusting specific parameters, making optimization of parameter tuning crucial for task implementation. In recent years, many scholars have proposed a series of GAN training techniques that have greatly facilitated their practical applications [11]. This paper integrates relevant research and, based on the characteristics of our study, employs the following training techniques:

(1) Avoid using fully connected neural networks except for the first layer of the generator and the last layer of the discriminator.
(2) For the generator's activation functions, use the ReLU function for all layers except the last one. For the last layer, select the activation function based on the data normalization range: use the tanh function if the range is [-1, 1], or the sigmoid function if the range is [0, 1].
(3) For the discriminator's activation functions, use the SeLU function for all layers except the last one. The last layer's activation depends on the data labeling method: for traditional GAN labeling (fake data labeled as 1, valid data as 0), use the sigmoid function; for labeling with gradient penalty (fake as 1, valid as -1, dummy as 0), use the tanh function.
(4) Use soft labels for data authenticity, avoiding simple 1 or -1 labels. Instead, add random noise in the range [0, 0.1], adjusting labels to random values between [-1, -0.9] and [0.9, 1].
(5) Add a batch normalization layer after each convolutional layer in the generator.
(6) For the WGAN-GP model, do not use batch normalization layers in the discriminator.
(7) Both the generator and discriminator should use a relatively large number of convolutional kernels. In this study's experiments, the maximum number of convolutional kernels reached 256.
(8) Avoid using pooling layers in both the generator and discriminator.
(9) The discriminator should not use overly deep convolutional networks; a depth of 2–3 layers is typically optimal, as excessively deep discriminators yield poor diagnostic performance.
(10) For each training round of the generator, train the discriminator n times, with n set to 3 in this study.

4 Experiments and Discussion

4.1 Dataset

The experimental data in this study were obtained from a robot posture perception system constructed in the laboratory. The system consists of several core components: a sensor network, a data acquisition module, a data processing unit, and control software.

The sensor network comprises various high-precision sensors designed to capture real-time physical parameters of the robot in different postures. The data acquisition module collects data from the sensor network and transmits it to the data processing unit for processing. The data processing unit performs preprocessing, feature extraction, and posture classification on the raw data. The control software provides a user-friendly interface for monitoring system status, adjusting parameters, and reviewing analysis results.

During data collection, the system samples data at an interval of 500 ms (0.5 s) to ensure the capture of dynamic features of posture changes. The collected data are stored in a local database for subsequent analysis and model training.

This dataset covers various robot posture categories and collects multiple parameters using high-precision sensor devices. The selection and arrangement of sensors have been optimized to ensure data accuracy and reliability.

The system collects parameters including trunk IMU triaxial acceleration, upper limb IMU angular velocity, lower limb IMU Euler angles, spinal curvature, bipedal pressure distribution, head IMU quaternion, knee joint angles, and elbow joint angles. The specific parameters are listed in the Table 1 below:

Table 1. Detailed measurement parameters

Parameter Name	Unit	Description
Trunk IMU Triaxial Acceleration	m/s^2	X, Y, Z-axis acceleration of the trunk
Upper Limb IMU Angular Velocity	rad/s	Angular velocity of the upper limbs
Lower Limb IMU Euler Angles	°	Euler angles (roll, pitch, yaw) of the lower limbs
Spinal Curvature	1/m	Degree of spinal curvature
Bipedal Pressure Distribution	Pa	Pressure distribution on the soles of both feet
Head IMU Quaternion	–	Quaternion representation of head posture
Knee Joint Angles	°	Bending angle of the knee joints
Elbow Joint Angles	°	Bending angle of the elbow joints

The dataset includes the following 8 robot posture categories, each corresponding to a specific action or state, as shown in the Table2 below:

Table 2. Detailed posture categories

Posture Category	Description
Standing (stan)	Robot standing upright
Walking (walk)	Robot walking at normal speed
Running (run)	Robot running at high speed
Jumping (jump)	Robot performing a jumping action
Bending (bend)	Robot bending to a certain angle
Head Turning (turn)	Robot turning its head
Waving (wave)	Robot waving its arm
Stationary (stat)	Robot remaining stationary

Data collection relies on a high-precision sensor network, including inertial measurement units (IMUs), pressure sensors, and angle sensors. These devices have been carefully calibrated and arranged to maximize the capture of features related to robot posture changes. The data acquisition module employs real-time transmission technology to ensure efficient data recording and storage.

By analyzing these data, significant support can be provided for research in areas such as robot posture perception, behavior recognition, and intelligent control.

4.2 Model Training

GAN training requires a certain amount of real data. In the experiment, each posture category was trained independently. For each posture category, 500 samples were selected to form the training set, with a batch size set to 200, and training was conducted for 100,000 epochs. Every 1,000 epochs, the generative model was saved, and a batch of data was generated using the generative model to evaluate the quality of the GAN model. This paper proposes using GAN to directly learn posture data and evaluates the quality of the generated data.

The deep learning algorithm was implemented using TensorFlow 2.6.0 and Python 3.9.7 within the PyCharm 2022 development environment. It utilizes CUDA 11.2 and cuDNN 8.1 libraries for GPU acceleration. The algorithm is executed on a graphics server equipped with an NVIDIA GeForce RTX 3080Ti GPU, Intel i9-11900K CPU, 64GB of RAM, and a 64-bit Windows 10 operating system.

4.3 Evaluation Based on MMD

To evaluate the quality of data generated by the GAN, this section uses the Maximum Mean Discrepancy (MMD) metric to assess the distribution differences between generated and real data. MMD is a method for measuring the discrepancy between two data distributions, where a smaller MMD value indicates a closer similarity between the distributions, thus verifying the proximity of generated data to real data.

This experiment analyzes the MMD of generated data corresponding to different training epochs to evaluate the GAN model's performance in learning robot pose data. The GAN model directly learns the raw pose data, with pose categories including Standing (Stan), Walking (Walk), Running (Run), Jumping (Jump), Bending (Bend), Head Turning (Turn), Waving (Wave), and Stationary (Stat).

Table3 presents the MMD values between generated data and real data for different pose categories. Each row represents the real data pose category, each column represents the generated data pose category, and the diagonal values indicate the MMD between generated and real data for the same pose category.

From Table3, it can be observed that for each pose category, the MMD values between generated and real data (diagonal values) are low, ranging from 0.05 to 0.09. This indicates that the GAN model effectively captures the distribution characteristics of real data when generating various pose data.

Although the MMD values for all poses are low, the difficulty of generating data varies across different poses. The following analysis examines the generation difficulty for each pose based on its complexity, motion dynamics, and sensor parameters.

Table 3. MMD values between generated and real data for different poses

	Stan	Walk	Run	Jump	Bend	Turn	Wave	Stat
Stan	**0.06**	0.96	0.83	0.81	0.83	0.80	0.75	0.70
Walk	0.96	**0.08**	0.98	1.00	0.52	0.62	0.94	0.67
Run	0.86	0.95	**0.09**	0.85	0.76	0.91	0.61	0.61
Jump	0.86	0.99	0.83	**0.07**	0.90	0.80	0.45	0.73
Bend	0.87	0.55	0.78	0.92	**0.06**	0.72	0.84	0.49
Turn	0.86	0.64	0.90	0.81	0.68	**0.07**	0.77	0.53
Wave	0.83	0.94	0.64	0.50	0.83	0.81	**0.07**	0.62
stat	0.81	0.71	0.62	0.80	0.48	0.58	0.63	**0.05**

(1) Standing (Stan): MMD Value: 0.06

Analysis: The standing pose is relatively simple, with the robot remaining stationary and minimal sensor data variation. The main parameters involved include trunk IMU triaxial acceleration and bipedal pressure distribution. Due to the small fluctuations in these parameters, the data distribution is relatively uniform, making it easy for the GAN model to learn its features. Thus, the MMD value is low, and the generation difficulty is minimal.

(2) Walking (Walk): MMD Value: 0.08

Analysis: The walking pose exhibits periodic motion characteristics, involving parameters such as lower limb IMU Euler angles, knee joint angles, and bipedal pressure distribution. These parameters show regular changes during walking, resulting in a predictable data distribution. The GAN model effectively captures this periodicity, with an MMD value of 0.08, indicating moderate generation difficulty.

(3) Running (Run): MMD Value: 0.09

Analysis: The running pose is more dynamic than walking, with larger motion amplitudes and higher speeds. Parameters such as trunk IMU triaxial acceleration, upper limb IMU angular velocity, and lower limb IMU Euler angles exhibit more significant changes. Although running has some periodicity, its data distribution is more complex, leading to slightly higher generation difficulty. The MMD value of 0.09 is the highest among all poses.

(4) Jumping (Jump): MMD Value: 0.07

Analysis: The jumping pose is a non-periodic dynamic action involving brief takeoff and landing phases. Sensor data, such as trunk IMU triaxial acceleration, bipedal pressure distribution, and knee joint angles, change sharply during the jump. Due to the abrupt and transient nature of the action, the data distribution is relatively complex, but the GAN model still effectively learns its features, resulting in an MMD value of 0.07 and moderate generation difficulty.

(5) Bending (Bend): MMD Value: 0.06

Analysis: The bending pose primarily involves changes in spinal curvature and trunk IMU triaxial acceleration, with slow and stable movements. The sensor data changes gradually, resulting in a simple distribution. The GAN model easily learns these features, yielding an MMD value of 0.06 and low generation difficulty.

(6) Head Turning (Turn): MMD Value: 0.07

Analysis: The head-turning pose mainly relies on changes in head IMU quaternion, with minimal variation in other sensor data. Due to the localized and simple nature of the action, the data distribution has low complexity, allowing the GAN model to accurately capture its features. The MMD value is 0.07, indicating low generation difficulty.

(7) Waving (Wave): MMD Value: 0.07

Analysis: The waving pose involves changes in upper limb IMU angular velocity and elbow joint angles, exhibiting some periodicity. The motion dynamics are moderate, and the data distribution has learnable patterns. The GAN model effectively generates samples close to real data, with an MMD value of 0.07, indicating moderate generation difficulty.

(8) Stationary (Stat): MMD Value: 0.05

Analysis: The stationary pose is similar to standing but may involve longer periods of stillness, with almost no changes in sensor data. The data distribution is extremely simple, with parameters such as trunk IMU triaxial acceleration and bipedal pressure distribution remaining stable. The GAN model generates highly accurate data, resulting in the lowest MMD value of 0.05 and the least generation difficulty among all poses.

Overall, the GAN model performs excellently in generating robot pose data, with MMD values for all pose categories ranging from 0.05 to 0.09, indicating a high degree of similarity between generated and real data distributions. Simple poses like Stationary (Stat) and Standing (Stan) have the lowest generation difficulty due to minimal sensor data variation, while dynamic poses like Running (Run) have relatively higher difficulty due to larger motion amplitudes and complex data distributions. Nevertheless, the GAN model effectively learns the features of all poses.

4.4 Evaluation Based on 1-NN

The quality assessment of GAN models remains an open research area, with no single authoritative metric capable of comprehensively evaluating the quality of generated data. Both the Maximum Mean Discrepancy (MMD) and 1-Nearest Neighbor (1-NN) metrics are highly effective evaluation methods. To achieve a more accurate assessment of experimental results, this study employs the 1-NN metric alongside the MMD metric and conducts a comprehensive analysis of the results to derive more reliable conclusions. Unlike MMD, the ideal value for the 1-NN metric is 0.5. Within the range [0.5, 1], lower values are better, but values below 0.5 indicate overfitting of the generated data, which is undesirable.

The following table presents the 1-NN values between generated and real data for different pose categories. The diagonal values represent the 1-NN values for generated data compared to real data of the same pose category.

From the Table 4, it is evident that the 1-NN values between generated and real data for each pose category range from 0.70 to 0.94, all above 0.5. This indicates that

Table 4. 1-NN values between generated and real data for different poses

	Stan	Walk	Run	Jump	Bend	Turn	Wave	Stat
Stan	**0.87**	1.00	0.99	1.00	1.00	1.00	1.00	1.00
Walk	1.00	**0.82**	1.00	1.00	0.99	1.00	1.00	1.00
Run	1.00	1.00	**0.82**	1.00	1.00	1.00	1.00	1.00
Jump	1.00	1.00	1.00	**0.94**	1.00	1.00	1.00	1.00
Bend	1.00	0.99	1.00	1.00	**0.78**	1.00	1.00	1.00
Turn	1.00	1.00	1.00	1.00	1.00	**0.78**	1.00	0.99
Wave	1.00	1.00	1.00	0.97	1.00	1.00	**0.83**	1.00
stat	1.00	1.00	1.00	1.00	1.00	0.96	1.00	**0.70**

the generated data do not exhibit overfitting. However, the relatively high 1-NN values suggest a significant distribution discrepancy between generated and real data, indicating room for improvement in the similarity of generated data.

The comprehensive evaluation shows that the GAN model performs well in capturing the overall distribution of robot pose data but falls short in generating local features. Future work could focus on optimizing model architecture, refining training strategies, or incorporating additional evaluation metrics to further enhance the quality of generated data.

5 Conclusion

In this study, we successfully applied Generative Adversarial Networks (GANs) to generate robot pose data, effectively addressing the challenge of data scarcity in intelligent diagnostics. Experimental results demonstrate that the GAN-based approach can accurately simulate the distribution characteristics of real pose data. Validated by evaluation metrics such as Maximum Mean Discrepancy (MMD) and 1-Nearest Neighbor (1-NN), the generated data closely align with real data in terms of both global distribution and local features. This capability makes the method a powerful tool for augmenting datasets in scenarios with limited or imbalanced data.

The ability of GANs to generate high-quality pose data significantly enhances the applicability of intelligent methods. By reducing reliance on large amounts of labeled data, this approach enables advanced diagnostic and control systems to be deployed in environments where data collection is challenging, thereby promoting the widespread adoption of intelligent methods in robotics and improving system robustness and adaptability.

However, the evaluation framework for generative models remains an immature research area, lacking a comprehensive assessment system. Future research could focus on developing a more robust evaluation framework that integrates factors such as distribution distance, diversity, and the preservation of unique pose data characteristics. This would further ensure the quality and reliability of GAN-generated data, solidifying its critical role in intelligent robotics applications.

References

1. Zhou, H., Yang, G., Wang, B., et al.: An attention-based deep learning approach for inertial motion recognition and estimation in human-robot collaboration. J. Manuf. Syst. **67**, 97–110 (2023)
2. Li, C., Zheng, P., Yin, Y., et al.: An AR-assisted deep reinforcement learning-based approach towards mutual-cognitive safe human-robot interaction. Robot. Comput.-Integr. Manuf. **80**, 102471 (2023)
3. Zheng, C., Wu, W., Chen, C., et al.: Deep learning-based human pose estimation: a survey. ACM Comput. Surv. **56**(1), 1–37 (2023)
4. Gulakala, R., Markert, B., Stoffel, M.: Generative adversarial network based data augmentation for CNN based detection of Covid-19. Sci. Rep. **12**(1), 19186 (2022)
5. Naaz, F., Herle, A., Channegowda, J., et al.: A generative adversarial network-based synthetic data augmentation technique for battery condition evaluation. Int. J. Energy Res. **45**(13), 19120–19135 (2021)
6. Cao, J., Mo, L., Zhang, Y., et al.: Multi-marginal wasserstein GAN. Adv. Neural inf. Process. Syst. **32** (2019)
7. Li, J., Niu, K., Liao, L., et al.: A generative steganography method based on WGAN-GP. In: proceedings of the International Conference on Artificial Intelligence and Security. Springer (2020)
8. Xu, Q., Huang, G., Yuan, Y., et al.: An empirical study on evaluation metrics of generative adversarial networks. arXiv e-prints (2018)
9. Gretton, A., Borgwardt, K., Rasch, M.J., et al.: A kernel method for the two-sample problem. arXiv e-prints, arXiv:0805.2368 (2008)
10. Ali, M.A., Hussain, A.J., Sadiq, A.T.: Human body posture recognition approaches: a review. ARO-The Sci. J. Koya Univ. **10**(1), 75–84 (2022)
11. Goodfellow, I.J., Pouget-Abadie, J., Mirza, M., et al.: Generative adversarial nets. Adv. Neural inf. Process. Syst. **27** (2014)

Optimal Electrode Configuration for Wrist sEMG-Based Gesture Recognition: A Systematic Evaluation of Number and Placement

Hai Wang[1,2,3], Ashirbad Pradhan[4], Xin Xia[1,2], Birong Dong[1,2], Ning Jiang[1,2,3], and Jiayuan He[1,2,3](✉)

[1] Center of Gerontology and Geriatrics, West China Hospital of Sichuan University, Chengdu 610041, Sichuan, China
jiayuan.he@wchscu.cn
[2] The National Clinical Research Center for Geriatrics, West China Hospital of Sichuan University, Chengdu 610041, Sichuan, China
[3] The Med-X Center for Manufacturing, Sichuan University, Chengdu 610041, Sichuan, China
[4] Department of Systems Design Engineering, University of Waterloo, Waterloo, Canada

Abstract. Wrist-worn surface electromyography (sEMG) presents a promising approach for unobtrusive gesture recognition in consumer wearables, but the absence of standardized electrode configurations poses a challenge for optimal system design. This study systematically investigates the relationship between electrode placement, channel selection, and machine learning performance by evaluating four classifiers which are linear discriminant analysis (LDA), k nearest neighborhood (KNN), support vector machine (SVM), and random forest (RF) with time-domain and autoregressive features. Our results reveal a consistent optimal 4-electrode symmetric configuration (positions 1, 2, 4, 5) across all models, achieving 62.1% cross-session accuracy (LDA) while minimizing hardware complexity and cost. Notably, the optimal channel selection is model-independent, suggesting generalizability across classifiers. The system demonstrates strong cross-session robustness, with less than 1% average accuracy degradation over 21 days for seven gross hand gestures encompassing common daily activities. Furthermore, we introduce a novel gesture-specific electrode optimization principle to enhance performance. These findings offer practical design guidelines for balancing accuracy and efficiency in sEMG-based wearable devices.

Keywords: Surface electromyography (sEMG) · Gesture recognition · Human-machine interface (HMI) · Electrode optimization · Wearable devices

1 Introduction

Traditional Human-Machine Interface (HMI) methods—such as physical buttons, graphical user interfaces (GUIs), and touchscreens—are well-established and reliable, but they suffer from notable limitations in adaptability and naturalness. These conventional interfaces are often rigid in function and require users to have good vision and fine motor skills. As modern industrial systems and software become increasingly complex, traditional HMIs tend to impose a heavier cognitive load on users [1]. While GUIs have improved flexibility to some extent, they have also introduced intricate interaction processes that further intensify cognitive demands [2]. For individuals with disabilities, traditional interfaces pose even greater challenges: those with restricted motor abilities may struggle to operate small buttons or perform touch gestures, and users with visual impairments cannot rely on visually based GUIs. In summary, the static and rigid nature of traditional input devices limit their functional scalability and accessibility, particularly in diverse user populations. These limitations drive the demand for next-generation "natural interaction" modalities.

Surface electromyography (sEMG) is a non-invasive technique for detecting muscle electrical activity. It only requires electrodes to be placed on the surface of the skin to capture muscle signals [3]. Compared to more complex technologies like brain-computer interfaces (BCIs), sEMG systems are simpler in hardware, lower in cost, and easier to operate without professional supervision. This makes them highly suitable for portable and wearable applications [4]. This technology offers significant advantages for next-generation interfaces due to its non-invasive nature and adaptability, benefiting both assistive applications for individuals with disabilities and general use by healthy populations [5]. With advances in miniaturized electronics and flexible materials, a variety of wearable sEMG devices have emerged—including armband-style sensors [6], fabric-integrated systems, and even "electronic tattoo" sensors [7]. These devices are lightweight, conform closely to the skin, and do not hinder natural movement. sEMG signals contain rich information about fine muscle control and can capture complex motion intentions such as hand gestures and postures. As a result, sEMG offers high bandwidth and strong adaptability, theoretically supporting a wide range of commands and continuous control—unlike buttons, which are limited to fixed outputs.

In wrist-worn sEMG gesture recognition systems, sensor placement is critical but lacks standardization. Two main strategies have been pursued: muscle-specific placement and equidistant electrode arrays. In the muscle-specific approach, electrodes are positioned over anatomically relevant forearm muscles. For example, Botros et al. compared forearm versus wrist placement using paired 4 + 4 electrode arrangements for gesture classification [8], and another study placed six electrodes targeting key muscles to decode hand joint angles with high correlation (Pearson correlation = 0.844) [9]. These anatomically-driven methods can capture strong localized signals but require precise sensor positioning and may vary with individual anatomy. By contrast, equidistant arrangements distribute electrodes uniformly around the wrist circumference. Yang and Liu, for instance, deployed eight evenly spaced electrodes to capture multi-axis wrist movements [10], while D'Accolti et al. used a cuff of eight bipolar sensors around the forearm to recognize flexion/extension, pronation/supination, and various hand grasps [11]. Such uniform layouts avoid the need for detailed muscle mapping and tend to be easier to don. Comparative evaluations suggest equidistant arrays can approach the performance of muscle-specific setups while offering practical benefits. He et al. reported that a six-electrode equidistant wrist band achieved approximately 92.4% of the accuracy of an eight-electrode forearm system for gesture classification, while significantly reducing setup time [12]. These findings indicate that uniform wrist arrays often match targeted placements in accuracy and consistency, with faster donning. In contrast, muscle-based setups may suffer from longer setup times and greater sensitivity to anatomical variability.

To validate these design considerations, this study systematically explores wrist-worn sEMG electrode configurations using data from the publicly available GrabMyo dataset [13] to systematically address the following key issues: 1. Is there an optimal symmetrical electrode configuration with the least number of electrodes that can achieve the best balance between performance and hardware cost in wrist sEMG gesture recognition? 2. Does this optimal configuration have model-independent, that is, perform consistently on different machine learning classifiers? 3. Does this configuration have cross-session long-term robustness to meet the application scenarios where devices need to be worn repeatedly in the real world?

We evaluate multiple symmetric and asymmetric electrode layouts under cross-session conditions to assess both recognition accuracy and long-term robustness. Building on these insights, the present study proposed a symmetric four-electrode wrist configuration (channels 1, 2, 4, and 5). This layout yielded a gesture recognition accuracy of ≈62.1% in our cross-session evaluation. Crucially, it respects practical design constraints: it uses only four electrodes on a typical 12–16 cm wrist circumference (below the usual six-electrode limit) and halves the channel count of standard forearm arrays [12], saving roughly €1.02 per electrode [14]. The reduced hardware simplifies donning and enhances user comfort. By balancing accuracy with anatomical and cost considerations, this symmetric arrangement offers a cost-effective and user-friendly configuration for wearable sEMG interfaces. Our results provide actionable guidelines for next-generation wrist sEMG-based HMI systems, particularly in wearable form factors that demand both accuracy and user comfort. Furthermore, to provide a potential mechanistic explanation for our findings, we introduce a novel conceptual hypothesis: the 'tendon symmetry conduction theory'. This framework proposes that sEMG signals at the wrist may be strongly influenced by the propagation of tension waves through tendons, rather than localized muscle activity as assumed in traditional forearm sEMG paradigms. Consequently, symmetric electrode arrangements more effectively capture tendon-driven kinematic patterns. Future work will build on this insight to develop fine-grained gesture recognition models tailored to this optimized configuration, advancing the feasibility and performance of wearable neural interfaces.

2 Methods

2.1 Data Acquisition and Processing

This study utilized the publicly available GRABMyo dataset (v1.1.0), a high-quality sEMG database collected by our research group and hosted on PhysioNet. The dataset comprises multi-day recordings from 43 healthy participants (23 males, 20 females; mean age 26.35 ± 2.89 years), including 38 right-handed and 5 left-handed individuals, with detailed anthropometric measurements (wrist circumference: 16.18 ± 1.21 cm; forearm length: 25.15 ± 1.74 cm). Data was collected across three sessions (Days

1, 8, and 29) to evaluate temporal robustness, with each session recording 16 static hand/wrist gestures (e.g., wrist flexion/extension, forearm pronation/supination, hand open/close, and fine digit movements) plus a REST condition, each repeated seven times (5-s holds, 10-s rest intervals). The dataset's rigorous design—featuring standardized electrode placement, controlled force levels, and intentional inter-session variability—ensures high signal quality (SNR: 14.565 ± 6.385 dB, CCN: 0.975 ± 0.041) and supports diverse applications, including gesture recognition, biometric authentication, and electrode configuration optimization. Compared to benchmarks like Ninapro DB2, GRABMyo demonstrates superior classification performance (AUC: 0.948 forearm, 0.941 wrist) and lower biometric error rates (EER: 0.028 forearm, 0.038 wrist), making it a valuable resource for developing robust sEMG-based systems.

In our study, we focused on a subset of seven gestures from the original dataset: wrist extension (WE), wrist flexion (WF), forearm supination (FS), forearm pronation (FP), hand open (HO), hand close (HC), and rest (RE). These gestures were selected due to their distinct, large-range movements, making them particularly suitable for sEMG-based gesture recognition. Importantly, we retained the original gesture acquisition protocol without modifications—our work repurposes this subset to investigate how different electrode arrangements influence classification performance. Specifically, we examined six electrode placement configurations around the wrist (Fig. 1) to assess their impact on recognition accuracy. In the original protocol, each gesture was held for 5 s per trial, with seven trials per gesture in each session.

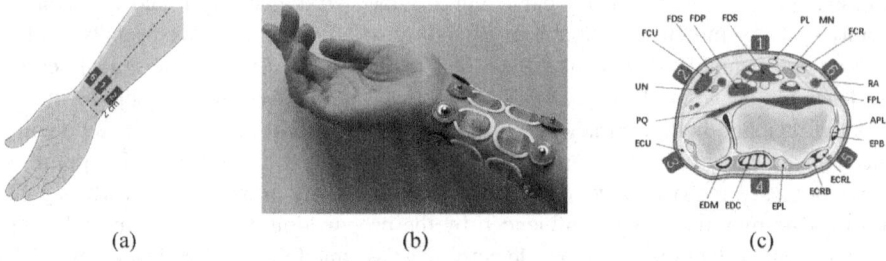

(a)　　　　　　　　　(b)　　　　　　　　　(c)

Fig. 1. Electrode placements. (a) The related wrist electrode positions. (b) Experimental setup for differential electrode configuration in this dataset recording experiment (c) The cross section of wrist muscles. APL, abductor pollicis longus; ECRB, extensor carpi radialis brevis; ECRL, extensor carpi radialis longus; ECU, extensor carpi ulnaris; EDC, extensor digitorum communis; EDM, extensor digiti minimi; EPB, extensor pollicis brevis; EPL, extensor pollicis longus; FCR, flexor carpi radialis; FCU, flexor carpi ulnaris; FDP, flexor digitorum profundus; FDS, flexor digitorum superficialis; FPL, flexor pollicis longus; PQ, pronator quadratus; RA, radial artery; UA, ulnar artery; UN, ulnar nerve.

The data were recorded by EMG-USB2 + equipment. The sample frequency of this machine is 2048Hz. The sEMG-USB2 + is a multichannel amplifier for bioelectrical signals designed by OT Bioelettronica, Torino, Italy. The gain of the device was set to 500, and the sampling rate was set to 2048 Hz. Pre-gelled skin-adhesive monopolar sEMG electrodes (AM-N00S/E, Ambu, Denmark) were used. The details of the electrode arrangement can be checked in [13].

2.2 Classification and Evaluation

To assess various wrist electrode arrangements, we employed the conventional machine learning approach of LDA (automatic shrinkage), KNN (5 neighbors), SVM (RBF kernel, C = 1.0, gamma = 'scale'), and RF (100 estimators). These methods are applied using four time domain features and six-order autoregressive coefficients for estimation purposes [15]. We use these four machine learning models to select the best electrodes arrangement of different numbers. And find whether the arrangements are common among different models. Four time domain features are mean absolute value (T_{MAV}), zero crossing (T_{ZC}), slope sign changes (T_{SSC}), and waveform length (T_{WL}), and their formulas are as follows:

(1) Mean absolute value (T_{MAV})

$$T_{\text{MAV}} = \frac{1}{N} \sum_{i=1}^{N} |x_i| \quad (1)$$

where N refers to the number of samples, x_i represents the sEMG value of one sample.

(2) Zero crossing value (T_{ZC})

$$T_{\text{ZC}} = \sum_{i=1}^{N-1} \delta\left(\text{sgn}_\theta(x_i) \neq \text{sgn}_\theta(x_{i+1})\right)$$

where $\text{sgn}(x) = \begin{cases} 1 & \text{if } x > 0 \\ 0 & \text{if } x = 0 \\ -1 & \text{if } x < 0 \end{cases}$ and $\delta(\text{condition}) = \begin{cases} 1 \text{ if condition is true} \\ 0 \text{ otherwise} \end{cases}$

(2)

where $\text{sgn}(x)$ is the sign function, δ is the indicator function.

(3) Slope sign change (T_{ssc})

$$T_{\text{SSC}} = \sum_{l=2}^{N-1} f[(x_i - x_{i-1}) \times (x_i - x_{i+1})]$$

$$f(x) = \begin{cases} 1, \text{ if } x \geq V_{\text{th}} \\ 0, \quad x < V_{\text{th}} \end{cases} \quad (3)$$

where V_{th} is the threshold to avoid the background noise in the sEMG signals.

(4) Waveform length (T_{WL})

$$T_{\text{WL}} = \sum_{i=1}^{N-1} |x_{i+1} - x_i| \quad (4)$$

This study analyzes wrist sEMG data from 43 participants performing 7 gesture trials. The data is preprocessed with bandpass (10-500 Hz) and bandstop (59-61 Hz) Butterworth filters to remove noise. Refer to [16, 17], the EMG data were segmented into a series of 200ms sliding windows with an increment part of 50ms. Five features are extracted from each segment: Mean Absolute Value, Zero Crossing, Slope Sign Change, Waveform Length, and 6th-order Autoregressive coefficients. Through every sliding window, one data sample with five features we have choosen is made for model training and testing. Feature extraction is performed for combinations of 1 to 6 electrodes. For classification, four machine learning models are used, with data scaled using standard nomalization. All data samples from session one is used to train the model firstly, and then the whole data samples from session two or three are used to test the model. A confusion matrix is generated to evaluate the model's performance across different classes. The results, including average accuracy for seven gestures and confusion matrices, are saved in an Excel file for each participant and electrode combination.

2.3 Anatomy and Channel Analysis

To complement the machine learning-based evaluation of electrode arrangements, we conducted anatomy analysis to understand how muscle activation patterns influence gesture recognition performance. This analysis focused on the underlying physiological mechanisms of the selected hand and wrist gestures and their relationship with sEMG signal characteristics. To further enhance the evaluation of electrode arrangements, we incorporated mutual information (MI) analysis between sEMG channels to quantify inter-electrode dependencies and assess the redundancy or complementary nature of signals from different electrode positions. This approach helps identify optimal electrode configurations that maximize discriminative information while minimizing redundant data.

For analyzing the channel information redundancy to explain the reason why choose these four channels, the mutual information is used to quantify the similarity of different channels. The mutual information calculation formula is as

$$I(x; y) = \sum_{x_i, y_j} P_{X,Y}(x_i, y_j) \log_u \frac{P_{X,Y}(x_i, y_j)}{P_X(x_i) P_Y(y_j)} \tag{5}$$

where X and Y are two discrete random variables (in this case, two sEMG channels). x_i, y_j are the discrete values (bins) that the random variables X and Y can take. $P_{X,Y}(x_i, y_j)$ is the joint probability distribution of X and Y. $P_X(x_i)$, $P_Y(y_j)$ are the marginal probability distributions of X and Y, respectively. The logarithm uses base 2 ($\log_2$) so that the resulting mutual information is measured in bits. The MI between sEMG channels ranges from 0 to 1, where values closer to 1 indicate higher similarity between signals. For temporal series X with N elements, histograms can be constructed using k bins uniformly partitioned across the range of X, with the value of k determined by the rice rule as

$$k = 2\sqrt[3]{N} \tag{6}$$

3 Results

3.1 Comprehensive Results of Different Models in Different Test Condition

To analyze which arrangement has the best performances of different electrode numbers. And prove out the good robustness of the arrangement, we have tested the performance of different arrangements in the long range of one month. The 1st day (which is called as S1) is used to train the four models and test the model performance in the 8th day (which is called as S2) and the 29th day (which is called as S3). And the results shown in the following table have displayed the suggested arrangement which has the best robustness in long time.

By careful observation of these tables, we can find although the change of the models and the test data, the best electrode arrangements are almost the same. Through intraclass correlation coefficient (ICC), we find that all ICC value larger than 0.9 and all p-calue less than 0.001, which means the change of model has no influence on electrode arrangement rankings. Table 1 provides a detailed comparison of model performance across different test datasets with varying numbers of electrodes. The first column specifies the number of electrodes used in each configuration. The third column presents the average classification accuracy across all possible electrode combinations for the 43 subjects. The fourth column reports the mean accuracy achieved by the optimal electrode configuration selected for the given number of electrodes. The fifth column indicates the p-value from a statistical significance test comparing the accuracy of the current optimal electrode configuration with that of the previous row (i.e., whether the improvement is statistically significant). The final column lists the specific electrode configuration identified as optimal for each case. The bold text highlights the optimal electrode configuration that differs from the most frequently selected arrangement across other models, while maintaining the same number of electrodes. And in Fig. 2, we can find that LDA performs the best among these four different models. More interestingly, there is an obvious elbow point in the curve of LDA which is the four-electrode arrangement (1, 2, 4, 5). As a result, it is more important to select the suitable electrode arrangement for the best performance.

Table 1. Performance comparison across electrode configurations.

Number of Electrodes	Model	Mean Accuracy (%)	Max Accuracy (%)	p-value	Best Combination
1	LDA (S1_S2)	42.95	46.71	–	1
2		50.77	56.79	0.0000	1, 4
3		54.03	59.92	0.0001	1, 2, 4
4		55.73	61.97	0.0069	1, 2, 4, 5
5		56.52	60.26	0.1566	1, 2, 3, 4, 5
6		57.26	57.26	0.1286	1, 2, 3, 4, 5, 6
1	LDA (S1_S3)	40.22	46.39	–	1
2		48.20	55.25	0.0000	1, 4
3		52.20	59.89	0.0000	1, 2, 4
4		54.73	62.07	0.0065	1, 2, 4, 5

(*continued*)

Table 1. (*continued*)

Number of Electrodes	Model	Mean Accuracy (%)	Max Accuracy (%)	p-value	Best Combination
5		56.20	61.67	0.5780	1, 2, 3, 4, 5
6		56.75	56.75	0.0063	1, 2, 3, 4, 5, 6
1	KNN(S1_S2)	38.92	41.47	–	4
2		45.37	50.54	0.0019	1, 4
3		48.07	52.01	0.0400	1, 2, 4
4		49.34	51.96	0.0748	1, 2, 4, 5
5		50.17	51.83	0.5537	1, 2, 3, 4, 5
6		50.81	50.81	0.3068	1, 2, 3, 4, 5, 6
1	KNN (S1_S3)	37.26	41.36	–	4
2		44.01	50.77	0.0000	1, 4
3		47.17	53.11	0.0109	1, 2, 4
4		49.18	53.16	0.3869	1, 2, 4, 5
5		50.77	52.83	0.6922	1, 2, 3, 4, 5
6		52.17	52.17	0.5707	1, 2, 3, 4, 5, 6
1	SVM(S1_S2)	41.68	45.03	–	1
2		48.41	55.13	0.0000	1, 4
3		51.15	57.39	0.0032	1, 2, 4
4		52.61	57.24	0.1633	1, 2, 4, 5
5		53.46	56.97	0.5278	1, 2, 3, 4, 5
6		53.98	53.98	0.1633	1, 2, 3, 4, 5, 6
1	SVM (S1_S3)	39.69	44.82	–	1
2		47.14	54.88	0.0002	1, 4
3		50.88	58.86	0.0002	1, 2, 4
4		53.08	59.23	0.1871	**1, 2, 3, 4**
5		54.56	59.38	0.0611	1, 2, 3, 4, 5
6		55.69	55.69	0.0259	1, 2, 3, 4, 5, 6
1	RF(S1_S2)	40.18	43.37	–	1
2		48.20	53.94	0.0003	1, 4
3		52.95	58.40	0.0833	**1, 4, 5**
4		56.24	60.33	0.0833	1, 2, 4, 5
5		58.75	60.54	0.3083	1, 2, 3, 4, 5
6		60.77	60.77	0.7948	1, 2, 3, 4, 5, 6
1	RF (S1_S3)	38.55	43.05	–	1
2		47.33	54.92	0.0001	1, 4
3		52.76	58.58	0.0014	1, 2, 4
4		56.55	60.73	0.1148	1, 2, 4, 5
5		59.28	60.91	0.7977	**1, 2, 4, 5, 6**
6		61.64	61.64	0.2088	1, 2, 3, 4, 5, 6

Columns show: (1) Number of electrodes, (2) The concrete testing condition of different models, for example, LDA_S1_S2 means training LDA by session 1 data and testing the model by session 2 data (2) Average accuracy over all combinations, (3) Accuracy of the optimal configuration, (4) p-value (vs. previous row's optimal), and (5) The best electrode setup. Bold highlights the different selected optimal configuration across models.

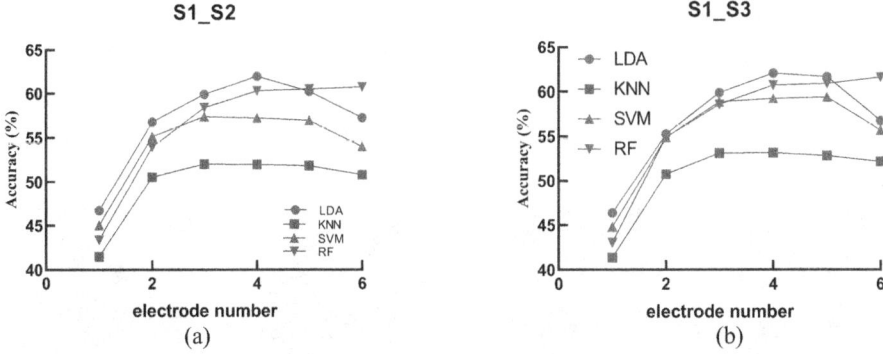

Fig. 2. The Classification accuracy of the best placement with different number of electrodes in different methods. (a) Trained in S1 and tested in S2. (b) Trained in S1 and tested in S3.

3.2 Concrete Confusion Matrix of Different Best Arrangements

Figure 3 presents the confusion matrices for the optimal four-electrode configuration (positions 1, 2, 4, 5) across all four machine learning models. Notably, the models exhibit consistent performance patterns, as evidenced by the similar distribution of values in corresponding matrix blocks. For example, RE has the largest accuracy in the confusion matrix, HC and WE are less, [WF, FS, FP, HO] are the least ones.

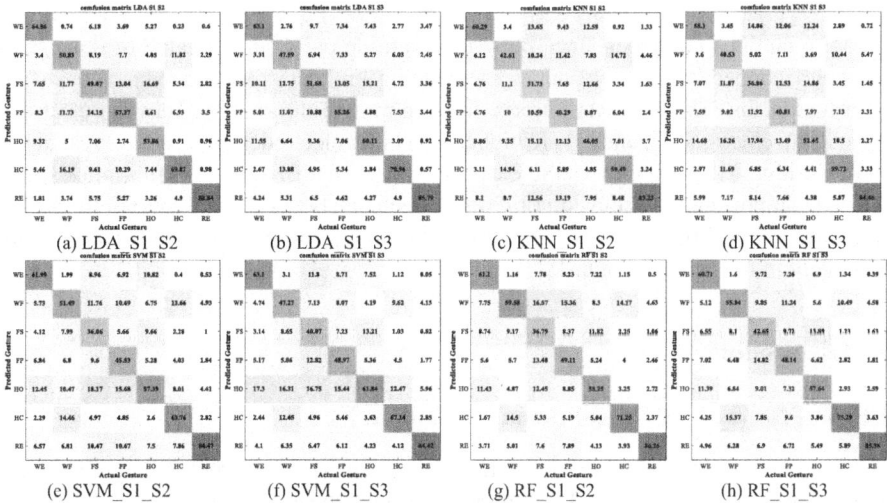

Fig. 3. Confusion matrices demonstrating the classification performance of the optimal four-electrode configuration (1, 2, 4, 5) across all machine learning models. (a) The performance of (1, 2, 4, 5) of LDA_S1_S2. (b) The performance of (1,2,4,5) of LDA_S1_S3. (c) The performance of (1, 2, 4, 5) of KNN_S1_S2. (d) The performance of(1,2,4,5) of KNN_S1_S3. (e) The performance of (1, 2, 4, 5) of SVM_S1_S2. (f) The performance of (1, 2, 4, 5) of SVM_S1_S3. (g) The performance of (1, 2, 4, 5) of RF_S1_S2. (h) The performance of (1, 2, 4, 5) of RF_S1_S3.

3.3 Channel Analysis

In this research, one trail of data has 10240 samples, so the value of k is about 43 by formula (6). Figure 4 is a group figure of the mutual information of different gestures in six channels.

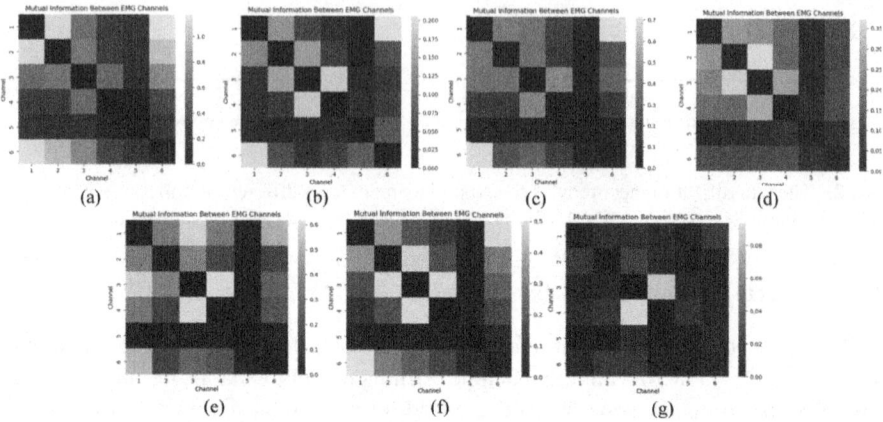

Fig. 4. Confusion matrix of the mutual information of different gestures in six channels. (a) Wrist flexion. (b) Wrist extension. (c) Forearm supination. (d) Forearm pronation. (e) Hand open. (f) Hand close. (g) Rest.

MI quantifies the dependence between electrode pairs: an MI value of 0 suggests complete independence, while values approaching 1 reflect strong redundancy or shared information. In Fig. 4, we can observe that the mutual information between electrode (1) and (6), electrode (3) and (4) are higher than other electrodes in most gestures. In our analysis, high MI between specific electrodes (e.g., (1)-(6) and (3)-(4)) implies signal overlap, supporting the exclusion of redundant channels (e.g., 3 and 6) to optimize the configuration. In brief, this is another proof that prove out the electrode (3) and (6) are redundant in the recognition task.

4 Discussion

4.1 The Necessity of Cross-Session Evaluation

This study adopts the cross-session evaluation scheme (for example, training the model with the data of the first day and conducting tests with the data of the 8th or 29th day). Its main purpose is to simulate the long-term usage scenarios of wearable devices in the real world. In practical applications, when users wear the device every day, the position of the electrode may slightly shift (electrode shift) due to wearing habits, and at the same time, physiological states such as skin resistance and muscle fatigue may also change over time. These factors can all lead to significant variations in the sEMG signal, which is a challenge that cannot be captured in the intra-session test in the laboratory environment.

If non-cross-day evaluation is adopted (that is, training and testing are conducted on the dataset of the same day), the recognition accuracy is usually much higher than approximately 62.1% reported in this study. However, this high accuracy rate is misleading because it fails to reflect the true performance of the system when facing the instability of real-world signals. Therefore, this study selects a more rigorous cross-day assessment, aiming to verify the long-term robustness and reliability of the proposed electrode configuration in practical applications. The research results show that the average accuracy rate of the four-electrode configuration (1, 2, 4, 5) we proposed decreased by less than 1% within a time span of up to 21 days.

This proves its potential as a practical solution.

4.2 Clarification on the 'Model-Independent' Nature of the Optimal Configuration

A central finding of this study is that the optimal four-electrode arrangement (1, 2, 4, 5) is largely 'model-independent'. It is crucial to clarify that this claim refers to the consistency in the selection of the optimal configuration across different classifiers, rather than uniformity in their absolute performance. As shown in Table 1 and Fig. 2, while the combination (1, 2, 4, 5) consistently ranked as the top performer for four electrodes across LDA, SVM, KNN, and RF models, the absolute accuracy achieved varied significantly, with LDA ($\approx$62.1%) outperforming others.

This performance disparity is expected and stems from the intrinsic properties of the models themselves. LDA, as a linear classifier, is particularly effective in finding a separating hyperplane for the time-domain and autoregressive features used, which appear to be reasonably linearly separable in this application. In contrast, models like KNN can be more sensitive to noise and the 'curse of dimensionality' in high-feature spaces, while RF and SVM employ different, more complex decision boundaries that may not have provided additional benefits for this specific feature set. The key takeaway from the model-independent finding is a practical one for hardware design: the consistent selection of configuration (1, 2, 4, 5) suggests that the physical design of an sEMG wearable can be optimized independently of the specific machine learning model ultimately deployed, which simplifies the design process and enhances modularity.

4.3 The Potential Reason from the Aspect of Anatomy

By the calculation of the appearance frequency of different best arrangements, the suggestion for 1 to 5 electrodes arrangements are(1), (1, 4), (1, 2, 4), (1, 2, 4, 5) and (1, 2, 3, 4, 5). Examining the anatomical structure of wrist muscles in Fig. 1, we aim to elucidate the distinct performances of electrodes in various positions during different gestures. By referencing the distribution of wrist muscles and the corresponding electrode arrangements, the anatomical basis for each change in accuracy can be discerned. In particular, electrode (1), positioned above the flexor digitorum superficialis, stands out. Its optimal performance when used in isolation can be attributed to the crucial role played by the flexor digitorum superficialis, in flexing four digits. In the execution of movements requiring such flexion, this muscle assumes an important function. This anatomically grounded analysis unveils the intricate relationship between electrode arrangement and the engagement of specific muscles. The emphasis on the flexor digitorum superficialis underscores its vital contribution to particular gestures, providing insight into the heightened accuracy observed when the electrode (1) operates independently. Further exploration into the connections between alternative electrode positions and diverse wrist muscles promises a nuanced understanding of the complex interplay between electrode configurations and muscular dynamics.

When utilizing a configuration of two electrodes, we observed that electrodes (1, 4) demonstrated the most effective performance. Notably, these two electrodes are positioned diametrically opposite each other. Specifically, electrode (4) is situated directly on the surface of the extensor digitorum communis. This observation implies that these two electrodes can collectively encapsulate a comprehensive set of information from the first electrode. Therefore, the optimal arrangement strategy involves situating one electrode on the surface of the flexor digitorum and the other on the surface of the extensor digitorum.

When using three electrodes in this task, electrodes (1, 2, 4) have the highest accuracy among other combinations. There are flexor carpi ulnaris and flexor digitorum superficialis under the electrode (4). This phenomenon explains that the flexor muscles seem play more significant roles in these seven gestures.

When using four electrodes, electrodes (1, 2, 4, 5) have the best performance. These four electrodes are symmetrically arranged with respect to the center of the wrist cross-section. By carefully observing Fig. 1, it can be seen that these four electrodes cover nearly all of the major muscles beneath them.

When using five electrodes, electrodes (1, 2, 3, 4, 5) have the best accuracy. By careful observation, extensor carpi ulnaris is under electrode (3). There is almost no functional part under electrode (6).

In this experiment, the performance of six electrodes is also calculated. From Fig. 2, we can find that the extended electrodes don't increase the accuracy except for the RF model. This proves that blindly increasing the number of electrodes does not significantly improve accuracy.

4.4 The Design of Real Wearable Equipment

As we have discussed before, a simple arrangement of sEMG electrodes as a kind of symmetrical arrangement for real applications should be recommended in real applications. The suggestions for different numbers of sEMG electrodes are provided in the previous section. But as some phenomena have been discussed in the results, (1, 2, 4, 5) is suggested to be arranged when embedded in wearable equipment. In the real application, engineers or scientists can place the electrodes on the relevant cross-section parts of the wrist.

For better surface fitness, flexible fabric electrodes can be used as sEMG electrodes. Some research has been done to testify the performance of flexible fabric electrodes, they are very suitable for embedding in wearable equipment.

4.5 Why Wrist sEMG with Fewer Electrodes?

The symmetric arrangement (1, 2, 4, 5) captures antagonistic muscle groups (flexors/extensors) more efficiently than forearm's muscle-specific placements, as wrist motion relies on coordinated tendon tension rather than individual muscle activation. Our experimental study on wrist-mounted electrode configurations revealed that a centrosymmetric four-electrode arrangement (selected from six circumferential positions) achieved optimal signal recognition rates about 62.1% and enhanced cross-day robustness.

Finally, we propose a new theory which is called the tendon symmetry conduction theory. A tendon tension wave refers to the changes in tension within a tendon that propagate in the form of waves when the muscle contracts or relaxes. Specifically, when a muscle contracts, the tendon, which connects the muscle to the bone, experiences varying degrees of stretching or compression. These changes in tension within the tendon create waves that can spread across different regions of the tendon. The propagation of these waves is similar to how physical waves spread, such as sound waves or seismic waves. When tension changes in the tendon, this variation is transmitted as a wave along the tendon and ultimately affects the connected bone or other tissues. These waves can propagate throughout the tendon, influencing the muscle and skeletal movement. In the context of sEMG signals, tendon tension waves might influence the signal generation. Traditional views attribute sEMG signals to the electrical activity of muscles, but this new theory suggests that these signals could also be influenced by the waves of tension in the tendon. In this way, the tension wave propagation within the tendon may affect sEMG signals, particularly when multiple muscles work together, as the tension waves from the tendon interact with the electrical activity of the muscles, influencing the resulting electromyography.

5 Conclusion

This study presents an optimized four-electrode symmetric configuration (positions 1, 2, 4, 5) for wrist-worn sEMG systems, achieving a balance between gesture recognition accuracy (62.1% with LDA) and practical wearable constraints. Systematic evaluation across four machine learning models demonstrates that this configuration reduces channel count by 50% compared to conventional forearm arrays while maintaining robust performance. Offline analysis using the GRABMyo dataset reveals three key advantages: (1) The centrosymmetric arrangement aligns with our proposed tendon symmetry conduction theory, suggesting wrist sEMG signals are governed by coordinated tendon tension waves; (2) Consistent performance across classifiers (ICC > 0.9) confirms model-agnostic reliability; and (3) Minimal accuracy degradation (<1% over 21 days) addresses critical challenges in long-term wearable use.

Current limitations in cross-session accuracy stem from inherent sEMG variability and traditional feature-based methods. Future work will focus on: (1) Developing real-time embedded systems with < 200 ms latency, leveraging the streamlined electrode setup; (2) Integrating domain adaptation techniques (e.g., CORrelation Alignment) to mitigate session-to-session variations; and (3) Expanding dynamic gesture recognition through multimodal sensor fusion. These advancements aim to bridge laboratory research and practical applications in assistive technologies and industrial HMIs, while the optimization framework can be adapted to other compact sEMG interfaces (e.g., ankle-worn systems). Some gestures (such as wrist flexion, forearm rotation, etc.) are more difficult to recognize because the muscle activation patterns in the wrist overlap or the signal sources are far away. This discovery is supported by Mutual Information (MI) analysis, which indicates that there are significant differences in the channel signal redundancy of different gestures. These results collectively point to an important future direction: developing an adaptive electrode configuration system that can adjust strategies according to specific tasks, thereby providing better solutions for high-precision application scenarios (such as rehabilitation training) while ensuring universality.The 'tendon symmetry conduction theory' introduced in this paper offers a plausible explanation for why symmetrical electrode placements are particularly effective for wrist-based gesture recognition. We must emphasize, however, that this theory is presented as a working hypothesis inspired by our empirical results, rather than a fully verified mechanism. The current study provides indirect support by showing a strong correlation between symmetric configurations and higher performance. Direct experimental validation is a crucial next step. Future work should aim to verify this hypothesis using multi-modal sensing approaches, for instance, by combining sEMG with high-frequency ultrasound imaging to simultaneously visualize tendon dynamics and measure electrical muscle activity. Such studies would be essential to confirm the role of tendon tension waves in the generation of sEMG signals at the wrist and would further solidify the theoretical foundation for designing next-generation wearable interfaces.

References

1. Zheng, M., Crouch, M.S., Eggleston, M.S.: Surface electromyography as a natural human-machine interface: a review. IEEE Sens. J. **22**(10), 9198–9214 (2022)
2. Villani, V., et al.: Towards modern inclusive factories: a methodology for the development of smart adaptive human-machine interfaces. In: 22nd IEEE International Conference on Emerging Technologies and Factory Automation (ETFA), Limassol, Cyprus (2017)
3. Jiang, N., et al.: Bio-robotics research for non-invasive myoelectric neural interfaces for upper-limb prosthetic control: a 10-year perspective review. Natl. Sci. Rev. **10**(5), nwad048 (2023)
4. Fang, Y., Hettiarachchi, N., Zhou, D., Liu, H.: Multi-modal sensing techniques for interfacing hand prostheses: a review. IEEE Sens. J. **15**(11), 6065–6076 (2015)
5. Farina, D., et al.: Man/machine interface based on the discharge timings of spinal motor neurons after targeted muscle reinnervation. Nat. Biomed. Eng. **1**(2) (2017)
6. Cao, J., Liu, Y., Han, L., Li, Z.: Finger tracking using wrist-worn EMG sensors. IEEE Trans. Mob. Comput. **23**(12), 14099–14110 (2024)
7. Li, C., et al.: Breathable, adhesive, and biomimetic skin-like super tattoo. Adv. Sci. **11**(40) (2024)
8. Botros, F.S., Phinyomark, A., Scheme, E.J.: Electromyography-based gesture recognition: is it time to change focus from the forearm to the wrist? IEEE Trans. Industr. Inf. **18**(1), 174–184 (2022)
9. Hai, W., Qing, T., Na, S., Xiaodong, Z.: Simultaneous estimation of hand joints' angles toward sEMG-driven human-robot interaction. IEEE Access **10**, 109385–109394 (2022)
10. Yang, D.P., Liu, H.: An EMG-based deep learning approach for multi-DOF wrist movement decoding. IEEE Trans. Industr. Electron. **69**(7), 7099–7108 (2022). (in English)

11. D'Accolti, D., Dejanovic, K., Cappello, L., Mastinu, E., Ortiz-Catalan, M., Cipriani, C.: Decoding of multiple wrist and hand movements using a transient EMG classifier. IEEE Trans. Neural Syst. Rehabil. Eng. **31**, 208–217 (2023)
12. He, J., Niu, X., Zhao, P., Lin, C., Jiang, N.: From forearm to wrist: deep learning for surface electromyography-based gesture recognition. IEEE Trans. Neural Syst. Rehabil. Eng. 1 (2023)
13. Pradhan, A., He, J., Jiang, N.: Multi-day dataset of forearm and wrist electromyogram for hand gesture recognition and biometrics. Sci. Data **9**(1) (2022)
14. Voorham, J., et al.: Cost effectiveness of emg biofeedback assisted pelvic floor muscle therapy for women with overact. Neurourol. Urodyn. **39**, S51–S53 (2020). (in English)
15. Hudgins, B., Parker, P., Scott, R.N.: A new strategy for multifunction myoelectric control. IEEE Trans. Bio-Med. Eng. **40**(1), 82–94 (1993)
16. Wang, H., Li, N., Gao, X., Jiang, N., He, J.: Analysis of electrode locations on limb condition effect for myoelectric pattern recognition. J. NeuroEng. Rehabil. **21**(1) (2024)
17. Wang, H., Tao, Q.: Deep forest model combined with neural networks for finger joint continuous angle decoding. In: Yang, H., et al. (eds.) ICIRA 2023. LNCS, vol. 14272, pp. 541–557. Springer, Cham (2023). https://doi.org/10.1007/978-981-99-6480-2_45

Robotic Grinding of Thin-Walled Parts: Reinforcement Learning-Based Chatter Suppression Method

Fuyong Zhang[1,2], Zhihao Xu[2(✉)], Yuming Li[2], Haifei Zhu[1], Zhaoyang Liao[2], Hongmin Wu[2], Xubin Lin[2], and Xuefeng Zhou[2(✉)]

[1] School of Electro-mechanical Engineering, Guangdong University of Technology, Guangzhou 510006, China
[2] Guangdong Key Laboratory of Modern Control Technology, Institute of Intelligent Manufacturing, Guangdong Academy of Sciences, GDAS, Guangzhou 510070, China
zh.xu@giim.ac.cn, xf.zhou@giim.ac.com

Abstract. To address chatter vibration in robotic thin-walled part grinding, this paper proposes a variable impedance control (VIC) method fusing deep deterministic policy gradient (DDPG) reinforcement learning with an imitation mechanism (IM). The method establishes dynamic mapping between vibration states and impedance parameters, which forms an integrated sensing-control scheme. Within the reinforcement learning (RL) framework, a multimodal state space is constructed by combining time-frequency domain features, including wavelet packet energy and force error. An imitation mechanism is introduced to generate state-action sample sets compliant with vibration dynamics for network pre-training, which effectively resolves the safety risks and training inefficiency issues encountered by reinforcement learning in real-world environments. Experimental results demonstrate that, compared with traditional impedance control (TIC), the proposed method suppresses characteristic chatter frequency amplitudes by over 34% and reduces force control errors by 50%. These results confirm its feasibility and effectiveness. This data-driven approach achieves closed-loop chatter detection and suppression without requiring precise system dynamics modeling, providing a novel solution for precision robotic machining in flexible manufacturing scenarios.

Keywords: Reinforcement Learning · Imitation Mechanism · Variable Impedance Control · Robotic Grinding · Thin-Walled Parts

1 Introduction

Industrial robots play a pivotal role in the transition from dedicated manufacturing systems to flexible automation, which effectively resolves inherent limitations of traditional production systems such as economic inefficiency and operational rigidity. While the widespread adoption of industrial robots has significantly enhanced manufacturing efficiency and adaptability, substantial technical challenges persist in thin-walled component processing. The intrinsic low-stiffness characteristics of these components often cause dimensional inaccuracies and surface defects during grinding operations, which critically degrade final product performance. Among these challenges, machining chatter emerges as the most prominent process defect, which not only degrades surface quality but also elevates energy consumption. Consequently, chatter suppression constitutes a fundamental technological bottleneck for achieving precision in thin-walled part machining.

Chatter monitoring serves as the fundamental prerequisite for chatter suppression. In this domain, researchers employ signal processing techniques to accurately identify and analyze chatter phenomena. Principal signal decomposition methods include but are not limited to: empirical mode decomposition (EMD), wavelet packet transform (WPT), variational mode decomposition (VMD), and fast fourier transform (FFT). These techniques enable effective extraction of discriminative features from complex vibration signals. Critical analytical metrics encompassing frequency-domain characteristics and time-domain features are subsequently introduced, which prove essential for chatter identification and classification.

Extensive research has been conducted on chatter monitoring. Fu et al. [1] proposed a methodology where vibration signals are first decomposed through EMD. Sub-bands are then selectively retained based on an energy confinement coefficient, prioritizing those with maximum energy concentration. The selected sub-bands are subsequently converted into frequency spectra, from which normalized energy ratios and variation coefficients are computed. These metrics are compared against predefined thresholds to achieve chatter identification. Liu et al. [2] developed a kurtosis-based automatic parameter selection method for VMD. By performing time-frequency analysis on the processed signals, their approach effectively identifies chatter frequency bands. Chatter states are subsequently classified through evaluation of the characteristic amplitude thresholds within these frequency bands. Chen et al. [3] proposed a methodology where vibration signals are first preprocessed using WPT. Two wavelet packets adjacent to the system's natural frequency are selected for signal reconstruction. Time-domain features and frequency-domain characteristics extracted from the reconstructed signals constitute the raw feature set for chatter identification. Chatter is subsequently detected through comparison with predetermined amplitude thresholds in the target frequency bands. Lamraoui et al. [4] applied multiband resonant filtering to preprocess vibration signals and extracted statistical features from the filtered data. Optimal features were selected based on relative entropy evaluation. These features were subsequently utilized as inputs to neural networks for chatter identification. Kumar et al. [5] proposed a chatter identification method using the mean square error of input signals as the chatter index parameter. They trained a chatter recognition model through an adaptive neuro-fuzzy inference system. However, most existing chatter monitoring methods primarily perform severity classification but do not establish continuous online suppression integrated with subsequent control processes.

Current chatter suppression methods predominantly target specific frequencies or limited bandwidths, falling into two categories: passive and active vibration control. Passive approaches utilize mechanical components to absorb and dissipate vibrational energy, typically effective only at predetermined frequencies. In contrast, active methods employ real-time controlled forces to neutralize vibrations, demonstrating broader bandwidth suppression capabilities. In chatter suppression research, Xu et al. [6] developed a passive vibration absorber based on electromagnetic induction principles. The device utilizes repulsive forces generated between permanent magnets and movable damping blocks to compensate for machining induced vibrations, thereby enhancing workpiece surface quality. Yuan et al. [7] developed a semi-active vibration absorber incorporating magnetorheological elastomer for robotic machining applications. The device, mounted on the robot spindle, demonstrates frequency selective chatter absorption capability through controlled current input, effectively mitigating vibration issues in robotic machining processes. Ding et al. [8] proposed a hybrid force/position control method for robotic processing applications. Their approach employs a proportional-integral controller to compute trajectory corrections along the surface normal vector, effectively suppressing chatter vibrations during the process. Wang et al. [9] developed an active chatter suppression strategy for flexible robots using piezoelectric ceramic actuators. Their approach incorporates a vibration suppressor with adaptive control schemes to mitigate chatter across varying frequency bands. Dai et al. [10] designed an active controller mounted at the robot end-effector, and developed an impedance matching control strategy that combines force and impedance control. The method dynamically adjusts controller parameters based on real-time system states to achieve vibration suppression through impedance matching.

Current vibration control methods exhibit two fundamental limitations: dependence on complete system knowledge requiring precise mathematical modeling. Restricted suppression bandwidth, and the installation of external devices significantly compromises robotic maneuverability in industrial applications. Furthermore, these methods demonstrate limited adaptability to frequency shifts that occur during position-dependent grinding operations.

To address these limitations, this paper proposes a RL-based intelligent control method that adopts a data-driven approach to learn optimal control policies directly from system input-output data. Our framework integrates chatter state detection with suppression while eliminating the need for complex prior environmental dynamics modeling. The key contributions as follows: (1)An RL framework establishes real-time correlations between robotic grinding states and control parameters, which directly transforms chatter states into impedance actions. This approach circumvents estimation biases inherent in manually-designed evaluation metrics. (2)For the scenario of robots grinding thin-walled parts, we introduce an IM to address RL deployment challenges, including low sampling efficiency and safety risks during direct robot-environment interaction. The mechanism collects demonstration data for network pre-training before full RL implementation.

2 Framework of the Proposed

2.1 Impedance-Based Dynamic Modeling

During thin-walled part grinding, the robot-workpiece system exhibits inherent instability. The rotating kinetic energy from the grinding head accumulates in the system, while structural damping dissipates energy. When the energy dissipation rate cannot match the accumulation rate, excess energy manifests as severe workpiece vibration. From an energy perspective, this study aims to suppress grinding chatter through controlled energy dissipation. Impedance control inherently possesses this capability by dynamically adjusting control parameters according to system states, thereby regulating energy conversion throughout the system. Figure 1 illustrates the overall control framework.

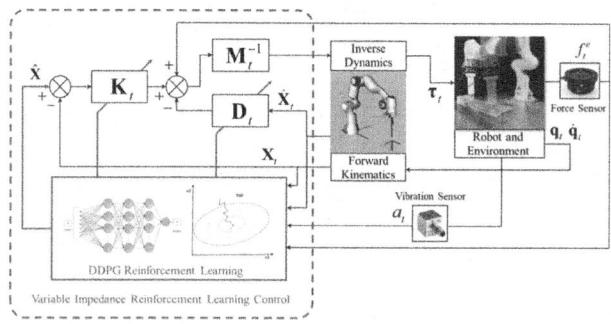

Fig. 1. Control framework.

Define the desired joint-space dynamic response of an n degree of freedom robot as a mass-damper-spring system:

$$M_d(\ddot{x} - \ddot{x}_d) + B_d(\dot{x} - \dot{x}_d) + K_d(x - x_d) = F - F_d, \tag{1}$$

where M_d, B_d, K_d represent the inertia, damping, and stiffness respectively; x_d, $\dot{x}_d$, and $\ddot{x}_d$ denote the desired trajectory, velocity, and acceleration in task space; x, $\dot{x}$, $\ddot{x}$ are the actual trajectory, velocity, and acceleration; F is the actual force, and F_d the desired force.

2.2 State Vector Construction in RL

The construction of state vectors is crucial for reinforcement learning control strategies, as they contain the system state information at each timestep during robotic grinding. Since chatter energy accumulates progressively, with its development dependent on both current and historical states, temporal features must be incorporated to characterize the process dynamics comprehensively. Wavelet packet decomposition (WPD) effectively decomposes vibration signals into time-frequency localized sub-bands, revealing energy distribution patterns across different frequency components. Specifically, for a vibration acceleration signal $a[n]$, the j-th level p-th sub-band coefficient $w_{j,p}[n]$ is computed through J-level decomposition:

$$w_{j,p}[n] = \begin{cases} \sum_m h[m - 2n] w_{j-1, \lfloor p/2 \rfloor}[m] & \text{for even } p, \\ \sum_m g[m - 2n] w_{j-1, \lfloor p/2 \rfloor}[m] & \text{for odd } p. \end{cases}$$

where:

- $h[m]$ and $g[m]$ denote low-pass and high-pass filter coefficients, respectively, satisfying $g[m] = (-1)^m h[1 - m]$
- Initial condition: $w_{0,0}[m] = x[m]$ (original signal)
- $\lfloor \cdot \rfloor$ represents the floor operation

The energy of the p-th sub-band at level j is calculated as:

$$E_{j,p} = \sum_{n=0}^{N/2^j - 1} |w_{j,p}[n]|^2. \tag{2}$$

At timestep t, the energy distribution across frequency bands is represented as:

$$\mathbf{E}_t = [E_{t,0}, E_{t,1}, \ldots, E_{t, 2^J - 1}] \in \mathbb{R}^{2^J}, \tag{3}$$

where J indicates the decomposition level, yielding 2^J energy sub-bands. Comparative analysis with initial states identifies energy variations across bands. A sub-band is designated as the chatter-developing band E_v when its cumulative energy increase exceeds 30%. Proper WPD level selection enables precise chatter frequency localization. Pre-chatter conditions manifest as energy concentration toward dominant frequencies, increasing signal orderliness. To quantify this phenomenon, we introduce wavelet packet energy entropy:

$$H = -\sum_{p=0}^{2^J - 1} p_p \log_2 p_p, \quad \text{where } p_p = \frac{E_{j,p}}{\sum_{q=0}^{2^J - 1} E_{j,q}}. \tag{4}$$

The end-effector force sensor directly monitors transient fluctuations in grinding forces, whose amplitude variations exhibit strong correlation with chatter intensity. The force error e_F, defined as the deviation between the real-time force signal $F(t)$ and steady-state reference force F_{ref}, is incorporated as a state input:

$$e_F = F(t) - F_{\text{ref}}. \tag{5}$$

A sequence of force errors over the most recent K timesteps is recorded as:

$$\mathbf{F}_t^e = [e_F(t), e_F(t-1), \ldots, e_F(t-K+1)] \in \mathbb{R}^K. \tag{6}$$

$$\mathbf{s}_t = [\mathbf{E}_t, \mathbf{F}_t^e] \in \mathbb{R}^{2^J + K} \tag{7}$$

The reinforcement learning state space $\mathbf{s}_t$ is constructed by fusing the WPD-derived spectral energy vector $\mathbf{E}_t$ with the force error sequence $\mathbf{F}_t^e$ to form an enriched state representation that captures multiple process characteristics

2.3 Impedance-Guided IM for RL Pretraining

RL requires extensive environmental interactions and exhibits substantial random exploration during initial stages. Direct deployment on robotic systems leads to inefficient learning and potential safety risks. Moreover, collecting large interaction datasets incurs significant time costs in practice. To address these challenges, we introduce an Imitation Mechanism that generates state-action pairs $\{(\mathbf{s}_i, \mathbf{a}_i)\}_{i=1}^N$ for network pre-training, as shown in Fig. 2. This produces a generalized model that undergoes subsequent task-specific fine-tuning to adapt to actual grinding conditions.

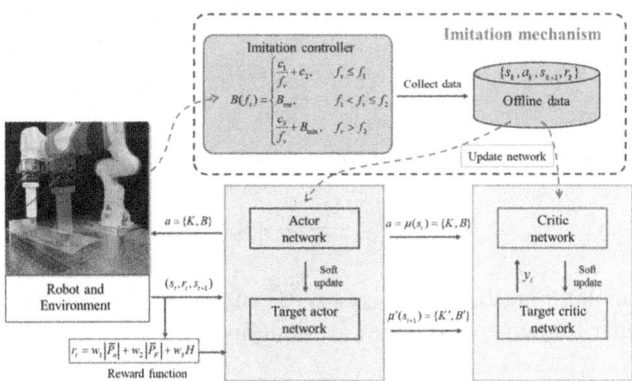

Fig. 2. The relationship between reinforcement learning and imitation mechanisms.

We develop a chatter frequency-damping matching mechanism. The impedance control system is modeled as:

$$M_d \ddot{x} + B\dot{x} + Kx = F_{\text{ext}}(t), \tag{8}$$

where $F_{\text{ext}}(t)$ contains chatter components $F_v(t) = A_v \sin(2\pi f_v t)$, with f_v estimated from the chatter band E_v. The Laplace-transformed frequency response function is:

$$H(j\omega) = \frac{X(j\omega)}{F_{\text{ext}}(j\omega)} = \frac{1}{-M_d\omega^2 + K + jB\omega}. \tag{9}$$

The vibration suppression requirement at chatter frequency $\omega_v = 2\pi f_v$ becomes:

$$|H(j\omega_v)| \leq \epsilon, \tag{10}$$

where ϵ is the allowable amplitude. This yields the suppression condition:

$$\frac{1}{\sqrt{(K - M_d\omega_v^2)^2 + (B\omega_v)^2}} \leq \epsilon. \tag{11}$$

low-frequency regime($\omega_v \ll \omega_n = \sqrt{K/M_d}$). The approximation $K - M_d\omega_v^2 \approx K$ simplifies the condition to:

$$B \geq \frac{\sqrt{1/\epsilon^2 - K^2}}{\omega_v}. \tag{12}$$

The required damping $B \propto 1/\omega_v$ indicates stiffness-dominated behavior requiring higher damping at lower frequencies. Resonance regime ($\omega_v \approx \omega_n$). With $K - M_d\omega_v^2 \approx 0$, the condition reduces to:

$$B \geq \frac{1}{\epsilon\omega_n}, \tag{13}$$

indicating frequency-independent damping requirements for peak suppression. High-frequency regime ($\omega_v \gg \omega_n$). The approximation $|K - M_d\omega_v^2| \approx M_d\omega_v^2$ leads to:

$$B \geq \frac{\sqrt{1/\epsilon^2 - M_d^2\omega_v^4}}{\omega_v}. \tag{14}$$

For sufficiently large ω_v, the asymptotic expansion becomes:

$$B \approx \frac{1}{\epsilon\omega_v} - \frac{M_d^2\omega_v^3}{2} + \mathcal{O}(\omega_v^{-5}). \tag{15}$$

The minimum damping $B_{\min} \geq 2\zeta_{\min}\sqrt{KM_d}$ ensures system responsiveness. The fuzzy controller implements a piecewise damping function:

$$B(f_v) = \begin{cases} \frac{c_1}{f_v} + c_2, & f_v \leq f_1 \quad \text{(low-frequency)} \\ B_{\text{res}}, & f_1 < f_v \leq f_2 \quad \text{(resonance)} \\ \frac{c_3}{f_v} + B_{\min}, & f_v > f_2 \quad \text{(high-frequency)} \end{cases} \tag{16}$$

where c_1, c_2, c_3 are boundary-determined constants, and $B_{\text{res}} = \frac{1}{2\pi\epsilon f_n}$ is the resonance damping. The mechanism generates state-action pairs (s_i, B_i) for pre-training the policy network.

2.4 RL Update Policy

For dynamic interaction tasks requiring real-time impedance parameter adjustment based on environmental vibration states, we formulate the parameter learning as a markov decision process. The state space $\mathbf{s}_t$ incorporates time-frequency features of vibration signals and end-effector force tracking errors. The action space is defined as $\mathbf{a}_t = \mathbf{z}_t = \{K, B\}$, where $\mathbf{z}_t$ represents the output impedance parameters. The reward function is designed as:

$$r_t = w_1|\bar{P}_a| + w_2|\bar{P}_F| + w_3 H, \qquad (17)$$

where:

- $\bar{P}_a$ denotes the normalized energy ratio of the top three sub-bands in $\mathbf{E}_t$, indicating dominant frequency content
- $\bar{P}_F$ represents the mean absolute force error from $\mathbf{F}_t^e$, reflecting force control accuracy
- w_1, w_2, w_3 are weighting coefficients for multi-objective optimization

We employ DDPG framework for end-to-end impedance parameter optimization with continuous action control. The architecture comprises:

- actor network $\mu_\phi(\mathbf{s})$ with parameters ϕ
- critic network $Q_\theta(\mathbf{s}, \mathbf{a})$ with parameters θ
- target networks $\mu_{\phi'}(\mathbf{s})$ and $Q_{\theta'}(\mathbf{s}, \mathbf{a})$
- experience replay buffer $\mathcal{D} = \{\mathbf{s}_t, \mathbf{a}_t, r_t, \mathbf{s}_{t+1}\}$

The actor network $\mu_\phi(\mathbf{s})$ generates deterministic actions by mapping states to impedance parameters, while the critic network $Q_\theta(\mathbf{s}, \mathbf{a})$ estimates long-term state-action values. Target networks ensure training stability through delayed parameter updates. The actor network $\mu_\phi(\mathbf{s})$:

- input dimension matches state space $\mathbf{s}_t$
- fully-connected hidden layers
- output dimension equals action space with safety constraints

The critic network $Q_\theta(\mathbf{s}, \mathbf{a})$:

- input dimension: state space + action space
- identical hidden structure to actor network
- single-neuron output for Q-value estimation

During each training iteration, sample mini-batch $\{\mathbf{s}_i, \mathbf{a}_i, r_i, \mathbf{s}_{i+1}\}_{i=1}^N$ from $\mathcal{D}$. The target value y_i is computed using the Bellman equation,

$$y_i = r_i + \gamma Q_{\theta'}(\mathbf{s}_{i+1}, \mu_{\phi'}(\mathbf{s}_{i+1})), \qquad (18)$$

miniming $\mathcal{L}_Q(\theta)$ ensures the critic's Q-values reflect the expected returns,

$$\mathcal{L}_Q(\theta) = \frac{1}{N} \sum_{i=1}^{N} (Q_\theta(\mathbf{s}_i, \mathbf{a}_i) - y_i)^2, \qquad (19)$$

θ are updated via gradient descent on this loss,

$$\theta \leftarrow \theta - \alpha_Q \nabla_\theta \mathcal{L}_Q(\theta). \qquad (20)$$

$\nabla_\phi J(\phi)$ guides the actor toward actions that maximize expected returns,

$$\nabla_\phi J(\phi) = \frac{1}{N}\sum_{i=1}^{N}\nabla_\theta Q_\theta(\mathbf{s}_i,\mathbf{a}_i)\nabla_\phi \mu_\phi(\mathbf{s}_i), \tag{21}$$

ϕ are updated via gradient ascent using this policy gradient,

$$\phi \leftarrow \phi + \alpha_\mu \nabla_\phi J(\phi). \tag{22}$$

Finally, perform a soft update on the target network:

$$\phi' \leftarrow \tau\phi + (1-\tau)\phi', \quad \theta' \leftarrow \tau\theta + (1-\tau)\theta', \tag{23}$$

where, y_i denotes the critic network's target value, γ is discount factor, α_Q and α_μ the learning rates for critic and actor networks respectively, and τ the soft update coefficient. The online reinforcement learning network is updated through the aforementioned policy. During the control process, the state vector $\mathbf{s}_t$ comprising wavelet packet energy of vibration signals and force error sequences serves as the input. The reinforcement learning module outputs optimized impedance parameters $\mathbf{z}_t$ that regulate the grinding process. This approach effectively suppresses machining chatter.

3 Experiment and Analysis

Fig. 3. Experimental scene of robot grinding thin-walled parts.

As illustrated in Fig. 3, the experimental platform consists of: end-effector force sensor, accelerometer, NI data acquisition module, grinding tool, thin-walled workpiece, Franka robot, and host computer.

In RL, the actor and critc networks use the same structure and both adopt a three-layer fully connected layer. After deploying the imitation-trained network in the reinforcement learning framework, we perform additional training using online-collected data. As shown in Fig. 4, the reward function values over 500 training episodes demonstrate rapid initial growth, indicating continuous optimization of the variable impedance strategy. The reward values stabilize around 8 after approximately 300 episodes, suggesting successful policy convergence. The trained reinforcement learning policy was deployed to the robot controller. Comparative experiments were conducted between the reinforcement learning based on variable impedance (RL-VI) strategy and TIC under identical working conditions, maintaining a fixed posture while grinding the same trajectory with a desired force of $F_d = 10$ N. The parameters of TIC are selected based on experience, and the impedance parameters with the most stable force error are chosen through repeated experiments.

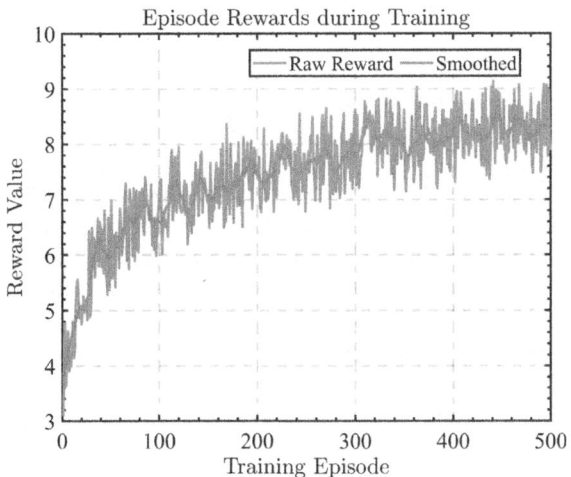

Fig. 4. Online RL-VI training curve.

We compared vibration levels and contact force, as depicted in Fig. 5, the blue line represents the end-effector force curve of grinding using TIC, where the impedance parameters are determined empirically. The red line corresponds to the end-effector force curve of the grinding process achieved through RL-VI. Upon comparison, it is evident that during the contact phase between the grinding tool and the workpiece, the force error of the RL-VI method is significantly lower than that of the TIC method.

During the grinding process, the end-effector force controlled by TIC primarily fluctuates between 8 N and 12 N, with a force error range of approximately ±2 N. In contrast, when employing the RL-VI method for grinding, the end-effector force mainly varies between 9 N and 11 N, with a force error range of approximately ±1 N. This represents a 50% reduction in force error compared to TIC. RL-VI improves force control stability during the grinding of thin-walled components. However, in the first 5 s, due to the large impact of the initial contact, the force error tracking of the two methods has large fluctuations.

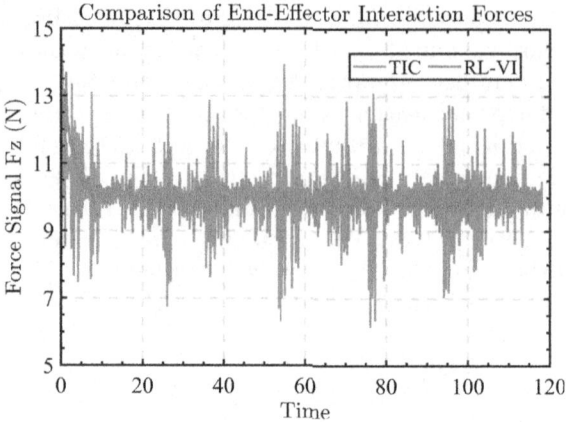

Fig. 5. Interaction force. (Color figure online)

As shown in Fig. 6, the blue and red curves respectively represent the superimposed short-time frequency spectra of TIC and RL-VI method. Spectral analysis indicates the conventional method exhibits significantly higher amplitudes at 95 Hz and 220 Hz, demonstrating severe chatter vibration in these bands, with amplitudes of 0.66 and 1.34 respectively, while RL-VI approach achieves substantially reduced peak amplitudes of 0.49 and 0.2 at these frequencies, over 34% amplitude reduction. Thereby effectively suppressing chatter vibration and maintaining stable grinding conditions throughout the process.

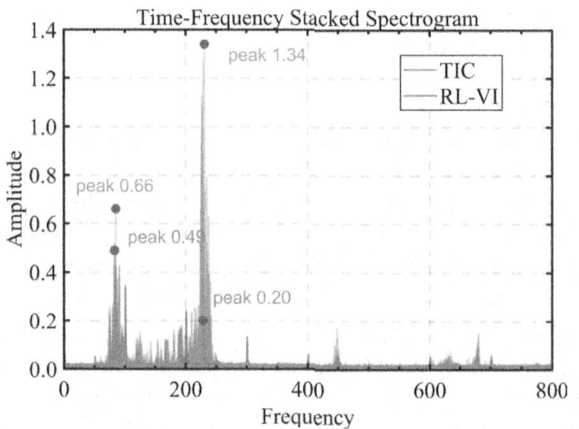

Fig. 6. Spectral comparison of vibration signals. (Color figure online)

4 Conclusion

This study addresses the chatter vibration problem in robotic grinding of thin-walled parts by proposing a RL-based adaptive variable impedance control framework. The framework combines imitation mechanismpriors with online RL-VI policy optimization to achieve chatter suppression and force control accuracy improvement. We develop a DDPG model for dynamic impedance parameter adjustment, where wavelet packet energy features and real-time contact force errors are jointly encoded into a multidimensional state space to enable real-time parameter optimization. A frequency-matched piecewise damping imitation controller is designed to generate state-action pairs that comply with thin-walled part dynamics, pre-training the network while eliminating the extensive environmental interactions required by conventional reinforcement learning. Experimental results confirm that the proposed method enhances grinding stability, effectively suppresses chatter vibration, and improves force control precision.

Acknowledgements. This work was supported by National Key R&D Program of China (2022YFF0607800), National Natural Science Foundation of China (22A20176 and 62203126), Guangdong Basic and Applied Basic Research Foundation (2025A1515011849 and 2022B1515120078), Young Talent Project of GDAS (2023GDASQNRC-0204), GDAS' Project of science and Technology Development (2024GDASZH-2024010102).

References

1. Fu, Y., et al.: Timely online chatter detection in end milling process. Mech. Syst. Signal Process. **75**, 668–688 (2016)
2. Liu, C., Zhu, L., Ni, C.: Chatter detection in milling process based on VMD and energy entropy. Mech. Syst. Signal Process. **105**, 169–182 (2018)
3. Chen, G.S., Zheng, Q.Z.: Online chatter detection of the end milling based on wavelet packet transform and support vector machine recursive feature elimination. Int. J. Adv. Manuf. Technol. **95**(1), 775–784 (2018)
4. Lamraoui, M., Barakat, M., Thomas, M., El Badaoui, M.: Chatter detection in milling machines by neural network classification and feature selection. J. Vibration Control: JVC (21-7) (2015)
5. Kumar, S., Singh, B.: Chatter prediction using merged wavelet denoising and anfis. Soft. Comput. **23**, 4439–4458 (2019)
6. Xu, D., Lu, X., Xu, B.: Design and modeling of a passive magnetic vibration absorber for robotic polishing process. J. Manuf. Process. **95**, 204–216 (2023)
7. Yuan, L., Sun, S., Pan, Z., Ding, D., Gienke, O., Li, W.: Mode coupling chatter suppression for robotic machining using semi-active magnetorheological elastomers absorber. Mech. Syst. Signal Process. **117**, 221–237 (2019)
8. Ding, Y., Min, X.: Force/position hybrid control method for surface parts polishing robot. J. Syst. Simul. **32**(5), 817–825 (2020)
9. Chen, X., Wang, H., Tao, W.: Experimental research on active vibration control of flexible robotic arms based on piezoelectric ceramics. J. Sens. Technol. **30**(5), 777–781 (2017)
10. Dai, J., Chen, C.Y., Zhu, R., Yang, G., Wang, C., Bai, S.: Suppress vibration on robotic polishing with impedance matching. Actuators **10**(3) (2021)

Electrode Shift-Robust Decomposition of Surface EMG Signals via Deep Learning: A Simulation Study

Zeyu Zhou[1], Yang Yu[1,2,3], and Xinjun Sheng[1,2,3(✉)]

[1] State Key Laboratory of Mechanical System and Vibration, Shanghai Jiao Tong University, Shanghai 200240, China
[2] Shanghai Key Laboratory of Intelligent Robotics, Shanghai Jiao Tong University, Shanghai 200240, China
[3] Meta Robotics Institute, Shanghai Jiao Tong University, Shanghai 200240, China
xjsheng@sjtu.edu.cn

Abstract. Real-time surface electromyography (sEMG) decomposition has emerged as a research hotspot, with applications spanning prosthetic control, medical rehabilitation, and beyond. However, the accuracy of decomposition algorithms is often compromised by electrode shifts. Here, we propose a deep learning-based (DL-based) decomposition method specifically for electrode shift interference. First, an electrode-shift-oriented data augmentation strategy is designed to enrich training data diversity for sEMG-to-motor unit spike train mappings. Subsequently, an spatiotemporal DL architecture with robustness to feature shift is constructed to learn mapping knowledge embedded in training data. Simulation evaluation results demonstrate that the proposed method outperforms the traditional DL-based method under 10 mm multidirectional electrode shifts, achieving an F_1-score of 0.917 ± 0.066 compared to 0.207 ± 0.306. Moreover, the proposed method requires only 0.0393 ± 0.0017 seconds per instance for decomposition, meeting real-time constraints. These outcomes enable reliable acquisition of neural drive information under electrode shift interference, thereby advancing the application of neural control interfaces.

Keywords: Motor unit · electrode shift · deep learning

1 Introduction

The motor unit (MU), the function entity consisting of a motor neuron and its innervated muscle fibers, encodes neural drive signals transmitted from the central nervous system to the muscle via spike trains [1]. Accurate identification of MU spike trains (MUSTs) has broad applications in clinical diagnosis [2], neurophysiology [3], and human-machine interface [4,5]. Surface electromyography (sEMG) enables non-invasive recording of multiple MU firing activities, making sEMG decomposition a prominent research focus. Application scenarios like prosthetic control and clinical diagnostics demanding real-time processing [6], giving real-time sEMG decomposition higher clinical utility compared to offline decomposition.

During real-world sEMG recordings, electrode shifts present significant challenges to real-time decomposition. Electrode repositioning, slippage, and motion-induced displacement between the skin and muscle can all lead to electrode shifts [7,8], thereby altering the mapping between sEMG signals and MUSTs. Decomposition models lacking robustness to such shifts typically require retraining to restore performance, imposing additional operational burdens on users. Thus, from a practical perspective, an ideal real-time sEMG decomposition method should exhibit robustness to electrode shifts.

Existing studies on electrode shifts primarily focus on control interfaces with direct sEMG-to-motion mapping [7–10]. Compared to end-to-end approach, neural control interfaces based on MUs offer superior effectiveness and interpretability [11]. Nevertheless, research on electrode shift robustness in sEMG decomposition remains scarce. Zhao et al. proposed a blind source separation-based (BSS-based) method where decomposition parameters are precomputed for different electrode positions and later selected based on real-time position analysis [12]. However, the BSS-based approach is inherently sensitive to noise due to their reliance on the whitening operation [13], leading to performance degradation when noise increase. In contrast, deep learning-based (DL-based) approach demonstrated strong noise robustness by training on diverse sEMG quality scenarios and avoiding the whitening operation [14]. Nevertheless, the robustness of DL-based decomposition to electrode shifts has yet to be investigated.

In this work, we propose a robust DL-based decomposition method designed to mitigate electrode shift effects. Specifically, we design a data augmentation strategy focusing on electrode shifts to enhance the training pipeline via varied sEMG-to-MUST mappings. Building upon this, we construct a decomposition model architecture that integrates spatiotemporal feature extraction capabilities with feature shift robustness. The decomposition accuracy and computational efficiency of the proposed method was evaluated using simulation data with ground-truth MUSTs.

2 Methods

2.1 Overview of the Decomposition Algorithm

The block diagram of the proposed method is illustrated in Fig. 1, comprising an offline stage for DL-based decomposition models training and an online stage for real-time sEMG decomposition. During the offline stage, central 6×6 grid sEMG signals were processed using BSS to identify the MUSTs of offline MUs [15]. Then, sliding window segmentation was applied to the offline sEMG signals to generate original training inputs, with the label of each input determined by the identified MUSTs. To enhance the robustness of the trained decomposition models against electrode shift, data augmentation was performed on the original training data using full-channel (8×8) sEMG signals. Finally, the DL-based decomposition model for each MU was trained using the augmented data. During the online stage, the real-time recorded sEMG signals were decomposed using the offline trained DL models to obtain original MUSTs. These MUSTs were then post-processed to eliminate redundant spikes, producing the final outputs.

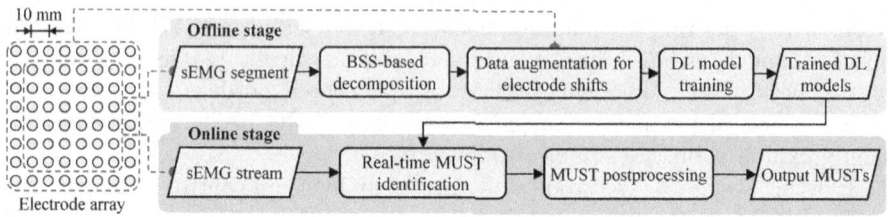

Fig. 1. Flowchart of the proposed method. The green section corresponds to the offline stage for training electrode shift-robust decomposition models. The blue section represents the online stage, where real-time decomposition of online sEMG stream is achieved using offline training models. The electrode array area involved in related steps is marked by grey dashed lines.

2.2 DL-Based Decomposition Models

The DL-based decomposition models were established individually for each MU. The architecture of the DL-based decomposition model is illustrated in Fig. 2. The input is a 40-sample 3D sEMG window data. The binary output represents the state of the target MU at the central timestamp of the input window, where 0 denotes the resting state and 1 indicates the firing state. Given that the input data contains both temporal and spatial features, the DL model first employs two 3D convolutional blocks for feature extraction, followed by a fully connected block for feature mapping. The kernel sizes of 3D convolutional and 3D max-pooling layers are specified in Fig. 2. Meanwhile, all the 3D convolutional layers used a stride of $1 \times 1 \times 1$ with $1 \times 1 \times 1$ padding, while the 3D max-pooling layers adopt a stride of $2 \times 2 \times 2$ without padding. Batch normalization is applied to enhance training stability. For nonlinearity, ReLU is used in intermediate layers to mitigate gradient vanishing, whereas sigmoid is applied at the final layer to produce binary output.

2.3 Training Pipeline

Since the decomposition models were MU-specific, the training data generation consequently adheres to the same unit-specific paradigm. The original input data for training was generated by sliding a 40-sample window with a 1-sample step over the offline sEMG segment. For each training input window, the label was the firing state of the target MU at the midpoint of the window, where the firing states were determined based on the MUSTs identified via offline BSS.

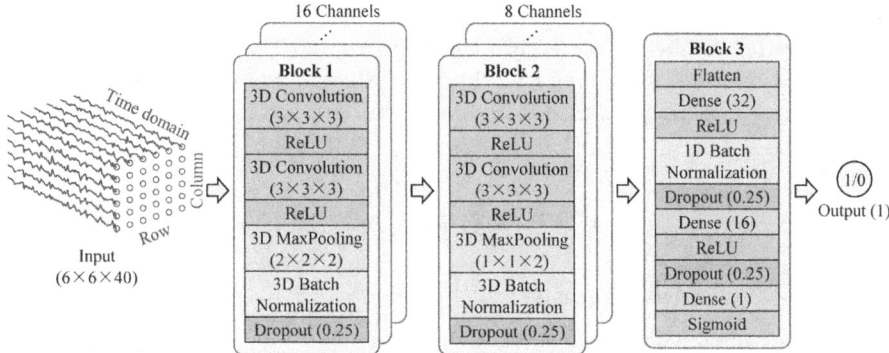

Fig. 2. DL model for real-time sEMG decomposition. The model processes a 40-sample 3D sEMG window data to output the firing state of the target MU at the midpoint of the input window. It consists of two CNN blocks for feature extraction and one FC block for feature mapping.

To enrich the training data with electrode-shift-related knowledge, each original training input was augmented by shifting original electrode array region upward, downward, leftward, rightward, and in their combined directions, as shown in Fig. 3. Each original training input yielded nine positional variants, all with the same label.

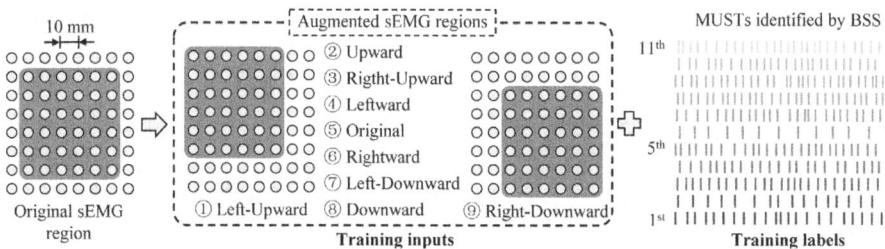

Fig. 3. Data augmentation for enhancing robustness against electrode shift. Nine augmented sEMG signals are obtained by shifting the original electrode array region leftward, rightward, upward, and downward, either singly or in combination. The training pipeline uses these augmented signals as inputs, with the MUSTs identified from the original sEMG signal via BSS serving as labels.

The training process employed MSELoss as the loss function, used the Adam optimizer, and ran for 100 epochs. Since firing states in a MUST is typically far less than resting states, the class imbalance was addressed by duplicating firing-state training samples to achieve a firing-to-resting ratio of approximately 1:8. During the validation process, the performance of each epoch model was evaluated via the F_1-score between the MUST identified by the DL model and that identified by BSS. The calculation of F_1-score is defined by Eq. 1, where TP represents the number of correctly identified spikes, FP denotes the number of incorrectly identified spikes, and FN indicates the number of missed spikes. The epoch model achieving the highest F_1-score was retained for real-time decomposition.

$$F_1\text{-score} = \frac{2 \cdot TP}{2 \cdot TP + FP + FN} \tag{1}$$

2.4 Real-Time Decomposition

During the online stage, the central 6×6 grid sEMG signals were decomposed every 0.125 s to identify MUSTs in real time. Upon completing the recording of the 0.125-second sEMG stream, sliding-window segmentation was applied with a window of 40 samples and a step size of 1 sample (consistent with the training process). The offline-trained decomposition models processed the windowed sEMG data as input, producing original real-time MUSTs with a length equal to the number of input windows. The small step size caused high similarity between adjacent input windows, which may lead to redundant spike predictions. To address this, the original real-time MUSTs underwent post-processing to eliminate potential false positives. The post-processing was performed independently for each MUST. First, consecutive spikes in the original MUST were grouped, where the distance between the first and last spike in a group does not exceed six sample intervals. Second, within each group, the candidate spike corresponding to the highest absolute sEMG value at the channel where the MUAP exhibits peak magnitude was retained, while all others were set as the resting state.

2.5 Performance Evaluation

The performance evaluation of the proposed method was primarily conducted on simulated data with available MUST ground-truth. The simulated sEMG signals were generated by convolving the action potential waveform of 100 MUs with their respective spike trains. There are a total of six 12.5-second simulation trials. Each trial followed a trapezoidal excitation pattern, which consisted of 1-second pre-rest, 2-second ramp-up, 6.5-second sustained contraction at 40% level, 2-second ramp-down, 1-second post-rest. The MUAP waveform of each MU was extracted from experimental sEMG signals recorded using an 8×8 electrode array with 10 mm inter-electrode distance. MUs were recruited in order of increasing action potential amplitude. Upon initial recruitment, the MU fired at 8 Hz, with firing rates increasing linearly at 0.3 Hz/excitation up to a maximum of 35 Hz. Inter-spike intervals followed a Gaussian distribution with 20% coefficient variation. To mimic experimental recording conditions, Gaussian white noise was added at an SNR of 30 dB.

The first two trials (25 s) of the simulated data were used as the offline sEMG segment, while the subsequent four trials (50 s) were reserved for decomposition test. The test process considered nine electrode shifts: left-upward, upward, right-upward, leftward, zero, rightward, left-downward, downward, and right-downward shift. For each shift condition, the decomposition method used the sEMG signals from the shifted 6×6 electrode grid as input, and the F_1-score was calculated between the identified MUSTs and ground-truth MUSTs. The comparative method was derived from the proposed method, employing the same DL model architecture but without implementing electrode shift-oriented data augmentation. It serves as a representative of existing DL-based decomposition studies that do not account for the impact of electrode shift on decomposition accuracy [14,16,17]. For clarity, the proposed and comparative methods are named 'DL-proposed' and 'DL-original', respectively.

All evaluations were conducted on a workstation equipped with an Intel Core i7-11700 CPU, NVIDIA GeForce RTX 2070 8 GB GPU, and 64 GB RAM.

3 Results

The decoded MUs of offline BSS were filtered using stringent quality thresholds (silhouette coefficient ≥ 0.8 and pulse-to-noise ratio ≥ 25) to ensure validity, ultimately resulting in the selection of 11 high-confidence MUs for performance evaluation. The overall F_1-score across all electrode shift conditions was 0.917 ± 0.066 for DL-proposed and 0.207 ± 0.306 for DL-original. Figure 4 illustrates the performance of both methods under each electrode shift condition. Figure 4(a) illustrates electrode shifts corresponding to the F_1-score matrix in Fig. 4(b), where 'Z', 'L', 'R', 'U', 'D' denote zero, leftward, rightward, upward, and downward shifts, respectively. As shown in Fig. 4(b), DL-proposed exhibited robustness to electrode shift, whereas DL-original maintained decomposition accuracy only for zero shift. Figure 5 visually compares the MUSTs identified by both methods for the first MU in the first test trial. The electrode shift codes 'Z', 'L', 'R', 'U', 'D' are the same as those defined in Fig. 4(a). The blue MUSTs identified by DL-proposed align closely with the green ground-truth MUST for all shifts, while the cyan MUSTs from DL-original show high consistency only for zero shift.

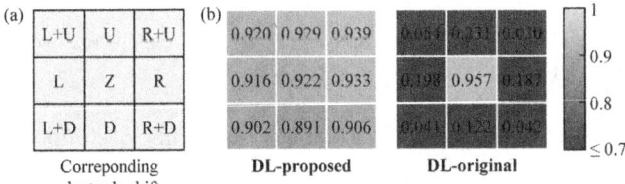

Fig. 4. Comparison of decomposition accuracy at different electrode positions. (a) Electrode shifts corresponding to the spatial distribution of F_1-score matrix, where 'Z', 'L', 'R', 'U', 'D' represent zero, leftward, rightward, upward, and downward shifts, respectively. (b) F_1-score matrix of the proposed method (DL-proposed) and the comparative method (DL-original).

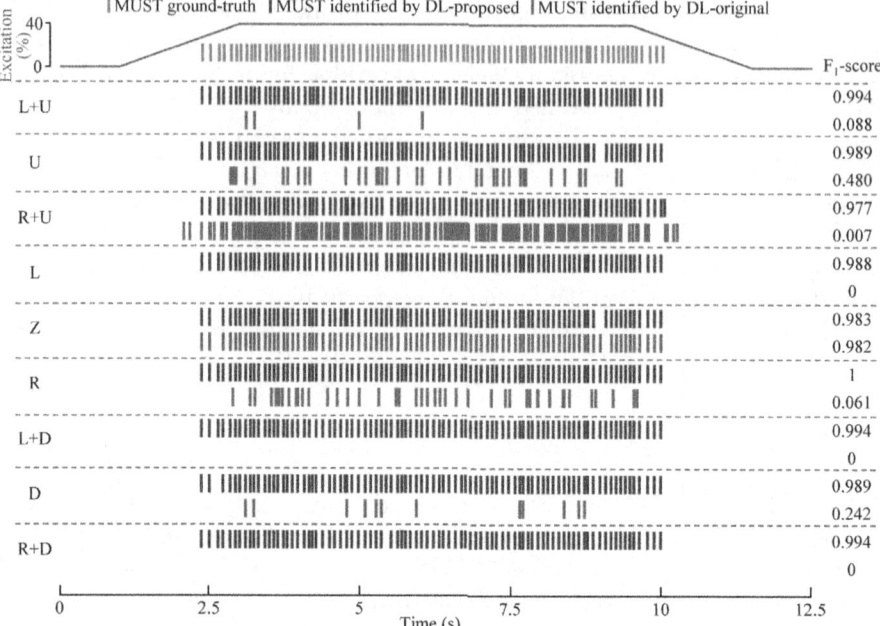

Fig. 5. Visual comparison of decomposition results for the first MU in a single trial. From top to bottom are the MUSTs identified by the proposed method (DL-proposed) and the comparative method (DL-original) at different electrode positions, where 'Z', 'L', 'R', 'U', 'D' represent zero, leftward, rightward, upward, and downward shifts, respectively. The rightmost column shows the F_1-score corresponding to the visualized MUSTs.

Regarding decomposition efficiency, the processing time per real-time decomposition window, involving DL model forward inference and MUST postprocessing, was 0.0393 ± 0.0017 seconds, averaging 0.0036 ± 0.0005 seconds per MU per window.

4 Discussion

This work presents a DL-based method for the real-time decomposition of sEMG under electrode shifts. The proposed method integrates a data augmentation strategy specifically designed to address electrode shifts with a spatiotemporal feature-capturing DL architecture. Evaluation results demonstrate that the proposed method maintains satisfactory decomposition accuracy under electrode shifts of up to 10 mm in any directions. In contrast, the traditional DL-based decomposition method can only work reliably in the absence of electrode shifts.

Electrode-shift-oriented data augmentation enhances DL-based decomposition model training by generating diverse mappings between shifted sEMG signals and MUSTs. Coupled with a well-constructed DL architecture capable of processing spatiotemporal features, the decomposition model effectively learned the above mappings and exhibited strong generalization. Notably, the robustness of the trained model stemmed not only from data augmentation but also from intrinsic architecture properties. The shift-equivariance of convolutional layers and the shift-invariance of max-pooling layers allow consistent extraction of discriminative features from shifted sEMG signals. These features maintain high compatibility with downstream mapping modules, thereby enabling reliable real-time decomposition across electrode position variations.

The decomposition performance degradation observed in the non-augmented method under electrode shift stems primarily from altered MU properties. Figure 6(a) presents the correlation coefficient matrix comparing shifted and original MU waveforms, while Fig. 6(b) illustrates extreme cases corresponding to the minimum and maximum correlation coefficient values. Notably, even unidirectional electrode shifts introduce significant waveform dissimilarities, which are further amplified by multidirectional shifts. These differences indicate the distribution mismatch between pre-shift training data and post-shift test data underlying, consequently beyond the generalization capability of trained decomposition models.

The training labels for DL-based decomposition models were derived from BSS techniques, thereby establishing the performance ceiling of BSS techniques as the theoretical upper bound for the proposed method under zero-shift conditions. Crucially, the separation vectors of BSS techniques exhibit strong correlation with MUAP waveforms [18]. This inherent correlation implies that morphological changes in MUAPs will inevitably compromise the validity of pre-optimized separation vectors. As Fig. 6 conclusively demonstrates the significant impact of electrode shift on MUAP waveforms, the superior robustness of the proposed method compared to BSS techniques under shift conditions becomes both theoretically justified and empirically demonstrable.

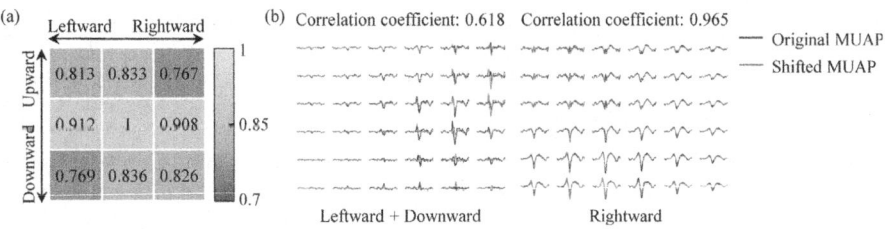

Fig. 6. Similarity between original and shifted MUAP waveforms. (a) Correlation coefficient matrix. (b) Visualization of MUAP waveforms corresponding to the minimum and maximum correlation coefficient values.

The human electromechanical response delay is about 0.25 s, while the real-time decomposition window length was set at 0.125 s. Hence, the processing time for decomposing a single real-time sEMG window data should be less than 0.125 s. Analysis of decomposition efficiency demonstrates that this real-time constraint was satisfactorily met, leaving a substantial temporal margin remaining for motion estimation based on real-time identified MUSTs.

This work has the following limitations. First, only a single shift distance (10 mm) was considered, while larger or smaller shifts may result in different decomposition difficulties. Second, the performance evaluation was conducted solely on simulated data. Future work may focus on the experimental evaluation of the decomposition accuracy of the proposed method under combined conditions of multiple shift directions and varying shift distances.

5 Conclusion

This study focuses on DL-based real-time sEMG decomposition under electrode shift interference. By designing an electrode-shift-oriented data augmentation strategy and constructing a 3D CNN-based DL architecture, the training pipeline incorporates rich sEMG-to-MUSTs mappings that can be effectively learned and generalized by trained decomposition models. The proposed method maintained decomposition accuracy under electrode shifts up to 10 mm. The outcomes enable reliable identification of neural drive information in scenarios prone to electrode shifts, thereby enhancing the practical utility of MU-based human-machine interfaces.

Acknowledgements. This work was supported in part by the National Natural Science Foundation of China under Grants 52205025 and 52175021.

References

1. Weinberger, M., Dostrovsky, J.O.: Motor Unit. Academic, Oxford (2010)
2. Holobar, A., Glaser, V., Gallego, J.A., et al.: Non-invasive characterization of motor unit behaviour in pathological tremor. J. Neural Eng. **9**(5), 056011 (2012)
3. Farina, D., Nergo, F., Diderisksen, J.L.: The effective neural drive to muscles is the common synaptic input to motor neurons. J. Physiol. **592**(16), 3427–3441 (2014)
4. Yu, Y., Chen, C., Sheng, X., et al.: Wrist Torque estimation via electromyographic motor unit decomposition and image reconstruction. IEEE J. Biomed. Health Inform. **25**(7), 2557–2566 (2021)
5. Chen, C., Yu, Y., Sheng, X., et al.: Non-invasive analysis of motor unit activation during simultaneous and continuous wrist movements. IEEE J. Biomed. Health Inform. **26**(5), 2106–2115 (2022)
6. Chen, C., Ma, S., Sheng, X., et al.: Adaptive real-time identification of motor unit discharges from non-stationary high-density surface electromyographic signals. IEEE Trans. Biomed. Eng. **67**(12), 3501–3509 (2020)
7. Wu, L., Zhang, X., Wang, K., et al.: Improved high-density myoelectric pattern recognition control against electrode shift using data augmentation and dilated convolutional neural network. IEEE Trans. Neural Syst. Rehabil. Eng. **28**(12), 2637–2646 (2020)
8. Ameri, A., Akhaee, M.A., Scheme, E., et al.: A deep transfer learning approach to reducing the effect of electrode shift in EMG pattern recognition-based control. IEEE Trans. Neural Syst. Rehabil. Eng. **28**(2), 370–379 (2020)

9. Li, Z., Zhao, X., Liu, G., et al.: Electrode shifts estimation and adaptive correction for improving robustness of sEMG-based recognition. IEEE J. Biomed. Health Inform. **25**(4), 1101–1110 (2021)
10. Gao, G., Zhang, X., Chen, X., et al.: Mitigating the concurrent interference of electrode shift and loosening in myoelectric pattern recognition using Siamese autoencoder network. IEEE Trans. Neural Syst. Rehabil. Eng. **32**, 3388–3398 (2024)
11. Yu, Y., Zhou, Z., Xu, Y., et al.: Toward hand gesture recognition using a channelwise cumulative spike train image-driven model. Cyborg Bionic Syst. **6**, 0219 (2025)
12. Zhao, H., Zhang, X., Chen, X., et al.: A robust myoelectric pattern recognition framework based on individual motor unit activities against electrode array shifts. Comput. Methods Programs Biomed. **257**, 108434 (2024)
13. Hyvarinen, A.: Fast and robust fixed-point algorithms for independent component analysis. IEEE Trans. Neural Netw. **10**(3), 626–634 (1999)
14. Clarke, A.K., Atashzar, S.F., Vecchio, A.D., et al.: Deep learning for robust decomposition of high-density surface EMG signals. IEEE Trans. Biomed. Eng. **68**(2), 526–534 (2021)
15. Nergo, F., Muceli, S., Castronovo, A.M., et al.: Multi-channel intramuscular and surface EMG decomposition by convolutive blind source separation. J. Neural Eng. **13**, 026027 (2016)
16. Wen, Y., Avrillon, S., Hernandez-Pavon, J.C., et al.: A convolutional neural network to identify motor units from high-density surface electromyography signals in real time. J. Neural Eng. **18**, 056003 (2021)
17. Lin, C., Chen, C., Cui, Z., et al.: A Bi-GRU-attention neural network to identify motor units from high-density surface electromyographic signals in real time. Front. Neurosci. **18**, 1306054 (2024)
18. Chen, C., Li, D., Xia, M.: A motor unit action potential-based method for surface electromyography decomposition. J. Neuroeng. Rehabil. **22**, 60 (2025)

Enhancing Softness Discrimination in Vision-Based Tactile Sensors via Modeling and Optimization of Gradient-Stiffness Elastomers

Lunwei Zhang, Zihao Wang, Yao Jiang(✉), and Tiemin Li

Tsinghua University, Beijing 100084, China
jiangyaonju@126.com

Abstract. Vision-based tactile sensors can provide robots with multiple tactile modalities simultaneously, representing a crucial solution of multimodal tactile perception for general-purpose robots. This study focuses on enhancing object softness discrimination capability through an improved elastomer design for vision-based tactile sensors. We observed that vision-based tactile sensors employing conventional homogeneous elastomers may exhibit sensitivity degradation in softness discrimination under specific conditions, especially when the object is smooth and homogeneous. To address this issue, we established a mechanical model of softness perception, theoretically revealing both the necessary and sufficient conditions for this sensitivity degradation phenomenon. Based on this theoretical framework, we developed quantitative sensitivity metrics to evaluate softness discrimination sensitivity and subsequently designed a gradient-stiffness elastomer through optimizing the sensitivity metric. Both finite element simulations and prototype experiments demonstrate that the improved elastomer significantly enhances the sensor's softness discrimination performance.

Keywords: softness discrimination · vision-based tactile sensor · tactile perception

1 Introduction

When human fingers press against objects, our powerful tactile perception enables us to discern their softness or hardness. This perceptual capability facilitates many daily tasks, such as assessing the quality of fruits or cushioning components based on their softness or hardness characteristics. Endowing robots with the ability to perceive softness through tactile sensing would enhance the application scenarios of general-purpose robots.

Typically, humans can judge an object's softness by detecting local deformation of the finger-object contact surface during interaction, without necessarily relying on proprioception [1, 2]. This approach reflects the material compliance (the inverse of elastic modulus), which we uniformly describe as "softness" throughout this paper.

To enable robots to perceive object softness, researchers have developed various tactile sensors. These sensors rely on different principles to identify softness, including

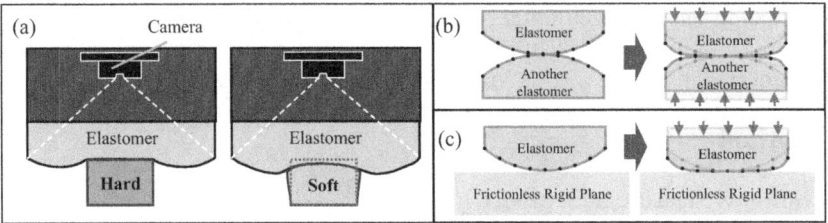

Fig. 1. (a) The deformation of the VBTS's elastomer exhibit difference when contacting hard and soft objects. (b) (c) The elastomer exhibits identical deformation processes when pressed against either a frictionless plane or another identical elastomer.

resonance response variations [3], contact force distribution characteristics [4–8], contact deformation signals [9–12], or force-displacement curve properties [13, 14]. Among these, vision-based tactile sensors (VBTS) [15] exhibit strong potential for multimodal tactile perception. They can simultaneously provide robots with softness information while retaining additional perception capability (e.g., contact force, contact area, and contact shape). Consequently, they have attracted widespread attention in tactile sensing solutions for general-purpose robots. This study also focuses on the softness perception capability of vision-based tactile sensors.

A vision-based tactile sensor consists of a transparent elastomer serving as a soft fingertip, with an embedded miniature camera capturing images of the elastomer's deformation during object contact [15]. By analyzing these images, the contact deformation field, distributed forces, and other tactile information can be reconstructed. The key to softness perception in VBTS lies in analyzing the deformation process of the elastomer when interacting with objects. The difference in deformation processes between soft and rigid objects upon contact provides critical information for discriminating softness [10] (as illustrated in Fig. 1(a)).

However, this study observed that a series of objects with specific combinations of shape and softness may induce nearly identical deformation processes in the elastomer. As illustrated in Fig. 1(b), when either a frictionless rigid plane or another identical elastomer presses against the sensor's elastomer, the resulting deformation processes are indistinguishable due to symmetry. Despite significant differences in the softness of these two objects, the tactile sensor cannot differentiate between them based on deformation information. This suggests that vision-based tactile sensors may experience a risk of softness discrimination sensitivity degradation when encountering specific objects.

To address this issue, this work conducts systematic theoretical research aiming to reveal the mechanical conditions under which the sensitivity degradation occurs, and propose methods to prevent such sensitivity loss in vision-based tactile sensors.

The main contributions of this study are:

(1) Establishing the model for measuring object softness using VBTS, revealing the conditions for softness discrimination sensitivity degradation;
(2) Developing quantitative metrics for evaluating softness discrimination sensitivity, providing guidance for elastomer design and optimization;

(3) Designing an optimized an elastomer that effectively prevents sensitivity degradation. Finite element analysis and experimental results demonstrate significant improvement.

2 Method

2.1 Softness Measurement Model

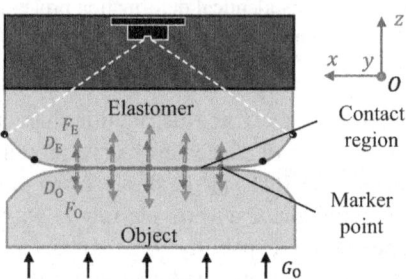

Fig. 2. Schematic diagram illustrating the force, deformation, and object displacement during elastomer-object contact.

The surface of VBTS's elastomer is typically printed with marker patterns. When the elastomer deforms upon contact, the sensor's measurement system tracks the 3D displacement of the feature points in pattern. In this study, we assume that the 3D displacements of the feature points can be precisely track in real-time.

The contact model is shown in Fig. 2, we consider n feature points uniformly distributed within the contact region. The displacements of the points in the sensor coordinate frame are represented as a column vector, denoted as $D_E = \left(D_{Ex}^T, D_{Ey}^T, D_{Ez}^T\right)^T$, where D_{Ex}, D_{Ey} and D_{Ez} represent the x, y, and z components. D_E can be measured by the tactile sensor directly. The contact forces acting on the neighborhoods of these feature points are represented as another column vector, denoted as $F_E = \left(F_{Ex}^T, F_{Ey}^T, F_{Ez}^T\right)^T$, where F_{Ex}, F_{Ey}, F_{Ez} represent the x, y, and z components. Assuming the elastic body is linear, the following relationships exists:

$$D_E = H_E F_E \quad (1)$$

where H_E is the elastomer's compliance matrix. Since D_E and F_E are described using the same set of points, H_E is symmetric and positive definite. Assuming no slip occurs at the contact interface, n corresponding points on the object's surface that coincide with the elastomer's feature points can be uniquely determined. Similarly to the elastomer, the object's deformation and contact force are also represented in the object's coordinate frame, denoted as $D_O = \left(D_{Ox}^T, D_{Oy}^T, D_{Oz}^T\right)^T$ and $F_O = \left(F_{Ox}^T, F_{Oy}^T, F_{Oz}^T\right)^T$. The contact forces on the elastomer and object are equal in magnitude but opposite in direction. The following relationships exists:

$$D_O = H_O F_O = -H_O F_E \quad (2)$$

where H_O is the object's compliance matrix. H_O may be positive definite or positive semi-definite.

During contact, the base of the elastomer is fixed, while the base of the object undergoes rigid displacement, denoted as $G_O = (g_x, g_y, g_z)^T$, without rotation. When the base of the object experiences a small change $\Delta G_O = (\Delta g_x, \Delta g_y, \Delta g_z)^T$ (where ΔG_O is sufficiently small such that changes in the contact region can be neglected), small changes in forces and deformations on both elastomer and object occur:

$$\Delta D_E = H_E \Delta F_E \tag{3}$$

$$\Delta D_O = H_O \Delta F_O = -H_O \Delta F_E \tag{4}$$

Here, ΔD_E, ΔF_E, ΔD_O and ΔF_O represent the incremental changes in D_E, F_E, D_O and F_O. We define a column vector $\Delta D_G = (\Delta G_x^T, \Delta G_y^T, \Delta G_z^T)^T$, where ΔG_x, ΔG_y, ΔG_z are vectors with all elements equal to Δg_x, Δg_x, Δg_z, respectively. ΔD_G represents the influence of the object's rigid displacement on all the contact points in the object frame. The relationship between ΔD_O and ΔD_E is given by:

$$\Delta D_O = -\Delta D_G + \Delta D_E \tag{5}$$

Solving the system of Eqs. (3)~(5), we obtain:

$$\Delta D_E = \left(H_O H_E^{-1} + I_{3n}\right)^{-1} \Delta D_G \tag{6}$$

where I_{3n} is a $3n$ identity matrix. Since H_E is a positive definite symmetric matrix and H_O is a positive definite or positive semi-definite symmetric matrix, the term $H_O H_E^{-1} + I$ is guaranteed to be invertible. Equation (6) describes the relationship between the incremental rigid-body displacement of the object ΔD_G and the resulting incremental deformation of the elastomer ΔD_E.

2.2 Conditions for Sensitivity Degradation

For a tactile sensor to effectively discrimination objects softness, it is crucial that the deformation trends ΔD_E of the elastomer should exhibit clear distinctions when in contact with soft objects and rigid bodies. Assuming that a rigid body with friction contacts the elastomer without any slip at the interface, the contact points undergo no deformation or displacement in the object coordinate frame. This is equivalent to $H_O = 0$. Substituting it into Eq. (6), we obtain:

$$\Delta D_E = \Delta D_G \tag{7}$$

This indicates that the displacement of the elastomer's contact surface matches exactly with the rigid body's displacement.

Next, we consider a soft object with a non-zero H_O induces a deformation in the elastomer that closely resembles that caused by a rigid-body. Suppose there exists a scaling factor $\lambda \in (0,1)$ such that:

$$\Delta D_E \approx \lambda \Delta D_G \tag{8}$$

Substituting (8) into (6) yields:

$$H_O H_E^{-1} \Delta D_G \approx \left(\frac{1}{\lambda} - 1\right) \Delta D_G \qquad (9)$$

Equation (9) indicates that $H_O H_E^{-1}$ has an eigenvector closely aligned with ΔD_G, which constitutes the necessary and sufficient condition for the elastomer to exhibit a nearly rigid-body displacement when in contact with a soft object. By rearranging (9) into (10), we can better interpret this condition:

$$H_E^{-1} \Delta D_G \approx \left(\frac{1}{\lambda} - 1\right) H_O^{-1} \Delta D_G \qquad (10)$$

Equation (10) suggests that the force vectors required to produce the same deformations on the elastomer and the object is proportional. The proportionality coefficient is $\frac{1}{\lambda} - 1$. This implies a strong mechanical similarity between the elastomer and the object. The straightforward scenario satisfying this condition occurs when H_E and H_O are approximately proportional:

$$H_O \approx \left(\frac{1}{\lambda} - 1\right) H_E \qquad (11)$$

Due to differences in surface curvature and material distribution along the z-axis, H_E and H_O typically do not maintain a strict proportionality. However, when the surface curvatures of the elastomer and object are large and their stiffness distributions in the x- and y-directions is similar, H_E and $\left(\frac{1}{\lambda} - 1\right) H_O$ will be numerically close. A typical scenario is a homogeneous elastomer presses against a homogeneous soft object with similar curvature.

In short, the similarity in the stiffness distributions of the elastomer and object within the contact region causes increasingly difficult to discern the object's softness.

2.3 Non-rigid Displacement Ratio

The deformation increment ΔD_E of the elastomer can be decomposed into orthogonal two parts: rigid-body displacement, denoted as $\Delta D_{E,r}$, and non-rigid components, denoted as $\Delta D_{E,nr}$. ΔD_E is present as a column vector $\Delta D_E = \left(\Delta D_{Ex}^T, \Delta D_{Ey}^T, \Delta D_{Ez}^T\right)^T$, where $\Delta D_{Ex}, \Delta D_{Ey}, \Delta D_{Ez}$ are column vectors denote the x, y, and z components. The rigid-body displacement component $\Delta D_{E,r}$ is:

$$\Delta D_{E,r} = \begin{pmatrix} \overline{\Delta D_{Ex}} \mathbf{1} \\ \overline{\Delta D_{Ey}} \mathbf{1} \\ \overline{\Delta D_{Ez}} \mathbf{1} \end{pmatrix} \qquad (12)$$

$\overline{\Delta D_{Ei}} \mathbf{1}$ are column vectors with the same dimension as $\overline{\Delta D_{Ei}}$, where all elements equal the mean value of ΔD_{Ei}. The non-rigid displacement component $\Delta D_{E,nr}$ is then calculated as:

$$\Delta D_{E,nr} = \Delta D_E - \Delta D_{E,r} \qquad (13)$$

For rigid body contact, the displacement at each point is identical, so $\Delta \boldsymbol{D}_E$ primarily consists of rigid displacement components. In contrast, when contacting soft objects, non-rigid displacement components should become prominent. Based on this, a metric called the Non-Rigid Displacement Ratio (NRDR), denoted as P_N, is proposed. NRDR is mathematically defined as the ratio of the L2 norms of the non-rigid displacement component and the total deformation increment $\Delta \boldsymbol{D}_E$:

$$P_N = \frac{\|\Delta \boldsymbol{D}_{E,\mathrm{nr}}\|}{\|\Delta \boldsymbol{D}_E\|} \tag{14}$$

When objects of different softness are in contact, the greater the variation in P_N values exhibited the higher the sensor's sensitivity in discriminating softness.

3 Elastomer Design and Optimization

3.1 Objectives of Design and Optimization

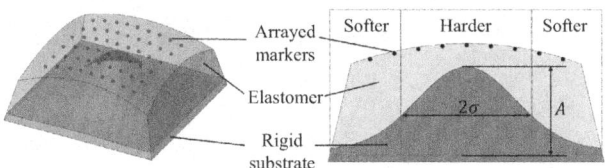

Fig. 3. The designed gradient-stiffness elastomer. The light blue portion features a concave structure at its base, creating a graded stiffness distribution. (Color figure online)

To avoid the sensitivity issue, the elastomer should exhibit stiffness distribution disparity relative to the contacted object. If the stiffness distribution of the elastomer in VBTS is altered from the conventional homogeneous form to a gradient-varying design, the likelihood of stiffness matching between the elastomer and the object will be significantly reduced.

In this study, we designed an elastomer as shown in Fig. 3. The upper surface of the elastomer features a convex spherical profile to simulate the rounded contour of a fingertip. The lower surface is recessed inward and fixed onto a rigid support substrate with mountain peak-like protrusions. This elastomer exhibits a thin-center-thick-edge structure, resulting in higher rigidity at the central region while demonstrating greater softness toward the edges. Its stiffness exhibits a gradient decrease from the center to the periphery. The gradient variation in the stiffness facilitates the generation of more pronounced non-rigid displacements when contacting compliant objects. We refer to this design as a gradient-stiffness elastomer.

The maximum thickness of this elastomer is 10 mm, and the radius of upper surface is 30 mm. The recessed lower surface is governed by Eq. (15):

$$z_L = A e^{-\left(\frac{x^2+y^2}{2\sigma^2}\right)} \tag{15}$$

Here, $x, y \in [-12, 12]$. The lower surface is a Gaussian surface. A represents the peak amplitude, which determines the stiffness difference between the center and edges. σ denotes the standard deviation, which represents the spatial extent of the high-stiffness region. By selecting appropriate values for A and σ, we may enhance the softness discrimination sensitivity. To achieve higher sensitivity in softness discrimination, there are expectations for elastomers with optimal A and σ:

1. When the elastomer contacting objects with varying softness, the difference in P_N values should be maximized to enable accurate discrimination.
2. For objects with identical softness, variations in P_N caused by differences in surface curvature or contact area should be minimized to ensure robust and consistent softness estimation.

3.2 Finite Element Method

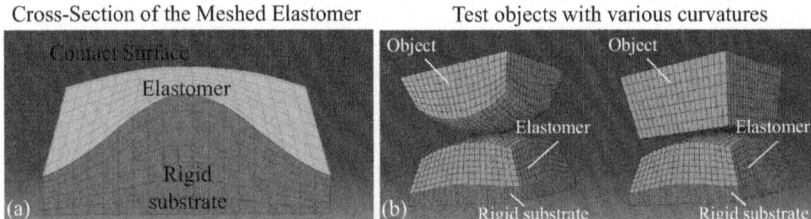

Fig. 4. (a) Mesh generation of the designed elastomer (cross-sectional view). (b) Objects with different surface curvatures used for pressing the elastomer.

To quantitatively determine the optimal peak amplitude A and standard deviation σ, we established a series of finite element models of the elastomers and objects for simulation testing. First, 81 finite element models of the elastomer with peak amplitude A ranging from 0 to 8 mm (in 1 mm increments) and standard deviations σ ranging from 2.0 to 6.0 mm (in 0.5 mm increments) are created. The elastomer's elastic modulus was set to $E_E = 0.38$ MPa, corresponding to a softness of $S_E = 2.63$ MPa^{-1}. The bottom surfaces of the elastomers were assigned a fixed constraint, while the convex spherical upper surface was designated for contact with objects. Then, 90 models of objects with softness S_O spanning 5.0, 3.3, 2.5, 1.7, 1.0, 0.50, 0.25, 0.13, 0.10 MPa^{-1} and top surface curvature radii R_O spanning 20, 30, 40, 50, 70, 90, 140, 230, 400, and 1000 mm are created (Fig. 4).

All the models were discretized into $20 \times 20 \times 8$ mesh elements. The contact regions between the elastomer and objects were defined as circular areas centered on their top surfaces, with radii R_C of 3, 4, 5, and 6 mm. Combining 81 elastomers configurations, 90 objects configurations, and 4 contact area variations, a total of 29,160 distinct contact conditions were tested.

The P_N value of each condition was calculated as follows: First, finite element analysis software Abaqus was employed to compute the global stiffness matrices for all elastomer and object models. The contact nodes were specified as finite element nodes within contact regions. Then, H_E and H_O were calculated using the method described in Section IV.A (Eqs. (23)–(27)) of the research [16]. The pressing direction between the elastomer and object was set along the z-axis. The global displacement vector for the pressing process was $\Delta D_G = \left(0^T, 0^T, 1^T\right)$. By substituting H_E, H_O, and ΔD_G into Eq. (6), we obtained ΔD_E. At last, P_N could be calculated from ΔD_E for all 29,160 contact conditions using Eq. (12)~(14).

4 Simulation

4.1 Optimal Parameter Selection

P_N Was calculated and analyzed for different elastomers and objects under varying contact areas to find better A and σ parameters for the elastomer. Figure 5 illustrates how changes in object softness S_O, object curvature radius R_O, and contact area radius R_C affect P_N values in elastomer characterized by different A and σ. P_N is expected to exhibit maximal variation with object softness changes, ensuring the sensor can sensitively distinguish object softness. Simultaneously, P_N should show minimal variation with changes in object surface curvature and contact radius, thereby enhancing consistency and robustness.

Figure 5(a) shows the variation of P_N values across different elastomer deformations when object softness changes from 0.1 to 5.0 MPa^{-1}. The elastomer with $A = 8.0$ mm and $\sigma = 6.0$ mm demonstrated the most significant P_N variation, indicating that this parameter combination provides optimal sensitivity for softness discrimination. Figure 5(b) presents the proportional change in P_N relative to the maximum P_N, calculated by $\Delta P_N/P_{N,\max}$, as object curvature radius R_O varies. The $A = 8.0$ mm, $\sigma = 6.0$ mm elastomer exhibited the smallest proportional P_N change. Figure 5(c) shows the proportional P_N change with varying contact area. The $A = 8.0$ mm, $\sigma = 2.5$ mm elastomer displayed the smallest $\Delta P_N/P_N$ ratio (0.46), though this was not substantially different from the 0.50 ratio shown by the $A = 8.0$ mm, $\sigma = 6.0$ mm elastomer. Notably, a $\Delta P_N/P_N$ of 0.5 represents significant variation, indicating that the P_N undergoes substantial changes with contact area variation. That is a serious drawback for softness estimation. However, data analysis revealed that P_N increases nearly linearly with increasing R_C. Given this near-linear relationship, we define a new normalized metric called Normalized Non-Rigid Displacement Ratio (N-NRDR), denoted as Q_N, by taking the ratio of P_N to R_C:

$$Q_N = \frac{P_N}{R_C} \quad (16)$$

The variation of Q_N with respect to object softness S_O and object curvature radius R_O follows the same trend as P_N. But its dependence on R_C is significantly reduced, as shown in Fig. 5(d). A comprehensive comparison across Fig. 5(a), (b), and (d) reveals that the elastomer with bottom indentation parameters $A = 8.0$ mm, $\sigma = 6.0$ mm exhibits the best performance. In subsequent discussions, the elastomer with these optimal parameters will be referred to as the optimized elastomer.

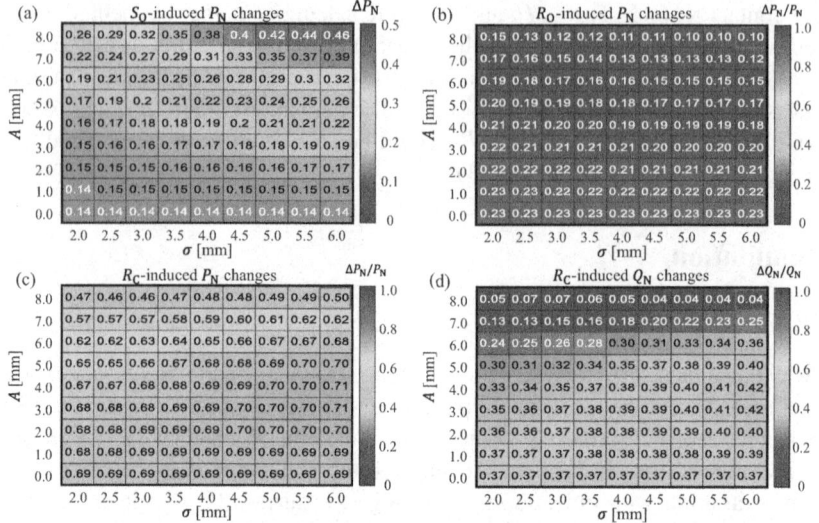

Fig. 5. Influence of object parameters on P_N and Q_N metrics for different elastomers: (a) Variation in P_N metric caused by changes in object softness S_O (larger variations desired) (b) Variation in P_N metric caused by changes in object surface curvature R_O (smaller variations desired) (c) Variation in P_N metric caused by changes in contact radius R_C (smaller variations desired) (d) Variation in Q_N metric caused by changes in contact radius R_C (smaller variations desired).

4.2 Verification

To verify the performance improvement of the optimized elastomer in object softness discrimination, finite element simulations were conducted to compare the performance of the optimized elastomer and a conventional homogeneous elastomer in object softness discrimination. Q_N values were calculated to evaluate the sensitivity of the sensors using two types of elastomers. Figure 6 shows that the Q_N values of the optimized elastomer are significantly higher than those of the conventional elastomer during contact, indicating that the optimized elastomer undergoes more pronounced non-rigid displacement when interacting with soft objects. Moreover, the Q_N values of the optimized elastomer also exhibit greater variation across objects of different softness levels. This suggests that, tactile sensor using the optimized elastomer can more sensitively discriminate between objects with similar softness compared to the sensors using conventional homogeneous elastomers.

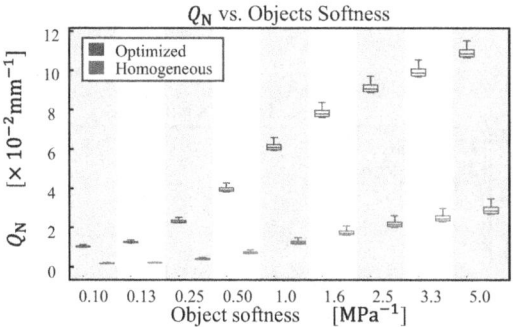

Fig. 6. Statistical distribution of Q_N from simulations when pressing objects of different softness using both optimized and conventional homogeneous elastomers. Each box plot represents 40 conditions with varying object curvature and contact radius.

5 Experiment

5.1 Setup

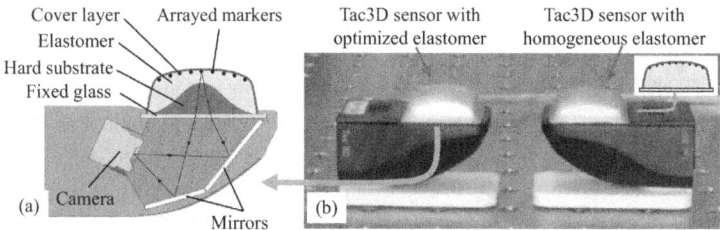

Fig. 7. (a) Cross-sectional structure of the Tac3D sensor employing a gradient-stiffness elastomer (b) Tac3D sensors used in the experiment: the left sensor uses an optimized gradient-stiffness elastomer, while the right sensor uses a conventional homogeneous elastomer.

In this study, we employed two Tac3D tactile sensors [17] as experimental platforms, which can measure the 3D deformation field and force distribution on the elastomer surface during contact. One Tac3D sensor (right one in Fig. 7(b)) uses a homogeneous elastomer as the fingertip, while the other Tac3D sensor (left one in Fig. 7(b)) uses an optimized gradient-stiffness elastomer as the fingertip. The structure of the optimized elastomer and the structure of the sensor are illustrated in the cross-sectional view in Fig. 7(a).

The gradient-stiffness elastomer is made of Dow Corning SYLGARD-184 PDMS with a curing agent to base ratio of 1:25, of which the elastic modulus is 0.4 MPa. The hard layer is made of the same PDMS but with a curing agent to base ratio of 1:10, resulting in elastic moduli of approximately 4 MPa. The elastic modulus of the hard substrate is much greater than that of the elastomer, and here we approximate the hard substrate as a rigid body. The elastomer and the hard substrate are separately fabricated using a casting method and then bonded to the glass using K-705 silicone adhesive. The cover layer with markers was prepared using spin-coating and laser engraving.

5.2 Result

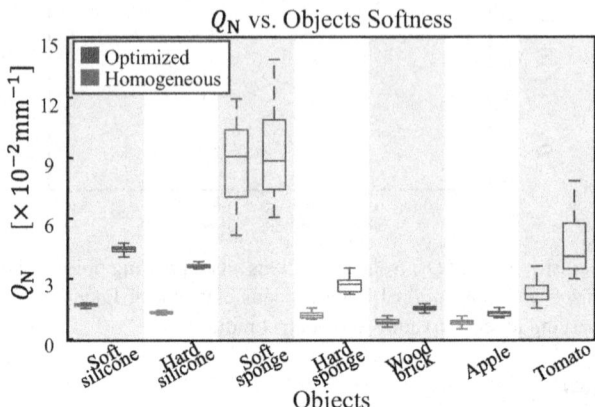

Fig. 8. Statistical distribution of Q_Ns from experimental tests using Tac3D sensors with both optimized and conventional elastomers pressing various objects. Each box plot represents 20 pressing trials.

In the experiments, multiple objects with varying degrees of softness were prepared, including a soft silicone block, hard silicone block, soft sponge, hard sponge, wooden brick, apple, and tomato. Each object was pressed 20 times against two Tac3D tactile sensors employing different elastomers. Figure 8 presents the statistical distribution of measured Q_N values for each object when pressed against both sensors. These Q_N values were calculated during the contact phase when the contact area ranged between $80\,\text{mm}^2$ and $120\,\text{mm}^2$. The statistical results demonstrate that variations in object softness induce more pronounced changes in Q_N values for the Tac3D sensor with the optimized elastomer. This indicates that the Tac3D sensor equipped with the optimized elastomer exhibits superior capability in discriminating object softness.

6 Conclusion

This study systematically investigates the issue of sharp sensitivity degradation in conventional vision-based tactile sensors when distinguishing object softness under specific conditions. First, based on elastic mechanics theory, we elucidate the underlying principles and necessary/sufficient conditions for this sensitivity degradation phenomenon. Specifically, it occurs when the stiffness distributions of the elastomer and the contacted object exhibit similarity. Building upon this finding, we propose two metrics (P_N and Q_N) to evaluate the softness discrimination sensitivity of vision-based tactile sensors. With the objective of maximizing the Q_N metric, we designed and optimized an elastomer with non-uniform stiffness distribution. Through simulations and experiments, we verified that the Tac3D tactile sensor employing this optimized elastomer demonstrates enhanced softness discrimination capability compared to conventional homogeneous elastomers in general application scenarios.

References

1. Di Luca, M. (ed.): Multisensory Softness: Perceived Compliance from Multiple Sources of Information. Springer, London (2014)
2. Srinivasan, M.A., LaMotte, R.H.: Tactual discrimination of softness. J. Neurophysiol. **73**, 88–101 (1995)
3. Omata, S., Murayama, Y., Constantinou, C.E.: Real time robotic tactile sensor system for the determination of the physical properties of biomaterials. Sens. Actuators A **112**, 278–285 (2004)
4. Kimoto, A., Matsue, Y.: A new multifunctional tactile sensor for detection of material hardness. IEEE Trans. Instrum. Meas. **60**, 1334–1339 (2011)
5. Fang, S., et al.: TactONet: tactile ordinal network based on unimodal probability for object hardness classification. IEEE Trans. Automat. Sci. Eng. **20**, 2784–2794 (2023)
6. Zhang, Z.: Hardness recognition of fruits and vegetables based on tactile array information of manipulator. Comput. Electron. Agric. (2021)
7. Wu, Y.Y., Shen, J.J.: A tactile sensor for measuring the hardness of soft materials. In: 2018 IEEE International Conference on Mechatronics, Robotics and Automation (ICMRA), pp. 141–144. IEEE, Hefei (2018)
8. Zhang, L., Ju, F., Cao, Y., Wang, Y., Chen, B.: A tactile sensor for measuring hardness of soft tissue with applications to minimally invasive surgery. Sens. Actuators A **266**, 197–204 (2017)
9. Yuan, W., Srinivasan, M.A., Adelson, E.H.: Estimating object hardness with a GelSight touch sensor. In: 2016 IEEE/RSJ International Conference on Intelligent Robots and Systems (IROS), pp. 208–215. IEEE, Daejeon, South Korea (2016)
10. Yuan, W., Zhu, C., Owens, A., Srinivasan, M.A., Adelson, E.H.: Shape-independent hardness estimation using deep learning and a GelSight tactile sensor. In: 2017 IEEE International Conference on Robotics and Automation (ICRA), pp. 951–958. IEEE, Singapore, Singapore (2017)
11. Nam, S., Jack, T., Lee, L.Y., Lepora, N.F.: Softness prediction with a soft biomimetic optical tactile sensor. In: 2024 IEEE 7th International Conference on Soft Robotics (RoboSoft), pp. 121–126. IEEE, San Diego, CA, USA (2024)
12. Pagnanelli, G., Ciotti, S., Lepora, N., Bicchi, A., Bianchi, M.: Model-based compliance discrimination via soft tactile optical sensing and optical flow computation: a biomimetic approach. IEEE Robot. Autom. Lett. **8**, 6611–6618 (2023)
13. Podbreznik, P., Potočnik, B.: Assessing the influence of temperature variations on the geometrical properties of a low-cost calibrated camera system by using computer vision procedures. Mach. Vis. Appl. **23**, 953–966 (2012)
14. Burgess, M., Zhao, J.: Learning object compliance via young's modulus from single grasps with camera-based tactile sensors (2024). http://arxiv.org/abs/2406.15304
15. Shimonomura, K.: Tactile image sensors employing camera: a review. Sensors **19**, 3933 (2019)
16. Zhang, L., Li, T., Jiang, Y.: Improving the force reconstruction performance of vision-based tactile sensors by optimizing the elastic body. IEEE Robot. Autom. Lett. **8** (2023)
17. Zhang, L., Wang, Y., Zhou, Y.H., Li, T., Jiang, Y.: Design, optimization and application of tactile sensor based on virtual binocular vision. SSRN J. (2022)

Filtering Selection for High-Density sEMG in Motor Unit Decomposition

Zeming Zhao[1], Zeyu Zhou[1], Weichao Guo[1,2], and Xinjun Sheng[1,2(✉)]

[1] State Key Laboratory of Mechanical System and Vibration, Shanghai Jiao Tong University, Shanghai, China
xjsheng@sjtu.edu.cn
[2] Meta Robotics Institute, Shanghai Jiao Tong University, Shanghai, China

Abstract. High-density surface electromyography (HD-sEMG) has become a valuable signal source in human-machine interface research due to its ability to non-invasively support motor unit (MU) decomposition. Although various filters have been proposed to enhance HD-sEMG signal quality, their effectiveness in improving MU decomposition performance remains unclear. In this study, we systematically evaluate five state-of-the-art filtering methods: Infinite Impulse Response (IIR), Wavelet Decomposition (WD), Variational Mode Decomposition (VMD), Ensemble Empirical Mode Decomposition (EEMD), Independent Vector Analysis (IVA), and a Hybrid filter. Their effects are assessed using two widely used MU decomposition algorithms, fastICA and LIBD-CKC. Both simulation and experimental results show that most filters, including WD, EEMD, VMD, and IVA, do not improve decomposition accuracy and can even degrade performance. The Hybrid filter provides meaningful improvement with statistically and practically relevant gains, although it incurs significant computational cost. Therefore, unless exceptionally high decomposition precision is required, advanced filtering methods are not recommended. In practical applications such as fingertip press estimation in this paper, HD-sEMG signal can be used directly without additional filtering.

Keywords: high-density surface electromyography · signal filtering · motor unit decomposition · human-machine interface

1 Introduction

Surface electromyography (sEMG) is a commonly used non-invasive signal in human–machine interface (HMI) systems, with wide applications in gesture recognition, medical diagnosis, and muscle fatigue monitoring [1]. The signal originates from action potentials generated when motor neurons activate muscle

---

This work is supported in part by the National Natural Science Foundation of China (Grant Nos. 52227808, 52175021), in part by State Key Laboratory of Robotics and Systems (HIT) (Grant No. SKLRS-2024-KF-01).

fibers during voluntary muscle contractions. These action potentials are transmitted through the skin and recorded as sEMG signals [2]. Each motor neuron, together with the muscle fibers it innervates, forms a motor unit (MU), which is the basic functional unit of neuromuscular control [3].

While conventional sEMG performs well in many applications, it is limited by a small number of channels and low spatial resolution, which makes it unsuitable for fine-grained analysis of MUs. To overcome this limitation, high-density surface electromyography (HD-sEMG) has been introduced. By increasing the spatial sampling density, HD-sEMG captures richer muscle activation information, making MU decomposition feasible. Several blind source separation (BSS) algorithms have been applied to MU decomposition based on HD-sEMG and have become a major research focus in this field [4–6].

However, these algorithms are highly sensitive to signal quality. The presence of noise and artifacts in HD-sEMG signals can significantly reduce decomposition accuracy. Therefore, effective filtering is a crucial preprocessing step to ensure reliable MU identification.

Although a variety of filtering techniques have been proposed for sEMG signal processing, there is still no established guideline for selecting filters specifically tailored to HD-sEMG in the context of MU decomposition. Filter selection often relies on subjective experience. This study aims to systematically compare the impact of different filtering methods on MU decomposition performance, with the goal of providing practical guidance for filter selection in HD-sEMG processing. The filters investigated include Infinite Impulse Response (IIR) filter [7], Wavelet Decomposition (WD) filter [8], Independent Vector Analysis (IVA) filter [9], Ensemble Empirical Mode Decomposition (EEMD) filter [10], Variational Mode Decomposition (VMD) filter [11], and a Hybrid filter [12]. The rationale behind selecting these filters is detailed in Sect. 2.2.2.

The organization of the remaining sections is as follows. Section 2 introduces the materials and methodology. Section 3 presents the results. In Sect. 4, the results are discussed in detail and the conclusions are presented.

2 Materials and Methodology

2.1 Databases

2.1.1 Noise Signals. In this study, three types of noise signals were considered: baseline and motion artifacts (BMA), powerline interference (PLI), and white Gaussian noise (WGN). These noise types are commonly encountered in HD-sEMG signal processing and were introduced into the simulated data to replicate real-world signal contamination scenarios.

BMA mainly arises from relative movement between the electrodes and the skin, as well as disturbances in the connecting wires. It varies slightly across different channels. To simulate this noise, Variable Mode Empirical Mode Decomposition (VME) [13] was applied to real 64-channel HD-sEMG recordings to extract signal components within the 0.1–10 Hz frequency band, which were used as the simulated BMA.

PLI is caused by electromagnetic interference from surrounding power supply systems and typically appears as a 50 Hz sinusoidal waveform. In this study, a synthetic 64-channel matrix of pure 50 Hz sine waves was generated to represent simulated PLI.

WGN is widely used to model random measurement noise in electrophysiological recordings. In this study, 11 sets of WGN were generated using the "wgn" function in MATLAB R2022b, each consisting of a 64-channel matrix with 50,000 samples per channel. These noise sets, labeled from 1 to 11, were used to simulate WGN.

Simulated Signals. Simulated HD-sEMG signals were generated using a multilayer cylindrical volume conductor model, with signals computed at 64 circular electrode sites arranged in an 8 × 8 grid. The specific parameters of the model are detailed in Table 1. For each motor unit (MU), its corresponding MU action potential (MUAP) and spike train (MUST) were computed based on the model. The spike trains were generated automatically according to different excitation levels and were determined by each MU's recruitment threshold and discharge rate. The recruitment order followed Henneman's size principle [14], with thresholds exponentially distributed and firing rates randomly drawn from a Gaussian distribution.

To simulate natural muscle contraction scenarios, the simulated signals were designed to follow a force line, as shown in Fig. 1. Two excitation levels were used: 10% and 30% of maximal excitation, ensuring distinct differences in both the number of recruited MUs and their discharge rates. To minimize the influence of specific MU model choices on the results, six different MU model libraries were used. For each library, two force levels were simulated, resulting in twelve sets of 64-channel HD-sEMG signals.

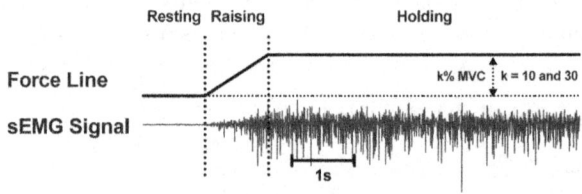

Fig. 1. An example of the simulated signals. The force line consists with three states: the resting state is between 0–1 s, the raising state is between 1–2 s, and the holding state with maximum value of k% MVC is between 2–7 s. The corresponding 64 channels sEMG signals are shown below (only 1st channel of sEMG signal is depicted here).

Furthermore, to better reflect real-world signal conditions and ensure practical filter evaluation, a noise mixture was added to the simulated signals. This mixture included 10 dB of BMA, 10 dB of PLI, and 40 dB of WGN. The WGN component corresponded to noise set 11 described in Sect. 2.1.1, while the other noise types were consistent with those described earlier in Sect. 2.1.1.

Table 1. Parameters of the volume conductor model

Symbol	Model Parameter	Value
R	Bone Radius	11 mm
r	Muscle Thickness	29 mm
h	Adipose Layer Thickness	4 mm
d	Skin Thickness	1 mm
G	Grid	8 × 8
a	Electrode Diameter	2 mm
IED	Inter-electrode Distance	10 mm
Fs	Sampling Frequency	2000 Hz
T	Signal Duration	20 s

Experimental Signals. Eight healthy subjects (six males and two females, aged 23–37 years), all right-handed and with no history of neurological or psychiatric disorders, participated in this study. Prior to the experiment, all participants were informed of the experimental procedures and signed written consent forms. The study protocol was approved by the Academic Ethics Committee of Shanghai Jiao Tong University (Approval No. B20200026I) and complied with the Declaration of Helsinki.

During the experiment, subjects were instructed to perform fingertip pressing tasks as prompted on a screen, while keeping their arms relaxed. Before the formal task, the maximum voluntary contraction (MVC) force of the index, middle, and ring fingers was measured and recorded individually. Each subject performed three sessions of the task, with each session repeated twice.

As illustrated in Fig. 2(c), each trial followed a predefined force trajectory: subjects gradually increased their fingertip force to 30% MVC over 5 s, maintained that force for 15 s, and then decreased it back to 0 over another 5 s. The target force trajectory thus formed an isosceles trapezoid. Fingertip force signals were synchronously recorded using a Pinchmeter P200 (Biometrics Ltd., UK).

HD-sEMG signals were simultaneously acquired using an 8 × 16 monopolar electrode grid (OT Bioelettronica, Torino, Italy) with an inter-electrode distance of 10 mm. The grid was aligned along the muscle fibers and positioned over the flexor digitorum superficialis (FDS) muscle. The reference and ground electrodes were placed separately on the elbow. The recording area for HD-sEMG placement is illustrated in Fig. 2(a). Prior to electrode placement, the skin surface was abraded with scrub cream and cleaned using alcohol wipes to reduce skin impedance.

sEMG signals were recorded using a home-made system equipped with RHD2164 ADC chips (Intan Technologies, California, USA), with a sampling rate of 2000 Hz. A bandpass filter with a bandwidth of 0.1–999 Hz was applied during acquisition to eliminate DC components and aliasing noise of the signal.

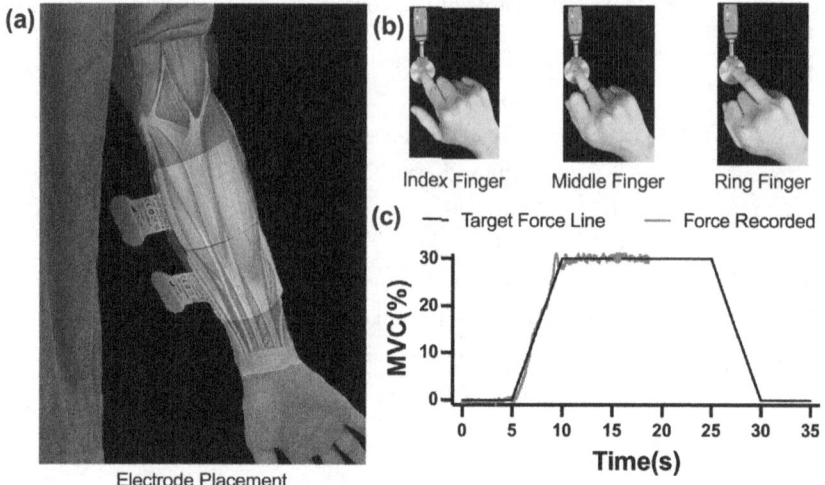

Fig. 2. Experimental Setup. (a) HD-sEMG recording placement. (b) pressure acquisition platform. (c) feedback interface to guide subjects with target and recorded fingertip force in real-time.

Contaminating Strategy. As shown in [15], WGN is the primary noise factor affecting MU decomposition performance in HD-sEMG. Other types of noise, including BMA and PLI do not significantly affect decomposition accuracy even at an SNR of 0 dB. Therefore, this study focuses solely on evaluating the effects of different filters under various SNR levels of WGN, without considering the influence of other noise sources.

In the simulation setup, a base mixture of noise was already added to approximate the noise characteristics of experimental recordings. On top of this, additional WGN was injected into the simulated signals to further vary the noise conditions. Specifically, WGN noise sets 1–10 (as described in Sect. 2.1) were added to all simulated signals at SNR levels of 0 dB, 10 dB, 20 dB, 30 dB, and a reference case with no additional noise. As a result, each signal segment was associated with 50 noisy versions.

It should be noted that the simulated signals already include an initial WGN component at 40 dB SNR. Thus, even in the "no additional noise" condition, the actual SNR of the signal is 40 dB.

2.2 Filtering and Decomposition Method

MU Decomposition Methods. In this study, we examine two MU decomposition algorithms: fastICA [6] and LIBD-CKC [5]. The parameter configurations for both algorithms are detailed in Table 2.

Table 2. Parameter settings for MU decomposition algorithms (LIBD-CKC and fastICA)

Algorithm	Symbol	Model Parameter	Value
LIBD-CKC	R	Extension Factor	10
	N_m	Number of Maximum Inner Loops	5
	h	Size of Spatial Window	3
	$thre_{CoV}$	CoV Threshold	0.45
	$thre_{PNR}$	PNR Threshold	25
fastICA	N_e	Percentage of Excluded Channels	10
	R	Extension Factor	8
	M	Number of MU Deconvolution Iterations	200
	N_N	Number of Maximum Inner Loops	20

Filtering Methods. As confirmed in [15], WGN is the dominant noise factor that affects the performance of MU decomposition in HD-sEMG. Consequently, any filter designed to suppress noise types other than WGN is theoretically unlikely to yield any improvement in decomposition accuracy. Therefore, this study focuses exclusively on filters capable of attenuating WGN components.

The WGN-suppressing filters considered in this study can be grouped into the following categories:

1) WD Filter: This method decomposes the signal into multiple wavelet sub-bands. A soft-thresholding strategy is then applied to suppress small-magnitude coefficients, resulting in signal smoothing. We adopt the filter proposed in [8], hereafter referred to as the WD filter.
2) VMD Filter: This approach performs spectral decomposition to extract variational mode functions (VMFs) across multiple frequency bands. An iterative interval thresholding (IIT) method is applied to remove small components for noise suppression [16].
3) EEMD Filter: This method performs spectral decomposition to extract intrinsic mode functions (IMFs) across multiple frequency bands. And a comparative study [10] shows that EEMD outperforms empirical mode decomposition (EMD) [16] in terms of noise suppression, and is therefore selected as the representative filter in this category.
4) IVA Filter: This method applies blind source separation (BSS) to decompose the signal into multiple source components. Components that fail to meet expected temporal characteristics are zeroed out to eliminate noise. According to results reported in [9], IVA outperforms other BSS-based methods such as canonical correlation analysis (CCA) [17] and independent component analysis (ICA) [18].
5) Hybrid Filter: Originally proposed in [12], this filter combines spectral decomposition and BSS. First, the signal is decomposed into IMFs. Then, each IMF is further separated into multiple source components using a BSS algorithm. Components that fail to meet time-frequency domain criteria are sequentially

zeroed out. This approach specifically targets Gaussian-distributed noise, which distinguishes it from the other methods.
6) IIR Filter: Additionally, the IIR filter has been widely used in existing MU decomposition studies. Therefore, we also implemented an IIR filter based on the configuration provided in [7].

The detailed parameter settings of each filter can be found in the respective reference papers and are not repeated here.

2.3 Performance Evaluation

For simulated signals, the ground truth of the MUSTs are known. Therefore, the quality of MU decomposition can be evaluated by comparing the number of MU (NMU) identified by the decomposition algorithm with the ground truth (Rate of Agreement ≥ 0.8). A greater value of NMU generally indicates better decomposition performance.

In the case of experimental signals, where the true discharge patterns of individual MUs are unknown, evaluation is performed using two complementary metrics: (1) the number of MUs decomposed by the algorithm, and (2) the fitting performance of the reconstructed MU activity to the measured fingertip pressing force. The quality of the fit is assessed using the correlation coefficient (R), which is computed as Eq. 1. A higher number of decomposed MUs, along with a higher R value, typically reflects superior decomposition accuracy and better physiological relevance.

$$R = \frac{\sum_{i=1}^{n}(x_i - \bar{x})(\hat{x}_i - \bar{\hat{x}})}{\sqrt{\sum_{i=1}^{n}(x_i - \bar{x})^2}\sqrt{\sum_{i=1}^{n}(\hat{x}_i - \bar{\hat{x}})^2}} \quad (1)$$

where x_i and $\hat{x}_i$ are the ground truth and estimated values at the i-th time point, respectively; $\bar{x}$ and $\bar{\hat{x}}$ are their respective means.

2.4 Statistical Analysis

For simulated signals, the results were categorized based on the MU decomposition algorithm and the MVC level. The filtering method and the SNR of added noise were treated as independent variables, while the number of motor units (NMU) served as the dependent variable for analysis. All data were confirmed to follow a normal distribution according to the Kolmogorov–Smirnov (KS) test ($p > 0.05$). A two-way analysis of variance (ANOVA) was conducted to examine the effects of the filtering method and SNR on MU decomposition performance. Statistical significance was set at a p-value below 0.05.

For experimental signals, due to the limited sample size, the results do not hold statistical significance. Therefore, only the mean and standard deviation of the relevant measures are reported.

3 Results

3.1 Simulated Results

Figure 3 illustrates the effects of various filters on MU decomposition under different decomposition algorithms and MVC levels. The red curve represents the MU decomposition results from unfiltered raw signals, serving as a baseline for comparison with the filtered signals.

The analysis covers two contraction intensities (10% and 30% MVC), two decomposition algorithms (fastICA and LIBD-CKC), and five levels of noise (0 dB, 10 dB, 20 dB, 30 dB, and 40 dB), resulting in a total of 20 distinct experimental scenarios.

We annotated the filters that demonstrated significant positive or negative impacts on MU decomposition performance across different scenarios, and a summary of these findings is provided in Table 3. The key observations are as follows:

Table 3. Summary of simulation results

Filtering Method	Positive Count	Negative Count
IIR Filter	0	0
WD Filter	1	**10**
EEMD Filter	3	3
IVA Filter	0	7
VMD Filter	4	3
Hybrid Filter	**10**	0

IIR filter: No significant impact on MU decomposition; **WD filter**: Provided improvement in 5% of cases but led to degradation in 50% of scenarios; **EEMD filter**: Showed positive effects in 15% of scenarios and negative effects in 15% of cases; **IVA filter**: No performance gain in any case and showed performance decline in 35% of scenarios; **VMD filter**: Demonstrated positive effects in 20% of scenarios and negative effects in 15% of scenarios; **Hybrid filter**: Improved MU decomposition in 50% of the cases and showed no negative impact in any scenario.

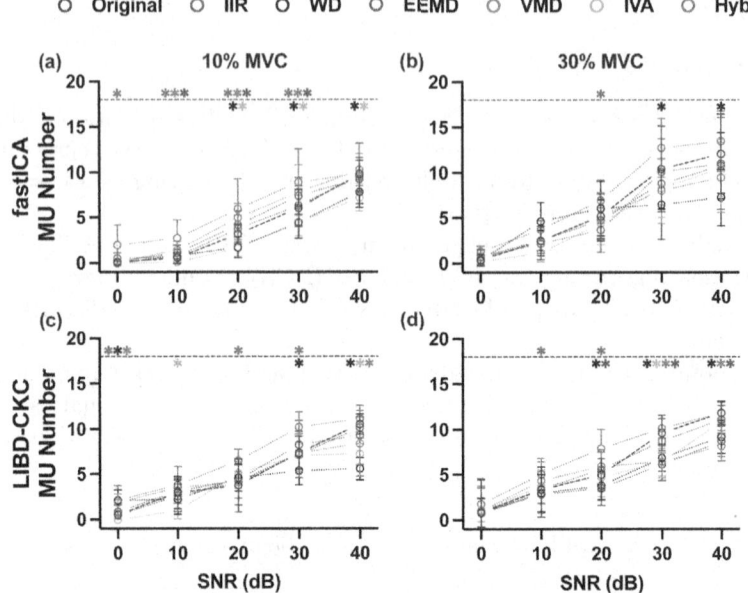

Fig. 3. Simulation results. The red line represents the MU decomposition results from the unfiltered signal. All other filter-based results are compared against this baseline. Asterisks (*) indicate statistically significant differences in MU decomposition results between the filtered and unfiltered signals at the corresponding SNR level ($p < 0.05$). Asterisks above the red line indicate that the corresponding filter yielded better MU decomposition performance than the unfiltered signal, while asterisks below the red line indicate worse performance. (Color figure online)

3.2 Experimental Results

Table 4 and 5 present the effects of different filters on MU decomposition outcomes under various decomposition algorithms. The results indicate that although slight differences exist between the decomposition results of LIBD-CKC and fastICA, the influence of each filter on MU decomposition remains largely consistent across both methods.

The Hybrid filter improves the number of decomposed MUs compared to the raw signal but does not yield a notable improvement in the force estimation R value. Although the IVA filter results in a reduction in the number of decomposed MUs, it does not significantly lower the corresponding R value. The IIR filter shows no change in either MU count or the R value relative to the raw signal. In contrast, the EEMD, VMD and Wavelet filters lead to reductions in MU count as well as a decrease in the force estimation R value.

Table 4. Number of MU (NMU) and force estimation accuracy (R) under different filtering conditions using fastICA algorithm

Subj.	Original		IIR		WD		EEMD		IVA		Hybrid		VMD	
	NMU	R	NMU	R	NMU	R	NMU	R	NMU	R	NMU	R	NMU	R
S1	9.15	0.79	8.77	0.79	6.76	0.78	7.98	0.78	8.09	0.80	10.72	0.80	7.62	0.77
S2	21.70	0.96	21.95	0.96	20.82	0.95	20.70	0.95	20.53	0.96	23.76	0.97	20.33	0.95
S3	14.89	0.94	15.17	0.95	12.80	0.92	13.53	0.91	13.08	0.95	16.38	0.96	14.52	0.93
S4	16.61	0.91	16.60	0.92	15.63	0.90	15.99	0.91	15.67	0.95	18.16	0.93	14.78	0.87
S5	11.34	0.96	11.06	0.96	9.43	0.93	9.47	0.95	9.77	0.95	11.69	0.98	9.95	0.94
S6	20.20	0.96	20.11	0.96	19.97	0.94	19.36	0.94	19.49	0.97	21.66	0.97	19.55	0.94
S7	19.53	0.97	19.28	0.96	18.25	0.96	17.96	0.95	17.53	0.99	20.80	0.96	18.99	0.96
S8	14.76	0.96	14.72	0.96	13.32	0.95	13.47	0.94	14.25	0.96	16.42	0.98	13.00	0.95
Mean	16.02	0.93	15.96	0.93	14.62	0.92	14.81	0.92	14.80	0.94	17.45	0.94	14.84	0.91
SD	4.38	0.06	4.51	0.06	5.00	0.06	4.56	0.06	4.42	0.06	4.63	0.06	4.61	0.07

Table 5. Number of MU (NMU) and force estimation accuracy (R) under different filtering conditions using LIBD-CKC algorithm

Subj.	Original		IIR		WD		EEMD		IVA		Hybrid		VMD	
	NMU	R	NMU	R	NMU	R	NMU	R	NMU	R	NMU	R	NMU	R
S1	11.15	0.79	12.01	0.79	10.83	0.78	9.69	0.77	9.62	0.81	12.63	0.80	10.07	0.77
S2	22.91	0.96	22.52	0.95	23.03	0.95	21.56	0.95	21.12	0.98	23.23	0.96	21.15	0.94
S3	17.45	0.95	16.48	0.96	17.33	0.95	15.33	0.92	16.27	0.95	18.17	0.96	15.87	0.96
S4	17.62	0.91	17.78	0.90	17.22	0.90	16.42	0.91	15.01	0.89	18.61	0.95	16.06	0.92
S5	10.90	0.96	10.79	0.94	14.55	0.98	9.14	0.97	8.85	0.97	11.59	0.97	10.38	0.96
S6	21.74	0.96	22.50	0.96	23.44	0.99	20.39	0.95	20.23	0.93	23.28	0.93	19.71	0.94
S7	21.03	0.98	20.47	0.96	18.99	0.96	19.92	0.96	19.10	0.97	22.13	0.98	19.98	0.97
S8	16.95	0.98	16.86	0.98	13.61	0.96	15.14	0.97	15.19	0.96	17.49	0.98	15.56	0.96
Mean	17.47	0.93	17.43	0.93	17.38	0.93	15.95	0.92	15.67	0.93	18.39	0.94	16.10	0.93
SD	4.53	0.06	4.40	0.06	4.41	0.07	4.69	0.07	4.57	0.06	4.50	0.06	4.19	0.06

4 Discussion and Conclusion

Inconsistencies were observed in the performance of several filters when applied to simulated versus experimental signals. A common feature among these filters is their dependence on a rest period as a reference for threshold estimation. The underlying cause of this discrepancy lies in the nature of the signals: in simulated data, the rest phase contains only artificial noise, whereas in experimental recordings, subjects are required to maintain forearm and hand posture even during rest, resulting in involuntary MU discharges and non-negligible sEMG signal segment.

Notably, the VMD filter, which yielded favorable results on simulated signals, exhibited similar behavior to the EEMD filter and WD filter in the experimental condition. Both filters led to a reduction in the number of decomposed MUs and a decline in the force estimation R-value. This reduction is primarily attributed to their shared mechanism of constructing smoothing thresholds based on noise power estimation. When the estimated threshold is excessively high, MU discharge waveforms may be attenuated or distorted, impairing the subsequent performance of blind source separation algorithms. In experimental conditions, the presence of low-level sEMG signals during the rest phase may be misclassified as noise, causing to overestimate the threshold and degrade MU decomposition performance.

Conversely, although the IVA filter also resulted in a reduced number of decomposed MUs, no corresponding decrease in the force estimation R-value was observed. This is likely due to the ability of filter to isolate components associated with MUs that remain active during the rest period. Because these components exhibit comparable power during both rest and contraction phases, they are suppressed during filtering and subsequently not identified by MU decomposition. However, given that these MUs do not contribute meaningfully to voluntary force estimation, their exclusion does not reduce the accuracy of force estimation.

This study compared the effects of multiple filters on MU decomposition performance. Based on both simulated and experimental results, it was found that filters designed for signal smoothing and WGN removal, such as WD, EEMD and VMD, not only failed to improve MU decomposition but in some cases introduced negative effects. This degradation is primarily due to the fact that smoothing may attenuate MU discharge waveforms, thereby reducing their detectability. Filters that rely solely on BSS and time-domain features, such as IVA, were observed to suppress waveforms from continuously active MUs. In contrast, the Hybrid filter was able to mitigate the limitations of both WGN-based smoothing and BSS-based suppression, resulting in improved MU decomposition outcomes. However, due to its high computational complexity, the Hybrid filter is not recommended for online applications. In most scenarios, IIR filtering or using unfiltered sEMG signals may provide the most appropriate balance between MU decomposition performance and computational efficiency.

References

1. Guo, W., et al.: Hand kinematics, high-density sEMG comprising forearm and far-field potentials for motion intent recognition. Sci. Data **12**(1), 445 (2025). https://doi.org/10.1038/s41597-025-04749-8
2. Farina, D., Holobar, A., Merletti, R.: The extraction of neural strategies from the surface EMG: an update. J. Neural Eng. **11**(6), 065003 (2014)
3. Heckman, C.J., Enoka, R.M.: Motor unit. J. Appl. Physiol. **104**(1), 1–2 (2008). https://doi.org/10.1152/japplphysiol.01137.2007
4. Holobar, A., Zazula, D.: Gradient convolution kernel compensation applied to surface electromyograms. In: Davies, M.E., James, C.J., Abdallah, S.A., Plumbley, M.D. (eds.) ICA 2007. LNCS, vol. 4666, pp. 617–624. Springer, Heidelberg (2007). https://doi.org/10.1007/978-3-540-74494-8_77

5. Xu, Y., Yu, Y., Xia, M., Zhu, X.: A novel and efficient surface electromyography decomposition algorithm using local spatial information. IEEE J. Biomed. Health Inform. **26**(9), 4501–4512 (2022). https://doi.org/10.1109/JBHI.2021.3135017
6. Dai, C., Hu, X.: Independent component analysis based algorithms for high-density electromyogram decomposition: systematic evaluation through simulation. Comput. Biol. Med. **109**, 237–245 (2019). https://doi.org/10.1016/j.compbiomed.2019.04.033
7. Luca, C.J., Gilmore, L.D., Kuznetsov, M., Roy, S.H.: Filtering the surface EMG signal: movement artifact and baseline noise contamination. J. Biomech. **43**(8), 1573–1579 (2010). https://doi.org/10.1016/j.jbiomech.2010.01.027
8. Rodríguez, H., Martínez, L., Pérez, F.: Comparing wavelet characterization methods for the classification of surface EMG. J. Neural Eng. Rehabil. **21**(2), 123–135 (2023)
9. Wang, K., Chen, X., Wu, L., Zhang, X., Chen, X., Wang, Z.J.: High-density surface EMG denoising using independent vector analysis. IEEE Trans. Neural Syst. Rehabil. Eng. (2020). https://doi.org/10.1109/TNSRE.2020.2987709
10. Li, Y., Wang, X., Li, J.: An improved filtering method based on EEMD and wavelet-threshold for modal parameter identification of hydraulic structure. Mech. Syst. Signal Process. **60–61**, 281–296 (2015). https://doi.org/10.1016/j.ymssp.2015.02.015
11. Ma, S., Lv, B., Lin, C., Sheng, X., Zhu, X.: EMG signal filtering based on variational mode decomposition and sub-band thresholding. IEEE J. Biomed. Health Inform. **25**(1), 47–58 (2021). https://doi.org/10.1109/JBHI.2020.2987528
12. Zhao, Z., Guo, W., Xia, M., Sheng, X.: A novel filtering framework for high-density sEMG based on variational mode decomposition and independent vector analysis. IEEE Sens. J. (2025). https://doi.org/10.1109/JSEN.2025.3532689
13. Nazari, M., Sakhaei, S.M.: Variational mode extraction: a new efficient method to derive respiratory signals from ECG. IEEE J. Biomed. Health Inform. **22**(4), 1059–1067 (2018). https://doi.org/10.1109/JBHI.2017.2734074
14. Gordon, T., Thomas, C., Munson, J., Stein, R.: The resilience of the size principle in the organization of motor unit properties in normal and reinnervated muscle. Can. J. Physiol. Pharmacol. **82**(8–9), 645–661 (2004)
15. Zhao, Z., Guo, W., Xu, Y., Sheng, X.: A biosignal quality assessment framework for high-density sEMG decomposition. Biomed. Signal Process. Control **90**, 105800 (2024). https://doi.org/10.1016/j.bspc.2023.105800
16. Kopsinis, Y., McLaughlin, S.: Development of EMD-based denoising methods inspired by wavelet thresholding. IEEE Trans. Signal Process. **57**(4), 1351–1362 (2009). https://doi.org/10.1109/TSP.2009.2013885
17. Hassan, M., Boudaoud, S., Terrien, J., Karlsson, B., Marque, C.: Combination of canonical correlation analysis and empirical mode decomposition applied to denoising the labor electrohysterogram. IEEE Trans. Biomed. Eng. **58**(9), 2441–2447 (2011). https://doi.org/10.1109/TBME.2011.2151861
18. Zheng, Y., Hu, X.: Interference removal from electromyography based on independent component analysis. IEEE Trans. Neural Syst. Rehabil. Eng. **27**(5), 887–894 (2019). https://doi.org/10.1109/TNSRE.2019.2910387

Sensory Input Shapes Motor Output: Decoding Corticomuscular Coherence Under Vibration-Induced Modulation

Xuefei Zhou[1,2], Huan Wen[2,3], Yueming Wang[2,3], Lin Yao[1,2,3,4(✉)], and Kedi Xu[2,3(✉)]

[1] College of Biomedical Engineering and Instrument Science, Zhejiang University, Hangzhou, China
lin.yao@zju.edu.cn
[2] Nanhu Brain-Computer Interface Institute, Hangzhou, China
[3] College of Computer Science and Technology, Zhejiang University, Hangzhou, China
xukd@zju.edu.cn
[4] MOE Frontiers Science Center for Brain and Brain-Machine Integration, State Key Laboratory of Brain-Machine Intelligence, Zhejiang University, Hangzhou, China

Abstract. This study investigates the frequency-dependent effects of vibratory stimulation on corticomuscular coherence (CMC) during isometric grip tasks. Synchronized EEG and high-density surface EMG (HD-sEMG) signals were recorded from six healthy subjects under four conditions: force-only, relaxation with 120 Hz vibration, force with 120 Hz vibration, and force with 40 Hz vibration. Results revealed a significant beta-band CMC peak over the contralateral motor cortex (C3) during force-only tasks, indicating dominant cortical control. Superimposing 120 Hz vibration abolished this peak during active contraction ($p = 0.0225$ vs. force-only), suggesting spinal reflex pathways (e.g., tonic vibration reflex) may partially mediate the motor output. In contrast, 40 Hz vibration preserved CMC synchrony ($p = 0.2506$). These findings demonstrate that high-frequency vibration attenuates corticomuscular functional connectivity via spinal mechanisms, providing insights for neuromodulation strategies in motor rehabilitation and neural interfaces.

Keywords: Corticomuscular coherence · Vibratory stimulation · Spinal reflex

1 Introduction

Corticomuscular coherence (CMC) is a measure of the strength of functional connectivity between the brain's motor cortex and target muscles. It reflects the transmission of motor cortical commands and the execution of actual movement in the target muscles during muscle contraction. CMC holds significant importance for understanding sensorimotor integration mechanisms, evaluating the effects of neuromodulation, and constructing closed-loop neural interface systems.

In 1991, McLachlan and Leung et al. [1] first discovered coherence in the gamma-band (32 Hz) between the primary sensorimotor cortex and muscles in epilepsy patients.

Subsequently, with the rapid development of neuromodulation techniques, the application of CMC in disease assessment has gained increasing attention, particularly in the fields of neurorehabilitation and movement disorders research. For example, in studies of children with unilateral cerebral palsy [2], the feasibility of CMC measurement was demonstrated. Research shows that children can complete CMC measurements and obtain stable results during goal-directed tasks. In studies of post-stroke movement disorders, researchers have also found [3] that CMC measurement can reflect the recovery of motor function after stroke by quantifying the interaction between motor cortical activity and the activity of controlled muscles. Furthermore, some researchers have used CMC as an indicator to evaluate the effectiveness of treatments for post-stroke sequelae [4], confirming that short-term NMES (Neuromuscular Electrical Stimulation) enhances corticomuscular functional connectivity and brain activation associated with motor tasks.

Neuromodulation is a technique that regulates physiological functions or treats diseases by intervening in the activity of the nervous system (including the brain, spinal cord, peripheral nerves, etc.). It influences the transmission of neural signals through physical, chemical, or biological means, thereby correcting abnormal neural activity to achieve the goal of alleviating symptoms or curing diseases.

Based on the intervention method, neuromodulation can be classified into two main categories: invasive and non-invasive. Invasive neuromodulation typically requires implanting electrodes into the brain or spinal cord to deliver electrical stimulation to target sites. This aims to suppress abnormal neural activity or block pain signal transmission, achieving therapeutic effects or symptom reduction. Examples include deep brain stimulation (DBS) and spinal cord stimulation (SCS). Acting directly on central or deep nerves, invasive neuromodulation offers the advantages of precise targeting and long-lasting efficacy, but carries surgical risks such as infection and hemorrhage. Non-invasive neuromodulation, in contrast, does not require penetration of the skin or skull, achieving neural regulation through external means. As a significant branch of non-invasive technology, vibratory stimulation applies mechanical vibration (e.g., low- or high-frequency vibration generated by transcutaneous vibratory devices) to superficial nerves, muscles, or specific body areas. This activates mechanoreceptors, sending signals to the central nervous system and thereby modulating neuronal excitability or neural circuit function.

Currently, vibratory stimulation has demonstrated its potential in improving spasticity [5, 6], muscle strengthening [7], and gait improvement [8]. Research has also shown that high-frequency (100~140 Hz) vibratory stimulation applied to tendons can elicit the tonic vibration reflex (TVR), activating spinal reflex pathways to improve prosthetic control [9].

However, systematic research is still lacking regarding how vibratory stimulation at different frequencies modulates CMC, its differential effects under active movement versus passive perception states, and its functional specificity in key sensorimotor regions such as C3 and C4. The C3 and C4 regions correspond to the primary motor and sensory cortices for the contralateral limbs (right and left, respectively). Coherence changes in these regions under different experimental conditions may reveal the brain's mechanisms for integrating sensory input and motor output, holding significant value for developing closed-loop neuromodulation interfaces.

This study systematically investigates the modulatory effects of vibratory input on CMC by synchronously acquiring EEG and high-density surface electromyography (HD-sEMG) signals. This is combined with a grip task-guided isometric contraction paradigm and multi-frequency vibratory stimulation (40 Hz and 120 Hz). The findings of this study will contribute to a deeper understanding of how sensory input influences motor control via corticospinal pathways and provide theoretical support for developing intelligent vibration feedback-based neural interface systems. In the future, such modulation strategies hold promise for application in areas including motor disorder rehabilitation, optimization of brain-computer interface (BCI) systems, and enhancement of neuroplasticity.

2 Materials and Methods

2.1 Subjects

Six healthy participants (Table 1) voluntarily participated in this study without a history of neurological disorders or injuries. The experimental protocol was clearly explained to the participants before the experiment, and written informed consent forms were received from all subjects.

Table 1. Subjects in experiments.

Number	Gender	Age
1	Male	23
2	Male	23
3	Male	27
4	Female	27
5	Male	26
6	Male	26

2.2 Experimental Setup

Signal Acquisition Device. Electroencephalography (EEG) data were collected using a Brain Products ActiCHamp system at 2000 Hz, with electrodes positioned according to the International 10–20 system and referenced to TP9 and TP10. Simultaneously, electromyography (EMG) data were acquired using an OT Bioelettronica Quattrocento amplifier at 2048 Hz. To precisely capture forearm muscle activity, three high-density surface EMG (HD-sEMG) electrode grids (each containing 64 channels) were positioned on the participant's right forearm: Grid 1 on the medial aspect targeting the flexor carpi ulnaris (FCU) and partially palmaris longus; Grid 2 on the lateral aspect covering the flexor carpi radialis; and Grid 3 on the dorsal aspect covering the extensor digitorum and wrist extensor group. This 192-channel HD-sEMG configuration ensured comprehensive monitoring of electrical activity during tasks. All electrodes were applied per manufacturer guidelines using conductive gel and adhesive tape to ensure optimal skin contact and minimize motion artifacts. Participants performed an isometric grip task using a dynamometer, with real-time grip force displayed as visual feedback to maintain constant contraction. LabStreamingLayer (LSL) ensured precise temporal synchronization between EEG and EMG data streams. All procedures were conducted in accordance with relevant ethical guidelines.

Vibration Stimulation Device. The vibratory stimulation was delivered using a custom-developed, high-frequency linear muscle vibrator. This device generated vibrations within a frequency range of 20–120 Hz and an amplitude range of 0–1 mm. The vibrator head was securely fastened to the medial aspect of the participant's forearm, specifically targeting the FCU muscle belly, using an adjustable strap to ensure consistent placement. Stimulation parameters were controlled via Bluetooth communication: a computer sent commands to an integrated controller unit, which subsequently delivered an alternating current to the vibration actuator. This current drove an electromagnetic coil assembly to generate an alternating magnetic field, which in turn induced reciprocating vertical motion in an embedded magnetic core. The resulting mechanical vibration was transmitted through the vibrator head to deliver transcutaneous vibratory stimulation to the underlying target muscle tissue (Fig. 1).

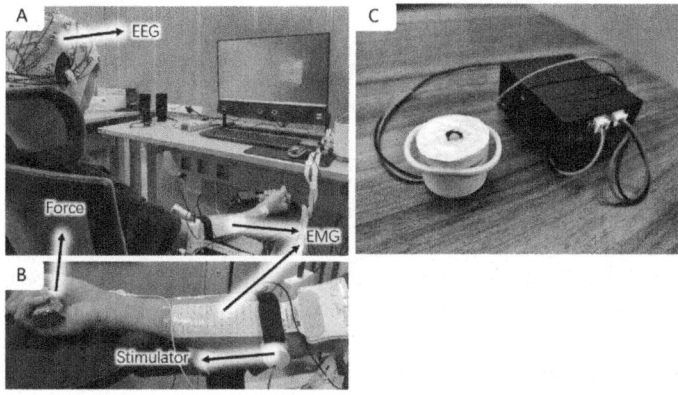

Fig. 1. Experimental Setup: (A) Acquisition of electroencephalography (EEG) and electromyography (EMG) signals; (B) Participant's right forearm equipped with three high-density surface EMG (HD-sEMG) electrode grids, a vibratory stimulator secured on the medial forearm targeting the flexor carpi ulnaris, and a dynamometer held in the hand for grip force measurement; (C) Custom-developed vibratory stimulation device used in the experiment, showing the vibration unit (left panel) and the control box (right panel).

2.3 Experimental Procedure

Participants sat comfortably in a chair, fitted with the EEG cap, EMG electrodes, and the vibratory stimulator. The right hand rested palm-up on a support platform attached to the chair armrest, holding the dynamometer. Prior to the main experiment, each participant's

Maximum Voluntary Contraction (MVC) was determined to establish their individual maximum grip force output. The formal experiment consisted of 3 identical blocks, with each block containing 24 trials. Trials were evenly distributed across 4 distinct experimental conditions and presented in a randomized order within each block. The timeline for a single trial/condition is depicted in Fig. 2. During the experiment, instructions were displayed on a screen. During the relaxation phase, participants were instructed to remain relaxed. During the grip phase, participants were required to maintain a constant isometric grip force at 15% of their pre-determined MVC. A visual feedback bar on the screen displayed the participant's real-time force output relative to the target force level to aid in maintaining the required contraction. A 5-min rest period was enforced between blocks to minimize muscle fatigue.

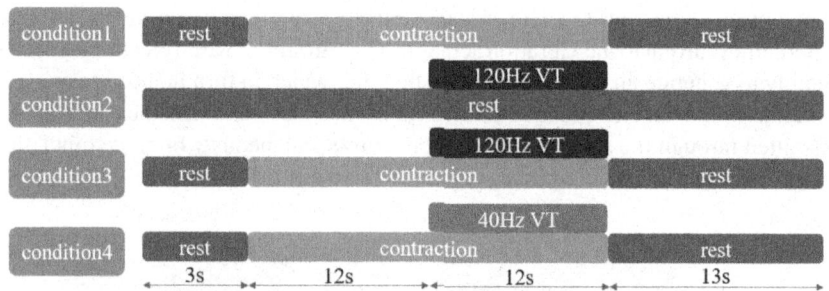

Fig. 2. The experimental process of a single trial

2.4 Data Analysis

EEG Data Preprocessing. EEG data preprocessing was performed using the EEGLAB toolbox. Raw data, recorded at 2000 Hz, were first loaded and Upsampled to 2048 Hz to match subsequent analysis requirements. The data were then re-referenced to the average of TP9 and TP10 (corresponding to channels 10 and 21) to reduce common-mode noise. A band-pass filter (1–50 Hz) was applied to remove low-frequency drift and high-frequency myogenic artifacts. Bad channel detection was performed based on the kurtosis coefficient (threshold = 5.5), and identified anomalous channels were reconstructed using spherical interpolation; the identities of these channels were recorded in separate files. To separate physiological artifacts (e.g., ocular, myogenic), Independent Component Analysis (ICA) was performed using the extended infomax algorithm (runica). Independent components corresponding to artifacts were identified and removed through manual inspection. Epochs were extracted from −15 s to +27 s relative to event triggers defined by the experimental paradigm (event types 1–4). Finally, within the analysis window, epochs containing artifacts were automatically rejected based on a voltage threshold of ±150 μV.

EMG Data Preprocessing. EMG signals were first processed by applying a band-pass filter (10–500 Hz) across all trials to remove low-frequency drift and high-frequency noise, preserving the physiologically relevant frequency band. Based on predefined event types (1–4), epochs were extracted from −15 s to +27 s relative to the event triggers. Epochs rejected during EEG preprocessing were synchronously excluded from the EMG data. Subsequently, multi-stage filtering was applied to mitigate laboratory line-frequency interference and stimulation-specific artifacts:

1. A universal 50 Hz notch filter (±3 Hz band-stop) was applied to suppress the fundamental power-line frequency and its harmonics (50–500 Hz).
2. Condition-specific notch filtering was then applied based on event type:
    a. For Event Types 2/3 (120 Hz vibration): A ±3 Hz band-stop filter centered on 120 Hz and its harmonics (120–480 Hz) was applied. This artifact removal strategy preserves motor unit activity information within the signal [10].
    b. For Event Type 4 (40 Hz vibration): A similar ±3 Hz band-stop filtering approach was implemented targeting 40 Hz and its harmonics.

The efficacy of all filtering steps was verified by inspecting spectrograms before and after application. Channel quality assessment was performed by detecting the standard deviation of the power spectrum within the 20–500 Hz band (threshold = 2.5); channels identified as anomalous were flagged and documented.

CMC Calculation. CMC was computed based on the cross-spectral density. The coherence $C_{xy}(f)$ between signals $x(t)$ (EEG) and $y(t)$ (EMG) is defined as:

$$C_{xy}(f) = \frac{|S_{xy}(f)|^2}{S_{xx}(f) \cdot S_{yy}(f)} \quad (1)$$

where $S_{xy}(f)$ is the cross-power spectral density estimate between $x(t)$ and $y(t)$, obtained by segmenting, windowing, and applying the Fourier transform:

$$S_{xy}(f) = \frac{1}{L} \sum_{i=1}^{L} X_i(f) \cdot Y_i^*(f) \quad (2)$$

Similarly, $S_{xx}(f)$ and $S_{yy}(f)$ are the auto-power spectral densities of $x(t)$ and. $y(t)$:

$$S_{xx}(f) = \frac{1}{L} \sum_{i=1}^{L} X_i(f) \cdot X_i^*(f) \quad (3)$$

In practice, CMC was estimated using the mscohere function (Matlab Signal Processing Toolbox). This function implements the Welch's averaged periodogram method: signals are divided into segments (using a Hamming window), each segment is Fourier transformed, and the power spectra are averaged. Coherence is calculated as the magnitude squared of the averaged cross-power spectrum normalized by the product of the averaged auto-power spectra. For each trial, the middle 10-s segment was used for analysis. The data were segmented using a 512-point (0.25 s) Hamming window with no overlap, yielding a frequency resolution of 4 Hz. CMC was calculated between every EEG channel and every EMG channel. The resulting coherence values were then averaged across the EMG channels for subsequent analysis.

3 Results

During analysis, the coherence data for the four experimental conditions were processed separately using the following steps: First, cross-coherence was calculated between the HD-sEMG and EEG signals for each participant. Second, the resulting coherence values were averaged across all EMG channels for each EEG channel. Finally, group-level analysis was performed on the average coherence data from the six participants. Given that prior research has established the association of the beta frequency band (14–30 Hz) with motor planning and execution [11], we generated beta-band coherence topographic maps (Fig. 3). This multi-layered averaging approach effectively captured the functional connectivity patterns between the motor cortex and muscles while mitigating the influence of individual variability and noise interference.

3.1 Topographic Map Changes Across Experimental Conditions

Condition 1 (Force Only - Right Hand): In the beta-band topographic map, a significant coherence peak was observed over the C3 region (contralateral motor cortex). This peak was markedly higher than coherence levels in other EEG regions (e.g., C4, Pz), indicating strong functional connectivity between the motor cortex and the right forearm muscle groups during contraction. This pattern aligns with the typical activation profile of the motor cortex during voluntary muscle contraction reported in the literature [12], confirming its dominant role in active motor control.

Condition 2 (Hand Relaxation + 120 Hz Vibration): In the beta-band topographic map, the coherence peak over the C3 region was significantly reduced. Furthermore, the overall topographic distribution exhibited relatively uniformly low coherence. This result suggests that while the 120 Hz vibratory stimulation activated spinal reflex circuits (e.g., the TVR [13]), it failed to establish effective functional connectivity between the cortex and muscles during muscle relaxation. This absence of connectivity may stem from the lack of active motor intent associated with muscle contraction, resulting in no corresponding motor cortical commands being generated [14].

Condition 3 (Force + 120 Hz Vibration): Most notably, the coherence peak over the C3 region was almost entirely abolished under this condition, resembling the pattern observed in Condition 2. This phenomenon was in marked contrast to Condition 1 ($p = 0.0225$, paired t-test), indicating that superimposing high-frequency vibration during active effort significantly weakened the cortical regulation of muscle activity.

The topographic map revealed that coherence was generally reduced not only over C3 but also across other EEG channels, resulting in a more uniformly low coherence distribution overall.

Condition 4 (Force + 40 Hz Vibration): In contrast to Condition 3, the coherence peak over the C3 region was preserved under this condition ($p = 0.2506$ vs Condition 1). Although slightly lower than in Condition 1, it remained significantly higher than in Conditions 2 and 3. The topographic coherence distribution pattern resembled that of Condition 1, albeit with a reduced peak magnitude. This indicates that low-frequency vibration stimulation did not severely disrupt the functional connectivity between the cortex and muscles during active contraction (Fig. 4).

Sensory Input Shapes Motor Output 347

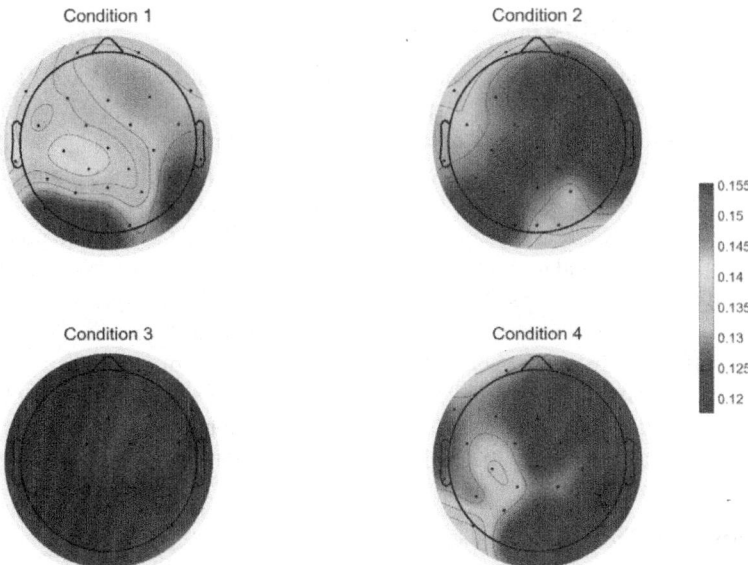

Fig. 3. Comparison of beta-band CMC across four conditions (averaged over 6 subjects)

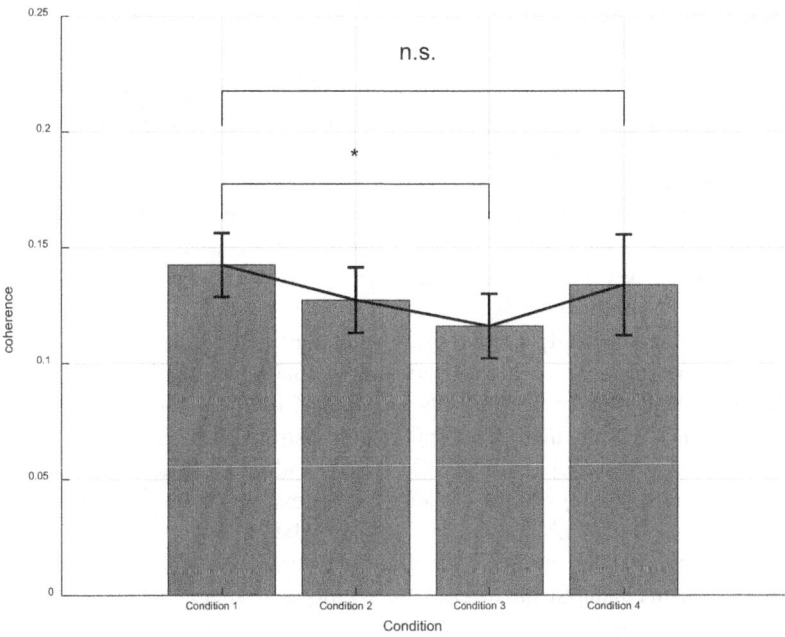

Fig. 4. Comparison of CMC in the C3 region at beta-band across four conditions

3.2 Relationship Between Vibration Frequency and CMC

As previously mentioned, high-frequency vibration stimulation elicits the TVR, activating Ia and II afferent fibers in muscle spindles. These fibers transmit signals about muscle length changes to the spinal cord, which, after spinal integration, further enhances muscle activation [15]. In the experiment, participants were required to maintain a constant grip force. In Condition 1, this grip force originated entirely from cortical control, thus demonstrating strong CMC. By contrast, both Condition 2 and Condition 3 used 120 Hz vibration stimulation, and no contralateral beta-band CMC peaks were observed in either the relaxed or force-applying states. This is because, although participants in Condition 3 also needed to maintain the same level of grip force, part of this force derived from spinal reflexes, partially substituting cortical descending control of muscles. This result supports the mechanism that high-frequency vibration directly regulates muscle activity via spinal reflexes, reducing cortical involvement. In Condition 4, low-frequency vibration did not induce the tetanic vibration reflex, and the coherence peak was preserved.

4 Conclusions

This study revealed the mechanism by which vibration frequency influences corticomuscular functional connectivity by analyzing coherence changes between EEG and EMG signals under different vibration stimulation conditions. The results showed that under the condition of right-hand force application only (Condition 1), the motor cortex (C3 region) and the right forearm muscles exhibited significant beta-band coherence peaks, indicating that the brain plays a central role in actively controlling muscle contraction. By contrast, when superimposed with 120 Hz high-frequency vibration stimulation (Condition 3), despite participants remaining in an active force-applying state, coherence in the C3 region significantly decreased. This suggests that high-frequency vibration may reduce direct cortical control of muscle activity by activating spinal reflex pathways. In contrast, low-frequency 40 Hz vibration stimulation (Condition 4) maintained high-level coherence in the C3 region, indicating that low-frequency vibration does not disrupt corticomuscular functional connectivity.

Taken together, this study found that high-frequency vibration (120 Hz) reduces corticomuscular coherence, possibly by activating spinal reflex mechanisms and thereby decreasing cortical involvement in muscle output. Low-frequency vibration (40 Hz), however, did not exhibit this effect and retained strong corticomuscular synchrony. These findings provide new evidence for understanding the role of vibration stimulation in neuromuscular regulation and offer theoretical support for its future application in fields such as motor rehabilitation and neural regulation. Follow-up studies could further integrate multiple physiological signals (e.g., fMRI, TMS) to explore the underlying neural mechanisms in depth and extend investigations to clinical populations to validate its application potential.

References

1. McLachlan, R.S., Leung, L.W.S.: A movement-associated fast Rolandic rhythm. Can. J. Neurol. Sci. **18**, 333–336 (1991)

2. Gangwani, R.R., et al.: Corticomuscular coherence in children with unilateral cerebral palsy: a feasibility and preliminary protocol study. J. Child Neurol. **38**, 357–366 (2023)
3. Zheng, Y., Peng, Y., Xu, G., Li, L., Wang, J.: Using corticomuscular coherence to reflect function recovery of paretic upper limb after stroke: a case study. Front. Neurol. **8**, 728 (2018)
4. Xu, R., Wang, Y., Wang, K., Zhang, S., He, C., Ming, D.: Increased corticomuscular coherence and brain activation immediately after short-term neuromuscular electrical stimulation. Front. Neurol. **9**, 886 (2018)
5. Liepert, J., Binder, C.: Vibration-induced effects in stroke patients with spastic hemiparesis – a pilot study. Restor. Neurol. Neurosci. **28**, 729–735 (2010)
6. Khosravani, S., et al.: Laryngeal vibration as a non-invasive neuromodulation therapy for spasmodic dysphonia. Sci. Rep. **9**, 17955–18011 (2019)
7. Rauch, F.: Vibration therapy. Dev. Med. Child Neurol. **51**, 166–168 (2009)
8. Rippetoe, J., Wang, H., James, S.A., Dionne, C., Block, B., Beckner, M.: Improvement of gait after 4 weeks of wearable focal muscle vibration therapy for individuals with diabetic peripheral neuropathy. J. Clin. Med. **9**, 3767 (2020)
9. Sagastegui Alva, P.G., Boesendorfer, A., Aszmann, O.C., Ibáñez, J., Farina, D.: Excitation of natural spinal reflex loops in the sensory-motor control of hand prostheses. Sci. Robot. **9**, eadl0085 (2024)
10. Xu, Y., et al.: Functional force stimulation alters motor neuron discharge patterns. Front. Neurosci. **17**, 1293017 (2023)
11. Kilner, J.M., Baker, S.N., Salenius, S., Hari, R., Lemon, R.N.: Human cortical muscle coherence is directly related to specific motor parameters. J. Neurosci. **20**, 8838–8845 (2000)
12. Little, S., Bonaiuto, J., Barnes, G., Bestmann, S.: Human motor cortical beta bursts relate to movement planning and response errors. PLoS Biol. **17**, e3000479–e3000479 (2019)
13. Burke, D., Hagbarth, K.E., Löfstedt, L., Wallin, B.G.: The responses of human muscle spindle endings to vibration during isometric contraction. J. Physiol. **261**, 695–711 (1976)
14. Brown, P.: Cortical drives to human muscle: the Piper and related rhythms. Prog. Neurobiol. **60**, 97–108 (2000)
15. Fallon, J.B., Macefield, V.G.: Vibration sensitivity of human muscle spindles and Golgi tendon organs. Muscle Nerve **36**, 21–29 (2007)

Adaptive Network Design for SSVEP/SSMVEP Classification via SE and Configurable Convolutions

Yichen Lin[1,2], Xiuyuan Wu[2], Xinyang Du[2], Haoran Zhang[2], Wenke Lu[1,2], Yu Zhu[2], Zengle Ren[2], Pengjie Qin[2], Jinke Li[2], and Yue Ma[2(✉)]

[1] College of Engineering, Southern University of Science and Technology, Shenzhen, China
`12433359@mail.sustech.edu.cn`
[2] Chinese Academy of Sciences, Shenzhen Institute of Advanced Technology, Shenzhen 518005, China
`yue.ma@siat.ac.cn`

Abstract. Electroencephalogram (EEG) signals are widely used in brain-computer interface (BCI) systems for their high temporal resolution and non-invasiveness. However, their non-stationarity, low signal-to-noise ratio (SNR), and complex spatiotemporal patterns pose significant challenges for classification. To address this, we propose a deep adjustable convolutional neural network that integrates the Squeeze-and-Excitation (SE) attention mechanism. The network features flexible depth adjustment, making it well-suited for complex tasks, particularly SSMVEP signal processing. Experiments on a self-built SSMVEP dataset and the public 12JFPM_SSVEP dataset demonstrate that our method surpasses mainstream models in accuracy, robustness, and scalability, showing strong potential for multi-class EEG classification and advancing BCI development.

Keywords: EEG · SSMVEP · Squeeze-and-Excitation · BCI

1 Introduction

EEG signals serve as a fundamental information source for BCIs, with wide applications in neural engineering and intelligent interaction. Compared to conventional SSVEP signals, SSMVEP signals offer milder stimulation, reducing visual fatigue and enhancing suitability for long-term use. However, their lower amplitude and weaker frequency-domain characteristics pose challenges for accurate recognition using traditional methods. Existing deep learning models lack specialized designs for these features, limiting their effectiveness.

To gain deeper insights into the frequency-domain features of SSMVEP signals, we performed Welch power spectral density (PSD) analysis on self-collected SSVEP and SSMVEP signals within the 8–13 Hz frequency band with 1 Hz intervals, under identical brightness and a stimulation duration of 20 s. As shown in Fig. 1, SSVEP signals exhibit more prominent spectral peaks at the target

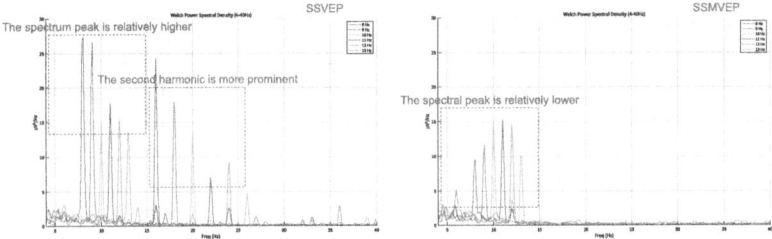

Fig. 1. Comparison of Power Spectral Density between SSVEP and SSMVEP signals

frequency and its harmonics, along with a higher signal-to-noise ratio, which facilitates feature extraction and classification. In contrast, SSMVEP signals display weaker spectral peaks and less distinct frequency-domain characteristics, increasing recognition difficulty and highlighting the need for more efficient classification models.

To enhance the recognition of weak EEG signals such as SSMVEP, this paper proposes a modular deep convolutional network integrated with the SE attention mechanism. The network features flexible depth adjustment and adaptive channel reweighting, which strengthens the representation of key frequency bands and channels, thereby improving the extraction of multi-channel spatiotemporal EEG features.

The proposed approach involves preprocessing the data followed by a sliding window operation, enabling the neural network to effectively capture class-specific features for accurate classification. The overall process is illustrated in Fig. 2.

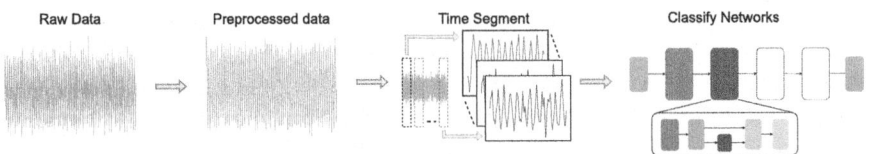

Fig. 2. Overview of the proposed data processing and classification pipeline

The main contributions of this paper are as follows:

1) A modular deep convolutional network is designed, supporting on-demand depth adjustment to enhance model generality and task adaptability;
2) The SE attention mechanism is integrated to improve the model's ability to capture key channel and dynamic visual features, especially enhancing the recognition performance of SSMVEP signals;

3) The proposed method is validated on both the self-built SSMVEP dataset and the publicly available 12JFPM_SSVEP dataset. On the self-built SSMVEP dataset, the highest accuracy reaches 90.98% within 1 s, while on the 12JFPM_SSVEP dataset, the highest accuracy reaches 98%. These results outperform several mainstream approaches, demonstrating strong classification performance and potential for practical applications.

The remainder of this paper is organized as follows. Section 2 reviews related work. Section 3 describes the dataset construction and the design of the deep learning model in detail. Section 4 presents and analyzes the experimental results. Section 5 discusses future research directions.

2 Related Work

Traditional methods for steady-state EEG recognition (SSVEP/SSMVEP), such as CCA [1], MsetCCA [2], FBCCA [3], TRCA [4], and PSDA, mainly rely on frequency-domain features and statistical correlations. They are computationally efficient and suitable for small samples and real-time decoding. However, their performance drops sharply with high channel counts, many stimulus targets, or low-quality signals, due to limited ability to capture complex EEG feature distributions, restricting their use in advanced brain-computer interfaces.

To overcome the performance bottlenecks of traditional methods, deep learning techniques have recently been introduced into SSVEP/SSMVEP decoding. Leveraging their powerful feature extraction capabilities, these methods demonstrate stronger robustness and generalization, especially in scenarios with short signal lengths or low-quality data.

With the development of deep neural networks, various architectures tailored for EEG signals have been proposed to improve SSVEP/SSMVEP recognition performance. Below is a brief introduction to some representative models:

EEGNet [5] is a lightweight convolutional neural network that combines temporal bandpass convolutions (DepthwiseConv2D) and frequency-domain separable convolutions (SeparableConv2D) to effectively extract cross-channel and cross-frequency EEG features. Its simple structure and small parameter size make it suitable for small-sample, low-power BCI systems and it has been widely validated across multiple EEG tasks including SSVEP.

C-CNN [6] is the first to transform EEG signals into the frequency domain (e.g., FFT) at the input stage, integrating temporal and spatial convolutions to jointly model spectral information and spatial distribution. It significantly improves classification accuracy in multi-target recognition tasks.

FBtCNN [7] introduces the filter bank concept by dividing EEG signals into multiple frequency bands for feature extraction, effectively addressing low SNR and complex spectral structures of signals like SSMVEP. This model is especially suitable for classification tasks with short time windows.

SSVEPformer [8], based on the Transformer architecture, incorporates temporal-channel attention mechanisms to learn key spatiotemporal features from raw signals. Its extended filter bank version further enhances recognition performance across subjects and frequencies, making it one of the current strong baselines.

DeepConvNet is a relatively deep convolutional neural network consisting of multiple sequential convolution-normalization-activation-pooling modules that progressively extract rich spatiotemporal features. Designed to model channel coupling and temporal sequences, it has good generalization ability and is often used as a standard baseline in EEG recognition research.

In recent years, attention mechanisms have enhanced EEG recognition by dynamically weighting feature channels or temporal points, improving robustness in noisy conditions. Widely successful in computer vision and NLP [9,10], attention is increasingly applied in EEG analysis [11].

Channel attention methods like SE [12] emphasize important EEG channels for better multi-frequency and multi-channel representation, while temporal attention captures time-response features, boosting performance under low SNR [13].

However, existing attention architectures still struggle with the weaker, less distinct features of SSMVEP signals. Developing efficient, SSMVEP-specific attention modules integrated with deep networks to enhance accuracy and practicality remains a key research challenge.

3 Method

3.1 Dataset Selection

To validate the effectiveness of the proposed method, we conducted experimental evaluations using one public SSVEP dataset and one self-built SSMVEP dataset.

In the SSVEP experiment, the public **12JFPM_SSVEP dataset** [14] was utilized to evaluate the performance of the proposed model. This dataset, curated by Nakanishi et al., includes EEG recordings from 10 healthy participants. The experimental paradigm employed twelve distinct visual stimulus targets, each modulated using joint frequency-phase modulation (JFPM) to enhance signal separability. The stimulation frequencies ranged from 9.25 Hz to 14.75 Hz in 0.5 Hz increments, ensuring dense frequency coverage within the low-frequency SSVEP range.

EEG signals were recorded using 8 electrodes positioned over the occipital region (Oz, O1, O2, POz, PO3, PO4, PO5, PO6), which is known to be most responsive to visual stimulation. The sampling rate was set at 256 Hz to capture the fine-grained temporal dynamics of brain responses. For each stimulus, 15 trials were conducted per subject, with each trial lasting approximately 4 s, resulting in a sufficiently large dataset for training and evaluation.

This dataset has been widely adopted in the literature for benchmarking SSVEP decoding methods, both traditional (e.g., CCA, FBCCA) and modern deep learning approaches. Its well-structured design, high signal quality, and balanced class distribution make it a standard reference in the BCI community for performance comparison and reproducibility.

Due to the lack of publicly available datasets specifically designed for SSMVEP, we constructed a new **self-built SSMVEP dataset**. This dataset was collected from six healthy participants (average age: 24 ± 2 years). During the experiments, a Quest 3 virtual reality headset was used to present periodic "contraction-expansion" checkerboard stimuli, simulating a multi-frequency visual evoked potential process. Six target frequencies (8–13 Hz with 1 Hz intervals) were used, and each frequency was repeated 10 times. Each trial consisted of a 2.5-second resting period, a 10-second visual stimulation period, and a 2.5-second post-stimulus rest. Participants were instructed to fixate on the center point of the checkerboard and sequentially focus on different frequency targets. EEG signals were recorded from occipital channels (O1, O2, Oz, and POz) at a sampling rate of 1000 Hz, ensuring high temporal resolution and signal quality. This dataset better simulates EEG responses under weak stimulation in complex environments and facilitates the evaluation of model robustness and generalization performance in SSMVEP tasks.

This dataset better simulates brain responses under weak stimuli in complex environments, helping to evaluate the robustness and generalization ability of models in SSMVEP tasks.

Figure 3 illustrates the overall process of the SSMVEP experiment, including the resting phase, stimulus presentation, and post-stimulus phase. In each trial, participants focused on stimulus targets with different frequencies to elicit visual evoked responses.

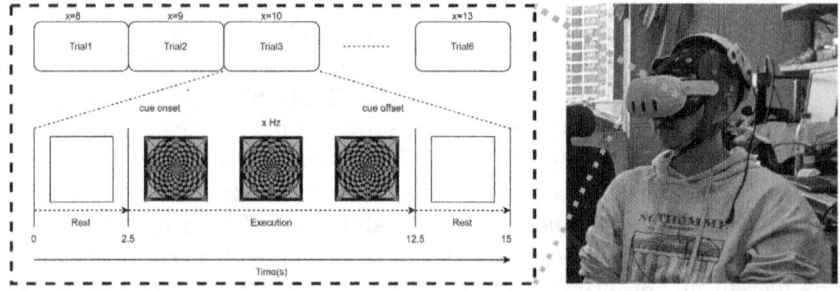

Fig. 3. Illustration of the SSMVEP experimental procedure and stimulus presentation

3.2 Design of Neural Networks

This network is based on the DeepConvNet architecture and adopts a modular design that supports flexible adjustment of the depth and width of convolutional blocks to accommodate diverse EEG signal processing needs. Users can configure the number of convolutional blocks and the number of kernels in each layer according to task complexity and hardware resources, thereby achieving a dynamic balance between model complexity and computational efficiency to enhance the model's applicability and scalability.

This network incorporates the SE attention mechanism module. This module performs global average pooling on the convolutional layer output channels and uses a two-layer fully connected network to adaptively learn channel weight distributions. It dynamically recalibrates channel responses of feature maps, effectively enhancing the model's representation of key spatial features and significantly improving discrimination performance and generalization.

The overall network consists of multiple convolutional blocks, each containing convolution operations, batch normalization, exponential linear unit (ELU) activation, an SE module, pooling layers, and dropout regularization. A fully connected layer at the end produces multi-class classification outputs. Figure 4 illustrates the overall network structure and core module relationships, clearly showing the processing flow from input EEG signals to final classification.

The first convolutional layer uses kernels of size $(1, k_t)$ with $k_t = 10$ to extract local temporal features:

$$\mathbf{F}_1 = \text{Conv2D}_{(1,k_t)}(\mathbf{X}). \tag{1}$$

Next, cross-channel convolution captures spatial correlations:

$$\mathbf{F}_2 = \text{Conv2D}_{(C,1)}(\mathbf{F}_1). \tag{2}$$

Each convolutional block embeds a SE module, applying global average pooling:

$$\mathbf{z} = \text{GAP}(\mathbf{F}), \tag{3}$$

followed by a two-layer fully connected network for feature recalibration:

$$\mathbf{s} = \sigma(\mathbf{W}_2\, \delta(\mathbf{W}_1 \mathbf{z})), \tag{4}$$

where δ is the activation function and σ the sigmoid function. The SE block adopts a bottleneck structure with a reduction ratio r, reducing the number of hidden units from C to C/r, and then restoring it:

$$\mathbf{W}_1 \in \mathbb{R}^{\frac{C}{r} \times C}, \quad \mathbf{W}_2 \in \mathbb{R}^{C \times \frac{C}{r}}. \tag{5}$$

In our implementation, we set the reduction ratio to $r = 4$.

Multi-level convolution and pooling reduce feature dimensionality while preserving key information. A final fully connected layer outputs multi-class probabilities:

$$\hat{\mathbf{y}} = \text{Softmax}(\mathbf{W}_{\text{fc}} \mathbf{f}). \tag{6}$$

Dropout and batch normalization are used to prevent overfitting and speed up training, balancing model expressiveness and efficiency.

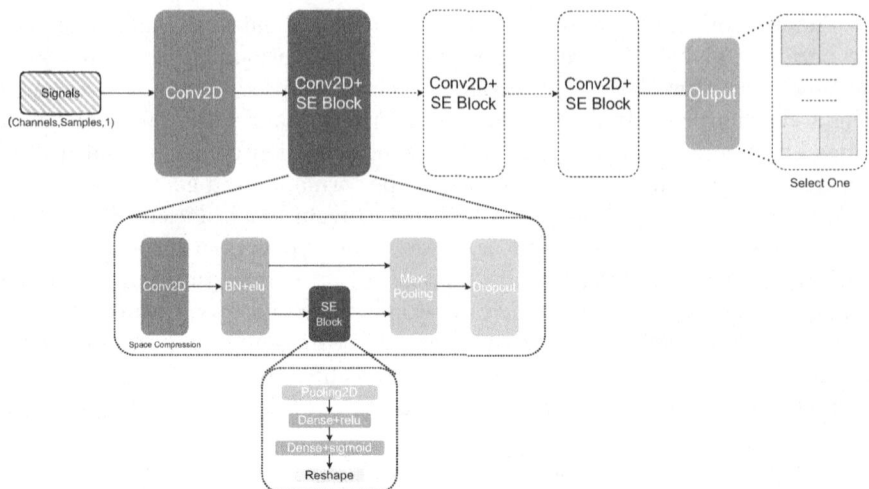

Fig. 4. Diagram of SE-Enhanced Adjustable Convolutional Network Architecture

4 Experimental and Results

4.1 Evaluation Metrics

In the 12JFPM_SSVEP dataset, the classification accuracy of each subject was used as the evaluation metric. The final performance was reported as the average accuracy across all subjects, which reflects the overall performance of the model on different individuals.

For the self-built SSMVEP dataset, both classification accuracy and Information Transfer Rate (ITR) were adopted as evaluation metrics. ITR measures the amount of information that a BCI system can transmit per unit time, taking into account both recognition accuracy and response speed. It is a crucial indicator for evaluating the real-time performance of BCI systems. The ITR is calculated as follows:

$$\text{ITR} = \frac{60}{T}\left[\log_2 N + P\log_2 P + (1-P)\log_2\left(\frac{1-P}{N-1}\right)\right], \quad (7)$$

where T represents the duration of a single trial (in seconds), N is the number of stimulus targets, and P denotes the classification accuracy (ranging from 0 to 1).

This metric effectively reflects the practicality and efficiency of the model in real-time decoding for SSVEP/SSMVEP tasks and serves as an important reference for the design of BCI systems.

4.2 Baseline Method Selection

To comprehensively evaluate the effectiveness and robustness of the proposed model, we conducted comparative experiments using multiple representative methods on both the 12JFPM_SSVEP dataset and the self-built SSMVEP dataset.

On the 12JFPM_SSVEP dataset, the comparison includes EEGNet, C-CNN, SSVEPformer, FBtCNN, and three improved models proposed in this paper (Ours-1CS, Ours-2CS, Ours-3CS). On the SSMVEP dataset, the comparative methods cover the traditional statistical approach CCA, deep neural networks such as DeepConvNet and EEGNet, as well as four proposed variants (Ours-3CS, Ours-4CS, Ours-5CS, Ours-6CS).

In the naming convention Ours-nCS, the number n denotes the number of convolutional layers used in the model. All variants consistently incorporate the SE channel attention mechanism to enhance feature selection. The design of this model series takes into account both the complexity of EEG signal patterns and the size of the available training data.

For relatively simple signals with dominant frequency components and limited spatial variation, as well as smaller datasets, shallower convolutional networks (e.g., Ours-1CS, Ours-2CS) are often sufficient for effective feature extraction while helping to prevent overfitting. In contrast, for more complex signals—such as those with rich spectral structures or distributed spatial features, like SSMVEP—as well as larger datasets that support greater model capacity, deeper architectures (e.g., Ours-5CS, Ours-6CS) are preferred. These deeper models enhance the ability to extract hierarchical features and improve representational power without sacrificing generalization.

Through comparison across configurations with different depths, we can investigate the influence of network depth on performance, and validate the structural design's effectiveness and generalizability across different types of EEG signals.

4.3 Experimental Procedure and Implementation Details

Due to differences in sampling methods, data volume, and task settings between the two datasets, all experiments were conducted independently on each dataset.

12JFPM_SSVEP Dataset: Experiments used a subject-dependent strategy. EEG signals were band-pass filtered (8–30 Hz) and z-score normalized. Inputs were $C \times T$ matrices ($C = 8$, $T \approx 1114$). Training employed the Adam optimizer with learning rate scheduling, batch size of 32, early stopping, and GPU acceleration. The model was compiled using the categorical cross-entropy loss function and evaluated with accuracy as the primary metric.

Self-built SSMVEP Dataset: To test generalization, the EEG data were split into training, validation, and testing sets with a ratio of 7.2:1.8:1. Data segmentation was performed using sliding windows of lengths 500, 1000, 1500, and 2000 points (corresponding to 0.5 s to 2 s) with a fixed step size of 100. For model training, 5-fold cross-validation was conducted on the training set, using a batch size of 32 and training for 200 epochs. In each fold, the model achieving the highest validation accuracy was saved, and subsequently evaluated on the held-out test set. The model was trained using the categorical cross-entropy loss function, and final performance results were reported as the average of the test performance across all folds.

All experiments ran in Python 3.9.21; 12JFPM_SSVEP experiments used PyTorch 1.10, SSMVEP experiments used TensorFlow 2.15. Training was performed on an NVIDIA RTX 4090 GPU for efficiency and stability.

4.4 Result Analysis on the 12JFPM_SSVEP Dataset

Figure 5 shows classification accuracy of various methods on the 12JFPM_SSVEP dataset for 10 subjects. The proposed models demonstrate high stability and robustness, with Ours-1CS achieving the best average accuracy of 98.00%, outperforming EEGNet (93.00%), C-CNN (93.67%), SSVEPformer (94.00%), and FBtCNN (89.33%). This indicates that a moderately deep, lightweight model with SE channel attention effectively enhances SSVEP feature extraction and recognition performance while maintaining efficiency.

By comparing the standard deviations of these models, we can observe that Ours-1CS has the smallest standard deviation, indicating that its performance fluctuates the least across multiple experiments, thus demonstrating stronger stability and generalization ability.

We also observed that as the number of module layers increases, the accuracy gradually decreases. For example, the accuracy of Ours-2CS is 95.33%, while that of Ours-3CS drops to 85.00%. We speculate that this is due to the limited size of the dataset, which leads to overfitting as the model depth increases.

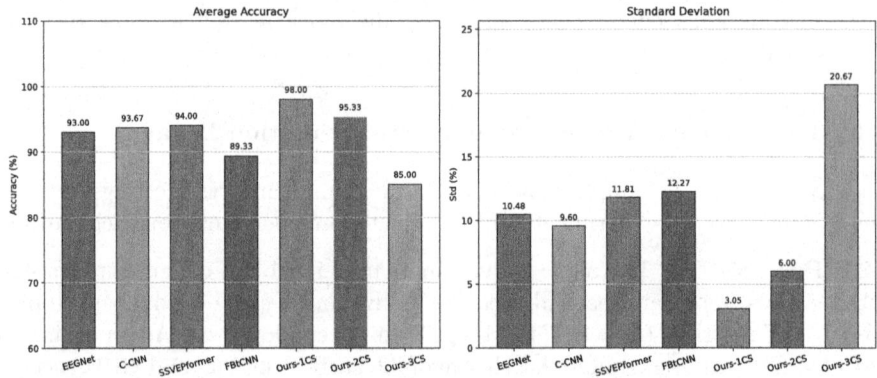

Fig. 5. Comparison of average accuracy and standard deviation of various methods on the 12JFPM_SSVEP dataset across 10 subjects

4.5 Results Analysis on the SSMVEP Dataset

Table 1 presents the classification accuracy and corresponding ITR of each method on the SSMVEP dataset under a 1-second window length. As shown in the results, the proposed Ours-6CS model achieves the best average classification accuracy of 90.98%, along with the highest ITR of 116.3 bits/min. It consistently outperforms other models across multiple subjects, demonstrating strong discriminative power and feature extraction capability for SSMVEP signals even under short time windows.

Although the Ours-6CS model delivers superior performance, its relatively complex architecture, larger number of parameters, and longer inference time pose limitations in practical applications where computational efficiency and real-time processing are critical. In contrast, the Ours-5CS model maintains competitive accuracy (average 90.85%) and ITR (115.9 bits/min), while offering faster inference and lower computational overhead. It also ranks second-best or even best for several subjects (e.g., Sub1, Sub5, Sub6). This balance between accuracy and efficiency makes Ours-5CS more suitable for deployment on edge devices or in real-time BCI systems, offering greater practical application value.

In the table, the highest accuracy or ITR value for each subject is highlighted in **bold**, while the second-best values are marked in dark green for intuitive comparison across subjects.

Table 1. Classification Accuracy (%) and ITR (bits/min) on SSMVEP Dataset (1 s Window)

	CCA	DeepConv-Net	EEGNet	Ours-3CS	Ours-4CS	Ours-5CS	Ours-6CS
Sub1	90.00	62.55	74.04	81.98	93.66	**93.90**	93.75
Sub2	55.00	35.65	61.50	68.27	80.28	81.81	**82.26**
Sub3	83.33	83.71	90.63	98.74	98.57	**99.28**	99.20
Sub4	66.67	56.63	68.41	77.34	89.33	**92.14**	91.19
Sub5	53.33	39.01	58.29	69.41	81.79	83.89	**84.68**
Sub6	66.67	59.66	70.76	75.85	92.36	94.05	**94.81**
Average	69.17	56.20	70.61	78.60	89.33	90.85	**90.98**
ITR	58.7	34.7	61.7	80.3	110.8	115.9	**116.3**

Taking the training process of Sub2 as an example, we conducted a comparative analysis of the performance variations across different networks. As shown in Fig. 6, the proposed model consistently outperformed EEGNet and DeepConvNet on the validation set throughout training, demonstrating faster convergence and superior generalization ability. Notably, in the later stages of training, the proposed method maintained stable accuracy and loss metrics, indicating strong robustness and efficient training dynamics.

4.6 Comparison of ITR Across Different Time Windows

To further evaluate the performance variation of the proposed model under different response times, we tested the Ours-5CS model on the SSMVEP dataset using four time window lengths: 0.5 s, 1 s, 1.5 s, and 2 s. The classification accuracy and corresponding ITR results are shown in Fig. 7.

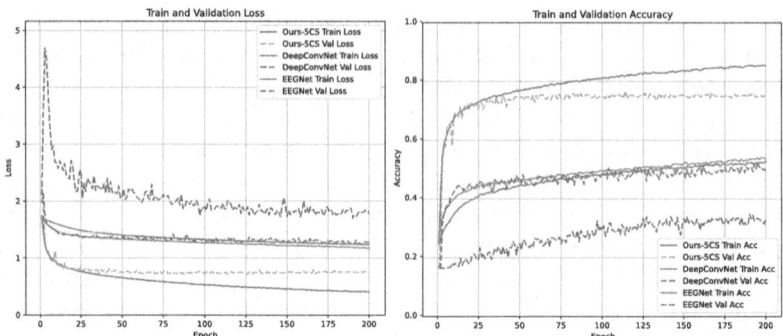

Fig. 6. Comparison of accuracy and loss during training on Sub2 using different networks

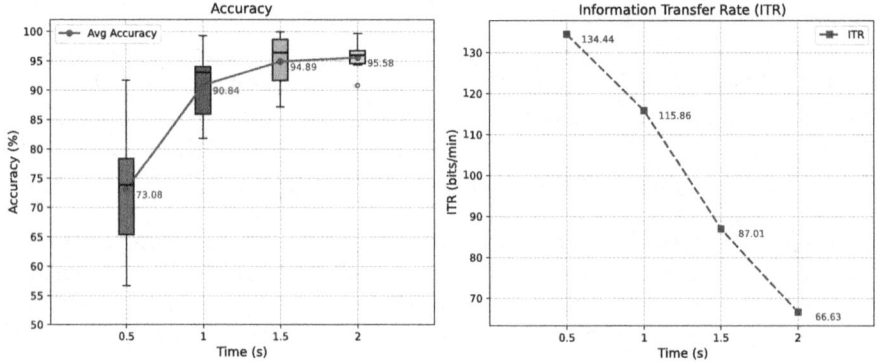

Fig. 7. Comparison of accuracy and ITR for the Ours-5CS model under different time windows

Although the highest ITR (134.44 bits/min) was observed with a time window of 0.5 s, the corresponding classification accuracy was relatively low (73.09%), indicating that the recognition performance was not sufficiently reliable for practical applications. This suggests that while shorter windows offer faster response times, they may not capture enough neural information for robust decoding.

When the time window was extended to 1 s, the accuracy significantly improved to 90.85%, while still maintaining a high ITR of 115.86 bits/min. This setting provides a favorable trade-off between speed and decoding performance, making it particularly suitable for real-time BCI applications where both responsiveness and reliability are crucial.

Further increasing the time window to 1.5 s and 2 s led to even higher accuracies of 94.89% and 95.58%, respectively. However, this improvement came at the cost of a noticeable decline in ITR, dropping to 87.01 and 66.63 bits/min. These results highlight a classic trade-off in BCI system design: longer windows enable more accurate decoding by leveraging more data, but they reduce the system's responsiveness, which may hinder user experience in interactive scenarios.

Overall, the 1-second time window emerges as the optimal choice, offering a practical balance between classification accuracy and communication speed. It ensures sufficient temporal information for reliable SSVEP recognition while keeping the system responsive enough for real-time interaction.

5 Conclusion

This paper proposes a deep adjustable CNN with an SE attention mechanism. Its modular design allows flexible adjustment of convolutional layers, balancing scalability and applicability. Experiments on the 12JFPM_SSVEP and self-collected SSMVEP datasets show superior accuracy, ITR, and robustness compared to state-of-the-art methods, demonstrating strong capability in extracting spatiotemporal EEG features and real-time potential.

Despite promising results, challenges remain in computational complexity and practical deployment. Future work will focus on: (1) optimizing the network to reduce resource use and improve real-time performance on embedded devices; (2) exploring multimodal EEG fusion for better adaptability; (3) applying transfer and self-supervised learning to enhance generalization across subjects and limited data; and (4) expanding applications to a wider range of brain-computer interface tasks. These efforts aim to make the method more practical and versatile for real-world use.

Acknowledgements. This work was supported by the Shenzhen Medical Research Fund (B2302002), the National Natural Science Foundation of China (Grant Nos. 62473359, U23A20344, 62403452), the Guangdong Basic and Applied Basic Research Foundation (2023A1515011321), and the Shenzhen Science and Technology Program (JCYJ20240813155852067).

References

1. Lin, Z., Zhang, C., Wu, W., Gao, X.: Frequency recognition based on canonical correlation analysis for SSVEP-based BCIs. IEEE Trans. Biomed. Eng. **53**(12), 2610–2614 (2006)
2. Zhang, Y., Zhou, G., Jin, J., Wang, M., Wang, X., Cichocki, A.: L1-regularized multiway canonical correlation analysis for SSVEP-based BCI. IEEE Trans. Neural Syst. Rehabil. Eng. **21**(6), 887–896 (2013)
3. Chen, X., Wang, Y., Nakanishi, M., Gao, X., Jung, T.-P., Gao, S.: High-speed spelling with a noninvasive brain–computer interface. Proc. Natl. Acad. Sci. **112**(44) (2015)
4. Nakanishi, M., Wang, Y., Chen, X., Wang, Y.-T., Gao, X., Jung, T.-P.: Enhancing detection of SSVEPs for a high-speed brain speller using task-related component analysis. IEEE Trans. Biomed. Eng. **65**(1), 104–112 (2018)

5. Lawhern, V.J., Solon, A.J., Waytowich, N.R., Gordon, S.M., Hung, C.P., Lance, B.J.: Eegnet: a compact convolutional neural network for EEG-based brain–computer interfaces. J. Neural Eng. 15(5), 056013 (2018)
6. Waytowich, N., et al.: Compact convolutional neural networks for classification of asynchronous steady-state visual evoked potentials. J. Neural Eng. 15(6), 066031 (2018)
7. Zhao, D., Wang, T., Tian, Y., Jiang, X.: Filter bank convolutional neural network for SSVEP classification. IEEE Access 9, 147 129–147 141 (2021)
8. Chen, J., Zhang, Y., Pan, Y., Xu, P., Guan, C.: A transformer-based deep neural network model for SSVEP classification. Neural Netw. 164, 521–534 (2023)
9. Vaswani, A., et al.: Attention is all you need (2017)
10. Wang, Q., Wu, B., Zhu, P., Li, P., Zuo, W., Hu, Q.: ECA-net: efficient channel attention for deep convolutional neural networks. In: 2020 IEEE/CVF Conference on Computer Vision and Pattern Recognition (CVPR), pp. 11 531–11 539 (2020)
11. Eldele, E., et al.: An attention-based deep learning approach for sleep stage classification with single-channel EEG. IEEE Trans. Neural Syst. Rehabil. Eng. 29, 809–818 (2021)
12. Hu, J., Shen, L., Sun, G.: Squeeze-and-excitation networks. In: 2018 IEEE/CVF Conference on Computer Vision and Pattern Recognition, pp. 7132–7141 (2018)
13. Li, M., Zheng, Y., Li, D., Wu, Y., Wang, Y., Fei, H.: MS-senet: enhancing speech emotion recognition through multi-scale feature fusion with squeeze-and-excitation blocks (2023)
14. Nakanishi, M., Wang, Y., Wang, Y.-T., Jung, T.-P.: A comparison study of canonical correlation analysis based methods for detecting steady-state visual evoked potentials. PLoS ONE 10(10), e0140703 (2015)

Multimodal Assessment of Visual-Motor Integration in Attention Deficit/Hyperactivity Disorder

Huan Wen[1,3], Mengyi Bao[4], Yucun Zhong[1,3], Haifeng Li[4], Lin Yao[1,2,3,5]([✉]), and Yueming Wang[2,3]

[1] MOE Frontiers Science Center for Brain and Brain-Machine Integration, Zhejiang University, Hangzhou 310058, China
lin.yao@zju.edu.cn
[2] The Nanhu Brain-Computer Interface Institute, Hangzhou 310027, China
[3] College of Computer Science and Technology, Zhejiang University, Hangzhou 310027, China
[4] Children's Hospital of Zhejiang University School of Medicine, Hangzhou 310051, China
[5] The Department of Neurobiology, Affiliated Mental Health Center and Hangzhou Seventh People's Hospital, Zhejiang University School of Medicine, Hangzhou 310029, China

Abstract. Attention Deficit/Hyperactivity Disorder (ADHD) is a prevalent neurodevelopmental condition that often leads to impairments in visual-motor integration (VMI), a function critical for the successful execution of many everyday tasks. Identifying and quantifying the differences in VMI performance between children with ADHD and their typically developing (TD) peers can contribute to a better understanding of the underlying neural mechanisms and support the development of objective assessment tools. Based on this motivation, we conducted an experiment involving 13 children with ADHD and 12 TD children who were asked to perform a static grip force control task in this study. Simultaneously recorded eye gaze and grip force were analyzed to assess their VMI abilities. The analysis revealed more obvious synchronization between eye gaze and grip force in the TD group compared to the ADHD group. Specifically, children with ADHD demonstrated greater variability in both eye gaze and grip force control. These findings suggest that the analysis of multimodal physiological data may offer a reliable method for evaluating the visual-motor integration abilities of children with ADHD.

Keywords: ADHD · visual-motor integration · eye gaze

1 Introduction

Attention Deficit/Hyperactivity Disorder is a common neurodevelopmental disorder, affecting approximately 5% of school-age children [10]. It is characterized by persistent inattention, hyperactivity, and impulsivity, which impair cognitive, emotional, and motor functions [11]. Among these challenges, visual-motor integration deficits are particularly critical, affecting everyday tasks such as reading, writing, and sports [2,9].

Mechanically, ADHD-related VMI impairments involve deficits in the integration of visual attention and motor control, with disruptions in neural circuits such as the frontoparietal [6] and corticospinal tracts [4]. Besides, children with ADHD also show more difficulties in force control tasks [9], weaker handwriting legibility [2], and lower precision in tasks such as table tennis [8], highlighting specific VMI impairments at both the neural and behavioral levels.

Visual-motor integration deficits in ADHD are widely recognized, whereas current assessments remain limited and lack comprehensive neurophysiological information. One promising method for assessing VMI abilities is the isometric grip force tracking paradigm. This force control task, commonly applied in both clinical and healthy groups, requires participants to align their force output with a visual target [5,13,14]. In the study [7], dynamic and static grip force tasks have been applied to evaluate the precision of force tracking in children with motor impairment via relative root mean square error (rRMSE).

However, visual-motor integration tasks are inherently complex, requiring the integration of visual input and motor output to achieve accurate movements [1]. Previous studies merely focused on behavioral motor output but ignored the neurophysiological features, which could reveal the neural basis of ADHD-related VMI deficits. The existing technological methods allow researchers to acquire various types of physiological data. For instance, eye-tracking data capture visual attention and fixation patterns, revealing how individuals process visual targets [12]. Meanwhile, grip force data quantify motor output precision and control [7,13]. Overall, eye-tracking data along with grip force offer insights into the peripheral mechanism of children with ADHD.

Under this circumstance, this study aims to explore the feasibility of using multimodal physiological data to assess and compare VMI abilities in ADHD and TD groups. By analyzing simultaneously recorded eye gaze data and grip force measurements during a static grip force task, this methodological enhancement enables a more comprehensive evaluation of the neural basis of their motor control deficits in ADHD.

2 Materials and Methods

2.1 Participants

Thirteen 6 to 10-year-old children with ADHD diagnosed by DSM-IV criteria (mean age = 8.59 ± 1.25 yrs, 2 girls) and twelve 6 to 11-year-old TD children (mean age = 8.38 ± 1.86 yrs, 7 girls) were recruited. Due to both recruitment limitations and the higher prevalence of ADHD in males, there was an imbalance in sex distribution within the ADHD group. This issue will be addressed in future studies through more balanced sampling strategies. The study was approved by the Medical Ethics Committee of Children's Hospital of Zhejiang University School of Medicine (approval number: 2022-IRB-0299-P-02).

2.2 Force Control Paradigm

The static grip force paradigm has been previously used in studies involving children with motor impairments, and it can provide valuable insights into their VMI abilities, reflecting their capacity for sustained force production and motor coordination [7,13]. For this reason, children were required to perform the similar force control task using the right forearm at different levels of their maximal isometric voluntary contraction (MVC) in this study. After a warm-up set, participants need to match their force output (a black dot) to a visual target (the red line) during the experimental task by executing three isometric voluntary contractions for 15 s at 10%, 20%, and 30% of their MVC, respectively. Only the 30% MVC task was included in the subsequent analysis, as the 10% and 20% MVC trials in the ADHD group were markedly reduced following data preprocessing and the exclusion of artifact-contaminated segments, resulting in an insufficient number of usable trials for valid group comparisons. Each trial involved a 3-second rest before and after the contraction. The illustration of the force control paradigm and the three levels of isometric voluntary contractions was shown in Fig. 1.

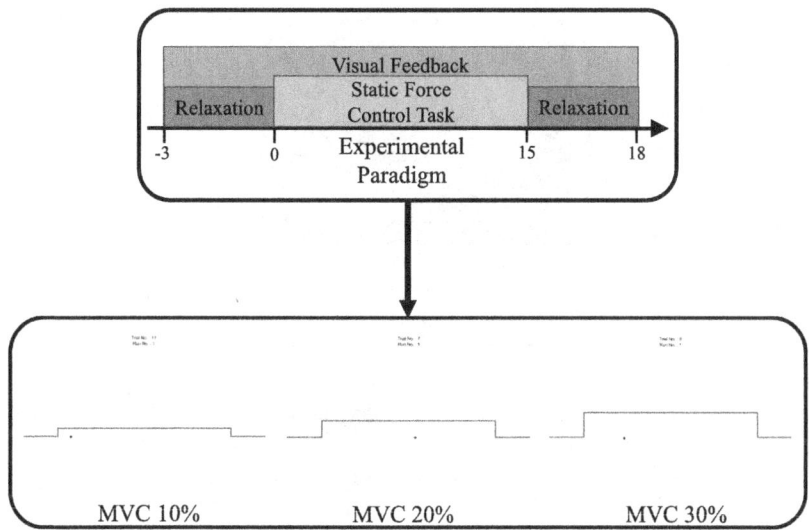

Fig. 1. Graphic illustration of static force control paradigm.

2.3 Data Acquisition and Preprocessing

In this study, eye gaze and grip force data collected by the force sensor were recorded simultaneously to investigate the relationship between visual attention and motor output. Figure 2 illustrates the overall data acquisition and processing pipeline. Specifically, it encompasses synchronized data collection, signal preprocessing, feature extraction, and statistical analysis procedures, providing a comprehensive overview of the methodological workflow.

1) Eye Gaze Behavior: Eye gaze behavior was recorded by a Tobii Pro Spectrum 300 eye tracker (Tobii, Stockholm, Sweden). This dataset consists of binocular eye-tracking data and pupil diameters at a sample rate of 300 Hz, and the average viewing distance was 65 cm with an accuracy of $1.0°$. The paradigm was displayed in full-screen mode on a 23.8-inch monitor (resolution: 1920 × 1080 pixels, refresh rate: 60 Hz). The pipeline for preprocessing raw eye gaze data included combining the left and right eye data, interpolation, and smoothing. In addition, pupil diameter data were smoothed and normalized.

2) Grip Force: This measurement was collected through a customized grip force sensor (measurement range: 0–500 N; data acquired via NI USB-6009 DAQ; analog signals were digitized and transmitted to a computer), and the sample rate was 5000 Hz. After acquisition, the raw data were notch filtered to remove 50 Hz and its harmonics and subsequently downsampled to 300 Hz. All participants were instructed to hold the grip force sensor with their right hand throughout the task to ensure consistency in motor data across subjects.

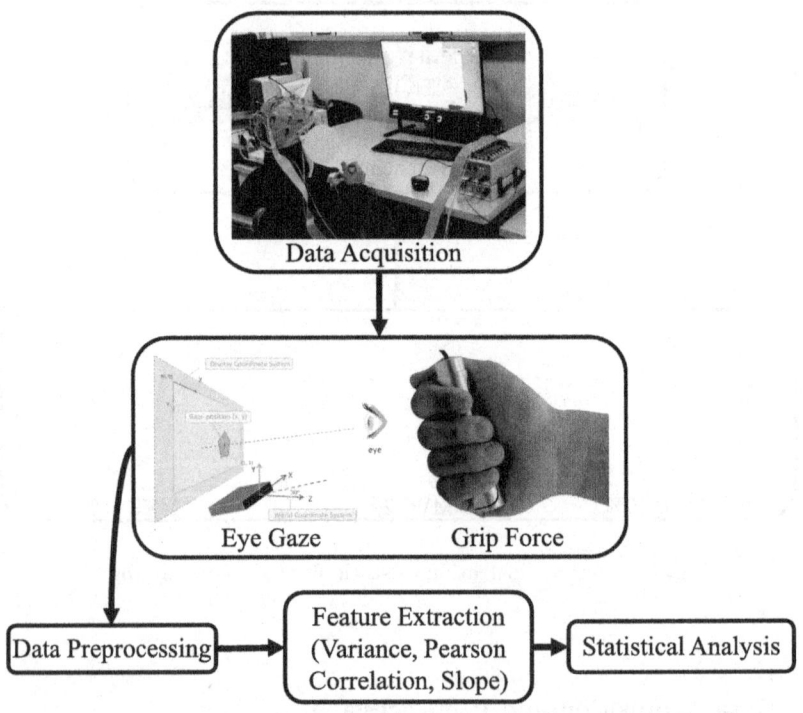

Fig. 2. Graphic illustration of analysis pipeline.

2.4 Feature Extraction

According to previous research, children with ADHD often exhibit difficulties in maintaining focus, sustaining attention, and inhibiting impulsive behaviors [11]. These impairments may manifest as irregular eye movement patterns and unstable motor control. In contrast, typically developing children tend to show more consistent vertical eye movements and steadier grip force control, reflecting superior visual attention and motor regulation abilities [3,12].

Based on these observations, this study aimed to investigate group differences by examining the variances in the grip force data and Y-coordinate of eye gaze, fixation time, pupil diameter, and the slope of the X-coordinate eye gaze over time, which may serve as physiological indicators distinguishing between two groups. In particular, the slope of the X-coordinate of eye gaze over time was calculated to assess whether participants' gaze followed the horizontal movement of the visual target. A positive slope indicated that the gaze trajectory shifted in the same direction as the moving stimulus, suggesting active visual tracking behavior. Meanwhile, fixation time and pupil diameter were included as supplementary indicators of attention, both of which were computed using the preprocessing scripts provided by the Tobii software suite. Longer fixation durations may reflect sustained cognitive engagement and attentional effort, providing further insight into attentional differences between groups.

Besides, the correlation between the Y-coordinate of eye gaze and grip force data may indicate the relationship between visual attention and body response, which would be utilized to distinguish the visual-motor integration of ADHD and TD. To quantify this relationship, the Pearson correlation coefficient of these two time series was calculated, as it effectively captures the linear association between continuous variables such as eye movement and grip force signals.

To study the differences between two groups, the definition of the variances, the slope, and correlation of the Y-coordinate of eye gaze data and grip force data were as follows:

$$Var = var(D_A) \tag{1}$$

$$slope = fit(D_{eye_{X-axis}}, time) \tag{2}$$

$$Corr = corr(D_{eye}, D_{force}) \tag{3}$$

where D_A refers to data from the Y-coordinate of eye gaze or grip force. $D_{eye_{X-axis}}$ refers to the X-coordinate of eye gaze, and Eq. 2 refers to the slope of the horizontal gaze position over time which is obtained by performing a first-order linear fit using MATLAB R2022b *polyfit* function. D_{eye} and D_{force} refer to the Y-coordinate of eye gaze and the grip force data respectively. *var* and *corr* refer to the calculation of the variance and pearson correlation separately.

2.5 Statistical Analysis

Prior to conducting statistical comparisons, all variables were tested for normality using the Shapiro-Wilk test. The results indicated that the data violated the assumption of normal distribution. Therefore, non-parametric analyses were applied. Specifically, the Mann-Whitney U test was used to assess group differences between children with ADHD and TD. The following variables mentioned above were compared between the two groups: (1) variance of grip force, (2) variance in the Y-coordinate of eye movements, (3) fixation time, (4) pupil diameter, (5) the slope of the X-coordinate eye gaze over time, and (6) the correlation between grip force trajectory and eye movement coordinates. All statistical tests were two-tailed with a significance threshold set at $p < 0.05$.

3 Results and Discussion

3.1 Eye Gaze and Grip Force

To investigate a comparative overview of motor output and visual tracking behavior between the two groups, the preprocessed eye gaze data and grip force data are mapped into the same coordinate.

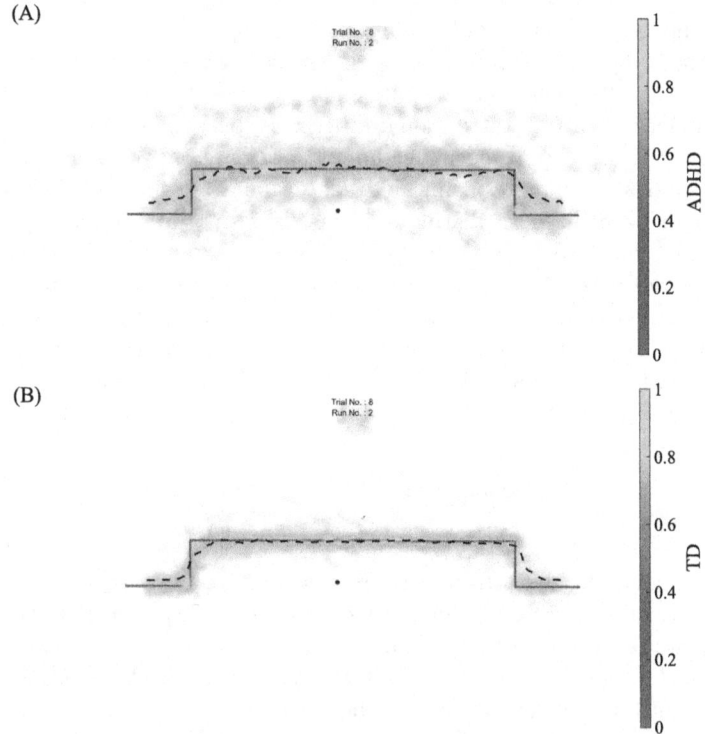

Fig. 3. Combined plot of the reference grip force trajectory, the actual grip force curve, and the preprocessed eye gaze from ADHD (A) and TD (B).

Figure 3 presents the combination figure of the reference grip force trajectory, the actual grip force curve, and the preprocessed eye gaze. The actual grip force

Multimodal Assessment of Visual-Motor Integration in ADHD 369

trajectory is obtained by averaging across all trials and participants within each group. For the eye gaze data, the number of gaze points falling within each vertical screen position is accumulated across all participants and trials, followed by normalization to a 0–1 range. The eye gaze data and actual grip force trajectory from the ADHD group (Fig. 3 (A)) are visibly more variable than those from the participant from TD (Fig. 3(B)). The relationship between eye gaze behaviors and grip force trajectories will be further examined in the following section.

3.2 Statistical Analysis in Multimodal Data

Note that during the motor execution period, there are significant differences in the variance of the actual grip force (Fig. 4(A)) and the Y-axis from the eye gaze data (Fig. 4(B)) between the ADHD and TD groups. Specifically, the ADHD group displays greater fluctuations in both eye gaze trajectory ($p = 0.0240$) and grip force data ($p = 0.0208$) significantly, suggesting more variability and potentially indicating less stable motor control compared to the TD group. These differences are particularly noticeable during certain phases of the motor task, such as force tapping, where the TD group exhibited more consistent and controlled movements [3].

However, when examining fixation time (Fig. 4(C)), pupil diameter (Fig. 4(D)), the slope of the X-coordinate eye gaze over time (Fig. 4(E)), and the correlation between eye gaze trajectory and grip force data (Fig. 4(F)), no statistically significant differences were observed between the ADHD and TD groups. Nevertheless, some observable trends emerged that may reflect underlying group differences. For instance, children in the TD group tended to exhibit slightly longer fixation durations (ADHD: 11.72 s ± 0.19, TD: 11.78 s ± 0.28) and more stable pupil diameters (ADHD: 3.14 ± 0.14, TD: 3.07 ± 0.08), which may suggest more sustained attention and cognitive engagement during the task. Similarly, the slope of the X-coordinate eye gaze over time in the TD group was generally more positive, indicating a more consistent tracking of the horizontally moving visual stimulus (ADHD: 0.14 ± 0.0035, TD: 0.147 ± 0.08). Additionally, the TD group showed marginally higher Pearson correlation coefficients between gaze and grip force signals, implying tighter visual-motor coordination (ADHD: 0.58 ± 0.0037, TD: 0.65 ± 0.029). Taken together, the above neurophysiological or their combined features allow for a preliminary differentiation between children with ADHD and TD as well as potential applications in clinical evaluation and intervention.

4 Conclusion and Future Work

This study explored the feasibility of evaluating the visual-motor integration abilities of children with ADHD using multimodal physiological data, including eye gaze behavior and grip force measurements. The comparison demonstrated that children with ADHD exhibited greater variability in both eye movement and grip force signals compared to typically developing children. These findings

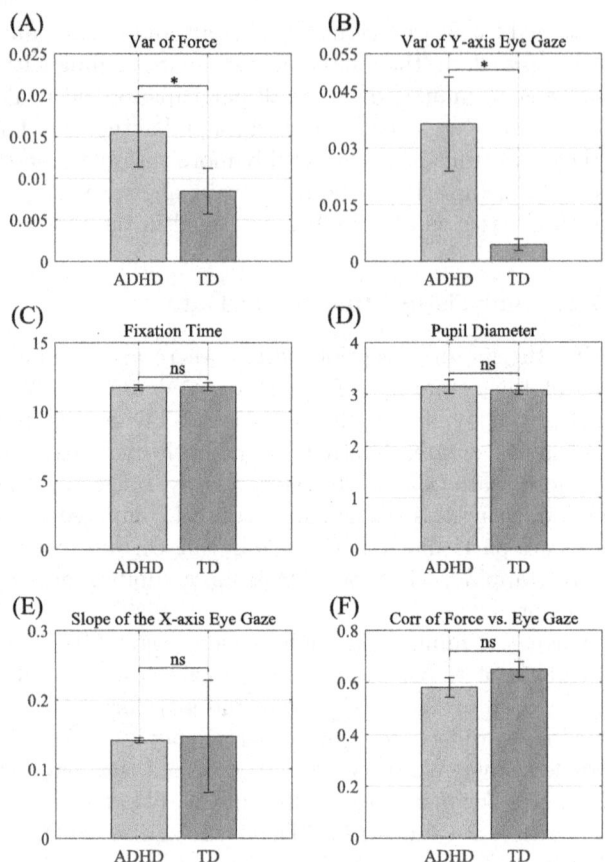

Fig. 4. Comparison between ADHD and TD in terms of the variance of the actual grip force (A) and the Y-axis from the eye gaze data (B), fixation time (C), pupil diameter (D), the slope of the X-axis eye gaze over time (E), and the correlation between the eye gaze trajectory and the actual grip force (F).

suggest that children with ADHD have less stable visual attention and reduced consistency in motor output, indicating impairments in visual-motor integration compared to their TD peers. Furthermore, the extracted features, such as gaze variance, fixation time, pupil diameter, grip force variability, and the correlation between eye movements and motor responses, provided a multifaceted perspective for analyzing and assessing the VMI abilities of children with ADHD. These indicators offer valuable insights into the underlying deficits in attention regulation and sensorimotor coordination. Nevertheless, it is also worth noting that the grip force paradigm employed in this study is relatively simple, serving as a preliminary step towards multimodal VMI assessment. Future studies will consider incorporating more complex experimental paradigms, such as dynamic or interactive grip tasks, and will aim to recruit a larger and more diverse sample population. These improvements are expected to enhance the ecological validity, generalizability, and robustness of the findings, paving the way for the development of an objective data-driven tool for the assessment of ADHD.

Acknowledgments. We thank all volunteers for their participation in the study. This work was supported in part by STI 2030—Major Projects under Grant 2021ZD0200400, in part by the National Natural Science Foundation of China under Grant 62336007, in part by the Key Research and Development Program of Zhejiang under Grant 2023C03003, in part by the Starry Night Science Fund of Zhejiang University Shanghai Institute for Advanced Study under Grant SN-ZJU-SIAS-002, in part by the Fundamental Research Funds for the Central Universities, in part by Zju-GenSci Children's Health Research and Development Center under Grant ZJU-GENSCI2024YB003, in part by the Technological Research Program of Zhejiang under Grant LBY21H170002, in part by the Project in Zhejiang's Provincial Key Disciplines (Traditional Chinese Medicine) under Grant 2024-XK-48, in part by the Project for Hangzhou Medical Disciplines of Excellence, and in part by the Key Project for Hangzhou Medical Disciplines.

Disclosure of Interests. The authors declare that there is no conflict of interest regarding the publication of this article. Submitting authors are responsible for coauthors declaring their interests.

References

1. Fabio, R.A., Andricciola, F., Caprì, T.: Visual-motor attention in children with ADHD: the role of automatic and controlled processes. Res. Dev. Disabil. **123**, 104193 (2022)
2. Farhangnia, S., Hassanzadeh, R., Ghorbani, S.: Handwriting performance of children with attention deficit hyperactivity disorder: the role of visual-motor integration. Int. J. Pediatr. (2020)
3. Hotham, E., Haberfield, M., Hillier, S., White, J.M., Todd, G.: Upper limb function in children with attention-deficit/hyperactivity disorder (ADHD). J. Neural Transm. **125**(4), 713–726 (2018)
4. Hyde, C., Fuelscher, I., Sciberras, E., Efron, D., Anderson, V.A., Silk, T.: Understanding motor difficulties in children with ADHD: a fixel-based analysis of the corticospinal tract. Prog. Neuropsychopharmacol. Biol. Psychiatry **105**, 110125 (2021)
5. Kurillo, G., Bajd, B.: Grip force control in healthy children and children with down syndrome. In: EUROCON 2005 - The International Conference on "Computer as a Tool", vol. 1, pp. 390–393 (2005)
6. Leisman, G., Melillo, R.: Front and center: maturational dysregulation of frontal lobe functional neuroanatomic connections in attention deficit hyperactivity disorder. Front. Neuroanat. **16**, 936025 (2022)
7. Lidstone, D.E., Miah, F.Z., Poston, B., Beasley, J.F., Mostofsky, S.H., Dufek, J.S.: Children with autism spectrum disorder show impairments during dynamic versus static grip-force tracking. Autism Res. **13**(12), 2177–2189 (2020)
8. Perochon, S., et al.: A tablet-based game for the assessment of visual motor skills in autistic children. NPJ Digit. Med. **6**(1), 17 (2023)

9. Pitcher, T.M., Piek, J.P., Barrett, N.C.: Timing and force control in boys with attention deficit hyperactivity disorder: subtype differences and the effect of comorbid developmental coordination disorder. Hum. Mov. Sci. **21**(5–6), 919–945 (2002)
10. Polanczyk, G.V., Willcutt, E.G., Salum, G.A., Kieling, C., Rohde, L.A.: ADHD prevalence estimates across three decades: an updated systematic review and meta-regression analysis. Int. J. Epidemiol. **43**(2), 434–442 (2014)
11. Shiels, K., Hawk, L.W.: Self-regulation in ADHD: the role of error processing. Clin. Psychol. Rev. **30**(8), 951–961 (2010)
12. Sotoodeh, M.S., Chien, S.H., Hadjikhani, N.: Visual attention modulates mu suppression during biological motion perception in autistic individuals. Eur. J. Neurosci. ejn.16596 (2024)
13. Svendsen, J.H., Samani, A., Mayntzhusen, K., Madeleine, P.: Muscle coordination and force variability during static and dynamic tracking tasks. Hum. Mov. Sci. **30**(6), 1039–1051 (2011)
14. Zhang, Z., et al.: Quantitative identification of ADHD tendency in children with immersive fingertip force control tasks. IEEE Trans. Neural Syst. Rehabil. Eng. **31**, 4561–4569 (2023)

Comparison of Propagation and Activation Characteristics of Motor Units Decomposed from Wrist and Forearm Surface Electromyography Signals

Lingyan Tian and Chen Chen(✉)

State Key Laboratory of Mechanical System and Vibration, School of Mechanical Engineering, Shanghai Jiao Tong University, Shanghai 200240, China
cedric_chen@sjtu.edu.cn

Abstract. Neural interfaces based on surface electromyography (sEMG) represent an important non-invasive approach for human-computer interaction. While most current interfaces based on sEMG focus on the forearm, the wrist may be a more suitable location for practical use. This study investigates the feasibility of wrist neural interfaces by comparing the propagation and activation characteristics of motor units (MUs) decomposed from forearm and wrist signals. First, the presence of MU propagation trends was determined by assessing wrist activation and innervation zone distribution. Second, the center of gravity of MU was calculated, and activation area was quantified to compare associations and differences between wrist and forearm signals. Experimental results indicate that MUs exhibiting propagation trends account for $61.9 \pm 8.7\%$ (wrist) and $59.0 \pm 10.4\%$ (forearm), $58.6 \pm 8.3\%$ (wrist) and $64.6 \pm 9.4\%$ (forearm) at two force levels, indicating forearm signals can propagate to the wrist via muscle fibers. Furthermore, MUs decomposed from wrist and forearm signals exhibit similar physiological behaviors and activation characteristics. These findings expand potential applications for wrist neural interfaces and wearable devices.

Keywords: Surface electromyography · wrist · forearm · motor unit · human-computer interaction

1 Introduction

Surface electromyography (sEMG) is an important non-invasive method for human-computer interaction [1], widely implemented in prostheses and other wearable devices based on forearm signals. With increasing demand for seamless and natural human-computer interfaces, the wrist may be more suitable for practical applications due to its higher user acceptance [2].

C. Chen—This work was supported by the National Natural Science Foundation of China under Grant 52205024

Recent studies have confirmed that wrist sEMG signals reflect neuromuscular activity and have further explored the feasibility of developing neural interfaces based on wrist sEMG [3, 4]. For instance, *Mendez et al.* [3] assessed the reliability of a far-field potential-based interface for motor neuron (MN) discharge estimation and used decoded MN activity to predict finger movements. It has been demonstrated that high accuracy can be attained in the classification of wrist and finger movements based on wrist sEMG signals [4, 5]. In addition, cross-day signal stability [6] and generalizability across subjects [7] have been validated, providing foundational support for wrist-worn interfaces.

Despite advances in exploring the feasibility of wrist-based interfaces, fundamental questions regarding the formation of wrist sEMG signals remain unresolved. Current studies primarily focus on signal stability metrics or pattern recognition results while neglecting electrophysiological connections between sEMG signals of wrist and forearm. By leveraging high-density surface electromyography (HD-sEMG) with high signal transmission rates and spatial resolution [8, 9], along with surface EMG decomposition techniques capable of identifying motor unit (MU) action potential trains [10], it is feasible to explore the relationship between far-field potentials and motor neuron discharges [3], as well as to investigate the correlation between motor unit activities recorded at the wrist and forearm [11]. However, studies on the mechanisms of sEMG signal propagation, as well as the physiological properties and activation characteristics of motor units at different sensing area, remains relatively limited. This gap hinders the development of wrist-based neural interfaces for clinical or commercial applications.

We systematically compare the propagation and activation characteristics of MUs decoded from wrist and forearm sEMG signals during grasping and finger movements. By analyzing the spatial distribution of MU activation zones and their physiological properties, we aim to investigate the feasibility of wrist neural interfaces.

2 Methods

2.1 Subject

Two healthy subjects (2 males; all right-handed; age: 19.6 ± 0.2 years) participated in this experiment. Both subjects had no history of neuromuscular disorders and provided written informed consent. The experimental protocol adhered to the Declaration of Helsinki and was approved by the local ethics committee (No. E20240248I).

2.2 Experimental Setup

HD-sEMG signals were recorded from the extensor and flexor muscles of the dominant arm using four grids of 64 equally spaced electrodes (8 × 8 array; inter-electrode distance: 10 mm; OT Bioelettronica, Italy). Two electrodes were placed below the ulnar styloid process on the extensor and flexor sides. Before the electrode placement, the skin was cleaned with alcohol. Signals were recorded in monopolar mode using a multichannel acquisition system (EMG-Quattrocento, OT Bioelettronica), with bandpass filtering (10–4400 Hz) and digitization at 2048 Hz. Force measurements were obtained using a hand grip dynamometer (G200, Biometrics Ltd, UK) for the first four grasping tasks and a pinchmeter (P200, Biometrics Ltd, UK) for the remaining tasks (Fig. 1).

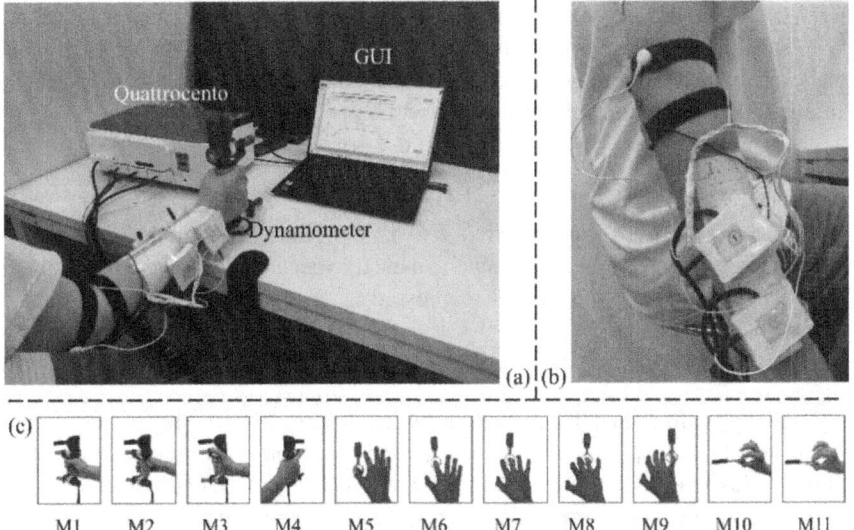

Fig. 1. Experimental setup and paradigm for surface electromyography (sEMG) recording. (a)(b) Setup for data acquisition; (c) 11 activities including cylindrical grasp, lumbrical grasp, oblique palmar grasp, intermediate power-precision grasp, individual finger press, two-finger pad-to-pad pinch, and three-finger pad-to-pad pinch.

2.3 Experimental Protocol

Subjects were positioned facing a laptop screen, with the right elbow supported on an armrest. They performed 11 daily activities with their dominant arm: cylindrical grasp, lumbrical grasp, oblique palmar grasp, intermediate power-precision grasp, individual finger press, two-finger pad-to-pad pinch, and three-finger pad-to-pad pinch (labeled M1–M11). Before the experiment, each task was explained in detail, and maximum voluntary contraction (MVC) force was measured. During each task, subjects followed a trapezoidal visual cue (2 s rest, 2 s ramp-up, 10 s steady contraction, 2 s ramp-down, 2 s rest) at two intensity levels (15% MVC and 30% MVC). Each task included three repetitions.

2.4 Data Analysis

sEMG Preprocessing. A 4th-order Butterworth bandpass filter (20–500 Hz) and a comb filter (50 Hz cutoff) were applied. Channels exhibiting excessive noise were excluded where the root mean square (RMS) of sEMG signals exceeded the average ± 3 standard deviations.

sEMG Decomposition. Preprocessed signals were decomposed into motor unit spike trains (MUSTs) using the Convolution Kernel Compensation (CKC) algorithm [12, 13]. The generative model of multi-channel EMG signals was formulated as a convolutive mixture of a series of impulses [13, 14]. The mixing process in matrix form can be described as:

$$y(n) = H\bar{t}(n) + w(n) \quad (1)$$

where $\bar{y}(n) = [y_1(n), \ldots, y_M(n)]^T$ is the surface electromyography signals of M channels, n is the discrete time as the sampling point, $\bar{t}(n)$ is the extended vector of n source signals, and H is the mixing matrix. The CKC method compensates the mixing matrix H in Eq. 1, estimating the pulse train of the jth motor unit as follows:

$$\hat{t}_j(n) = c_{tjy}^T C_{yy}^{-1} y(n) \tag{2}$$

where $C_{yy} = E(y(n)y^T(n))$ is the correlation matrix of the EMG signal, C_{tjy}^T is the cross-correlation vector, where $E(\cdot)$ is the mathematical expectation. Suppose the estimation of the pulse train $w_j = C_{yy}^{-1} c_{tjy}$ can be expressed as:

$$\hat{t}_j(n) = w_j^T y(n) \tag{3}$$

MUSTs were discarded if their average discharge rate (DR, ratio between spike count of a MU and its active period measured in seconds) calculated over the interval between the first and last discharge timings was <5 Hz or >35 Hz, or if the coefficient of variation [17] (CoV, ratio between the standard deviation of interspike intervals to their average value) during steady contraction exceeded 1.

MUAP Extraction. MU action potentials (MUAP) waveforms (16 × 8 channels) were extracted via spike-triggered averaging (STA) [15]. For each channel, signals within a 50 ms window centered on MU discharge times were averaged.

2.5 Physiological Analysis

The number of MUs, pulse-to-noise ratio [16] (PNR, mean of the detected spiking activity divided by the mean baseline of the estimated source expressed in dB), CoV of the inter spike intervals, and DR of MUs were calculated for wrist and forearm signals. Statistical analyses were performed to compare physiological properties. After conducting normality tests on the results, independent t-tests and Mann-Whitney U tests were respectively applied for significance testing of normally and non-normally distributed data ($p < 0.05$).

2.6 Analysis of Activation and Propagation Characteristics

Analysis of Propagation Characteristics. To compare the information of wrist and forearm signals, we analyzed the propagation characteristics of MUs. Firstly, based on the MUAPs derived from decomposition results at different sensing locations, effective channels on the extensor and flexor sides were identified, and further it is determined whether there are activated areas in the wrist. The innervation zone (IZ) positions on both sides were localized, and MUs with valid channels in the wrist and an IZ in the forearm were classified as having a propagation trend. Statistical analyses were performed on these propagating MUs.

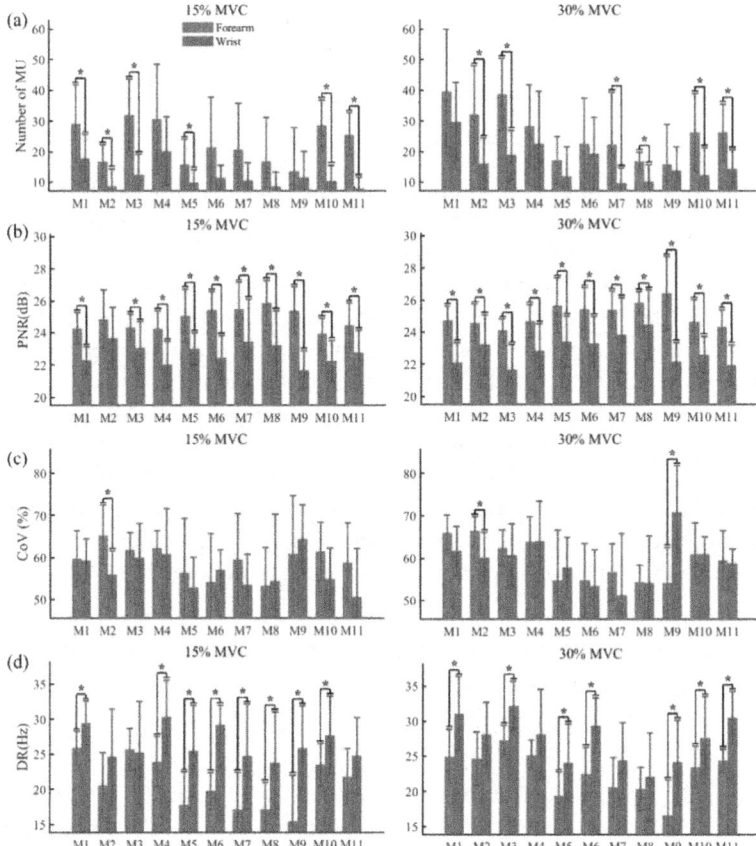

Fig. 2. Physiological analysis of the decoded motor units from the wrist and forearm for 15% and 30% force levels. (a)(b)(c)(d) respectively show the number of MUs, pulse-to-noise ratio (PNR, dB), coefficient of variation (CoV, %), and discharge rate (DR, Hz) decomposed from wrist and forearm signals under different movements at two force levels.

For the MUAP waveform recorded at each electrode, the baseline noise was defined as the standard deviation of the first 15 ms and last 15 ms in the spike-triggered averaging interval. A channel was deemed effective if its MUAP peak amplitude exceeded four times the baseline noise [18]. Wrist activation was confirmed if at least one effective channel was present in each of the four rows of wrist electrodes.

The IZ reflects the region where motor neurons innervate muscle fibers and marks the initiation position of MUAPs [19]. The IZ localization procedure was as follows: Based on the decomposition results of wrist and forearm signals, MUAPs from all 16 × 8 channels were obtained. The peak-to-peak value (PPV) of effective channels were normalized by dividing them by the maximum PPV. Channels with normalized amplitudes > 0.2 were retained; otherwise, the MU was marked as invalid. For columns with at least four consecutive effective channels, the lagged cross-correlation between adjacent rows in the bipolar MUAP was calculated using the formula:

$$R(k, \tau) = \frac{1/N \sum_{i=1}^{N}(x_{k,i} - \bar{x}_k) \times (x_{k+1,i+\tau} - \bar{x}_{k+1})}{1/N \sqrt{\sum_{i=1}^{N}(x_{k,i} - \bar{x}_k)^2 \times \sum_{i=1}^{N}(x_{k+1,i} - \bar{x}_{k+1})^2}} \quad (4)$$

where $R(k, \tau)$ is the lagging cross-correlation value with τ phase shift in the kth pair of data, $x_{i,k}$ is the ith data point in the kth pair of data, N is the number of data points, and τ is the time phase shift between two adjacent signals. The maximum lagged cross-correlation vector was formed by retaining the signed maximum amplitudes from each valid column. The IZ position was identified as the channel number corresponding to the minimum lag between two adjacent peaks in this vector. If no peaks were detected, the channel with the minimum lag was selected. To avoid misclassification of noised channels, the correlation coefficient between the monopolar MUAP and its adjacent channels was required to exceed 0.9[20]. In this study, if the monopolar MUAP at the IZ position meets the correlation condition with any adjacent channel in the column, it is considered to be an effective identification. The final IZ position was calculated as the weighted average of coordinates using the normalized PPV of the identified IZ channels. If there are no valid columns, the channel with the highest normalized PPV is assigned as the IZ.

Analysis of Activation Characteristics. To compare the MU composition between wrist and forearm signals, we first calculated the center of gravity (CoG) of multi-channel MUAPs and analyzed MU activation patterns using the estimated activation area.

Compared to the surface EMG centroid, the MUAP CoG provides a more stable evaluation of MU activation zones [21]. The CoG calculation steps were: An activation map of MUAPs was constructed based on normalized PPV. Faulty channels were replaced via linear interpolation using their 8-neighboring electrodes [22]. Channels with PPV exceeding 80% of the maximum value were selected, and the CoG was calculated using a weighted average method.

The activation area, an effective indicator of spatial MU activation patterns [23], was defined in this study as regions where normalized PPV in effective channels exceeded the average value of all effective channels. Prior to calculation, faulty channels were interpolated. Activation boundaries were determined by fitting an ellipse [24] to the boundary points using an ellipse detection method, with the major and minor axes respectively constrained to 16 cm and 1 cm. The ellipse area was used to quantify the MU activation area. The specific fitting process was: All point pairs were iterated to form candidate major axis endpoints. Ellipse parameters including center coordinates were calculated for each pair. For each third point, the minor axis length was calculated, and the points were filtered based on predefined major/minor axis limits. The optimal minor axis length was determined using a 1D accumulator. The ellipse area was derived as the estimated MU activation area.

3 Results

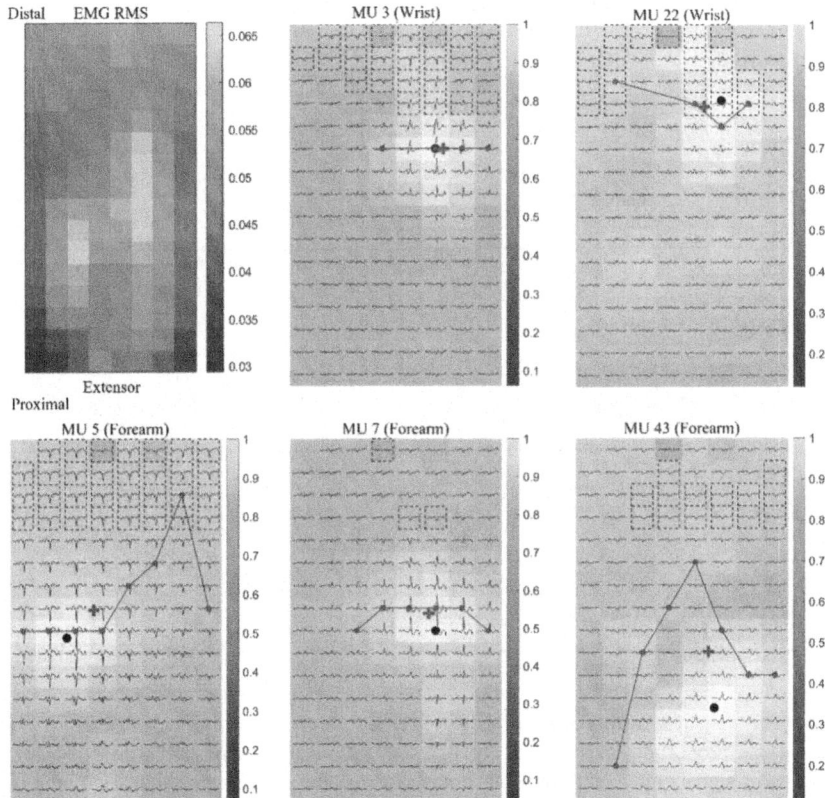

Fig. 3. Spatial distribution of EMG signal RMS values and normalized MUAP PPV. The black dots indicate the position of the center of gravity and the dashed box marks the activation channels in the wrist. Red dots represent the IZ positions calculated based on valid columns, while red crosses denote the IZ positions obtained through weighted averaging. Missing MUAP waveforms resulted from channel removal during sEMG signal preprocessing.

Figure 2 displays the physiological indices derived from the decomposition of wrist and forearm sEMG signals. A certain number of MUs were successfully decomposed for each movement task. Across all tasks and both force levels, the PNR was 24.9 ± 0.6 dB and 25.1 ± 0.7 dB for forearm signals, with CoV of 59.4 ± 3.6% and 59.5 ± 4.8%. For wrist signals, the PNR was 22.7 ± 0.6 dB and 22.9 ± 0.9 dB, with CoV of 56.7 ± 4.0% and 59.5 ± 5.4%. The DR of MUs from both wrist and forearm signals ranged between 5–35 Hz, consistent with the physiological behavior of motor units. Statistical analysis revealed significantly higher PNR values for forearm signals across different tasks, while MU discharge rates derived from wrist signals were significantly higher.

Figure 3 shows the root mean square (RMS) activation map of sEMG signals for one subject performing task M1 at 15% MVC, along with examples of MUAPs derived from wrist and forearm signal decomposition that exhibit or lack propagation trend. MUs were considered to exhibit propagation characteristics if the IZ position was located on the forearm and an activation area was present at the wrist. MU3 from wrist signal and MU5 from forearm signal exhibit propagation trend.

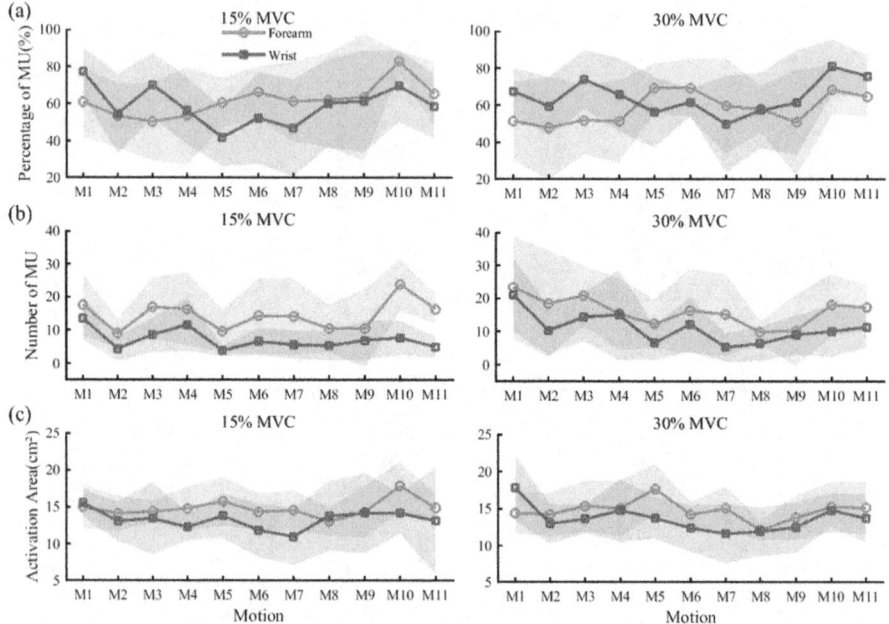

Fig. 4. The statistical results of the propagation trend and the activation area of each MU. (a)(b) represent the proportion and number of MUs with propagation trends decomposed from wrist and forearm signals under different movements at two force levels; (c) activation area size of decomposed MUs.

Figure 4 presents the results for the number of MUs exhibiting propagation trend and the activation area derived from wrist and forearm signal decomposition. At 15% MVC, the number of MUs with propagation characteristics was 15 ± 4 and 7 ± 3 for wrist and forearm signals, accounting for 61.9 ± 8.7% and 59.0 ± 10.4% of decomposed MUs. The activation area sizes were 14.8 ± 1.2 cm^2 and 13.3 ± 1.2 cm^2. At 30% MVC, the number was 16 ± 4 and 11 ± 5, accounting for 58.6 ± 8.3% and 64.6 ± 9.4%, with activation area of 14.7 ± 1.3 cm^2 and 13.6 ± 1.7 cm^2.

Figure 5 illustrates the spatial distribution of the CoG derived from wrist and forearm signal for one subject across the 11 different movement tasks. The results show overlapping activation areas for MUs derived from both signal sources across all tasks, and the activation areas exhibit differences between tasks.

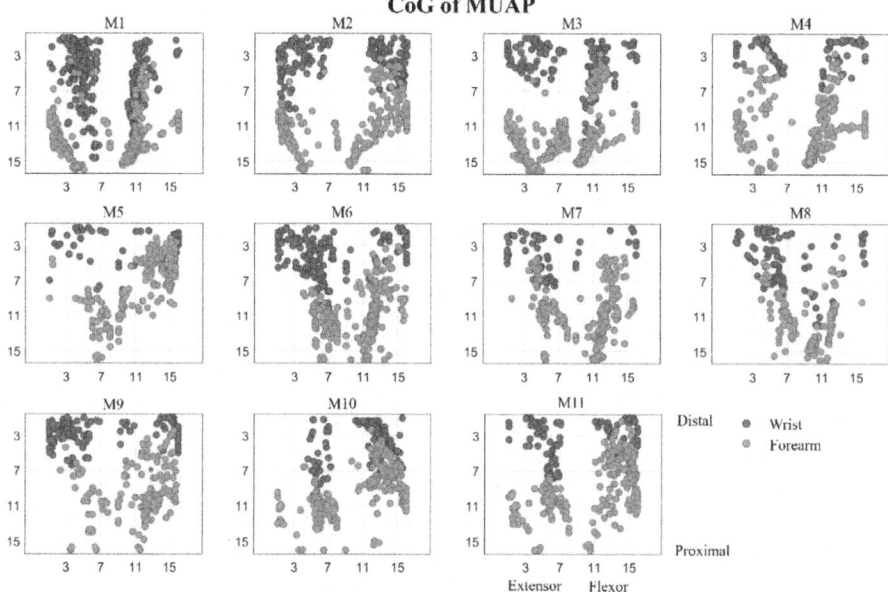

Fig. 5. The CoG distribution of eleven movements of one subject. Each subplot represents the CoG distribution calculated from signals corresponding to each movement at two force levels.

4 Discussion

In this study, we conducted a comparative analysis of propagation and activation characteristics for MUs derived from wrist and forearm sEMG signals, based on decoded MU activities. The results demonstrate similarities between wrist and forearm signals, with forearm signals propagating to the wrist via muscle fibers.

The physiological indices derived from wrist and forearm sEMG signals demonstrated similarity and were consistent with the physiological behavior of motor units, indicating that both signals are valid for decomposition.

While prior studies assessed wrist MU reliability by spike-triggered averaging of forearm signals using wrist-derived discharge timings [3], our approach applied decomposition to both signals. We further integrated innervation zone localization to determine MU propagation trends. The results show that at 15% MVC, the trend in the number of MUs exhibiting propagation characteristics was similar for both signals. Given the similar number of MUs, the proportion exhibiting propagation trend was higher for the first four grasp tasks decoded from wrist signals. This demonstrates that forearm signals can propagate to the wrist, confirming that wrist signals effectively reflect neuromuscular activities. At 30% MVC, wrist signals yielded higher proportions of MUs exhibiting propagation characteristics than forearm signals for most tasks. This indicates that wrist signals retain information from neurons with higher recruitment thresholds. As the level of activation increases, the information on motor units retained by the wrist signals also increases, which aligns with Henneman's size principle [25].

CoG provides a stable method for characterizing MU activation regions. While previous work typically computed CoG by triggering on decomposed spikes from the same signal domain[21], our method utilized the decomposed MUSTs from either wrist or forearm decomposition to trigger MUAP averaging across the entire recording region. The CoG distribution indicates that for different tasks, wrist signal retained a portion of MUs with the activation area extended to the forearm, while forearm signal decomposition also resolved a portion of MUs active at the wrist. This confirms that wrist signals can be decomposed to obtain MUs with spike trains similar to those decoded from forearm signals, validating the reliability of wrist signal decomposition. It further indicates that although information attenuation and waveform distortion occur during sEMG signal propagation, a portion can still propagate to the wrist via muscle fibers and be effectively recorded. Furthermore, activation areas for different tasks exhibited distinct spatial patterns identifiable in decomposition results from either wrist or forearm signals. This discriminability of different tasks aligns with findings from wrist-based classification studies employing diverse methodologies including time-domain features [4, 5] and MU features [4, 11], providing theoretical support for wrist signal pattern recognition and interface development.

There are several limitations in this study. During decomposition, MU propagation characteristics were analyzed separately for extensors and flexors, overlooking potential neuromuscular coordination between these muscle groups. The experimental protocol was also constrained. Future research should explore signal propagation across different muscle regions and further elucidate the propagation mechanisms from forearm to wrist. Additionally, research targeting diverse populations and dynamic gestures is required to further assess the feasibility of wrist neural interfaces.

5 Conclusion

This study conducted a comparative analysis of motor unit propagation and activation characteristics between wrist and forearm sEMG signals during grasping and finger movements. The analysis was based on motor unit action potential propagation trends and activation area distribution. High-density surface electromyography with 256 channels was used to record muscle activation in the extensors and flexors, which was then decomposed into MUAPs. The results demonstrate that motor units derived from wrist and forearm signals exhibit similar physiological behavior and possess overlapping activation areas. Furthermore, analysis of MU propagation characteristics demonstrates forearm-to-wrist signal propagation via muscle fibers. These findings are conducive to clarifying mechanisms underlying wrist sEMG signal formation and support the development of wrist-based neural interfaces and wearable devices.

References

1. Ahmadizadeh, C., Khoshnam, M., Menon, C.: Human machine interfaces in upper-limb prosthesis control: a survey of techniques for preprocessing and processing of biosignals. IEEE Signal Process. Mag. **38**(4), 12–22 (2021)
2. Fang, Y.M., Chang, C.C.: Users' psychological perception and perceived readability of wearable devices for elderly people. Behav. Inf. Technol. **35**(3), 225–232 (2016)

3. Guerra, I.M., Barsakcioglu, D.Y., Vujaklija, I., Wetmore, D.Z., Farina, D.: Far-field electric potentials provide access to the output from the spinal cord from wrist-mounted sensors. J. Neural Eng. **19**(2), 026031 (2022)
4. Jiang, S., et al.: Feasibility of wrist-worn, real-time hand, and surface gesture recognition via sEMG and IMU sensing. IEEE Trans. Ind. Inf. **14**(8), 3376–3385 (2017)
5. Botros, F.S., Phinyomark, A., Scheme, E.J.: Electromyography-based gesture recognition: is it time to change focus from the forearm to the wrist? IEEE Trans. Ind. Inf. **18**(1), 174–184 (2020)
6. Botros, F.S., Phinyomark, A., Scheme, E.J.: Day-to-day stability of wrist EMG for wearable-based hand gesture recognition. IEEE Access **10**, 125942–125954 (2022)
7. Ctrl-labs at Reality Labs, Sussillo, D., Kaifosh, P., Reardon, T.: A generic noninvasive neuromotor interface for human-computer interaction. Biorxiv, 2024-02 (2024)
8. Farina, D., Merletti, R., Enoka, R.M.: The extraction of neural strategies from the surface EMG. J. Appl. Physiol. **96**(4), 1486–1495 (2004)
9. Li, D., Kang, P., Yu, Y., Shull, P.B.: Graph-driven simultaneous and proportional estimation of wrist angle and grasp force via high-density emg. IEEE J. Biomed. Health Inform. **28**(5), 2723–2732 (2024)
10. Chen, C., Yu, Y., Sheng, X., Zhu, X.: Non-invasive analysis of motor unit activation during simultaneous and continuous wrist movements. IEEE J. Biomed. Health Inform. **26**(5), 2106–2115 (2021)
11. Yang, X., De Oliveira, D.S., Braun, D.I., Ponfick, M., Farina, D., Del Vecchio, A.: Non-invasive neural interfacing for tetraplegic individuals using residual motor neuron activity decoded at the forearm or wrist. IEEE J. Biomed. Health Inf. 1–9 (2025)
12. Holobar, A., Zazula, D.: Multichannel blind source separation using convolution kernel compensation. IEEE Trans. Signal Process. **55**(9), 4487–4496 (2007)
13. Holobar, A., Zazula, D.: Gradient convolution kernel compensation applied to surface electromyograms. In: International Conference on Independent Component Analysis and Signal Separation, pp. 617–624. Springer, Heidelberg (2007)
14. Negro, F., Muceli, S., Castronovo, A.M., Holobar, A., Farina, D.: Multi-channel intramuscular and surface EMG decomposition by convolutive blind source separation. J. Neural Eng. **13**(2), 026027 (2016)
15. Farina, D., Holobar, A., Merletti, R., Enoka, R.M.: Decoding the neural drive to muscles from the surface electromyogram. Clin. Neurophysiol. **121**(10), 1616–1623 (2010)
16. Holobar, A., Minetto, M.A., Farina, D.: Accurate identification of motor unit discharge patterns from high-density surface EMG and validation with a novel signal-based performance metric. J. Neural Eng. **11**(1), 016008 (2014)
17. Holobar, A., Minetto, M.A., Botter, A., Negro, F., Farina, D.: Experimental analysis of accuracy in the identification of motor unit spike trains from high-density surface EMG. IEEE Trans. Neural Syst. Rehabil. Eng. **18**(3), 221–229 (2010)
18. Quiroga, R.Q., Nadasdy, Z., Ben-Shaul, Y.: Unsupervised spike detection and sorting with wavelets and superparamagnetic clustering. Neural Comput. **16**(8), 1661–1687 (2004)
19. Dai, C., Hu, X.: Extracting and classifying spatial muscle activation patterns in forearm flexor muscles using high-density electromyogram recordings. Int. J. Neural Syst. **29**(01), 1850025 (2019)
20. Masuda, T., Sadoyama, T.: Skeletal muscles from which the propagation of motor unit action potentials is detectable with a surface electrode array. Electroencephalogr. Clin. Neurophysiol. **67**(5), 421–427 (1987)
21. Xia, M., Chen, C., Xu, Y., Li, Y., Sheng, X., Ding, H.: Extracting individual muscle drive and activity from high-density surface electromyography signals based on the center of gravity of motor unit. IEEE Trans. Biomed. Eng. **70**(10), 2852–2862 (2023)

22. Nizamis, K., Rijken, N.H., Van Middelaar, R., Neto, J., Koopman, B.F., Sartori, M.: Characterization of forearm muscle activation in duchenne muscular dystrophy via high-density electromyography: a case study on the implications for myoelectric control. Front. Neurol. **11**, 231 (2020)
23. Jiang, X., et al.: Quantifying spatial activation patterns of motor units in finger extensor muscles. IEEE J. Biomed. Health Inform. **25**(3), 647–655 (2020)
24. Xie, Y., Ji, Q.: A new efficient ellipse detection method. In: 2002 International Conference on Pattern Recognition, vol. 2, pp. 957–960. IEEE (2002)
25. Henneman, E.: Relation between size of neurons and their susceptibility to discharge. Science **126**(3287), 1345–1347 (1957)

High-Discrimination Multi-level Electrotactile Feedback via Compound Perception Descriptors and Efficient Calibration

Chen Yang[1], Naixing Gao[1], Xiaoxin Wang[1], Qiming Zeng[1], Bangquan Xie[2], Hongwei Zhang[1], and Yixuan Sheng[1]($\boxtimes$)

[1] State Key Laboratory of Robotics and System, Harbin Institute of Technology Shenzhen, Shenzhen 518055, China
24B953039@stu.hit.edu.cn, shengyixuan@hit.edu.cn
[2] Dongguan Key Laboratory of Intelligent Equipment and Smart Industry, School of Advanced Engineering, Great Bay University, Dongguan 523000, China

Abstract. Existing electrotactile systems face challenges in reliably distinguishing multiple levels using a single channel. This limitation reduces their practicality in real-world applications. This study introduces a new framework to address these challenges. Four predefined levels were designed using compound perception descriptors based on intensity, frequency, and sensation quality. Each level ensures at least two distinct perceptual dimensions. Additionally, a rapid calibration method was developed, combining preset parameters with a GUI-guided adjustment process. Furthermore, subjective evaluations were conducted to assess urgency, annoyance, valence, and arousal for the four levels, providing insights for application-specific designs. The calibration process was efficient, with an average completion time of 7.2 min. Final tests demonstrated a classification accuracy of 96.1%, confirming the system's ability to reliably distinguish the four levels. This framework provides a simple and effective solution for single-channel multi-level electrotactile feedback. The approach has potential applications in medical devices, virtual reality systems, and other human-computer interaction fields.

Keywords: Electrotactile Feedback · Multi-level Coding · Compound Perception Descriptors · Calibration Efficiency

1 Introduction

Tactile feedback plays a key role in human-computer interaction. Electrotactile feedback uses electrical currents or voltages to stimulate sensory nerves in the skin, creating tactile sensations in the brain [1]. Compared to traditional mechanical vibrotactile methods, electrotactile feedback has several advantages. It consumes less energy, responds faster,

---

This work was supported by the National Key R&D Program of China (Grant No.2022YFB4700200), the National Natural Science Foundation of China (Grant No.62403170), and the Shenzhen Science and Technology Program (Grant No. GXWD20231129102014001).

costs less to produce, and is more wearable [2]. These features make it promising for applications like medical rehabilitation [3, 4], sensory substitution [5, 6], and virtual reality [7, 8].

When electrotactile sensations are distinct enough, users can learn to associate specific sensations with different pieces of information [9]. For example, Tim Duente [10] developed a wrist-worn system that provided electrotactile feedback for smartwatches. Encoding strategies for electrotactile feedback typically fall into two categories: spatial coding and single-channel parametric coding. Spatial coding employs multiple electrodes to convey information through spatial variation [11], but it is limited by its large skin coverage requirements and higher implementation costs. In contrast, single-channel coding operates on a single electrode by adjusting electrical parameters such as pulse amplitude (PA), pulse frequency (PF), and pulse width (PW) [12]. These parameters can be used independently or combined with spatial approaches, like Strbac's spatiotemporal system for prosthetic feedback [13].

Choosing the right encoding method is critical for ensuring users can understand the information. However, current methods lack strong theoretical foundations. Most studies focus on how electrical stimulation parameters affect subjective perception. This often involves measuring "perceptual intensity" as a single dimension. For instance, one study used high-frequency pulse trains to create three intensity levels with over 85% accuracy [9]. Another study [14] proposed using a sensitivity index (SI) to quantify intensity and tested multi-level discrimination, pointing out that the accuracy cannot be guaranteed when the number of levels is more than 3. Beyond intensity, research [15] explored perceptual frequency as another dimension, though multi-level validation is missing. Sensation quality, such as prickling or vibrating, is another important attribute but has been studied less [15]. One study explored the perceived qualities of electrotactile feedback, but only one sensation was identified with more than 50% accuracy [10].

Thus, developing a reliable multi-level single-channel electrotactile feedback system faces several challenges. One major issue is the characterization of perception. Current metrics, such as numeric intensity scales, are overly simplistic and lack consistency across users. Physiological differences, such as variations in skin properties, further complicate the relationship between electrical stimulation parameters and perception. External factors, such as sweating or electrode displacement, also affect performance. To address these issues, proper perceptual descriptors and efficient calibration methods are both essential for practical applications.

This study proposes a framework for single-channel multi-level electrotactile feedback. The framework combines compound perceptual descriptors with an efficient calibration process, achieving over 96% discrimination accuracy across four levels. The main contributions are summarized as follows:

- **Compound perceptual descriptors.** We propose an innovative approach to represent electrotactile feedback by introducing triaxial perceptual descriptors. Unlike traditional single-attribute representations, these descriptors integrate three perceptual dimensions: intensity, frequency, and sensation quality. These dimensions are captured using qualitative natural-language labels, enabling intuitive communication and

enhancing the interpretability of feedback. Experimental results confirm that the proposed simple, yet multidimensional representation method effectively distinguishes stimulation levels.
- **Efficient calibration protocol.** We present a novel calibration protocol that integrates key parameter presets, such as pulse frequency and pulse width, with a graphical user interface (GUI) to facilitate guided personalization. This approach simplifies the calibration process and the calibration time was measured at an average of 7.2 min, highlighting the efficiency and practicality of the proposed method.
- **Perceptual level profiling.** Feedback levels are evaluated using four dimensions—urgency, annoyance, valence, and arousal. These evaluations provide actionable guidelines for designing context-aware feedback sequences and applications.

2 Methods

2.1 Subjects and Stimulation System

Eight healthy adults (aged 22–31 years; 6 males, 2 females) participated in this study, referred to as S1–S8. Informed consent was obtained from all participants, and the study was approved by the Ethics Committee of Harbin Institute of Technology (Approval No. HIT-2023055). All experimental procedures adhered to the ethical standards outlined in the 1964 Declaration of Helsinki and its subsequent amendments.

The electrical stimulation system was adapted from a previous design [16] and consisted of a constant-current monophasic pulse generator paired with a graphical user interface (GUI). During the experiments, currents were delivered via hydrogel electrodes (diameter: 20 mm) placed on the right gastrocnemius muscle (Fig. 1). The large surface area of the electrodes minimized skin-electrode impedance [14, 17]. Subjects interacted with the GUI using a mouse while wearing ear protection.

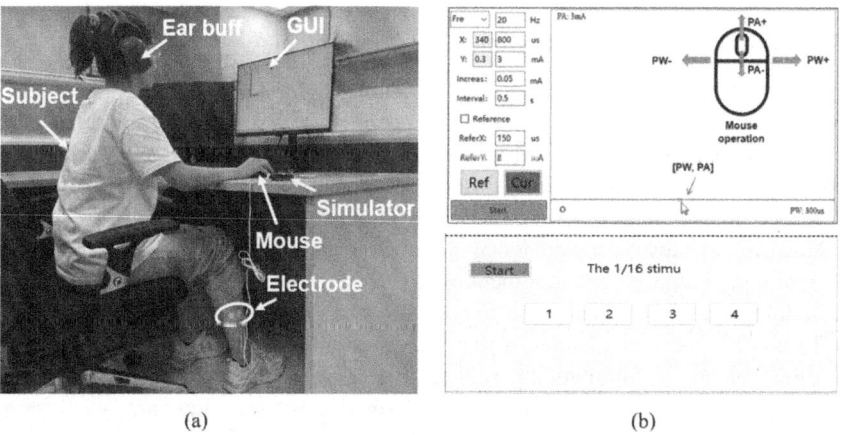

Fig. 1. Calibration and Experimental Platform. (a) Experimental setup. (b) Graphical user interface.

2.2 Compound Perceptual Descriptors

To enhance characterization of electrotactile sensations, this study introduced compound natural-language descriptors as an alternative to conventional unidimensional intensity metrics. Inspired by advancements in large language models that unify vision and language [15], this approach hypothesizes that qualitative verbal descriptors provide superior discrimination and inter-user consistency in electrotactile feedback.

Three perceptual dimensions were selected: intensity, frequency, and sensation quality. Intensity and frequency were chosen based on prior studies [15], while sensation quality was informed by research on tactile perception [10]. Each dimension was operationalized using qualitative descriptors: intensity (light, moderate, moderately strong), frequency (intermittent, rapid, continuous), and quality (pulsating, vibrating, tingling, buzzing).

To ensure inter-level discriminability, each pair of consecutive levels was designed to differ across at least two perceptual dimensions. Through a small-scale pre-experiment, four electrotactile feedback levels were empirically established (Table 1). Numerical indices (Levels 1–4) serve as categorical identifiers without implying a progressive relationship of any perception.

Table 1. Compound Descriptors for Multi-Level Electrotactile Stimuli

Level	Intensity	Frequency	Quality
1	Moderately strong	Intermittent	Pulsating
2	Light	Rapid	Vibrating
3	Moderately strong	Rapid	Vibrating + Tingling
4	Moderate	Continuous	Buzzing

2.3 Calibration Protocol for Stimulation Parameters

Physiological variability in skin properties among individuals creates subject-specific mappings between electrical parameters and perceptual responses. Temporal instability further complicates this relationship due to dynamic factors including sweating, electrode migration, or detachment. Consequently, personalized and temporally resilient calibration is essential for reliable electrotactile feedback deployment.

However, exhaustive parameter-by-parameter calibration proves prohibitively time-consuming, risking user abandonment of electrotactile devices. An efficient calibration methodology is therefore critical for practical adoption.

To address these challenges, a two-step calibration method was developed. First, predefined electrical stimulation parameters were used to narrow the calibration range. Second, personalized adjustments were performed to optimize the parameters for each subject.

Parameter Presets. Previous studies have highlighted the relationship between perceptual frequency and pulse frequency (PF). For instance, [15] demonstrated that perceptual frequency is strongly correlated with PF, with a stronger perceptual response observed in the lower frequency range. Additionally, [18] reported that the distinction in frequency perception becomes less pronounced above 10 Hz. Research conducted by [19] indicated that human perception of pulse frequency tends to saturate around 50 Hz. Furthermore, experimental data from [19] revealed that buzzing sensations were predominantly reported at stimulation frequencies exceeding 50 Hz. Based on these findings, the initial PF values were set at 2 Hz, 10 Hz, and 50 Hz to optimize frequency perception distinction.

Pulse widths exceeding 500 μs were avoided due to their association with pain [20]. As established in [21], stimulation intensity is jointly governed by pulse amplitude (PA) and pulse width (PW), with their product defining charge transfer. Thus, for Level 3's tingling sensation, a higher PW preset (350 μs) was selected to activate neural pathways linked to tingling.

Conversely, for Level 1, a lower PW preset (150 μs) was implemented to elicit the "pulsating" descriptor while avoiding pain-inducing activation. Levels 2 and 4 received intermediate PW values (250 μs).

Table 2. Initial Parameter Presets for Multi-level Compound Perception Descriptors

Level	Compound perceptual descriptors	PF_0(Hz)	PW_0(μs)
1	Moderately strong + Intermittent + Pulsating	2	150
2	Light + Rapid + Vibrating	10	250
3	Moderately strong + Rapid + Vibrating + Tingling	10	350
4	Moderate + Continuous + Buzzing	50	250

Personalized Calibration Protocol. Calibration was conducted using the GUI (Fig. 1), where PF values were directly input, PW adjusted via mouse movement, and pulse amplitude (PA) modulated through mouse wheel scrolling (0–9 mA range). Stimulation parameters were logged upon mouse-click when descriptor-matched sensations were confirmed. The specific calibration was as follows:

Calibration Preparation. The subjects were asked to sit in front of a computer screen and stick electrodes. The system and operation method were introduced to the subjects, and simple training was conducted. The subjects were told that all sensations should be within their acceptable range. This process took about 5 min.

Calibration Process. Calibration iterated through each level (1–4), starting with predefined PF/PW values (Table 2). PA was incrementally increased (0.05 mA steps) until the target perception matched the descriptor or pain onset occurred. PW was increased by 100 μs (PA reset to 0) for up to two iterations if sensations failed to match.

The time from the start to the end of calibration was recorded for each subject. It should be emphasized that in the experiment, the parameters can only be recorded after confirming that the current feeling is consistent with the description; "light" should also be clearly felt, rather than vague.

2.4 Electrotactile Feedback Level Discrimination Experiment

This experiment quantified subjects' ability to discriminate four electrotactile feedback levels (Table 1) using individualized stimulation parameters calibrated in Sect. 2.3. Following calibration, subjects underwent a 3-min rest period before commencing the discrimination experiment. During the 5-min preparation phase, subjects familiarized themselves with the experimental protocol via practice trials. Identical electrode placement was maintained across calibration and testing sessions to ensure stimulation site consistency.

Each experimental session comprised 16 randomized trials (4 stimuli per level × 4 levels), preceded by a cued replay of all four stimulus levels (2 s duration, 3 s interstimulus interval) to reinforce perceptual templates. To prevent discomfort, stimuli during formal trials followed identical timing parameters (2 s ON, 3 s OFF). Subjects classified each stimulus by clicking corresponding buttons (1–4) on the response interface immediately after offset.

Three identical sessions were conducted with 1-min inter-session rests.

2.5 Multimodal Subjective Assessment of Feedback Levels

To enable context-aware mapping of electrotactile levels to real-world notifications, subjects rated each feedback level across four psychometric dimensions adapted from [21]: perceived urgency, annoyance, valence and arousal. Perceived urgency is important where messages of different importance need to be communicated. Annoyance refers to whether the user feels uncomfortable or irritated due to stimulation. Valence refers to the degree to which the user's emotions are positive or negative towards stimulation. Arousal refers to the degree of physiological or psychological activation (calm vs. excitement).

Immediately following the discrimination task, subjects completed 7-point Likert scales for each level, with anchors standardized as: Urgency: 1 (Not urgent) – 7 (Extremely urgent); Annoyance: 1 (Not annoying) – 7 (Extremely annoying); Valence: 1 (Very unpleasant) – 7 (Very pleasant); Arousal: 1 (Very calm) – 7 (Very excited).

3 Results

3.1 Calibration Time

Personalized calibration leveraging literature-based presets succeeded for all calibrated subjects (8/8), with each achieving descriptor-matched Perception. Calibration durations (Fig. 2) ranged from 4.4 min to 9.5 min (mean: 7.2 min).

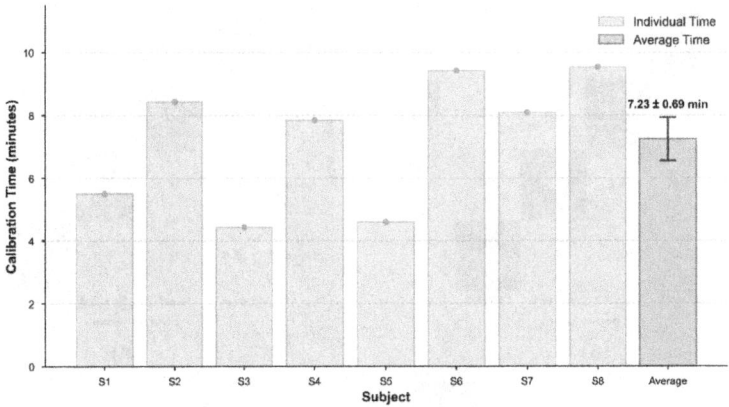

Fig. 2. Calibration time distribution.

3.2 Feedback Level Discrimination Accuracy

All eight subjects completed three sessions of electrotactile stimulation, each comprising 16 randomized trials (4 stimuli × 4 levels). Subjects classified stimulus levels after each delivery.

Mean session accuracy across subjects ranged from 87.5% to 100% (individual profiles: S1 = 100%, S2 = 97.9%, S3 = 91.7%, S4 = 93.8%, S5 = 95.8%, S6 = 87.5%, S7 = 93.8%, S8 = 91.7%, overall mean = 94.0%). The average accuracy of the 8 subjects in the first session was 91.4%, the average accuracy in the second session was 94.5%, and the average accuracy in the third session was 96.1%. The confusion matrix of the judgment results in each session is shown in Fig. 3 (Fig. 4).

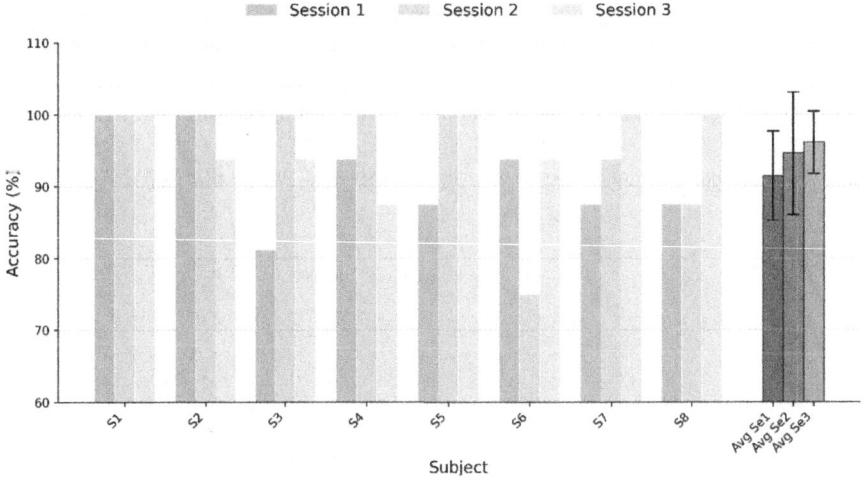

Fig. 3. Feedback level discrimination accuracy.

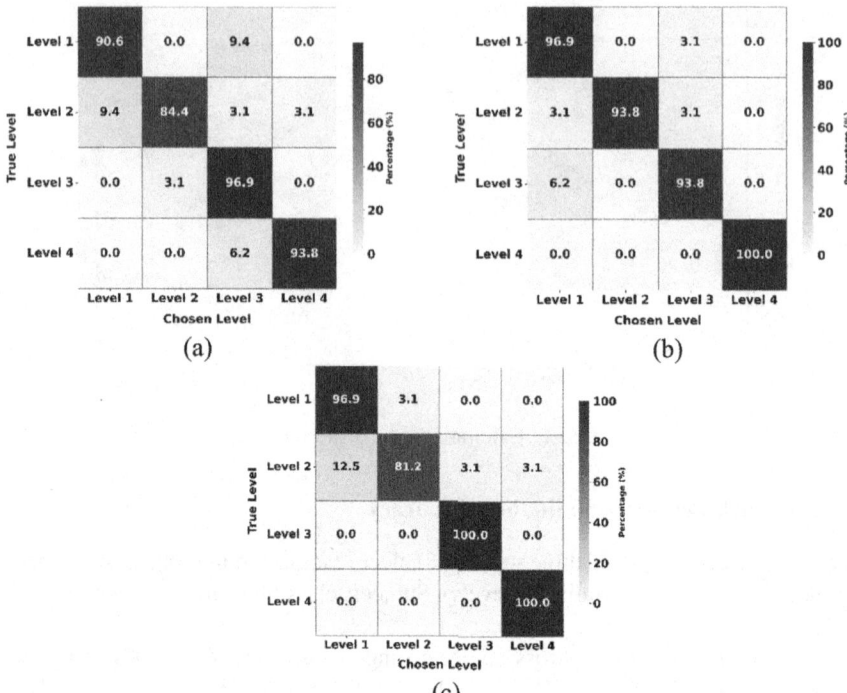

Fig. 4. Confusion matrix of discrimination accuracy. (a) session 1. (b) session 2. (c) session 3.

3.3 Multimodal Subjective Assessment of Feedback Levels

Following the classification experiment, subjects immediately completed a four-dimensional subjective evaluation questionnaire for each electrotactile feedback level. The dimensions assessed were urgency, annoyance, valence, and arousal, measured using 7-point Likert scales. Individual ratings across all eight subjects are visualized in Fig. 5, while Table 3 summarizes the mean scores and standard deviations per level.

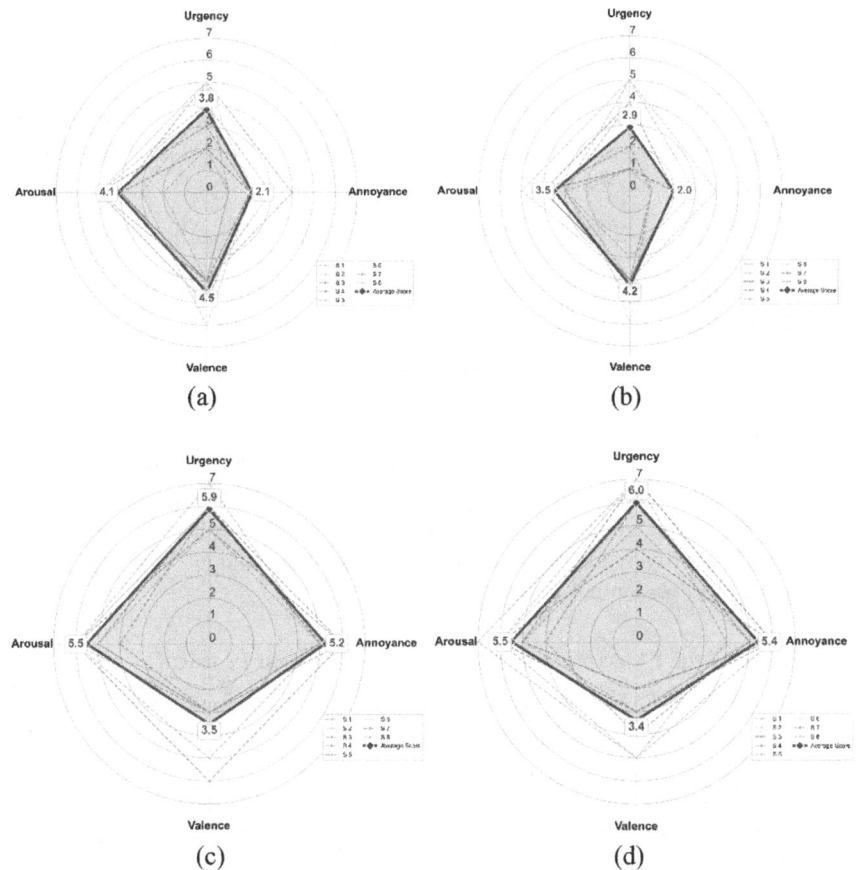

Fig. 5. Subjective Assessment. (a) level 1. (b) level 2. (c) level 3. (d) level 4.

Table 3. Mean scores and standard deviations per level

Level	Urgency	Annoyance	Valence	Arousal
1	3.75 ± 1.28	2.13 ± 0.99	4.50 ± 0.76	4.13 ± 1.13
2	2.87 ± 1.81	2.00 ± 1.07	4.25 ± 0.89	3.50 ± 0.93
3	5.88 ± 0.64	5.25 ± 0.46	3.50 ± 1.31	5.50 ± 0.76
4	6.00 ± 1.07	5.38 ± 0.74	3.38 ± 1.19	5.50 ± 0.93

4 Discussion

4.1 Validity of Compound Perceptual Descriptors

The eight calibrated subjects all successfully elicited perceptions matching the predefined descriptors during calibration. This confirms that the descriptors are both intuitively comprehensible and reliably inducible through electrical stimulation.

The average accuracy rate for discriminating electrotactile feedback levels reached 96.1% in the third session, demonstrating that the compound perception descriptors enable highly discriminable multi-level electrotactile coding (compared to > 85% for three levels in [9] and > 80% for four levels in [14]). Furthermore, accuracy increased progressively across sessions (Session 1: 91.4%; Session 2: 94.5%; Session 3: 96.1%). We conjecture this improvement stems from two factors:

- Subjects' growing familiarity with the experimental interface reduced operational errors.
- Repeated judgments might reinforce perceptual memory traces of level-specific sensations, strengthening sensation-level associations.

This suggests deliberate learning may enhance perceptual discrimination of feedback levels, warranting further investigation in future work.

The confusion matrices reveal that Level 2 was more frequently confused across all three sessions. We attribute this to two factors: Level 2's lower intensity descriptor ("Light") may have compromised subjects' frequency perception discrimination to some extent [15]. Shared parameters between Levels 2 and 3 – identical frequency descriptor ("Rapid") and partially overlapping quality descriptor (both include "Vibrating") – likely reduced inter-level perceptual distinctiveness.

4.2 Validity of the Electrotactile Parameter Calibration Protocol

Building upon established literature regarding parameter-perception relationships, we derived presets for electrical stimulation parameters. All eight subjects successfully elicited target sensations using the preset PF and PW values (Table 2), confirming the presets' physiological plausibility. Notably during Level 3 calibration, subjects consistently reported emergent tingling sensations with increasing PA, suggesting progressive activation of nociceptive nerve fibers at higher charge injections. Despite higher mean PA values in Level 1 versus Level 3, no tingling occurred in Level 1, which aligns with our design intent.

Calibration duration ranged from 4.4 min to 9.5 min (mean: 7.2 min). We conjecture further time reduction is achievable with operator familiarity. Efficient parameter calibration could facilitate real-world adoption of electrotactile feedback technology.

4.3 Subjective Assessment of Feedback Levels

Mean subjective ratings across all eight subjects revealed distinct perceptual-emotional profiles: Levels 1 and 2 exhibited similarly low urgency, low annoyance, and neutral valence/arousal ratings, with Level 2 perceived as marginally less urgent. These levels could be suitable for binding to routine notifications. Levels 3 and 4 demonstrated comparably elevated urgency, annoyance, and arousal, suggesting applicability for urgent scenario alerts. Furthermore, it should be noted that while levels 3 and 4 were perceived as mildly "unpleasant," they remained within an acceptable range, as participants were explicitly informed prior to calibration that no stimuli would induce strong discomfort. The framework proposed in this study may support practical adoption of electrotactile feedback in medical wearables, VR interfaces, and related human-computer interaction domains.

4.4 Limitation

The number of subjects in the experiment was relatively small (8 individuals), which is acceptable in human-machine interaction studies. However, a larger sample size would enhance the generalizability of the conclusions. Additionally, one participant exhibited extreme cutaneous sensitivity, reporting pain at minimal current levels, and therefore did not participate in subsequent calibration and experimental procedures. This suggests that the electrical stimulation feedback method may have limitations for individuals with heightened sensitivity to electrical stimuli.

5 Conclusion

This study presents a practical framework for achieving high-discrimination multi-level electrotactile feedback. By integrating compound perceptual descriptors with an efficient calibration protocol (average calibration time: 7.2 min), the approach demonstrated a 96.1% discrimination accuracy for four-level coding using a single-channel setup. Subjective profiling further identified distinct perceptual and emotional patterns, with Levels 1–2 suited for routine notifications and Levels 3–4 optimized for urgent alerts. The proposed framework offers promising potential for real-world applications, including medical wearables, VR interfaces, and other human-computer interaction domains.

References

1. Chouvardas, V.G., Miliou, A.N., Hatalis, M.K.: Tactile displays: overview and recent advances. Displays **29**(3), 185–194 (2008)
2. Kourtesis, P., et al.: Electrotactile feedback applications for hand and arm interactions: a systematic review, meta-analysis, and future directions. IEEE Trans. Haptics **15**(3), 479–496 (2022)
3. Isaković, M., et al.: Electrotactile feedback improves performance and facilitates learning in the routine grasping task. Eur. J. Transl. Myol. **26**(3), 6069 (2016)
4. Štrbac, M., et al.: Short-and long-term learning of feedforward control of a myoelectric prosthesis with sensory feedback by amputees. IEEE Trans. Neural Syst. Rehabil. Eng. **25**(11), 2133–2145 (2017)
5. Saunders, F.A.: Information transmission across the skin: high-resolution tactile sensory aids for the deaf and the blind. Int. J. Neurosci. (1983)
6. Blamey, P.J., Clark, G.M.: Psychophysical studies relevant to the design of a digital electrotactile speech processor. J. Acoust. Soc. Am. **82**(1), 116–125 (1987)
7. Germani, M., Mengoni, M., Peruzzini, M.: Electro-tactile device for material texture simulation. Int. J. Adv. Manuf. Technol. (2013)
8. Keef, C.V., et al.: Virtual texture generated using elastomeric conductive block copolymer in a wireless multimodal haptic glove. Adv. Intell. Syst. **2**(4), 2000018 (2020)
9. Parsnejad, S., et al.: Investigating Distinct intensity levels in electrotactile machine-to-human communication. In: 2022 IEEE International Symposium on Circuits and Systems (ISCAS), pp. 1–5. IEEE (2022)
10. Duente, T., et al.: Colorful electrotactile feedback on the wrist. In: Proceedings of the 22nd International Conference on Mobile and Ubiquitous Multimedia, pp. 1–10 (2023)

11. Dosen, S., et al.: Multichannel electrotactile feedback with spatial and mixed coding for closed-loop control of grasping force in hand prostheses. IEEE Trans. Neural Syst. Rehabil. Eng. **25**(3), 183–195 (2016)
12. Paredes, L.P., et al.: The impact of the stimulation frequency on closed-loop control with electrotactile feedback. J. Neuroeng. Rehabil. **12**, 1–16 (2015)
13. Štrbac, M., et al.: Integrated and flexible multichannel interface for electrotactile stimulation. J. Neural Eng. **13**(4), 046014 (2016)
14. Zhou, Z., et al.: Perceptual properties of fingertips under electrotactile stimulation. In: Intelligent Robotics and Applications, LNCS, vol. 9999, pp. 1–13. Springer, Cham (2022)
15. Kaczmarek, K.A., et al.: Interaction of perceived frequency and intensity in fingertip electrotactile stimulation: dissimilarity ratings and multidimensional scaling. IEEE Trans. Neural Syst. Rehabil. Eng. **25**(11), 2067–2074 (2017)
16. Zhou, Z., et al.: Explore electrotactile parametric properties using an electrical stimulation system. IEEE Sens. J. **22**(7), 7053–7062 (2022)
17. Zhou, Z., et al.: Mathematical model of fingertip skin under constant-current electrotactile stimulation. IEEE Trans. Haptics **16**(1), 3–12 (2022)
18. Kaczmarek, K.A., et al.: The afferent neural response to electrotactile stimuli: preliminary results. IEEE Trans. Rehabil. Eng. **8**(2), 268–270 (2000)
19. Graczyk, E.L., et al.: Frequency shapes the quality of tactile percepts evoked through electrical stimulation of the nerves. J. Neurosci. **42**(10), 2052–2064 (2022)
20. Butikofer, R., Lawrence, P.D.: Electrocutaneous nerve stimulation-II: stimulus waveform selection. IEEE Trans. Biomed. Eng. **2**, 69–75 (2007)
21. Alotaibi, Y., Williamson, J.H., Brewster, S.A.: First steps towards designing electrotactons: investigating intensity and pulse frequency as parameters for electrotactile cues. In: Proceedings of the 2022 CHI Conference on Human Factors in Computing Systems, pp. 1–13 (2022)

Cross-Task EEG Mental Workload Detection in Aviation: An LSTM Framework Leveraging Task-Invariant Neural Signatures

Huanpeng Ye[1], Yumeng Li[2], Bo Lv[3], Peiru An[2], and Yang Xu[2](✉)

[1] Shenyang Aircraft Design and Research Institute, Shenyang 110035, China
yehuanpeng@126.com
[2] The School of Intelligent Medicine, China Medical University, Shenyang 110122, China
xuyang74@cmu.edu.cn
[3] State Key Laboratory of Robotics and Intelligent Systems, Shenyang Institute of Automation, Chinese Academy of Sciences, Shenyang 110169, China
lvbo@sia.cn

Abstract. Monitoring of pilots' mental workloads is crucial for flight safety. Given the scarcity of flight data, developing transferable mental workload detectors trained on accessible paradigms like the n-back task represents a critical advancement toward deployable neuroadaptive systems in aviation. In this work, we developed an LSTM framework that extracts task-invariant neural signatures from spectral power of EEG rhythms using a controlled n-back paradigm and transfers detection to flight simulations without retraining. The model achieved 79.25% ± 4.07% accuracy on n-back data, with hierarchical F1-scores revealing state-dependent efficacy: rest (0.858) > severe workload (0.773) > mild workload (0.750). When applied to professional pilots (n = 2) during flight scenarios of graded difficulty, workload detection ratios scaled increasing with perceived difficulty. This cross-task validity—validated despite limited flight labels—confirms that EEG workload markers transcend task boundaries. The proposed approach enables deployable neuroadaptive systems for real-time cognitive state monitoring.

Keywords: mental workload · EEG · flight simulation · LSTM

1 Introduction

When commercial pilots navigate congested airspace, they must simultaneously monitor navigation systems, respond to air traffic control, and manage cockpit alerts while maintaining aircraft stability leading the mental labor intensity continues to rise [1]. Empirical analyses of aviation incident databases reveal

---

H. Ye and Y. Li—The two authors contribute equally to this work.

that over 60% of safety occurrences involve interruption-induced errors, with cascading failures contributing to catastrophic outcomes [2]. Consequently, rigorous assessment of cognitive workload is imperative for accident prevention, as excessive workload critically undermines human task performance [3].

Current mental workload assessment methodologies comprise three principal approaches: subjective evaluations, behavioral performance metrics, and physiological measurements [4]. Traditional assessment approaches face inherent constraints. Subjective evaluations like NASA-TLX suffer from recall bias and disrupt task continuity; behavioral performance metrics provide lagging indicators. Different from traditional assessment approaches, physiological evaluation methods using electroencephalogram (EEG), electrocardiogram (ECG) or electromyography (EMG), offer distinct advantages, including preservation of experimental continuity, high objectivity, and real-time monitoring capabilities [5–10]. Among physiological techniques, EEG emerges as a particularly promising modality, offering direct access to cortical dynamics at millisecond resolution. Its capacity to decode cognitive states—from stress biomarkers (elevated β-band power) to attentional engagement (θ/α phase coupling)—has been validated across neuroergonomic studies [11].

While EEG has become the preferred modality for characterizing cognitive states in targeted assessments [12–15], the scarcity of flight simulation data poses significant challenges for model development. Consequently, establishing robust methods to leverage accessible paradigms,such as gamified n-back tasks, for training transferable workload detectors holds critical implications for aviation safety. Long Short-Term Memory (LSTM) networks offer distinct advantages for EEG-based cognitive workload detection by inherently modeling the nonstationary temporal dynamics intrinsic to neural signals [16]. Unlike static classifiers (e.g., SVMs) that treat EEG epochs as independent snapshots, LSTMs capture evolving neurophysiological patterns across extended time series—critical for identifying workload escalation during complex tasks like aviation emergencies. This capability proves particularly valuable given EEG's millisecond-scale fluctuations in spectral power that correlate with shifting attentional demands [17,18]. Furthermore, LSTMs automatically learn hierarchical representations, enabling robust generalization across inter-subject neuroanatomical variations. When processing multi-channel EEG inputs, bidirectional LSTMs leverage contextual information from past and future states to resolve ambiguous workload transitions. These attributes collectively position LSTMs as the optimal architecture for translating noisy, high-dimensional EEG streams into reliable cognitive state metrics in ecological settings.

In this study, we developed an LSTM framework to achieve cross-task mental workload detection. The model was further validated using publicly available datasets [19], training exclusively on EEG data from a controlled n-back paradigm (n=16 subjects) and transferring the model to professional pilots (n=2) during ecologically validated flight simulations. While the limited sample size of simulated flight data constrained precise quantitative assessment, the proposed model nevertheless demonstrated robust capacity for cross-task parameter transfer to aviation-relevant scenarios.

2 Methods and Materials

In this study, we trained an LSTM model for multi-level classification of mental workload states in a continuous performance task test. The model, trained on data from the N-back task, is intended to establish a generalizable representation of cognitive workload. This model was subsequently applied to predict pilots' mental workload during the simulated flight task. The schematic of the overall experimental framework is presented in Fig. 1.

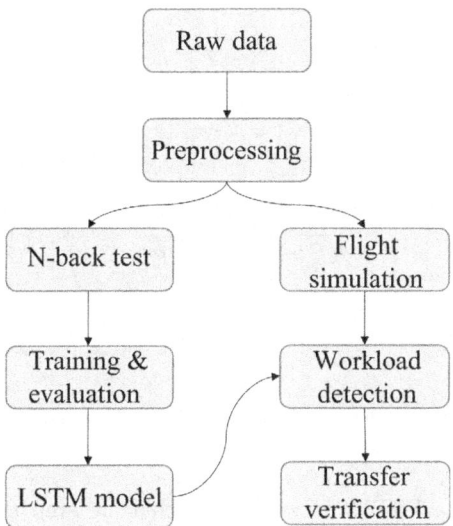

Fig. 1. The schematic of the overall experimental framework.

2.1 Data Preprocessing

The EEG preprocessing workflow comprised the following steps:

(1) Data were re-referenced to the common average reference;
(2) A dual-notch filter at 50 Hz and 60 Hz is used to remove power frequency interference;
(3) The signals were filtered between 0.5 Hz and 64 Hz using a 4-order Butterworth bandpass filter to attenuate low-frequency drift and high-frequency noise;
(4) The EEG recordings were partitioned into 40-s epochs with 30-s overlap [20]. Subsequently, the power band for the major brain rhythms (theta: 4–8 Hz, alpha: 8–12 Hz, beta low: 12–18 Hz, beta high: 18–25 Hz and Gamma: >25 Hz) of each channel were extracted from each window.

2.2 Model Architecture: Long Short-Term Memory (LSTM) Network

To effectively capture the temporal dependencies inherent in the EEG data, an LSTM network was employed as the core architecture for classifying neural tension levels. The LSTM model is particularly well-suited for sequential data, as it can selectively remember or forget information over extended time periods through its memory cells and gating mechanisms. The architecture of the LSTM model used in this study is illustrated in Fig. 2.

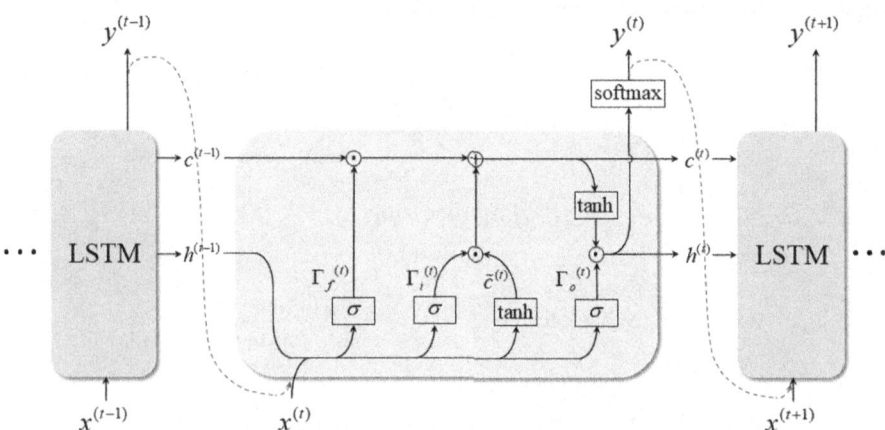

Fig. 2. The schematic of the LSTM framework.

The input to the LSTM network at each time step t is a 70-dimensional vector $\mathbf{x}^{(t)} = [F_1(t), F_2(t), \ldots, F_{70}(t)]$, representing the EEG features extracted from the 14 channels and 5 frequency bands. The LSTM layer consists of a sequence of LSTM units, each processing the input vector $\mathbf{x}^{(t)}$ along with the hidden state $\mathbf{h}^{(t-1)}$ and cell state $\mathbf{c}^{(t-1)}$ from the previous time step. The internal structure of each LSTM unit includes three key gates: the forget gate $\mathbf{f}^{(t)}$, the input gate $\mathbf{i}^{(t)}$, and the output gate $\mathbf{o}^{(t)}$, which are computed as follows:

$$\mathbf{f}^{(t)} = \sigma(\mathbf{W}_f \cdot [\mathbf{h}^{(t-1)}, \mathbf{x}^{(t)}] + \mathbf{b}_f), \tag{1}$$

$$\mathbf{i}^{(t)} = \sigma(\mathbf{W}_i \cdot [\mathbf{h}^{(t-1)}, \mathbf{x}^{(t)}] + \mathbf{b}_i), \tag{2}$$

$$\mathbf{o}^{(t)} = \sigma(\mathbf{W}_o \cdot [\mathbf{h}^{(t-1)}, \mathbf{x}^{(t)}] + \mathbf{b}_o), \tag{3}$$

where σ denotes the sigmoid activation function, $\mathbf{W}_f$, $\mathbf{W}_i$, and $\mathbf{W}_o$ are the weight matrices, and $\mathbf{b}_f$, $\mathbf{b}_i$, and $\mathbf{b}_o$ are the bias terms for the respective gates. The candidate cell state $\tilde{\mathbf{c}}^{(t)}$ is computed using the hyperbolic tangent (tanh) activation function:

$$\tilde{\mathbf{c}}^{(t)} = \tanh(\mathbf{W}_c \cdot [\mathbf{h}^{(t-1)}, \mathbf{x}^{(t)}] + \mathbf{b}_c). \tag{4}$$

The cell state $\mathbf{c}^{(t)}$ is then updated by combining the forget gate and input gate outputs:

$$\mathbf{c}^{(t)} = \mathbf{f}^{(t)} \odot \mathbf{c}^{(t-1)} + \mathbf{i}^{(t)} \odot \tilde{\mathbf{c}}^{(t)}, \tag{5}$$

where $\odot$ denotes element-wise multiplication. Finally, the hidden state $\mathbf{h}^{(t)}$ is computed as:

$$\mathbf{h}^{(t)} = \mathbf{o}^{(t)} \odot \tanh(\mathbf{c}^{(t)}). \tag{6}$$

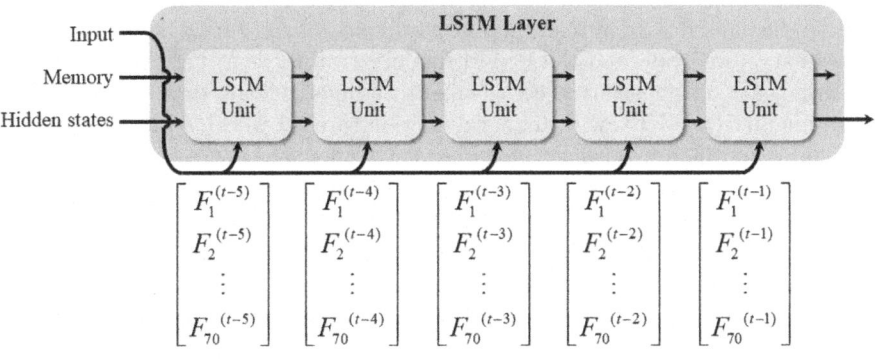

Fig. 3. The data flow of the LSTM Layer.

The LSTM layer processes the sequence of input vectors $\mathbf{x}^{(t-5)}, \mathbf{x}^{(t-4)}, \ldots, \mathbf{x}^{(t-1)}$ over a fixed time window of 5 time steps, as shown in Fig. 3. The hidden state $\mathbf{h}^{(t)}$ at the final time step is passed through a fully connected layer with a tanh activation function to produce a latent representation. This representation is then fed into a softmax layer to generate the output probabilities $\mathbf{y}^{(t)}$, corresponding to the predicted neural tension levels. The softmax function is defined as:

$$\mathbf{y}_i^{(t)} = \frac{\exp(\mathbf{z}_i)}{\sum_j \exp(\mathbf{z}_j)}, \tag{7}$$

where $\mathbf{z}$ is the output of the fully connected layer, and i indexes the possible classes of neural tension (e.g., low, medium, high).

2.3 Training and Validation Using N-Back-Test Data

The LSTM model was implemented using the PyTorch framework and trained on a dataset comprising EEG recordings from 16 subjects, with each subject contributing approximately 10 min of data. To evaluate the model's performance, a leave-one-out (LOO) cross-validation strategy was employed. In this approach, the model was trained on the data from 15 subjects and tested on the data from the remaining subject, iterating over all 16 subjects to ensure each subject served as the test set exactly once. The model was trained using the Adam optimizer with a learning rate of 0.001 and a batch size of 32. The cross-entropy loss function was used to measure the discrepancy between the predicted probabilities and the ground truth labels. To prevent overfitting, early stopping was applied with a patience of 10 epochs, and a dropout rate of 0.3 was introduced in the fully connected layer. The performance of the model was evaluated using standard metrics, including accuracy, precision, recall, and F1-score, averaged across all iterations of the LOO cross-validation.

2.4 Task Transfer Evaluation Using Flight Simulator Data

Due to the absence of direct mental workload labels during simulated flight experiments, we evaluated the LSTM model's transfer learning capability using validated surrogate measures. Experiments findings indicate that increased flight task difficulty correlates with higher detection rates of workload classes [20]. We therefore quantified mental workload levels by calculating the ratio of detections in two workload-associated classes (mild workload and severe workload) to rest class detections across varying flight difficulty conditions. Three workload indices were computed: (i) mild/rest, (ii) severe/rest, and (iii) (mild + severe)/rest, where mild and severe represent detection counts for low- and high-intensity workload states, respectively, and rest denotes baseline resting-state detections.

2.5 Experimental Setup

All experiments were conducted on a computing system equipped with an NVIDIA RTX 3090 GPU and 64 GB of RAM. The EEG data were processed in real-time using a custom pipeline developed in Python, integrating libraries such as MNE-Python for EEG preprocessing and PyTorch for model implementation.

3 Dataset Description

The data used for the algorithm validation were selected from an dataset collection for Mental Workload Predictions, which collected 14 channels EEG signals according to the International 10/20 System [19]. The dataset comprises two components: an N-back task and a simulated flight task. The placement of 14-electrodes is shown in Fig. 4(a), while the experimental protocols of N-back task and simulated flight task are described in Fig. 4(b)–(c). For the N-back task, participants were 16 male individuals aged 20–60 years. Each participant performed the N-back task at three difficulty levels (low, medium, and high), followed by completion of the NASA-Task Load Index (NASA-TLX) questionnaire to provide subjective workload labels. In the simulated flight task, participants were two professional pilots. Five distinct flight scenarios were simulated, representing graded difficulty levels from low to high.

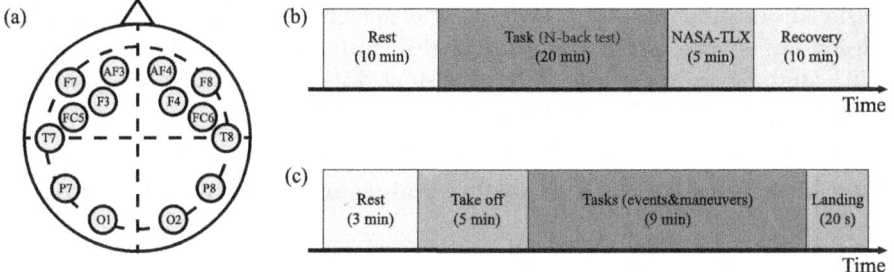

Fig. 4. The experiment paradigm. (a) The placement of electrodes for the EEG signals. (b) The timeline of the N-back test experimental. (c) The timeline of the simulated flight experimental.

4 Results

4.1 Indicators for Evaluating the Results of N-Back Test

During the N-back task used for model training, the mean accuracy across the 16 subjects was 79.25%, with a standard deviation of 4.07%. Table 1 presents the per-class and macro-averaged precision, recall, and F1-score, providing a detailed assessment of the model's performance across the three classes: rest, mild workload, and severe workload.

Table 1. Per-Class and Macro-Averaged Metrics for Mental Workload Classification

Class	Precision	Recall	F1-Score
Rest	0.867	0.85	0.858
Mild Workload	0.722	0.78	0.750
Severe Workload	0.798	0.75	0.773
Macro-Average	**0.796**	**0.793**	**0.794**

The per-class metrics reveal distinct performance patterns across the three classes. The rest class achieved the highest performance, with a precision of 0.867, recall of 0.85, and F1-score of 0.858, indicating that the model is highly effective at identifying the rest state, likely due to its distinct EEG features compared to the tension states. In contrast, the mild tension class exhibited the lowest performance, with a precision of 0.722, recall of 0.78, and F1-score of 0.750, reflecting the challenge of distinguishing mild tension from both rest and severe tension, possibly due to overlapping EEG features. The severe tension class showed moderate performance, with a precision of 0.798, recall of 0.75, and F1-score of 0.773, suggesting that the model struggles to differentiate severe tension from mild tension, which is expected given the continuum of neural tension levels. The macro-averaged metrics, with a precision of 0.796, recall of 0.793, and F1-score of 0.794, are consistent with the overall mean accuracy, confirming the robustness of the model across the three classes.

4.2 Indicators for Task Transfer Evaluation Using Flight Simulator Data

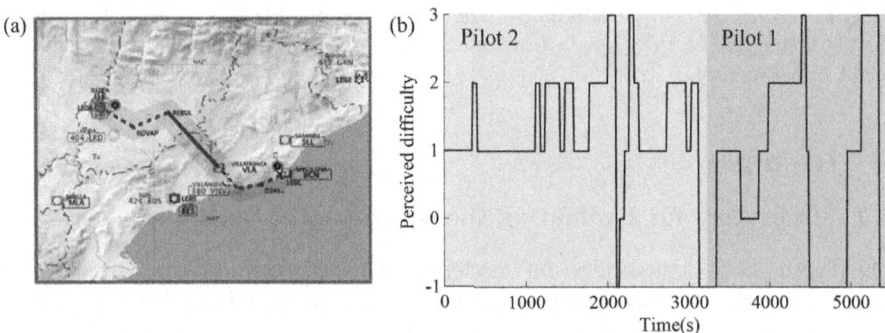

Fig. 5. The paradigm of simulated flight experimental. (a) The flight simulation route. (b) Task difficulty across experimental sessions.

Figure 5 depicts the flight simulation route and the temporal variations in task difficulty across experimental sessions for the two professional pilots during the simulated flight task. The perceived difficulty ratings ranged from 0 to 3 in Fig. 5, corresponding to easy, medium, medium-hard, and hard conditions respectively, with a rating of –1 denoting the baseline state. The mild and severe workload detection percentages are shown as a function of the perceived task difficulty in Fig. 6 and Fig. 7, respectively. Figure 8 demonstrates increasing mental workload detection percentages with escalating perceived task difficulty for both pilots, as quantified by bar plots.

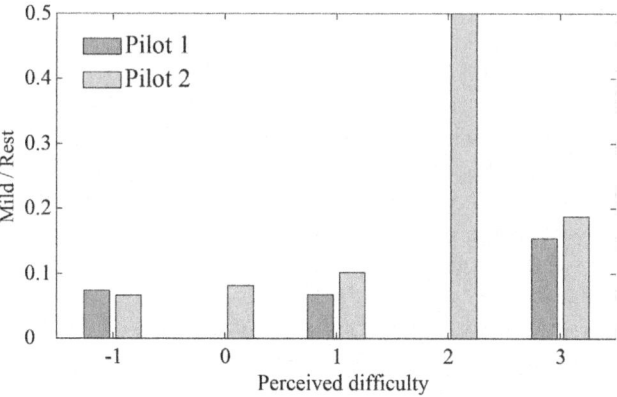

Fig. 6. Mild workload detection percentages scale with task difficulty.

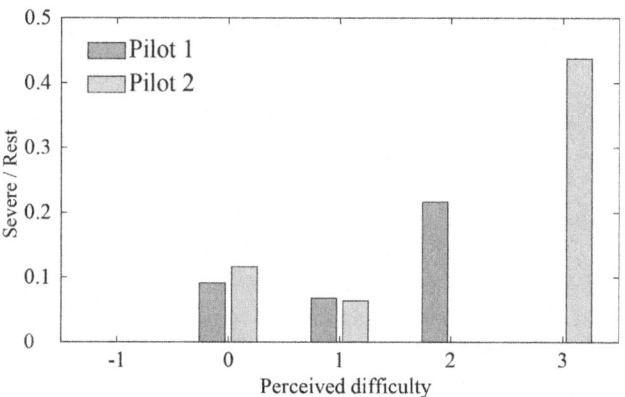

Fig. 7. Severe workload detection percentages scale with task difficulty.

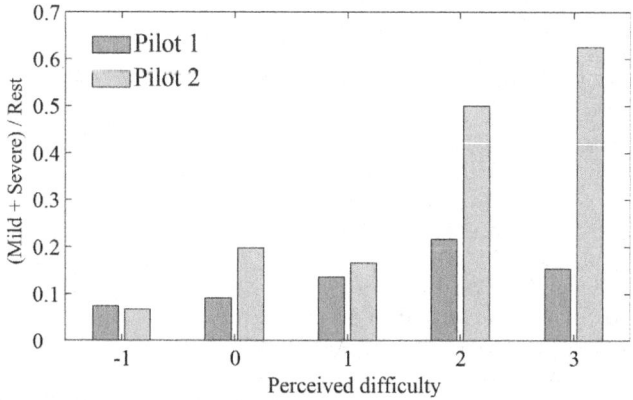

Fig. 8. All Workload detection percentages scale with task difficulty.

5 Conclusion

This study establishes an LSTM framework capable of generalizing mental workload detection across distinct task domains. The model demonstrated robust performance on the n-back task (mean accuracy: 79.25% ± 4.07%). Critically, using only n-back training data, the model effectively predicted pilot workload states in high-temporal-resolution flight simulations, with detection rates scaling monotonically with perceived task difficulty. This cross-task validity—achieved without aviation-specific calibration—confirms that EEG-derived workload signatures transcend task boundaries, providing a robust foundation for adaptive neuroergonomic systems in safety-critical operations.

While the framework demonstrates cross-task validity, several limitations warrant attention. Mild workload misclassification (F1: 0.750) persists due to neurophysiological overlaps at low cognitive-strain thresholds. The assessment of cross-task model transferability remains constrained by the limited sample size of flight simulation data (2 pilots) and the absence of ground-truth mental workload labels—factors hindering rigorous validation of predictive accuracy in aviation contexts.

Acknowledgments. This study was funded by Liaoning Doctoral Research Startup Fund (Grant Nos.:2025-BS-0607 and 2024-BSBA-50).

References

1. Kirmeyer, S.L.: Coping with competing demands: interruption and the type A pattern. J. Appl. Psychol. **73**(4), 621 (1988)
2. Shappell, S., Detwiler, C., Holcomb, K., et al.: Human error and commercial aviation accidents: an analysis using the human factors analysis and classification system. In: Human Error in Aviation, pp. 73–88. Routledge (2017)
3. Reinerman-Jones, L.E., Hughes, N., D'Agostino, A., et al.: Human performance metrics for the nuclear domain: a tool for evaluating measures of workload, situation awareness and teamwork. Int. J. Ind. Ergon. **69**, 217–227 (2019)
4. Radüntz, T.: Dual frequency head maps: a new method for indexing mental workload continuously during execution of cognitive tasks. Front. Physiol. **8**, 1019 (2017)
5. Jiang, G., Chen, H., Wang, C., et al.: Mental workload artificial intelligence assessment of pilots' EEG based on multi-dimensional data fusion and LSTM with attention mechanism model. Int. J. Pattern Recogn. Artif. Intell. **36**(11), 2259035 (2022)
6. Wanyan, X., Zhuang, D., Lin, Y., et al.: Influence of mental workload on detecting information varieties revealed by mismatch negativity during flight simulation. Int. J. Ind. Ergon. **64**, 1–7 (2018)
7. Jiang, Z., Zhang, K., Wu, K., et al.: Mental workload recognition using ECG and machine learning in simulated flight tasks. In: 2022 IEEE 6th Advanced Information Technology, Electronic and Automation Control Conference (IAEAC), pp. 1560–1565. IEEE (2022)
8. Fallahi, M., Motamedzade, M., Heidarimoghadam, R., et al.: Effects of mental workload on physiological and subjective responses during traffic density monitoring: a field study. Appl. Ergon. **52**, 95–103 (2016)

9. Xu, Y., Yu, Y., Xia, M., et al.: A novel and efficient surface electromyography decomposition algorithm using local spatial information. IEEE J. Biomed. Health Inf. **27**(1), 286–295 (2022)
10. Xu, Y., Yu, Y., Zhao, Z., et al.: Decoding multi-DoF movements using a CST-based force generation model with single-DoF training. IEEE Trans. Neural Syst. Rehabil. Eng. **32**, 974–982 (2024)
11. Zhou, Y., Huang, S., Xu, Z., et al.: Cognitive workload recognition using EEG signals and machine learning: a review. IEEE Trans. Cogn. Dev. Syst. **14**(3), 799–818 (2021)
12. Belt, S., Gai, Y., Gururajan, S., Tamilselvan, G., Bollock, N.K.: Exploring pilot workload during professional pilot primary training and development: a feasibility study. In: Nunes, I.L. (ed.) AHFE 2021. LNNS, vol. 265, pp. 193–201. Springer, Cham (2021). https://doi.org/10.1007/978-3-030-79816-1_24
13. Zhang, P., Wang, X., Chen, J., You, W., Zhang, W.: Spectral and temporal feature learning with two-stream neural networks for mental workload assessment. IEEE Trans. Neural Syst. Rehabil. Eng. **27**, 1149–1159 (2019)
14. Lee, D.H., Jeong, J.H., Kim, K., Yu, B.W., Lee, S.W.: Continuous EEG decoding of pilots' mental states using multiple feature block-based convolutional neural network. IEEE Access **8**, 121929–121941 (2020)
15. Wu, E.Q., Peng, X., Zhang, C.Z., Lin, J., Sheng, R.S.: Pilots' fatigue status recognition using deep contractive autoencoder network. IEEE Trans. Instrum. Meas. **68**, 3907–3919 (2019)
16. Graves, A., Graves, A.: Long short-term memory. Superv. Seq. Label. Recurrent Neural Netw. 37–45 (2012)
17. Safari, M.R., Shalbaf, R., Bagherzadeh, S., et al.: Classification of mental workload with EEG analysis by using effective connectivity and a hybrid model of CNN and LSTM. Comput. Methods Biomech. Biomed. Eng. 1–15 (2024)
18. Sharma, S., Gupta, R., Kumar, J., et al.: EEG-based mental workload estimation using bidirectional LSTM. In: 2024 4th International Conference on Technological Advancements in Computational Sciences (ICTACS), pp. 1082–1086. IEEE (2024)
19. Hernández-Sabaté, A., Yauri, J., Folch, P., et al.: EEG dataset collection for mental workload predictions in flight-deck environment. Sensors **24**(4), 1174 (2024)
20. Hernández-Sabaté, A., Yauri, J., Folch, P., et al.: Recognition of the mental workloads of pilots in the cockpit using EEG signals. Appl. Sci. **12**(5), 2298 (2022)

Wearable Robots for Assistance, Augmentation and Rehabilitation of Human Movements

A Physiology-Informed Training Protocol for Cross-Paradigm Transfer Learning in ErrP-Based Brain-Computer Interface

Ruijie Luo[1], Yuxuan Wei[1], Ximing Mai[1], Guangye Li[1,2], and Jianjun Meng[1,2(✉)]

[1] Institute of Robotics, School of Mechanical Engineering, Shanghai Jiao Tong University, Shanghai, China
mengjianjunxs008@sjtu.edu.cn
[2] State Key Laboratory of Mechanical System and Vibration, Shanghai Jiao Tong University, Shanghai, China

Abstract. In recent years, the application of error-related potentials (ErrPs) in brain-computer interfaces (BCIs) has expanded the amount of information available for decoding user intent. To extract users' preferences of BCI control outcomes from ErrP across a wide range of control scenarios, researchers seek to rapidly deploy ErrP decoding models to new BCI paradigms. However, variability in ErrP waveform characteristics across paradigms limits the direct application of pre-trained classifiers in novel paradigms. Existing transfer learning approaches for cross-paradigm ErrP decoding lack a necessary physiological foundation and therefore cannot provide physiologically meaningful reference-state data for transfer learning. To address this limitation, we propose that EEG responses recorded under a neutral condition which is free from task-related expectations can be utilized as physiology-informed reference data for cross-paradigm transfer learning. Significant cross-paradigm correlations between this neutral condition responses and ErrP responses in both the latency and amplitude of waveforms support the reference value of this neutral condition. Furthermore, we introduce a Neutral Condition Aligned Training Protocol (NCTP) for cross-paradigm ErrP data alignment. The significant improvements in the balanced accuracy of cross-paradigm decoding demonstrate the effectiveness of this NCTP approach.

Keywords: ErrP · Cross-paradigm decoding · Transfer learning · Human-machine interaction

1 Introduction

Research on error-related potentials (ErrP) has attracted growing attention within the field of brain-computer interfaces (BCIs) in the last few years [1, 2]. ErrP is elicited by feedback outcome stimuli either violate or confirm expectations that are formed by task-related rules. The difference in event-related potentials (ERPs) elicited by these expected (correct condition) versus unexpected (erroneous condition) feedback outcome stimuli is defined as the ErrP. As ErrP-based BCI applications expand across diverse experimental and real-world scenarios, it has been shown that various feedback types can evoke ErrPs [3]. However, these ErrPs often exhibit considerable variability in their ERP components across paradigms [4, 5].

This variability presents a significant challenge for ErrP decoding in new paradigms, which necessitates the collection of correct and erroneous EEG data through pseudo-control experiments to retrain classifiers. Such procedures substantially increase user burden and limit the practicality of ErrP-based BCIs. To address this challenge, researchers have proposed applying transfer learning techniques for cross-paradigm ErrP decoding [6, 7]. Theoretically, transfer learning across paradigms requires building a domain adaptation model that aligns EEG data from a target paradigm to the feature space of a source paradigm [8, 9]. Once this alignment is established, a classifier trained on the source paradigm can be used to decode ErrPs in the target paradigm.

An existing limitation of cross-paradigm ErrP transfer learning methods lies in the lack of ErrP-independent physiological reference-state data. On the one hand, prior research has identified various paradigm-related factors such as task difficulty and control workload potentially contributing to ErrP variability [10, 11]. However, these factors have not demonstrated quantifiable correlations with cross-paradigm ErrP changes, which limits their predictive value and usefulness as the reference-state data. On the other hand, while some studies have attempted to align latency-based ERP features [12] or covariance-based representations of ERP [6] across paradigms, they typically rely on correct and erroneous conditions data from the new paradigm as reference-state data. This approach still depends on ErrP-related data which is recorded from pseudo-control experiments.

The hierarchical nature of outcome processing mechanisms underlying ErrP generation suggests that a task-free neutral condition can be used as a physiologically grounded reference state. Specifically, the early stages of outcome processing which is prior to any expectation-based outcome comparison reflect a relatively neutral and stimulus encoding related process [13]. Since outcome comparisons across different paradigms are typically dichotomous, either matching or mismatching the expectations, the early stages of processing are more susceptible to paradigm-specific factors like environmental settings or visual presentation. Consequently, the EEG responses after this early processing can naturally provide the reference-state data to characterize the initial ERP responses across different paradigms. By systematically recording these neutral condition responses under different paradigms, we can obtain EEG signals that are intrinsically free of task-related outcome expectations. Leveraging these neutral-state responses for transfer learning may provide a physiological reference for aligning data across paradigms, thus addressing the key limitation in current ErrP cross-paradigm decoding research.

In this study, we design three experimental paradigms and record EEG signals under a neutral condition in which task-related outcome expectations are removed. We analyze the cross-paradigm correlations between the neutral condition and both correct and erroneous conditions in terms of ERP latency and amplitude. Based on these findings, we propose a transfer learning training protocol that leverages EEG responses from this neutral condition. The results demonstrate that this physiology-informed training protocol significantly enhances the performance of cross-paradigm ErrP decoding.

2 Methods

2.1 Subjects and Experimental Setup

Ten healthy adults (aged 20–30 years) with normal or corrected-to-normal vision participated in the study. Before the experiment, all participants were fully informed of the experimental procedures and provided written informed consent. The study protocol was approved by the Institutional Review Board of Shanghai Jiao Tong University (IRB HRP E2021216I). EEG signals were recorded at a sampling rate of 1024 Hz using a 64-channel BioSemi ActiveTwo system (BioSemi, Netherlands). Electrode placement followed the international 10–20 system, with Common Mode Sense (CMS) and Driven Right Leg (DRL) electrodes serving as reference and ground, respectively. Data acquisition and stimulus presentation were conducted using the BCI2000 platform [14].

2.2 Experimental Design

Participants performed three cursor control paradigms that varied in movement dimensions and control modes: one-dimensional movement discrete control (Experiment I), two-dimensional movement discrete control (Experiment II), and two-dimensional movement continuous control (Experiment III) (see Fig. 1(a)). In each paradigm, participants used keyboard inputs to control the direction of a red cursor to hit a red target block. To introduce errors, 30% of input commands were randomly executed in incorrect directions. Task failure was defined as either hitting a gray block or exceeding the movement limit (16 moves). Participants were instructed to complete each task trial successfully by avoiding these conditions.

To record EEG responses related solely to outcome stimuli, task-free idle trials were embedded as a neutral condition. In these idle trials, all blocks were gray and participants had no specific goals or outcome expectations (see Fig. 1(b)). Keyboard input was replaced with spacebar presses, and cursor movement followed random directions—left or right in Experiment I, and all four directions in Experiments II and III. Idle trials replicated the visual and motor dynamics of task trials but eliminated goal-directed expectations, allowing for the recording of purely stimulus-driven EEG responses. Each paradigm included idle trials to ensure coverage across feedback contexts.

The time course of each paradigm is illustrated in Fig. 1(c). Each participant completed one session per paradigm, with four runs per session. Each run included 18 trials: 12 task and 6 idle. Idle trials were interleaved after every two task trials to minimize fatigue effects. The order of paradigms was pseudo-randomized across participants. Before each paradigm, participants received standardized instructions and were asked to maintain visual attention on the monitor while minimizing physical movement throughout the experiment.

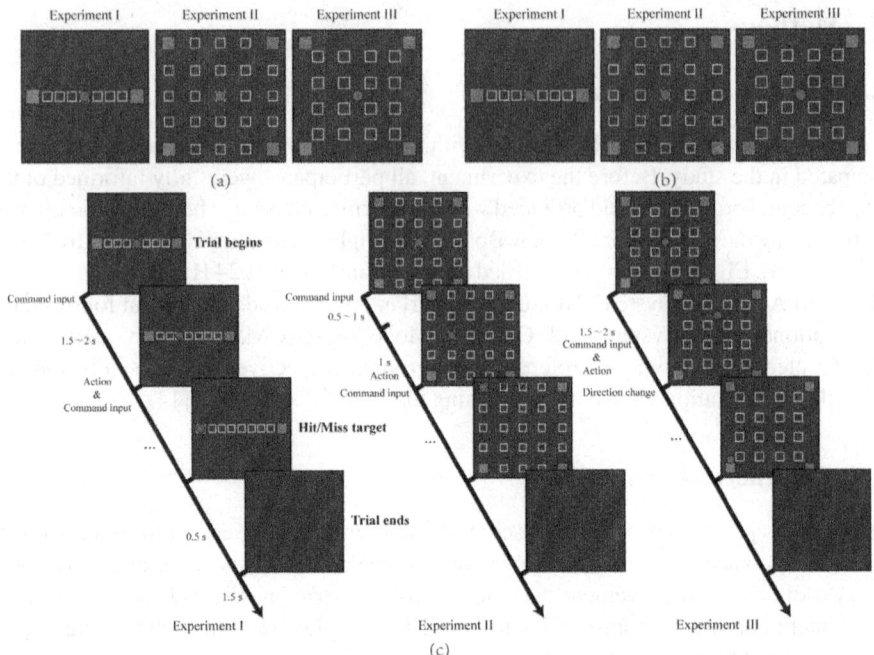

Fig. 1. Illustration of experimental design. (a) Task trials for Experiments I, II, and III. (b) Idle trials for Experiments I, II, and III. (c) Time course of each experimental paradigm.

2.3 Signal Processing and ERP Analysis

EEG data were band-pass filtered between 1 and 30 Hz using a zero-phase finite impulse response (FIR) filter. Continuous recordings were segmented into epochs ranging from −0.3 to 1 s, time-locked to cursor movement onset in Experiments I and II, or to cursor direction changes in Experiment III. Epochs containing any data point that deviated by more than ± 5 standard deviations from the mean across all epochs were rejected. To reduce contamination from ocular artifacts, signals from anterior frontal (AF) electrodes were removed. The remaining EEG channels were re-referenced to the common average. A baseline correction was applied by subtracting the mean signal within the [−0.3, 0] s window, and all epochs were subsequently downsampled to 256 Hz.

The extracted epochs were categorized according to the characteristics of cursor movement into three conditions: correct, erroneous, and neutral conditions. Correct trials reflected cursor movements aligned with the participant's keyboard input during task trials, erroneous trials involved movements that deviated from the keyboard input. Correspondingly, neutral trials corresponded to cursor movements during idle trials without task-related movement expectations. Epochs corresponding to each condition were averaged for each participant. A permutation-based F-test [15] was then performed at each time point within the [0, 1] s window, focusing on the FCz electrode.

We further quantify the ERPs' correlation between correct-neutral conditions and erroneous-neutral conditions by latency and amplitude of ERP waveforms. Cross-correlation analysis was employed to estimate the overall latency difference between the two paradigms. Let $X_i^I, X_i^{II} \in \mathbb{R}^{N_c \times N_s}$ represent the averaged ERP epochs for participant i in Experiment I and Experiment II, respectively, where N_c denotes the number of channels and N_s the number of time points. The latency difference $D_i^{I,II}$ between the two paradigms of participant i can be computed as:

$$d_k = \arg\max_d (xcorr(x_k^I, x_k^{II}(t-d))) \tag{1}$$

$$D_i^{I,II} = [d_1 \ldots d_{N_c}] \tag{2}$$

where x_k^I and x_k^{II} are the averaged ERP at channel k for Experiment I and II, respectively. Thus, the latency difference between the two experimental paradigms was extracted by $D_i^{I,II}$, $D_i^{I,III}$, and $D_i^{II,III}$ for the subsequent correlation analysis. Correspondingly, amplitude difference was quantified by the latency corrected ERPs of two paradigms. Let $\widehat{X_i^{II}}$ denotes the ERPs of X_i^{II} after correcting the latency difference according to $D_i^{I,II}$. The amplitude difference between Experiment I and II can be obtained from:

$$A_i^{I,II} = \widehat{X_i^{II}} - X_i^I \tag{3}$$

The amplitude difference was further smoothed by averaging through a 40 ms window without overlap for each ERP.

To evaluate whether the cross-paradigm ERP variations in correct and erroneous conditions are correlated with those observed in the neutral condition, mixed-effects linear regression (MELR) was employed. The MELR model was constructed for each channel to assess latency difference. The latency difference MELR models for correct and erroneous conditions were established as:

$$d_k^{Correct} \sim d_k^{Neutral} + (1|subject) + \epsilon \tag{4}$$

$$d_k^{Erroneous} \sim d_k^{Neutral} + (1|subject) + \epsilon \tag{5}$$

For amplitude difference correlation analysis, the MELR model was constructed for each channel at each sampling point. Thus, the MELR model of correct and erroneous conditions were:

$$a_{km}^{Correct} \sim a_{km}^{Neutral} + (1|subject) + \epsilon \tag{6}$$

$$a_{km}^{Erroneous} \sim a_{km}^{Neutral} + (1|subject) + \epsilon \tag{7}$$

where a_{km} is the element in k-th channel and m-th sampling point of A_i. The significance of each MELR analysis was accessed by Scatterthwaite's approximation for degrees of freedom of t statistics.

2.4 Neutral Condition Aligned Training Protocol

We employed cross-paradigm transfer learning decoding to evaluate the feasibility of applying data from the neutral condition as reference-state data for decoding correct-vs-erroneous trials across paradigms. The aforementioned preprocessed EEG epochs were downsampled to 64 Hz, and data from 20 channels located near the fronto-central and centro-parietal regions (i.e., F3, F1, Fz, F2, F4, FC3, FC1, FCz, FC2, FC4, C3, C1, Cz, C2, C4, CP3, CP1, CPz, CP2, CP4) within the 0.2–0.8 s window were extracted for cross-paradigm decoding.

Given that covariance-based feature extraction methods have been demonstrated to be superior to power- or amplitude-based methods in cross-data decoding [9, 16], we adopted a covariance-based approach for feature extraction. Let $Z \in \mathbb{R}^{N_c \times N_s}$, $N_c = 20$, $N_s = 39$ denotes the epoch data after preprocessing. The covariance matrix C of this epoch is defined as:

$$C = \frac{1}{N_s} ZZ^T \tag{8}$$

Since C is a symmetric matrix, only the upper triangular elements were vectorized to uniquely represent the covariance features.

Previous research has shown that Riemannian geometry can be utilized to align data across paradigms [6]. However, such alignment requires reference-state data [17]. To this end, we proposed the Neutral Condition Aligned Training Protocol (NCTP) for cross-paradigm data alignment. As illustrated in Fig. 2(a), we assume that the variations of correct and erroneous trials across paradigms originate from changes in the neutral condition, and the changes relative to the neutral condition are consistent across paradigms. Centering the covariance matrix with respect to the paradigm-specific neutral condition will only keep the changes relative to the neutral condition according to the congruence invariance property of symmetric positive definite (SPD) matrices. Thus, a transformation matrix $\overline{R}$ describing the centering process (see Fig. 2(b)) can be estimated from the covariance matrices of the neutral condition:

$$\overline{R} = \arg\min_{C} \sum_{i=1}^{N_t} \delta^2(C_i^{Neutral}, C) \tag{9}$$

where $C_i^{Neutral}$ is the covariance matrix for i-th epoch of the neutral condition, and N_t is the number of neutral condition epochs. This transformation matrix $\overline{R}$ will be estimated for each paradigm. The matrix $\overline{R}$ is then applied to align the covariance matrices of the correct and erroneous condition epochs in corresponding paradigms (see Fig. 2(c)):

$$\widetilde{C}_i^{Correct} = \overline{R}^{\frac{1}{2}} logm\left(\overline{R}^{-\frac{1}{2}} C_i^{Correct} \overline{R}^{-\frac{1}{2}}\right) \overline{R}^{\frac{1}{2}} \tag{10}$$

$$\widetilde{C}_i^{Erroneous} = \overline{R}^{\frac{1}{2}} logm\left(\overline{R}^{-\frac{1}{2}} C_i^{Erroneous} \overline{R}^{-\frac{1}{2}}\right) \overline{R}^{\frac{1}{2}} \tag{11}$$

where $logm$ denotes the logarithm of a matrix. The aligned covariance matrices $\widetilde{C}_i^{Correct}$ and $\widetilde{C}_i^{Erroneous}$ are subsequently vectorized to form feature vectors for decoding in the target paradigm.

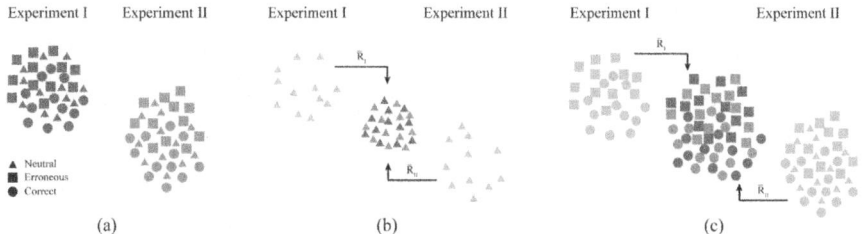

Fig. 2. Neutral condition aligned training protocol. (a) Raw data of two experiments. (b) Aligning the data of neutral condition. (c) Transformation of erroneous and correct events

Cross-paradigm decoding was conducted between every pair of paradigms. In each case, feature vectors from one paradigm were normalized using [0,1] min-max scaling and used to train a shrinkage linear discriminant analysis (s-LDA) classifier. This classifier was then applied to feature vectors from the other paradigm to assess cross-paradigm decoding performance. Due to the class imbalance between correct and erroneous samples in the dataset, decoding performance was evaluated using balanced accuracy (bACC) [4]:

$$bACC = \frac{TPR + TNR}{2} \quad (12)$$

where TPR and TNR denote the true positive rate and true negative rate of cross-paradigm decoding. By comparing decoding performance with and without the use of NCTP, we examined the effectiveness of leveraging information from the neutral condition to improve cross-paradigm decoding of ErrP.

3 Results

3.1 Cross-Paradigm Variability of ERPs

ERPs for the correct, erroneous, and neutral conditions across the three paradigms were first examined to confirm whether ERP responses change with paradigm variation. As shown in Fig. 3, ERP waveforms at the FCz channel exhibit a consistent trend of increased latency as the experimental paradigm shifts from one-dimensional to two-dimensional movement and from discrete to continuous control. In addition, amplitudes of these ERPs tend to increase within the [0.3, 0.5] s time window. Statistical analysis revealed significant cross-paradigm differences for all three conditions, with the significant time intervals consistently falling within the [0.3, 0.5] s range.

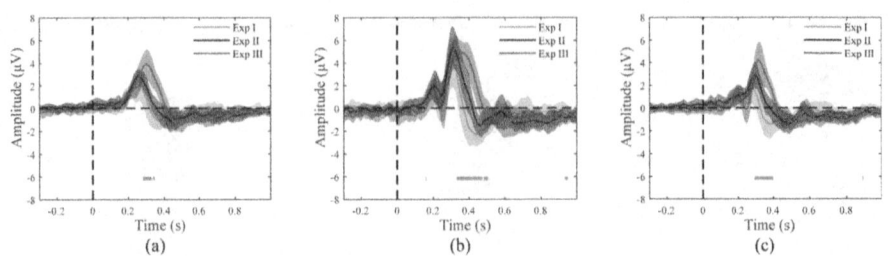

Fig. 3. The ERP waveforms at channel FCz. (a) Correct condition. (b) Erroneous condition. (c) Neutral condition. The grey shaded areas indicate the significant ($p < 0.05$) difference time period across three experimental paradigms.

3.2 Latency and Amplitude Correlation Between ERP Responses

Figure 4(a) and 4(b) showed the results of the latency difference correlation between the correct and neutral conditions, and between the erroneous and neutral conditions, respectively. Significant correlations were observed in the fronto-central, centro-parietal, and bilateral parietal regions. These findings indicated that ERP latency differences across paradigms in both the correct and erroneous conditions were significantly associated with those in the neutral condition in these regions. Moreover, differences in beta values suggested that the correct condition exhibited stronger correlations with the neutral condition than the erroneous condition did.

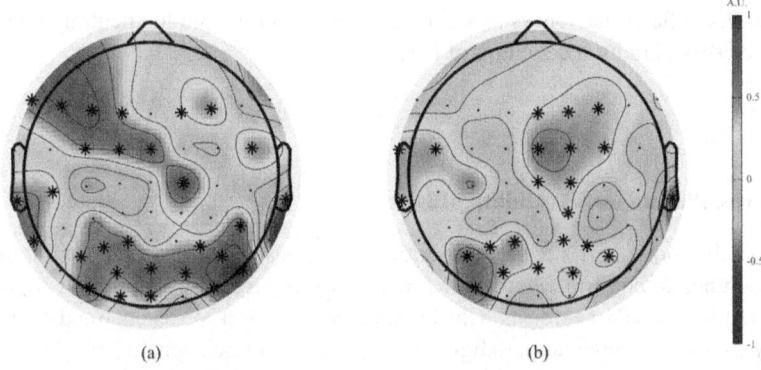

Fig. 4. The topographies of latency correlation beta values estimated by MELR. (a) Correlation between correct and neutral conditions. (b) Correlation between erroneous and neutral conditions. The significantly correlated channels are marked as * in the topographies.

Figure 5 illustrated the cross-paradigm correlation results for amplitude differences. Both the correct and erroneous conditions exhibited significant correlations with the neutral condition in the fronto-central, centro-parietal, and bilateral parietal regions within the [0.6, 0.9] s time window. Additionally, the correct condition showed significant correlations in these regions during the [0.26, 0.34] s interval, whereas no such correlations were observed for the erroneous condition in this period. Conversely, the erroneous condition demonstrated significant correlations in the frontal region around 0.22 s, which were absent in the correct condition. These results confirmed that both correct and erroneous conditions exhibited significant spatial and temporal correlations with the neutral condition. However, the distributions of these correlations differ between correct and erroneous conditions.

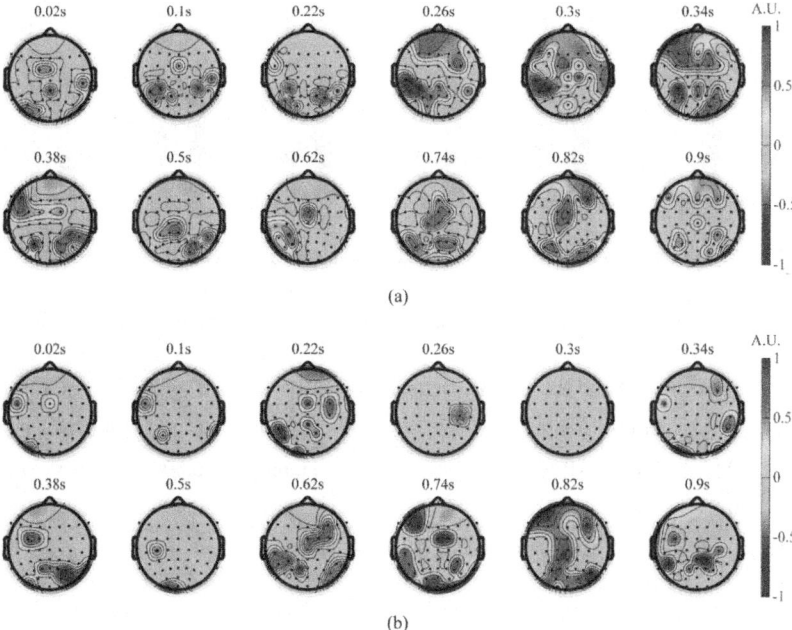

Fig. 5. The topographies of amplitude difference correlation estimated by MELR. (a) Correlation between correct and neutral conditions. (b) Correlation between erroneous and neutral conditions. Only significant beta values ($p < 0.05$) of MELR are shown in the topographies.

3.3 Cross-Paradigm Decoding Performance

Cross-paradigm decoding performance is depicted in Fig. 6. All six cross-paradigm training–testing configurations showed a noticeable increase in bACC after applying the NCTP method. Among them, the configurations from Experiment II to I, Experiment III to II, Experiment I to III, and Experiment III to I exhibited statistically significant bACC improvements. The most prominent enhancement was observed in the Experiment II to I setting, where the bACC of ErrP decoding increased by 11%. These significant improvements in cross-paradigm decoding performance confirm that NCTP effectively aligned EEG data of correct and erroneous conditions across different paradigms.

Participants were divided into two groups, HC (7 participants) and LC (3 participants), based on the magnitude of the maximum cross-correlation coefficient at the FCz channel between the neutral conditions of the two paradigms (see Table 1). The decoding accuracy in the HC group is higher than that in the LC group. This difference suggests that NCTP leverage the reference property of the neutral condition.

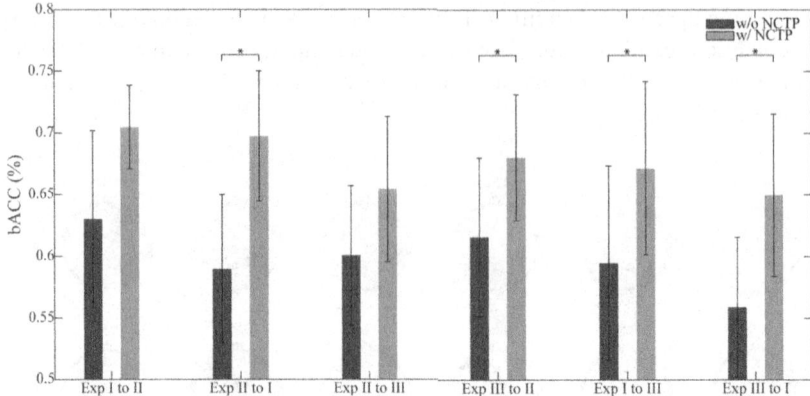

Fig. 6. Balanced accuracy of cross-paradigm classification without and with NCTP.

Table 1. Cross-paradigm classification with NCTP for different groups of participants

Group	Experiment I and II			Experiment II and III			Experiment I and III		
	r	I to II	II to I	r	II to III	III to II	r	I to III	III to I
HC	0.82	0.71	0.71	0.87	0.67	0.69	0.80	0.68	0.67
LC	0.55	0.68	0.67	0.73	0.61	0.66	0.49	0.64	0.61

HC: high correlation coefficient group; LC: low correlation coefficient group.

4 Discussion

This study introduced a novel training protocol based on the physiological mechanisms underlying ErrP generation to address the lack of physiological grounding in existing transfer learning approaches for cross-paradigm decoding of ErrP. Specifically, we proposed that a neutral condition, which removed task-related expectations, can be used to trace cross-paradigm variations in EEG responses associated with correct and erroneous outcomes. We confirmed the correlation between the stimulus-related neutral condition and task-related correct and erroneous conditions in ERPs' latency and amplitude using MELR analysis. Building upon these findings, we developed a transfer learning training protocol named NCTP to improve cross-paradigm decoding. The enhanced decoding performance demonstrated the effectiveness of the neutral condition in facilitating transfer learning for ErrP decoding.

Unlike previous studies, which lacked quantitative analysis of how proposed factors influence cross-paradigm variability in correct and erroneous EEG responses [4, 10, 11], this work introduced a physiological marker, the EEG response under the neutral condition, and established its quantitative correlation with the correct and erroneous responses. Notably, the brain regions exhibiting significant correlations in latency and amplitude aligned with cognitive regions known to be involved in ErrP generation [18].

Moreover, existing cross-paradigm decoding methods heavily relied on collecting correct and erroneous EEG data under the new paradigm using pseudo-control experiments [6, 19]. This requirement imposed additional training time and cognitive effort on participants and limited practical applicability. In contrast, the proposed NCTP method enhances cross-paradigm decoding performance without EEG data from correct or erroneous conditions in the new paradigm, thereby enabling data-efficient transfer learning without condition-specific data acquisition.

5 Conclusion and Future Work

This study proposes a novel physiology-informed training protocol for transfer learning in cross-paradigm ErrP decoding. The significant correlations observed in ERP responses and the improvement in cross-paradigm decoding accuracy demonstrate the effectiveness and superiority of the proposed NCTP method.

In the future, we should further investigate EEG-based physiological indicators to elucidate the underlying mechanisms contributing to the effectiveness of the proposed NCTP protocol. The current MELR analysis results only demonstrate a correlation between ERP changes in the neutral condition and those in the correct and erroneous conditions, but lack evidence of causality. Further physiological investigations, such as source localization and brain network analysis, are needed to complement these findings. Additionally, collecting data from a larger sample of participants will be essential to validate the generalizability of its cross-paradigm decoding performance for the general population.

Funding. This work was supported in part by the Science and Technology Commission of Shanghai Municipality (STCSM, Grant No. 24YL1900200) and the National Natural Science Foundation of China (Grant No. 52175023).

References

1. Tao, T., Jia, Y., Xu, G., Liang, R., Zhang, Q., Chen, L., et al.: Enhancement of motor imagery training efficiency by an online adaptive training paradigm integrated with error related potential. J. Neural Eng. **20**(1), 016029 (2023)
2. Wimmer, M., Weidinger, N., Veas, E., Müller-Putz, G.R.: Multimodal decoding of error processing in a virtual reality flight simulation. Sci. Rep. **14**(1), 9221 (2024)
3. Iwane, F., et al.: Customizing the human-avatar mapping based on EEG error related potentials. J. Neural Eng. **21**(2), 026016 (2024)
4. Yasemin, M., Cruz, A., Nunes, U.J., Pires, G.: Single trial detection of error-related potentials in brain-machine interfaces: a survey and comparison of methods. J. Neural Eng. **20**(1), 016015 (2023)
5. Abu-Alqumsan, M., Kapeller, C., Hintermüller, C., Guger, C., Peer, A.: Invariance and variability in interaction error-related potentials and their consequences for classification. J. Neural Eng. **14**(6), 066015 (2017)
6. Aydarkhanov, R., Uscumlic, M., Chavarriaga, R., Gheorghe, L., Millan, J.D.: Spatial covariance improves BCI performance for late ERPs components with high temporal variability. J. Neural Eng. **17**(3), 036030 (2020)

7. Cruz, A., Pires, G., Nunes, U.J.: Spatial filtering based on Riemannian distance to improve the generalization of ErrP classification. Neurocomputing **470**, 236–246 (2022)
8. She, Q., Cai, Y., Du, S., Chen, Y.: Multi-source manifold feature transfer learning with domain selection for brain-computer interfaces. Neurocomputing **514**, 313–327 (2022)
9. Wu, D., Xu, Y., Lu, B.-L.: Transfer learning for EEG-based brain–computer interfaces: a review of progress made since 2016. IEEE Trans. Cogn. Dev. Syst. **14**(1), 4–19 (2022)
10. Omedes, J., Iturrate, I., Minguez, J., Montesano, L.: Analysis and asynchronous detection of gradually unfolding errors during monitoring tasks. J. Neural Eng. **12**(5), 056001 (2015)
11. Iturrate, I., Chavarriaga, R., Montesano, L., Minguez, J., Millán, J.D.R.: Latency correction of event-related potentials between different experimental protocols. J. Neural Eng. **11**(3), 036005 (2014)
12. Iturrate, I., Grizou, J., Omedes, J., Oudeyer, P.Y., Lopes, M., Montesano, L.: Exploiting task constraints for self-calibrated brain-machine interface control using error-related potentials. PLoS ONE **10**(7), e0131491 (2015)
13. Spreng, R.N., Stevens, W.D., Chamberlain, J.P., Gilmore, A.W., Schacter, D.L.: Default network activity, coupled with the frontoparietal control network, supports goal-directed cognition. Neuroimage **53**(1), 303–317 (2010)
14. Schalk, G., McFarland, D.J., Hinterberger, T., Birbaumer, N., Wolpaw, J.R.: BCI2000: A general-purpose, brain-computer interface (BCI) system. IEEE Trans. Biomed. Eng. **51**(6), 1034–1043 (2004)
15. Oostenveld, R., Fries, P., Maris, E., Schoffelen, J.-M.: FieldTrip: open source software for advanced analysis of MEG, EEG, and invasive electrophysiological data. Comput. Intell. Neurosci. **2011**, 1–9 (2011)
16. Wan, Z., Yang, R., Huang, M., Zeng, N., Liu, X.: A review on transfer learning in EEG signal analysis. Neurocomputing **421**, 1–14 (2021)
17. Zanini, P., Congedo, M., Jutten, C., Said, S., Berthoumieu, Y.: Transfer learning: a riemannian geometry framework with applications to brain–computer interfaces. IEEE Trans. Biomed. Eng. **65**(5), 1107–1116 (2018)
18. Ullsperger, M., Fischer, A.G., Nigbur, R., Endrass, T.: Neural mechanisms and temporal dynamics of performance monitoring. Trends Cogn. Sci. **18**(5), 259–267 (2014)
19. Iwane, F., Iturrate, I., Chavarriaga, R., Millán, J.D.R.: Invariability of EEG error-related potentials during continuous feedback protocols elicited by erroneous actions at predicted or unpredicted states. J. Neural Eng. **18**(4), 046044 (2021)

Design and Implementation of Thermoplastic Composite Robotic Winding System

Huangchao Chen[1], Tianming Li[2], Dailin Zhang[1(✉)], Xingwei Zhao[1(✉)], and Bo Tao[1]

[1] The State Key Laboratory of Intelligent Manufacturing Equipment and Technology, Department of Mechanical Science and Engineering, Huazhong University of Science and Technology, Wuhan 430074, China
zhaoxingwei@hust.edu.cn, mnizhang@mail.hust.edu.cn
[2] Hubei Sanjiang Aerospace Jiangbei Mechanical Engineering Co., Ltd., Xiaogan 432100, China

Abstract. Thermoplastic composites are widely used in the manufacturing of composite components due to their fast molding speed and excellent mechanical properties. This paper proposes a robotic winding system based on the collaboration between a six-axis industrial robot and a positioner, aiming to achieve the automated winding of thermoplastic composites. The system integrates multi-physics control modules (tension, temperature, pressure) with an offline programming module, and combines the winding path generated by CADWIND to enable coordinated motion planning of the robot's end-effector posture and the mandrel rotation angle. Traditional methods, when generating trajectories, assume a certain yarn suspension length, which may lead to the roller detaching from the mandrel and failure in molding. To address this issue, a geometry-based trajectory generation method is proposed to ensure constant contact between the roller and the mandrel. Experimental results demonstrate that the developed system can effectively complete winding tasks on complex surfaces, such as pressure vessel with elliptical domes, highlighting the potential of the system for automated thermoplastic composite winding applications.

Keywords: Thermoplastic Composite · Robotic Winding · Motion Planning

1 Introduction

Thermoplastic composites offer advantages such as in-situ molding, excellent mechanical properties, and recyclability, making them widely attractive in fields such as aerospace and transportation. Fiber winding is one of the most widely used composite material manufacturing techniques [1,2]. By winding continuous reinforcement fibers on a mandrel, a layer with clear fiber direction and precise positioning is created, which helps maximize fiber strength [3]. Thanks to the material properties, the thermoplastic composite winding process eliminates the need for a curing step after winding, significantly reducing manufacturing time [4].

In the in-situ molding process of thermoplastic composite materials, a small portion of the prepreg and substrate is rapidly heated to its melting temperature and pressed together by a roller. As the heat source moves, the prepreg continuously deposits onto the substrate, while the previously heated section cools and solidifies [5]. During the winding process, it is necessary to adjust the direction of the prepreg to ensure it deposits at the specified winding angle. Furthermore, the mandrel is continuously rotated to ensure the uniform distribution of prepregs. Both CNC machine tools and robotic systems can be developed and used to implement the aforementioned process. Compared to CNC machine tools, the latter offers higher flexibility and lower cost [6]. Specifically, a robot is used to drive the placement tool along the predefined trajectory, while a positioner rotates the mandrel. In addition, the placement tool typically needs to integrate re-feeding unit, cutting unit, tension control unit, pressure control unit and heating device to meet the requirements of automation [7,8].

In the winding process, the design of the winding pattern directly determines the path and coverage of the fibers on the mandrel, which affects the structural load-bearing efficiency, stress distribution uniformity, and fatigue resistance of the finished part [9]. Two design approaches are commonly used: 1) model-based methods [1,10,11] and 2) discrete methods [12,13] On the other hand, trajectory generation involves converting the geometric path into motion commands for the winding machine/robot. Traditional commercial CAD/CAM software (such as CADWIND, CADfil, CADPATH, etc.) uses geometry mapping algorithms to generate geodesic or non-geodesic paths. These software programs also reserve a safety distance by maintaining a segment of suspended fiber to prevent collisions between the pay-out eye and the mandrel, a practice that has become well-established in conventional winding processes [14]. However, due to the specific requirements of thermoplastic composite winding processes—particularly the need for the roller to maintain a constant contact pressure with the mandrel to achieve resin melting, infiltration, and interlaminar bonding [15]—the trajectory generated based on the suspended yarn can lead to instability in the contact pressure distribution. This, in turn, can cause defects such as increased porosity and reduced interlaminar shear strength [5,16]. Furthermore, during winding, the fibers need to change direction at the dome and be tangent to the pole hole, which means the winding angle will vary [17]. In summary, the winding trajectory must not only satisfy the normal contact constraints between the roller and the mandrel but also account for variations in the winding angle at the dome.

This paper focuses on the development and implementation of a thermoplastic composite robotic winding system using industrial robot and positioner. The study involves the construction of a six-axis robot-positioner collaborative platform, integrating multiple control modules such as pressure, temperature, and tension, to build an integrated control architecture for multi-physics field collaboration during the winding process. The winding path is generated using

CADWIND, and through geometric relations, it is converted into coordinated commands for the robot end-effector posture and positioner rotation angle. The primary contribution of this work is the development of a thermoplastic composite robotic winding system and a feasible trajectory generation method.

This paper is organized as follows: Sect. 2 presents the overall design of the robotic winding system. Section 3 introduces the trajectory generation method. Section 4 provides experimental results. Section 5 gives conclusion.

2 The Overall Design of The Robotic Wingding System

2.1 Process Flow

Figure 1 illustrates the process flow of the robotic winding system. After the system is started, the robot first moves from its initial pose to the preset trajectory starting point. When the robot's end-effector reaches the trajectory starting point, the roller forms an initial contact state with the mandrel. At this point, the system sequentially activates the following modules: 1) The preheating heater is powered on to perform preliminary heating of the prepreg; 2) The re-feeding unit performs the feeding action, accurately delivering the pretreated prepreg to the roller-mandrel contact point (nip point).

Subsequently, the system enters the collaborative motion stage. The robot and the positioner begin collaborative motion based on the offline-programmed trajectory. During this process, three key control units operate in sync: 1) The tension control unit adjusts the unwind tension of the prepreg in real-time to maintain material tightness; 2) The laser adjusts the output power through closed-loop temperature feedback to ensure the resin matrix reaches the optimal flow state; 3) The pressure control unit dynamically compensates for the roller contact force to ensure inter-layer bonding strength. After the planned trajectory is completed, the system sequentially shuts down the preheating heater, tension control unit, laser, and pressure control unit following safety protocols. The cut-off unit then activates to cut the prepreg. Finally, the robot resets to its initial position, completing the entire winding process cycle.

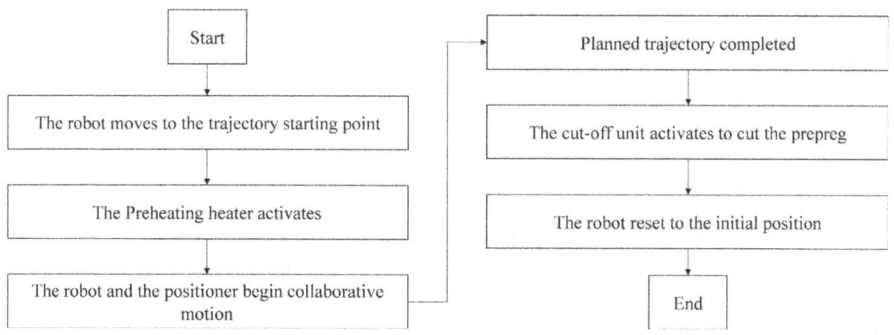

Fig. 1. The process flow of the robotic winding system.

2.2 Hardware Setup

The system includes a positioner, a six-axis robotic arm, a placement tool, and its dedicated controller to carry out the winding process. In the constructed system, thermocouple preheating and laser heating methods are used to heat the prepreg to their melting temperature. Tension and pressure are controlled by a tension wheel and an air-floating device, respectively. Additionally, a cutting unit and a re-feeding unit are integrated.

The winding system uses the robotic arm to drive the placement tool, tracking changes in the winding angle and the surface normal vector of the curved surface. The positioner continuously rotates the mandrel, ensuring the material is evenly deposited on the mandrel. The laser, as part of the placement tool, emits laser beams at an angle at the interface with the mandrel. The controller can precisely adjust key parameters, such as winding speed, laser power, and pressure. Figure 2(a) demonstrates the primary forming principle: the laser beam heats the prepreg and substrate to a molten state, followed by the roller applying pressure to compress the molten portion. Meanwhile, as the roller moves, the prepreg is continuously fed out until the winding process is complete.

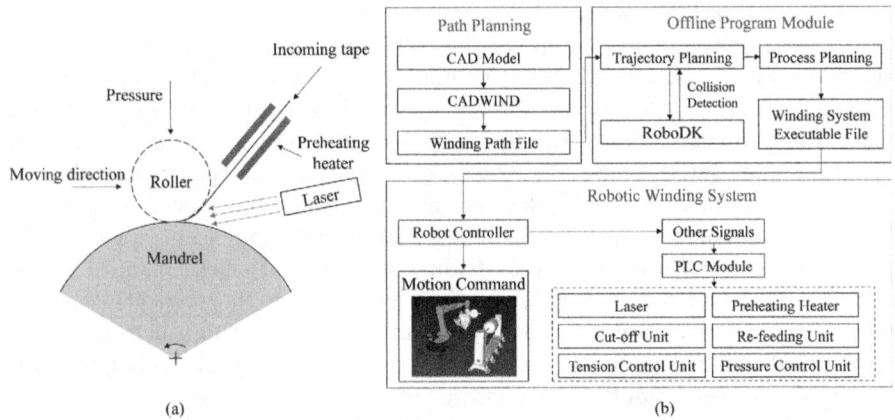

Fig. 2. The overall design of the robotic winding system. (a) Forming principle and (b) Integrated control architecture.

2.3 Integrated Control Architecture

Figure 2(b) illustrates the integrated control architecture. The CAD model of mandrel is used as input, and the parameters are imported into CADWIND software to design the winding pattern and generate the path file. The exported path file is then input into the offline programming module for trajectory generation. The trajectory is input into RoboDK for motion simulation, and the feasibility of the trajectory is determined based on collision check results. Finally, an executable file for the winding system is generated, which drives the robot and positioner and controls modules such as the laser according to the process flow.

The offline programming module runs on an external device and transmits the executable file to the robot controller via Ethernet protocol. The robot controller parses and distributes the received executable file, with motion commands sent to the robot and positioner, while other control commands are sent to the PLC module. The PLC module then sends control signals to devices such as the laser and tension wheel.

2.4 Process Limitations and Operational Stability Analysis

Based on the process flow, the prepreg tape must be heated to its melting point to ensure successful consolidation, which requires sufficient irradiation time. Excessive winding speed shortens heating time, leading to incomplete melting and reduced placement quality, thus imposing an upper limit on the system's maximum winding speed. Moreover, since the roller and mandrel must remain in contact, winding over the dome section may cause collisions between the placement tool and the mandrel fixtures. A thorough collision check must therefore be performed before operation to verify mandrel compatibility.

Laser power, tension, and pressure are the three critical parameters in the winding process. To maintain their stable output, the laser employs built-in temperature and power sensors with closed-loop PID control to compensate for fluctuations; the tension roller integrates force sensors and an air-bearing feedback mechanism for high-speed tension adjustments; and the roller assembly uses pressure sensors coupled with a servo controller for dynamic pressure regulation. All parameters are displayed on a centralized monitoring interface with real-time values and trend charts. Should any parameter exceed predefined thresholds, the system automatically transitions to a safe or paused state, ensuring continuous and reliable operation throughout the winding cycle.

3 The Generation of Winding Trajectory

In CADWIND, users can either create a new model based on mandrel parameters or directly import existing models. Subsequently, winding patterns can be designed according to process requirements while exporting relevant winding path. The winding path file contains critical information including the total number of cycles and the coordinates of winding path points. As an example, the process of calculating the reference trajectory of the robot and the positioner based on the winding path will be introduced, using a pressure vessel with elliptical domes.

For convenience, the workpiece coordinate system is aligned with the built-in coordinate system of CADWIND, as shown in the Fig. 3. The origin of the coordinate system is located at the center of the circle at the right end of the mandrel's cylindrical section. The Y-axis is aligned along the mandrel's axial direction, pointing toward the left end of the cylindrical section, and the Z-axis is directed vertically upwards. The tool coordinate system's origin is located at the center of the roller, with the Y-axis aligned with the Y-axis of the workpiece coordinate system. The Z-axis points toward the robot flange.

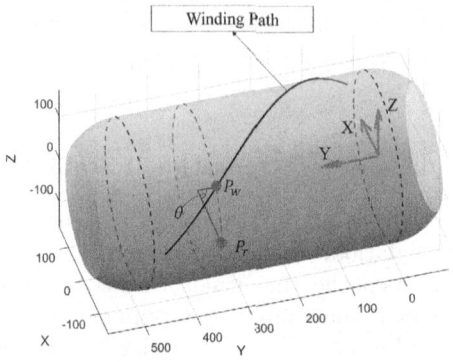

Fig. 3. Schematic of workpiece coordinate system and winding path. The boundaries of the dome section and the cylindrical section are marked with black dashed lines. Two points are located on the cross-sectional circle indicated by the red dashed line: P_w represents the winding path point, P_r denotes the corresponding robot path point, with an angle of θ. (Color figure online)

In this paper, we reference the motion mode of a 4-axis winding machine, where the roller does not move along the Z-axis of the workpiece coordinate system. Meanwhile, the posture is adjusted to match the variation of the winding angle while maintaining normal contact between the roller and the mandrel. Therefore, the roller exhibits motion in the following directions: 1) movement along the X-axis and Y-axis of the workpiece coordinate system; 2) rotation around the Z-axis of the tool coordinate system to align with the normal vector; 3) rotation around the X-axis of the tool coordinate system to match the winding angle.

Let the Z-coordinate of the robot's path point be z_0, and assume the roller is located in the negative direction of the X-axis. Based on the aforementioned assumptions and the set motion model, for any winding path point $\boldsymbol{P}_w = [P_{wx}\ P_{wy}\ P_{wz}]^T$, it can be rotated counterclockwise around the Y-axis. When the Z-coordinate first equals z_0, this point corresponds to the robot path point $\boldsymbol{P}_r$, and the angle of rotation is the corresponding positioner's angle displacement. Based on the geometric relationship, we have:

$$\begin{cases} \boldsymbol{P}_r = \boldsymbol{R} \cdot \boldsymbol{P}_w \\ \theta = \mathrm{acos}\left(\dfrac{P_{wz}}{\sqrt{P_{wx}^2+P_{wz}^2}}\right) - \mathrm{acos}\left(\dfrac{z_0}{\sqrt{P_{wx}^2+P_{wz}^2}}\right) \end{cases} \qquad (1)$$

where

$$R = \begin{bmatrix} \cos\theta & 0 & \sin\theta \\ 0 & 1 & 0 \\ -\sin\theta & 0 & \cos\theta \end{bmatrix} \quad (2)$$

Next, it is necessary to determine the posture of the tool coordinate system relative to the workpiece coordinate system. During the winding process, the roller must be adjusted such that the deposition direction aligns with the path direction and is also aligned with the normal vector to maintain contact. For any winding path point P_w, its tangent vector along the path can be approximated using the backward difference method, and its normal vector can be obtained analytically from the surface expression, thereby determining the roller's posture R_w at that point. For the ith path point P_w^i in the winding path, the tangent vector along the path is:

$$\vec{t} = \frac{P_w^i - P_w^{i-1}}{\|P_w^i - P_w^{i-1}\|} \quad (3)$$

When the path point is located on the cylindrical section, its normal vector is the line connecting the point and the center of the section's circular cross-section $P_{w0} = \begin{bmatrix} 0 & P_{wy}^i & 0 \end{bmatrix}^T$, i.e.,

$$\vec{n} = \frac{P_w^i - P_{w0}^i}{\|P_w^i - P_{w0}^i\|} \quad (4)$$

When the path point is located on the dome section, its normal vector can be expressed as:

$$\vec{n} = \begin{bmatrix} \frac{2P_{wx}}{Ra^2} & \frac{2P_{wy}}{Rb^2} & \frac{2P_{wz}}{Rc^2} \end{bmatrix}^T \quad (5)$$

The binormal vector of this path point is:

$$\vec{b} = \vec{t} \times \vec{n} \quad (6)$$

According to the coordinate system correspondence, the Y-axis of the tool coordinate system is aligned with $\vec{t}$, the Z-axis is aligned with $\vec{n}$, and the X-axis is aligned with $\vec{b}$. Thus, the rotation matrix of the tool coordinate system can be determined as follows:

$$R_w = \begin{bmatrix} \vec{b} & \vec{t} & \vec{n} \end{bmatrix} \quad (7)$$

Since P_r is derived by rotating P_w, the corresponding the rotation matrix of roller R_r satisfies:

$$R_r = R \cdot R_w \quad (8)$$

4 Experiments

The developed robotic winding system hardware consists mainly of a 6-axis industrial robot (KUKA KR210-R2100 extra), a positioner (KUKA) with a stroke of 3500 mm and a maximum load of 2000 kg, and a self-developed placement tool. The main technical parameters of the system are shown in the Table 1. Relevant programs have been written in MATLAB to automatically generate executable file for the winding system.

Table 1. Technical Parameters of the Winding System.

Parameters	Value
Winding Bandwidth	6.35 mm–12.7 mm
Maximum Winding Speed	800 mm/s
Maximum Heating Temperature	500 °C
Tension Range	10 N–120 N

After careful tuning and calibration, we used the system for winding experiments. The considered substrate is a metallic pressure vessel composed of a cylindrical section and two elliptical domes at each end. The cylinder has a diameter of 508 mm and a length of 375 mm, while the depth of each elliptical head is 130 mm. The winding pattern design was completed in CADWIND and the path was exported, as shown in Fig. 4. The bandwidth is 6.35 mm, the winding angle is 53°, the coverage is 110%, and the total number of winding turns is 167.

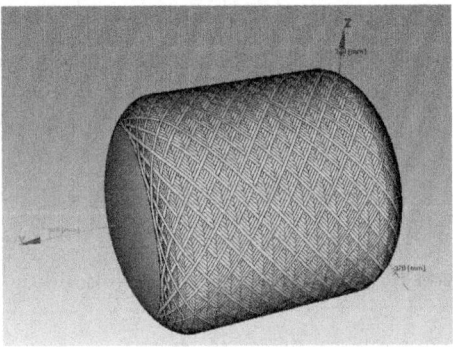

Fig. 4. The winding pattern generated by CADWIND. The gray solid represents the mandrel, which is uniformly and fully covered by the prepreg tape. (Color figure online)

The generated trajectory is shown in Fig. 5, where the black line represents the robot's motion path and the red arrows indicate the normal vectors. The generated trajectory was imported into RoboDK for collision detection, and the results showed no collisions during the operation. Subsequently, the generated executable file was imported into the winding system for actual winding. Figure 6 illustrates the finished product after winding, where the fibers are tightly arranged and evenly covered on the mandrel. The winding experiment demonstrates the application potential of the developed winding system and the effectiveness of the proposed trajectory generation method.

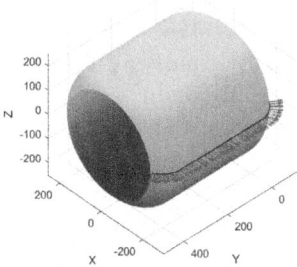

Fig. 5. The generated trajectory: the black line represents the reference position and the red arrows indicate the normal vectors. (Color figure online)

Fig. 6. The winding process.

5 Conclusion

This paper presents the design and implementation of a robotic winding system for thermoplastic composites based on a collaborative control architecture between a six-axis industrial robot and a positioner. A hardware system integrated with multi-physics field control modules was developed, supporting real-time regulation of tension, temperature, and pressure. A trajectory generation method based on geometric mapping is proposed to address the issue of lacking contact constraints in traditional method. Experimental results validate the effectiveness of the developed system in pressure vessel winding tasks.

The primary limitation at this stage is the absence of quantitative metrics to evaluate the final product's performance. Future work will focus on optimizing winding process parameters and conducting hydraulic burst tests to improve both the system's manufacturing capabilities and product performance.

Acknowledgments. This work was funded by the Major Program (JD) of Hubei Province (2023BAA004), the National Key Research and Development Program of China (2023YFB3408603) and the National Science Foundation of China (Nos. 52275020 & 62293514).

References

1. Zu, L., Xu, H., Zhang, Q., Jia, X., Zhang, B., Li, D.: Design of filament-wound spherical pressure vessels based on non-geodesic trajectories. Compos. Struct. **218**, 71–78 (2019). https://doi.org/10.1016/j.compstruct.2019.03.045
2. Liang, J., et al.: Design of continuous transition line pattern between layers of composite pressure vessel. J. Reinforced Plastics Compos. 07316844241226548 (2024). https://doi.org/10.1177/07316844241226548.
3. Guo, K., et al.: Design of winding pattern of filament-wound composite pressure vessel with unequal openings based on non-geodesics. J. Eng. Fibers Fabr. **15**, 1558925020933976 (2020). https://doi.org/10.1177/1558925020933976
4. Mack, J., Schledjewski, R.: 7 - Filament winding process in thermoplastics. In: Advani, S.G., Hsiao, K.-T. (eds.) Manufacturing Techniques for Polymer Matrix Composites (PMCs), pp. 182–208. Woodhead Publishing (2012). https://doi.org/10.1533/9780857096258.2.182.
5. Donough, M.J., Shafaq, St John, N.A., Philips, A.W., Gangadhara Prusty, B.: Process modelling of In-situ consolidated thermoplastic composite by automated fibre placement – a review. Compos. Part A: Appl. Sci. Manuf. **163**, 107179 (2022). https://doi.org/10.1016/j.compositesa.2022.107179.
6. Gao, J., Pashkevich, A., Cicellini, M., Caro, S.: Optimization of robot and positioner motions in manufacturing of high-pressure composite vessels. IFAC-PapersOnLine. **51**, 44–49 (2018). https://doi.org/10.1016/j.ifacol.2018.11.516
7. Zhang, Z., et al.: Laser-assisted thermoplastic composite automated fiber placement robot for bonding GF/PP unidirectional composites and braided composites. Compos. B Eng. **287**, 111798 (2024). https://doi.org/10.1016/j.compositesb.2024.111798

8. Carosella, S., Hügle, S., Helber, F., Middendorf, P.: A short review on recent advances in automated fiber placement and filament winding technologies. Compos. B Eng. **287**, 111843 (2024). https://doi.org/10.1016/j.compositesb.2024.111843
9. Lisbôa, T.V., Almeida Jr, J.H.S., Dalibor, I.H., Spickenheuer, A., Marczak, R.J., Amico, S.C.: The role of winding pattern on filament wound composite cylinders under radial compression. Polym. Compos. **41**, 2446–2454 (2020). https://doi.org/10.1002/pc.25548
10. Zu, L., Xu, H., Wang, H., Zhang, B., Zi, B.: Design and analysis of filament-wound composite pressure vessels based on non-geodesic winding. Compos. Struct. **207**, 41–52 (2019). https://doi.org/10.1016/j.compstruct.2018.09.007
11. Wang, Y., Xu, H., Song, H., Li, K., Hu, J.: Design method of variable slippage coefficient non-geodesic filament-wound composite pressure vessels. Polym. Compos. **45**, 3950–3964 (2024). https://doi.org/10.1002/pc.28036
12. Fu, J.H., Yun, J.D., Jung, Y.H.: Winding trajectory generation for composite products. AMM. **541–542**, 407–411 (2014). https://doi.org/10.4028/www.scientific.net/AMM.541-542.407
13. Wang, J., Tang, J., Yan, W., Xin, S., Xu, J.: A fast and precise filament winding path planning method based on discrete non-iterative semi-geodesic algorithm for all applicable mandrel. Compos. Commun. **40**, 101620 (2023). https://doi.org/10.1016/j.coco.2023.101620
14. Sofi, T., Neunkirchen, S., Schledjewski, R.: Path calculation, technology and opportunities in dry fiber winding: a review. Adv. Manuf. Polymer Compos. Sci. **4**, 57–72 (2018). https://doi.org/10.1080/20550340.2018.1500099
15. Miao, L., et al.: An analytical model for pressure distribution in automated fiber placement on irregular surfaces and its application in aeronautical manufacturing. J. Manuf. Process. **106**, 102–116 (2023). https://doi.org/10.1016/j.jmapro.2023.09.057
16. Cheng, L., Zheng, C., Wang, H., Dong, H., Ke, Y.: Pressure control for pneumatic pressing roller in automated fiber placement. J. Reinforced Plastics Compos. 07316844231205077 (2023). https://doi.org/10.1177/07316844231205077.
17. Wang, Y., Xu, H., Song, H., Li, K., Hu, J.: Determining the optimal dome shape using a novel variable slippage coefficient non-geodesic. Polym. Compos. **45**, 11730–11742 (2024). https://doi.org/10.1002/pc.28594

A Stretchable Resistive Electronic Skin for Shape Sensing of End Continua of Flexible Surgical Instruments

Lizhi Pan[1,2], Tianze Zhang[1,2], Jianmin Li[1,2], and Jinhua Li[1,2(✉)]

[1] Key Laboratory of Mechanism Theory and Equipment Design of Ministry of Education, School of Mechanical Engineering, Tianjin University, Tianjin 300350, China
[2] Institute of Medical Robotics and Intelligent Systems, Tianjin University, Tianjin 300072, China
lijinhua@tju.edu.cn

Abstract. With the increasing application of continuum surgical robots, accurate shape sensing has become essential for the successful execution of surgical tasks. Previous studies have primarily focused on shape sensing in industrial soft robots with relatively large diameters. In this work, we propose a stretchable resistive electronic skin composed of three meander-pattern strain sensing units to realize shape sensing of the end continua of flexible surgical instruments. Each strain sensing unit is designed with a conductive structure prepared by a mixture of polydimethylsiloxane (PDMS), multiwalled carbon nanotubes (MWCNTs), and graphene (GR), showing excellent sensing and mechanical properties, including high linearity (0.98), good sensitivity (GF = 2.95), rapid response (188 ms) under 0–70% strain, and great stability and durability (1000 tensile cycles). Three pieces of such e-skin are integrated onto the end continuum of a compact flexible surgical instrument (9 mm diameter, 110 mm length) to verify shape sensing performance. The average shape sensing error is less than 6 mm. The current study offers a novel perspective for shape sensing of end continua in medical applications.

Keywords: PDMS/MWCNTs/GR · e-skin · shape sensing · continua

1 Introduction

Most animals interact accurately with their surroundings due to their flexible and accurate environment perception. Similarly, intelligent robots require accurate environment perception to make precise decisions and execute complex behaviors. Soft robots, with unlimited degrees of freedom and enhanced mobility [1], are widely used in medical applications [2], agriculture [3], disaster response, and manufacturing [4]. However, their flexibility poses challenges for accurate closed-loop control [5].

Flexible surgical instruments with continuum structures offer advantages in minimally invasive surgical techniques [6], yet their motion control relies on precise shape perception [7]. Early shape sensing methods depended on mechanical and kinematic models [8], but these models exhibited limited accuracy due to factors like friction [9] and deformation [10]. Researchers then explored other techniques. Optical fibers can reconstruct continuum shapes based on curvature and strain [11,12] and have been applied in flexible surgical instruments [12,13]. Electromagnetic sensors and intraoperative imaging techniques like fluoroscopy [14], endoscopy [15,16], and ultrasound [17] also provide shape sensing capabilities. However, optical fibers are constrained by their stiffness and high cost; electromagnetic sensors are susceptible to interference in complex surgical environments; and imaging techniques pose challenges such as radiation exposure and incomplete spatial information. In recent years, flexible sensors have been applied for shape sensing in large-diameter industrial robots due to their high stretchability, biocompatibility, flexibility, and low cost [18,19]. Despite extensive research in this area, there are few applications in surgical robots due to the small diameters and stringent requirements for biocompatibility and accuracy.

This study presents a meander-pattern flexible resistive strain sensor for shape sensing in flexible surgical instruments. The sensor, fabricated from PDMS, MWCNTs, and graphene, possesses a strain range of 70% and can estimate large-angle bending. It is integrated onto TPU film and encapsulated as a stretchable e-skin with four functional layers. Three such e-skins are mounted on the end continuum of a flexible surgical instrument, achieving an average shape estimation error of less than 6 mm.

2 Experimental Section

2.1 Materials

Multi-walled carbon nanotubes (MWCNTs, purity $\geq$ 95%, inner diameter 3–5 nm, outer diameter 8–15 nm, tube length 3–12 μm), graphene (GR, purity $\geq$ 99.5%), polydimethylsiloxane (PDMS, including base and curing agent), dispersant silicone oil, and thermoplastic polyurethane elastomer (TPU, with surface protected by a double-layer PET film).

2.2 Manufacturing

The fabrication process of the flexible sensing unit is illustrated in Fig. 1. Initially, 10 g of PDMS and 0.67 g of curing agent (15:1) were mixed for 10 min. Meanwhile, 0.75 g of MWCNTs and 0.083 g of GR (9:1) were ultrasonicated in ethanol for 15 min and then added to the PDMS mixture. Subsequently, 0.375 g of silicone oil (MWCNTs:silicone oil = 2:1) was added to enhance conductivity. The resulting conductive ink was printed onto a 50 μm TPU film using a flexible microelectronic printer. Three sensor patterns (rectangular, S-shaped, meander pattern; dimensions: 26 mm × 8 mm) were printed. The printed sensors were

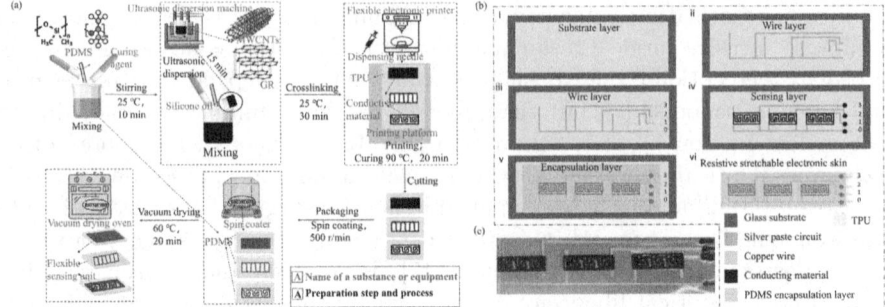

Fig. 1. (a) Preparation process of the flexible resistive strain sensing unit [25]; (b) Fabrication process of the stretchable resistive e-skin; (c) Photograph of the fabricated stretchable resistive e-skin.

then cured at 90 °C for 20 min and encapsulated using spin-coated PDMS at 500 rpm. A final curing step was performed at 60 °C for 20 min in a vacuum [21,23].

Based on comparative analysis, the meander-pattern unit was selected for integration. The e-skin consists of four functional layers: substrate, wire, sensing, and encapsulation. As shown in Fig. 1(b), the fabrication process involves: (i) Placing the TPU film on a glass substrate; (ii) Printing 200 µm-thick silver paste circuits; (iii) Attaching copper wires for electrical connections and heating at 90 °C; (iv) Printing the sensing layer, reinforcing junctions with conductive filler and curing at 60 °C; (v) Spin-coating a 50 µm PDMS encapsulation layer and heating t at 60 °C; (vi) Cutting the final stretchable resistive e-skin to 30 mm × 120 mm. A photo of the fabricated device is shown in Fig. 1(c).

2.3 Characterization and Integration of E-Skin for Continuum Shape Sensing

A sensing platform was established to evaluate the performance of the flexible resistive sensing units, as shown in Fig. 2(a). It consists of a tensile testing machine, LABRD software, a custom fixture, a personal computer, a signal processing circuit, an MCC acquisition card with DAQ software, and Quick Macro software. This platform enables comprehensive evaluation of sensor performance, including linearity, sensitivity, response speed, repeatability, and stretchability. During testing, the sensing unit was fixed using the clamp, and Quick Macro software was applied to simultaneously trigger both LABRD and DAQ software, ensuring synchronized data acquisition. As the sensing unit stretched, its resistance changed. The resistance was converted into a voltage signal via the signal processing circuit and recorded by the MCC acquisition card.

The integration of the e-skin onto the continuum is shown in Fig. 2(b). The continuum is a self-developed device, with a diameter of 9 mm and a length of 110 mm. Three e-skin units were coated with J-527S silica gel and wrapped isoperimetrically around the continuum. The assembly was left to cure at room temperature for 24 h. The experimental setup for shape sensing using the stretchable resistive e-skin is depicted in Fig. 2(c). It consists of the PMAC system,

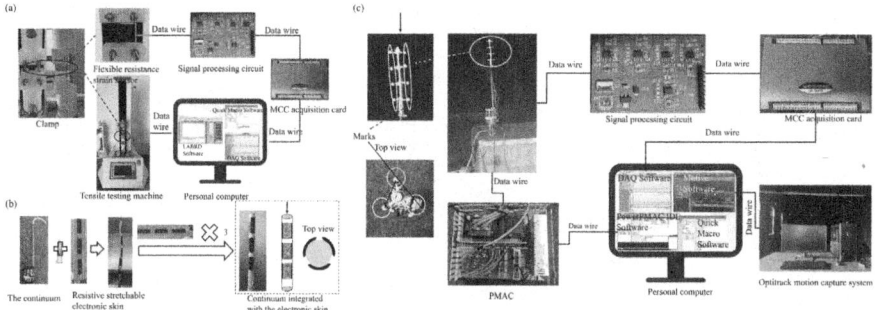

Fig. 2. (a) Sensing platform for characterizing the flexible resistance strain sensor; (b) Integration of the stretchable resistive e-skin with the continuum; (c) Experimental setup for continuum shape sensing.

continuum, signal processing circuit, MCC acquisition card, Optitrick, and a personal computer. The PMAC system controlled the continuum to perform bending motions. A total of 12 reflective markers (3 × 4) were attached to the continuum for OptiTrack-based shape measurement, evenly distributed on both sides of the sensing units. As the continuum bent, the resistance of the e-skins changed accordingly. This resistance was converted to a voltage signal via the signal conditioning circuit and captured by the MCC acquisition card, which then transmitted the data to the personal computer for processing.

3 Result and Disscussion

3.1 Structure and Properties

Particle-filled polymers exhibit a typical percolation behavior, influenced by filler purity, aspect ratio, conductivity, and dispersion uniformity. For MWCNTs in PDMS, the percolation threshold is 4–5 wt% [22,23], necessitating filler content above this threshold to ensure conductivity. In strain sensors, stretchability is a critical performance indicator. Figure 3(a) shows the elongation of flexible sensors with varying PDMS/curing agent and MWCNTs contents. A mass ratio of 10:1 (PDMS to curing agent) is commonly adopted in flexible sensor fabrication. Generally, a lower curing agent ratio enhances PDMS stretchability [24], though it may prolong the curing time. However, the incorporation of conductive fillers into the PDMS matrix can mitigate this effect, allowing for enhanced stretchability without significantly increasing curing time. To evaluate maximum elongation, a series of PDMS samples with curing agent ratios of 10:1 to 20:1 were tested. A 15:1 ratio achieved 102% strain (without fillers). This ratio was used to investigate the effect of varying MWCNTs mass fractions above the percolation threshold. Subsequently, samples with MWCNTs contents ranging from 6 $wt\%$ to 9 $wt\%$ were fabricated and tested. At 7.5 wt%, the flexible sensor demonstrated a tensile strain of 94.5%, indicating a favorable balance between conductivity and stretchability.

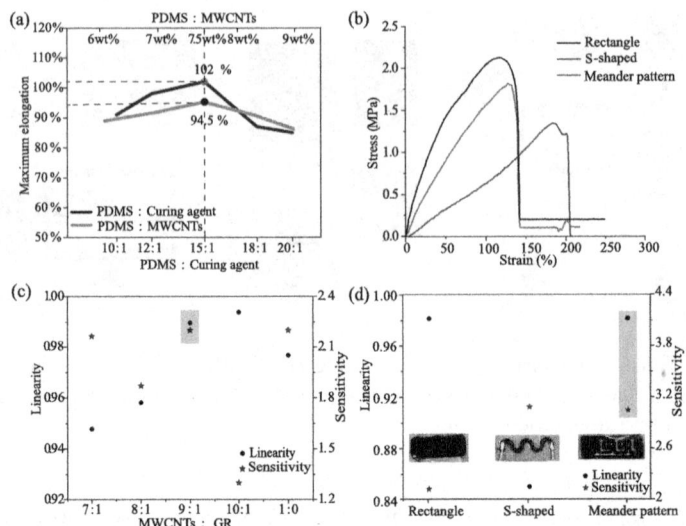

Fig. 3. (a) Elongation of flexible sensors with varying PDMS/curing-agent and MWCNT contents; (b) Stress-strain diagrams of rectangular, S-shaped, and meander pattern flexible sensors at $m_{MWCNTs}:m_{GR} = 9:1$; (c) Comparison of sensitivity and linearity of flexible sensors with different ratios of MWCNTs and GR at $m_{PDMS}:m_{MWCNTs} = 100:7.5$; (d) Comparison of linearity and sensitivity of flexible sensors in rectangular, S-shaped, and meander pattern at $m_{MWCNTs}:m_{GR} = 9:1$.

Flexible sensors with three different patterns were subjected to stress-strain characterization, as illustrated in Fig. 3(b). The rectangle flexible sensor exhibited the highest tensile stress but the lowest stretchability. In contrast, the S-shaped sensor demonstrated greater stretchability and lower tensile strength. The meander-pattern sensor, combining the advantages of both rectangle and S-shaped, exhibited a higher stretchability than the rectangle sensor and a greater tensile strength than the S-shaped one, achieving 1.76 MPa tensile strength and 128% elongation. Furthermore, the sensor packaged with PDMS is not affected by liquid in the human body.

Sensitivity and linearity are key performance indicators for flexible sensors. MWCNTs, with their high aspect ratio and flexibility, readily form conductive networks but suffer from poor dispersion. To improve dispersion and network connectivity, a small amount of GR, a two-dimensional nanomaterial, was introduced. This GR enhanced network continuity by bridging gaps and reducing voids through synergistic effects with MWCNTs. To investigate this behavior, samples were fabricated with 7.5 wt% MWCNTs in PDMS and varying MWCNT:GR mass ratios from 7:1 to 1:0. Excessive GR content disrupted conductive paths, resulting in unstable signals, whereas moderate GR significantly improved performance. As shown in Fig. 3(c), a ratio of 9:1 yielded optimal performance, with linearity of 0.99 and sensitivity of 2.16. Based on this composition, sensors with rectangular, S-shaped, and meander patterns were evaluated for linearity and sensitivity. Among them, the meander-pattern sensor demonstrated the highest performance, achieving a linearity of 0.98 and sensitivity of 2.95 across a strain range of 0–70%, as shown in Fig. 3(d).

3.2 Sensing Characteristics

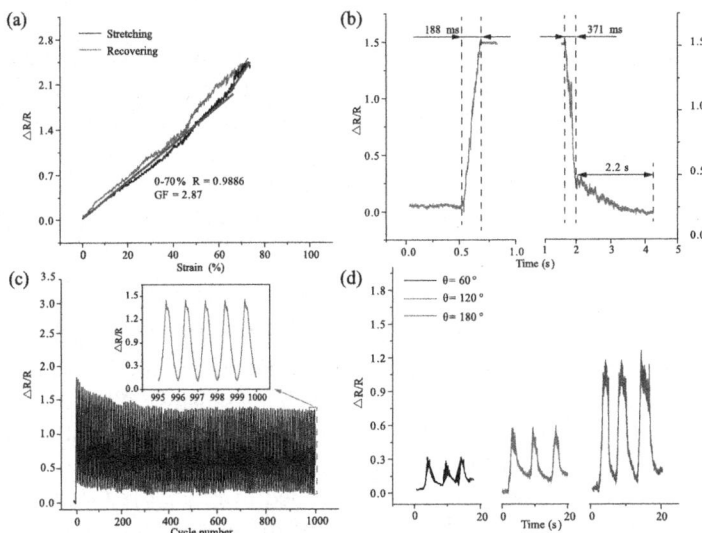

Fig. 4. (a) Relative resistance change of the flexible resistive strain sensor during stretching and recovering; (b) Response speed of the flexible resistive strain sensor at 60% strain during stretching and recovering; (c) 1000 repetitive tests of the flexible resistive strain sensor at 60% strain; (d) Dynamic response of the flexible resistive strain sensor at different bending angles.

The meander-pattern flexible resistive strain sensor exhibited a distinct hysteresis loop under 80% strain, as shown in Fig. 4(a). The response can be divided into two phases: from 0–70%, $\frac{\Delta R}{R}$ increases linearly with a low GF, as the contact between conductive networks undergoes less significant changes and less disruption of the conductive paths. Beyond 70%, the PDMS matrix material enters into a highly stretched state, breaking connection points of MWCNTs and GR conductive networks and increasing the gap between fillers, which decreases the conductive paths, resulting in an increase in $\frac{\Delta R}{R}$. At higher strain, the resistance would show a sharp increase, and the conductive mechanism gradually changes from the original contact conductivity (tunneling effect and percolation network) to intermittent conductivity (part of the path is completely disconnected).

The sensor showed asymmetric response dynamics at 60% strain, as shown in Fig. 4(b), with a rapid response time of 188 ms during stretching but a longer recovery time of 371 ms to return to $\frac{\Delta R}{R} = 0.25$, and up to 2.2 s to baseline. This hysteresis stems from PDMS viscoelasticity, irreversible network changes, and energy dissipation. While stretching involves fast elastic deformation and minor network adjustment, recovery is hindered by molecular relaxation, contact loss, and interfacial friction, reducing network reconstruction efficiency.

During cyclic testing, as shown in Fig. 4(c), initial resistance increased significantly due to network reorganization, filler slippage, and contact point breakage. However, with repeated loading cycles, the network became progressively stabilized, interfacial friction was reduced, and the response was dominated by elastic deformation. As a result, resistance variation became more consistent and repeatable, demonstrating improved mechanical and electrical reliability.

As shown in Fig. 4(d), the sensor exhibited increased $\frac{\Delta R}{R}$ with greater bending angles (60°, 120°, 180°), showing good correlation and repeatability, with similar signal amplitudes under repeated bending.

3.3 E-Skin for Shape Sensing of the Continuum

Shape Sensing Principle. Figure 5 illustrates the working principle of the flexible resistive strain sensor for continuum shape sensing. When the continuum shows deformation under tensile force, the flexible resistive strain sensors on its surface will experience synchronous deformation, which can be used to measure the bending angle of the continuum. As defined in Fig. 7(a), L and K represent the initial length of the flexible resistive strain sensor and the corresponding neutral axis length of the continuum when there is no bending, respectively; k, l, r, and θ represent the length of the flexible resistive strain sensor after bending of the continuum, the corresponding neutral axis length, the bending radius, and the bending angle corresponding to the neutral axis length k, respectively; ϵ is the strain of the flexible sensor; D is the diameter of the continuum. Assuming that the neutral axis length of the continuum does not change during bending, the following relationship can be obtained based on the arc length, bending angle, and diameter:

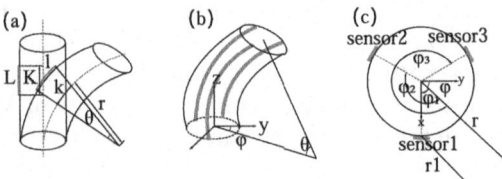

Fig. 5. Shape sensing of the continuum with the proposed flexible resistance strain sensor [26]. (a) Measurement of the continuum bending angle in a single direction; (b) Axonometric diagram for measuring the three-dimensional bending angle of the continuum; (c) Top view for measuring the three-dimensional bending angle of the continuum.

$$L = K = k = \theta \times r \tag{1}$$

$$l = \theta \times \left(r + \frac{D}{2}\right) \tag{2}$$

With in 70% strain range, the resistance change and strain have a certain linear relationship, obtained as:

$$l - L = \varepsilon = \theta \times \frac{D}{2} = a \times \frac{\Delta R}{R} \tag{3}$$

$$\theta = \frac{2a}{D} \times \frac{\Delta R}{R} \tag{4}$$

$$l = a \times \frac{\Delta R}{R} + L \tag{5}$$

where $\frac{\Delta R}{R}$ represents the relative resistance change and a represents the scale factor.

As shown in Figs. 5(b) and 5(c), three flexible sensing units are uniformly distributed around the circumference to realize multi-directional sensing. Then we have:

$$r_i = r - \frac{D}{2\cos\varphi_i} \tag{6}$$

$$l_i = k - \frac{D}{2\theta\cos\varphi_i}, (l = \theta \times r) \tag{7}$$

$$l_2 - l_1 = \frac{D}{2}\theta\left(\cos\varphi_1 - \cos\varphi_2\right), l_3 - l_2 = \frac{D}{2}\theta\left(\cos\varphi_2 - \cos\varphi_3\right) \tag{8}$$

where φ represents the angle between the bending direction and the y-axis, r_i represents the bending angle corresponding to the ith sensor, φ_i represents the bending direction at the ith sensor, and l_i represents the length of the ith flexible sensor. The relationship between φ_i and φ can be expressed as:

$$\varphi_i(i = 1, 2, 3); \varphi_1 = 90° - \varphi, \cdot\varphi_2 = 210° - \varphi, \cdot\varphi_3 = 330° - \varphi \tag{9}$$

By combining Eq. (6), the relationship between the bending direction and the length of the flexible resistance strain sensor can be obtained as:

$$\sqrt{3}\cos\varphi l_1 + \left(\frac{3}{2}\sin\varphi - \frac{\sqrt{3}}{2}\cos\varphi\right)l_2 - \left(\frac{3}{2}\sin\varphi + \frac{\sqrt{3}}{2}\cos\varphi\right)l_3 = 0 \tag{10}$$

$$\tan\varphi = \frac{-2\sqrt{3}l_1 + \sqrt{3}l_2 + \sqrt{3}l_3}{3l_2 - 3l_3} \tag{11}$$

$$\varphi = \arctan(\frac{-2\sqrt{3}l_1 + \sqrt{3}l_2 + \sqrt{3}l_3}{3l_2 - 3l_3}) \tag{12}$$

By combining Eq. (7) and Eq. (11), the relationship among bending angle, sensor length, and bending direction can be obtained as:

$$\theta = \frac{2(k-l_1)}{D\cos\varphi_1} \tag{13}$$

$$l_1 + l_2 + l_3 = 3k - \frac{D}{2}\theta(\cos\varphi_1 + \cos\varphi_2 + \cos\varphi_3) \tag{14}$$

$$k = \frac{l_1 + l_2 + l_3}{3} \tag{15}$$

$$\theta = \frac{2l_2 + 2l_3 - 4l_1}{3D\sin\varphi} \tag{16}$$

Finally, the continuum shape can be sensed when multiple groups of sensing units are arrayed across the continuum.

Experiment Results. In the validation experiment, as introduced in Sect. 2.3, a total of 12 marker points ($3 \times 4 = 12$) were affixed to the surface of the continuum, and the spatial positions of each point was captured using the Optitrick. Based on the three markers arranged circumferentially, the center position of each cross-sectional circle was calculated in MATLAB to reconstruct the actual shape. Meanwhile, each axial group consisting of four markers was arranged in pairs to determine the corresponding length of each flexible resistive sensor in the column. After integrating the stretchable resistive e-skins onto the distal segment of the continuum, a calibration process was conducted. During calibration, each e-skin were subjected to bending in six distinct directions, and each bending direction was repeated three times. The values of $\frac{\Delta R}{R}$ and the relative length change ($\frac{\Delta L}{L}$) of the sensors were collected during the stretching and compression.

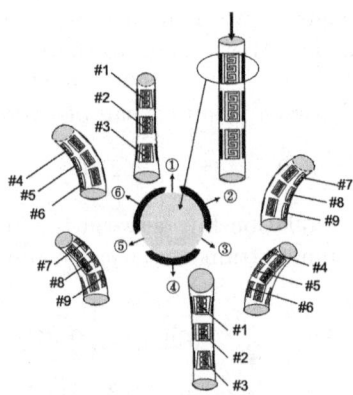

Fig. 6. The bending direction of the end continuum during calibration of the e-skin and the experiment.

A Stretchable Resistive Electronic Skin for Shape Sensing of End Continua

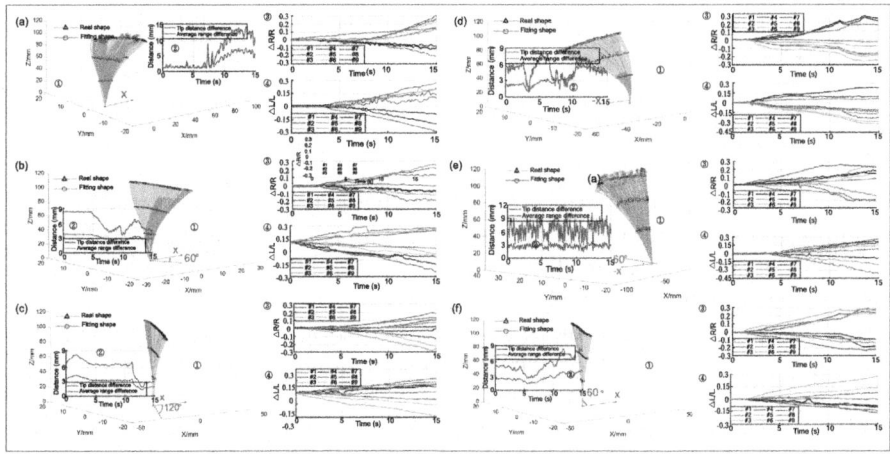

Fig. 7. ① The shape of the continuum predicted by MATLAB according to the actual shape measured by the Optitrack; ② Tip error and average shape error of actual shape and predicted shape; ③ Changes in the relative resistance of each sensor when the continuum is bent. The relative change in length predicted by the relative change in resistance. (a) Forward bending; (b) Bending at the axial clockwise rotation of 60°; (c) Bending at the axial clockwise rotation of 120°; (d) Bending at the axial clockwise rotation of 180°; (e) Bending at the axial clockwise rotation of 240°; (f) Bending at the axial clockwise rotation of 300°.

After calibration, the continuum integrated with e-skins was actuated to perform multi-directional bending with equal angles, following the scheme in Fig. 6. Due to limited training data, a machine learning toolbox in MATLAB was employed to predict $\frac{\Delta L}{L}$ from $\frac{\Delta R}{R}$. Key point coordinates were derived using Eq. (11) and (15), and shape reconstruction was achieved via polynomial fitting. This approach addressed the sensor's nonlinear response over the full strain range, enhancing prediction accuracy and robustness.

Figure 7 presents experimental results for six-direction bending, including dynamic shape evolution, predicted versus actual tip positions, and sensor responses. Generally, $\frac{\Delta L}{L}$ is positively correlated with $\frac{\Delta R}{R}$: an increase in $\frac{\Delta L}{L}$ leads to a rise in $\frac{\Delta R}{R}$, while a decrease in $\frac{\Delta L}{L}$ results in a reduction in $\frac{\Delta R}{R}$. However, variations exist due to sensor anisotropy and mechanical differences under complex loading. Sensors aligned with the bending direction experience dominant tensile/compressive stress, while others undergo shear, leading to different resistance changes. The tip position error reached up to 15 mm but remained within 10 mm in most cases, with overall shape reconstruction errors under 6 mm.

Several limitations remain in the current study. Although the proposed e-skin approach shows potential, its sensing accuracy is still lower than that of mature techniques such as optical fiber sensing and electromagnetic tracking. A key issue is the calibration assumption of uniaxial strain, while actual deformations involve anisotropic and complex loading. Future designs may consider isotropic geometries (e.g., cylindrical sensors) to improve consistency and resilience under multidirectional strain.

4 Conclusions

In this work, a meander-pattern flexible resistive strain sensor was prepared by a simple and low-cost method. The flexible sensor has excellent mechanical and sensing properties, with excellent linearity (0.98), high sensitivity (GF = 2.95), fast tensile response (188 ms), good stability and durability (1000 cycles). A stretchable resistive electronic skin composed of three meander pattern strain sensing units can sense the shape of the end continuum with a tip error of less than 15 mm, an average shape error of less than 6 mm, and a high Pearson's correlation coefficient of greater than 0.8. Although there remains a gap in accuracy compared with clinical requirements for surgical robotics, this study offers a promising strategy for future shape sensing of flexible surgical instruments.

Acknowledgments. The authors thank all the participants in the experiment. This work was supported by the National Key Research and Development Program of China under Grant 2022YFB4700801.

References

1. Xie, Z., Yuan, F., Liu, J., et al.: Octopus-inspired sensorized soft arm for environmental interaction. Sci. Rob. **8**(84), eadh7852 (2023)
2. Rusu, D.M., Mândru, S.D., Biri, C.M., et al.: Soft robotics: a systematic review and bibliometric analysis. Micromachines **14**(2), 359 (2023)
3. Wang, Y., Wang, Y., Mushtaq, R.T., et al.: Advancements in soft robotics: a comprehensive review on actuation methods, materials, and applications. Polymers **16**(8), 1087 (2024)
4. Ambaye, G., Boldsaikhan, E., Krishnan, K.: Soft robot design, manufacturing, and operation challenges: a review. J. Manuf. Mater. Process. **8**(2), 79 (2024)
5. Shih, B., et al.: Electronic skins and machine learning for intelligent soft robots. Sci. Robot. **5**, eaaz9239 (2020)
6. Gilbert, H.B., et al.: Concentric tube robots: the state of the art and future directions. In: Proceedings of International Symposium and Robotics Research, pp. 253–269 (2016)
7. Shi, C., Luo, X., Qi, P., et al.: Shape sensing techniques for continuum robots in minimally invasive surgery: a survey. IEEE Trans. Biomed. Eng. **64**(8), 1665–1678 (2016)
8. Chirikjian, G.S.: Conformational modeling of continuum structures in robotics and structural biology: a review. Adv. Robot. **29**, 817–829 (2015)
9. Jones, B.A., Walker, I.D.: Practical kinematics for real-time implementation of continuum robots. IEEE Trans. Robot. **22**(6), 1087–1099 (2006)
10. Rucker, D.C., et al.: A geometrically exact model for externally loaded concentric-tube continuum robots. IEEE Trans. Robot. **26**(5), 769–780 (2010)

11. Cao, Y., Liu, Z., Yu, H., Hong, W., Xie, L.: Spatial shape sensing of a multi-section continuum robot with integrated DTG sensor for maxillary sinus surgery. IEEE/ASME Trans. Mechatron. **28**(2), 715–725 (2022)
12. Wang, F., Jiang, Q., Li, J.: Shape sensing for continuum robots using FBG sensors array considering bending and twisting. IEEE Sens. J. **24**(2), 1546–1554 (2023)
13. Chen, X., Qian, J., Yu, Y., et al.: Shape detection of thin diameter flexible sensors with non-uniform gratings. Meas. Sci. Technol. **35**(4), 045117 (2024)
14. Zhong, X., Hoffmann, M., Strobel, N., Maier, A.: Semi-automatic basket catheter reconstruction from two x-ray views. In: Gall, J., Gehler, P., Leibe, B. (eds.) GCPR 2015. LNCS, vol. 9358, pp. 379–389. Springer, Cham (2015). https://doi.org/10.1007/978-3-319-24947-6_31
15. Liu, X., et al.: Multi-interface strain transfer modeling for flexible endoscope shape sensing. IEEE Rob. Autom. Lett. **9**(3), 2670–2677 (2024)
16. Lv, B., Qin, Y., Shi, Y., et al.: Fluoroscopy-free tip shape estimation for flexible endoscope using permanent magnet positioning. IEEE Trans. Instrument. Meas. **73**, 4011409 (2024)
17. McDonald-Bowyer, A., Syer, T., Retter, A., Stoyanov, D., Stilli, A.: Autonomous control of an ultrasound probe for intra-operative ultrasonography using vision-based shape sensing of pneumatically attachable flexible rails. Int. J. Comput. Assist. Radiol. Surg. **19**(7), 1391–1398 (2024)
18. Li, J., et al.: Three-dimensional graphene structure for healable flexible electronics based on Diels—Alder chemistry. ACS Appl. Mater. Interfaces. **10**, 9727–9735 (2018)
19. Zou, Y., et al.: A bionic stretchable nanogenerator for underwater sensing and energy harvesting. Nat. Commun. **10**, 2695 (2019)
20. Zhao, H., O'Brien, K., Li, S., et al.: Optoelectronically innervated soft prosthetic hand via stretchable optical waveguides. Sci. Rob. **1**(1), eaai7529 (2016)
21. He, Y., Wu, D., Zhou, M., et al.: Wearable strain sensors based on a porous polydimethylsiloxane hybrid with carbon nanotubes and graphene. ACS Appl. Mater. Interfaces **13**(13), 15572–15583 (2021). https://doi.org/10.1021/acsami.0c22823
22. Zhong, F., et al.: Piezoresistive design for electronic skin: from fundamental to emerging applications. Opto-Electron Adv. **5**, 210029 (2022)
23. Zhao, X., Mei, D., Tang, G., et al.: Strain and pressure sensors based on MWCNT/PDMS for human motion/perception detection. Polymers **15**(6), 1386 (2023)
24. Li, S., Zhang, J., He, J., et al.: Functional PDMS elastomers: bulk composites, surface engineering, and precision fabrication. Adv. Sci. **10**(34), 2304506 (2023)
25. Yan, H., et al.: Cable-driven continuum robot perception using skin-like hydrogel sensors. Adv. Funct. Mater. **32**, 2203241 (2022)
26. Yang, J.K.: Research on flexible bending sensors for soft robots. Mechanical Engineering, Tianjin University (2022)
27. So, J., Kim, U., Kim, Y.B., et al.: Shape estimation of soft manipulator using stretchable sensor. Cyborg Bionic Syst. (2021)

An Intelligent Process Decision-Making Method for Robotic Grinding Random Defects via Incremental Learning and Database

Tao Ding[1,2], Hao Wu[1,2], Guibin Xu[3], Zebin Hu[3], and Dahu Zhu[1,2(✉)]

[1] Hubei Key Laboratory of Advanced Technology for Automotive Components, Wuhan University of Technology, Wuhan 430070, China
dhzhu@whut.edu.cn
[2] Hubei Collaborative Innovation Center for Automotive Components Technology, Wuhan University of Technology, Wuhan 430070, China
[3] Hubei Central China Technology Development of Electric Power Co., Ltd., Wuhan 430070, China

Abstract. Industrial robots, leveraging their high flexibility and reconfigurability, are widely applied in grinding large complex components. But for variable defects like splattered welding slags on automotive body-in-white, existing robotic grinding strategies cannot adjust dynamically, causing unstable quality. To effectively remove random defects, this paper proposes an intelligent process decision-making method via incremental learning and database. First, orthogonal experiments and F-test are employed to screen out effective modeling data. Subsequently, an incremental support vector regression (SVR) algorithm is developed to establish an upgradable robotic grinding roughness model and material removal model. On this basis, a weighted case-based reasoning (CBR) method combined with an improved multi-objective grey wolf optimizer (MOGWO) is employed to determine optimal process parameters under complex grinding conditions. Meanwhile, the residual height of weld slags after grinding is predicted by the material removal model, thereby supporting secondary grinding and reducing the need for repeated measurements. Experimental results demonstrate that random weld slags can be effectively removed. The average surface roughness (Ra) of the processed areas can reach 0.95 μm, with an average prediction error of only 9.0%, validating the effectiveness of the proposed intelligent process decision-making method.

Keywords: Robotic Grinding · Welding Slags · Materials Removal · Process Database · Intelligent Process Decision-Making

1 Introduction

Intelligent manufacturing represented by robotic machining technology has deeply integrated information technology with advanced manufacturing technologies, and is widely applied in fields such as aerospace [1], rail transit [2], and automotive manufacturing [3]. In grinding of large complex components like automotive body, robots effectively enhance the accuracy, efficiency, and product consistency of grinding through multi-sensor fusion, configuration of flexible end-effectors, and integration with information technology [4]. However, welding slags on automotive body feature random distribution, size variation, inconsistent grinding allowance, and variable removal difficulty. When robots are used for grinding, on the one hand, the traditional schemes with fixed paths and static process parameters are difficult to achieve efficient and high-quality grinding, and their models are not capable of being updated with the changing scenarios. On the other hand, the lack of process databases hinders systematic case management, starving robotic grinding applications for random defects of critical empirical support. Therefore, for random welding slag removal, the digital management and utilization of process cases as well as the decision-making of optimal processes are crucial to the application of robot grinding.

Extensive research is conducted in three aspects for enhancing robotic grinding quality: material removal modeling, process database development, and intelligent process decision-making.

Among model-based approaches, the material removal depth model based on the Preston equation [5–7] is the most prevalent. Hertzian contact theory [8] is also widely used in robotic grinding modeling. For example, Zhang et al. [9] established a contact stress-force model via simulation and Hertz theory, then constructed a robotic blade grinding model using multiple regression. Material removal research also involves finite element analysis [10], the tribological Archard equation [11], tool wear studies [12], and machine learning integration [13]. Surface roughness studies focus on two directions: predicting roughness from process parameters [14] and real-time sensor monitoring [15], both effective for surface quality control. While existing models fit specific grinding scenarios, they overlook material/abrasive variations, limiting application scope and reliability under changing conditions.

Fixed-scenario grinding process databases emerged earlier. For example, Choi et al. [16] and Cai et al. [17] developed GIGAS and IGA, respectively. GIGAS recommends process parameters based on models and empirical data using heuristic rules, while IGA relies on CBR for parameter recommendation. However, these databases fail to adjust parameters during machining, prompting the proposal of intelligent process databases. Wang et al. [18] developed the EconG© expert system, which integrates grinding process database and parameter recommendation modules, monitors system electrical data, and uses neural networks to optimize grinding strategies in real time. Jian et al. [19] developed an intelligent lathe monitoring system that records chatter thresholds via a database, compensates thermal expansion in real time, mitigates chatter, and enhances product quality while prolonging tool life.

Decision-making algorithms are crucial for acquiring process parameters. They can be directly used for decision-making or embedded in process databases to integrate historical case experience. Early methods relied on orthogonal experiments and statistical analysis [20], but showed limited adaptability to frequent changes. Intelligent approaches have since emerged, mainly through two perspectives: CBR [21] and process optimization [22]. While effective, these methods face limitations in addressing random welding slag defects: CBR lacks suitable process databases and struggles to adapt historical cases to new problems; process optimization methods often fail to efficiently derive optimal solutions due to random initial parameter generation.

Thus, scenario-adaptive models, optimal-solution decision algorithms, and intelligent case-managed process databases are pivotal to overcoming the bottleneck of robotic random defect grinding.

2 Material Removal Characteristic Model for Robotic Grinding

2.1 Support Vector Regression Incremental Learning Algorithm

This study collected grinding data of four materials through orthogonal experiments: aluminum alloys 6061-T6 and 7075-T6, stainless steel 304, and carbon structural steel Q235. Subsequently, F-test is used to identify factors significantly influencing robotic grinding quality. Factors with p-values below 0.05 are regarded as significant, and their data are used to build the grinding characteristic model.

Robotic grinding is affected by numerous mutually coupled factors with complex interactions. The SVR algorithm, featuring strong generalization ability, handles complex nonlinear problems via kernel function construction. Incremental Learning (IL) updates pre-trained models with new data without full retraining, avoiding catastrophic forgetting. This paper proposes SVR-IL by integrating replay-based IL to optimize SVR:

$$\min \frac{1}{2}\|\omega\|^2 + C \sum_{i=1}^{n} \left(\zeta_i + \zeta_i^*\right) \tag{1}$$

$$s.t. \begin{cases} y_i - \omega^T \phi(x_i) - b \leq \varepsilon + \zeta_i \\ \omega^T \phi(x_i) + b - y_i \leq \varepsilon + \zeta_i^* \\ \zeta_i, \zeta_i^* \geq 0, i = 1, \ldots, n \end{cases} \tag{2}$$

where, ζ_i, ζ_i^* is the penalty term, C is the penalty coefficient, and $\phi(x_i)$ is the kernel function. The dual form is transformed as:

$$\min_{\alpha, \alpha^*} \frac{1}{2} (\alpha - \alpha^*)^T Q (\alpha - \alpha^*) + \varepsilon (\alpha + \alpha^*) - y^T (\alpha - \alpha^*) \tag{3}$$

$$s.t. \begin{cases} e^T (\alpha - \alpha^*) = 0 \\ 0 \leq \alpha_i, \alpha_i^* \leq C \\ i = 1, \ldots, n \end{cases} \tag{4}$$

where Q is a positive semidefinite matrix, and $Q_{ij} = K(x_i, x_j) = \phi(x_i)^T \phi(x_j)$. Due to the influence of abrasive belt wear in the robotic grinding process, which is time-related, the $\phi(x_i)$ is constructed as a composite kernel based on the RBF kernel and PER kernel:

$$K(x, x') = \theta_1^2 \exp\left(-\frac{(x-x')^2}{2\theta_2^2}\right) + \theta_3^2 \exp\left(-\frac{2}{\theta_4^2} \sin^2\left(\frac{\pi(x-x')}{T_{\text{ker}}}\right)\right) \tag{5}$$

where, $\theta_1, \theta_2, \theta_3, \theta_4$ and T_{ker} are hyperparameters.

This paper employs sample replay, combining new samples with partial old ones for joint training during updates. The SVR-IL algorithm follows these updating steps:

(1) Compute similarity between new and old samples, then sort support vector samples and non-support vector samples in ascending order. The similarity is calculated by:

$$d_j^{(i)} = \sum_{k=1}^{m} \left| x_j^{(i)} - x_k^{new} \right| F_{kp}^T + \sum_{k=1}^{m} \left| x_j^{(i)} - x_k^{new} \right| F_h^T \qquad (6)$$

where $x_j^{(i)}$ is the feature vector of the j-th sample in the i-th generation, x_k^{new} is the feature vector of the k-th sample in the new samples, F_{kp} is the feature weight vector related to k_p, and F_h is the feature weight vector related to the grinding depth. The feature weight vector consists of weight coefficients for each feature variable. The weight coefficient $F^{(i)}$ is calculated as:

$$F^{(i)} = \frac{1}{e^{p_i}} \bigg/ \sum_{j=1}^{n} \frac{1}{e^{p_j}} \qquad (7)$$

where p is calculated by the F-test between the feature variable and the target variable;

(2) Calculate the number of old samples extracted from each generation of samples:

$$M_{old}^{(n)} = \frac{M^{(n)} M_{old}}{\sum_{i=1}^{m} M^{(i)}}. \qquad (8)$$

where $M_{old}^{(n)}$ is the number of samples extracted from the n-th generation, $M^{(n)}$ is the number of samples introduced when updating the n-th generation model, and M_{old} is the total number of old samples composing the training set. For each generation's extracted samples, the proportion of support vectors and non-support vectors is determined by their total number ratio.

(3) Combine new samples with top-ranked support and non-support vector samples from each generation to form the new training set X_{new}.
(4) Train the model with X_{new}, and record the support vector samples and non-support vector samples in the new samples.

2.2 Robotic Grinding Removal Depth Model and Roughness Model

The Preston equation, describing the relationship between process parameters and material removal, finds extensive applications in grinding, cutting, etc. Moreover, as the grinding wheel's outer layer is rubber and welding slag is metal, Hertzian contact condition is satisfied. Based on Preston equation, Hertzian contact theory, and SVR-IL algorithm, the robotic grinding material removal depth model is derived as:

$$H = \frac{K_p(x) F_n^a V_s^b}{V_f^c} \left[\frac{9\pi E^*(A+B)}{64 k^2 \varepsilon(k)} \right]^d \qquad (9)$$

where H represents the grinding removal depth. $K_p(x)$ is the mapping model, built by the SVR - IL algorithm, relating machining feature variables to k_p (a fixed wear coefficient). F_n is the normal grinding force, V_s is the linear velocity, V_f is the feed rate), A, B are the relative principal curvatures of the contact point, and a, b, c and d are correction coefficients. x, the input for $K_p(x)$, includes working condition features like force, velocities, grit size, belt service time, and workpiece material properties. When training $K_p(x)$, first compute k_p per data point. Then, use the F-test to check if factors significantly affecting grinding depth also impact k_p. If conditions are met, these features calculate the wear coefficient model:

$$K_p(x) = \omega_{kp}^T \phi(x) + b_{kp} \tag{10}$$

where, ω_{kp} is the weight coefficient of the variable, and b_{kp} is the bias term. By transforming (9) into a linear model and using the K_p calculated by the $K_p(x)$ to replace the original wear coefficient k_p, the linear model of the removal depth model is constructed by combining with other inputs as training samples:

$$\ln H = a \ln F_n + b \ln V_s - c \ln V_f + d \ln \left[\frac{9\pi E^*(A+B)}{64 k^2 \varepsilon(k)} \right] + \ln K_p \tag{11}$$

During training, the loss function is defined based on the incremental learning regularization paradigm as:

$$L = \alpha \frac{1}{n} \sum_{i=0}^{n} \left(\omega_{new}^T x_{new} - y_{new} \right)^2 + \beta \frac{1}{n} \sum_{i=0}^{n} \left(\omega_{old}^T x_{new} - y_{new} \right)^2 \\ + \lambda \left(\|\omega_{new}\|^2 + \|\omega_{old}\|^2 + \|\omega_{new} - \omega_{old}\|^2 \right) \tag{12}$$

where ω_{new} is the coefficient matrix of the new model, ω_{old} is the coefficient matrix of the old model, x_{new} is the feature vector of the training samples, y_{new} is the actual output of the training samples, λ is the regularization coefficient, and α, β are the incremental coefficient, with the calculation formula:

$$\begin{cases} \alpha = \dfrac{M_{old}}{M_{old} + M_{new}} \\ \beta = \dfrac{M_{new}}{M_{old} + M_{new}} \end{cases} \tag{13}$$

where M_{old} is the total number of old samples and M_{new} is the total number of new samples. The coefficients a, b, c, and d are obtained via stochastic gradient descent training, and substituting them into (9) yields the modified removal depth model.

Due to the lack of a universal physical model for surface roughness, this paper directly employs the SVR-IL algorithm to fit the robotic grinding surface roughness model. The modeling steps are shown in Fig. 1.

Using the F-test, factors significantly influencing surface roughness are identified and integrated into input features. SVR hyperparameters (C, ε, Γ) and kernel function parameters ($\theta_1, \theta_2, \theta_3, \theta_4, T_{ker}$) are optimized via random search with predefined ranges. Samples are split 80%/20% for training/testing with 50 search iterations. All samples

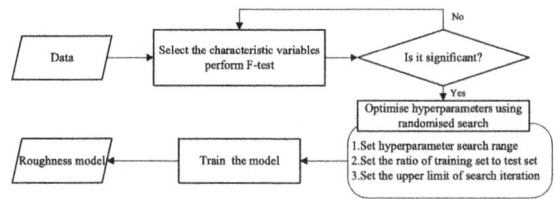

Fig. 1. Robotic grinding surface roughness modelling process.

are input into the training process to obtain the surface roughness model, which can be expressed as:

$$R_a(x) = \omega_{R_a}^T \phi_{R_a}(x) + b_{R_a} \tag{14}$$

where, ω_{R_a} represents the feature weights of the model, $\phi_{R_a}(x)$ denotes the kernel function, and b_{R_a} is the bias term. When updating the model, the optimal hyperparameter combination is also searched according to the original settings before training.

3 Intelligent Process Decision-Making Based on Database

After deriving the robotic grinding model, intelligent optimizers recommend process parameters, but their stochastic nature challenges parameter regulation. This paper establishes a case database and proposes a hybrid method integrating weighted-CBR and MOGWO. Comprising four steps—case retrieval, reuse, revision, and learning—it uses Analytic Hierarchy Process (AHP) for factor weights, weighted CBR for case matching, improved MOGWO for optimization, and updates the model by adding new cases.

The weighted CBR method constructs a hierarchical feature model, builds a judgment matrix using F-test p-values to calculate feature weights, normalizes them via geometric mean, and validates consistency (CR < 0.1) to achieve weighted case matching and optimization. When historical cases retrieved via case matching fail to meet machining requirements for new process problems, case revision is performed. This paper enhances the GWO for robotic grinding parameter optimization, with steps as follows:

(1) Initial population: To enhance efficiency, optimized process parameters are extracted from the top 10 case-based reasoning cases to form individual positions. Remaining population positions are determined by:

$$x = \sum_{i=1}^{m} \alpha_i x_i + \frac{1}{2} x_{rand} \tag{15}$$

where, x_i is the individuals derived from case-based reasoning, α_i denotes random numbers within [0, 1) that sum to 1, and x_{rand} is a vector randomly generated within the value range.

(2) Fitness function: To ensure the surface quality of the workpiece after grinding, the removal depth and surface roughness are taken as the optimization objectives, so the

fitness function is modified as:

$$\min fitness_h = h_{exp} - H(X) \\ \min fitness_{Ra} = R_a(X) - Ra_{exp} \quad (16)$$

where, h_{exp} is the target removal depth, Ra_{exp} is the expected surface roughness, $H(X)$ and $R_a(X)$ are the established robotic grinding removal depth model and surface roughness model, respectively. X is the input vector of the model formed by combining the population individual x and the existing descriptions of the new process problem.

(3) Multi-objective Ranking: Non-dominated sorting of NSGA-II[23] efficiently solves each layer of the Pareto front. However, direct integration of NSGA-II into GWO has three drawbacks: crowding distances set to infinity for extreme values lead to local optima; randomness occurs in α wolf selection when there are only two solutions in the Pareto front; priorities of optimization objectives are not considered in practical applications. To address the above issues, this study optimizes the multi-objective ranking method: 1) Normalize fitness values of each individual; 2) Use fast non-dominated sorting on normalized values to derive non-dominated frontiers; 3) Compute comprehensive SCORE for each individual; 4) Sort frontiers by ascending SCORE. The comprehensive *SCORE* is calculated as follows:

$$SCORE_i = e^{1-t}f_h^i + e^{t-1}f_{Ra}^i \quad (17)$$

where, f_h is the normalized value of $fitness_h$, f_{Ra} is the normalized value of $fitness_{Ra}$, and t is the machining factor. Set t = 0 for rough machining (focused on allowance removal) and t = 1 for finish machining (demanding lower surface roughness). The formula balances sample diversity and machining requirements, offering an optimal ranking criterion for robotic grinding optimization.

4 Experimental Verification

4.1 Experimental Setup

To validate the proposed intelligent decision-making method for robotic grinding, a random welding slag robotic grinding experimental platform was constructed as shown in Fig. 2. System hardware includes a scanner (PowerScan-Pro2.3M), roughness tester (Mitutoyo SJ-210), force sensor (ATI Omega160 SI-1500-240), and industrial robot (ABB IRB 6700-200/2.6). Software components comprise RobotStudio simulation software, PowerPac path planning plug-in, TestSignalViewer force monitoring software, and the developed process database.

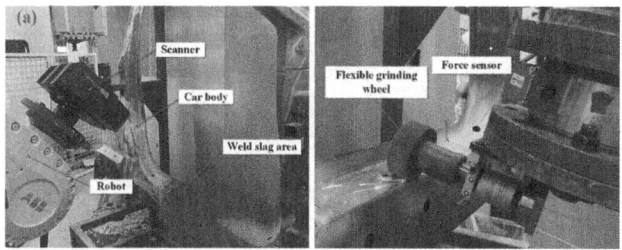

Fig. 2. Random defects intelligent process decision grinding experimental platform. (a) Weld slag measurement, (b) grinding experiments.

4.2 Preparation for Grinding

To verify the grinding effect of robot on welding slags of varying heights, the slag point cloud is secondarily clustered using the method in [24] based on position and height. Machining areas are divided, and the shortest path is solved via an improved genetic algorithm to derive the grinding trajectory in Fig. 3, where regions denote to-be-ground areas classified by maximum slag height.

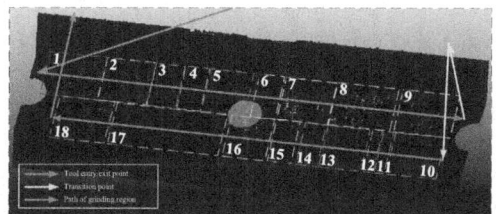

Fig. 3. Weld slag clustering and trajectory planning result.

As shown in Fig. 4, the measured maximum slag height and other factors are fed into the process database, which performs concurrent case and model matching. Matched models predict grinding quality: parameters are applied directly if predictions meet requirements; otherwise, case revision optimizes them. The optimized strategy updates the case library.

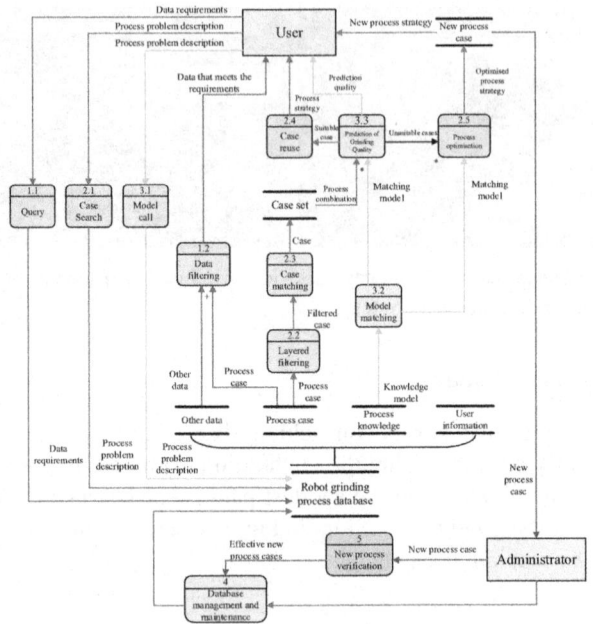

Fig. 4. Process parameter decision-making data flow.

The decision results specify two grinding passes: the first uses a 120-grit abrasive belt for roughing, with parameters and predicted results detailed in Table 1. The second machining is determined by rough machining predictions. As shown, machining areas 1, 3, 4 have incomplete slag removal, and all areas have excessive roughness. A 240-grit abrasive belt is used for fine machining, with parameters in Table 2.

Table 1. Rough grinding process decision-making results.

Region	Maximum slag height (mm)	Process parameters			H_{pre}(mm)	Ra_{pre}(μm)
		F_N(N)	V_s(m/s)	V_f(mm/s)		
1	0.561	20.1	8.8	23.3	0.489	1.646
2	0.399	11.5	8.5	7.9	0.549	1.998
3	0.573	26.3	15.1	12.9	0.507	2.132
4	0.673	29.2	12.9	18.3	0.645	1.941
5	0.426	20.0	7.6	6.8	0.638	2.040
6	0.673	15.1	15.7	18.6	0.703	1.936
7	0.556	33.3	10.1	9.7	0.629	2.017
8	0.624	18.4	8.5	12.8	0.661	1.967
9	0.538	11.2	8.5	8.0	0.756	1.999
10	0.673	10.8	11.3	13.0	0.681	1.990

(*continued*)

Table 1. (continued)

Region	Maximum slag height (mm)	Process parameters			H_{pre}(mm)	Ra_{pre}(μm)
		F_N(N)	V_s(m/s)	V_f(mm/s)		
11	0.292	9.3	15.6	19.0	0.371	1.877
12	0.673	33.5	12.3	12.5	0.726	2.058
13	0.292	8.9	20.3	16.0	0.293	1.997
14	0.340	29.7	6.1	23.5	0.341	1.636
15	0.147	14.0	9.7	11.1	0.261	2.022
16	0.515	24.2	11.8	21.4	0.558	1.817
17	0.469	19.5	10.8	14.5	0.521	1.966
18	0.422	19.8	9.9	9.8	0.461	2.080

Table 2. Fine grinding process decision-making results.

Region	Weld slag allowance (mm)	Process parameters			Ra_{pre}(μm)
		F_N(N)	V_s(m/s)	V_f(mm/s)	
1	0.072	16.6	25.2	22.8	0.960
3	0.066	23.5	17.6	26.6	0.935
4	0.028	13.3	17.6	32.3	0.909
Else	0	14.8	13.2	31.3	0.844

4.3 Analysis of Experimental Results

As depicted in Fig. 5(a), the pre-machining automotive body is covered with numerous welding slags, with the slag heights being notably higher in the head and tail regions. Figure 5(b) illustrates the post-grinding condition, where randomly distributed small slags have been entirely removed; however, partial residues persist in machining areas 1, 10, and 17. The post-grinding slag point cloud is presented in Fig. 5(c). In machining area 1, the remaining slag allowance is relatively substantial, reaching a maximum height of 0.1315 mm, whereas the heights of other residual slags are all below 0.1 mm.

In machining areas 1 and 10, significant force fluctuations at initial contact cause motor power to exceed the rated value, reducing rotation speed below the set value and weakening grinding ability, leading to slag residues. In area 17, an uneven body bottom and calibration errors prevent the grinding wheel from clinging to the workpiece, causing local insufficient grinding. However, these partial residues do not affect the verification of grinding process decision results.

In all machining areas obtained by slag point cloud clustering, the surface roughness was measured. During measurement, a 0.8 mm line segment is randomly sampled along the tangential direction of the grinding wheel linear velocity. In areas 1, 3, and 4 (incompletely slag-removed), three random positions were measured and averaged. For fully removed areas, three points at the front, middle, and end of the path were measured and averaged. Results are shown in Table 3.

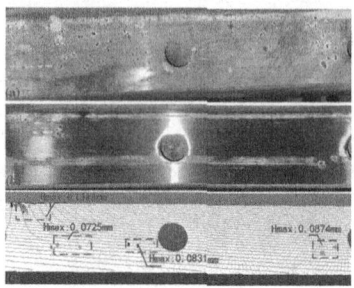

Fig. 5. Comparison of welding slag region before and after grinding. (a) Welding slag area before grinding, (b) welding slag area after grinding, (c) point cloud of welding slag area after grinding.

Table 3. Surface roughness measurement results of grinding surface.

Grinding area	Predicted Ra (μm)	Measured Ra (μm)	Errors
1	0.960	1.1	13.1%
3	0.935	1.0	4.2%
4	0.909	0.8	7.5%
Incomplete removal areas	0.844	1.0	17.1%
Other areas	0.844	0.8	2.9%

The experimental measurements generally align with the predicted results. For the normally removed slag, the maximum error is 7.5% and the minimum is 2.9%; for the incompletely removed parts due to equipment limitations, the maximum error is 17.1% and the minimum is 13.1%, with an average roughness error of 9.0%.

When comparing the actual slag removal height and surface roughness with the predicted values, although experimental errors result in incomplete slag removal, the results validate that the established material removal characteristic model for robotic grinding of vehicle body welding slag can guide grinding processes. This demonstrates that the proposed intelligent process decision-making method for robotic grinding is applicable to practical robotic grinding operations.

5 Conclusion

This study presents an intelligent robotic grinding decision method via incremental learning and self-updating database, enabling adaptation to random defects, optimal parameter delivery, and continuous updating. Experimental verification is carried out for the robotic grinding and removal scenario of automotive body welding slags, and the following conclusions are drawn:

(1) The SVR-IL-based material removal and roughness models can not only reflect the relationship between multiple factors and machining quality, but also enable continuous learning, addressing the issue of significant application scenario limitations in traditional models.
(2) The database-driven intelligent decision-making method integrates weighted CBR and improved MOGWO for case matching and parameter optimization, resolving limitations of traditional methods—their inflexibility and suboptimal machining performance under complex conditions.
(3) The robotic grinding experiment on automotive welding slags validates the method: random defects are effectively removed, post-machining roughness (Ra) stays within 1.2 μm (avg. 0.95 μm), and the 9.0% average prediction error confirms model accuracy and decision-making feasibility.

The method applies to automotive body local defects repair and can be adapted for other scenarios via simple modifications, such as 3D putty or paint film defects on high-speed railway white body. However, the accuracy of tool calibration requires improvement. Future work will focus on enhancing tool calibration to improve machining stability.

Acknowledgements. The authors would like to gratefully acknowledge the financial support from the National Nature Science Foundation of China (No. 52375509).

References

1. Zhang, B., Wu, S., Wang, D., Yang, S., Jiang, F., Li, C.: A review of surface quality control technology for robotic abrasive belt grinding of aero-engine blades. Measurement **220**, 113381 (2023)
2. Yang, Z., Xu, X., Wang, X., Cai, W., Yan, S., Ge, S.: Optimal configuration for mobile robotic grinding of large complex components based on redundant parameters. IEEE Trans. Ind. Electron. **71**(8), 9287–9296 (2024)
3. Wang, S., Xu, Z., Wu, C., Lin, H., Zhu, D.: Towards region-based robotic machining system from perspective of intelligent manufacturing: a technology framework with case study. J. Manuf. Syst. **70**, 451–463 (2023)
4. Zhu, D., et al.: Robotic grinding of complex components: a step towards efficient and intelligent machining – challenges, solutions, and applications. Rob. Comput.-Integrat. Manuf. **65**, 101908 (2020)
5. Yang, Z., et al.: Prediction and analysis of material removal characteristics for robotic belt grinding based on single spherical abrasive grain model. Int. J. Mech. Sci. **190**, 106005 (2021)
6. Lv, Y., Peng, Z., Qu, C., Zhu, D.: An adaptive trajectory planning algorithm for robotic belt grinding of blade leading and trailing edges based on material removal profile model. Rob. Comput.-Integrat. Manuf. **66**, 101987 (2020)
7. Deja, M.: The use of Preston equation to determine material removal during lap-grinding with electroplated CBN tools. Wear 528–529 (2023)
8. James, G.: Analysis of elliptical Hertzian contacts. Tribol. Int. **30**(3), 235–237 (1997)

9. Zhang, H., Li, L., Zhao, J., Zhao, J., Gong, Y.: Theoretical investigation and implementation of nonlinear material removal depth strategy for robot automatic grinding aviation blade. J. Manuf. Process. **74**, 441–455 (2022)
10. Yang, Z., Huang, Z., Wang, H., Wang, L., Yang, H.: Process parameter optimization model for robotic abrasive belt grinding of aero-engine blades. Int. J. Adv. Manuf. Technol. **131**(5), 2039–2054 (2024)
11. Zhang, W., et al.: Modeling of material removal depth in robot abrasive belt grinding based on energy conversion. J. Manuf. Process. **97**, 76–86 (2023)
12. Syreyshchikova, N.V., Pimenov, D.Y.: Wear of a flexible abrasive tool. J. Frict. Wear **40**(2), 139–145 (2019)
13. Zhang, X., Kuhlenkötter, B., Kneupner, K.: An efficient method for solving the Signorini problem in the simulation of free-form surfaces produced by belt grinding. Int. J. Mach. Tools Manuf **45**(6), 641–648 (2005)
14. Qu, C., Lv, Y., Yang, Z., Xu, X., Zhu, D., Yan, S.: An improved chip-thickness model for surface roughness prediction in robotic belt grinding considering the elastic state at contact wheel-workpiece interface. Int. J. Adv. Manuf. Technol. **104**(5–8), 3209–3217 (2019)
15. Kassubeck, M., Malek, T., Mühlhausen, M., Kappel, M., Castillo, S., Dittrich, M.A.: Optical quality control for adaptive polishing processes. In: 2020 IEEE Southwest Symposium on Image Analysis and Interpretation, SSIAI, pp. 90–94. IEEE, Albuquerque (2020)
16. Choi, T., Shin, Y.H.: Generalized intelligent grinding advisory system. Int. J. Prod. Res. **45**(8), 1899–1932 (2007)
17. Cai, R., Rowe, W., Moruzzi, J.L., Morgan, M.N.: Intelligent grinding assistant (IGA(©)) - system development part I intelligent grinding database. Int. J. Adv. Manuf. Technol. **35**(1–2), 75–85 (2007)
18. Wang, J., Tian, Y., Hu, X., Fan, Z., Han, J., Liu, Y.: Development of grinding intelligent monitoring and big data-driven decision making expert system towards high efficiency and low energy consumption: experimental approach. J. Intell. Manuf. **35**(3), 1013–1035 (2024)
19. Jian, B., Hsieh, C., Guo, Y.: Intelligent integrated monitoring system for lathe equipment. J. Low Freq. Noise Vib. Active Control **40**(2), 978–992 (2021)
20. Siddiquee, A.N., Fan, P., Mallick, Z.: Grey relational analysis coupled with principal component analysis for optimisation design of the process parameters in in-feed centreless cylindrical grinding. Int. J. Adv. Manuf. Technol. **46**(9–12), 983–992 (2010)
21. Huo, Y., Liu, J., Xiong, J., Xiao, W., Zhao, J.F.: Machine learning and CBR integrated mechanical product design approach. Adv. Eng. Inf. **52**, 101611 (2022)
22. Tsai, J., Chou, P., Chou, J.: Color filter polishing optimization using ANFIS with Sliding-level particle swarm optimizer. IEEE Trans. Syst. Man Cybern. Syst. **50**(3), 1193–1207 (2020)
23. Zhao, F., Huan, L., Zhang, Y., Ma, W., Zhang, C.: A novel multi-objective optimization algorithm based on differential evolution and NSGA-II. In: 2018 IEEE 22nd International Conference on Computer Supported Cooperative Work in Design, CSCWD, pp.570–575. IEEE, Nanjing (2018)
24. Ding, T., Ouyang, P., Zhang, H., Feng, X., Hua, L., Zhu, D.: 3D vision-guided robotic grinding framework for repairing random defects. IEEE Trans. Autom. Sci. Eng. **22**, 15819–15831 (2025)

Knee Prosthesis Stair Ascending with Adaptive Clearance and Foot Placement

Wenduo Zhu, Mengchen Cai, Haofei Hou, Shunyi Zhao, Lecheng Ruan[✉], and Qining Wang[✉]

School of Advanced Manufacturing and Robotics, Peking University, Beijing 100871, China
ruanlecheng@ucla.edu, qiningwang@pku.edu.cn

Abstract. Stair ascent control for powered knee prostheses during swing phase presents a multi-objective challenge, requiring simultaneous optimization of foot clearance and placement. Existing Finite State Machine (FSM) based approaches struggle to effectively integrate multi-source information and balance competing control objectives. This paper proposes a novel optimization-based framework that transforms environmental and human motion information into objective-oriented representations through a chest-mounted camera and leg-mounted IMUs. These representations are then integrated into a unified optimization framework to generate prosthetic trajectories that simultaneously satisfy both clearance and foot placement objectives. Experimental results demonstrate that our approach achieves superior performance in maintaining appropriate clearance while ensuring optimal foot placement compared to traditional FSM-based methods, offering a more systematic solution for powered prosthetic stair ascent control.

Keywords: Powered Prosthesis · Stair Ascending · Optimization

1 Introduction

Stair ascent represents a crucial task for powered knee prostheses [1,2], demonstrating significant implications for enhancing the mobility capabilities and autonomy of individuals with limb loss in activities of daily living [3]. Among various control challenges, the swing phase control is particularly demanding, as it requires active motion control to accommodate variations in both stair parameters and human movement characteristics [4]. This challenge is further complicated by the dynamic nature of human-prosthesis interaction and the diverse environmental conditions encountered during stair climbing.

The control objectives during the swing phase can be formulated as a multi-objective problem. First, the prosthesis must maintain appropriate clearance

---

W. Zhu and M. Cai—Contributed equally to this work.

during the swing phase to successfully clear the stair step for different heights [5]. Second, it needs to actively position the prosthetic foot to achieve proper foot placement, avoiding collisions while ensuring comfortable step-over distances for varying stair depths [6]. These objectives are inherently coupled and often competing, requiring sophisticated control strategies to achieve optimal performance.

Existing research has demonstrated various approaches to enable prosthetic stair ascent [2,7–9]. The predominant methodology employs Finite State Machine (FSM)-based approaches, where motion phases are identified and predefined fixed actions are switched based on proprioceptive information from the prosthesis [10]. However, this basic FSM framework necessitates substantial redesign and recalibration for different stair configurations and individual users [11].

To enhance adaptability, subsequent studies have attempted to incorporate thigh motion into the FSM framework by establishing mapping relationships between thigh movements and prosthetic trajectories [12,13]. While these approaches indirectly address both clearance and foot placement objectives, they lack direct constraints on these control goals. Moreover, the effectiveness of such mapping rules can be compromised by user fatigue and variations in movement patterns [14]. Gergg et al. [15] attempted to directly incorporate environmental information (prosthesis-stair distance) into FSM control. While this approach directly addresses the clearance objective, it reveals the limitation of rule-based methods in balancing multiple objectives - achieving sufficient clearance while avoiding excessive lift.

The limitations of existing approaches can be attributed to two fundamental challenges in FSM-based control frameworks. Firstly, current frameworks struggle to establish direct relationships between multi-source information (human motion, prosthesis states, and environmental parameters) and control objectives. The complexity of designing state transition conditions increases significantly with the incorporation of additional indirect information sources, making it difficult to effectively utilize all available data [14]. Secondly, the rule-based nature of FSM approaches inherently limit their capability to systematically balance multiple competing objectives. As the number of objectives increases, designing rules that simultaneously satisfy all requirements becomes increasingly challenging.

To address these limitations, we propose a novel optimization-based control framework consisting of: (1) a front-end perception module that leverages a chest-mounted camera [16] and leg-mounted IMUs to transform environmental and human motion information into objective-oriented representations for clearance and foot placement control; (2) a back-end optimization module that integrates these representations into a unified framework to generate prosthetic trajectories satisfying both clearance and foot placement objectives simultaneously.

In the following sections, we describe our proposed framework in Sect. 2. Section 3 and Sect. 4 shows the verification setup and experiment results. Section 5 concludes the paper with a summary of contributions and future directions.

2 Methodology

(See Fig. 1).

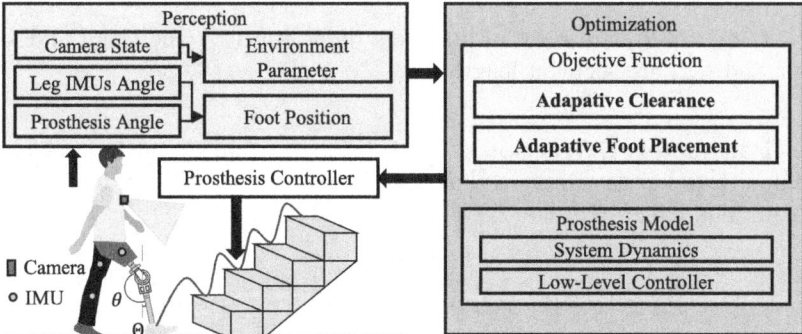

Fig. 1. Proposed Framework. The framework consists of: (1) A front-end perception module that processes prosthesis, environmental and human motion data to objective-related information, and (2) A back-end optimization module that generates prosthetic trajectories considering both clearance requirements and foot placement adaptation.

2.1 Perception

The perception module aims to extract and transform multi-source information (human motion, environment, and prosthesis states) into objective-oriented representations for clearance control and foot placement optimization. This section details how we process sensor data to obtain these essential parameters.

Foot Position Estimation. Foot position directly reflects the states of both the intact limb and the prosthetic leg during stair clearance. We derive this through a kinematic chain using CoM position, leg lengths, and joint angles. The process begins with global state estimation using a chest-mounted camera:

The kinematic state of the camera $\boldsymbol{\xi}_C = \langle \boldsymbol{p}_C(t), \boldsymbol{v}_C(t), \boldsymbol{\theta}_C(t) \rangle$ at time t is calculated by solving:

$$\min_{\boldsymbol{\xi}_k^C} \left(\mathcal{L}_\mathcal{P} + \mathcal{L}_\mathcal{B} + \mathcal{L}_\mathcal{F} + \mathcal{L}_\mathcal{D} + \mathcal{L}_{\mathcal{D}_h} \right), \tag{1}$$

where, $\mathcal{L}_\mathcal{P}$ represents the prior cost, $\mathcal{L}_\mathcal{B}$ is the IMU-preintegration cost, $\mathcal{L}_\mathcal{F}$ and $\mathcal{L}_\mathcal{D}$ remain as the visual feature and depth measurement costs, and $\mathcal{L}_{\mathcal{D}_h}$ represents the co-visible projection cost.

Then the CoM position can be determined by:

$$\boldsymbol{p}_{\text{CoM}} = \boldsymbol{p}_C + \Delta \boldsymbol{p}, \tag{2}$$

where p_C is the position of the camera, and Δp is the predefined offset between the camera and the CoM.

The foot positions p_{foot} are calculated through forward kinematics:

$$p_{\text{foot}} = p_{\text{com}} + R_1(\theta_t) \cdot l_t + R_2(\theta_s) \cdot l_s, \tag{3}$$

where $R(\theta_t)$, $R(\theta_s)$ are rotation matrices determined by the thigh and shank angles, and l_t, l_s are segment lengths.

Stair Parameter Extraction. For collision avoidance and foot placement planning, three key environmental parameters are extracted from the depth camera data. The integrated map $\mathcal{M}$ is constructed by:

$$\mathcal{M} = \sum_{j=0}^{n_{I_{\mathcal{D}}}} \text{R}(\theta j^{\mathcal{C}}, pj^{\mathcal{C}})^{4 \times 3} \left[pj, 1^{I_j^{\mathcal{D}}} \; pj, 2^{I_j^{\mathcal{D}}} \; \ldots \; pj, np^{I_j^{\mathcal{D}}} \right]^{3 \times n_p}, \tag{4}$$

To identify staircases, the walking direction $\bar{v}_c$ is used to align analysis, with the normal vector defined as:

$$n = \bar{v}_c \times g. \tag{5}$$

The projected points for analysis are obtained as:

$$(p_d^j)' = p_d^j - \left[(p_d^j - p_d^k) \cdot n \right] \cdot n, \tag{6}$$

From this analysis, we extract: (1) The vertical plane positions q through RANSAC-based plane detection. (2) Step heights calculated by:

$$h_{st} = \lambda \cdot \bar{w}_{st}, \quad h_{nr} = \lambda \cdot \bar{w}_{nr}, \tag{7}$$

where $\bar{w}st$ and $\bar{w}_{nr}$ are mean vertical positions of standing and nearest planes. (3) Stair depth determined by:

$$d_{str} = \lambda \cdot \left| q_{min}^{nr} - q_{min}^{st} \right|, \tag{8}$$

where q_{min}^{nr} and q_{min}^{st} are minimum horizontal positions of nearest and standing planes.

2.2 Prosthetic Dynamics Model

To enable trajectory optimization, we model the powered knee prosthesis as a second-order dynamic system:

$$M\ddot{\theta}(t) + D\dot{\theta}(t) + K\theta(t) = K_p[\theta_{\text{tar}}(t) - \theta(t)] + K_d[\dot{\theta}_{\text{tar}}(t) - \dot{\theta}(t)] - mgl\sin\Theta(t), \tag{9}$$

where M, D, K are inertia, damping and stiffness parameters respectively, K_p, K_d are PD control gains, and $mgl\sin\Theta(t)$ represents gravitational torque.

Defining state vector $\boldsymbol{x}(t) = [\theta(t)\ \dot\theta(t)]^\top$ and control input $\boldsymbol{u}(t) = [\theta_{\text{tar}}\ \dot\theta_{\text{tar}}]^\top$, the system can be written in state-space form:

$$\dot{\boldsymbol{x}}(t) = \boldsymbol{A}\boldsymbol{x}(t) + \boldsymbol{B}\boldsymbol{u}(t) + \boldsymbol{B}_\omega \omega(t), \tag{10}$$

where $\omega(t) = \sin[\Theta(t)]$ and system matrices are:

$$\boldsymbol{A} = \begin{bmatrix} 0 & 1 \\ -\frac{K_p+K}{M} & -\frac{D+K_d}{M} \end{bmatrix}, \boldsymbol{B} = \begin{bmatrix} 0 & 0 \\ \frac{K_p}{M} & \frac{K_d}{M} \end{bmatrix}, \boldsymbol{B}_\omega = \begin{bmatrix} 0 \\ -\frac{mgl}{M} \end{bmatrix}. \tag{11}$$

The discretized system with sampling time T is:

$$\boldsymbol{x}(k+1) = \boldsymbol{A}_d \boldsymbol{x}(k) + \boldsymbol{B}_d \boldsymbol{u}(k) + \boldsymbol{B}_{\omega,d}\omega(k), \tag{12}$$

where discrete matrices $\boldsymbol{A}_d$, $\boldsymbol{B}d$, and $\boldsymbol{B}\omega, d$ are obtained through standard discretization.

Through the prosthesis model, we can predict the angle θ corresponding to input series u.

2.3 Optimization

Building upon the objective-oriented representations from our perception module, we formulate a multi-objective optimization framework that directly addresses the two key challenges in prosthetic stair ascent: clearance control and foot placement optimization.

Clearance Optimization. The clearance objective ensures sufficient but not excessive step clearing height. Using the environmental parameters extracted from our perception module, we quantify the horizontal and vertical clearances as:

$$\begin{aligned} d_x^{\text{clr}} &= [\boldsymbol{p}_{\text{foot}}^{\text{pros}}]_x - q_i \\ d_z^{\text{clr}} &= [\boldsymbol{p}_{\text{foot}}^{\text{pros}}]_z - h_i \end{aligned} \tag{13}$$

where q_i represents the current vertical plane position and h_i is the step height.

The clearance objective function is formulated as:

$$J_{\text{clr}} = \lambda_1^{\text{clr}} \left(\frac{1}{(d_x^{\text{clr}})^2 + \epsilon_x} + \frac{1}{(d_z^{\text{clr}})^2 + \epsilon_z} \right) + \lambda_2^{\text{clr}} \|\boldsymbol{u}\|^2, \tag{14}$$

where ϵ_x, ϵ_z are small positive constants, and the second term penalizes control effort.

Foot Placement Optimization. The foot placement optimization serves two crucial purposes: ensuring collision-free prosthetic foot placement and facilitating comfortable stepping for the intact limb. For collision avoidance with the next step:

$$J_{\text{plm}}^{\text{col}} = \lambda_{\text{col}} \left(\frac{1}{(d_x^{\text{clr}})^2 + \epsilon_x} \right) \tag{15}$$

More importantly, the prosthetic foot placement should be optimized to enable natural and comfortable stepping of the intact limb. Based on the method in [17], we predict the intact leg's next heel strike position using CoM trajectory and current foot positions, where heel strike (hs) represents the moment when the foot contacts the ground:

$$\boldsymbol{p}_{\text{foot}}^{\text{int,hs}}[k+1] = 2\boldsymbol{p}_{\text{foot}}^{\text{int,hs}}[k] - \boldsymbol{p}_{\text{foot}}^{\text{int,hs}}[k-1] \qquad (16)$$

where superscript 'int' denotes the intact limb.

The deviation from step center is calculated as:

$$d_{\text{center}} = \boldsymbol{p}_{\text{foot}}^{\text{int,hs}}[k+1] - (q_i^{\text{int}} + d_{\text{str}}/2) \qquad (17)$$

where q_i represents the horizontal position of the nearest vertical plane (step) relative to the prosthetic foot or intact foot, and d_{str} is the stair depth. By incorporating this deviation into our optimization, we adjust the prosthetic foot placement to ensure the intact limb can maintain a comfortable step length without being forced to awkwardly adjust its landing position to avoid stair edges:

$$J_{\text{plm}}^{\text{sym}} = \lambda_{\text{sym}} |[\boldsymbol{p}_{\text{foot}}^{\text{pros}}]x - (q_i^{\text{pros}} + d_{\text{center}})|^2 \qquad (18)$$

Fig. 2. Simulation. (a) The human-prosthesis hybrid model. (b) Showcase of the proposed framework in successful ascending of stair.

Reference Guidance. To enhance optimization convergence, we incorporate a nominal reference trajectory based on level-ground walking patterns:

$$J_{\text{ref}} = \sum_{k=0}^{N-1} \lambda_{\text{ref}} |\theta_{\text{tar}}(k) - \theta_{\text{ref}}(k)|^2, \qquad (19)$$

where $\theta_{\text{ref}}(k)$ is generated using ZMP-based planning [18] for its balance between computational efficiency and stability [19].

Full Optimization Problem. The complete optimization problem is formulated as:

$$\begin{aligned}\min_{u} J &= J_{\text{clr}} + J_{\text{plm}} + J_{\text{ref}}, \\ \text{subject to} & \\ \dot{\boldsymbol{x}}(t) &= \boldsymbol{A}\boldsymbol{x}(t) + \boldsymbol{B}\boldsymbol{u}(t) + \boldsymbol{B}_\omega \omega(t) \\ \boldsymbol{M}\boldsymbol{Z} &\leq \boldsymbol{\Gamma}\end{aligned} \qquad (20)$$

The state vector $x(t) = [\theta(t), \dot{\theta}(t)]^\top$ represents the prosthesis knee angle and angular velocity. The control input $u(t) = [\theta_{\text{tar}}(t), \dot{\theta}_{\text{tar}}(t)]^\top$ defines the target angle and angular velocity. System matrices A, B, B_ω follow the definitions in Sect. 2.2. State and input constraints ensure physical feasibility of the generated trajectory. The constraint vector Z combines states and inputs, where $MZ \leq \Gamma$ represents physical limitations including joint angle range, velocity limits, and corresponding bounds on target states, ensuring the generated trajectory remains within the prosthetic device's mechanical capabilities.

3 Verification Setup

In this section, we would like to evaluate the performance of the proposed method with diverse stair heights and depths. The preliminary verification is conducted in simulation.

3.1 Simulation Settings

Table 1 provides critical parameters for simulation. To address the optimization problem, we employ the OSQP solver [20] from the cvxpy library, which utilizes the ADMM framework for efficient handling of large-scale and sparse problems.

Table 1. Critical parameters for simulation.

Parameter	Value	Parameter	Value
S_z	1.0 m	D	10 N.m.s/rad
T_{step}	0.65 s	l	0.2 m
T	0.01 s	λ_{ref}	10000
L_{step}	0.3 m	λ_1^{clr}	100000
M	0.4 kg.m^2	λ_2^{clr}	diag{1000, 1000}
K	100 N.m/rad	λ_{col}	50000

3.2 Simulator Establishment

We use the Isaac Gym [21] simulation environment to validate the proposed strategy. It contains a realistic physical engine and can thus effectively verify the controller stability. The amputee-prosthesis model includes 28 Degree of Freedom (DoF) and 14 rigid bodies, as shown in Fig. 2(a). The powered knee prosthesis has one DoF, modeled as a motor-driven joint, while the ankle on the amputated side is a passive joint with three DoF. One RGB-D camera on the chest and IMUs on legs are used to capture human and environment information.

A key challenge in prosthesis simulation is realistic human motion modeling. We address this through a human-prosthesis hybrid model where the amputee's control policy π_h is derived from a bipedal model [11]. In particular, the amputee's walking strategy π_h is generated by

$$\max_{\pi_h} \mathbb{E}_{\zeta \sim \pi_h} \left[\sum_{t=0}^{T} \gamma^t R_t \right], \tag{21}$$

where γ is the discount factor, R_t is the similarity with human motion, and ζ is the sampled trajectory. The training follows

$$\pi_h \leftarrow \pi_h + \alpha \cdot \mathbb{E}_{\zeta \sim \pi_h} \left[\sum_{t=0}^{T} A_t \cdot \nabla_{\pi_h} \log \pi_h(a_t|s_t) \right], \tag{22}$$

where $A_t = \sum_{k=t}^{T} \gamma^{k-t} R_k - \mathbb{E}_{\pi_h} \left[\sum_{k=t}^{T} \gamma^{k-t} R_k \mid s_t \right]$ is the advantage function and α is the learning rate. Notice that the human model training does not involve any information about the prosthesis control in this paper.

3.3 Protocol

To evaluate our optimization-based method, which achieves (1) an appropriate clearance for stepping over stairs of varying heights and (2) an optimal foot placement that adjusts the position of the next stair as well as the comfort of the intact side during stepping, the following experimental protocol is designed.

First, we conduct clearance generalization tests to assess the adaptability of the prosthetic leg when stepping over stairs of various heights. In this test, 15 cm, 20 cm, and 25 cm stair heights are used to simulate real-world variations in stair height.

Second, we perform foot placement tests to investigate the prosthetic leg's performance in selecting appropriate foot placements on stairs of varying depth. Stair depths are varied in 15 cm, 20 cm, and 25 cm.

In each test we conduct the baseline comparison, we utilize a recently published prosthetic obstacle avoidance strategy [15]. In this method, the knee joint angle is adjusted dynamically based on the distance between the prosthetic foot's landing point and the obstacle. The baseline knee angle trajectory $\theta_b(t)$ is defined as:

$$\theta_b(t) = \theta_{\text{ref}} + w_b \cdot \max(d_{\text{safe}} - d_x^s, 0), \tag{23}$$

where $\theta_b(t)$ is the target knee angle trajectory, θ_{ref} is the reference knee angle, w_b is the avoidance weight, d_x^s is the horizontal distance between the foot and the obstacle during the stance phase, and d_{safe} is the predefined safe distance.

4 Experiment Results

4.1 Clearance Generalization Tests

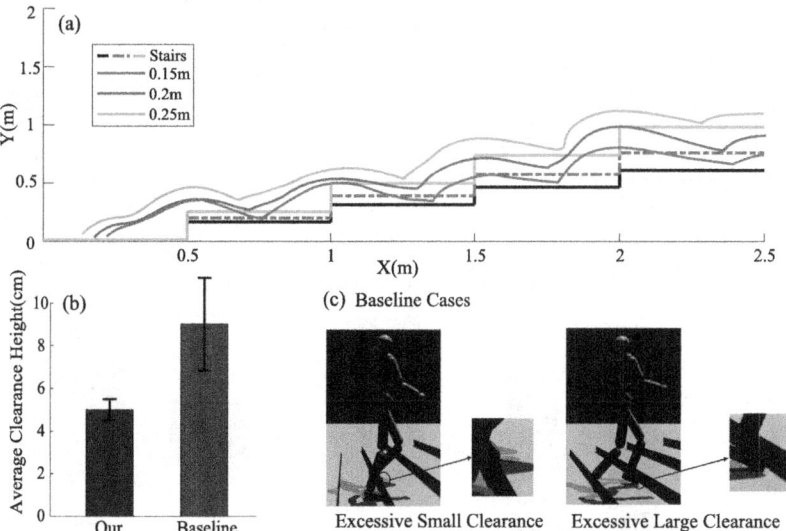

Fig. 3. Foot trajectories for stair ascending. (a) Foot trajectories for the proposed and the baseline methods. (b) Foot-stair distance at trajectory peak for the proposed and the baseline methods. (c) Two defective cases with the baseline methods: excessive small clearance leads to inability to step over, and excessive large clearance causes being too close to the next step.

The results demonstrate our method's superior adaptability to varying stair heights while maintaining efficient clearance control. As shown in Fig. 3, our approach successfully navigated stairs ranging from 15 cm to 25 cm without collision. The average toe clearance maintained by our method was 5.04 cm, providing sufficient safety margin while avoiding excessive lift. In contrast, the baseline method exhibited significant limitations in generalization. As shown in Fig. 3(c), with smaller tuning weights, the method failed to generate sufficient clearance for higher stairs, leading to potential collisions. Conversely, when the weights were increased to ensure clearance over the highest stairs, it resulted in excessive lift for lower steps, risking collision with the next step's edge. Even with optimally tuned parameters, the baseline method generated an average clearance of 9.11 cm, approximately 44.68% higher than our method.

4.2 Foot Placement Tests

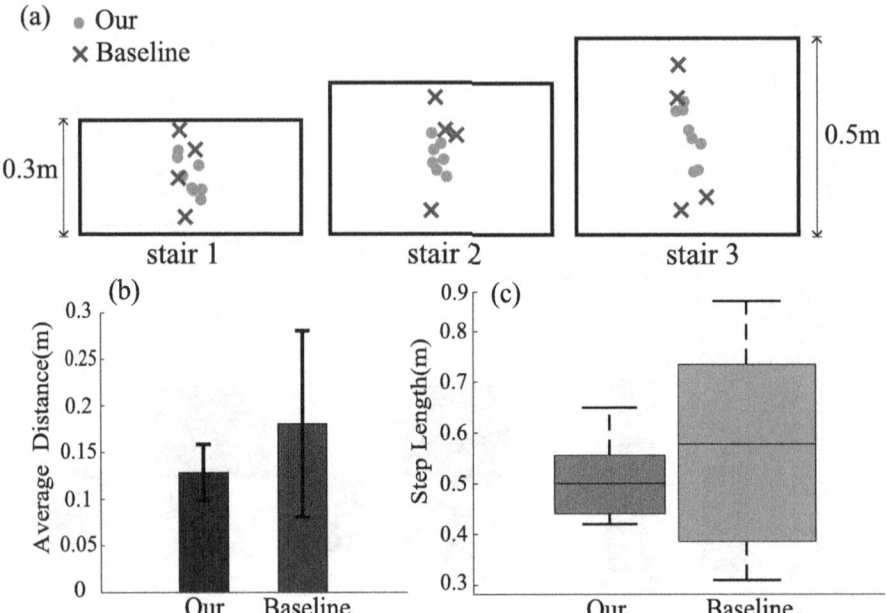

Fig. 4. **Foot Placement for stair ascending.** (a) Foot placement on stairs with different widths for the proposed and the baseline methods. (b) Average vertical distance between the prosthetic foot and step center for the proposed and the baseline methods. (c) Average step length of the intact limb during stair ascent for the proposed and the baseline methods.

The foot placement optimization results highlight our method's capability to handle varying stair depths while ensuring both no-collision stepping and intact-limb stable gait. As illustrated in Fig. 4 (a), our method consistently positioned the prosthetic foot within the central region of each step, with an average deviation of 0.13 m from the step center. This central placement ensures stability and reduces the risk of edge contact. In comparison, the baseline method showed significant limitations in foot placement control, the prosthetic foot placement varied considerably, with deviations up to 0.18 m from step center, as shown in Fig. 4 (a). As shown in Fig. 4 (c), our method enabled the intact limb to maintain natural and consistent stepping patterns, with an average step length of 0.50 m ± 0.11 m. In contrast, subjects using the baseline method frequently needed to make compensatory adjustments to their gait, resulting in highly variable step lengths ranging from 0.31 m to 0.86 m. These results demonstrate that our optimization-based approach successfully balances environmental constraints with natural gait requirements, maintaining both reliable stair clearance and comfortable stepping patterns across diverse stair configurations.

5 Discussion and Conclusion

This paper presents an optimization-based framework for powered prosthetic stair ascent, addressing the limitations of traditional fixed-trajectory and rule-based methods. Rule-based approaches rely heavily on predefined mappings or manually designed rules, which often struggle to adapt to variable environments and user-specific characteristics [22]. These methods face significant challenges in tasks requiring the simultaneous satisfaction of multiple objectives, such as stair clearance and suitable foot placement. Furthermore, the complexity of rule-based systems grows exponentially with the addition of new objectives or environmental factors, making them difficult to generalize across diverse scenarios.

In contrast, the proposed framework leverages optimization to dynamically integrate diverse inputs, including environmental, prosthesis and human information, into a unified control strategy. A key innovation of our approach lies in its ability to simultaneously consider both human motion characteristics and environmental constraints within a single optimization framework. This integration is crucial as successful stair ascent requires not only adaptation to varying stair geometries but also synchronization with the user's natural gait patterns and comfort preferences. The front-end perception module processes real-time information about stair geometry (e.g., height, depth, and position) and user kinematics (e.g., center of mass and foot positions), providing a comprehensive representation of the task environment. This information is embedded in a back-end optimization module, which systematically balances multiple objectives to generate adaptive and efficient trajectories.

Simulation results validate the effectiveness of the proposed method, showing that it can reliably navigate stairs with varying dimensions while maintaining natural step coordination with the intact limb. The framework's ability to simultaneously optimize for both environmental constraints and human motion patterns leads to more natural and efficient stair ascent.

The optimization framework also demonstrates superior scalability. By formulating stair ascent as a multi-objective optimization problem, the framework can seamlessly incorporate additional goals like energy consumption [23] and different prosthesis model [24] without significant changes to its structure. In future work, we plan to implement and validate this optimization framework on physical prosthetic systems. This will involve addressing key challenges in real-time computation efficiency, environmental perception, and human-machine interaction. We will focus on evaluating the framework's performance under actual sensor noise and latency conditions, and refine the method through user interaction studies to ensure its reliability and practicality in real-world applications.

Acknowledgment. This work was supported by the National Natural Science Foundation of China under Grant 52475001. The authors thank Beijing Super Cloud Computing Center for their support of computational resources.

References

1. Fu, G., et al.: A robotic transtibial prosthesis with equilibrium-adjustable parallel springs to improve energy efficiency in slope walking. IEEE/ASME Trans. Mechatron. **30**, 2210–2221 (2024)
2. Hoover, C.D., Fulk, G.D., Fite, K.B.: Stair ascent with a powered transfemoral prosthesis under direct myoelectric control. IEEE/ASME Trans. Mechatron. **18**(3), 1191–1200 (2012)
3. Riener, R., Rabuffetti, M., Frigo, C.: Stair ascent and descent at different inclinations. Gait Posture **15**(1), 32–44 (2002)
4. Cheng, S., Bolívar-Nieto, E., Welker, C.G., Gregg, R.D.: Modeling the transitional kinematics between variable-incline walking and stair climbing. IEEE Trans. Med. Rob. Bionics **4**(3), 840–851 (2022)
5. Reznick, E., et al.: Lower-limb kinematics and kinetics during continuously varying human locomotion. Sci. Data **8**(1), 282 (2021)
6. McFadyen, B.J., Winter, D.A.: An integrated biomechanical analysis of normal stair ascent and descent. J. Biomech. **21**(9), 733–744 (1988)
7. Ledoux, E.D., Goldfarb, M.: Control and evaluation of a powered transfemoral prosthesis for stair ascent. IEEE Trans. Neural Syst. Rehabil. Eng. **25**(7), 917–924 (2017)
8. Lenzi, T., Cempini, M., Hargrove, L., Kuiken, T.: Design, development, and testing of a lightweight hybrid robotic knee prosthesis. Int. J. Rob. Res. **37**(8), 953–976 (2018)
9. Lawson, B.E., Varol, H.A., Huff, A., Erdemir, E., Goldfarb, M.: Control of stair ascent and descent with a powered transfemoral prosthesis. IEEE Trans. Neural Syst. Rehabil. Eng. **21**(3), 466–473 (2012)
10. Sup, F., Varol, H.A., Mitchell, J., Withrow, T.J., Goldfarb, M.: Self-contained powered knee and ankle prosthesis: initial evaluation on a transfemoral amputee. In: 2009 IEEE International Conference on Rehabilitation Robotics, pp. 638–644. IEEE (2009)
11. Hou, H., Zhu, W., Ruan, L., Wang, Q.: Prosthetic control by learning: a multi-agent cooperative game framework. In: 2025 International Conference On Rehabilitation Robotics (ICORR), pp. 1–6. IEEE (2025)
12. Hood, S., Gabert, L., Lenzi, T.: Powered knee and ankle prosthesis with adaptive control enables climbing stairs with different stair heights, cadences, and gait patterns. IEEE Trans. Rob. **38**(3), 1430–1441 (2022)
13. Cortino, R.J., Bolívar-Nieto, E., Best, T.K., Gregg, R.D.: Stair ascent phase-variable control of a powered knee-ankle prosthesis. In: 2022 International Conference on Robotics and Automation (ICRA), pp. 5673–5678. IEEE (2022)
14. Cortino, R.J., Best, T.K., Gregg, R.D.: Data-driven phase-based control of a powered knee-ankle prosthesis for variable-incline stair ascent and descent. IEEE Trans. Med. Rob. Bionics **6**(1), 175–188 (2023)
15. Cheng, S., Laubscher, C.A., Gregg, R.D.: Automatic stub avoidance for a powered prosthetic leg over stairs and obstacles. IEEE Trans. Biomed. Eng. **71**, 1499–1510 (2023)
16. Zhao, S., et al.: A learning-free method for locomotion mode prediction by terrain reconstruction and visual-inertial odometry. IEEE Trans. Neural Syst. Rehabil. Eng. **31**, 3895–3905 (2023)
17. Mobbs, R.J., et al.: Gait metrics analysis utilizing single-point inertial measurement units: a systematic review. Mhealth **8**, 9 (2022)

18. Park, J., Youm, Y.: General zmp preview control for bipedal walking. In: Proceedings 2007 IEEE International Conference on Robotics and Automation, pp. 2682–2687. IEEE (2007)
19. Erbatur, K., Kurt, O.: Natural zmp trajectories for biped robot reference generation. IEEE Trans. Ind. Electron. **56**(3), 835–845 (2008)
20. Stellato, B., Banjac, G., Goulart, P., Bemporad, A., Boyd, S.: Osqp: an operator splitting solver for quadratic programs. Math. Program. Comput. **12**(4), 637–672 (2020)
21. Makoviychuk, V., et al.: Isaac gym: high performance gpu-based physics simulation for robot learning. arXiv preprint arXiv:2108.10470 (2021)
22. Zhu, W., Cai, M., Hou, H., Zhao, S., Ruan, L., Wang, Q.: Obstacle avoidance for knee prostheses via direct integration of environment information. In: 2025 The 44th Chinese Control Conference (CCC), pp. 1–6. IEEE (2025)
23. Zhu, W., Mai, J., Wang, Q.: Effects of modulation coefficient adjustment on energy regeneration of damping torque controlled transtibial prosthesis. In: 2022 9th IEEE RAS/EMBS International Conference for Biomedical Robotics and Biomechatronics (BioRob), pp. 1–6. IEEE (2022)
24. Zhu, W., Ju, Z., Fu, G., Ruan, L., Wang, Q.: Design of a mode-switchable elastic actuator towards interactive robotic applications. In: International Conference on Intelligent Robotics and Applications, pp. 133–146. Springer, Heidelberg (2024). https://doi.org/10.1007/978-981-96-0780-8_10

A Hybrid FES-Soft Exosuit System to Improve Interlimb Symmetry in Post-stroke Patients

Xingyu Lu[1], Yanwei Zhao[1], Zhengbo Wang[1], Yu Xia[1], Shuxiao Jin[3], Chunfang Wang[3], Gang Liu[3], Jianda Han[1,2], Ying Zhang[3], and Weiguang Huo[1,2(✉)]

[1] College of Artificial Intelligence, Nankai University, Tianjin 300350, China
weiguang.huo@nankai.edu.cn
[2] Shenzhen Research Institute, Nankai University, Shenzhen 518083, China
[3] Rehabilitation Medical Centre, Tianjin Union Medical Centre, Tianjin 300121, China

Abstract. Post-stroke hemiplegic gaits are typically characterized by a decrease in forward propulsion and dorsiflexion angle, resulting in decreased mobility and an increased risk of falling. To address these issues, we design a hybrid assistive system that integrates functional electrical stimulation (FES) and a soft exosuit. This hybrid system synergistically combines biomechanical support with neuromuscular activation. Moreover, we propose a shank-angle-guided control strategy for the hybrid FES-soft exosuit system, ensuring stable assistance across various walking speeds. Clinical trials involving two post-stroke patients demonstrated that the developed hybrid system significantly reduced interlimb propulsion asymmetry and enhanced interlimb dorsiflexion angle symmetry during the swing phase, resulting in a significant increase in interlimb symmetry. These results highlight the potential of the hybrid system to simultaneously address hemiplegic gaits in post-stroke patients.

Keywords: FES · Soft exosuit · hybrid system · post-stroke patient · interlimb symmetry · rehabilitation

1 Introduction

Stroke is an acute disease characterized by a high morbidity and disability rate [7]. It can lead to walking disorders and seriously affect the quality of life of the patient [4]. Walking disorders in stroke patients are essentially a complex coupling of neurological control deficits and biomechanical compensations, which are mainly manifested in asymmetrical walking patterns and increased interstride variability [11]. Most patients show a large interlimb difference in forward propulsion during the stance phase, along with a compound deficit of insufficient ankle dorsiflexion angle in the swing phase, leading to reduced walking speed, increased energy consumption, and increased risk of falls in patients [18].

Many assistive devices, such as ankle exoskeletons and functional electrical stimulation(FES), have also matured in research. Both of them have been demonstrated to be effective when used in clinical settings [14,19]. Ankle exoskeletons are used to provide movement assistance for stroke patients, providing weight support and strength assistance during repeated gait rehabilitation exercises [14]. However, traditional rigid exoskeletons have high inertia and restrict the range of motion [15]. To better adapt to daily activities and patients' individual needs, some soft exosuits have been proposed. These exosuits aim to enhance ankle strength during the plantar flexion phase, thereby improving the patient's walking disorder [1–3]. Louis N. Awad et al. [1] used a soft robotic exosuit to improve walking in post-stroke patients, effectively reducing interlimb differences in forward propulsion and decreasing walking metabolic consumption. FES is a technique that uses low-frequency current pulses to stimulate the patient's muscles to produce functional movements, which can increase muscle strength and improve locomotion, inducing changes in neuroplasticity [13]. Given the inherent limitations of traditional FES systems in achieving efficient modulation of ankle dorsiflexion during gait cycles, closed-loop control strategies and adaptive stimulation profiles have emerged as preferred approaches in the recent literature. These methodological advancements have exhibited statistically significant improvements in correcting insufficient dorsiflexion angles during the swing phase, thereby mitigating fall risks in post-stroke patients [9].

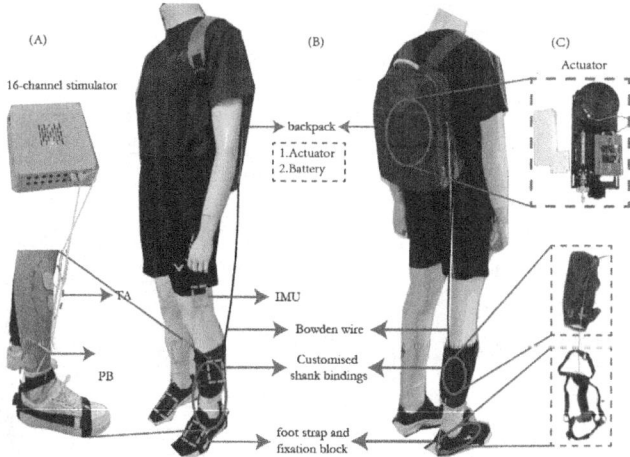

Fig. 1. Overview of the design of the FES-soft exosuit system. (a) The 16-channel electrical stimulator and electrode placements. (b) The hybrid FES-soft exosuit system donned on a mannequin. (c) The mechanical design of the actuator of the soft exosuit, as well as the shank binding and foot strap.

Integration of functional electrical stimulation (FES) with the soft exosuit reduces the requirement for motor-driven actuation components, thereby reducing the system weight while simultaneously providing neuromuscular activation benefits for gait rehabilitation. In contrast, the soft exosuit compensates for the limitations of FES during plantarflexion tasks, where excessive stimulus intensity induces rapid muscle fatigue. By combining the advantages of the above assistive devices, we designed a hybrid FES-soft exosuit system for post-stroke patients, which was well-suited to address the gait disorder of post-stroke patients in gait cycles. In our previous study [12], we improved the walking ability of stroke patients using a hybrid system of FES-soft exosuit. However, only walking speed-related indicators were mentioned in that study, and the underlying reasons were not analyzed.

In this paper, we propose a shank angle-guided control strategy for the hybrid FES-soft exosuit system. To address the limitations of traditional control strategies in delivering consistent assistance during different speeds across patients, [1,12], we proposed a shank-angle-guided control strategy that replaces temporal parameters with shank angular measurements as dynamic inputs. This approach enables optimized assistance profiles for the FES-soft exosuit system, eliminating reliance on time-based synchronization while ensuring effective assistance across diverse walking conditions. Two post-stroke patients participated in clinical trials. The experimental results showed that the proposed method significantly reduced the interlimb difference in forward propulsion force and improved the interlimb dorsiflexion angle symmetry of the swing phase during walking. The FES-soft exosuit was able to significantly increase the overall interlimb symmetry and improve walking in post-stroke patients.

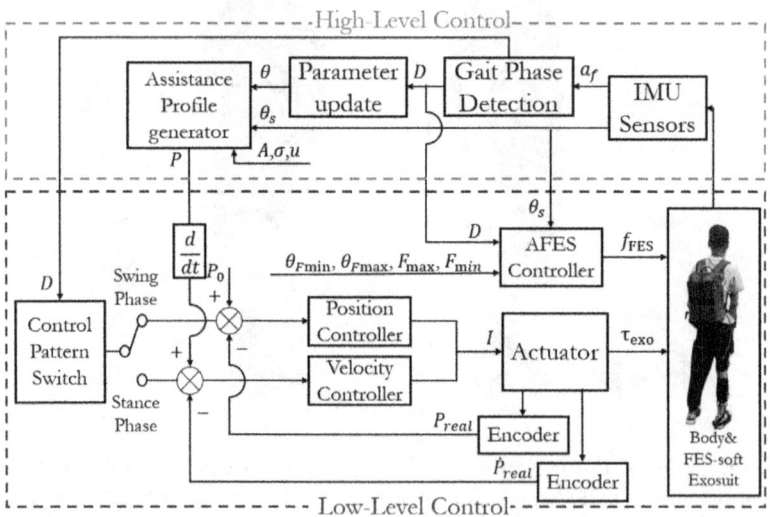

Fig. 2. Schematic Block Diagram of Hybrid FES-Soft Exosuit Control Framework. p_0 represents the initial position.

2 Design and Control Method of FES-Soft Exosuit

2.1 System Design

Figure 1 shows the design of the hybrid FES-soft exosuit system. For the FES, the system incorporates a customized 16-channel functional electrical stimulator (FES) that generates electrical stimulation currents in two channels, which are selected to act on the tibialis anterior and peroneus brevis muscles. For the soft exosuit, a DC motor (AK80-8, T-Motor, China) coupled with a Bowden cable transmission system provides mechanical actuation. Customized shank binding and foot strap were used to secure the soft exosuit to the subject's body. A fixation block connecting the end of the Bowden Cable to the foot strap is placed at the heel, increasing and transmitting the assisted moment of plantar flexion at the ankle joint. For the gait phase detection and angle measurement, five IMUs (Xsens, Netherlands) are mounted on the thigh, shank, and foot segments of the affected limb, as well as the shank and foot of the unaffected limb, respectively.

2.2 Control Strategy of FES-Soft Exosuit

The present study proposed a hybrid controller for the FES-Soft exosuit system (see Fig. 2), which is designed to provide efficient assistance to patients. The hybrid controller is a hierarchical controller that consists of two control loops. The high-level controller detects key events during the gait phase based on an IMU placed on the foot and generates an assistive profile based on gait phases and shank angle. The low-level controller directly controls the functional electrical stimulation (FES) and motor actuation: during the stance phase, it engages velocity control mode to drive the motor for a precise assistance profile, while switching to position control mode during the swing phase to maintain the Bowden cable in a relaxed state and simultaneously activate the FES.

Gait Phase Detection. Precise gait phase detection is an essential prerequisite for the FES-soft exosuit system to be able to provide accurate and stable assistance. A gait phase detection algorithm, which was capable of detecting both initial contact (IC) and toe-off (TO) events [9], is used in this study.

Control Strategy of Soft Exosuit. Human locomotion during everyday activities is characterized by inherently variable gait speeds. To address this problem, we propose an efficient assistance profile generation strategy.

In traditional control methods, time was usually used as an intermediate variable because its relationship to joint dynamics information can be easily obtained through offline analysis of kinetic data. Several studies have explored the feasibility of using joint angle information as an intermediate variable instead of time [16–18]. All of these show that the shank angle is one of the promising intermediate variables for representing the assistance profile, and the measurement requires only one IMU sensor.

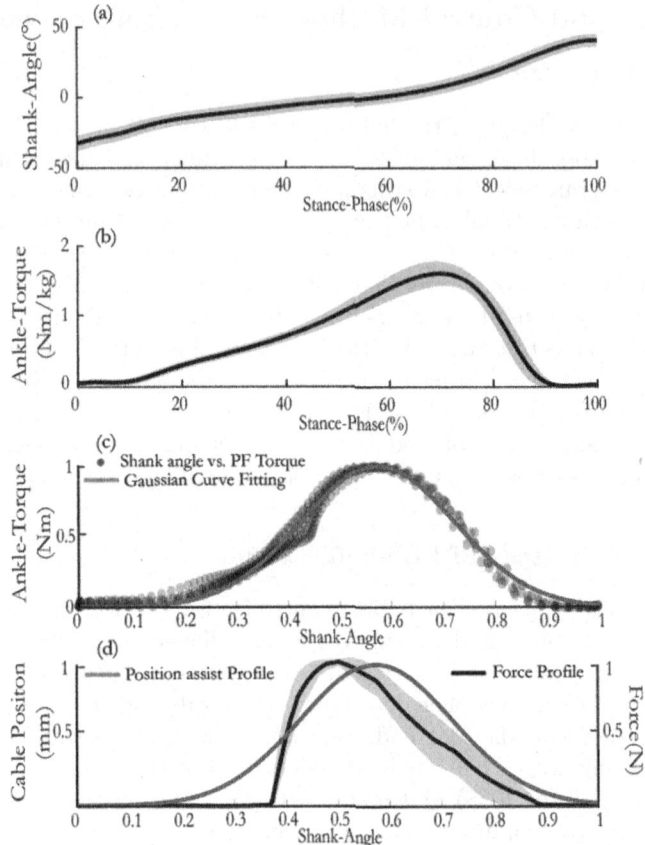

Fig. 3. Biomechanical data and Gaussian fitting results. (a) Shank angle in the stance phase. (b) Angle torque in stance phase (c) Gaussian function fitting for shank angle and ankle torque in six subjects (all data from [5]). Shank angle and ankle torque were both normalized. (d) A force profile generated by the novel assistance strategy used in healthy subjects.

While the adjustment of the assistance profile can be dynamically modulated through real-time shank angle, the amplitude characteristics of the assistance profile require precise definition to ensure biomechanical efficacy. An assistance profile with control parameters tuned based on ankle torque has been shown to have the ability to improve human walking [6]. So ankle torque profile can be viewed as an effective assistance profile for ankle joint function enhancement. A public biomechanical dataset [5] was used to analyze the relationship between shank angle and ankle torque as described above. We normalized the shank angle and ankle torque to reduce the impact of individualized differences between people on the analysis results. The curve of the ankle torque versus shank angle during the stance phase and the well-fitted Gaussian function curve are shown in Fig. 3. The fitted Gaussian function curve is as follows:

$$\tau_n(\theta_{sn}) = Ae^{-\frac{(\theta_{sn}-\mu)^2}{2\sigma^2}} \qquad (1)$$

where τ_n is the normalized ankle torque, θ_{sn} is the normalized shank angle, A is the amplitude, μ is the mean, and σ is the standard deviation. The profile depicted in Fig. 3 represents a continuous mathematical relationship where output varies with the shank angle throughout the gait cycle. Based on Eq. (1), a novel soft exosuit assistance profile (shown in Fig. 4) is developed that maintains time independence while replicating the ankle torque characteristics observed in human locomotion, as follows:

$$P(\theta_s) = Ae^{-\frac{(\theta_s - (\theta\mu + \theta_{Emin}))^2}{2(\theta\sigma)^2}} \qquad (2)$$

A, μ, and σ are concerned with the control of form and define the shape of the assistance profile. θ_s is the shank angle. θ represents the motion range of shank ($\theta_{Emax} - \theta_{Emin}$). The θ_{Emax} and θ_{Emin} in Eq. (2) denote the maximum and minimum values of the shank angle within the complete gait, respectively. This parameter is updated at an interval of three steps.

This novel assistance profile was evaluated on healthy subjects to assess its efficacy (as shown in Fig. 3). During the experimental trial, participants were instructed to imitate post-stroke gait patterns while quantifying the applied assistance force through instrumented force sensors.

Adaptive FES Assistance. The main goal of the FES assistance is to compensate the patients' foot-drop during the swing phase. To mitigate accelerated muscle fatigue caused by conventional trapezoidal FES protocols, the proposed FES stimulation profile dynamically adjusts stimulus intensity: it reduces stimulus intensity during mid-swing to decelerate fatiguing effects, while gradually reinstating maximal intensity to counteract heightened plantar flexor co-contraction in the late swing [9]. To reduce the control variables of the FES-soft exosuit system, the shank angle was used to adaptively modulate the proposed profile (shown in Fig. 4), as follows:

$$f = f_a(\theta_s, \theta_{Fmax}, \theta_{Fmin}, F_{\max}, F_{\min}, D)$$
$$+ f_{\text{ramp}}(F_{\max}, F_{\min}, D) \qquad (3)$$

where

$$f_a = D(k)((F_{\max} - F_{\min})\lambda + F_{\min}), \qquad (4)$$

$$f_{\text{ramp}} = \begin{cases} D(k)(F_{\max}\operatorname{sat}(t_1/0.05) - f_a) & \text{for } t_1 \leq 0.08 \\ (1 - D(k))F_{\max}(1 - t_2/0.1) & \text{for } t_2 \leq 0.1 \\ 0 & \text{otherwise}, \end{cases} \qquad (5)$$

with
$$\lambda = \frac{1}{2}\left(\operatorname{sat}\left(\frac{2\theta_{Fmin}(\theta_{Fmax}-\theta_s)}{\theta_s(\theta_{Fmax}-\theta_{Fmin})}-1\right)+1\right) \tag{6}$$

where f_{ramp} represents the ramp-up and down stimulation at the beginning and the end of the swing phase, and f_a represents the adaptive period stimulation profile. $F_{\max}$ and $F_{\min}$ show the maximum and minimum values of the stimulus intensity. θ_{Fmax} and θ_{Fmin} show two shank angle thresholds. The swing detection $(D(k))$ of the stance and the swing can be obtained by computing the period between TO and IC (1 for swing and 0 for stance) [9]. t_1 and t_2 show the time (s) after the TO and IC event during one stride, respectively. sat() denotes the saturation function.

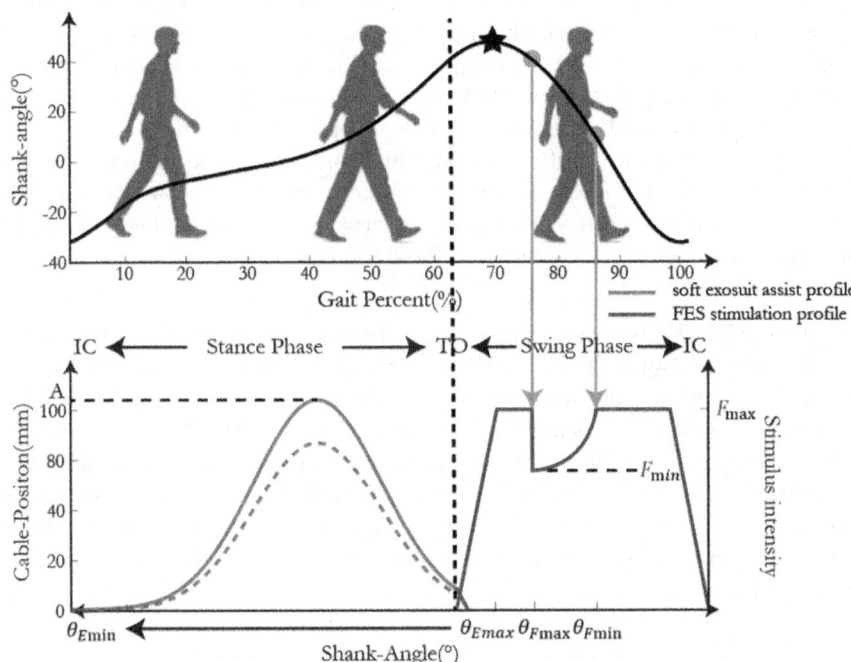

Fig. 4. The FES-soft exosuit control method. Synchronized actuation strategy combining: soft exosuit assist profile (solid red line) during stance phase, and FES stimulation profile (solid blue line) during swing phase. (Color figure online)

3 System Validation

3.1 Experimental Setup

Two patients were recruited to participate in the system performance validation (see Table 1). After fully understanding the experimental protocol and signing the informed consent form, subjects participating in the experiment will wear the FES-soft exosuit system and IMUs. The FES outputs stimulation signals through two designated electrical stimulation channels with pulse widths and frequencies of $500us$ and 50 Hz, respectively. A total of five IMUs (sampling frequency: 100 Hz) were used in this study. Ground reaction force data were recorded by two three-dimensional force plates (Bertec, USA, sampling frequency: 500 Hz) in the walking test field. The study was approved by the institutional review board of Nankai University (approval number: NKUIRB2024101).

3.2 Experimental Protocol

The overall experimental protocol was divided into two parts: parameter calibration and self-select speed walking test. The experimental protocol is described in detail below:

Parameter Calibration

FES Threshold Setting. The subject was asked to sit relaxed, and the amplitude of the electrical stimulation was gradually increased. The amplitude capable of inducing a tremor in the dorsiflexion of the ankle joint of the subject was designated as F_{min}, while the amplitude capable of achieving the maximum dorsiflexion angle of the ankle joint was set at F_{max}. The electrical stimulation parameters of all subjects who participated in the experiment are shown in Table 1.

Table 1. Subject Information and Control Parameters

No.	Brunnstrom Score	Affected Side	Muscles	F_{max}	F_{min}	θ_{Fmax}	θ_{Fmin}	A	μ	σ
1	IV	right	TA	25 mA	17 mA	35°	5°	100	0.58	0.15
			PB	15 mA	8 mA	35°	5°			
2	V	left	TA	30 mA	23 mA	35°	5°	80	0.58	0.15
			PB	17 mA	10 mA	35°	5°			

IMUs Calibration. The joint angle is a key parameter in the verification of system performance and system control. Consequently, it is necessary to perform a series of operations that enable IMUS to obtain precise relative kinematic information of the human body through the algorithm [10].

Soft Exosuit Parameter Selection. After completing the above calibration, the subject was asked to complete a 5–10 min habilitation exercise to adapt to the walking assistance provided by the FES-soft exosuit system. During the process, the amplitude of personal-based assistive will be set (shown in Table 1).

Self-select Speed Walking Test. Some foam pads and two three-dimensional force plates were used to lay out the walking field as shown in Fig. 5 to serve as the experimental field for the self-select speed walking test. After parameter calibration, subjects were then asked to carry out five walking tests on the field, with each walking test needing to include round-trip walking. Both unassisted and assisted conditions are included in this process.

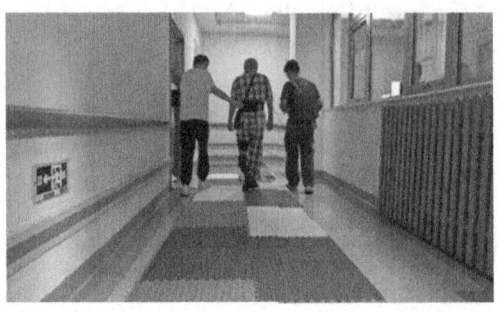

Fig. 5. Experiments with a post-stroke patient on the walking field.

3.3 Experimental Results

Motion Analysis

Interlimb Propulsion Asymmetry. Subjects walked on the walking field with two three-dimensional force plates (Bertec) to independently measure GRFs for each limb. GRFs were used to calculate the primary kinetic outcome of this study: interlimb propulsion asymmetry(IPA). Interlimb propulsion asymmetry was calculated as follows:

$$IPA = \frac{PP_h - PP_a}{PP_h} \tag{7}$$

where, PP_h and PP_a are the propulsive pulses (PP) on the unaffected and affected sides of the subject, respectively. The propulsive pulse is the integral of forward propulsive force over time.

Interlimb Dorsiflexion Angle Symmetry. The unaffected and affected sides' ankle angles were used to calculate the primary kinematic outcome of this study: correlation coefficient (CC) and interlimb dorsiflexion angle symmetry (IDAS). CC quantifies interlimb coordination by analyzing dorsiflexion kinematic synchrony between unaffected and affected limbs during gait cycles. IDAS was evaluated using the Euclidean distance-based similarity. The normalized distance for the maximum amplitude of the swing phase in the healthy side ankle angles is:

$$d(p_h, p_a) = \frac{\sqrt{\sum_{n=1}^{m}(p_h(n) - p_a(n))^2}}{\max(|p_h|)} \tag{8}$$

where p_h and p_a represent the ankle angle for the entire swing phase of the healthy and affected sides of the subject, respectively. Consequently, the similarity score is:

$$IDAS = \frac{1}{1 + d\left(p_h, p_a\right)} \qquad (9)$$

IDAS score approaching 1 indicates better interlimb symmetry.

Analysis Result. Figure 6 depicts the excellent effect of the FES-soft exosuit system in reducing interlimb propulsion asymmetry. With the assistance of the FES-soft exosuit system, the two subjects showed a 38% and 21% significant decrease ($t-test$, $p < 0.05$) in IPA, respectively. This shows the significant effect of this hybrid system in enhancing ankle strength during the stance phase.

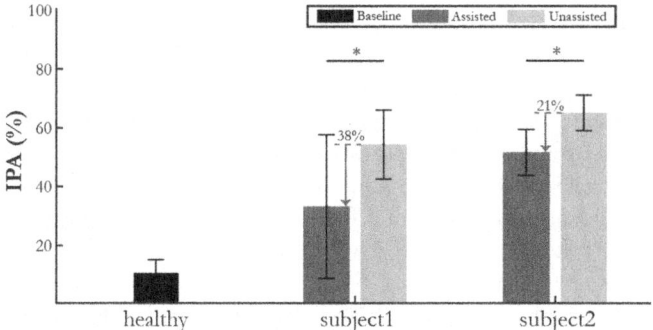

Fig. 6. Average changes of individual subjects in Interlimb propulsion asymmetry (IPA), GRFs for five complete gait cycles of both subjects were collected to calculate the final IPA. (*) represents $p < 0.05$.

For each subject, we chose the angle data from the 10-step gait cycle to calculate the final IDAS and CC. Figure 7 demonstrates the positive impact of the FES-soft exosuit system in increasing interlimb dorsiflexion angle symmetry. Subject-specific analysis revealed divergent response patterns to the intervention: Subject 1 exhibited an 11% improvement in IDAS score alongside a significant increase in CC value ($t-test$, $p < 0.001$), while Subject 2 demonstrated a significant enhancement (12%) in IDAS score ($t-test$, $p < 0.01$). As demonstrated by the ankle angle profile in Fig. 7, the FES-soft exosuit system significantly enhances both patients' range of motion (ROM) and peak dorsiflexion angle of the ankle joint during the swing phase.

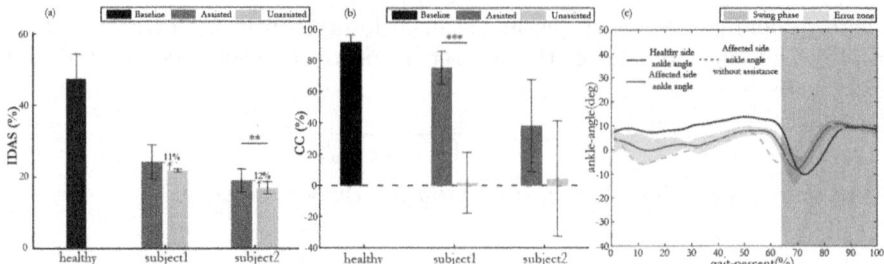

Fig. 7. Subjects' experimental results. (a) Average changes of individual subjects in IDAS. (b) Average changes of CC between the healthy and affected sides of subjects with and without assistance. (c) The ankle angle profile with assistance. (**) represents $p < 0.01$. (***) represents $p < 0.001$.

4 Conclusion

In this paper, we propose a hybrid control strategy for an FES-soft exosuit system to efficiently provide adaptive FES assistance and ankle plantarflexion assistance, both of which are based on shank angle and gait phase. Clinical trials with post-stroke patients have demonstrated that the hybrid system reduces interlimb propulsion asymmetry and enhances interlimb dorsiflexion angle symmetry in post-stroke patients, effectively increasing interlimb symmetry. These results highlight the potential of the FES-soft exosuit to improve post-stroke gait disorders. The developed hybrid system has great potential for assisting patients with foot drop walking in home and community settings due to its lightweight design and high efficiency. A new venture has been established to commercialize the system for widespread patient use.

Acknowledgment. This study was supported in part by the National Key Research and Development Program of China (2022YFB4700200), the National Natural Science Foundation of China (62373202), the Science and Technology Program of Tianjin (23JCYBJC01200, 24JCZXJC00340, and 22JCZDJC00060), and the Fundamental Research Funds for the Central Universities of China.

References

1. Guan, T., et al.: Rapid transitions in the epidemiology of stroke and its risk factors in china from 2002 to 2013. Neurology **89**(1), 53–61 (2017)
2. Coleman, E.R., et al.: Early rehabilitation after stroke: a narrative review. Curr. Atheroscler. Rep. **19**, 1–12 (2017)
3. Lin, P.-Y., et al.: The relation between ankle impairments and gait velocity and symmetry in people with stroke. Arch. Phys. Med. Rehabil. **87**(4), 562–568 (2006)
4. Weerdesteijn, V.G.M., et al.: Falls in individuals with stroke. J. Rehabil. Res. Dev. **45**(8), 1195 (2008)

5. Wu, C.-H., et al.: The effects of gait training using powered lower limb exoskeleton robot on individuals with complete spinal cord injury. J. Neuroeng. Rehabil. **15**, 1–10 (2018)
6. Murray, S.A., et al.: An assistive control approach for a lower-limb exoskeleton to facilitate recovery of walking following stroke. IEEE Trans. Neural Syst. Rehabil. Eng. **23**(3), 441–449 (2014)
7. Nazari, F., et al.: Applied exoskeleton technology: a comprehensive review of physical and cognitive human-robot interaction. IEEE Trans. Cogn. Dev. Syst. **15**(3), 1102–1122 (2023)
8. Bae, J., et al.: A lightweight and efficient portable soft exosuit for paretic ankle assistance in walking after stroke. In: 2018 IEEE International Conference on Robotics and Automation (ICRA), pp. 2820–2827. IEEE (2018)
9. Bae, J., et al.: A soft exosuit for patients with stroke: Feasibility study with a mobile off-board actuation unit. In: 2015 IEEE International Conference on Rehabilitation Robotics (ICORR), pp. 131–138. IEEE (2015)
10. Awad, L.N., et al.: A soft robotic exosuit improves walking in patients after stroke. Sci. Transl. Med. **9**(400), eaai9084 (2017)
11. Marquez-Chin, C., et al.: Functional electrical stimulation therapy for restoration of motor function after spinal cord injury and stroke: a review. Biomed. Eng. Online **19**(1), 34 (2020)
12. Huo, W., et al.: Adaptive FES assistance using a novel gait phase detection approach. In: 2018 IEEE/RSJ International Conference on Intelligent Robots and Systems (IROS), pp. 1–9. IEEE (2018)
13. Ma, Y., et al.: A hybrid FES-soft exosuit system for assisting post-stroke patients during walking. In: 2024 30th International Conference on Mechatronics and Machine Vision in Practice (M2VIP), pp. 1–6. IEEE (2024)
14. Sugar, T., et al.: Phase plane analysis of walking with applications in controlling bipeds and prostheses. Int. Rob. Auto J. **6**(1), 53–58 (2020)
15. Holgate, M.A., et al.: A novel control algorithm for wearable robotics using phase plane invariants. In: 2009 IEEE International Conference on Robotics and Automation, pp. 3845–3850. IEEE (2009)
16. Tan, X., et al.: A time-independent control system for natural human gait assistance with a soft exoskeleton. IEEE Trans. Robot. **39**(2), 1653–1667 (2022)
17. Fukuchi, C.A., et al.: A public dataset of overground and treadmill walking kinematics and kinetics in healthy individuals. PeerJ **6**, e4640 (2018)
18. Grimmer, M., et al.: Comparison of the human-exosuit interaction using ankle moment and ankle positive power inspired walking assistance. J. Biomech. **83**, 76–84 (2019)
19. Huo, W., et al.: Fast gait mode detection and assistive torque control of an exoskeletal robotic orthosis for walking assistance. IEEE Trans. Rob. **34**(4), 1035–1052 (2018)

Digital Twin Modeling and Performance Evaluation of a Gimbal Servo System

Yulong Xia[1], Mubang Xiao[1(✉)], Zhijie Wen[1], Lianfeng Liu[2], and Huimin Cai[2]

[1] The College of Intelligence Science and Technology, National University of Defense Technology, Changsha 410073, China
xiaomubang@nudt.edu.cn
[2] Tianjin Jinhang Institute of Technical Physics, Tianjin 300308, China

Abstract. The modeling of high-precision servo mechanisms is complicated by friction nonlinearities, torque fluctuations, and sensor errors, making it difficult to theoretically determine key nonlinear parameters. To address these challenges, a dynamic model of a two-axis servo system incorporating nonlinear parameters was developed. Both inertial and joint nonlinear parameters were identified through system identification. Then, a digital twin model of the servo system was constructed, with its accuracy evaluated using correlation coefficient metrics. Experimental validation was performed on a two-axis test platform by comparing time- and frequency-domain data. The results demonstrate that the digital twin model accurately captures the dynamic characteristics of the system, confirming the effectiveness of the proposed modeling methodology and providing a reliable approach for performance evaluation and control design in high-precision applications.

Keywords: Gimbal Servo System · Dynamics model · Parameter Identification · Digital Twin

1 Introduction

As the tracking accuracy and bandwidth requirements for optoelectronic gimbal servo systems increase, a comprehensive analysis of system dynamics across the whole frequency domain becomes essential. High-precision servo modeling is hindered by friction nonlinearities, torque disturbances, and sensor errors, particularly at low frequencies where nonlinear effects are pronounced, and at high frequencies where traditional models fail to capture actual dynamics. Moreover, nonlinear parameters are difficult to quantify analytically, and the strong nonlinear coupling of servo mechanisms further complicates accurate modeling. Consequently, input-output data-driven identification methods, while effective for capturing global behavior, offer limited insight into the system's internal dynamic characteristics.

Digital twins are becoming increasingly essential in control engineering due to their ability to mirror physical systems and enable bidirectional interaction and government operations virtually [1]. First introduced by Professor Michael Grieves [2], the concept has been widely applied across the field. Tao Fei et al. [3] proposed a six-level maturity model and a five-dimensional framework—comprising physical entities, virtual models, connectivity, twin data, and service layers—emphasizing the importance of virtual–honest feedback, data fusion, and iterative decision-making optimization. Wu Dongyang et al. [4] developed a quadrotor digital twin by integrating multiple modeling approaches and validating its performance through real-time experiments. Sun J.Y. [5] constructed a photodetector digital twin using transfer-function modeling and Bayesian inference. At the same time, Liu Z.S. et al. [6] developed a digital twin for the safety assessment of steel structures incorporating support vector machines. For servo and CNC systems, advanced digital twin strategies have focused on integrating kinematic and dynamic data to address frictional effects and disturbances. Xu et al. [7] employed multi-physics simulation to develop a digital-twin-driven cam servo motion system, thereby enhancing trajectory planning and control precision. Xue et al. [8] proposed a hybrid modeling and data-fusion method coupled with ensemble learning for robust fault diagnosis in CNC machine tools. Jiang Jing [9] established kinematic digital twins using 3D workstation models and performance calibration, while Jiang Xianliang et al. [10] implemented a hybrid control framework that synchronizes model parameters with real-time sensor data, significantly improving disturbance rejection and system resilience. These studies collectively demonstrate the rapid evolution and growing sophistication of digital-twin methodologies, which are proving indispensable for accurate modeling, advanced analytics, and adaptive control in complex engineering systems.

Despite recent advances, deploying digital twins in motion control remains challenging due to the complexity of accurately modeling physical systems and maintaining real-time synchronization with their physical counterparts [11]. Effective digital twins must continuously integrate sensor data to enable dynamic model calibration, allowing for both real-time monitoring and bidirectional interaction. Such coherence is crucial for advanced functions—including data management, state estimation, predictive control, and safety monitoring—that support adaptive and resilient control strategies [12, 13].

This paper first develops a comprehensive dynamics model of a two-axis optoelectronic stabilized servo mechanism, explicitly incorporating key nonlinearities. A hybrid identification scheme is then applied to estimate both linear and nonlinear model parameters. Drawing on the dependency of torque output on angular position and velocity, a detailed simulation model of the dual-axis servo system is constructed, and the correlation coefficient is introduced to rigorously assess model fidelity. Finally, a dedicated two-axis experimental platform is assembled to empirically validate the proposed modeling and identification methodology.

2 Two-Axis Gimbal Servo System

2.1 Definition of the Coordinate System

In this study, a two-axis gimbal servo mechanism with external in-azimuth pitching is analyzed. The structure of the gimbal servo mechanism is shown in Fig. 1.

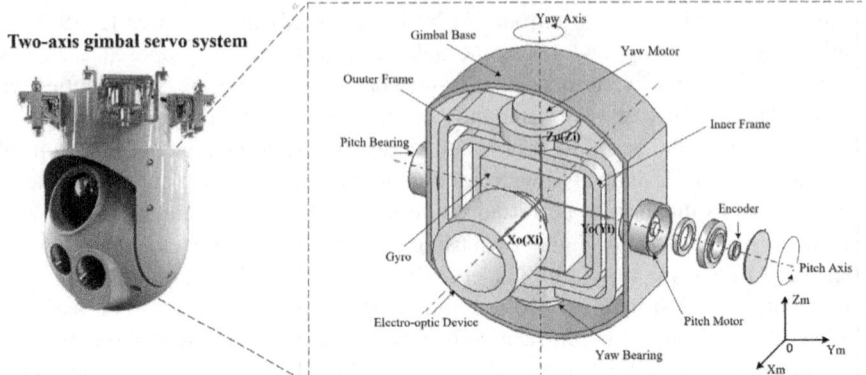

Fig. 1. An illustration of the two-axis gimbal servo system.

The transformation of its frame coordinate system is carried out as follows:

$$o_m x_m y_m z_m \xrightarrow[o_m z_m]{\theta_p} o x_o y_o z_o \xrightarrow[o z_o]{\theta_y} o x_i y_i z_i$$

where θ_p represents the pitch angle, θ_y represents the yaw angle, $o_m x_m y_m z_m$ is the coordinate system fixed to the carrier, $o x_o y_o z_o$ is the outer frame coordinate system, and $o x_i y_i z_i$ is the inner frame coordinate system.

2.2 Gimbal's Kinematics Equations

The spatial relationship between the carrier and the servo mechanism, combined with the principle of composite motion, provides a clear understanding of the system's kinematics. Specifically, the motion of the outer frame is the result of the superposition of the carrier's motion and the relative motion of the outer frame. Similarly, the motion of the inner frame is a composite of the motions of the carrier, the outer frame, and the inner frame itself. The carrier angular velocity must be defined in the carrier coordinate system projection vector as $\omega_m(t) = \begin{bmatrix} \omega_{mx} & \omega_{my} & \omega_{mz} \end{bmatrix}^T$, The angular velocity vector of the outer frame coordinate system is $\omega_o(t) = \begin{bmatrix} \omega_{ox} & \omega_{oy} & \omega_{oz} \end{bmatrix}^T$, The angular velocity vector of the inner frame coordinate system is $\omega_i(t) = \begin{bmatrix} \omega_{ix} & \omega_{iy} & \omega_{iz} \end{bmatrix}^T$, Depending on the Gestalt relationship, there is:

$$\begin{bmatrix} \omega_{ox} \\ \omega_{oy} \\ \omega_{oz} \end{bmatrix} = \begin{bmatrix} \omega_{mx} \cos \lambda_y - \omega_{mz} \sin \lambda_y \\ \omega_{my} + \dot{\lambda}_y \\ \omega_{mx} \sin \lambda_y + \omega_{mz} \cos \lambda_y \end{bmatrix} \quad (1)$$

$$\begin{bmatrix} \omega_{ix} \\ \omega_{iy} \\ \omega_{iz} \end{bmatrix} = \begin{bmatrix} \omega_{ox} \cos \lambda_z + \omega_{oy} \sin \lambda_z \\ -\omega_{ox} \sin \lambda_z + \omega_{oy} \cos \lambda_z \\ \omega_{oz} + \dot{\lambda}_z \end{bmatrix} \quad (2)$$

2.3 Gimbal's Dynamics Equations

The carrier coordinate system rotates and translates in inertial space, the frame rotates with respect to the carrier coordinate system, and there is an unbalanced mass in the frame whose center of rotation does not coincide with the center of mass. Therefore, the motion of the frame should be equivalent to the rotation of a rigid body around a moving point, and the dynamic behavior of the pointing mechanism should be modeled using the momentum moment theorem for the rotation of a rigid body around a moving point.

In a translational coordinate system $ox_g y_g z_g$, the momentum theorem for a system of masses rotating around a moving point can be expressed as

$$\frac{dL'_o}{dt} = M_o + \rho_c \times (-ma_o) \tag{3}$$

In the translational coordinate system $ox_g y_g z_g$, the momentum of the frame is denoted by L'_o. The moment of the external force acting on the frame at the moving point O is denoted by M_o. The moment of the implicated inertial force on the moving point O of the point of mass, where all the mass is concentrated at the center of mass, is denoted by $\rho_c \times (-ma_o)$. This is also known as the mass imbalance moment of the frame. The implicated acceleration on the moving point o is denoted by a.

Let $[a_x, a_y, a_z]$ be the overload acceleration of the carrier, and from the spatial relationship between the airline and the platform, as well as the principle of compound motion, the implicated acceleration of the moving point o is:

$$\begin{bmatrix} a_{ox} \\ a_{oy} \\ a_{oz} \end{bmatrix} = \begin{bmatrix} \left(-\omega_{my}^2 \rho - \omega_{mz}^2 \rho + a_x\right) \cos \lambda_y - \left(\dot{\omega}_{my}\rho + a_z\right) \sin \lambda_y \\ \dot{\omega}_{mz}\rho + a_y \\ \left(-\omega_{my}^2 \rho - \omega_{mz}^2 \rho + a_x\right) \sin \lambda_y + \left(\dot{\omega}_{my}\rho + a_z\right) \cos \lambda_y \end{bmatrix} \tag{4}$$

Therefore, using the Moment of Moment Theorem for a rigid body rotating about a moving point for the inner frame, the dynamical equations for the inner frame can be found to be:

$$M_{iz} = J_{iz}\dot{\omega}_{iz} + (J_{iy} - J_{ix})\omega_{ix}\omega_{iy} + J_{ixy}(\omega_{ix}^2 - \omega_{iy}^2) + J_{iyz}(\dot{\omega}_{iy} + \omega_{ix}\omega_{iz})$$
$$+ J_{ixz}(\dot{\omega}_{ix} - \omega_{iy}\omega_{iz}) + (\rho_{cix}a_{oiy} - \rho_{ciy}a_{oix})m_i \tag{5}$$

where: M_{iz} represents the external moment acting on the pitch axis; J_{iy}, J_{ix}, J_{iz} is the moment of inertia of the inner frame about the active axis; $J_{ixy}, J_{iyz}, J_{ixz}$ is the inertia product of the inner frame; m_i denotes the mass of the inner frame; and ρ_{ci} is the vector from the origin to the center of mass of the inner frame in its coordinate system $ox_i y_i z_i$.

The external moments acting on the pitch axis generally include the motor driving moment and various nonlinear interference moments. Among them, the nonlinear interference moments mainly include the elastic drag interference moments and friction moments of the wires, etc., so that Eq. (5) can be expressed as:

$$J_{iz}\dot{\omega}_{iz} = M_{motor\_iz} - M_{f\_iz} - M_{wire\_iz} - M_{J\_iz} - M_{b\_iz} \tag{6}$$

In the equation, M_{motor_iz} is the pitch axis motor driving moment, M_{f_iz} is the pitch axis a nonlinear friction moment, M_{wire_iz} is the pitch axis nonlinear wire interference moment, and $M_{J_{-iz}}$ is the inertia coupling moment of the inner frame.

Similarly, the kinetic equation of the outer frame can be expressed as

$$J'_{oy}\dot{\omega}_{oy} = M_{m\_oy} - M_{f\_oy} - M_{ub\_oy} - M_{wire\_oy} - M_{J\_oy} \tag{7}$$

3 Model Parameter Identification

A system of differential equations has been formulated to describe the dynamics of both the inner and outer frames of the servo mechanism, facilitating the regulation of the control mechanism. The complexity of the system is heightened by the presence of multiple coupling effects. To improve the accuracy of parameter identification, it is essential to simplify the motion model, highlight key parameters, and reduce the interference caused by inertial coupling between the carrier and the frame. This can be achieved by carefully designing experimental conditions.

3.1 Dynamic Model of a Uniaxial Servo Mechanism

To minimize the effects of inertial coupling between the inner and outer frames, this study employs static base and single-axis locking as experimental conditions. The static base experiment refers to tests conducted while the mechanism is mounted on a non-moving platform, thereby eliminating motion errors induced by carrier dynamics. Single-axis locking refers to constraining all but one axis during testing—for example, when evaluating the roll (or Elevation) axis, the orthogonal axis is fixed in place, to eliminate inertial coupling effects between the two axes.

Under the above constraints, the linear part of the servo system can be simplified to an inertia-damping link with the dynamics modeled as:

$$J\ddot{\theta} + B\dot{\theta} = T_m - T_{d1} - T_{d2} \tag{8}$$

J is the total rotational inertia of the frame load, θ, $\dot{\theta}$, and $\ddot{\theta}$ are the rotational angle, angular velocity, and angular acceleration, respectively, T_m is the motor driving torque, T_{d1} and T_{d2} represent the friction interference torque and unbalanced mass interference torque, respectively.

The servo system power amplifier operates in current closed-loop mode, and its bandwidth is much higher than the normal operating bandwidth of the servo system, which can be simplified as the DC motor model:

$$T_m = K_a K_t \bar{u} \tag{9}$$

3.2 Linear Partial Model Parameter Identification

The input to the servo system is the power amplifier command signal u, and the output is the load-side speed signal ω. Under high-frequency excitation conditions, the friction effect is negligible, and the system behaves as a first-order inertial structure equivalently.

$$G(s) = \frac{1}{Js + B} \tag{10}$$

To minimize the impact of nonlinear factors, high-frequency sinusoidal excitation signals u1(k) and -u1(k) with equal amplitude and opposite phase are employed. The corresponding outputs, w1(k) and w2(k), are recorded. The average difference between the pairs of input and output signals is then computed and used as the new dataset for analysis. The system inertia J is subsequently identified using the least squares algorithm. The specific identification procedure is as follows:

(1) Apply high-frequency excitation signals u1(k) and -u1(k);
(2) Record the response signals w1(k) and w2(k), calculate (u1(k)-(-u1(k)))/2 and (w1(k)-w2(k))/2;
(3) Least squares parameter estimation was performed with the above data to obtain an estimate of the inertia;
(4) Verify the identification results, if it does not meet the accuracy requirements, then optimize the excitation signal and repeat the identification.

3.3 Nonlinear Partial Model Parameter Identification

In friction dynamics modeling, the coupling of static-kinetic friction transition processes, directional dependence, and physical effects is central to the nonlinear characterization of the system. First, the friction force is linearized, and the Coulomb friction force is equated to the input moment. The friction model is expressed as follows.

As the system speed approaches zero, the friction is balanced against the external load but does not exceed the maximum static friction threshold:

$$T_f = \begin{cases} -\min(T_{c,z}, |T_L|), & \text{if } T_L \geq 0 \\ \min(T_{c,f}, |T_L|), & \text{if } T_L < 0 \end{cases} \tag{11}$$

where $T_{c,z}$, and $T_{c,f}$ are forward and backward static friction, respectively.

When the system is in motion, friction consists of Coulomb friction, spring forces, and viscous friction:

$$T_f = \begin{cases} -T_{c,z} - K_w q - Bv, & \text{if } v > 0 \\ T_{c,f} - K_w q - Bv, & \text{if } v < 0 \end{cases} \tag{12}$$

where Kw is the system connection stiffness, and B is the viscous friction coefficient.

The uniaxial kinetic equations were Laplace transformed to obtain the transfer function model expression:

$$\theta(s) = \frac{1}{s(Js + B)}[K_t K_a \bar{u}(s) - T_{d1}(s) - T_{d2}(s)] \tag{13}$$

The steps of nonlinear model parameter identification are as follows.

(1) A low-frequency white noise signal is designed as the excitation input to the system u1(k);
(2) Under the velocity closed-loop condition, a PI controller is used and the response signal w1(k) of the system under u1(k) excitation is captured;
(3) The identification model shown above is built in MATLAB, where the inertia J is a fixed value obtained by linear parameter identification;
(4) Validate the initial identification results. If the results do not meet the requirements, redesign the excitation signal and perform another identification until the accuracy requirements are met.

4 Digital Twin Modeling

Based on the previous theoretical derivation and parameter identification, the two-axis servo mechanism simulation model shown in the figure below is established by combining linear and nonlinear parameter identification (Fig. 2).

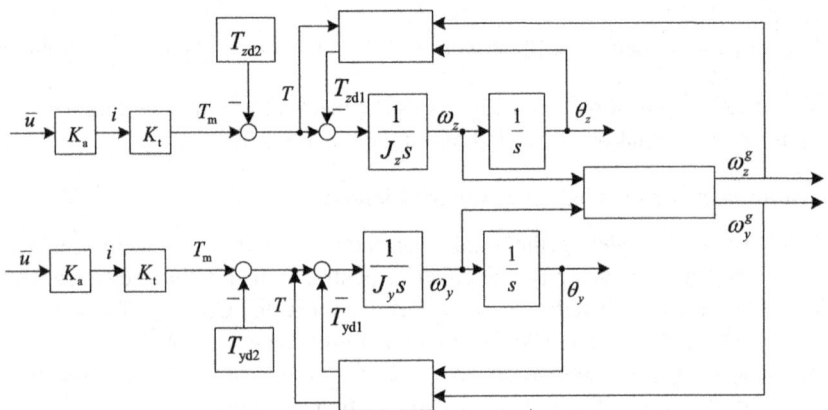

Fig. 2. Two axis servo mechanism model

To measure the rate of roll and elevation, a mathematical model of the gyroscope is established based on the coordinate transformation between the frames. Combined with the actual system characteristics, the established model includes sensor delay, noise, bias, low-pass filtering, and gyroscope dynamics, and the specific structure is shown in Fig. 3.

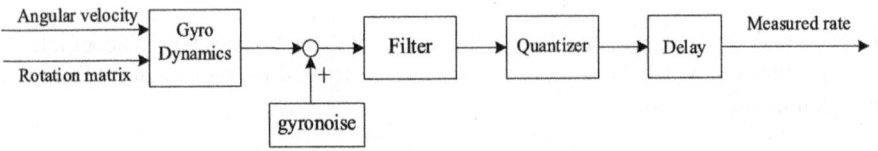

Fig. 3. Model of the gyroscope

4.1 Virtual-Real Interaction

To optimize the dynamic performance of the twin model in the two-axis optoelectronic servo system, a control scheme is designed based on prior theoretical derivations and parameter identification, incorporating both linear and nonlinear parameter identification techniques. As shown in Fig. 4, the scheme describes the linkage between the actual physical system and the digital twin model, achieving the integration of the virtual and real worlds. Accurate sensor measurements are utilized to implement velocity closed-loop feedback for the twin model, which ensures that the same control voltage is applied to both the twin model and the actual physical system. Simultaneously, the equivalent torque of the friction model is updated in real time using actual sensor data, enabling real-time closed-loop interaction between the virtual and real environments, thereby further validating the accuracy of the model.

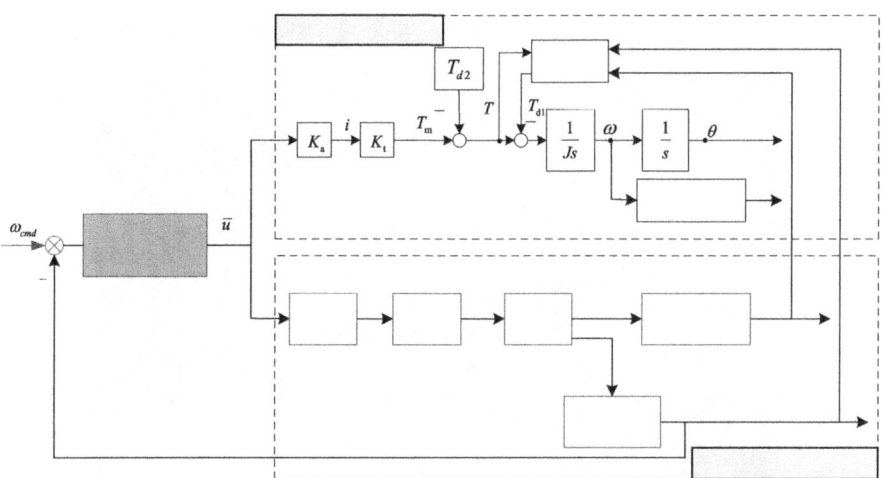

Fig. 4. Digital Twin Program

4.2 Digital Twin Model Accuracy Evaluation Metrics

In the design and realization of the digital twin system, the accuracy of the model and the identification of the parameters are key to ensuring accuracy of the system. In order to evaluate the performance of the system, the model prediction results need to be compared with the experimental data to verify the validity of the model. To quantify the accuracy of the digital twin model, a correlation coefficient metric is introduced, with values ranging from 0 to 1. The more the correlation coefficient converges to 1, the better the data fit, and the value obtained by multiplying the correlation coefficient by 100% measures the accuracy of the model's time-domain response, defined as follows:

$$I_r = \frac{\sum_{i=1}^{N} y_{\text{sim}}(i) \cdot y_{\text{mea}}(i)}{\sum_{i=1}^{N} y_{\text{mea}}(i)^2} \times 100\% \tag{14}$$

where N is the total sample length, simulation model measurements are $y_{\text{sim}}(i)$, and physical prototype measurements are $y_{\text{mea}}(i)$.

5 Experimental Verification

To verify the accuracy and feasibility of the digital twin model, an experimental test platform for the direct-drive servo system of the torque motor is constructed, as shown in Fig. 5. The servo performance test experiment is conducted using the realtime semi-physical simulation platform, and the actual speeds collected by the sensors are compared and analyzed with the twin speeds.

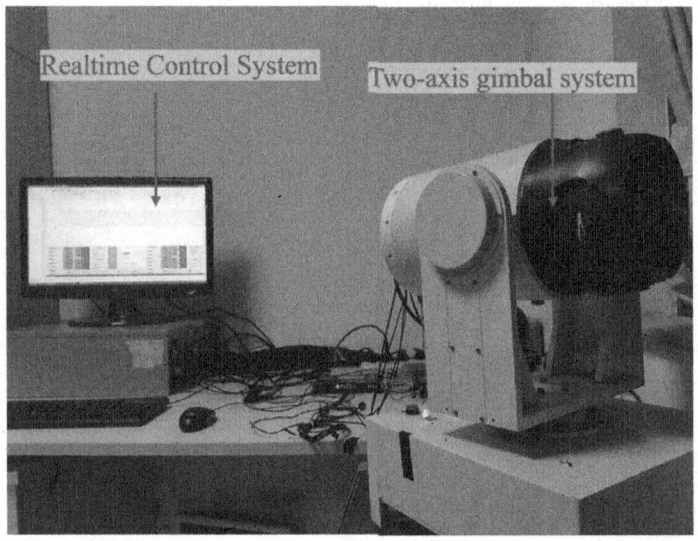

Fig. 5. The experimental environment for servo performance evaluation.

According to Sect. 3, combining linear and nonlinear parameter identification, the model parameters of the inner and outer frames are identified respectively, and the model parameters of the two-axis servo system are obtained as shown in Table 1:

Table 1. The parameters obtained by recognizing

Parameters	Inner frame value	Outer frame value
Inertia $J(kg \cdot m^2)$	0.0819	0.12
Forward friction $T_{mf}(N \cdot m)$	0.0091	0.0999
Backward friction $T_r(N \cdot m)$	0.1608	0.0363
Viscous friction $b(N \cdot m \cdot s \cdot rad^{-1})$	0.0034	0.0047
Cable Stiffness $K_w(N \cdot m/rad)$	0.0052	0.00466

(*continued*)

Table 1. (*continued*)

Parameters	Inner frame value	Outer frame value
Load torque $T_d (N \cdot m)$	-0.0422	0.1680

5.1 Experimental Validation of the Twin Model

In order to evaluate the frequency domain accuracy of the established digital twin model, the digital twin model and the experimental system are simultaneously swept for frequency tests and the Bode plots of the inner and outer frames are obtained, as shown in Fig. 6. By comparing the amplitude and phase frequency response curves of the model simulation and measurement, the accuracy indexes are calculated separately, and the amplitude frequency accuracy of the inner frame is 98.93% and the phase frequency accuracy is 94.24%; the amplitude frequency accuracy of the outer frame is 97.37% and the phase frequency accuracy is 99.85%, which indicates that the digital twin model can reflect the dynamic characteristics of the system within 40 Hz.

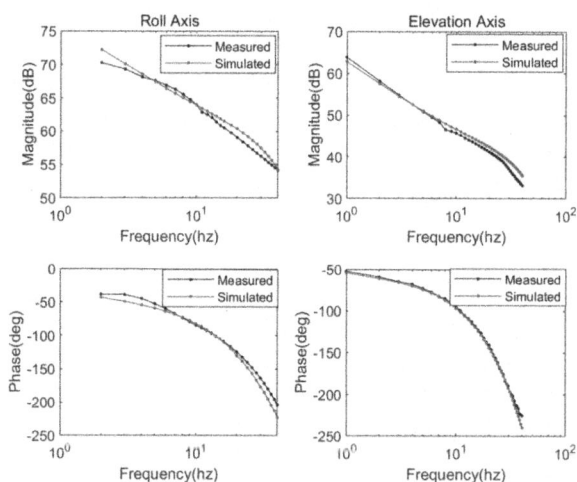

Fig. 6. Open-loop frequency response

In the velocity closed-loop control scheme shown in Fig. 4, sinusoidal input signals with varying amplitudes and frequencies are applied to the system at time 0s. As demonstrated in Table 2, the model and the experimental velocity responses are in good agreement, with the model accuracy exceeding 87%. Figure 7 presents a comparison of the experimental and simulated sinusoidal command responses of the inner and outer frames under closed-loop conditions.

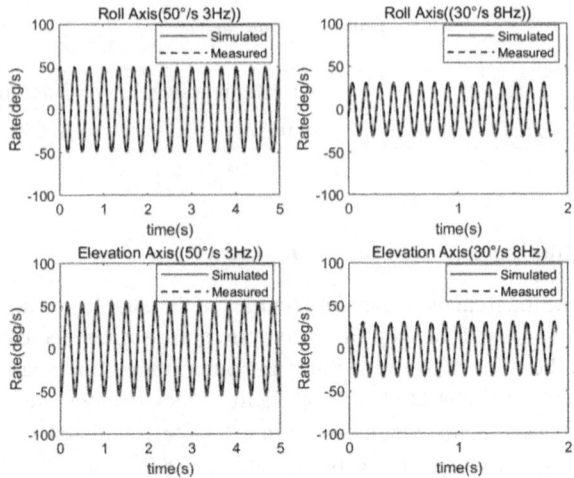

Fig. 7. Closed-Loop Time Domain Responses

Table 2. Speed control test results

Test Serial Number	Speed command	Inner frame accuracy	Outer frame accuracy
1	50°/s 1 Hz	88.7%	95.5%
2	50°/s 2 Hz	89.4%	91.8%
3	50°/s 3 Hz	99.3%	91.3%
4	50°/s 4 Hz	99.6%	90.6%
5	40°/s 6 Hz	97.1%	88.8%
6	30°/s 8 Hz	96.8%	97.6%
7	25°/s 10 Hz	94.8%	95.6%
8	15°/s 15 Hz	91.3%	95.6%
9	10°/s 20 Hz	89.5%	99.7%

By comparing the accuracy of open-loop frequency-domain response and velocity closed-loop time-domain response, the accuracies are all in the range of 85–100%, the model is able to effectively predict the response characteristics of the servo mechanism, and the accuracy of the digital twin model is in line with the modeling requirements of the digital twin mechanism model.

6 Conclusion

Aiming at the challenges in modeling high-precision gimbal servo systems, this paper proposes a digital twin modeling method based on friction parameter identification. By establishing a digital twin model that incorporates nonlinear friction characteristics and constructing a servo platform experimental test system, comparative validation experiments are conducted to validate the system.

The open-loop frequency domain response test and velocity sinusoidal response test experiments show that the output response of the digital twin model shows good consistency with the measured data of the actual system, and the correlation coefficients between the sinusoidal response curve and the theoretical response curve are all greater than 85%, which is a quantitative index that fully verifies the effectiveness of the digital twin model. This result provides a strong experimental basis for the application of digital twin technology in the field of servo control.

References

1. Mi, X.: Research on displacement cooperative control of electro-hydrostatic actuator (EHA) based on digital twin. North Central University (2023)
2. Grieves, M., Vickers, J.: Digital twin: mitigating unpredictable, undesirable emergent behavior in complex systems. Transdisciplinary Perspectives on Complex Systems, pp. 85–113 (2017)
3. Tao, F., Zhang, C., Qi, Q., et al.: Digital twin maturity model. Comput. Integr. Manuf. Syst. **28**(5), 1267–1281 (2022)
4. Wu, D., Dou, J., Li, J.: Design of digital twin system for quadrotor. Comput. Eng. Appl. **57**(16), 237–244 (2021)
5. Sun, J.: A photodetector applied in optical communication system and its performance prediction under mathematical model. J. Nanoelectronics Optoelectron. **15**(10), 1260–1268 (2020)
6. Liu, Z., Bai, W., Du, X., Zhang, A., Xing, Z., Jiang, A.: Digital Twin-based Safety Evaluation of Prestressed Steel Structure. Advances in Civil Engineering. September, pp. 1–10 (2020)
7. Xu, J., Guo, T.: Application and research on digital twin in electronic cam servo motion control system. Int. J. Adv. Manuf. Technol. **112**(3–4), 1145–1158 (2021)
8. Xue, R., Zhang, P., Wang, J., Huang, Z.: Digital twin-driven fault diagnosis for CNC machine tool. Int. J. Adv. Manuf. Technol. **131**(11), 5457–5470 (2024)
9. Jiang, J.: Research on CNC machine tool machining path optimization method based on digital twin. Wuhan University of Technology, Hubei (2019)
10. Jiang, X., Chen, L., Zheng, J., Tan, R., Li, B., Fan, D.: High-precision control method of direct drive components based on digital twin model. J. Mech. Eng. **57**(17), 98–109 (2021)
11. Wang, X., Wu, Y., Zhang, E., et al.: Characteristic model-based adaptive controller with discrete extended state observer for servo systems. Proc. Inst. Mech. Eng.Part I J. Syst. Control Eng. **231**(4), 259–27012 (2017)
12. Guo, F., Liu, J., Zou, F., et al.: Research on the state-of-art, connotation and key implementation technology of assembly process planning with digital twin. J. Mech. Eng. **55**(17), 110–132 (2019)
13. LNCS Homepage. http://www.springer.com/lncs. Accessed 21 Nov 2016

Kinematics and Calibration of a Continuum Manipulator Considering Nonconstant Elasticity

Mubang Xiao[1], Xinrui Zhan[1], Huimin Cai[2], Zhijie Wen[1]([✉]), and Shixun Fan[1]

[1] The College of Intelligence Science and Technology, National University of Defense Technology, Changsha 410073, China
wenzhijie@nudt.edu.cn
[2] Tianjin Jinhang Institute of Technical Physics, Tianjin 300308, China

Abstract. Present methods of modeling a continuum manipulator do not pay much attention to nonconstant elasticity along the length, such as tensile or bending stiffness. In this paper, we develop a modified constant strain model based on the constant internal wrench and piecewise constant elasticity assumption. Section length and section compliance, which are the inverse of section stiffness, are set as the section kinematic parameters, and internal wrench as the kinematic variable. The explicit error model and the identify matrix of these kinematic parameters are derived in the product-of-exponentials (POE) formula. Redundancy and identifiability are discussed based on the identify matrix. The parameters are identified by minimizing the pose error through a nonlinear optimization algorithm, and effectiveness of the calibration is verified through experiments. The work can be beneficial for improving the modeling accuracy of a general continuum manipulator with complex structures and material properties.

Keywords: Continuum robot · Nonconstant Elasticity · Parameters Calibration

1 Introduction

Soft robots have been extensively studied for locomotion and manipulation in constrained environments. Continuum manipulators, a type of soft robot with elastic structures, can bend continuously with infinite degrees of freedom [1]. Representative examples include Octarm, active cannulae, and underwater soft robots studied in [2–4]. Comprehensive reviews [1, 5] introduce various kinematic models for continuum manipulator motion.

Constant Curvature (CC) and Piecewise Constant Curvature (PCC) models [6] are prevalent methods for continuum manipulator modeling and control. These models approximate the robot as segments of circular arcs, with arc length, curvature, and orientation angle defined as joint variables. This establishes a direct mapping from actuator space to joint space and task space [1]. Despite CC model limitations, its computational efficiency enables real-time motion control [7, 8] and dynamic modeling [9, 10]. Alternative approaches incorporate Euler-Bernoulli beam theory-based compensation for elastic deflections [11].

The continuous Cosserat rod theory employs variable curvature formulations with infinitesimal curves to derive the equilibrium equations under external forces while accounting for shear and torsion [12, 13]. This enables accurate spatial motion modeling at the expense of high computational complexity. Renda extended this framework to the piecewise constant strain (PCS) model [14], which discretizes continuum manipulators into finite segments assuming uniform strain distribution per segment. These discretized segments correspond to revolute/prismatic joints in traditional rigid robotics. Notably, the PCC model's circular arcs generalize into screw arcs with fixed axis/pitch in PCS formulations.

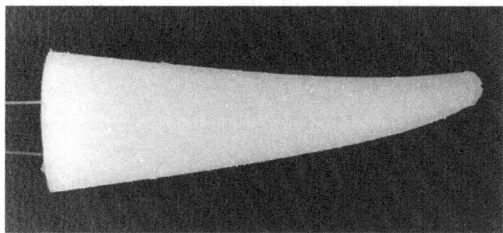

Fig. 1. A prototype of a cone-like cable driven continuum robot

It is critical to note that conventional CC/constant strain (CS) models assume homogeneous elasticity (e.g., constant tensile/bending stiffness), which lacks real-world generality. For instance, the tip of a conical cable-driven continuum robot (Fig. 1) exhibits lower stiffness than the base, leading to greater strain under external wrenches. The constant internal wrench (CIW) assumption demonstrates broader applicability since cable/pneumatic actuators inherently generate constant wrenches [6, 15], degenerating to CC/CS models when stiffness remains uniform along the length. Our work introduces a piecewise constant elasticity (PCE) assumption: through linear constitutive laws, segment strain equals internal wrench normalized by stiffness. As stiffness parameters depend solely on material properties and geometry, they become identifiable constants. This differs from serial-link D-H parameters [16] where geometric link dimensions define kinematics; here, segment stiffnesses determine deformation responses under known internal wrenches. Notably, the number of elasticity parameters correlates directly with the spatial discretization resolution.

Recent studies have explored parameter identification for continuum robots. Active cannulas were modeled using the minimum energy principle with dynamic parameters of a 2-DOF prototype identified through pose data fitting [3, 17, 18]. Geometric calibration of a two-section pneumatic manipulator based on the PCC model was conducted in [19]. Flexural rigidity and viscous parameters for planar bending soft grippers were identified in [20]. Alternative elasticity identification methods include force-strain ratio or torque-angle measurements [9, 21]. These studies demonstrate improved accuracy post-identification/calibration. However, explicit error propagation models from parameter uncertainties to pose errors remain absent, precluding rigorous analysis of parameter redundancy and identifiability. To our knowledge, no systematic investigation exists for full-dimensional elasticity identification in continuum manipulators incorporating shear and torsion effects.

Established calibration methodologies for serial-link robots offer reference frameworks. Park et al. [22] formulated an explicit error model for joint twist calibration using the product-of-exponentials (POE) formula. Parameter redundancy and identifiability in serial robots were investigated in [23], with analytical methods proposed to eliminate redundant error parameters [24].

This paper aims to establish an explicit elasticity error model for continuum manipulators and identify complete kinematic parameters. Section 2 develops POE-based kinematic/error models under CIW-PCE assumptions. Section 3 analyzes parameter redundancy and identifiability. Section 4 details the calibration procedure, with experimental validation presented in Sect. 5.

2 Kinematic and Error Model

A continuum manipulator with all strain components is analyzed based on the constant internal wrench (CIW) and piecewise constant elasticity (PCE) assumptions. The kinematic model could be extended to a more precise piecewise constant internal wrench (PCIW) model, where the equilibrium is considered between the section boundary wrenches [14]. However, it is more difficult to derive the explicit error model.

2.1 Kinematic Model of One Discretized Section

In [14], configuration of the continuum's micro-solid at axial length $X \in [0,L]$ is defined as a Lie group $g(X)$, L is the total length of the manipulator (Fig. 2). $g(X)$ is written as:

$$g(X) = \begin{bmatrix} R & u \\ 0 & 1 \end{bmatrix} \in SE(3) \tag{1}$$

where R is the rotation matrix, and u is the position vector. Strain twist $\xi \in \mathbb{R}^6$ in the local frame of the continuum body is defined as the tangent vector field of $g(X)$ along the length X, introduced in [14], ξ is given by:

$$\hat{\xi} = g^{-1} \frac{\partial g}{\partial X} = \begin{bmatrix} \tilde{k} & q \\ 0 & 0 \end{bmatrix} \in se(3), \xi = (k^T, q^T)^T \tag{2}$$

where $k \in \mathbb{R}^3$ represents the angular strains, and $q \in \mathbb{R}^3$ the linear strains, the tilde $\sim$ means the skew symmetric matrix.

A linear elastic constitutive model at length X is given by:

$$\mathcal{F} = \Sigma(\xi - \xi^0) \tag{3}$$

where $\mathcal{F} = [\mathcal{M}^T, \mathcal{N}^T]^T \in \mathbb{R}^6$ is the constant internal wrench, M is the internal torque vector and N is the force vector. Σ is the constant screw stiffness matrix of this section, given by $\Sigma = \mathrm{diag}([EJ_x, EJ_y, GI_z, GA, GA, EA])$, where E is the Young modulus, G

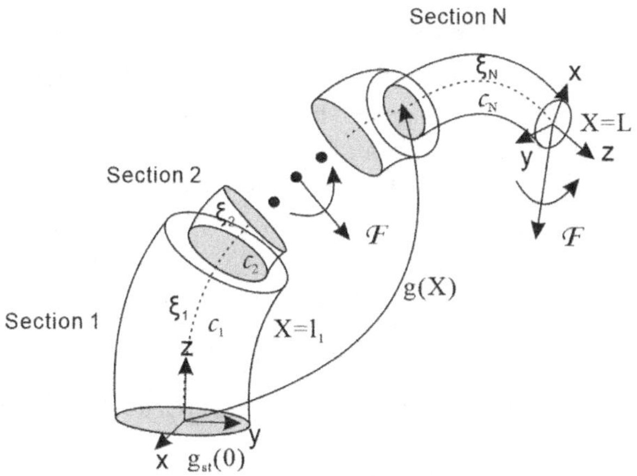

Fig. 2. The piecewise constant strain model of N sections based on the constant interna wrench (CIW) and piecewise constant elasticity (PCE) assumptions.

is the shear modulus, J_x, J_y, I_z is the bending and torsion second moment of inertia, respectively. A is the section area, and ξ_0 is the initial straight configuration.

Then the strain twist of a single section equals to:

$$\xi = \xi^0 + \Sigma^{-1} \mathcal{F} \tag{4}$$

Since the stiffness matrix of a rigid body is infinite and cannot be identified, the inverse of stiffness matrix is identified instead. Then (4) can be rewritten as:

$$\xi = \xi^0 + C \cdot \mathcal{F} = \xi^0 + \mathcal{C} \cdot \text{diag}(\mathcal{F}) \tag{5}$$

where C is stated as the section compliance vector, given by:

$$\mathcal{C} = [g_x, g_y, g_z, e_x, e_y, e_z]^T \in \mathbb{R}^6 \tag{6}$$

The configuration of the end-effector in the POE formula is given by:

$$g = \exp(\hat{\xi} \cdot L) g_{st}(0) \tag{7}$$

where $g_{st}(0)$ is the initial configuration, $\hat{\xi}$ is se(3) of the strain twist ξ. If the internal wrench F and the compliance vector C are known, using (5), $\hat{\xi}$ can then be written as:

$$\hat{\xi} = \begin{bmatrix} \tilde{k} & q \\ 0 & 0 \end{bmatrix} = \begin{bmatrix} 0 & -k_z & k_y & q_x \\ k_z & 0 & -k_x & q_y \\ -k_i & k_x & 0 & q_z \\ 0 & 0 & 0 & 0 \end{bmatrix} = \begin{bmatrix} 0 & -m_z g_z & m_y g_y & n_x e_x \\ m_z g_z & 0 & -m_x g_x & n_y e_y \\ -m_y g_y & m_x g_x & 0 & 1 + n_z e_z \\ 0 & 0 & 0 & 0 \end{bmatrix} \tag{8}$$

The exponential term of (7) can be calculated in a direct way as below:

$$\exp(\hat{\xi} \cdot L) = I_4 + L \cdot \hat{\xi} + \frac{1}{\theta^2}(1 - \cos(\theta L)) \cdot \hat{\xi}^2 + \frac{1}{\theta^3}(\theta L - \sin(\theta L)) \cdot \hat{\xi}^3 \tag{9}$$

2.2 Kinematic Model of N Sections

The 6 DOFs continuum manipulator is discretized into N sections. Section lengths are given by $l = [l_1, \cdots, l_N]^T$, with the total length L. According to the PCE assumption, compliance vector defined in (6) is constant in the ith section, denoted by $\mathcal{C}_i$. Using the CIW assumption and Eq. (5), strain twist is also constant in the ith section, denoted by ξ_i. $\mathcal{C}_i$ and ξ_i are given by:

$$\mathcal{C}_i = [g_{xi}, g_{yi}, g_{zi}, e_{xi}, e_{yi}, e_{zi}]^T \in \mathbb{R}^6 \tag{10}$$

$$\xi_i = \xi^0 + \mathcal{C}_i \cdot \text{diag}(\mathcal{F}) \tag{11}$$

For a N-sections model, the configuration of the end-effector is given by:

$$g = \prod_{i=1}^{N} \exp(\widehat{\xi}_i \cdot l_i) g_{st}(0) \tag{12}$$

where the exponential terms can be calculated using (9).

In this research, the internal wrench F or the strain twist of the reference section ξ_{ref} can be regard as the joint variable belonging to se(3). The section compliance vector $\mathcal{C}_i$ and the section length l_i can be regard as the joint kinematic parameters.

2.3 Kinematic Error Model

Suppose there is no error in the initial configuration $g_{st}(0)$, the Lie group of the end-effector pose error in the base frame can be expressed by linearizing the forward kinematic Eq. (12) given by:

$$\delta g \cdot g^{-1} = (\frac{\partial g}{\partial \xi} \delta \xi + \frac{\partial g}{\partial l} \delta l) g^{-1} \tag{13}$$

where $\xi = [\xi_1^T, \cdots, \xi_N^T]^T \in \mathbb{R}^{6N}$ is the total strain twists and $l = [l_1, \cdots, l_N]^T$ is the total section lengths. Using the differential of (11), the pose error twist can be derived as:

$$\begin{aligned}\delta \mathcal{Y} = [\delta g \cdot g^{-1}]^{\vee} &= [(\frac{\partial g}{\partial \xi} \cdot \text{diag}(\mathcal{F})\delta \mathcal{C} + \frac{\partial g}{\partial l} \cdot \delta l) g^{-1}]^{\vee} \\ &= J \cdot [\delta \mathcal{C}_1^T, \delta l_1, \cdots, \delta \mathcal{C}_N^T, \delta l_N]^T = J \cdot \delta \mathcal{X}\end{aligned} \tag{14}$$

where $[\cdot]^{\vee}$ is the twist of $\cdot$, $\delta \mathcal{Y}$ is the pose error twist, $J = [J_1, \cdots, J_N] \in \mathbb{R}^{6 \times 7N}$ is the identification matrix, and $J_i \in \mathbb{R}^{6 \times 7}$ is the identification block associated with the ith element of the total kinematic parameters X, given by $\mathcal{X} = [\mathcal{C}_1^T, l_1, \cdots, \mathcal{C}_N^T, l_N]^T$.

(14) shows that the pose error results from the parameters error of section compliance vectors $\mathcal{C}_i$ and section lengths l_i.

Now we derive the identification matrix J of $\delta \mathcal{C}_i$ and δl_i. According to the parameter identification work of a serial link robot introduced in [22, 23], using the differential of (12), we have:

$$\begin{aligned}[\delta g \cdot g^{-1}]^{\vee} = &[(\delta \exp(\widehat{\xi}_1 l_1)) \exp(-\widehat{\xi}_1 l_1)]^{\vee} \\ &+ \sum_{k=2}^{N} Ad(\prod_{i=1}^{k-1} \exp(\widehat{\xi}_i l_i))[(\delta \exp(\widehat{\xi}_k l_k)) \exp(-\widehat{\xi}_k l_k)]^{\vee}\end{aligned} \tag{15}$$

where

$$\text{Ad}(g) = \begin{bmatrix} R & 0 \\ \tilde{u}R & R \end{bmatrix}$$

is the adjoint transformation of g.

The error model of the compliance vector C_k, internal wrench F and section length lk is now established. Suppose there is no error in measuring the internal wrench F, according to (15) and (16), jacobian block J_k of the identify matrix J is derived:

$$J_k = \begin{cases} [A_1 \text{diag}(\mathcal{F}), \xi^0 + \text{diag}|(\mathcal{F})C_1] \ k = 1 \\ \text{Ad}(\prod_{i=1}^{k-1} \exp(\hat{\xi}_i l_i)) \cdot \\ [A_k \text{diag}(\mathcal{F}), \xi^0 + \text{diag}(\mathcal{F})C_k] \ 1 < k \leq N \end{cases} \quad (16)$$

3 Calibration Process

There are total 7N unidentified kinematic parameters, $\mathcal{X} = [C_1^T, l_1, \cdots, C_N^T, l_N]^T$. Suppose there are m measured poses, satisfying $6m >> 7N$, then we can expand the error model (14) into:

$$\delta \overline{y} = \overline{J} \cdot \delta \mathcal{X} \quad (17)$$

where $\delta \overline{y} = [\delta y_1^T, \cdots, \delta y_m^T]^T \in \mathbb{R}^{6m}$ is the total pose error and $\overline{J} = [J^{(1)}, \cdots, J^{(m)}]^T$ is the total identify matrix of the m poses. If $\overline{J}$ is column full rank, the update value of kinematic parameters $\mathcal{X}$ in this iterative step can be calculated by using the pseudo-inverse method:

$$\delta \mathcal{X} = (\overline{J}^T \overline{J})^{-1} \overline{J}^T \cdot \delta \overline{y} \quad (18)$$

What need to be measured in the calibration process is the end-effector pose g_a and the internal wrench F. The pose error twist is given as:

$$[\delta g \cdot g^{-1}]^\vee = [(g_a - g) \cdot g^{-1})]^\vee \in \mathbb{R}^6 \quad (19)$$

where g is the predicted nominal pose of the end-effector calculated by (12) using the measured internal wrench F, and the nominal kinematic and elastic parameters C and l defined above.

Let $[\delta g^{(i)} \cdot (g^{(i)})^{-1}]^\vee$ be the ith error of the measured poses, $i = 1,\ldots,m$. The pose error squares is given by:

$$E = \frac{1}{m} \sum_{i=1}^{m} \left\| [\delta g^{(i)} \cdot (g^{(i)})^{-1}]^\vee \right\|_Q^2 \quad (20)$$

where Q is a positive definite matrix, and $\|u\|_Q = (u^T Q u)^{\frac{1}{2}}$ is a norm of vector u, then the weights of the angular and position error can be adjusted. The parameters identification work is equivalent to finding the global optimal $C = [C_1^T, \cdots, C_N^T]^T$ to minimize the pose error squares E.

$$\min_{C=[C_1^T,\cdots,C_N^T]^T} E = \frac{1}{m} \sum_{i=1}^{m} \left\| [\delta g^{(i)} \cdot (g^{(i)})^{-1}]^\vee \right\|_Q^2 \tag{21}$$

The calibration process start with the number of sections $N = 1$, when the accuracy after calibration is not satisfying, $N = N + 1$ is tried for the next optimization. The block diagram of the calibration process is shown in Fig. 3. As there are 4 m independent quadratic terms in the quadratic sum E, number of the poses m should satisfy: $4m \geq 6N$. Thus $\lceil m \geq 3N/2 \rceil \lceil \ \rceil$, is the ceil function.

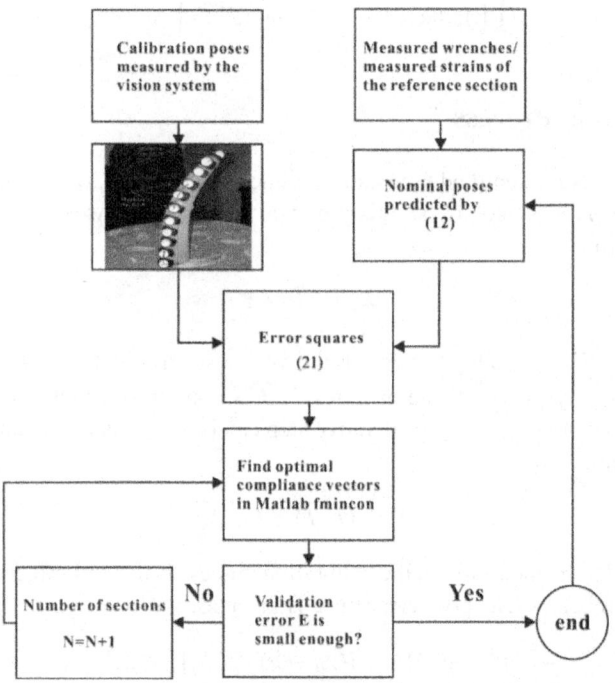

Fig. 3. The calibration process of the kinematics and elastic parameters of a continuum robot.

Except the pseudo-inverse method given in (19), nonlinear optimization algorithms without calculating the inverse of $\overline{J}^T \overline{J}$ can be used to deal with the least-squares problem, including gradient descent algorithms, genetic algorithm, etc.

4 Experimental Results

Two examples are studied here. In the first numerical experiment, effectiveness of the calibration, parameter redundancy are investigated. In the second example, compliance vectors of a cone-like cable driven manipulator are identified.

4.1 Experiment I

A dimensionless numerical calibration of a continuum manipulator with the actual number of sections N = 3 and total length L = 200 is experimented in Matlab 2017. Actual values of the compliance vectors C_i and the section lengths l_i, (i = 1, 2, 3) are present in Table 1. 50 samples are generated for identification and additional 50 samples are generated for verification by setting random internal wrenches F. End-effector pose and internal wrench of each sample are recorded. Manipulator configurations under four different internal wrenches are shown in Fig. 4. To inspect the robustness of the calibration, sensor noise in the range of $[-0.1, 0.1]$, $[-0.002, 0.002]$, and $[-0.005, 0.005]$ is added to the end-effector position, orientation and internal wrench. The total compliance vector $\mathcal{C} = [\mathcal{C}_1^T, \mathcal{C}_2^T, \mathcal{C}_3^T]^T \in \mathbb{R}^{18}$ is optimized by utilizing Matlab's fmincon toolbox to minimize the error squares given in (21), with weights matrix Q set as diag(50, 50, 50, 1, 1, 1). BFGS algorithm is used here to avoid the identification matrix singularities. The initial nominal values of C are given in Table 1. The lower and upper estimation bound of C is set to be 0 and 20.

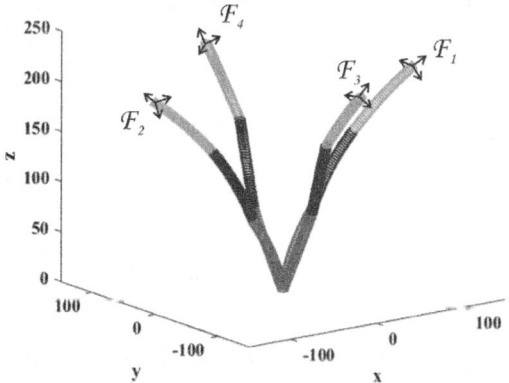

Fig. 4. Static configurations of the continuum manipulator.

In case I, C is identified without noise. In case II and III, C is identified with different section lengths. Errors after calibration are compared to test the redundancy of the section lengths l. Parameter identification results are shown in Table 1, with the set parameters value written in a bold font.

Table 1. Actual and Calibrated Values of Examples I.

	Section 1	Section 2	Section 3
Actual Values	$[C_1,l_1]=$ [4.3,4.1,0.5, 0.4,0.2,0.2, **80**]	$[C_1,l_1]=$ [3.5,3.6,0.9, 0.2,0.2,0.3,**40**]	$[C_1,l_1]=$ [3.1,2.8,0.7, 0.4,0.3,0.2,**80**]
Case I: Without Noise	$[C_1,l_1]=$ [4.348,4.146,0.489, 0.4,0.203,0.198,**80**]	$[C_1,l_1]=$ [3.58,3.553,0.787, 0.282,0.205,0.263,**40**]	$[C_1,l_1]=$ [3.052,2.741,0.7, 0.397,0.312,0.199, **80**]
Case II: With Section Lengths 1	$[C_1,l_1]=$ [4.284,4.076,0.698, 0.362,0.091,0.202,**80**]	$[C_1,l_1]=$ [3.497,3.69,0.015, 0.382,0.677,0.249,**40**]	$[C_1,l_1]=$ [3.106,2.78,0.964, 0.34,0.168,0.225,**80**]
Case III: With Section Lengths 2	$[C_1,l_1]=$ [4.335,4.124,0.784, 0.359,0.075,0.202,**66.7**]	$[C_1,l_1]=$ [3.571,3.593,0.174, 0.377,0.48,0.231,**66.7**]	$[C_1,l_1]=$ [3.061,2.724,1.048, 0.336,0.163,0.228, **66.7**]

We find that, in noise free case I, parameters identification results converge nearly to the actual values, even though the error of initial guesses is large. In case II, a small deviation from the actual values occurs because of the external noise. A different identification result is obtained in case III because of changed section lengths. However, error squares of case II and III after calibration both keep very small, E = 0.123 (Fig. 5).

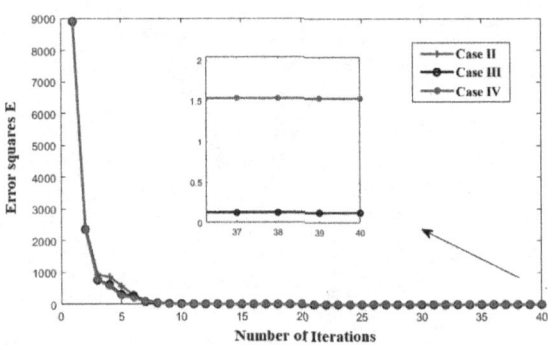

Fig. 5. Static configurations of the continuum manipulator.

Now other three cases with different number of sections N = 1, 2, 4 are calibrated. Errors after calibration are compared in Fig. 6 to find how does N influence the accuracy. It is observed that N = 3 (the actual number of sections) result in least error. The error of N = 3 calibrated case is far less than the error of the uncalibrated case, and is about 10 times smaller than error of the N = 1 calibrated case. In general, more refined sections division of the manipulator can result in a more accurate model, however, computation complexity should be made a trade-off. It is found in our experiment that convergence of the error becomes slow and local optimum problem will happen when the number of sections N is large.

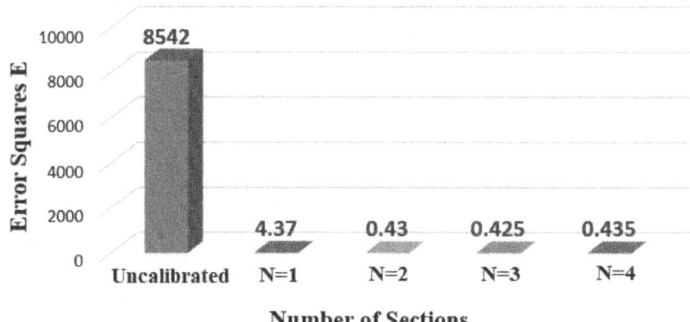

Fig. 6. Error squares of the Uncalibrated and N = 1, 2, 3, 4 calibrated cases of Example I.

4.2 Experiment II

A cone-like 3-cables driven silicone continuum manipulator with two directions planar bending is given in this example. The radius of the top and the bottom is respectively 5 mm and 15 mm, the total length is 150 mm. Axial stretching, shear and torsion can be neglected as the corresponding deformations are very small, therefore g_z, e_x, e_y, e_z are set as 0, and only the bending compliance vectors g_x and g_x should be calibrated. Further, taking full advantage of the symmetry of the manipulator, g_x can be regard as equivalent to g_y, and g_x can be calibrated by only testing 2-dimensional bending samples in the yz plane.

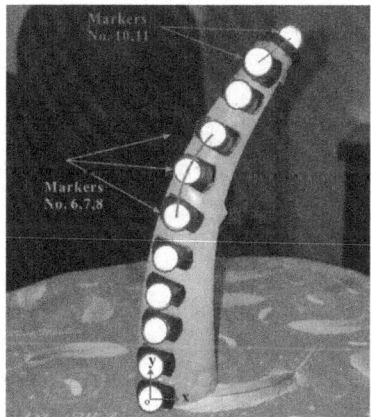

Fig. 7. Experiment a cone-like cable driven robot of Example II.

The whole experimental system is shown in Fig. 7, including the binocular camera and 11 tracking markers installed on the manipulator surface at an interval of 15 mm.

The binocular camera's intrinsic and extrinsic parameters are calibrated using Matlab's stereo camera calibrator toolbox. In the image processing step, the markers are projected into the bending plane of the manipulator to obtain the bending profile curve. The pose of the end-effector is estimated by locating the last two tracking markers, NO: 10, 11, and the bending torque m_x can be approximately substituted by the estimated bending curvature k_x^{ref} of the reference section (detailed in Sect. 2.2), which is determined by the arc consists of three arbitrarily chosen tracking markers, for instance, the markers NO. 6, 7, 8.

30 samples are generated for calibration and other 20 samples are generated for verification by exerting random tractions on one cable, and the bending plane is defined as the yz plane. The error of vision measurement is about 1 mm. The weights matrix Q is set as diag[50 mm/rad, 50 mm/rad, 50 mm/rad, 1, 1, 1]. Other conditions are the same as in Experiment I. Error squares E with unit mm^2 after calibration of different number of sections N = 1, 2, 3, 4 are compared in Fig. 8, it is clear that N = 3, 4 both result in very small error. Identification results of gx are given in Table 2.

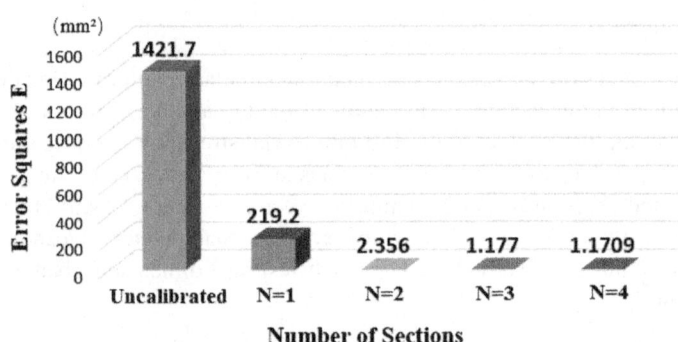

Fig. 8. Error squares of the Uncalibrated and N = 1, 2, 3, 4 calibrated cases of Example II.

Table 2. Calibrated Values of g_x in Examples II.

Initial Value	N = 1	N = 2	N = 3
[1]	[0.55]	[0.027; 1.546]	[0. 276; 0.084 2.017]

Before calibration, initial value of the bending compliance g_x is set as 1, it is simply a constant curvature model of which the curvature equals to the measured one k_x^{ref}. In this case a large error squares E = 1421.7 mm^2 occurs. In contrast, the accuracy has been significantly improved after calibration of g_x even in the N = 1 case, where E is 219.2. In more refined piecewise constant curvature cases when N = 2 and N = 3, the error squares E = 1.18 mm^2 and E = 1.17 mm^2 are much smaller. An illustration of the profile curves of different N cases is shown in Fig. 9. Identification results also shows that g_x is larger at the tip than that at the bottom, this can be explained properly as the compliance increases when the manipulator radius decreases.

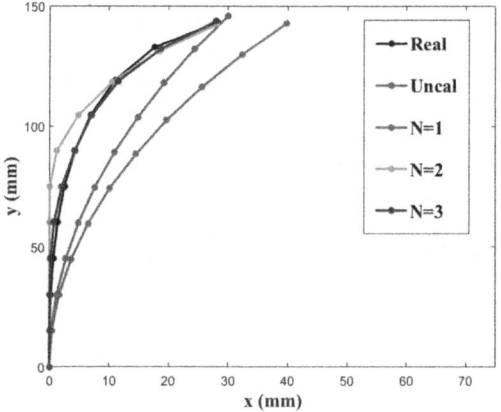

Fig. 9. Error squares of Uncalibrated and N = 1, 2, 3 calibrated cases in Example II.

5 Conclusion

Continuum manipulators with nonconstant elasticity cannot be simply modeled using the constant curvature or constant strain assumption. In this letter, a kinematic model of a whole 6-dimensional continuum manipulator is presented in the POE formula based on the constant internal wrench and piecewise constant elasticity assumptions. The pose of the end effector is calculated using the linear elastic constitutive laws. Compliance vectors are defined as the minimal kinematic parameters and internal wrench the kinematic variable. The POE based identification methods of a serial link robot is applied to identifying the compliance vectors of the continuum manipulator. Results of a numerical experiment and a planar bending manipulator experiment show that all the compliance vectors can be identified quickly and robustly, and modeling accuracy has been significantly improved after calibration. Our model can be applied to a large class of continuum robots with complex structures and material properties.

In the future work, kinematic and calibration work need to be extended to a more precise model considering the wrenches equilibrium. Besides, the experiment should be verified on a 6 DOFs continuum manipulator with shear and torsion.

References

1. Webster, R.J., Jones, B.A.: Design and kinematic modeling of constant curvature continuum robots: a review. Int. J. Robot. Res. **29**(13), 1661–1683 (2010)
2. Trivedi, D., Lotfi, A., Rahn, C.D.: Geometrically exact models for soft robotic manipulators. IEEE Trans. Robot. **24**(4), 773–780 (2008)
3. Webster, R.J., Romano, J.M., Cowan, N.J.: Mechanics of precurved-tube continuum robots. IEEE Trans. Robot. **25**(1), 67–78 (2009)
4. Serchi, F.G., Arienti, A., Corucci, F., Giorelli, M., Laschi, C.: Hybrid parameter identification of a multi-modal underwater soft robot. IOP Sci. **12**(2), 025007 (2017)
5. Sadati, S.M.H., et al.: Mechanics of continuum manipulators, a comparative study of five methods with experiments. In: Conference Towards Autonomous Robotic Systems (2017)

6. Jones, B.A., Walker, I.D.: Kinematics for multisection continuum robots. IEEE Trans. Robot. **22**(1), 43–55 (2006)
7. Bailly, Y., Amirat, Y.: Modeling and control of a hybrid continuum active catheter for aortic aneurysm treatment. In: InternationalConference on Robotics and Automation (2005)
8. Marchese, A.D., Rus, D.: Design, kinematics, and control of a soft spatial fluidic elastomer manipulator. Int. J. Robot. Res. **35**(7), 840–869 (2015)
9. Falkenhahn, V., et al.: Dynamic modeling of bellows-actuated continuum robots using the Euler-Lagrange formalism. IEEE Trans. Robot. **31**(6), 1483–1496 (2015)
10. Marchese, A.D., et al.: Dynamics and trajectoryoptimization for a soft spatial fluidic elastomer manipulator. Int. J. Robot. Res. **35**(8) (2015)
11. Mahvash, M., Dupont, P.E.: Stiffness control of a continuum manipulator in contact with a soft environment. In: IEEE/RSJ International Conference on Intelligent Robots and Systems (2010)
12. Antman, S.S.: Nonlinear Problems of Elasticity. Springer, New York (1995)
13. Kratchman, L.B., et al.: Guiding elastic rods with a robot-manipulated magnet for medical applications. IEEE Trans. Robot. **33**(1), 227–233 (2017)
14. Renda, F., et al.: Screw-based modeling of soft manipulators with tendon and fluidic actuation. ASME J. Mech. Robot. **9**(4), 041012 (2017)
15. Li, C., Rahn, C.D.: Design of continuous backbone, cable-driven robots. ASME J. Mech. Des. **124**, 265–271 (2002)
16. Hayati, S.: Robot arm geometric parameter estimation. In: Proceedings of 22ndIEEE International Conference on Decision and Control (1983)
17. Rucker, D.C., et al.: Equilibrium conformations of concentric-tube continuum robots. IEEE Int. J. Robot. Res. **29**(10), 1263–1280 (2010)
18. Rucker, D.C., et al.: A geometrically exact model for externally loaded concentric-tube continuum robots. IEEE Trans. Robot. **26**(5), 769–780 (2010)
19. Escande, C., et al.: Kinematic calibration of a multisection bionic manipulator. IEEE/ASME Trans. Mechatron. **20**(2), 663–674 (2015)
20. Wang, Z., Hirai, S.: Soft gripper dynamics using a line-segment model with an optimization-based parameter identification method. IEEE RAL **2**(2), 624–631 (2017)
21. Deutschmann, B., et al.: A method to identify the nonlinear stiffness characteristics of an elastic continuum mechanism. IEEE RAL **3**(3), 1450–1457 (2018)
22. Okamura, K., Park, F.C.: Kinematic calibration using the product of exponentials formula. IEEE Trans. Robot. **14**(4), 415–421 (1996)
23. He, R., et al.: Kinematic-parameter identification for serial-robot calibration based on POE formula. IEEE Trans. Robot. **26**(3), 411–423 (2010)
24. Chen, G., Wang, H., Lin, Z.: Determination of the identifiable parameters in robot calibration based on the POE formula. IEEE Trans. Robot. **30**(5), 1066–1077 (2014)

Predictive Modeling of Robot Deformation Errors via Incremental Learning

Ze-Sheng Guo[1,2], Zhao-Yang Liao[1(✉)], Zi-Wei Lu[1], Zhi-Hao Xu[1], Hong-Min Wu[1], and Xue-Feng Zhou[1]

[1] Institute of Intelligent Manufacturing, Guangdong Academy of Sciences, Guangdong Key Laboratory of Modern Control Technology, Guangzhou, China
zy.liao@giim.ac.cn
[2] Wuyi University, Jiangmen, China

Abstract. Robot deformation errors caused by force exhibit strong nonlinearity and significant spatiotemporal variation, making accurate prediction challenging for traditional models. This paper proposes an incremental learning model based on GWO-XGBoost to improve prediction accuracy amid changing workspaces and operating times. First, Grey Wolf Optimization (GWO) tunes XGBoost hyperparameters to build an initial prediction model. XGBoost then maps 6D joint angles, 3D theoretical positions, and 3D force data to deformation errors. An online incremental learning mechanism dynamically updates the model with real-time data to adapt to load variations. Experiments show MSE drops from 0.758 to 0.416 and MAE from 0.587 mm to 0.346 mm under new loads, demonstrating strong fitting and predictive performance for enhancing robot deformation accuracy.

Keywords: Industrial robots · Incremental learning · Error prediction · Deformation error

1 Introduction

Industrial robots are widely used in precision manufacturing sectors such as aerospace and high-speed train welding due to their flexibility, large workspace, and cost-effectiveness [1]. However, under continuous high-load conditions, non-geometric errors—stemming from limited structural rigidity, joint compliance, and dynamic load coupling—significantly hinder their precision applications [2]. These errors are primarily attributed to the weak rigidity transmission in serial open-chain structures, where loads propagate through the kinematic chain, causing joint deformation, link vibration, and interference from gear backlash, friction, and thermal expansion, ultimately resulting in substantial end-effector deviations.

This work was co-supported by the National Natural Science Foundation of China [U22A20176], Guangdong Basic and Applied Basic Research Foundation [2025A1515011849], Young Talent Project of GDAS [2024GDASQNRC-0318], GDAS' Project of Science and Technology Development [2024GDASZH-2024010102].

© The Author(s), under exclusive license to Springer Nature Singapore Pte Ltd. 2026
T. Matsuno et al. (Eds.): ICIRA 2025, LNAI 16074, pp. 509–521, 2026.
https://doi.org/10.1007/978-981-95-2095-4_42

Excessive end-effector loads exacerbate absolute positioning errors, especially in lightweight collaborative robots like the UR16e, which suffer from stiffness degradation and pronounced elastic deformation in joints and links. In long-reach operations, such errors are amplified and exhibit strong nonlinear coupling with joint angles and load magnitude [3, 4]. For instance, Berezny et al. demonstrated the complex nonlinear nature of such errors in force-controlled robots, offering a theoretical basis for compensation strategies [5].

Current compensation approaches fall into two categories: Model-based methods rely on stiffness analysis or kinematic modeling to quantify load-deformation mappings. For example, Wu proposed a joint error identification method using laser trackers [6], while Zhang et al. validated theoretical models via trajectory error compensation [7]. These methods, however, depend heavily on precise structural calibration and are limited in adapting to dynamic, nonlinear load effects [8]. Data-driven methods employ machine learning to model joint angle–position error relationships. Xu et al. combined crayfish optimization with Gaussian Process Regression for non-geometric error prediction [9]. Though accurate under fixed conditions, such models degrade over time due to data drift, as they lack adaptability to load variations and evolving paths [10, 11].

To overcome these limitations, online adaptive modeling has gained traction. Incremental Learning has shown promise in non-stationary environments like equipment monitoring and time-series prediction, enabling continuous model updates with real-time data. Yuan et al. proposed a few-shot class incremental learning method to mitigate concept drift [12], while Liu et al. applied iterative learning control to reduce path tracking errors [11]. Moreover, the Grey Wolf Optimizer (GWO) has been integrated with XGBoost for cross-domain tasks, offering strong nonlinear fitting and efficient global search. For instance, Wang et al. used GWO-XGBoost in network link prediction [13], and Asemi et al. applied it to EEG emotion recognition [14], demonstrating its versatility.

Nonetheless, applying such frameworks to robot deformation error prediction presents two key challenges. Multi-source feature fusion: Integrating joint angles, theoretical positions, and force data requires preserving spatiotemporal relationships. Zhang et al. emphasized the value of multimodal fusion for robustness [15], and a laser-tracker system [17] supports our experimental setup. Incremental update strategy: Balancing convergence and real-time efficiency remains difficult. Existing retraining or fine-tuning methods often fail to meet the operational demands of robotic systems [18].

To address these issues, this study proposes an online robot deformation error prediction model based on XGBoost with Incremental Learning. The model dynamically incorporates real-time joint and force data, mitigating the limitations of static models during prolonged tasks. GWO is employed to optimize hyperparameters, enhancing training efficiency and applicability in high-precision manufacturing.

The remainder of the paper is structured as follows: Sect. 2 explains the deformation mechanism and the GWO-XGBoost incremental learning model. Section 3 presents experimental validation. Section 4 concludes with key insights on prediction accuracy, generalization, and engineering value.

2 Method

To address the limitations of static models in predicting nonlinear deformation, this paper proposes an incremental learning framework based on GWO-XGBoost. By dynamically fusing force sensor signals and laser tracker data, the model establishes a mapping between multi-source inputs and deformation errors. Its online learning mechanism updates weight parameters in real time, improving generalization under varying conditions and reducing the need for extensive data collection. The overall architecture is shown in Fig. 1.

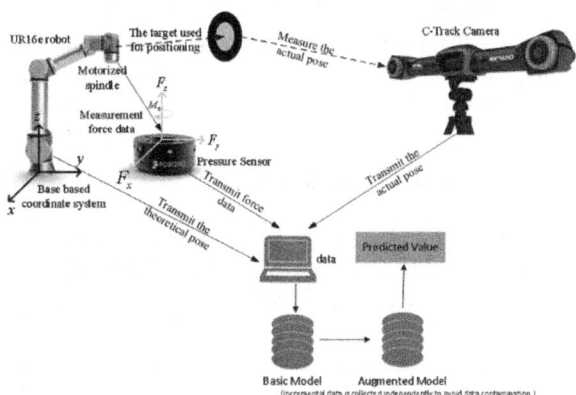

Fig. 1. System Structure.

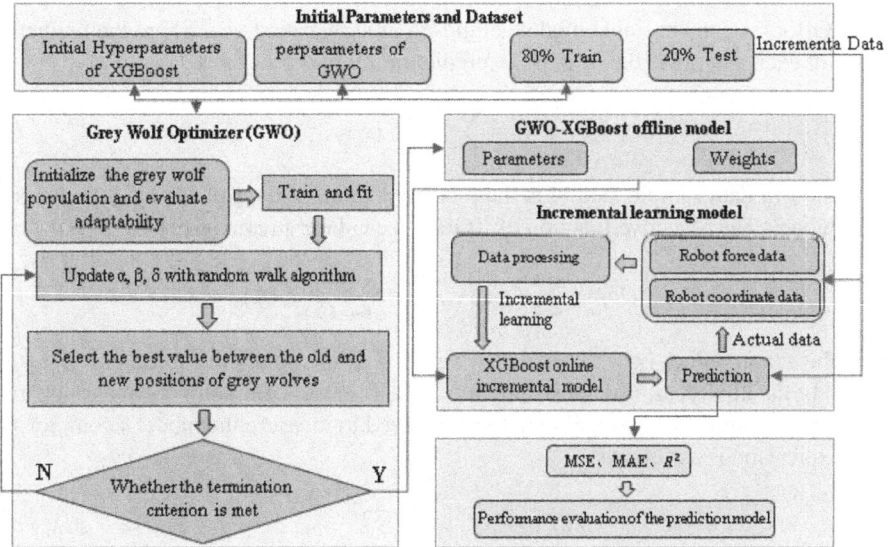

Fig. 2. Training Process of Increment GWO-XGBoost model.

The framework integrates Grey Wolf Optimization (GWO), XGBoost, and incremental learning in a cyclic structure to predict deformation errors and enable dynamic model updates. GWO iteratively refines XGBoost hyperparameters via a random walk strategy, selecting optimal parameter sets (α, β, δ) based on population positions. These optimized parameters initialize the offline XGBoost model.

Augmented force and pose data are then fed into the online incremental model, which retains prior knowledge while updating its tree structure with new data to adapt to evolving scenarios. Prediction performance is assessed in real time using MSE, MAE, and R^2. If accuracy drops below a set threshold or working conditions shift significantly, GWO re-optimization is triggered.

This study focuses on algorithm validation; actual incremental environments are simulated by segmenting the dataset into different working regions, forming a closed-loop of offline tuning, incremental learning, and dynamic recalibration. The detailed model structure is illustrated in Fig. 2.

2.1 eXtreme Gradient Boosting (XGBoost)

The robot end-effector deformation error prediction model constructed in this paper employs the XGBoost [18], which enhances nonlinear modeling by integrating multiple regression trees within a gradient boosting framework. Key strengths include high-order optimization, regularization, and engineering efficiency.

The model inputs a 12-dimensional feature vector combining multi-source robot data: 6D joint angles (θ_1–θ_6), 3D theoretical end-effector position (X, Y, Z), and 3D external force (F_x, F_y, F_z). By explicitly including joint states, loads, and positions, the model effectively captures nonlinear stiffness deformation and pose coupling for precise structural deformation prediction.

XGBoost is an ensemble model composed of k decision trees, where the predicted value of each sample is the sum of the prediction scores of all trees:

$$\widehat{y_i} = \sum_{k=1}^{K} f_k(x_i) \tag{1}$$

x_i is the i-th data sample, and $\widehat{y_i}$ is the predicted value of the i-th sample. k is the kth base model. The objective function of XGBoost can be expressed as:

$$Obj = \sum_{i=1}^{m} L(y_i, \widehat{y_i}) + \sum_{k=1}^{K} \omega(f_k) \tag{2}$$

y_i is the actual value, $\widehat{y_i}$ is the predicted value, K is the number of trees, and f_k is the model of the kth tree. L is the loss function, which is most commonly the mean squared error (MSE), and ω is the regularization term used to measure the model's complexity. The expression is as follows:

$$\omega(f) = \gamma T + \frac{1}{2}\lambda \sum_{j=1}^{T} \omega_j^2 \tag{3}$$

γ is the gamma coefficient controlling pruning, λ is the L_2 regularization coefficient, and T is the number of branches and the weight of internal split trees. Next, the objective function is minimized by adding the t-th decision tree. To find the optimal tree in the t-th iteration, the objective function is solved:

$$\hat{y}_i^t = \hat{y}_i^{t-1} + f_t(x_i) \tag{4}$$

$$\text{Obj}^{(t)} = \sum_{i=1}^{n} L\left(y_i, \hat{y}^{t-1} + f_t(x_i)\right) + \omega(f_t) \tag{5}$$

$\hat{y}_i^{(t-1)}$ is the predicted value of the model on the previous t-1 trees, and $f_t(x_i)$ is the tree model added at the t-th time. After that, XGBoost uses the second-order Taylor method to minimize the loss function. Expanding it gives:

$$\text{Obj}^{(t)} \approx \sum_{i=1}^{n} \left[L\left(y_i, \hat{y}^{t-1}\right) + g_i f_t(x_i) + \frac{1}{2} h_i f_t^2(x_i) \right] + \omega(f_t) \tag{6}$$

By merging the same function values for the same leaf node, we obtain:

$$w_j = -\frac{G_j}{H_j + \lambda} \tag{7}$$

G_j and H_j represent the sums of the first- and second-order loss function derivatives. After removing constants, the objective function depends only on these derivatives. Substituting and simplifying w_j yields the final objective function:

$$\text{Obj}^{(t)} = -\frac{1}{2} \sum_{j=1}^{T} \frac{G_j^2}{H_j + \lambda} + \gamma T \tag{8}$$

2.2 Random Walk Grey Wolf Optimizer

The Grey Wolf Optimizer (GWO), proposed by Mirjalili et al. in 2014 [19], is a bio-inspired algorithm structured around four key stages: hierarchy establishment, prey tracking, encirclement, and attack. The process begins with random initialization of wolves in the decision space, followed by ranking individuals by fitness into four levels: α (best), β (second-best), δ (third-best), and ω (others). The hierarchy guides the pack's encirclement and attack on the prey, driving the optimization process as detailed below:

$$Q(t+1) = Q_p(t) - (2a \cdot p_1 - a)\left(2p_2 \cdot Q_p(t) - Q(t)\right) \tag{9}$$

$$a = 2 - 2 \cdot it/MAX\_IT \tag{10}$$

t is the iteration number, and $Q_p(t)$ denotes the prey's position, i.e., the current optimal XGBoost hyperparameter set (n_estimators, learning_rate, gamma). $Q_p(t)$ i is the gray wolf's position vector, representing the candidate hyperparameter for the next iteration. Random coefficients $p1$ and $p2$ are drawn from [0, 1]. The second equation is used to calculate a. In (10), it represents the current number of iterations, MAX_IT represents the maximum number of iterations. In each iteration, GWO retains three optimal solutions and updates the positions of other wolves through the model.

The Random Walk Grey Wolf Optimizer (RWGWO), proposed by Gupta et al. in 2019 [20], is an improved version of the Grey Wolf Optimizer (GWO). Its core innovation lies in introducing random walk perturbations to the top three optimal solutions (α/β/δ wolves), which enhances the exploration capability to avoid the premature convergence of traditional GWO into local optima. The process is as follows:

$$W_N = \sum_{i=1}^{N} s_i = \sum_{i=1}^{N-1} s_i + X_N = W_{N-1} + s_N \qquad (11)$$

Among them, W^N and W^{N-1} are random walking states. s_i is the random step size that can be obtained from any random distribution.

2.3 GWO-XGBoost Incremental Learning Model

(1) GWO for Hyperparameter Optimization: XGBoost performance heavily depends on hyperparameters, particularly gamma (regularization), learning_rate, and n_estimators (number of base learners) [13, 21, 22]. Gamma controls model complexity and should not be too large to avoid underfitting. A higher learning_rate speeds up convergence but must be balanced with n_estimators to maintain generalization. Increasing n_estimators can improve accuracy but risks overfitting. Traditional grid search methods are exhaustive and computationally intensive, often falling into local optima. To address this, GWO is employed to optimize these parameters, mapping position vectors to hyperparameter sets and iteratively identifying optimal configurations.

(2) Initialization of GWO-XGBoost Model: The model is built by feeding the GWO-optimized hyperparameters into XGBoost for training [23]. The process starts by setting default hyperparameters, defining search ranges, initializing the population, and specifying parameters like population size and iteration count. Model performance is evaluated using MSE as the fitness metric.

After each iteration, the top three solutions are retained, and random walk strategies are applied to guide the next generation. New hyperparameter sets are used to retrain and re-evaluate the model. The iteration continues until stopping criteria are met—such as reaching the maximum iterations or early stopping—at which point the best hyperparameters are used to finalize the GWO-XGBoost prediction model.

2.4 XGBoost Incremental Learning

Aiming at the dynamic data characteristics of robot position prediction, this paper adopts an incremental learning mechanism to continuously optimize the model. Specifically, this strategy retains the tree structure of the existing prediction model, updates knowledge by recalculating leaf node weights, and dynamically adds new trees based on data increments. This approach not only preserves the knowledge accumulation from early training but also adaptively incorporates real-time input data of the robot, enabling the incremental model to have both good accuracy and generalization ability. The number of new trees is jointly determined by the scale of the initial dataset and input dataset, the number of initial model trees, and the scaling parameter ρ, where ρ is used to regulate the incremental update degree of the initial model. The parameter adjustment formula for ρ is as follows:

$$T_{\text{Incre}} = \frac{D_{\text{Input}}}{D_{\text{Basic}}} \times T_{\text{Basic}} \times \rho \quad (12)$$

3 Experiment

To analyze robot deformation error distribution, a 6 mm nylon rope (46 kg load capacity) is used to simulate concentrated milling loads. One end is fixed to the UR16e flange, the other to a force sensor. Latin hypercube sampling is applied for uniform sampling of end-effector positions. Through communication between the robot, computer, C-Track, and force sensor, joint angles, end positions, and force data are collected. These are then used as inputs to build the deformation error prediction model.

The experiment uses a UR16e collaborative robot (±0.03 mm repeatability) equipped with a Robotiq FT300 force sensor (±0.1 N accuracy) and a Creaform vxTrack vision system (±0.02 mm accuracy, 30 Hz) to capture end-effector pose. A total of 400 samples are collected via Latin hypercube sampling within the workspace x ∈ [−650, −400], y ∈ [−400, 150], z ∈ [200, 500]. Each sample includes 12 input features (6 joint angles, 3 theoretical positions, 3 force components simulating 0–5 kg loads) and 3 output labels (pose errors). Data is split into training and test sets at a 4:1 ratio. For incremental learning, 160 additional samples are collected from new workspace regions, ensuring no overlap with initial data to prevent leakage and preserve metric validity. Hyperparameters are empirically set to γ = 0, learning_rate = 0.1, and n_estimators = 200.

3.1 Experimental Results

(1) Performance Comparison of Optimization Algorithms

To investigate the convergence efficiency and performance of the Grey Wolf Optimizer (GWO), comparisons are made with the Particle Swarm Optimization (PSO), Whale Optimization Algorithm (WOA), and Sparrow Search Algorithm (SSA). Both the population size and the number of iterations are set to the default value of 20.

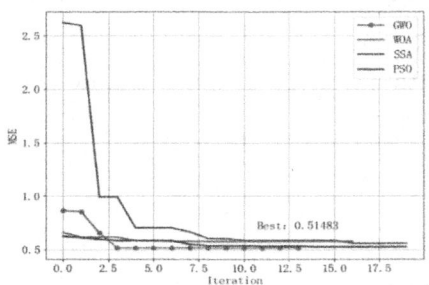

Fig. 3. Iteration results of optimization algorithm.

The test training results are shown in Fig. 3 The Grey Wolf Optimizer (GWO) performs best, achieving stability at the 4th iteration and triggering early stopping, ending at the 14th round. Other algorithms also perform well after 20 iterations. As shown in Table 1, the Grey Wolf algorithm exhibits the best effect and the shortest calculation time. Hyperparameter analysis indicates that the algorithm requires more trees to achieve optimal fitting, and the gamma value is close to 0, suggesting that no pruning of the tree structure is needed.

Table 1. Comparison of running results between Wolf and otheroptimization.

Name	Best N	Best Eta	BestGamma	Run	MSE	Time/s
Whale	1280	0.1409	0	16	0.53148	940
Sparrow	1405	0.1825	6.54×10^{-5}	20	0.54137	2221
Particle	1459	0.1777	6.49×10^{-9}	20	0.55176	973
Wolf	1253	0.1646	0	14	0.51483	703

(2) Deformation Error Prediction of GWO-XGBoost

To enhance interpretability, XGBoost's built-in feature importance analysis was used to identify key factors affecting deformation error (see Table 2). For the UR16e robot, Y-axis position is the most influential factor, significantly affecting structural stability under complex tasks. Y-direction force ranks second, as it can induce displacement in joints and links. The forearm joint (A4) also plays a major role; under load, its motion can cause local stress concentration and stiffness degradation, leading to increased deformation [8]. Base joint A1 and wrist joint A5 contribute as well—A1 alters the moment arm of end loads, amplifying torque effects, while A5 affects force transmission paths near the end-effector. In contrast, forces in the X/Z directions and other joint angles have relatively minor impact.

Table 2. Importance analysis of factors influencing deformation error.

Rank	Feature	Importance Score	Rank	Feature	ImportanceScore
1	Y	2.9931	7	A3	0.1789
2	Fy	0.617	8	Fx	0.1513
3	A4	0.5554	9	A2	0.1406
4	Fz	0.3982	10	Z	0.1076
5	A1	0.2609	11	A6	0.1063
6	A5	0.2005	12	X	0.0665

Model Performance Comparison: To investigate the performance of the GWO-XGBoost model, this section introduces comparative models including Random Forest, Multilayer Perceptron (MLP), and Support Vector Regression (SVR). As shown in Table 3, GWO-XGBoost significantly outperforms other models in terms of the R^2 correlation coefficient, demonstrating excellent overall performance. SVR performs worst in MSE, indicating its deficiency in prediction accuracy; MLP shows the poorest performance in MAE, validating its limitations in handling complex data.

Table 3. Performance comparison between GWO-X GBoost and different models.

Name	MSE	MAE	MSLE	R^2	Time/s
GWO-XGBoost	0.55568	0.36561	0.05148	0.59319	1.234 s
LP	1.05313	0.72026	0.12499	−0.20698	0.424 s
RF	0.89142	0.40385	0.06312	−1.33826	0.469 s
SVR	1.22038	0.51140	0.05295	0.38687	0.229 s

(3) Deformation Error Prediction Results

This section demonstrates the prediction performance of the GWO-XGBoost model by predicting the robot's deformation errors. A total of 73 error samples were randomly selected from the test samples, and force-induced deformation errors of the sample points in the X, Y, and Z directions were predicted. The specific results are shown in Fig. 4. The prediction error range in the X direction is [−0.99 mm, 1.03 mm] with a mean absolute error (MAE) of 0.26 mm; in the Y direction, the error range is [−1.94 mm, 1.38 mm] with an MAE of 0.44 mm; and in the Z direction, the error range is [−0.26 mm, 0.15 mm] with an MAE of 0.05 mm.

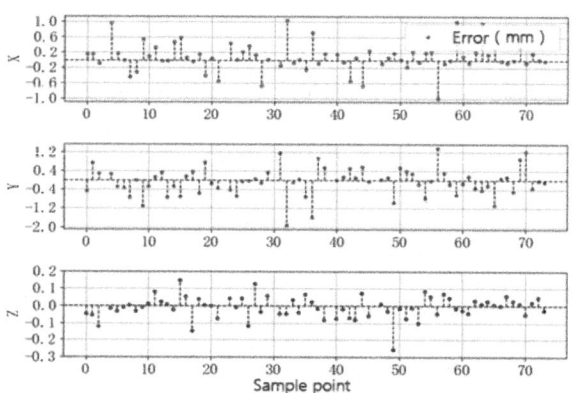

Fig. 4. Error between predicted and actual deformation error value.

Thus, it can be seen that the force-induced deformation error in the Z direction is the most stable, while the error variance in the Y direction is larger. Additionally, the model exhibits good prediction performance and stability in all three directions.

3.2 Incremental Learning Prediction Experiment

To evaluate the adaptability of the incremental learning module to new tasks and scenarios, two experimental schemes were designed. Scheme 1: Based on data from an initial processing point A, 50 new samples were collected at a different point B—25 for fine-tuning and 25 for testing. Three methods were compared: no prediction, prediction with the original model, and prediction with the incrementally updated model. Scheme 2: The UR dataset was divided into five subsets, each incrementally added in sequence and tested on a fixed test set.

As shown in Fig. 5, the original model performed poorly on new samples, while the incrementally fine-tuned model achieved significantly better prediction accuracy. Results for Scheme 2 are shown in Table 4. During the initial incremental learning rounds, the model's performance improved markedly—MSE dropped from 0.75807 to 0.47389, and MAE from 0.58748 to 0.37425 within the first two rounds. From the third round onward, improvements plateaued: MSE only decreased slightly to 0.41582, MAE fluctuated around 0.34, and MSLE increased from 0.05226 to 0.06435. This indicates the model nearing convergence, with limited gains and potential overfitting risks, highlighting the need for further optimization.

Table 4. Incremental learning prediction result of GWO-XGBoost, option 2.

Run	MSE	MAE	MSLE	R^2
1	0.75807	0.58748	0.07938	0.45183
2	0.47389	0.37425	0.05699	0.55862
3	0.43069	0.33961	0.05226	0.57294
4	0.41452	0.33368	0.05250	0.61824
5	0.41582	0.34610	0.06435	0.61581

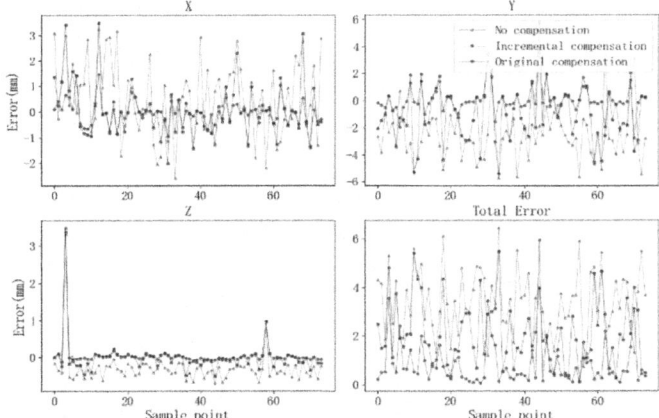

Fig. 5. Incremental learning prediction result of GWO-XGBoost, option 1.

3.3 Ablation Study

This section evaluates the contributions of GWO, XGBoost, and incremental learning by comparing models with specific modules removed. Without incremental learning, two models are tested: the initial GWO-XGBoost and one with periodic full retraining. Without GWO, three XGBoost variants are tested: initial-data, periodic retraining, and incremental learning. Replacing XGBoost, a random forest with incremental learning serves as a baseline.

Results (Table 5, Fig. 6) show the GWO-XGBoost incremental model achieves the best performance. The incremental model without GWO adapts slower initially but converges quickly. Models trained only on initial data underfit due to limited data and trees, while periodic retraining improves accuracy close to the GWO-XGBoost model. Although random forest supports incremental learning, its generalization is weaker because it only adjusts leaf weights without increasing tree numbers. Overall, GWO-XGBoost outperforms all alternatives in both accuracy and effectiveness.

Table 5. Performance comparison of ablation research for GWO-XGBoost.

Name	MSE	MAE	MSLE	R^2
Basic_op	2.6183	1.6418	0.2274	43.651%
All_op	0.5557	0.3656	0.0514	59.368%
Basic_no_op	2.7382	1.6813	0.2616	41.871%
All_no_op	0.5718	0.3961	0.0598	58.394%
Incre_begin_no_op	2.5157	1.7279	0.2416	42.157%
Incre_end_no_op	0.4891	0.3677	0.0653	60.614%
Random_Forest	6.5281	2.8177	0.5173	46.821%
GWO-incre_begin	0.7580	0.5875	0.0793	45.183%
GWO-incre_end	0.4158	0.3461	0.0644	61.581%

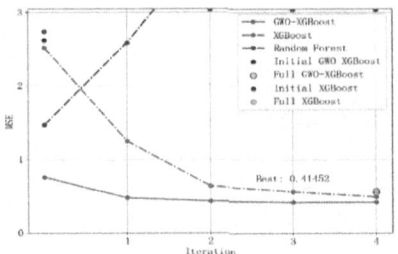

Fig. 6. Experimental results of ablation study for GWO-XGBoost.

4 Conclusion

This paper tackles nonlinear deformation error prediction in industrial robots caused by weak structural rigidity and load coupling, proposing an incremental learning framework based on GWO-XGBoost. The Grey Wolf Optimizer (GWO) optimizes XGBoost hyperparameters to build an initial prediction model, which is then iteratively updated via dynamic node adjustment using real-time joint angles, end-effector positions, and force data. Experiments demonstrate strong generalization in new scenarios, reducing MSE from 0.758 to 0.416 and MAE from 0.587 mm to 0.346 mm under varying loads. Compared to traditional methods like Random Forest and MLP, the model improves accuracy by over 30% and training speed by 50%. The incremental learning approach overcomes the inefficiency of batch training. Results confirm its effectiveness and engineering feasibility for enhancing robot positioning accuracy in complex industrial settings. Future work will employ time-series cross-validation with strictly separated incremental data to further validate robustness in dynamic environments.

References

1. Chen, Y.T., Liu, C.S., Lee, B.K.: Trajectory positioning error compensation and verification for six-axis industrial robot. Int. J. Adv. Manufact. Technol. **137**(9), 5205–5212 (2025)
2. Zou, J., Yang, F.: Efficient fabric defect detection based on lightweight model. Eng. Res. Exp. (2025)
3. Huang, S., Yang, J., Hu, P., et al.: High stiffness 6-DOF dual-arm cooperative robot and its application in blade polishing. IEEE Trans. Autom. Sci. Eng. (2023)
4. Dambly, V., Olivier, B., Rivière-Lorphèvre, E., et al.: Iterative offline trajectory correction based on dynamic model for compensating robot-dependent errors in robotic machining. Robot. Comput.-Integr. Manufact. **94**, 102960 (2025)
5. Berezny, N., Ahmadi, M.: Improving robotic force control performance in devices with force measurement and modelling error. IEEE Trans. Instrum. Measur. (2025)
6. Wu, H., Huang, N., Pi, J., et al.: Sequential identification of joint-dependent geometric errors for industrial robots using a laser tracker. Precis. Eng. (2025)
7. Zhang, J., Lin, J., Gao, Y., et al.: Efficient positioning error compensation for robots in wire arc hybrid manufacturing systems. Robot. Comput.-Integr. Manuf. **95**, 103040 (2025)
8. Zerun, Z., Chen, C., Fangyu, P., et al.: Identification of joint position-dependent stiffness parameters and analysis of robot milling deformation. Int. J. Adv. Manuf. Technol. 1–15 (2022)

9. Xu, S., Jia, X., Liu, J., et al.: Hierarchical compensation of robot positioning error: addressing geometric and non-geometric influences. IEEE Trans. Instrum. Meas. (2025)
10. Li, S., Liu, F., Jiac, L., et al.: Prompt-based concept learning for few-shot class-incremental learning. IEEE Trans. Circuits Syst. Video Technol. (2025)
11. Liu, Y., Li, Y.: Continuous path tracking of robots based on positioning error compensation with iterative learning control. IEEE Trans. Instrum. Meas. (2025)
12. Yuan, J., Chen, H., Tian, S., et al.: Prompt-based learning for few-shot class-incremental learning. Alex. Eng. J. **120**, 287–295 (2025)
13. Wang, Z., Yuan, F., Li, R., et al.: Hidden AS link prediction based on random forest feature selection and GWO-XGBoost model. Comput. Netw. **262**, 111164 (2025)
14. Asemi, H., Farajzadeh, N.: Improving EEG signal-based emotion recognition using a hybrid GWO-XGBoost feature selection method. Biomed. Signal Process. Control **99**, 106795 (2025)
15. Zhang, Y., Li, A., Li, H., et al.: Robust positioning in extreme environments: a tightly coupled GNSS-vision-inertial-wheel odometer framework. Sensor Rev. (2025)
16. Tan, C.S., Mohd-Mokhtar, R., Arshad, M.R.: Expected-mean gamma-incremental reinforcement learning algorithm for robot path planning. Expert Syst. Appl. **249**, 123539 (2024)
17. Xu, K., Xu, S., Qi, Q.: Research on high-precision positioning method of robot based on laser tracker. Intel. Serv. Robot. **16**(3), 361–371 (2023)
18. Chen, T., Guestrin, C.: Xgboost: a scalable tree boosting system. In: Proceedings of the 22nd ACM SIGKDD International Conference on Knowledge Discovery and Data Mining, pp. 785–794 (2016)
19. Kaushal, A., Sharma, A.K., Gupta, K.: Decentralised coordination in swarm robots through xgboost-enhanced colour light communication. Arab. J. Sci. Eng. **49**(12), 16253–16269 (2024)
20. Mirjalili, S., Mirjalili, S.M., Lewis, A.: Grey wolf optimizer. Adv. Eng. Softw. **69**, 46–61 (2014)
21. Zhou, S.: Gwo-ga-xgboost-based model for Radio-Frequency power amplifier under different temperatures. Expert Syst. Appl. **278**, 127439 (2025)
22. Gu, Z., Cao, M., Wang, C., et al.: Research on mining maximum subsidence prediction based on genetic algorithm combined with XGBoost model. Sustainability **14**(16), 10421 (2022)
23. Pan, S., Zheng, Z., Guo, Z., et al.: An optimized XGBoost method for predicting reservoir porosity using petrophysical logs. J. Petrol. Sci. Eng. **208**, 109520 (2022)

Soft Robotics

Design and Analysis of a Morphing Wing Based on Corrugated-Honeycomb Structure for UAV

Guang Yang, Chunlong Wang, Yuqi Li, Hong Xiao(✉), and Hongwei Guo

Harbin Institute of Technology, Harbin 150001, Heilongjiang, China
xiaohong@hit.edu.cn

Abstract. The cambered span morphing wing for unmanned aerial vehicle (UAV) can greatly improve its flight efficiency. In this work, a new flexible morphing wing that can achieve variable bending driven by shape memory alloy (SMA) is designed. The Morphing wing is composed of several morphing units with the same structure in series. The morphing unit is composed of two kinds of 0 Poisson's ratio honeycomb structures and corrugated plate. The honeycomb structures have the same shape and different thickness. The theoretical models of 0 Poisson's ratio honeycomb structures and corrugated plate structure are established and analyzed. The effects of different honeycomb structure thickness and corrugated structure thickness on the cambered ability of morphing wing is analyzed and verified by finite element simulation.

Keywords: morphing wing · honeycomb structure · corrugated structure

1 Introduction

Unmanned aerial vehicle (UAV) will face different environments in flight. In order to achieve the best aerodynamic performance in different flight states, it is necessary to change the wing shape. In the course of flight, the change of morphing wing dihedral angle can significantly improve the flight efficiency and enhance the maneuverability and stability of the UAV [1–3].

Morphing wing are composed of morphing skeleton, actuator and morphing skin. The actuator provides power for the deformation of wing, the morphing skin bears aerodynamic force. The morphing skeleton provides support for the skin to ensure the wing stiffness. The morphing skeleton needs to meet the requirements of deformation capacity, load-bearing capacity and low mass [4, 5].

The traditional morphing skeleton realizes the deformation by truss structure. VC Sherrer et al. [6] achieved wing bending by designing a combined truss wing mechanism to act as an elastic hinge. S. Lucato et al. [7] designed a high authority shape morphing plate which is connected by a tetrahedral truss core and consists of a Kagome truss. Pennsylvania State University [8] proposed a flexible honeycomb truss connected by flexible joints to achieve continuous and stable deformations in the wing span direction. University of Florida [9] developed a seagull-like morphing wing based on the truss structure.

In recent years, corrugated structures and honeycomb structures have been widely used in the field of morphing wing due to their anisotropy. Yokozeki et al. [10] developed a variable bending machine structure with corrugated plate structure, which can be applied to front and rear edges. Olympio et al. [11] designed a morphing skin with honeycomb structure, and carried out theoretical analysis and finite element verification on the mechanical properties of honeycomb.

In order to achieve the simple structure, less drive and modularization of morphing wing, a new flexible morphing wing that can achieve variable bending driven by shape memory alloy (SMA) is designed in this paper. The morphing wing is composed of several morphing units with the same structure in series. The morphing unit is composed of two kinds of 0 Poisson's ratio honeycomb structures and corrugated plate. The honeycomb structures have the same shape and different thickness. The theoretical models of 0 Poisson's ratio honeycomb structures and corrugated plate structure are established and analyzed. The effects of different honeycomb structure thickness and corrugated structure thickness on the cambered ability of morphing wing is analyzed by finite element simulation.

2 Design of Morphing Wing

The main goal of this work is to design a new variable camber morphing wing for UAV. According to the deformation requirement, a new morphing wing based on corrugated-honeycomb structure is proposed, as shown in Fig. 1. The morphing wing is composed of several morphing units with the same structure in series. The morphing unit is composed of two kinds of 0 Poisson's ratio honeycomb structures and corrugated plate. The honeycomb structures have the same shape and different thickness.

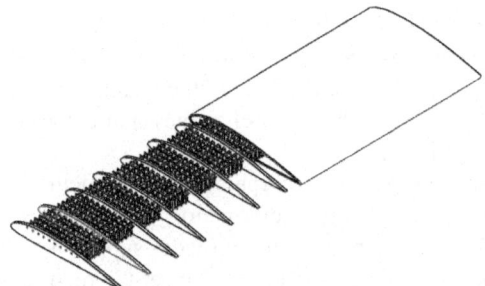

Fig. 1. The cambered span morphing wing.

The morphing wing is designed by modularization, which is composed of several meta-modules with the same structure in series, and the number of series is set by the structure.

As shown in Fig. 2, the morphing unit is a symmetrical structure which is represented by two rib plate and the corrugated-honeycomb structure. The wing ribs are connected to the honeycomb through corrugated plates. If only corrugated plates are used to connect the ribs, it is necessary to add honeycomb and SMA in the corrugated plate to enhance the flexural rigidity of the wing because the bending rigidity of the corrugated plate is low and the wing is easy to bend under the action of aerodynamic force.

The corrugated plates divide the honeycomb structure into two parts. The two parts have the same honeycomb shape, but the thickness of walls is different so that the elastic modulus of the upper and lower sides of the corrugated plates are different. The distance between wing ribs is shortened by pulling the shape memory alloy wire across the midline of the corrugated plate. However, the different elastic moduli between the upper and lower parts of the corrugated plate will cause the ribs to bend.

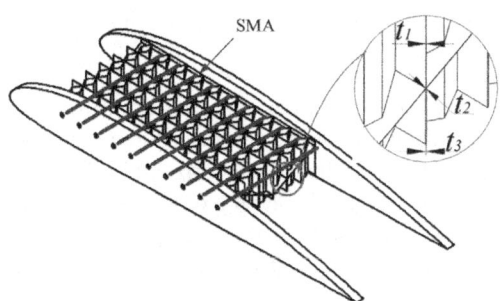

Fig. 2. The morphing unit.

In this work, in order to ensure the simple structure of corrugated plate, the commonly used triangular corrugated plate is selected. The honeycomb structure has the characteristics of light weight and high out-of-plane stiffness. According to Poisson's ratio, the honeycomb can be divided into positive Poisson's ratio honeycomb, zero Poisson's ratio honeycomb and negative Poisson's ratio honeycomb. However, when the positive and negative Poisson's ratio honeycomb is subjected to bending stress, the honeycomb will warp in different shapes. In order to ensure that the structures in other directions do not change during the deformed wing-span bending deformation, the most commonly used honeycomb with zero Poisson's ratio is accordion honeycomb.

3 Analytical Model

The wing ribs are connected to the honeycomb through corrugated plates, in which the upper and lower honeycomb structures are the same, but the wall thickness is different. The effects of honeycomb thickness, corrugated plate thickness and angle on the modulus of elasticity of deformed wing cells are analyzed theoretically.

3.1 Mechanical Properties of Honeycomb

The plane sketch and cell size of the filled accordion honeycomb are shown in Fig. 3. Honeycomb cell structure is horizontally symmetrical. Cell size can be expressed by the length of honeycomb wall S_1 and b_1, the thickness of honeycomb wall t_1, the height of honeycomb wall H_1 and the angle between honeycomb wall α.

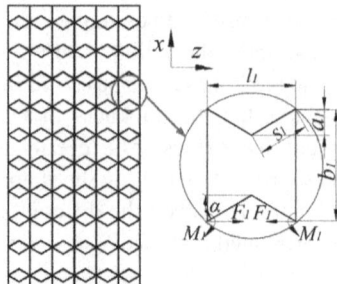

Fig. 3. The plane sketch and cell size of honeycomb.

A theoretical prediction model of transverse tensile stiffness of honeycomb is established based on the second card theorem. The shear force is neglected, and a transverse tensile load F_1 is assumed to be applied at the horizontal ends of honeycomb. The internal force component on the z-direction section of honeycomb can be expressed by the axial force $F(x)$ and the bending moment $M(x)$.

The deformation displacement of corrugated structure under load F_1 is obtained as follows:

$$\delta_{1z} = \frac{1}{EA}\int N\frac{\partial N}{\partial F}ds + \frac{1}{EI}\int M\frac{\partial M}{\partial F}ds \tag{1}$$

In which (1):

$$N = F_1 \sin\alpha \tag{2}$$

$$M_z = F_1 s \cos\alpha - \frac{F_1 S_1 \cos\alpha}{2} \tag{3}$$

From (1), (2) and (3), we obtain in the global coordinate system:

$$\delta_{1z} = \frac{F_1 S_1 \sin^2\alpha}{EA} + \frac{F_1 S_1^3 \cos^2\alpha}{12EI} \tag{4}$$

In which (4):

$$F_1 = \frac{\sigma_{1z} b_1 H_1}{2} \tag{5}$$

$$I = \frac{H_1 t_1^3}{12} \tag{6}$$

$$A = H_1 t_1 \tag{7}$$

From (4), (5), (6) and (7), we obtain:

$$\delta_{1z} = \sigma_{1z}(\frac{b_1 S_1 \sin^2\alpha}{2Et_1} + \frac{b_1 S_1^3 \cos^2\alpha}{2Et_1^3}) \tag{8}$$

In the analysis of elastic modulus, the equivalent variation and equivalent force of honeycomb can be rewritten as:

$$\varepsilon_{1z} = \frac{\delta_{1z}}{S_1 \sin \alpha} \tag{9}$$

$$E_{1z} = \sigma_{1z}/\varepsilon_{1z} \tag{10}$$

From (8), (9) and (10), we obtain the Equivalent elastic modulus:

$$E_{1z} = \frac{2Et_1^3 \sin \alpha}{b_1(t_1^2 \sin^2 \alpha + S_1^2 \cos^2 \alpha)} \tag{11}$$

The honeycomb structure above the corrugated plate is similar to that below the corrugated plate. The Young's modulus of the honeycomb structure below the corrugated plate is obtained by using similar deduction process:

$$E_{3z} = \frac{2Et_3^3 \sin \alpha}{b_1(t_3^2 \sin^2 \alpha + S_1^2 \cos^2 \alpha)} \tag{12}$$

In this work, the effect of honeycomb thickness on elastic modulus is analyzed. The geometric parameters of honeycomb cell are as follows: $b_1 = 50$ mm, $S_1 = 23.095$ mm, $\alpha = 60°$.

3.2 Mechanical Properties of Corrugated Plate

The plane sketch and structural dimensions of corrugated plates between ribs are shown in Fig. 4. The structure of corrugated plate is vertical and symmetrical. Its size can be expressed by the length S2 and height H2 of corrugated plate, the thickness of corrugated plate t2, and the angle between corrugated plate and horizontal direction θ.

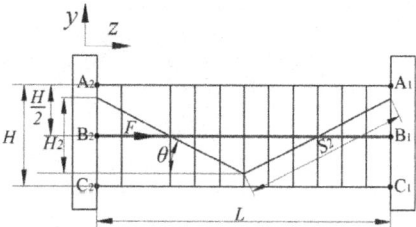

Fig. 4. Component unit of morphing wing.

Similarly, the theoretical prediction model of transverse tensile stiffness of corrugated plate is established based on the second theorem of the card. The modulus of elasticity in z- direction of corrugated plate is:

$$E_{2z} = \frac{Et_2^3 \cos \theta}{(H_2 + t_2)(t_2^2 \cos^2 \theta + S_2^2 \sin^2 \theta)} \tag{13}$$

When $\theta = 0°$, the elasticity modulus of corrugated plate in z-direction is the material elasticity modulus. The geometric parameters of corrugated cell are as follows: $H = 80$ mm, $L = 240$ mm.

3.3 Analysis of Equivalent Models

For corrugated-honeycomb structures, the z-direction equivalent modulus E_z can be expressed as the sum of the contributions of the upper honeycomb structure, the lower honeycomb structure and the hollow corrugated plate.

$$E_z = \lambda_1 E_{1z} + \lambda_2 E_{2z} + \lambda_3 E_{3z} \tag{14}$$

In which (14), the volume percentages of upper honeycomb structure, corrugated plate structure and lower honeycomb structure in cells are expressed $\lambda_1, \lambda_2, \lambda_3$.

4 Finite Element Modeling

In order to analyze the effects of different honeycomb thickness ratios ($K_{31} = t_3/t_1$), corrugated plate thickness ratios ($K_{21} = t_2/t_1$) and corrugated plate angle θ on the flexural properties of flexible wing, the elastic modulus of deformed wing element in z-direction was numerically analyzed by using finite element software WOEKBENCH.

The finite element model adopts the actual proportional model, as shown in Fig. 5. The wing rib plate is made of aluminium alloy, and the corrugated plate is made of ABS-PUS material printed in 3D for the convenience of honeycomb structure. The boundary condition of deformed wing element is fixed constraint on the right rib plate and driving force F on the left rib shape memory alloy mounting hole.

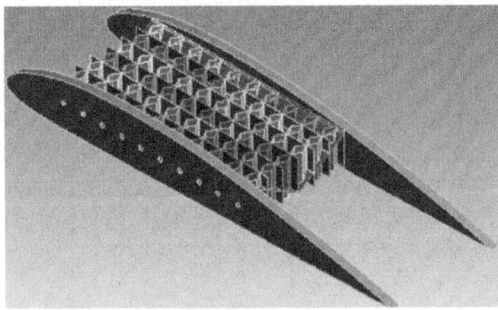

Fig. 5. Component unit of morphing wing.

In this work, the bending function of morphing wing is simulated and verified by finite element method. The morphing wing model is composed of three morphing element modules in series. Fixed constraints are applied at the root of morphing wing. Driving force is applied at the installation holes of shape memory alloy connection rib plate. The results of finite element simulation of morphing wing bending deformation are shown in Fig. 6.

Fig. 6. Bending deformation of morphing wng.

5 Results and Discussions

In this work, the dimensionless Young's modulus of honeycombs with different geometric shapes is parameterized by the finite element numerical simulation. According to the different corrugated shapes, the morphing wing element modules are divided into the following four types, as shown in Fig. 7 named as (a) $\theta = 0°, K_{21} = 0$, (b) $\theta = 0°, K_{21} = 1$, (c) $\theta = 30°, K_{21} = 1$, (d) $\theta = -30°, K_{21} = 1$.

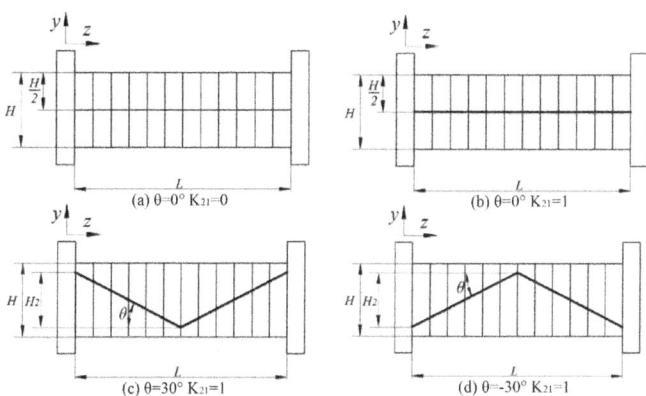

Fig. 7. Four different morphing unit.

5.1 Simulation Comparisons of Extensional Elasticity Modulus

In order to analyze the elastic modulus of different corrugated shape, the four elements shown in Fig. 8 are analyzed by the finite element analysis. The numerical simulation results of Young's modulus E_z in z-direction with different thickness ratios of honeycomb and honeycomb on corrugated plate are shown in Figs. 8(a), (b), (c) and (d).

As shown in Fig. 8(a) and Fig. 8(b), when the corrugated plate is not or flat, the deformation of point B_2 in z-direction decreases gradually with the increase of K_{31}, while the deformation of point B_2 in z-direction increases proportionally with the increase of driving force.

As shown in Fig. 8(c), it can be seen that the deformation of point B_2 in z-direction decreases with the increase of K_{31} value, and increases in proportion with the increase of driving force. The deformation of point B_2 in z-direction reaches its maximum at $K_{31} = 1$.

As shown in Fig. 8(d), it can be seen that the deformation of point B_2 in z-direction decreases first and then increases with the increase of K_{31}, while the deformation of point B_2 in z-direction increases proportionally with the increase of driving force. The overall the deformation of point B_2 in z-direction reaches the maximum at $K_{31} = 1$ and the minimum at $K_{31} = 5$.

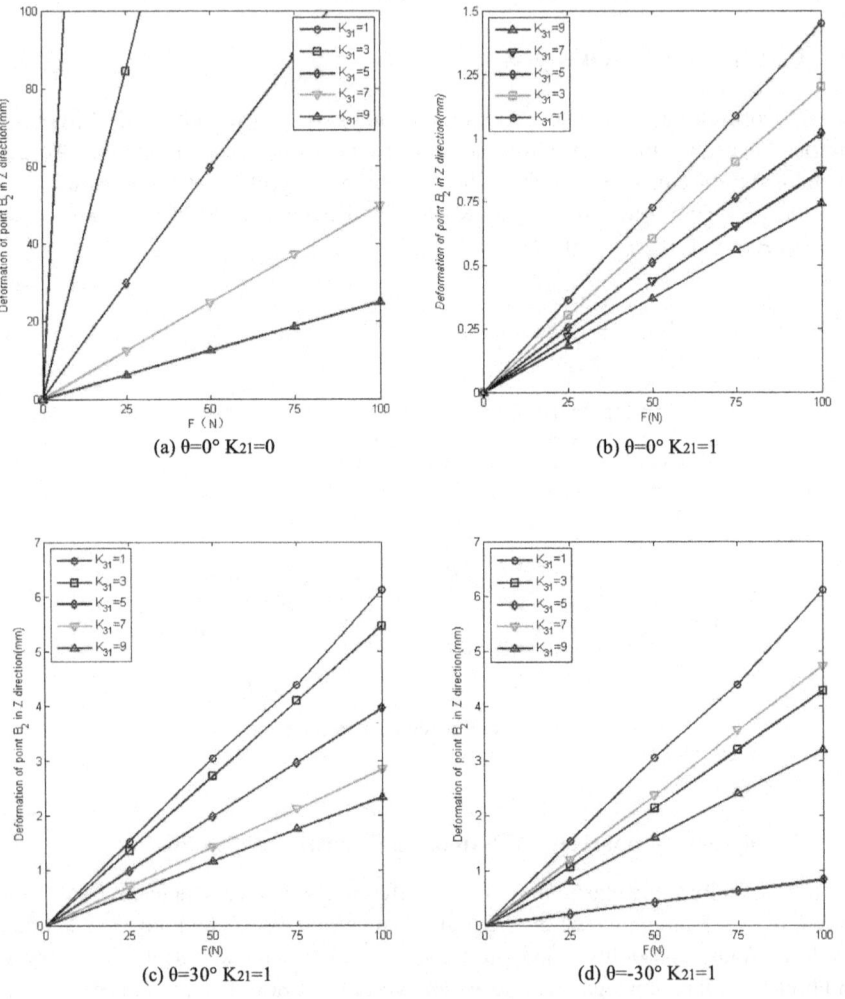

Fig. 8. Simulation comparisons of extensional elasticity modulus.

As shown in Fig. 8(a), Fig. 8(b) and Fig. 8(c), when the morphing wing element relies only on honeycomb structures, the elastic modulus is too low to withstand large loads.

As shown in Fig. 8(c) and Fig. 8(d), when the thickness ratio K_{31} of morphing wing element is the same, the elastic modulus at $\theta = 30°$ and $\theta = -30°$ is different.

Compared with Fig. 8, it can be seen that the different bending angles and directions of corrugated plates have different effects on the z-direction moving distance of morphing wing elements.

5.2 Simulation Comparison of Deflection Angle

In this work, the upside and downward bending state of morphing wing can be realized by inverted ripple-honeycomb structure, so only the upside bending state of morphing wing when $t_2 = 0.1$mm, $t_1 = 0.1$mm, $K_{21} = 1$ is analyzed. The bending angles of morphing elements with different honeycomb thickness ratios K_{31} and corrugated plate angle θ are shown in Fig. 9. According to the different corrugated angle θ, the morphing wing elements are divided into three types, namely (a) $\theta = 0°$, (b) $\theta = 30°$, (c) $\theta = -30°$.

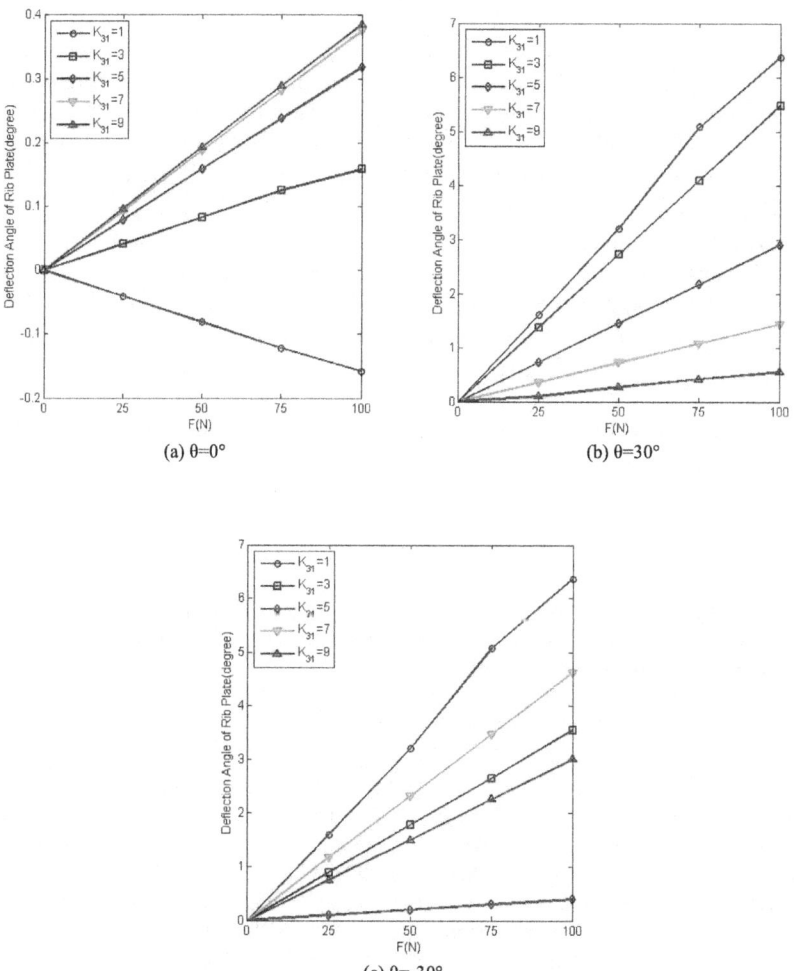

Fig. 9. Simulation comparison of deflection angle.

As shown in Fig. 9(a), it can be seen that the bending angle of morphing wing element increases gradually with the increase of K_{31}, while the bending angle of morphing wing element increases proportionally with the increase of driving force, but the overall bending angle is smaller.

As shown in Fig. 9(b), it can be seen that the bending angle of morphing wing element decreases with the increase of K_{31} value, and increases in proportion with the increase of driving force. The bending angle reaches its maximum at $K_{31} = 1$.

As shown in Fig. 9(c), it can be seen that the bending angle of morphing wing element decreases first and then increases with the increase of K_{31}, while the bending angle of deformed wing element increases proportionally with the increase of driving force. The overall bending angle reaches the maximum at $K_{31} = 1$ and the minimum at $K_{31} = 5$.

6 Conclusions

In this work, a new type of flexible morphing wing driven by shape memory alloy (SMA) is designed by combining 0-Poisson's ratio honeycomb with corrugated plates. The honeycomb structures have the same shape and different thickness. The theoretical modeling of 0-Poisson's ratio honeycomb structure and corrugated plate structure is carried out to calculate the elasticity modulus. The finite element model was established to analyze the effects of different honeycomb thickness ratios K_{31}, corrugated plate thickness ratios K_{21} and corrugated plate angle θ.

As the results of simulation shown, corrugated plate can greatly enhance the z-direction elastic modulus of morphing wing element. Different angles θ of corrugated plate have a greater impact on the z-direction elastic modulus and bending angle. When $K_{31} = 1$, z-direction moving distance and bending angle of morphing wing elements is the largest at $\theta = 30°$ and $\theta = -30°$. The different K_{31} and θ has a great influence on the bending angle of the morphing unit. This will be helpful for application of the morphing wing and more work will to be done in the future.

References

1. Valasek, J.: Morphing Aerospace Vehicle and Structure, New York, CA: Hoboken (2012)
2. Thill, C., Etches, J., Bond, I., et al.: Morphing skins. Aeronaut. J. **112**(1129), 117–139 (2008)
3. Barbarino, S., Friswell, M., Inman, D., et al.: A review of morphing aircraft. J. Intell. Mater. Syst. Struct. **22**(9), 823–877 (2011)
4. Ajaj, R., Beaverstock, C., Friswell, M.: Morphing aircraft: the need for a new design philosophy. Aerosp. Sci. Technol. **49**, 154–166 (2016)
5. Kota, S., et al.: Design and application of compliant mechanisms for morphing aircraft structures. Smart Struct. Mater. **5054**(2), 24–33 (2003)
6. Sherrer, V., Hertz, T., Shirk, M.: Wind tunnel demonstration of aeroelastic tailoring applied to forward swept wings. J. Aircr. **18**(11), 976–983 (2015)
7. Lucato, S., Wang, J., Maxwell, P., et al.: Design and demonstration of a high authority shape morphing structure. Int. J. Solids Struct. **41**(13), 3521–3543 (2004)
8. Ramrkahyani, D.: Morphing aircraft structures using tendon actuated compliant cellular truss. Master's degree thesis of Pennsylvania State University, Pennsylvania (2005)

9. Abdulrahim, M.: Maneuvering control and configuration adaptation of a biologically inspired morphing aircraft. Doctor's degree thesis of University of Florida, Gainesville (2007)
10. Yokozeki, T., Takeda, S., Ogasawara, T., et al.: Mechanical properties of corrugated composites for candidate materials of flexible wing structures. Compos. Part A Appl. Sci. Manuf. **37**(10), 1578–1586 (2006)
11. Olympio, K., Gandhi, F.: Flexible skins for morphing aircraft using cellular honeycomb cores. J. Intell. Mater. Syst. Struct. **21**(17), 1719–1735 (2010)

Design and Analysis of a Novel Metamaterial with Tunable Coefficient of Thermal Expansion

Chunfeng Li[1], Hong Xiao[1]([✉]), Guang Yang[1], Hongwei Guo[1], Yan Xia[2], Runchao Zhao[1], Jianguo Tao[1], and Rongqiang Liu[1]

[1] National Key Laboratory of Aerospace and Mechanism, Harbin Institute of Technology, Harbin 150001, China
xiaohong@hit.edu.cn

[2] China Academy of Launch Vehicle Technology, The First Academy of China Aerospace Science and Technology Corporation, Beijing 100000, China

Abstract. In fields such as flexible electronics and aerospace engineering, where dimensional accuracy demands precise control of thermal deformation, mechanical metamaterials with tunable thermal expansion properties are gaining significant attention. These materials enable thermal expansion matching with surrounding components, ensuring high thermo-mechanical stability under temperature variations. This paper presents the design and analysis of a metamaterial capable of achieving tunable coefficients of thermal expansion (CTE), including positive, zero and negative thermal expansion, through internal bending deformation. A pseudo-rigid-body model is developed to establish a theoretical thermo-mechanical performance model, which is verified by finite element analysis (FEA). The proposed model was employed to conduct parametric analysis on the metamaterial, elucidating the correlation between structural parameters and effective thermomechanical properties, while simultaneously establishing a novel modeling methodology applicable to other mechanical metamaterials. Both theoretical and FEA results demonstrate the capability of the proposed metamaterials to serve as structural or functional components in engineering systems for avoiding undesired thermal expansion mismatch.

Keywords: Metamaterial · Coefficient of thermal expansion · Pseudo-rigid body model

1 Introduction

High-performance and high-precision devices in aerospace fiels are susceptible to suffer large temperature fluctuation and undesired thermal expansion [1, 2]. For example, the surface temperature of hypersonic cruise vehicles may exceed 1000 °C, which makes thermal expansion mismatch and the resulting thermal stresses a critical issue [3]. In morphing wing system, a thermal environment of 2–300 °C leads to movement stuck and structure failure [4]. Addressing thermal expansion mismatch issues requires precise tuning of materials' coefficients of thermal expansion (CTE). Materials with zero thermal expansion (ZTE) and negative thermal expansion (NTE) properties hold significant practical value in advanced engineering applications [5].

© The Author(s), under exclusive license to Springer Nature Singapore Pte Ltd. 2026
T. Matsuno et al. (Eds.): ICIRA 2025, LNAI 16074, pp. 536–546, 2026.
https://doi.org/10.1007/978-981-95-2095-4_44

Metamaterials refer to engineered materials that can regulate mechanical properties by their microstructural geometries rather than by the base materials conventionally. Among them, tunable CTE metamaterials achieve large-scale control of effective CTE through the reasonable arrangement of two materials with different coefficients of thermal expansion. Jefferson et al. proposed reconfigurable thermal expansion structures based on planar hexagonal and square grids. By incorporating flexible structural designs, they achieved isotropic near-zero and negative CTE, where the global expansion is counterbalanced by internal bending deformation [6]. Zhang et al. designed and analyzed a bi-layer rib unit cell, which can be assembled into two-component triangular lattice metamaterials [7]. Chen et al. classified programmable CTE metamaterials into three categories: end-to-end Connection (EC), side-to-side Connection (SC), and the newly proposed Zigzag Connection (ZC), where ZC configuration enables ultra-low thermal stress [8]. The aforementioned studies primarily focus on 2D metamaterials. In the realm of 3D metamaterials, Pasini et al. demonstrated, fabricated, and thermally characterized octet-truss lattice bi-material structures (Al6061-Ti-6Al-4V), which can be tuned to cover a wide range of CTE values [9]. Xu proposed a novel 3-D structure with tunable Poisson's ratio and adjustable thermal expansion by adding the reinforcing rods into the original 2-D star-shaped structure [10]. Peng designed a class of three-dimensional lattice structures of cubic symmetry by spatially assembling and merging a number of two-dimensional re-entrant honeycomb structures, which can exhibit large negative Poisson's ratios and isotropic negative CTE [11].

The theoretical modeling of metamaterials is rather complex, and its analysis and verification mainly rely on the finite element method. Zhang predicted the effective CTE effective stiffness and Poisson's ratio by the stiffness matrix method [12]. Chen establishing the unified and simplified CTE and thermal stress equations for bi-material beams based on the theory of elasticity mechanics [13]. PRBM is a parametric approximation in which the flexural link is modeled as two rigid links joined by a torsional spring. The stiffness coefficient of the spring is determined by the material properties and geometry of the compliant segment [14]. The application of PRBM to metamaterials can achieve efficient analysis of their mechanical properties.

In this paper, we propose a new type of three-dimensional metamaterial element. Then, pseudo-rigid-body model is applied to establish a theoretical model to predict its thermo-mechanical performance. The finite element analysis results verify the accuracy of the theoretical CTE. The effective CTE of this metamaterial cell can be programmed by controlling the geometric parameters and material properties. This metamaterial can be applied as a structural or functional component in engineering systems to avoid unwanted thermal expansion mismatches.

2 Design of Novel Tunable CTE Metamaterial

The main concept examined in this paper relates to the possibility of utilizing flexural bending deformation of the truss member accommodating the overall expansion of the proposed metamaterial. A continuous honeycomb mesh structure is composed of material 1 with relatively low CTE. Material 2 with higher CTE is inserted into each cell, as shown in Fig. 1.

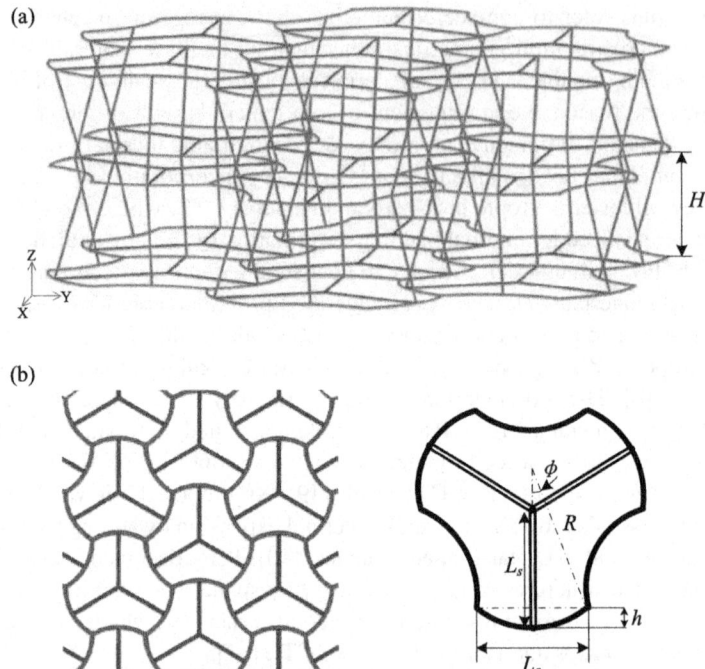

Fig. 1. Design concept of 3-D tunable CTE metamaterial. (a) Schematic reprensentation of the metamaterial; (b) Illustration of the unit cell of the lattice panel.

According to Fig. 1(b), the panel can be difined by honeycomb edge length L_c, the insert support rod L_s, and the arc radius of the edge R. When the temperature rises, the insert support rods expand more thermally, causing the honeycomb edges to bend. The reduced honeycomb size due to bending offsets the overall expansion of the structure. As seen from its structural illustration, this metamaterial exhibits transverse isotropy, meaning its thermal expansion is isotropic within the x-y plane but differs along the z-direction.

3 Analysis and FEA Validation

In this section, we establish the mode to predict its thermal expansion behavior by using pseudo-rigid-body model, thereby providing a theoretical foundation for thermal expansion matching design in advanced engineering applications.

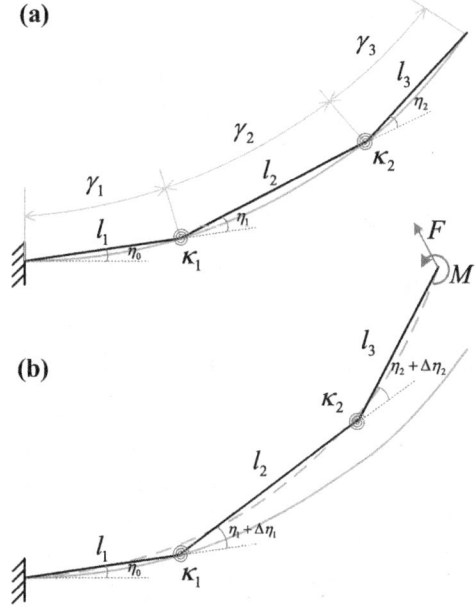

Fig. 2. 2R PRBM model for the curved beam.

3.1 2R PRBM

The 2R PRBM for a curved beam with fix-free segment is shown in Fig. 2. The 2R PRBM consists of three rigid linkages and two torsional spring joints. These two joints separate the beam by length ratio $\gamma_1, \gamma_2, \gamma_3$. Their summation is equal to one. The lengths of the three linkages are represented by l_1, l_2, l_3. And the angles between each linkage are η_1 and η_2. η_0 is the angle between the first linkage and the x-axis. The spring stiffness at the two pin joints can be expressed using dimensionless quantities $k_{\eta i}$ and beam properties EI/L.

$$K_i = k_{\eta i} \frac{EI}{L} \tag{1}$$

The kinematic equations of the 2R PRBM be derived as follows.

$$\begin{bmatrix} x_{tip} \\ y_{tip} \end{bmatrix} = R(\eta_0) \begin{bmatrix} l_1 \\ 0 \end{bmatrix} + R(\eta_0 + \eta_1 + \Delta\eta_1) \begin{bmatrix} l_2 \\ 0 \end{bmatrix} + R(\eta_0 + \eta_1 + \Delta\eta_1 + \eta_2 + \Delta\eta_2) \begin{bmatrix} l_3 \\ 0 \end{bmatrix} \tag{2}$$

$$R(\eta) = \begin{bmatrix} \cos(\eta) & -\sin(\eta) \\ \sin(\eta) & \cos(\eta) \end{bmatrix}$$

$$\begin{bmatrix} x_{tip} \\ y_{tip} \end{bmatrix} = \begin{bmatrix} l_1 \cos(\eta_0) + l_2 \cos(\eta_0 + \eta_1 + \Delta\eta_1) + l_3 \cos(\eta_0 + \eta_1 + \Delta\eta_1 + \eta_2 + \Delta\eta_2) \\ l_1 \sin(\eta_0) + l_2 \sin(\eta_0 + \eta_1 + \Delta\eta_1) + l_3 \sin(\eta_0 + \eta_1 + \Delta\eta_1 + \eta_2 + \Delta\eta_2) \end{bmatrix} \tag{3}$$

Differentiating the kinematic equations in Eq. (3) with respect to joint rotation $\Delta\eta_1$ $\Delta\eta_2$ yields the Jacobian matrix, and the static relationship between external load F, external moment M and joint rotation is expressed as:

$$\begin{bmatrix} K_1 \Delta \eta_1 \\ K_2 \Delta \eta_2 \end{bmatrix} = \mathbf{J}^T \begin{bmatrix} F \cos(\phi) \\ F \sin(\phi) \end{bmatrix} + \begin{bmatrix} M \\ M \end{bmatrix} \quad (4)$$

$$\mathbf{J} = \begin{bmatrix} -l_2 \sin(\eta_0 + \eta_1 + \Delta \eta_1) - l_3 \sin(\eta_0 + \eta_1 + \eta_2 + \Delta \eta_1 + \Delta \eta_2) & -l_3 \sin(\eta_0 + \eta_1 + \eta_2 + \Delta \eta_1 + \Delta \eta_2) \\ l_2 \cos(\eta_0 + \eta_1 + \Delta \eta_1) + l_3 \cos(\eta_0 + \eta_1 + \eta_2 + \Delta \eta_1 + \Delta \eta_2) & l_3 \cos(\eta_0 + \eta_1 + \eta_2 + \Delta \eta_1 + \Delta \eta_2) \end{bmatrix} \quad (5)$$

When K_1, K_2, F, and M are given, these nonlinear equations can be easily solved numerically to obtain $\Delta \eta_1$ and $\Delta \eta_2$. The characteristic parameters of the 2R PRBM were obtained from the optimization model, which is derived by Wang [14].

3.2 Theoretical Model of the Metamaterial

For the honeycomb panels, due to the inherent symmetry of the periodic unit cell, their effective thermal expansion in X-Y plane shows isotropic characteristics, which can obtained through the position of point Q within the periodic frame. The pseudo-rigid body model of the minimum repeating unit of the honeycomb and the representative cell of the metamaterial is shown in Fig. 3.

In the model, the center O is regarded as fixed. Due to symmetry, point Q is constrained to have only degrees of freedom along the diagonal direction OQ. In addition, the moment M acting on point Q is zero, and the direction of the external force F is perpendicular to OQ. In PRBM, the unit cell of the metamaterial is treated as a compliant mechanism. Point O is the fixed origin point of the unit cell. The difference in the coefficient of thermal expansion between different materials is regarded as the linear driving distance of the OP rod. Q coordinate can be expressed as follows.

$$\begin{bmatrix} Q_x \\ Q_y \end{bmatrix} = \begin{bmatrix} P_x \\ P_y \end{bmatrix} + \begin{bmatrix} x_{tip} \\ y_{tip} \end{bmatrix}, \quad Q_y = -\sqrt{3} Q_x \quad (6)$$

$$l_1 = 2R \sin \frac{\gamma_1 \phi}{2}, \quad l_2 = 2R \sin \frac{\gamma_2 \phi}{2}, \quad l_3 = 2R \sin \frac{\gamma_3 \phi}{2}, \quad \eta_0 = \frac{\gamma_1 \phi}{2}, \quad \eta_1 = \frac{\gamma_1 + \gamma_2 \phi}{2}, \quad \eta_2 = \frac{\gamma_2 + \gamma_3 \phi}{2} \quad (7)$$

$$\theta = \arcsin \frac{2\xi}{1+\xi^2}, \quad \xi = \frac{2h}{L} \quad (8)$$

The insert support rod composed of the second material drives point P to move along the y-axis in thermal condition. The coordinates of point P and the arc radius of the curved edge R can be calculated as follows:

$$P = \begin{bmatrix} P_x \\ P_y \end{bmatrix} = \begin{bmatrix} 0 \\ \frac{\sqrt{3}L}{2}(1+\xi)(1+\Delta T \alpha_2) \end{bmatrix} \quad (9)$$

$$R = \frac{\sqrt{3}L(1+\xi^2)(1+\Delta T \alpha_1)}{4\xi} \quad (10)$$

The torsional spring moment at the hinge position balances the moment generated by the external force F at this location. The force equilibrium equation can be derived from Eq. (4), (5). In the PRBM, the external moment M acting on point Q is zero.

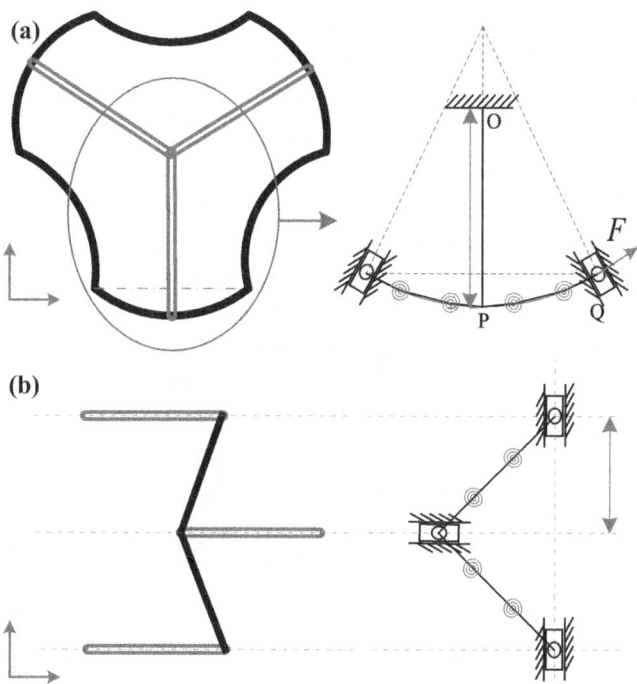

Fig. 3. PRBM for the tunable CTE metamaterial. (a) PRBM for the unit cell of honeycomb panel. (b) PRBM for the stand column in Z-Y plane.

In Z-Y plane, stand column is the rod connect point P in adjacent honeycomb layer as shown in Fig. 3(b). The inclination angle μ_0 are defined by arc depth h and layer height H. And the position equation can be derived as follows.

$$\begin{bmatrix} y^c_{tip} \\ z^c_{tip} \end{bmatrix} = \begin{bmatrix} l_{c1}\cos(\mu_0) + l_{c2}\cos(\mu_0 + \Delta\mu_1) + l_{c3}\cos(\mu_0 + \Delta\mu_1 + \eta_{c2} + \Delta\mu_2) \\ l_{c1}\sin(\mu_0) + l_{c2}\sin(\mu_0 + \Delta\mu_1) + l_{c3}\sin(\mu_0 + \Delta\mu_1 + \eta_{c2} + \Delta\mu_2) \end{bmatrix} \quad (11)$$

$$l_{c1} = \gamma_1 L_c, \quad l_{c2} = \gamma_2 L_c, \quad l_{c3} = \gamma_3 L_c, \quad L_c = \sqrt{H^2 + 4h^2}, \quad \mu_0 = \arctan(\frac{H}{2h}) \quad (12)$$

By combining Eqs. (6) (9) and (11), Q_x, Q_y, Q_z can be derived. Then, the CTE of the metamaterial can be written as $\alpha_{m-inplane} = (2Q_x/L - 1)/\Delta T$, and $\alpha_{m-outplane} = (Q_z - H)/H/\Delta T$.

3.3 FEA Validation

The proposed metamaterial CTE was analyzed using finite element analysis (FEA) in ANSYS Workbench to validate the accuracy of the theoretical model. The default geometric parameters were set as L = 20 mm, H = 10 mm. Stainless steel, Titanium alloy and Aluminum alloy were selected as the base materials. Beam188 elements was applied on the metamaterial with 1mm radius circle cross section. The simulation results are shown in Fig. 4. Figure 4(b) shows the deformation of the unit cell of the honeycomb panel when ξ is 0.4, and the base materials are Steel and Al under 600K. It is clearly seen that the material expand with effective CTE $\alpha_{m-inplane} = 3.83 \times 10^{-6}$. Figure 4(c) shows deformation of the unit cell composed of Ti and Al, which exhibit a negative effective CTE $\alpha_{m-inplane} = -2.23 \times 10^{-6}$.

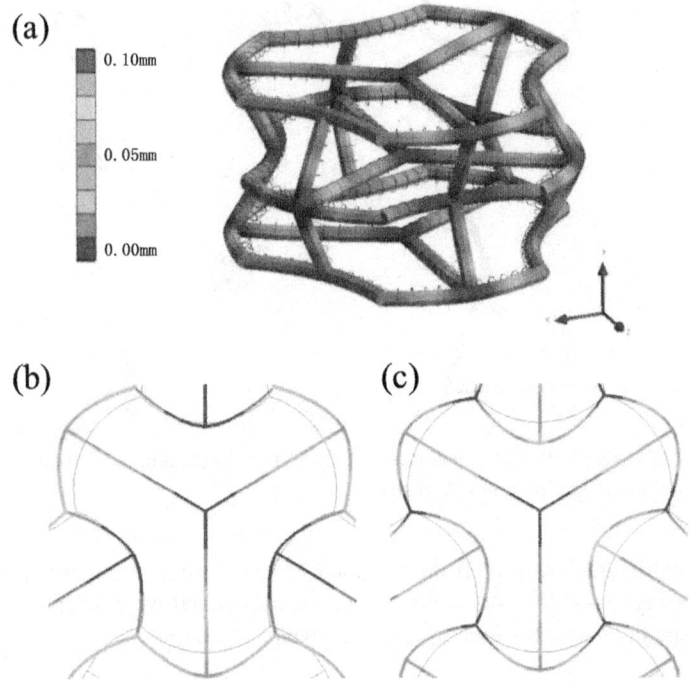

Fig. 4. FEA results of the tunable CTE metamaterial. (a) The unit cell of metamaterial: $\xi =$ 0.2.Ti-Al. (b) The unit cell of honeycomb panel: $\xi = 0.4$, Steel-Al. (c) The unit cell of honeycomb panel:.$\xi = 0.4$, Ti-Al

Figure 5 shows the relative CTE from theoretical and FEA, for various combines of fundamental materials. With these parameters specified, the curvature amplitude $\xi = 2h/L$ is varied to control the structure's CTE. The insets in Fig. 7 schematically illustrate the periodic structure for selected y0 values. For large ξ values, the curvature interferes with adjacent cells.

The results show that the thermal expansion coefficient of the superstructure obtained from theoretical calculations is highly consistent with the simulation results. It can be used to guide the design of structural parameters.

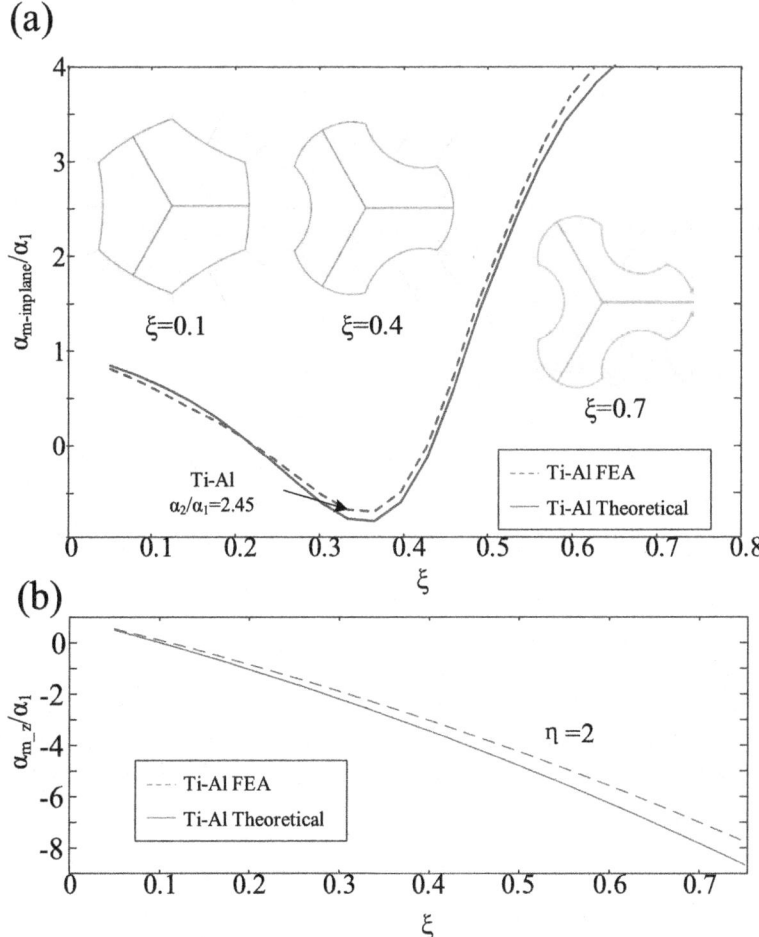

Fig. 5. FEA results of the tunable CTE metamaterial. (a) The unit cell of metamaterial: $\xi = 0.2$.Ti-Al. (b)The unit cell of honeycomb panel: $\xi = 0.4$, Steel-Al. (c) The unit cell of honeycomb panel: $\xi = 0.4$, Ti-Al

4 Parametric Study

To explore the feasible range of material and geometric parameters, a parametric influence analysis was conducted on the metamaterial unit cell. The accuracy of the PRBM has been previously verified. This section investigates the effects of material properties and geometric parameters on the metamaterial's CTE. Figure 6 presents the effective thermal expansion of the metamaterial under different CTE ratios of base materials, as obtained through theoretical calculations. Notably, the minimum CTE occurs near $\xi = 0.35$. This is because when theta is greater than 30°, the reaction force F at point Q exerts a clockwise torque on the curved beam, causing the curved beam to be straightened. Consequently, increasing ξ does not appear to offer practical benefits.

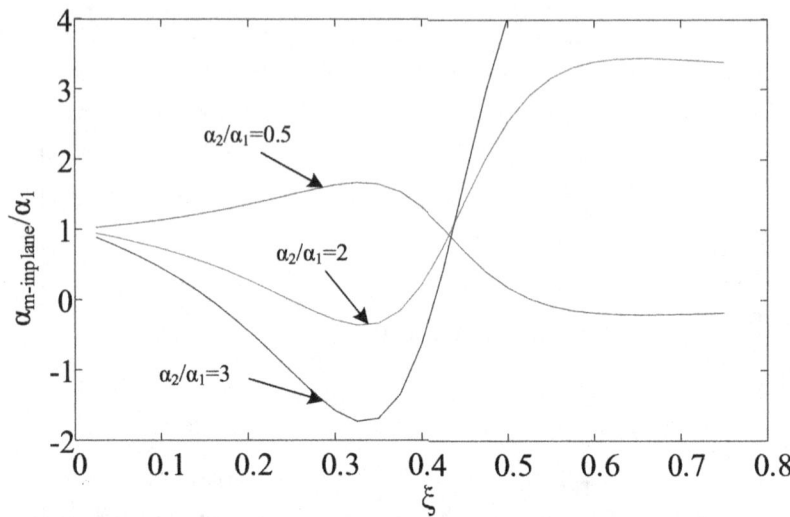

Fig. 6. Effective inplane expansion of a unit cell of honeycomb panel for selected constituent CTE ratios.

Figure 7 illustrates the metamaterial's effective thermal expansion in the z-direction under varying ξ and η values, as derived from theoretical computations. Where $\eta = 2H/L$. As the η value increases (indicating larger panel spacing), the reduction in column inclination angle leads to a z-direction thermal expansion coefficient that asymptotically approaches the intrinsic CTE of the constituent material. When the η value remains

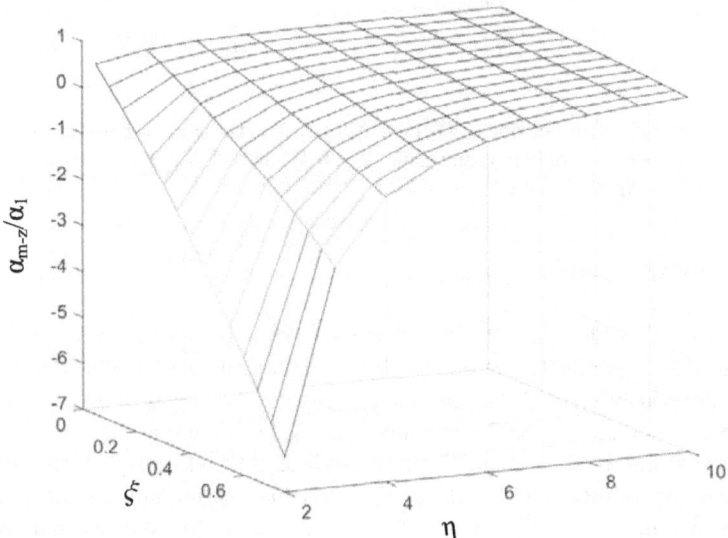

Fig. 7. Variations of effective expansion in z-direction of the metamaterial with different xi and eta.

constant and the ξ value increases, the column inclination angle increases, resulting in a reduction of the metamaterial's z-direction CTE.

5 Conclusion

A three-dimensional tunable coefficient of thermal expansion (CTE) transverse isotropy metamaterial is proposed. A simplified thermal expansion model of the superstructure is established based on the pseudo-rigid-body model, and its accuracy is verified through finite element analysis (FEA). The results demonstrate that the theoretical thermal expansion coefficient of the superstructure closely matches the simulation results. Both theoretical and FEA analyses confirm the proposed metamaterial's capability to serve as structural or functional components in engineering systems, mitigating undesired thermal expansion mismatch. In the future, further analyses will be conducted on the stiffness, strength and failure modes of the proposed structure to provide a theoretical basis for the practical application of this metamaterial.

References

1. Kai, W., Yong, P., et al.: Three dimensional lightweight lattice structures with large positive, zero and negative thermal expansion. Compos. Struct. **188**, 287–296 (2018)
2. Sigmund, O., Torquato, S., et al.: Design of materials with extreme thermal expansion using a three-phase topology optimization method. In: Smart Structures & Materials International Society for Optics and Photonics (1997)
3. Steeves, C.A., Evans, A.G.: Evans, optimization of thermal protection systems utilizing sandwich structures with low coefficient of thermal expansion lattice hot faces. J. Am. Ceram. Soc. **94**(s1), s55–s61 (2011)
4. Chunfeng, L., Jianguo, T., et al.: Thermoelastic dynamic model for a telescopic wing system based on an absolute nodal coordinate formulation deployable thin plate element. Thin-Walled Struct. **213**, 113372 (2025)
5. Sigmund, O., Torquato, S.: Design of materials with extreme thermal expansion using a three-phase topology optimization method. J. Mech. Phys. Solids **45**(6), 1037–1067 (1997)
6. Jefferson, G., Parthasarathy, T.A., Kerans, R.J.: Tailorable thermal expansion hybrid structures. Int. J. Solids Struct. **46**(11–12), 2372–2387 (2009)
7. Zhang, Y.C., Liang, Y.J., Liu, S.T., et al.: A new design of dual-constituent triangular lattice metamaterial with unbounded thermal expansion. Acta. Mech. Sin. **35**(3), 507–517 (2019)
8. Chen, J., Wei, K., Wang, Z., et al.: Metamaterials with modulated coefficient of thermal expansion and ultra-low thermal stress. Int. J. Mech. Sci. **269**, 109072 (2024)
9. Xu, H., Pasini, D.: Structurally efficient three-dimensional metamaterials with controllable thermal expansion. Sci. Rep. **6**, 34924 (2016)
10. Xu, N., Liu, H.T.: A novel 3-D structure with tunable Poisson's ratio and adjustable thermal expansion. Compos. Commun. **22**(1782), 10043 (2020)
11. Peng, X.L., Bargmann, S.: Tunable auxeticity and isotropic negative thermal expansion in three-dimensional lattice structures of cubic symmetry. Extreme Mech. Lett. **43**, 101201 (2021)
12. Zhang, Q., Sun, Y.: Novel metamaterial structures with negative thermal expansion and tunable mechanical properties. Int. J. Mech. Sci. **261**, 108692 (2023)

13. Chen, J., Xu, W., Wei, Z., et al.: Stiffness characteristics for a series of lightweight mechanical metamaterials with programmable thermal expansion. Int. J. Mech. Sci. **202–203**, 106527 (2021)
14. Weishen, W., Mohui, J., et al.: Two PRBMs of Euler spiral segments and their chained models for analyzing general curved beams in compliant mechanisms. Mech. Mach. Theory **204**, 105838 (2024)

Neural Implicit Embedded PWM Control Approach for Dielectric Elastomer Actuators with Rate-Dependent Viscoelasticity

Xuning Gou[1,2], Xingyu Chen[1,2], Guoying Gu[1,2], and Jiang Zou[1,2(✉)]

[1] Robotics Institute, School of Mechanical Engineering, Shanghai Jiao Tong University, Shanghai 200240, China
zoujiang@sjtu.edu.cn
[2] State Key Laboratory of Mechanical System and Vibration, School of Mechanical Engineering, Shanghai Jiao Tong University, Shanghai 200240, China

Abstract. The precise control of dielectric elastomer actuators (DEAs) usually relies on cumbersome power devices to generate continuous and complex control signals, hindering the miniaturization of DEA-based soft robots. To solve the above problem, a Neural Implicit Embedded Pulse Width Modulated (PWM) Controller (NEPC) is proposed to generate multilevel PWM signals to compensate for the rate-dependent viscoelasticity and mechanical vibration of DEAs. To this end, we first establish a lumped-parameter dynamic model to characterize the nonlinear dynamic responses of the DEA, which is used to generate data for controller training. Next, the NEPC, composed of three parts: (1) the Neural Implicit Embedded Controller (NEC) module, (2) the PWM generator, and (3) an end-to-end training framework, is developed and trained to generate multilevel PWM signals. Finally, different tracking experiments are conducted to verify the effectiveness of our control method. The experimental results of different frequencies and trajectories demonstrate that the NEPC can eliminate the rate-dependent viscoelasticity and mechanical vibration of DEAs. The maximum tracking error and root mean square error are reduced by 37.39% and 19.57% at 5 Hz, respectively.

Keywords: Dielectric elastomer actuator · Soft robotics · Learning-based control · Multilevel PWM · Rate-dependent viscoelasticity

1 Introduction

Dielectric elastomer actuators (DEAs) have garnered significant attention in soft robotics due to their high energy density, large deformation, fast response speed,

---

X. Gou and X. Chen—Contributed equally to this work.
This work was supported in part by Natural Science Foundation of Shanghai under Grant 24511103602, and in part by National Natural Science Foundation of China under Grant 52275024.

and lightweight structure [1–3]. With the increasing deployment of DEA-based robots–such as climbing robots [4], underwater explorers [5], aerial robots [6], and wearable devices [7]–high-precision and untethered tracking control of DEA systems has become more and more important. However, due to the viscoelasticity and mechanical vibration, the dynamic responses of DEAs usually suffer from serious nonlinearity, leading to a great challenge. Especially, for the untethered DEA-based robots, limited control hardware cannot generate the desired continuous control signal, further increasing the difficulty of control.

In previous work, three categories of control methods have been proposed: (1) Direct inverse hysteresis control is based on phenomenological models, such as Prandtl-Ishlinskii [8,9] and Backlash models [10]. Phenomenological models use fewer parameters and rely solely on experimental data, giving them strong extensibility. These controllers can effectively address rate-dependent viscoelasticity. However, their operating frequency typically remains below the DEA's natural frequency, because phenomenological models cannot capture the mechanical resonance. (2) Nonlinear controllers, such as nonlinear PID, adaptive sliding-mode control and H-infinity control [11–13], depend on lumped-parameter models capable of describing viscoelasticity, mechanical resonance, and their coupling. They can accurately track static or low-frequency periodic trajectories. However, as the frequency increases, the coupling between viscoelasticity and mechanical vibration degrades performance and limits the usable bandwidth of these controllers. (3) Learning-based controllers, such as NARX neural network based control, GRU neural network based control and neural implicit embedded control (NEC) [14–16], leverage neural networks' strong nonlinear fitting capability to train directly on experimental data without complex mathematical derivations, effectively eliminating the DEA's nonlinearity, including viscoelastic hysteresis and creep. However, their performance remains constrained by network size and data volume. These methods above output continuous voltage to drive the DEAs, imposing stringent requirements on high-voltage amplifier bandwidth and resolution. Hence, they are ill-suited for integrated, miniaturized designs.

Existing portable high-voltage power supplies for DEAs typically output square wave signals and cannot simultaneously deliver high voltage and high frequency [17,18]. Achieving precise DEA control via PWM signals, which are better suited to the integrated design, is therefore an urgent challenge. One possible approach is carrier-comparison based on the area equivalence principle, which directly converts a continuous control voltage output by controllers above into a PWM signal [19]. Under the converted PWM signal, a pure inertial load yields a substantially similar dynamic response [20,21]. However, DEAs cannot be accurately modeled as a pure inertial element because of the complex dynamics. Consequently, directly applying the converted PWM signal to the DEA introduces substantial control errors. To eliminate the errors, we can introduce a learning-based approach that leverages the end-to-end optimization capability of neural networks. In consideration of the NEC's demonstrated ability to adapt to variations in the frequency and amplitude of desired trajectories, we adopt the NEC framework, resulting in the Neural Implicit Embedded Pulse Width Modulated (PWM) Controller (NEPC). First, we develop an equivalent dynamic model of the DEA to generate a large volume of stable training data. Next, we design the NEPC architecture, comprising three modules: (1) the NEC module, which generates a continuous intermediate voltage; (2) the PWM generator, which employs an adaptive carrier-generation scheme and gradient-preserving carrier comparison to produce a multilevel PWM voltage; and (3) the end-to-end training framework, in which a tailored loss function is evaluated and gradients are propagated through both the NEC and PWM modules to optimize parameters. Subsequent experiments demonstrate that the proposed controller can adaptively track trajectories with varying amplitudes and frequencies.

The remainder of this paper is organized as follows. Section 2 presents the experimental setup and formalizes the problem definition. Section 3 details the architecture and design of the NEPC. Section 4 describes the experimental procedures and analyzes the results to demonstrate the controller's performance. Finally, Sect. 5 concludes the paper.

2 System Description

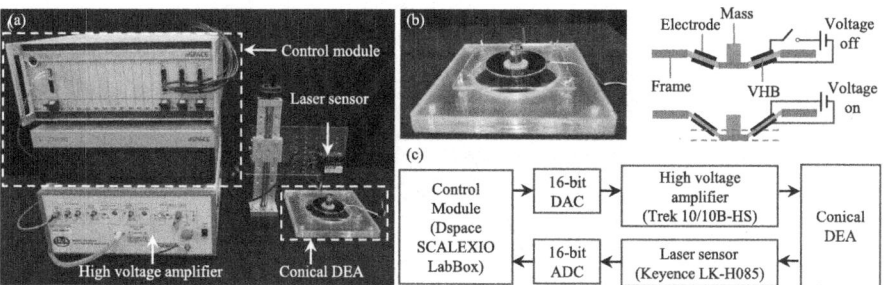

Fig. 1. Experimental setup. (a) Experimental equipment. (b) Conical DEA used in this work. (c) Block diagram representation.

2.1 Experimental Setup

To characterize the dynamic responses of the DEAs and verify the effectiveness of our control strategy, we establish an experimental setup, shown in Fig. 1(a) and (b). A conical DEA is fabricated for proof-of-concept testing. The actuator consists of an equibiaxially prestretched DE membrane (VHB4910, prestretched by a factor of 3), a mass, and an acrylic mounting frame. Control signals are generated by a dSPACE SCALEXIO LabBox, which drives a Trek 10/10B-HS high-voltage amplifier with a gain of 1000. The output voltage of the amplifier is limited to no more than 5 kV to ensure safe operation below the DEA breakdown threshold (approximately 6 kV). The conical DEA is positioned below a Keyence LK-H085 laser displacement sensor. During operation, the laser sensor converts the measured displacement into an analog signal, which is routed back into the LabBox via a 16-bit ADC. Figure 1(c) presents the block diagram of the system.

2.2 Characterization of Dynamic Responses

Based on the above experimental setup, we firstly investigate the dynamic responses of DEAs under sinusoidal voltages with different frequencies, as shown in Fig. 2. The resulting hysteresis loops vary with frequency, exhibiting pronounced rate-dependent behavior and asymmetry. Notably, at 3.94 Hz, 4.5 Hz, and 5 Hz, some portions of the displacement fall below 0, a consequence of operating near the actuator's resonance frequencies. In addition, the inherent viscoelasticity of the DEA gives rise to creep [22]. Therefore, achieving high precision control of the DEA requires two key mitigations:

(1) Nonlinear, rate-dependent hysteresis compensation, to extend the actuator's usable bandwidth;
(2) Viscoelastic creep reduction, to suppress time-dependent drift in the dynamic response and maintain consistent performance over prolonged operation.

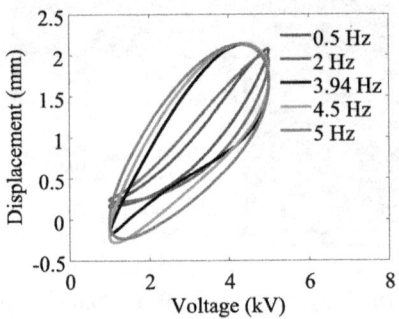

Fig. 2. Hysteresis loops of the DEA in several frequencies. The input voltage is sinusoidal voltage.

2.3 Dynamic Modeling

To accurately capture the complex dynamic behavior of DEA, we adopt the lumped-parameter model from [12]. The structure of the dynamic model can be expressed as follows:

$$m\ddot{x} + \eta_0 \dot{x} + px + qx^2 + \sum_{i=1}^{n} k_i z_i = U^2(ax^2 + bx + c) \qquad (1)$$

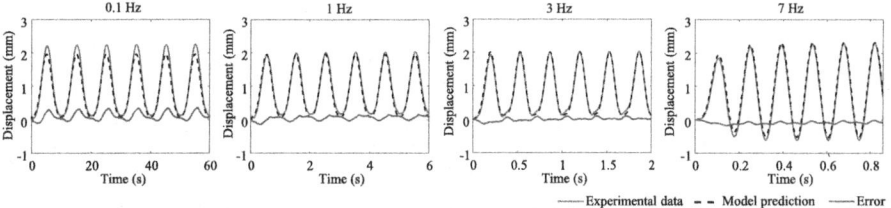

Fig. 3. The identification results in several test frequencies.

Table 1. Identified parameters of the dynamic model

Parameter	Value	Parameter	Value	Parameter	Value
m	0.0842	q	0	η_4	93.7505
a	0	η_0	0.0046	k_1	19.5557
b	0.0022	η_1	0.1810	k_2	123.1417
c	0.0081	η_2	2.6794	k_3	0.5387
p	103.1931	η_3	3.1911	k_4	0.0396

$$k_i z_i = \eta_i (\dot{x} - \dot{z}_i) \tag{2}$$

where m and η_0 denote the mass and damping coefficient, respectively; a, b, c, p and q are constant model parameters; k_i and z_i represent the stiffness and displacement of the spring within the i-th rheological unit; η_i is the damping coefficient of the damper within the i-th rheological unit; n is the total number of rheological units; U is the input voltage, and x is the output displacement.

We apply twelve sinusoidal voltage inputs–each with amplitude ranging from 1 kV to 5 kV at distinct frequencies–sampled at 1 kHz for 60 s, to the physical conical DEA, recording its displacement response. Using the collected data, all parameters of the equivalent dynamic model are identified based on the Bayesian optimization algorithm. The result is listed in Table 1. The fit of the model at several representative frequencies is shown in Fig. 3. As can be seen, the identified model accurately reproduces the dynamic response of the DEA.

2.4 Problem Definition

Building upon the identified dynamic model, we define the control problem as follows:

$$(\theta_i^*)_{1 \times m} = \arg\min_{\theta_1, \theta_2, ..., \theta_m} \| M(U_e | \theta_1, \theta_2, ..., \theta_m) - x_e \| \tag{3}$$

$$U_p = P(x_d | \lambda_1, \lambda_2, ..., \lambda_n) \tag{4}$$

$$x_p = M(U_p | \theta_1^*, \theta_2^*, ..., \theta_m^*) \tag{5}$$

$$(\lambda_j^*)_{1\times n} = \underset{\lambda_1,\lambda_2,...,\lambda_n}{\arg\min} \ (L(x_d, x_p)) \tag{6}$$

where M denotes the equivalent dynamic model, U_e is the excitation voltage used during system identification, x_e is the measured displacement, P represents the PWM controller model, U_p is the PWM voltage generated by the controller, x_d is the desired displacement trajectory, and x_p is the predicted displacement produced by the dynamic model. L denotes the defined loss function used to evaluate the tracking performance. The core problem is to develop a differentiable PWM conversion module that transforms the NEC's continuous voltage output into a multilevel PWM signal while preserving gradient flow to enable end-to-end network training. To address this problem, we propose the following Neural Implicit Embedded PWM Controller.

3 Design of NEPC

Based on the voltage conversion and gradient preservation issues outlined in Section II, we design the NEPC.

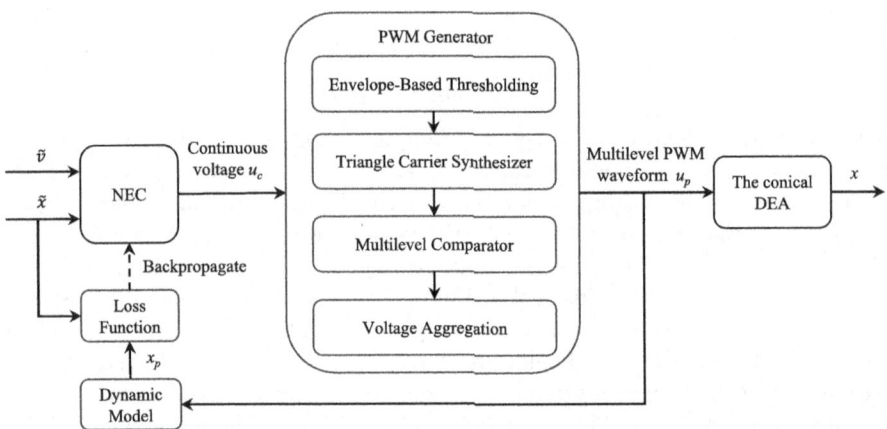

Fig. 4. Schematic diagram of the NEPC

To enable automatic end-to-end parameter optimization while constraining the output waveform, we propose an architecture comprising three main parts, as illustrated in Fig. 4: (1) The NEC module [16]. The NEC produces a continuous intermediate voltage U_c tailored to the desired displacement trajectory. (2) The PWM Generator. Inspired by multilevel carrier comparison techniques in power electronics [19], our approach transforms the continuous reference U_c into a multilevel PWM U_p via triangle carrier comparison. (3) The end-to-end training framework. Compute the DEA displacement output using the equivalent dynamic model, then evaluate the loss with the loss function and perform backpropagation to optimize the network parameters.

3.1 Carriers Generation Method

The generation of the triangular carriers is divided into two main steps. First, to ensure that the carrier's amplitude is compatible with the amplitude of the continuous voltage U_c output by the NEC, we compute the envelope signal $A(t)$ of the U_c via the Hilbert transform. Then, the 95th-percentile value of $A(t)$ is selected as the maximum amplitude of the PWM voltage $U_{\max}$. Second, triangular carriers are generated based on $U_{\max}$, as shown in Eqs. (7)–(10)

$$\Delta v = \frac{U_{\max}}{L} \tag{7}$$

$$\alpha = \frac{2}{T} \times (t \bmod T) \tag{8}$$

$$B_j = (j-1) \times \Delta v \, , j = 1, ..., L \tag{9}$$

$$C_j(t) = B_j + \Delta v(1 - |\alpha - 1|) \, , j = 1, ..., L \tag{10}$$

where L denotes the number of carriers, Δv is the amplitude of each triangular carrier, α is the phase, T is the carrier period, B_j is the valley level of the j-th carrier, $C_j(t)$ denotes the value of the triangular carrier.

3.2 Gradient Preserving PWM Conversion

The PWM conversion is also conducted in two steps. In the first step, a multilevel comparator converts the NEC's output U_c into a set of binary switching signals by comparing it against a bank of triangular carriers C_j. Specifically, each carrier produces a corresponding logic output $b_j(t)$, as shown in Eq. (11):

$$b_j(t) = \begin{cases} 1, & U_c(t) > C_j(t) + \delta_j(t) \\ 0, & otherwise \end{cases} , j = 1, ..., L \tag{11}$$

where $\delta_j(t)$ is an offset term proportional to the first derivative of U_c. However, Eq. (11) is a piecewise constant function, which interrupts the gradient flow from b_j to U_c and thus hinders gradient-based optimization. To enable end-to-end training, we replace it with the differentiable approximation given in Eq. (12):

$$s_j(t) = sigmoid(k \times [U_c(t) - C_j(t) - \delta_j(t)]) \, , j = 1, ..., L \tag{12}$$

$$b_j(t) = round(s_j(j)) \, , j = 1, ..., L \tag{13}$$

where $k > 0$ is a constant coefficient, *sigmoid* is the logistic activation function, and *round* is the rounding operator. As k increases, *sigmoid* more closely approximates the ideal comparator output. We then obtain the binary switching signal $b_j(t)$ according to Eq. (13). To preserve gradient flow during backpropagation, we employ a Straight-Through Estimator (STE) [23], taking the gradient of the comparator from *sigmoid* instead of *round*. Thus, although b_j is discrete in the forward pass, meaningful gradients still propagate back to U_c in the backward pass.

In the second step, the PWM output is generated by voltage aggregation based on the binary signals $b_j(t)$, as shown in Eq. (14):

$$U_p(t) = \sum_{j=1}^{L} b_j(t) \Delta v \tag{14}$$

where Δv is the carrier amplitude.

Finally, the generated PWM signal $U_p(t)$ is fed into the equivalent dynamic model M to produce the predicted displacement trajectory. We then compute the loss using the designed loss function. This loss is backpropagated through the entire network, including the differentiable PWM conversion module, to update the network parameters and minimize the trajectory tracking loss.

4 Experiments

4.1 Implementation

Network Hyperparameters: The temporal sampling window length is set to 20, and the training batch size is 30. The learning rate schedule follows Eq. (15). The loss function is defined in Eq. (16), where $c_1 = 50$ and $c_2 = 4000$. These weights are chosen to balance the difference in order of magnitude between displacement and velocity errors. The number of network layers and the dimensions of the convolutional kernel are chosen according to the values reported in [16].

$$lr = 8 \times 10^{-4} \times 0.971^{epoch} \tag{15}$$

$$loss = c_1 \times L1\left(x_d, x_p\right) + c_2 \times L1(v_d, v_p) \tag{16}$$

Dataset: With the identified model, we generate a displacement data set under sinusoidal voltage inputs. To avoid mechanical resonance, we restrict the training frequency range to 0.1–4.9 Hz. Because the lowest and highest training frequencies differ by nearly a factor of 50, we allocate different recording durations to each segment so that all segments cover approximately the same number of cycles under limited computational resources: (1) 0.1–0.5 Hz for 30 s. (2) 0.5–1 Hz for 15 s. (3) 1–3 Hz for 7.5 s. (4) 3–4.9 Hz for 9 s. To ensure consistency across all segments, the sampling interval is fixed at 0.0025 s.

PWM Parameters: To reduce the instantaneous voltage span, the PWM is configured with discrete levels $L = 5$, and the carrier period is set to 20 times the sampling interval to ensure sufficient PWM resolution.

Hardware and Software: All network training and testing are implemented in PyTorch and execute on an RTX 3090 GPU with a 24 core CPU.

Evaluation Metrics: We evaluate both training and experimental performance using MAE (Mean Absolute Error), RME (Relative Maximum Error), RMAE (Relative Mean Absolute Error), and RRMSE (Relative Root Mean Square Error) [16].

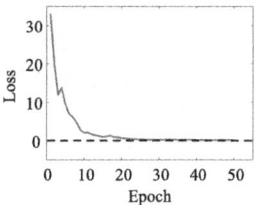

Fig. 5. The training loss over 50 epochs.

4.2 Voltage Generation

The training target trajectories consist of a series of sinusoidal trajectories at specific frequencies. During training, the loss decreases rapidly and approaches zero as illustrated in Fig. 5, demonstrating convergence. The resulting voltage outputs are shown in Fig. 6(a). Once the model is trained, it can generate 3600 feedforward control voltages for a given trajectory in just 75 ms, using only about 755 MB of GPU memory. Due to its fast inference speed and low memory consumption, the model has the potential to be deployed on small embedded devices for real-time inference. However, this depends on the specific hardware configuration and can be explored in future work.

Table 2. Tracking errors on training and test datasets

Frequency/Hz	Training Duration (≤ 15 s)			Test Duration (40 s)			Without Controller		
	RME/%	RMAE/%	RRMSE/%	RME/%	RMAE/%	RRMSE/%	RME/%	RMAE/%	RRMSE/%
1.000	16.07	5.18	6.24	24.53	7.63	9.75	31.00	8.49	11.37
2.000	21.90	5.32	7.55	22.91	6.98	9.26	38.68	11.42	14.27
3.000	21.71	6.13	7.53	25.45	7.50	9.54	47.78	14.22	18.21
4.000	14.60	4.43	5.67	17.67	7.05	8.56	49.85	17.20	20.18
1.307	19.23	5.84	7.22	21.43	6.40	8.09	32.51	8.89	12.06
2.410	24.80	6.77	8.50	23.11	7.10	8.88	42.38	11.75	15.94
3.940	16.21	4.65	5.76	24.43	5.70	7.18	46.79	16.14	19.07
5.000	13.62	4.56	5.73	18.18	7.72	8.97	51.01	22.67	25.30

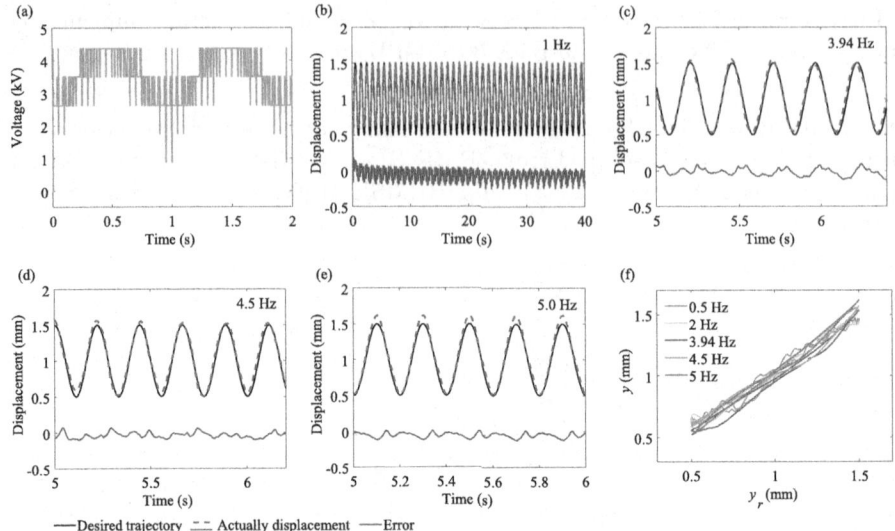

Fig. 6. Experimental results of tracking sinusoidal trajectories. (a) Control voltage generated by the controller for tracking a 1 Hz sinusoidal trajectory; (b) Experimental results in 1 Hz; (c) Experimental results in 3.94 Hz; (d) Experimental results in 4.5 Hz; (e) Experimental results in 5 Hz; (f) The hysteresis loops of the NEPC.

4.3 Experimental Testing

In feedforward experiments, we evaluate the controller's ability to track sinusoidal trajectories at various frequencies on the physical conical DEA. The resulting displacement outputs are shown in Fig. 6. These results demonstrate that NEPC effectively mitigates the inherent nonlinearities of the DEA. In a 1 Hz long-duration test, the controller also successfully eliminates viscoelastic creep.

To further validate the controller's generalization, we test several frequencies that are not included in the training dataset–both within and beyond the original training duration. The detailed tracking errors are listed in Table 2. Even in the feedforward situation, our controller achieves precise tracking for both training and test frequencies, confirming its frequency-domain generalization capability. In addition, when tested over durations that exceed those used in training, the controller continues to maintain accurate trajectory tracking, indicating that it has learned and compensated for time-dependent creep, thus exhibiting time-domain generalization. When comparing the hysteresis loops in Fig. 2 (without control) with those in Fig. 6(f) (with NEPC), there is a marked reduction in loop width, demonstrating effective suppression of rate-dependent hysteresis.

Beyond sinusoidal signals, we also track triangular and frequency-sweep trajectories, as shown in Fig. 7. The results confirm that the controller can accurately track signals throughout the continuous frequency band of its operational range.

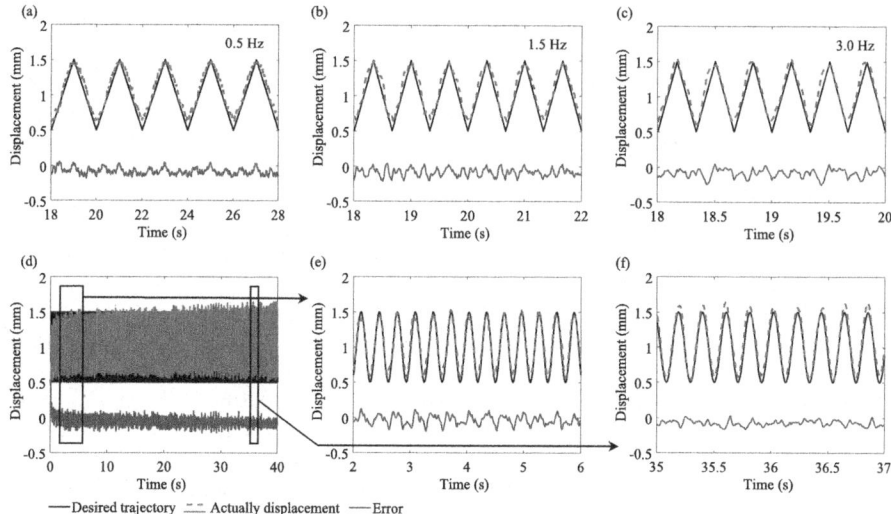

Fig. 7. Experimental results of tracking different complex trajectories through the NEPC. (a) The triangular wave in 0.5 Hz; (b) The triangular wave in 1.5 Hz; (c) The triangular wave in 3 Hz; (d) Sweep signals (3 to 5 Hz); (e) The sweep signal between 2 s and 6 s (3.1 to 3.3 Hz); (f) The sweep signal between 35 s and 37 s (4.75 to 4.85 Hz).

5 Conclusion

In this work, we propose a Neural Implicit Embedded PWM controller for DEAs' precise tracking control. First, a lumped-parameter model is identified to capture the DEA's complex dynamic response. Based on this model, an NEPC is designed to generate PWM signals that eliminate the nonlinearity of DEAs. In experiments, the controller successfully tracks sinusoidal, triangular, and frequency-sweep trajectories, demonstrating that our feedforward-based approach can effectively eliminate the DEA's rate-dependent viscoelasticity and mechanical vibration. In future work, we will leverage larger datasets, further optimize carrier parameters, and adapt the method to the performance constraints of embedded hardware to accelerate its practical applications.

References

1. Pelrine, R., et al.: High-speed electrically actuated elastomers with strain greater than 100%. Science **287**(5454), 836–839 (2000)
2. Gu, G., et al.: A survey on dielectric elastomer actuators for soft robots. Bioinspir. Biomim. **12**(1), 011003 (2017)
3. Wang, Y., et al.: Bio-inspired transparent soft jellyfish robot. Soft Rob. **10**(3), 590–600 (2023)
4. Gu, G., et al.: Soft wall-climbing robots. Sci. Robot. **3**(25), eaat2874 (2018)
5. Li, G., et al.: Self-powered soft robot in the mariana trench. Nature **591**(7848), 66–71 (2021)

6. Chen, Y., et al.: Controlled flight of a microrobot powered by soft artificial muscles. Nature **575**(7782), 324–329 (2019)
7. Zhao, H., et al.: A wearable soft haptic communicator based on dielectric elastomer actuators. Soft Rob. **7**(4), 451–461 (2020)
8. Zou, J., Gu, G.: Feedforward control of the rate-dependent viscoelastic hysteresis nonlinearity in dielectric elastomer actuators. IEEE Robot. Autom. Lett. **4**(3), 2340–2347 (2019)
9. Zou, J., Gu, G.: High-precision tracking control of a soft dielectric elastomer actuator with inverse viscoelastic hysteresis compensation. IEEE/ASME Trans. Mechatron. **24**(1), 36–44 (2018)
10. Li, Z., et al.: Development of a butterfly fractional-order backlash-like hysteresis model for dielectric elastomer actuators. IEEE Trans. Industr. Electron. **70**(2), 1794–1801 (2023)
11. Rizzello, G., et al.: Robust position control of dielectric elastomer actuators based on LMI optimization. IEEE Trans. Control Syst. Technol. **24**(6), 1909–1921 (2016)
12. Zou, J., et al.: A generalized motion control framework of dielectric elastomer actuators: dynamic modeling, sliding-mode control and experimental evaluation. IEEE Trans. Rob. **40**, 919–935 (2023)
13. Ye, Z., Chen, Z.: Modeling and control of a 2-DoF dielectric elastomer diaphragm actuator. IEEE/ASME Trans. Mechatron. **24**(1), 218–227 (2019)
14. Huang, P., et al.: Self-sensing motion control of dielectric elastomer actuator based on narx neural network and iterative learning control architecture. IEEE/ASME Trans. Mechatron. **29**(2), 1374–1384 (2023)
15. Zhang, Y., et al.: Inverse dynamics modelling and tracking control of conical dielectric elastomer actuator based on GRU neural network. Eng. Appl. Artif. Intell. **118**, 105668 (2023)
16. Chen, X., et al.: Dynamic model based neural implicit embedded tracking control approach for dielectric elastomer actuators with rate-dependent viscoelasticity. IEEE Robot. Autom. Lett. **9**(10), 9031–9038 (2024)
17. Shao, Q., et al.: Portable, high-frequency, and high-voltage control circuits for untethered miniature robots driven by dielectric elastomer actuators. arXiv preprint arXiv:2502.06166 (2025)
18. Schlatter, S., et al.: Peta-pico-voltron: an open-source high voltage power supply. HardwareX **4**, e00039 (2018)
19. Baimel, D., et al.: A review of carrier based PWM techniques for multilevel inverters control. WSEAS Trans. Power Syst. **12**, 165–170 (2017)
20. Jiang, D., et al.: Advanced pulse-width-modulation: With freedom to optimize power electronics converters. Springer (2021)
21. Erickson, R.W., Maksimovic, D.: Fundamentals of power electronics. Springer (2007)
22. Yan, P., et al.: Mitigating the coupled effects of rate-dependent viscoelasticity and mechanical resonance in dielectric elastomer actuators via modified repetitive control. IEEE/ASME Trans. Mechatron. (2024)
23. Bengio, Y., et al.: Estimating or propagating gradients through stochastic neurons for conditional computation. arXiv preprint arXiv:1308.3432 (2013)

Design of a Rigid–Elastic–Soft Coupled DELTA Mechanism with Variable Cartesian Stiffness

Xingyue Zhu[1], Zhenkun Liang[1], Hao Yuan[2], Hao Wang[1], and Genliang Chen[1,2(✉)]

[1] State Key Laboratory of Mechanical Systems and Vibration, Shanghai Jiao Tong University, Shanghai 200240, China
[2] Meta Robotics Institute, Shanghai Jiao Tong University, Shanghai 200240, China
leungchan@sjtu.edu.cn

Abstract. To meet the dual requirements of precise positioning and passive compliance in variable-stiffness robots, we propose a rigidelasticsoft coupled DELTA mechanism. The mechanism replaces the traditional DELTA's active revolute joints with a plug-and-play pneumaticmotor hybrid drive module: the motor actuator provides precise positioning, while the serially connected fabric origami chamber achieves programmable compliance via internal pressure control. Benefiting from the module's redundant actuation and precisely modelable forcedisplacement characteristics, the system introduces a 27% increase in variable stiffness without altering its original size or maximum stiffness. Based on a kinetostatic analysis, we established a forceequilibrium model incorporating external loads, which reveals the differences in output force and stiffness of the fabric origami chamber under varying internal pressures at the same configuration. Furthermore, we developed a stiffness model of the DELTA mechanism under three independently adjustable stiffness actuation units. A prototype was designed and tested, demonstrating that the vertical stiffness at the end effector increases from 4.71 N/mm to 5.99 N/mm as the internal pressure of the chamber increases from 0 kPa to 20 kPa. This work provides a generalizable path for upgrading traditional rigid mechanisms into high-precision, adaptive robots and demonstrates a new paradigm for parallel robots in collaborative manufacturing, precision tasks, and rapid environment switching.

Keywords: rigidelasticsoft coupling · DELTA mechanism · variable stiffness · origami pneumatic · hybrid actuation

1 Introduction

Robots now require tunable stiffness to balance precision and safety: high stiffness enables accurate positioning and force, while low stiffness improves compliance in unstructured settings. Fixed-stiffness robots cannot satisfy both simultaneously. Variable-stiffness mechanisms embed elastic or soft elements into joints or drives to adjust stiffness on the fly.

These mechanisms fall into three categories: pure rigid, pure soft, and rigid-soft hybrids. Pure rigid designs use mechanical structures for discrete or continuous stiffness adjustment, offering fast response and high precision but limited compliance range and higher complexity and weight [1–6]. Pure soft designs exploit material property changes (e.g., granular jamming [7,8], phase-change materials [9]) or embedded structures [10,11], yielding excellent compliance and safety but limited maximum stiffness and slower response.

Rigid–soft hybrids combine a rigid frame with flexible actuators to achieve wide stiffness range with maintained precision. For example, Zhu et al. [12] developed a pneumatic–tendon actuator (0.7–23.6 N), and Zhang et al. [13,14] used fabric origami chambers for multimodal motion and stiffness tuning. However, hybrid compliance complicates drive coordination and demands precise force–displacement modeling for control.

The fabric origami chamber offers programmable deformation and precise force–displacement modeling, making it ideal for rigid–elastic–soft hybrid drives. Its soft yet unstretchable fabric guides inflation directionally while remaining strong and lightweight [15,16], enabling high-force, large-stroke, fast-response actuators. Rigid origami creases prevent unwanted bulging, improving motion accuracy [17–19]. For example, Gao et al. [20] used fabric–TPU skins and paper creases to achieve durable pure bending, and Long et al. [21] combined an elastic plate with asymmetric origami to build a pneumatic actuator with 22.5 N output and 2 mm precision.

Building on our previous rigid–elastic–soft pneumatic actuator [21], this study applies it to a conventional DELTA mechanism. We designed a parallel drive for each DOF using a motor and pneumatic actuator, and extended the chamber's kineto-static model to include external loads. We then developed both the chamber's variable-stiffness model and the DELTA's global stiffness model, built a prototype, and measured a stiffness increase of approximately 27% at a fixed pose. This variable-stiffness DELTA shows strong potential for collaborative assembly, millimeter-level positioning, and rapid rigid–soft transitions, markedly improving safety and efficiency in electronic component insertion and biological sample handling.

2 Design

2.1 Overall DELTA Mechanism Design

On the basis of the traditional rigid parallel DELTA mechanism, to achieve the effect of rigid–elastic–soft coupling drive, the traditional active revolute joint is replaced by a pneumatic–motor hybrid drive module, as shown in Fig. 1. Unlike the conventional guide-rail slider four-bar mechanism, this module uses the slider as the linear input end, and its input link is replaced by a rigid–elastic–soft coupled pneumatic actuator, which integrates passive compliance and active driving functionality. This replacement introduces redundant actuation to the mechanism.

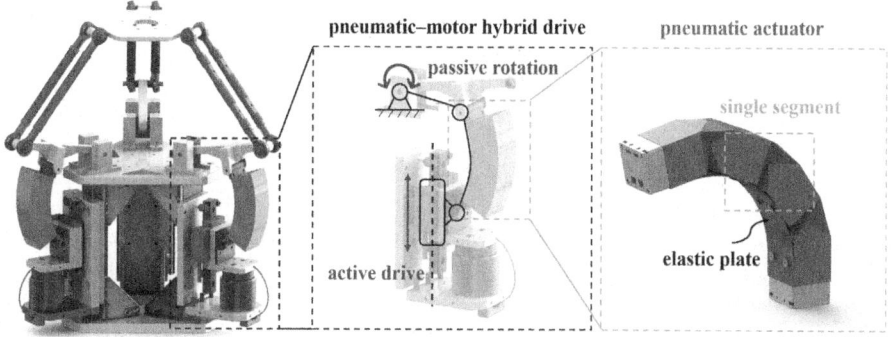

Fig. 1. Design of the DELTA mechanism.

The advantage of the pneumatic–motor hybrid drive is that, after the motor actuator drives the pneumatic actuator to a specified pose, by controlling the internal air pressure, the elastic plate undergoes active deformation, which macroscopically is equivalent to changes in the length and stiffness of the replaced rigid link. This change enables the passive rotation output of the pneumatic–motor hybrid drive to actively adjust both rotation angle and torsional stiffness; these adjustments are superimposed on the stiffness and displacement control of the motor actuator itself, thereby endowing the DELTA mechanism's end-effector with active compliance in stiffness and position control. Notably, the pneumatic–motor hybrid drive is plug-and-play: in any traditional rigid mechanism, replacing the original active revolute drive with a compliant four-bar module driven collaboratively by a motor actuator and a pneumatic actuator preserves the original rigidity and precision while enhancing the overall compliance and stiffness adaptability.

2.2 Design of the Pneumatic Actuator

The pneumatic actuator is composed of three serially connected single segments of the chamber. Each chamber segment is fabricated by combining a fabric origami chamber with a soft but unstretchable fabric chamber, and its sidewalls are bolted to an elastic plate to achieve directional bending under asymmetric stiffness. Detailed manufacturing process can be found in [21], which ensures precise positioning of the origami facets and thus improves the motion accuracy of the chamber.

Differing from previous work, and based on the DELTA mechanism's required drive range and size constraints, we adjusted the overall dimensions of the chamber by reducing the length of the bolted connection blocks on the top and bottom segments, thereby achieving a larger bending-angle range within the limited link length. Moreover, to prevent the chamber from bending in the opposite direction under internal mechanism forces when in its initial straight state, we mounted the chamber onto a carbon-fiber elastic plate with an inherent curvature. Although this modification reduces the overall rotation-angle and stiffness-variation range of the chamber, it ensures reliable motion of the entire mechanism.

3 Analysis

To validate that, at the same pose of the DELTA mechanism, the pneumatic–motor hybrid drive design can further enhance end-effector stiffness beyond the motor actuator's stiffness adjustment alone, we further derived the kineto-static characteristics of a single segment of the chamber, extending the original no-external-force static-equilibrium kinematics to include external forces. This derivation verifies that, under an identical pose, the output force exerted by the single segment of the chamber on the environment varies with different internal pressures.

3.1 Kineto-Static and the Stiffness of a Single Segment of the Chamber

Soft actuators' stiffness often depends on their inputs (pressure, magnetic field, etc.), exhibiting strong nonlinearity and anisotropy, which poses challenges for precise modeling. In prior work, we used axis–angle decomposition and POE modeling to derive the kineto-static model of an elastic plate [22], equivalently representing the plate's planar motion as a series of discrete rotational joints each with stiffness k. Each joint's rotation angle θ is an unknown solved via a gradient-based algorithm for large-deflection equilibrium. We then used the chamber's force on the elastic plate, F_{chamber}, as an intermediate variable, applying energy methods to derive the chamber's force–displacement relationship and POE modeling to derive the elastic plate's force–displacement relationship, thereby obtaining the kineto-static model of an entire single segment of the chamber [21]. Our kineto-static model assumes quasi-static equilibrium and neglects fluid compressibility and thermal effects, but remains broadly applicable under typical operating conditions where temperature variations are small.

Unlike the aforementioned study, when the pneumatic actuator is integrated into the mechanism, its end also experiences an external force F_{add}, as shown in Fig. 2. This external force, together with F_{chamber}, balances the internal force generated by the elastic plate's stiffness. Therefore, the new static-equilibrium equation can be written as:

$$\mathbf{f}(\theta, \alpha, r) = \begin{bmatrix} K\theta - J^T F_{\text{chamber}}^T - J^T F_{\text{add}}^T \\ \log\left(g_t g_{st}^{-1}\right)^\vee \end{bmatrix} = \begin{bmatrix} \chi \\ \tau \end{bmatrix} = \mathbf{0}_{(N+6)\times 1} \quad (1)$$

where the first row enforces the position constraint and the second row enforces the moment equilibrium.

For gradient-based solution of (1), the Jacobian

$$\nabla \mathbf{f} = \frac{\partial \mathbf{f}}{\partial(\theta,\alpha,r)} = \begin{bmatrix} \frac{\partial \chi}{\partial \theta} & \frac{\partial \chi}{\partial \alpha} & \frac{\partial \chi}{\partial r} \\ \frac{\partial \tau}{\partial \theta} & \frac{\partial \tau}{\partial \alpha} & \frac{\partial \tau}{\partial r} \\ \frac{\partial \tau}{\partial \theta} & \frac{\partial \tau}{\partial \alpha} & \frac{\partial \tau}{\partial r} \end{bmatrix} \in \mathbb{R}^{(N+6)\times(N+2)}, \quad (2)$$

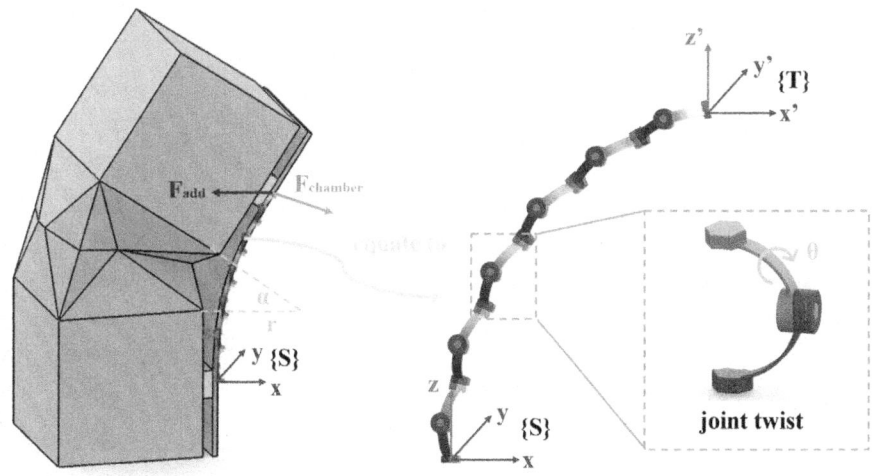

Fig. 2. Kineto-static analysis of a single segment of the chamber.

remains unchanged in the first row and in the last two columns of the second row, since F_{add} does not depend on the chamber's shape parameters α and r. The only changing term is $\partial \tau / \partial \theta$, which under external loading becomes:

$$\frac{\partial \tau}{\partial \theta} = K - K_J - K_F, \tag{3}$$

where K is the stiffness matrix of the equivalent elastic joints;

$$K_J = \frac{\partial J^T}{\partial \theta} F$$

denotes the configuration-dependent term of the Jacobian; and K_F is the configuration-dependent term of the force, expressed as

$$K_F = J^T \frac{\partial F}{\partial \theta}, \tag{4}$$

where $F = F_{add} + F_{chamber}$ is the resultant force.

On this basis, the end-effector stiffness of a single segment of the chamber under different external force equilibria can be numerically evaluated. Let the equilibrium joint angle solution be θ^*, and denote the corresponding end-effector position by $\mathbf{p}_0$. Small perturbation forces $\pm \Delta F$ are then applied along the x and y directions, yielding measured end-effector displacements Δx and Δy. The compliance matrix is constructed as

$$C = \begin{pmatrix} \frac{\Delta x}{\Delta F} & \frac{\delta x_y}{\Delta F} \\ \frac{\delta y_x}{\Delta F} & \frac{\Delta y}{\Delta F} \end{pmatrix}. \tag{5}$$

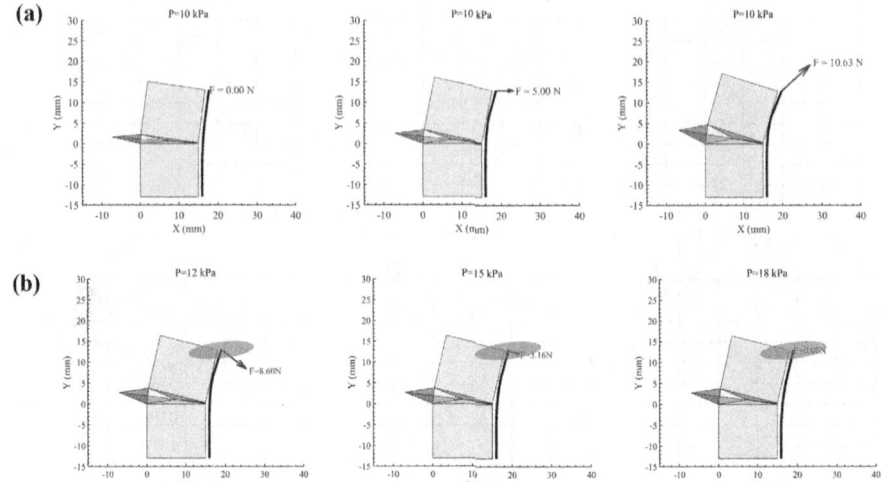

Fig. 3. Kineto-Static calculation results for a single segment of the chamber: (a) deformation modes under 0 N, 5 N, and 10.63 N external loads at 10 kPa; (b) static equilibrium poses at different pressures for the same configuration, with the orange region denoting the end-effector stiffness ellipse.

Next, we perform eigen decomposition of the compliance matrix:

$$C = V \operatorname{diag}(\mu_1, \mu_2), \tag{6}$$

where μ_1 and μ_2 are the lengths of the semi-axes of the stiffness ellipse. Finally, a planar stiffness ellipse can be plotted at the chamber's end effector to visualize its directional compliance characteristics.

Upon obtaining the kineto-static analysis of a single segment of the chamber under external loading, we performed the following theoretical calculations based on that model, as shown in Fig. 3.

First, we computed the deformation modes under identical internal pressure but different external forces. As illustrated in Fig. 3a, with the chamber pressure fixed at 10 kPa, external loads of 0 N, 5 N, and 10.63 N were applied at the end effector to demonstrate the variation in end-effector displacement under different load conditions. It can be seen that, at the same pressure, the end-effector pose varies within a certain range depending on the applied force; hence, given an operating range of end-effector forces, the chamber's motion mode can be solved accordingly.

Next, to verify that the output force differs at the same configuration when internal pressure changes, we used the equilibrium pose at $P = 18$ kPa with 0 N external load as the reference. We then numerically traversed the static equilibrium poses at $P = 12$ kPa and $P = 15$ kPa, obtaining two solutions whose poses closely match the reference, as shown in Fig. 3b. This confirms that, at the same end-effector pose, the chamber exhibits different output force characteristics under different internal pressures.

Furthermore, in Fig. 3b we plot the numerically computed stiffness ellipses at the end effector. These ellipses provide a visual representation of the directional anisotropy of stiffness, where the major axis points to the softest direction and the minor axis to the stiffest. Since the stiffness variation of a single segment is small, the three ellipses appear similar. The calculated major-axis stiffness values are 5.652 N/mm at $P = 8$ kPa and 5.777 N/mm at $P = 12$ kPa, yielding a stiffness difference of approximately 2.2%. Notably, the end-effector stiffness slightly decreases as pressure increases, which may be due to the need to overcome the elastic plate's reaction force in this particular configuration.

3.2 The Stiffness of the DELTA Mechanism

To evaluate the stiffness at the moving-platform center P of the DELTA mechanism, we first perform forward kinematic analysis as illustrated in Fig. 4a. Given the three drive angles θ_i ($i = 1, 2, 3$), the upper-arm end positions B_i are uniquely determined by θ_i, L_1, and R. Due to the DELTA mechanism's inherent three-degree-of-translation characteristic, the platform connector points C_i can be expressed in terms of $P = (x, y, z)$. Finally, by enforcing the three link-length constraints

$$\|C_i - B_i\| = L_2,$$

we solve for $P = (x, y, z)$.

After obtaining P for different sets of θ_i, the end-effector stiffness matrix K_{end} can be computed. Let K_{θ_i} denote the stiffness of branch i corresponding to drive angle θ_i. The parallel-mechanism end stiffness is then the sum of all branch contributions:

$$K_{\text{end}} = \sum_{i=1}^{3} K_i = \sum_{i=1}^{3} J_i^{-T} K_{\theta_i} J_i^{-1} \in \mathbb{R}^{3 \times 3}, \qquad (7)$$

where each branch stiffness contribution K_i depends on K_{θ_i} and the branch Jacobian J_i, which maps drive-angle increments to end-effector displacements.

The Jacobian of branch i is obtained by numerical perturbation of its drive angle:

$$J_i = \frac{\partial P}{\partial \theta_i} \in \mathbb{R}^{3 \times 1}. \qquad (8)$$

Similarly, the end-effector stiffness matrix at the moving-platform center P can be visualized as stiffness ellipsoids. When the three pneumatic–motor hybrid drives have equal stiffness, the computed ellipsoids at various configurations are shown in Fig. 4b. By assigning three distinct stiffness values to the drives, one can directly observe how the stiffness ellipsoid changes with configuration: notably, when the drive angles are identical, the ellipsoid's major axis aligns vertically, indicating that the DELTA mechanism is "softest" in the vertical direction, thus validating the accuracy of our stiffness computation.

Moreover, at a fixed configuration, unequal stiffness values for the three pneumatic–motor hybrid drives yield the ellipsoids depicted in Fig. 4c. These

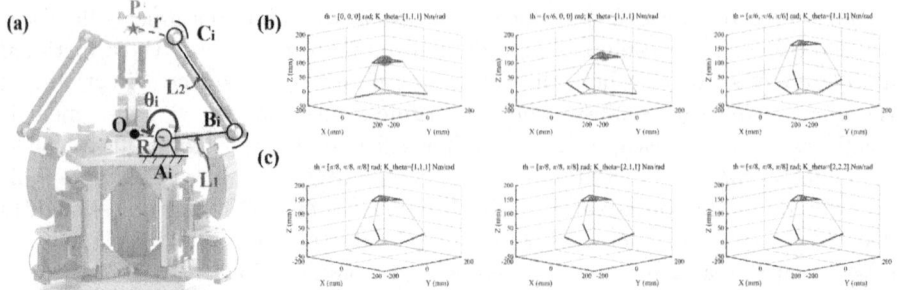

Fig. 4. Calculation of the stiffness of the DELTA mechanism: (a) schematic of the kinematic and stiffness computation; (b) end-effector stiffness ellipsoids at various configurations with equal pneumatic–motor hybrid drive stiffness; (c) stiffness ellipsoids at a fixed configuration with unequal pneumatic–motor hybrid drive stiffness values.

results demonstrate that altering individual drive stiffness can rotate the principal axis direction, while proportionally scaling all three drives changes the overall stiffness magnitude without affecting the principal direction. This confirms that tuning the output stiffness of the pneumatic–motor hybrid drives has a significant impact on the global stiffness behavior of the mechanism.

4 Experiments

To validate that the designed DELTA mechanism, under active drive by the pneumatic–motor hybrid drive, can achieve variable end-effector stiffness at the same motor actuator position through active control of the pneumatic actuator, we designed and fabricated a prototype and conducted preliminary experimental verification.

4.1 Prototype Fabrication

A prototype DELTA Mechanism is shown in Fig. 4(a). The linear slider in each pneumatic–motor hybrid drive module is actuated by a Voice Coil Motor, featuring high-speed response and an 18 mm stroke. The pneumatic actuator is designed as a three-section chamber, with its dimensions adjusted to suit the mechanism; together, the three chambers drive approximately 10 mm of vertical motion at the DELTA Mechanism's end-effector.

On the actuation side, the three Voice Coil Motor drivers are daisy-chained via Ethernet to a single PLC, which communicates directly with the PC-based upper-level controller for motion control. Each pneumatic actuator's inlet is regulated by a proportional pressure valve interfaced to an Arduino Mega 2560 microcontroller running a PID control algorithm for precise pressure regulation; the microcontroller in turn communicates with the upper-level controller over a serial link.

4.2 Variable Stiffness Testing

During end-effector stiffness testing, a force sensor was mounted on a UR robot to allow real-time adjustment of its position, as shown in Fig. 5a. The sensor tip was aligned with the DELTA mechanism's end effector to measure the output force.

In the experiment, the chamber pressure was set to 0 kPa, 10 kPa, and 20 kPa sequentially, while maintaining the DELTA mechanism in the same pose (the voice-coil motor remained fixed, and the end effector and force sensor tips were co-located). The force sensor was then lowered in the vertical direction from 0 to 5 mm in 1 mm increments, and the corresponding force data were recorded. This yielded force–displacement curves at each pressure level for three repetitions, as shown in Fig. 5b.

It is noteworthy that without any external constraint (i.e., in the free state), increasing chamber pressure causes the pneumatic actuator to bend more, lowering the DELTA mechanism's end effector. Therefore, the free-state position at 20 kPa was chosen as the fixed test pose, resulting in an initial force of 0 N at 20 kPa. As pressure decreases to 10 kPa and 0 kPa, the force exerted on the external sensor increases, because the chamber's force on the elastic plate diminishes while the plate's reaction force on the environment grows.

The experimental data were fitted linearly, with the slope corresponding to the vertical stiffness of the mechanism in that pose. The measured stiffness values at 0 kPa, 10 kPa, and 20 kPa were 4.71 N/mm, 5.66 N/mm, and 5.99 N/mm, respectively. This represents a 27.18% increase in stiffness when the chamber is pressurized to 20 kPa compared to the unpressurized state. These results confirm that the pneumatic–motor hybrid drive module, even under pneumatic actuation alone, can modulate both force and stiffness at the end effector. In future applications, combining this effect with the motor actuator will further enhance passive compliance while broadening the mechanism's range of stiffness and force output.

5 Discussion

The designed pneumatic–motor hybrid drive, by replacing the rigid drive, endows the traditional rigid mechanism with passive compliance while simultaneously broadening its stiffness output range, as verified in experiments. Moreover, since the proposed pneumatic actuator has a precisely modelable force–displacement characteristic, control of the pneumatic–motor hybrid drive can be significantly simplified. Therefore, the pneumatic–motor hybrid drive, as an active hybrid-drive functional module, can be modularly substituted for existing rigid-drive modules in traditional mechanisms, offering broad application potential. Compared with the pneumatic–tendon actuator in [12] and the origami–motor hybrid gripper in [14], our module adds significantly less mass (about 50 g per joint) for the same package volume.

In future research, we plan to investigate the following aspects: at the design level, perform inverse geometric parameter design of the pneumatic–motor

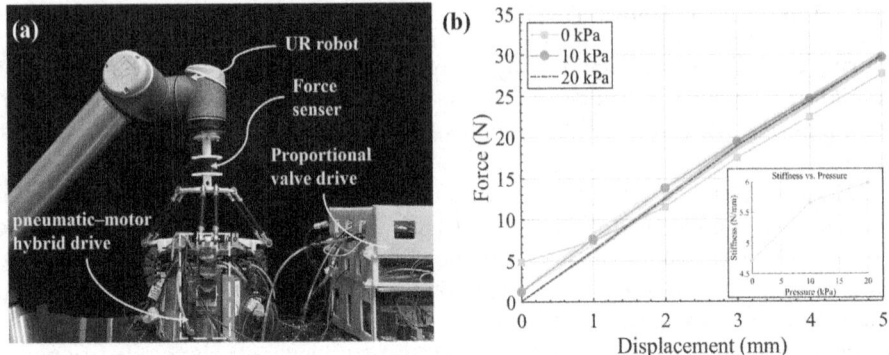

Fig. 5. Prototype stiffness testing of the DELTA mechanism: (a) setup showing the UR-mounted force sensor and end-effector alignment; (b) force–displacement curves with shaded regions indicating mean ± one standard deviation for three trials at 0 kPa, 10 kPa, and 20 kPa, and inset showing the stiffness trend.

hybrid drive based on actual application requirements (e.g., output rotation range and torque range) to enhance its plug-and-play capability—these geometric parameters include, but are not limited to, origami chamber facet dimensions, number of segments, elastic plate length, elastic plate initial curvature, and motor actuator stroke; at the analysis level, extend the force–displacement characteristics of a single segment of the chamber to multi-segment chambers and develop a comprehensive mechanical model of the full pneumatic–motor hybrid drive; at the control level, further design and refine the electro-pneumatic hybrid control strategy to achieve enhanced compliance control, thereby concretely demonstrating the performance improvements enabled by rigid–elastic–soft coupling.

Acknowledgments. This research was supported in part by the National Key Research & Development Program of China under the Grant 2019YFA0709000 and the Natural Science Foundation of China (NSFC) under the Grant 52022056.

Author contributions.
Xingyue Zhu: Conceptualization, Methodology, Investigation, Validation, Writing – original draft, Visualization.
Zhenkun Liang: Methodology, Investigation, Validation.
Hao Yuan: Methodology, Investigation, Visualization.
Yanjun Wang: Validation. **Hao Wang:** Resources, Funding acquisition. **Genliang Chen:** Writing - review & editing, Visualization, Methodology, Investigation, Conceptualization, Funding acquisition.

Data Availibility Statement. Data will be made available on request.

Declaration of Competing Interest. The authors declare that they have no conflict of interest or financial conflicts to disclose.

References

1. Salman, M., Niu, Z., Singh, R., Kshetrimayum, L., Hussain, I.: Robust control of a compliant manipulator with reduced dynamics and sliding perturbation observer. Sci. Rep. **15**(1), 8934 (2025)
2. Hussain, I., Albalasie, A., Awad, M.I., Seneviratne, L., Gan, D.: Modeling, control, and numerical simulations of a novel binary-controlled variable stiffness actuator (BcVSA). Front. Robot. AI **5**, 68 (2018)
3. Toubar, H., Awad, M.I., Boushaki, M.N., Niu, Z., Khalaf, K., Hussain, I.: Design, modeling, and control of a series elastic actuator with discretely adjustable stiffness (SEADAS). Mechatronics **86**, 102863 (2022)
4. Zhong, Y., Ruxu, D., Guo, P., Haoyong, Yu.: Investigation on a new approach for designing articulated soft robots with discrete variable stiffness. IEEE/ASME Trans. Mechatron. **26**(6), 2998–3009 (2021)
5. Yang, S.K., Chen, P., Wang, D.Q., Yi, Yu., Liu, Y.W.: Design and analysis of a 2-DOF actuator with variable stiffness based on leaf springs. J. Bionic Eng. **19**(5), 1392–1404 (2022)
6. Ohe, T., Alemayoh, T.T., Lee, J.H., Okamoto, S.: Feedforward operational stiffness modulation and external force estimation of planar robots equipped with variable stiffness actuators. Intell. Serv. Robot. **15**(2), 179–192 (2022)
7. Yang, B., et al.: Reprogrammable soft actuation and shape-shifting via tensile jamming. Sci. Adv. **7**(40), eabh2073 (2021)
8. Zhang, Z., et al.: Layer jamming skin-based bionic webbed foot soft gripper with variable stiffness and envelopment. Compos. Struct. **341**, 118215 (2024)
9. Manti, M., Cacucciolo, V., Cianchetti, M.: Stiffening in soft robotics: a review of the state of the art. IEEE Robot. Autom. Mag. **23**(3), 93–106 (2016)
10. Lotfiani, A., Zhao, H., Shao, Z., Yi, X.: Torsional stiffness improvement of a soft pneumatic finger using embedded skeleton. J. Mech. Robot. **12**, 011016 (2019)
11. Li, X., Hao, Y., Zhang, J., Wang, C., Li, D., Zhang, J.: Design, modeling and experiments of a variable stiffness soft robotic glove for stroke patients with clenched fist deformity. IEEE Robot. Autom. Lett. **8**(7), 4044–4051 (2023)
12. Zhu, J.Q., MengHao, P., Chen, H., Yi, X., Ding, H., ZhiGang, W.: Pneumatic and tendon actuation coupled muti-mode actuators for soft robots with broad force and speed range. SCIENCE CHINA Technol. Sci. **65**(9), 2156–2169 (2022)
13. Zhang, Z., et al.: Bioinspired rigid-soft hybrid origami actuator with controllable versatile motion and variable stiffness. IEEE Trans. Rob. **39**(6), 4768–4784 (2023)
14. Zhang, Z., et al.: Hybrid-driven origami gripper with variable stiffness and finger length. Cyborg Bionic Syst. **5**, 0103 (2024)
15. Zhang, Z., Long, Y., Chen, G., Wu, Q., Wang, H., Jiang, H.: Soft and lightweight fabric enables powerful and high-range pneumatic actuation. Sci. Adv. **9**(15), eadg1203 (2023)
16. Long, Y., et al.: Lightweight and powerful vacuum-driven gripper with bioinspired elastic spine. IEEE Robot. Autom. Lett. **8**(12), 8136–8143 (2023)
17. Yang, D., et al.: Soft multifunctional bistable fabric mechanism for electronics-free autonomous robots. Sci. Adv. **11**(5), eads8734 (2025)
18. Changchun, W., Liu, H., Lin, S., Lam, J., Xi, N., Chen, Y.: Shape morphing of soft robotics by pneumatic torsion strip braiding. Nat. Commun. **16**(1), 3787 (2025)
19. Chen, G., et al.: A non-electrical pneumatic hybrid oscillator for high-frequency multimodal robotic locomotion. Nat. Commun. **16**(1), 1449 (2025)

20. Gao, S., et al.: Tri-prism origami enabled soft modular actuator for reconfigurable robots. Soft Robot. (2025)
21. Long, Y., Xingyue Zhu, P., Shi, Q.L., Wang, Y., Wang, H., Chen, G.: A high-performance elastic-soft hybrid pneumatic actuator with origami structure. Int. J. Mech. Sci. **287**, 109935 (2025)
22. Chen, G., Zhang, Z., Wang, H.: A general approach to the large deflection problems of spatial flexible rods using principal axes decomposition of compliance matrices. J. Mech. Robot. **10**, 031012 (2018)

Pneumatic Kirigami Actuators with Programmable Motion for Versatile Robotic Functionalities

Yang Yu, Yanqi Yin, Ruiyu Bai, and Bo Li(✉)

Shaanxi Key Laboratory of Intelligent Robots, School of Mechanical Engineering, Xi'an Jiaotong University, Xi'an 710049, China
liboxjtu@xjtu.edu.cn

Abstract. Kirigami, an oriental art of paper cutting, involves creating patterned cuts on a flat, thin sheet to achieve bending, buckling as well as extra elongation when an external stimulus is applied. In this study, we propose a series of kirigami-based pneumatic actuators utilizing laser cutting and stacking fabrication approach. This method allows for rapid prototyping of pneumatic actuators through strategic cut designs, eliminating 3D manufacture of air chambers. The motion mode of the proposed kirigami actuator is programmable in terms of expanding, bending and twisting with corresponding cut patterns. The proposed bending actuator can deform over 200° and possess an end blocking force of up to 20 N at a pressure of 20 kPa. For instance of robotic functions, a soft gripper is illustrated by employing a bending actuator capable of lifting objects up to 20 times its own weight. Moreover, we demonstrate the potential for these actuators to be assembled into a crawling robot. This new soft actuator shall enrich the design strategy of soft robots by expanding kirigami from mechanical design to kinematic motion.

Keywords: pneumatic actuator · programmable · kirigami

1 Introduction

Soft actuators and robotics have received an increasing development in recent years, demonstrating tremendous potential cross various fields due to their inherent compliance and adaptability to unstructured environments [1]. These applications include human-machine interaction [2], wearable devices [3, 4] robotic locomotion [5–8], and manipulation [9–12]. Among the diverse actuation strategies, such as magnetic, optical and electrical [13–18], pneumatic-actuated soft actuators [19] have garnered considerable attention for their simple and human-friendly interaction. The predominant fabrication techniques for these pneumatic soft actuators are 3D printing [20–22] and molding [23–27]. However, these methods are often time consuming and costly, as they involve constructing complex air channel or multiple casting steps. Meanwhile, the used soft materials in molding or 3D printing typically possess a low Young's modulus, which allows for high compliance, but can lead to excessive deformation or even failure when continuous increased pressure is applied, resulting in irreversible and irreparable damage. Additionally, these actuators generally produce only a single motion mode such as bending. By integrating structural designs with actuating strategies, basic motion modes like bending, twisting, contraction and elongation have been achieved [28–33], enabling the realization of versatile soft robotics. However, these often result in limited output forces or motion modes, restricting their practical applications. Consequently, there is a critical need to develop new soft actuators capable of generating multiple motion modes towards programmability while maintaining a high output force.

Kirigami, an oriental art of paper cutting, involves creating patterned cuts on a flat and thin sheet to achieve significant deformation [34–36] and complex motions when subjected to external stimuli [37–40]. This technique demonstrates considerable potential in the development of soft actuators. Despite the advantages of kirigami, challenges remain in arranging the cut patterns and selecting appropriate actuation strategies to achieve desired motion modes and high output force.

In this study, we introduce a novel design for programmable soft pneumatic actuators based on kirigami. This design employs a planar laser cutting and sequential stacking approach, allowing for the construction of pneumatic actuators through cut design rather than the creation of complex air channels. We propose three actuators capable of fundamental motion modes: expanding, bending, and twisting. To further explore their potential, we evaluate the performance of the bending actuator, which is implemented as a soft gripper and a crawling robot. This innovative approach to soft pneumatic kirigami actuators enhances the design strategy of soft robots by extending kirigami from mechanical design to kinematic motion.

2 Design and Fabrication

The proposed pneumatic kirigami actuators are fabricated through a planar laser cutting and sequential stacking approach. The actuator mainly consists of eight layers corresponding different laminate materials stacked sequentially. Specifically, thermoplastic polyurethane (TPU) layers (soft and extensible material with a thickness 0.2 mm) are used as inflatable pockets, the nylon layers are (soft but not as extensible as TPU with a thickness 0.05 mm) are utilized as limiting layers, hot melt adhesive films are utilized to bond the layers on both sides of them. An additional internal polyethylene terephthalate (PET) layer (thickness 0.2 mm) mask is utilized as the air channel between the two bonded TPU layers. In addition, the PET layer is also utilized to regulate the actuator for non-symmetric deformation upon pressure for different motion modes (e.g., bending and twisting). As depicted in Fig. 1(a), the process of fabricating a pneumatic kirigami actuator can be divided into three steps: 1) Cutting each layer of the corresponding laminate materials with a laser cutter. 2) Manually aligning and stacking the layers to construct the desired actuator. 3) Utilizing a heat press to form the air channel network, leaving a small boundary unsealed for air pipe insertion. All pneumatic kirigami actuators with different motion modes sharing the same manufacturing process.

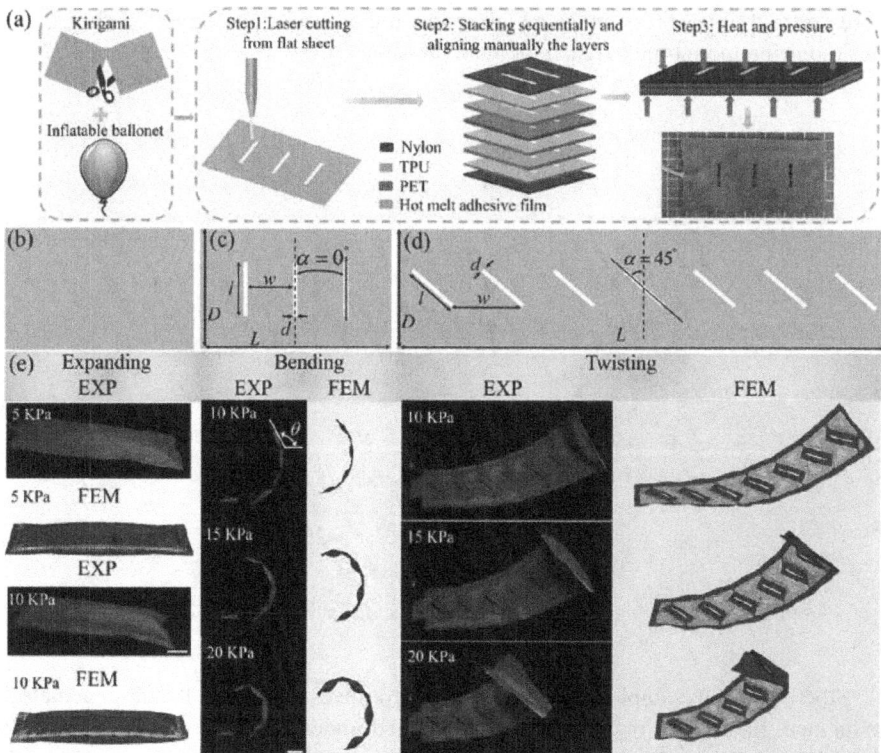

Fig. 1. (a) Schematic illustration of the fabrication processes of the actuator. (b) Schematic illustration of the expanding actuator. (c) Schematic illustration of the bending actuator. (d) Schematic illustration of the twisting actuator. (e) Snapshots of experimental observations and simulated deformations identified by FEM of the expanding, bending and twisting actuator's deformation status under varying pressure. Scale bar: 30 mm.

Figure 1(b) - Fig. 1(d) demonstrate three actuators with distinct motion modes. The geometric parameters of the cuts play a pivotal role in controlling the motion mode, which can be programmed by adjusting the tilt angle α (angle between the axis of the cuts and the vertical line). Specifically, actuator without cuts (Fig. 1(b)) results in an expanding motion mode (i.e., no bending or twisting motions), and a bending motion mode occurs when the axis of the cuts is parallel to the vertical line (i.e. tilt angle $\alpha = 0°$, Fig. 1(c)), while a twisting motion mode is induced when the axis of the cuts is not parallel to the vertical line (i.e. tilt angle $\alpha > 0°$, Fig. 1(d)). The deformation status of the proposed actuators under varying pressure are experimentally identified and validated using the finite element method (FEM) in Fig. 1(e). The experimental and FEM results are in good agreement.

The proposed bending actuator can respond rapidly when inflated. Figure 2 shows that a bending actuator of 200 mm in length can reach its fully bent state in approximately 400 ms under the input pressure of 15 kPa. The response time of the bending actuator increases with input pressure, as a higher pressure necessitates a larger bending angle, thus requiring more time to reach the final position.

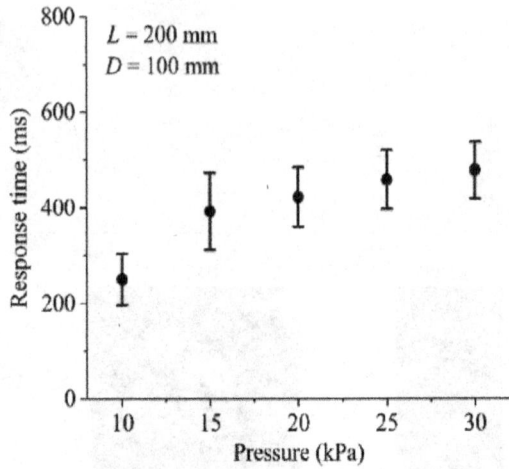

Fig. 2. A bending actuator's response time under varying pressure inputs.

Moreover, ten samples were fabricated to investigate the bending actuator's endurance. Each actuator was repeatedly inflated under the input pressure of 20 kPa and then deflated until failure. Table 1 presents the endurance cycles of the investigated actuators, revealing that the majority exhibit endurance exceeding 500 cycles. The premature failure of sample 5 after only 208 cycles may be attributed to inherent random errors introduced during the fabrication process.

Table 1. Ten bending actuators' endurance cycles

Sample	1	2	3	4	5	6	7	8	9	10
Cycles	568	602	621	676	208	761	1249	820	957	863

3 Results

A kinematic model is established for the bending actuator. We assume the actuator is non-stretchable upon inflation and then, approximate the inflated actuator using a series of rigid links with revolute joints. As shown in Fig. 3(a), l_i ($i = 1, 2, 3...$) denotes the length of the i-th link between the (i-1)-th joint and i-th joint ($i = 1, 2, 3...$), θ_i denotes the corresponding rotation angle between the (i-1)-th and i-th links.

For a bending actuator, the homogeneous coordinate transformation matrix T_i^{i-1} from the joint i-1 to the joint i can be expressed as:

$$T_i^{i-1} = Rot(z_{i-1}, \theta_i) \times Trans(x_i, l_i) = \begin{pmatrix} \cos\theta_i & -\sin\theta_i & 0 & l_i \cos\theta_i \\ \sin\theta_i & \cos\theta_i & 0 & l_i \sin\theta_i \\ 0 & 0 & 1 & 0 \\ 0 & 0 & 0 & 1 \end{pmatrix} \quad (1)$$

The the length of the i-th link of the actuator can be approximated as:

$$l_i = w + d \quad (2)$$

Hence, the position of the terminal joint (x, y, z) in the base coordinate can be calculated from its position in its own coordinate (x_n, y_n, z_n) and the total transformation matrix can be written as:

$$\begin{pmatrix} x \\ y \\ z \\ 1 \end{pmatrix} = T_n^0 \begin{pmatrix} x_n \\ y_n \\ z_n \\ 1 \end{pmatrix} = \prod_{i=1}^{n} T_i^{i-1} \begin{pmatrix} 0 \\ 0 \\ 0 \\ 1 \end{pmatrix} \quad (3)$$

Six bending actuators ($L = 180$ mm, $D = 90$ mm) were fabricated to investigate the effect of width d and length l of the cut on the bending angle θ (the angle between the end of the actuator and the horizontal line, marked in Fig. 1(e)). These actuators were divided into two groups: one group consisted of three actuators with identical cut width d ($d = 2$ mm) but different cut length l ($l = 30, 40$ and 45 mm respectively), while the other group comprised three actuators with identical cut length l ($l = 35$ mm) but different cut width d ($d = 2, 4$ and 8 mm respectively). The experimental results, corroborated by the FEM simulations, indicate a clear trend that the bending angle tends to increase with an increase in the cut length l (Fig. 3(a)), and decrease with an increase in cut width d (Fig. 3(b)). Compared to previously developed pneumatic bending actuators [20, 41–48], the proposed kirigami bending actuator achieves a higher blocking force and a large bending angle, as shown in Fig. 4.

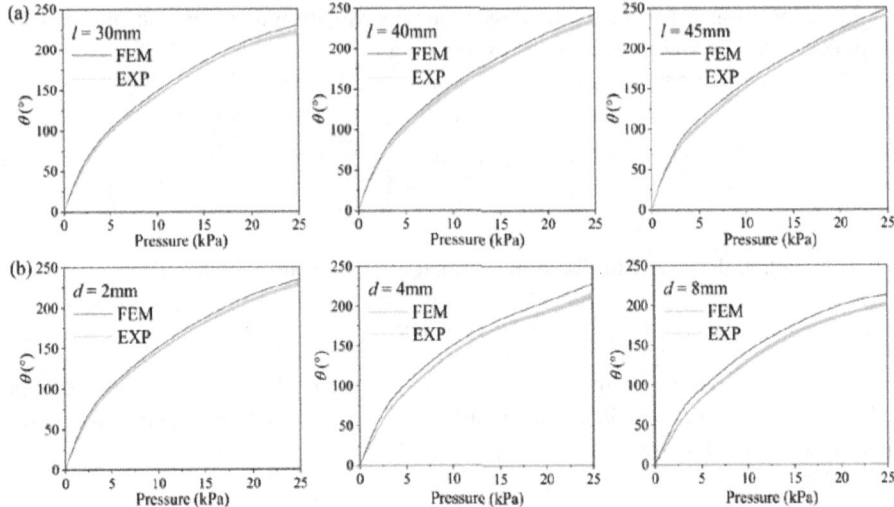

Fig. 3. (a) The effect of length l of the cut on the bending angle: comparison of FEM and experimental results. (b) The effect of width d of the cut on the bending angle: comparison of FEM and experimental results.

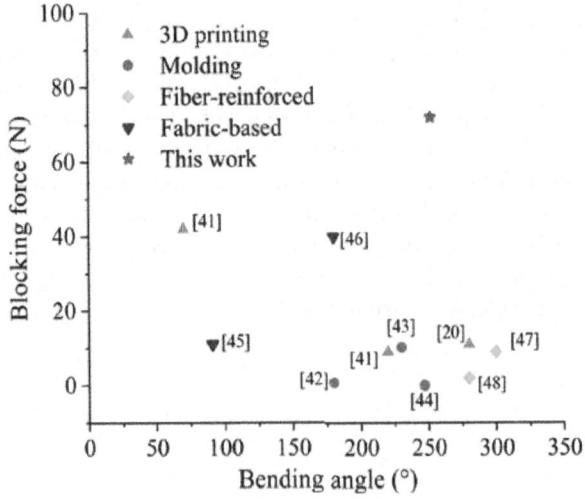

Fig. 4. A comparison of the proposed kirigami bending actuator with existing actuators.

In addition to the unidirectional bending motion mode, a bidirectional bending motion mode can be readily achieved utilizing two unidirectional bending actuators. Figure 5(a) illustrates the schematic illustration and experimental results of a bidirectional bending actuator. Specifically, two unidirectional bending actuators bend in opposite directions are bonded in a parallel manner, forming a bidirectional bending actuator. Each unidirectional bending actuator can be controlled independently, allowing the bending direction of the bidirectional actuator to be determined by selecting which actuator to be inflated.

Moreover, cuts with different tilt angles can be integrated on a single actuator to accomplish more complex motions. As shown in Fig. 5(b), the cuts are labeled into two groups along the vertical direction, defining different tilt angles. Upon inflation, the actuator exhibits both actuation modes (bending and twisting, bending and expanding). Note that more complex motion types can be readily achieved by arranging cuts with different tilt angles on a single actuator as needed owing to the convenience from the three-step fabrication process. In addition, the actuators manufactured through the planar laser cutting and sequential stacking approach demonstrate high reliability as evidenced by various experiments conducted in extreme environments. To assess the reliability, a bending actuator was subjected to both high and low temperature conditions. The actuator, with a 50 g load attached to its end, was placed in a refrigerator with a low temperature of $-10\,°C$ and a thermostat with a high temperature of 80 °C. After 30 min, the actuator normally bent when inflated, as illustrated in Fig. 5(c).

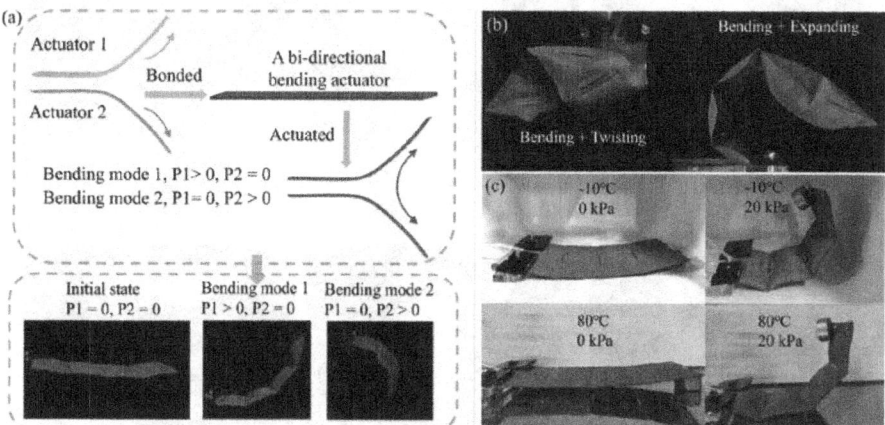

Fig. 5. (a) Schematic illustration and experimental observations on the bending modes of a bidirectional bending actuator. (b) Experimental observations on a bending-twisting and bending-expanding actuator. (c) Operation ability in a low (−10°C) /high (80 °C) temperature environment of the bending actuator.

4 Robotic Applications

4.1 Kirigami Gripper

To further leverage the advantages of the actuator, a gripper utilizing the bending motion mode was designed, and a series of grasping tests were conducted to assess its practical performance. The gripper, as illustrated in Fig. 6(a), demonstrates its ability to grasp a pen container under an actuation pressure of 30 kPa. By alternating between the inflated and deflated states of the actuator, the gripper can swiftly transition between picking and placing tasks. As shown in Fig. 6(b), the gripper is capable of grasping small, light objects (e.g., a plush toy, 50 g) as well as large, heavy objects (e.g., a bottle of water, 600 g). Remarkably, the actuator, with a self-weight of 30 g, can lift objects up to 20 times its own weight.

Fig. 6. (a) Grasping, picking up and moving a pen container. (b) Grasping different objects with weights ranging from 40 g to 600 g.

4.2 A Crawling Robot

A crawling robot was presented here, which consists of three independently controlled bending actuators, demonstrated versatile motion capabilities. The crawling robot is 216 mm long, 150 mm wide and 1.5 mm high. The robot was capable of realizing different motion modes such as moving forward, turning left and turning right by selecting which actuator to inflate. For instance, inflating actuator 1 propels the robot forward, while inflating actuator 2 causes it to turn right, and inflating actuator 3 results in a left turn. To further validate its agility, a maze experiment was conducted, as shown in Fig. 7. In this experiment, the robot was placed at the entrance of a simple maze and successfully navigated through it by inflating different actuators to move forward, turn left, or turn right, ultimately exiting the maze.

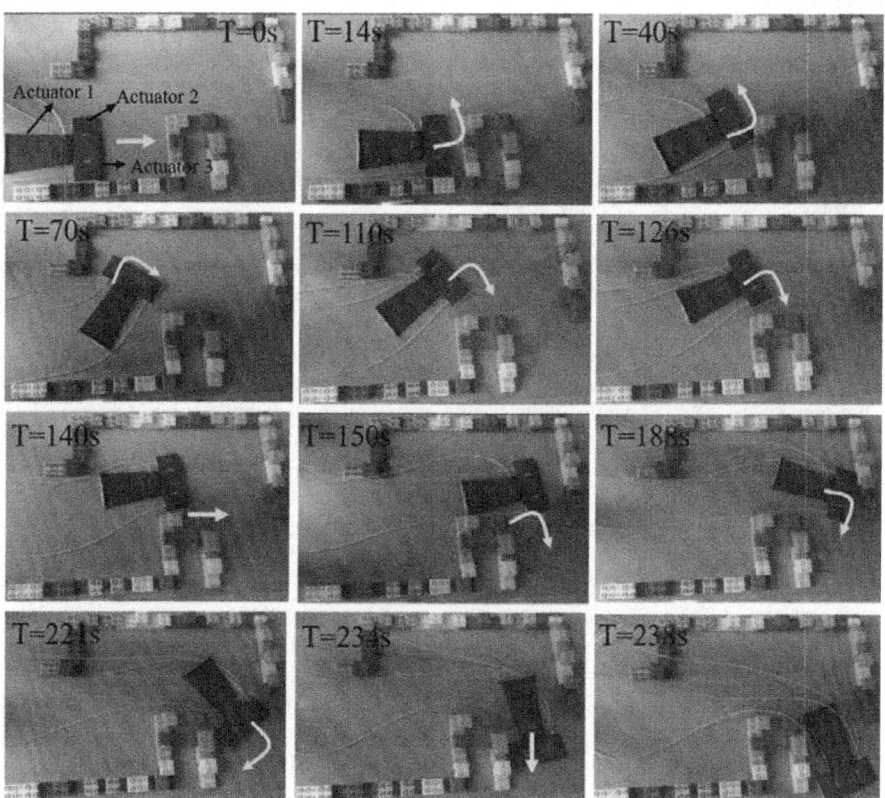

Fig. 7. The robot crawls out of the maze. Scale bar: 70 mm.

5 Discussion and Conclusion

This paper introduces three types of kirigami pneumatic actuators, which capable of performing expanding, bending and twisting motion mode respectively. The motion mode of the actuator is programmable and combinable by changing the geometric parameters of the cuts, enabling versatile functionality. Among the proposed designs, the bending actuator exhibits a powerful output force and is utilized as a soft gripper and a crawling robot. Note that more motion mode such as contraction can be achieved by arranging different cuts on the kirigami actuator. Utilizing the kirigami with advanced manufacturing, it is promising to apply the kirigami from laboratory prototypes to large-scale production and commercialization. While pneumatic kirigami actuators offer several advantages, challenges persist, particularly in miniaturization, a common hurdle for soft pneumatic actuators in general. Current soft pneumatic actuators are typically fabricated on a centimeter scale, largely due to limitations in existing processing technologies (e.g. 3D printing or molding). Future advancements in manufacturing processes will likely be crucial for achieving significant miniaturization of soft pneumatic actuators.

References

1. Rus, D., Tolley, M.T.: Design, fabrication and control of soft robots. Nature **521**, 467–475 (2015)
2. Zhao, H., O'Brien, K., Li, S., Shepherd, R.F.: Optoelectronically innervated soft prosthetic hand via stretchable optical waveguides. Sci. Robot. **1**, eaai7529 (2016)
3. Shveda, R.A., et al.: A wearable textile-based pneumatic energy harvesting system for assistive robotics. Sci. Adv. **8**(34), eabo2418 (2022)
4. In, H., Kang, B.B., Sin, M., Cho, K.-J.: Exo-glove: a wearable robot for the hand with a soft tendon routing system. IEEE Robot. Autom. Mag. **22**, 97–105 (2015)
5. Ze, Q., et al.: Spinning-enabled wireless amphibious origami millirobot. Nat. Commun. **13**, 3118 (2022)
6. Zhang, S., Ke, X.X., Jiang, Q., Ding, H., Wu, Z.G.: Programmable and reprocessable multifunctional elastomeric sheets for soft origami robots. Sci. Robot. **6**, eabd6107 (2021)
7. Chen, S., et al.: Soft crawling robots: design, actuation, and locomotion. Adv. Mater. Technol. **5**(2), 1900837 (2020)
8. Lee, W.-K., et al.: A buckling-sheet ring oscillator for electronics-free, multimodal locomotion. Sci. Robot. **7** (2022)
9. Decker, C.J., et al.: Programmable soft valves for digital and analog control. Proc. Natl. Acad. Sci. USA **119**, e2205922119 (2022)
10. Sun, J., Lerner, E., Tighe, B., Middlemist, C., Zhao, J.: Embedded shape morphing for morphologically adaptive robots. Nat. Commun. **14**, 6023 (2023)
11. Zhang, S., Ke, X., Jiang, Q., Chai, Z., Wu, Z., Ding, H.: Fabrication and functionality integration technologies for small-scale soft robots. Adv. Mater. **34**, e2200671 (2022)
12. Shintake, J., Cacucciolo, V., Floreano, D., Shea, H.: Soft robotic grippers. Adv. Mater. **30**, 1707035 (2018)
13. Novelino, L.S., Ze, Q., Wu, S., Paulino, G.H., Zhao, R.: Untethered control of functional origami microrobots with distributed actuation. Proc. Natl. Acad. Sci. USA **117**, 24096–24101 (2020)
14. Cheng, Y.C., Lu, H.C., Lee, X., Zeng, H., Priimagi, A.: Kirigami-based light-induced shape-morphing and locomotion. Adv. Mater. **32**(7), 1906233 (2020)
15. Kellaris, N., Venkata, V.G., Smith, G.M., Mitchell, S.K., Keplinger, C.: Peano-HASEL actuators: muscle-mimetic, electrohydraulic transducers that linearly contract on activation. Sci Robot. **3**, eaar3276 (2018)
16. Li, S., et al.: Digital light processing of liquid crystal elastomers for self-sensing artificial muscles. Sci. Adv. **7**(30), eabg3677 (2021)
17. Mao, G.Y., et al.: Soft electromagnetic actuators. Sci. Adv. **6**, eabc0251 (2020)
18. Wang, X.Q., et al.: Somatosensory, light-driven, thin-film robots capable of integrated perception and motility. Adv. Mater. **32**, e2000351 (2020)
19. Gorissen, B., Reynaerts, D., Konishi, S., Yoshida, K., Kim, J.-W., De Volder, M.: Elastic inflatable actuators for soft robotic applications. Adv. Mater. **29**, 1604977 (2017)
20. Guo, J., et al.: Kirigami-inspired 3D printable soft pneumatic actuators with multiple deformation modes for soft robotic applications. Soft Robot. **10**, 737–748 (2023)

21. Zhai, Y.C., et al.: Desktop fabrication of monolithic soft robotic devices with embedded fluidic control circuits. Sci. Robot **8**, eadg3792 (2023)
22. Schaffner, M., Faber, J.A., Pianegonda, L., Ruhs, P.A., Coulter, F., Studart, A.R.: 3D printing of robotic soft actuators with programmable bioinspired architectures. Nat. Commun. **9**, 878 (2018)
23. Rafsanjani, A., Zhang, Y., Liu, B., Rubinstein, S.M., Bertoldi, K.: Kirigami skins make a simple soft actuator crawl. Sci. Robot. **3**, eaar7555 (2018)
24. Pal, A., Goswami, D., Martinez, R.V.: Elastic energy storage enables rapid and programmable actuation in soft machines. Adv. Funct. Mater. **30**, eaar7555 (2019)
25. Martinez, R.V., Fish, C.R., Chen, X., Whitesides, G.M.: Elastomeric origami: programmable paper-elastomer composites as pneumatic actuators. Adv. Func. Mater. **22**, 1376–1384 (2012)
26. Jin, L., Yang, Y., Maldonado, B.O.T., Lee, S.D., Figueroa, N., Full, R.J., Yang, S.: Ultrafast, programmable, and electronics-free soft robots enabled by snapping metacaps. Adv. Intell. Syst. **5**(6), 2300039 (2023)
27. Cui, Y., Liu, X.-J., Dong, X., Zhou, J., Zhao, H.: Enhancing the universality of a pneumatic gripper via continuously adjustable initial grasp postures. IEEE Trans. Rob. **37**, 1604–1618 (2021)
28. Zhang, Z., Long, Y., Chen, G., Wu, Q., Wang, H., Jiang, H.: Soft and lightweight fabric enables powerful and high-range pneumatic actuation. Sci. Adv. **9**, eadg1203 (2023)
29. Belding, L., et al.: Slit tubes for semisoft pneumatic actuators. Adv. Mater. **30**, 1704446 (2018)
30. Quevedo-Moreno, D., Roche, E.T.: Design and modeling of fabric-shelled pneumatic bending soft actuators. IEEE Robot. Autom. Lett. **8**, 3110–3117 (2023)
31. Zhang, C., et al.: Plug & play origami modules with all-purpose deformation modes. Nat. Commun. **14**, 4329 (2023)
32. Ma, K., Chen, X., Zhang, J., Xie, Z., Wu, J., Zhang, J.: Inspired by physical intelligence of an elephant trunk: biomimetic soft robot with pre-programmable localized stiffness. IEEE Robot. Autom. Lett. **8**, 2898–2905 (2023)
33. Wu, S., Ze, Q., Dai, J., Udipi, N., Paulino, G.H., Zhao, R.: Stretchable origami robotic arm with omnidirectional bending and twisting. Proc. Natl. Acad. Sci. USA **118**, e2110023118 (2021)
34. An, N., Domel, A.G., Zhou, J., Rafsanjani, A., Bertoldi, K.: Programmable hierarchical kirigami. Adv. Funct. Mater. **30**, 1906711 (2019)
35. Yu, Y., et al.: Reprogrammable multistable ribbon kirigami with a wide cut. Appl. Phys. Lett. **123**, 011701 (2023)
36. Tang, Y.C., Yin, J.: Design of cut unit geometry in hierarchical kirigami-based auxetic metamaterials for high stretchability and compressibility. Extreme Mech. Lett. **12**, 77–85 (2017)
37. Zhu, H., Wang, Y., Ge, Y., Zhao, Y., Jiang, C.: Kirigami-inspired programmable soft magnetoresponsive actuators with versatile morphing modes. Adv. Sci. **9**, 2203711 (2022)
38. Jin, L., Forte, A.E., Deng, B., Rafsanjani, A., Bertoldi, K.: Kirigami-inspired inflatables with programmable shapes. Adv. Mater. **32**, e2001863 (2020)
39. Yang, Y., Vella, K., Holmes, D.P.: Grasping with kirigami shells. Sci. Robot. **6**, 6426 (2021)
40. Duhr, P., Meier, Y.A., Damanpack, A., Carpenter, J., Studart, A.R., Rafsanjani, A., Demirors, A.F.: Kirigami Makes a Soft Magnetic Sheet Crawl. Adv. Sci. (Weinh) **10**, e2301895 (2023)
41. Liu, X., Zhao, Y., Geng, D., Chen, S., Tan, X., Cao, C.: Soft humanoid hands with large grasping force enabled by flexible hybrid pneumatic actuators. Soft Robot. **8**, 175–185 (2021)
42. Yoon, J., Yun, D.: Geometrical parameters investigation of a zig-zag soft pneumatic actuators. Adv. Eng. Mater. **26**, 2400560 (2024)
43. Cheng, P., Ye, Y., Yan, B., Lu, Y., Wu, C.: Eccentric high-force soft pneumatic bending actuator for finger-type soft grippers. J. Mech. Robot. **14**, 060908 (2022)

44. Gariya, N., Kumar, P., Prasad, B., Singh, T.: Soft pneumatic actuator with an embedded flexible polymeric piezoelectric membrane for sensing bending deformation. Mater. Today Commun. **35**, 105910 (2023)
45. Lee, K., Bayarsaikhan, K., Aguilar, G., Realmuto, J., Sheng, J.: Design and characterization of soft fabric omnidirectional bending actuators. Actuators **13**, 112 (2024)
46. Lee, H., Oh, N., Rodrigue, H.: Expanding pouch motor patterns for programmable soft bending actuation: enabling soft robotic system adaptations. IEEE Robot. Autom. Mag. **27**, 65–74 (2020)
47. Wei, Q., Xu, H., Sun, F., Chang, F., Chen, S., Zhang, X.: Biomimetic fiber reinforced dual-mode actuator for soft robots. Sens. Actu. A: Phys. **344**, 113761 (2022)
48. Wirekoh, J., Parody, N., Riviere, C.N., Park, Y.-L.: Design of fiber-reinforced soft bending pneumatic artificial muscles for wearable tremor suppression devices. Smart Mater. Struct. **30**, 015013 (2020)

Stress Monitoring and Adaptive Grasping for Robotic Grippers Using Distributed Optical Fiber Sensing

Baijin Mao[1,2], Xulong Shi[1,2], Yuyaocen Xiang[1,2], Yedong Huang[1,2], and Juntian Qu[1,2(✉)]

[1] Shenzhen International Graduate School, Tsinghua University, Shenzhen 518055, China
[2] Shenzhen Key Laboratory of Advanced Technology for Marine Ecology, Tsinghua University, Shenzhen 518055, China
juntian.qu@sz.tsinghua.edu.cn

Abstract. Reliable and adaptive grasping in robotic systems remains challenging due to the lack of real-time structural feedback and multi-directional stress awareness. To address this, we propose a novel dexterous manipulation system that integrates distributed optical fiber sensing and fuzzy logic-based adaptive control. A strain rosette structure, formed by embedding fiber Bragg gratings (FBGs) in robotic fingers, enables high-resolution two-dimensional (2D) stress field reconstruction with a sensitivity of -0.2091 pm/N and linearity of 0.99. Crucially, instead of relying on conventional single-axis force, the system employs real-time maximum principal stress as a feedback signal to ensure structural safety and enable adaptive grasp force regulation. The fuzzy controller dynamically adjusts control gains to accommodate objects with varying stiffness and damping characteristics. Experimental results demonstrate that this approach reduces steady-state force error to within 6.5 kPa and improves response speed by 18% compared to conventional PID control. This work establishes a closed-loop framework that tightly couples structural integrity assessment and intelligent control, offering a promising solution for safe and efficient robotic grasping in dynamic environments.

Keywords: Optical fiber sensing · 2D stress monitoring · Dexterous manipulation · Fuzzy control · Robotic gripper

1 Introduction

With the rapid advancement of intelligent manufacturing [1,2] and robotics [3,4], robotic hand has become key actuators for achieving automated and dexterous operations [5,6]. Their force sensing capabilities are now critical for enhancing operational precision and safety [7,8]. In complex environments, manipulators are required not only to detect contact forces but also to accurately perceive multi-directional and multi-dimensional stress distributions to avoid overload-induced damage and to improve operational stability. However, most current force sensing systems are limited to single-dimensional contact force measurement [9,10], lacking the ability to capture two-dimensional or three-dimensional stress field distributions in real time. Furthermore, they do not provide real-time structural safety assessment of the manipulator [11], which significantly limits their safety and stability during interactions involving heavy objects and constrains the further development of intelligent control.

To address this technical bottleneck, extensive research has been conducted globally, employing technologies such as flexible sensors [12,13], piezoelectric materials [14,15], and strain gauges [16,17] to improve force sensing systems. Among them, fiber Bragg grating (FBG) sensors have emerged as a promising solution due to their high sensitivity, immunity to electromagnetic interference, and capability for distributed sensing [18–20]. However, existing research primarily focuses on point-wise or single-axis force detection and has not yet established a complete sensing and control system for internal two-dimensional stress fields within robotic manipulators.

This study proposes a dexterous manipulation system that integrates 2D stress field sensing with adaptive force feedback using a fuzzy logic-tuned PID controller. A distributed FBG array is embedded in the robotic finger, and a 2D stress sensing structure based on FBG strain rosettes is developed with finite element analysis. The system achieves high sensitivity (-0.2091 pm/N) and excellent linearity (0.99), enabling real-time stress mapping. Using maximum principal stress as feedback, the fuzzy PID controller adapts grasping force for objects with varying stiffness while ensuring structural safety. Experiments show the system reduces steady-state error, improves response speed, and enhances grasp stability compared to traditional PID control. In summary, the main innovations of this study include:

(1) The development and implementation of a 2D stress field sensing structure based on FBG strain rosettes, overcoming the limitations of traditional single-dimensional force sensing and establishing a theoretical method for real-time structural monitoring of manipulators.
(2) In contrast to conventional tactile feedback approaches, this study innovatively employs real-time maximum principal stress as the feedback basis. On the premise of ensuring structural safety, it proposes and implements an adaptive intelligent control strategy based on fuzzy logic, effectively meeting the grasping demands of diverse objects and significantly enhancing control performance and system response efficiency.

This system holds great potential for future applications in industrial automation, medical rehabilitation, and service robotics, enhancing the adaptability and operational safety of robotic manipulators when interacting with diverse objects.

2 Principle of FBG Sensing and System Setup

The Fiber Bragg Grating (FBG) sensing system operates based on the principle of selective reflection of specific wavelengths. As shown in Fig. 1, An FBG

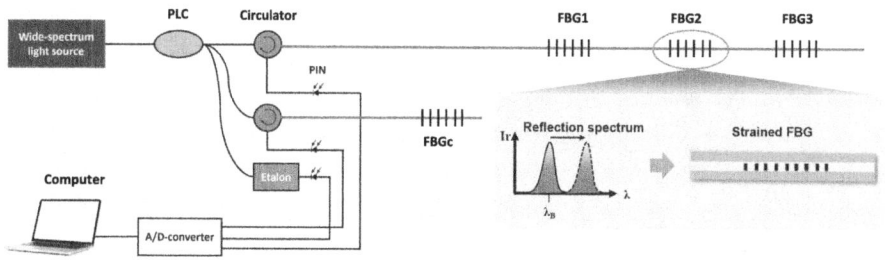

Fig. 1. The sensing principle and system composition of fiber Bragg grating sensors.

sensing system typically consists of several key components: a broadband light source providing a continuous spectrum, a planar lightwave circuit (PLC) splitter enabling multi-channel signal distribution, an optical circulator controlling the propagation path of light to ensure directional transmission of the reflected signal, a photodetector (PD) converting the reflected optical signal into an electrical signal, an analog-to-digital (A/D) converter digitizing the signal, and a computer for data acquisition, demodulation, and analysis.

When broadband light sources inject light into the fiber, the FBG structure reflects only the light centered at the Bragg wavelength, while other wavelengths are transmitted. The fundamental relationship governing this principle is described by the Bragg condition equation:

$$\lambda_B = 2n_{eff}\Lambda \tag{1}$$

Here, λ_B denotes the reflected Bragg wavelength, n_{eff} represents the effective refractive index of the fiber core, and Λ is the grating period of the fiber Bragg grating structure. Fiber Bragg gratings are sensitive to both temperature and strain variations. The overall change in the Bragg wavelength can be quantitatively expressed as follows:

$$\Delta\lambda_B = \lambda_B \left[P_\lambda \cdot \Delta\varepsilon + (\alpha + \gamma) \cdot \Delta T \right] \tag{2}$$

$\Delta\lambda_B$ denotes the variation in the Bragg wavelength, P_λ refers to the strain sensitivity coefficient related to the Bragg wavelength, $\Delta\varepsilon$ represents the change in strain, α is the thermal expansion coefficient of the optical fiber material, γ indicates the thermo-optic coefficient describing how the refractive index varies with temperature, and ΔT corresponds to the temperature change.

FBG sensors also possess distributed sensing capabilities, allowing multiple gratings to be inscribed along a single fiber for the simultaneous measurement of multiple physical parameters. Therefore, they have been widely applied in fields such as structural health monitoring. To address the issue of cross-sensitivity between strain and temperature, a dual-fiber configuration was adopted, as illustrated in Fig. 1. One optical fiber (FBG1–FBG3) is embedded within the robotic manipulator for structural monitoring, while the other optical fiber (FBGc), isolated from mechanical stress, is used solely for temperature compensation.

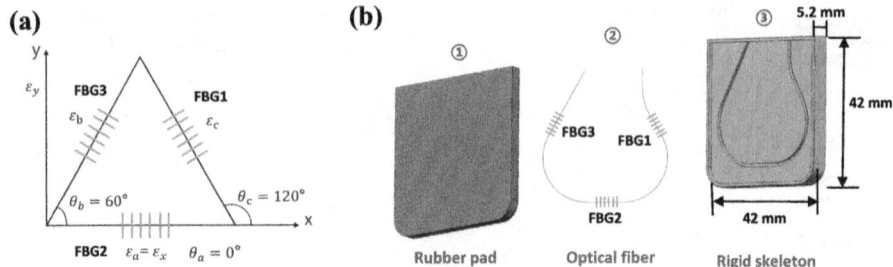

Fig. 2. (a) Schematic diagram of 60° strain variation. (b) Exploded view of the robotic finger embedded with FBG strain rosette.

3 Design of FBG -Embedded Robotic Finger

3.1 Principle and Formula Derivation of Stress Field Monitoring

The fiber Bragg grating (FBG) strain rosette enables multi-axial strain sensing by embedding three FBGs at 60° intervals within the robotic finger's rigid structure (Fig. 2). This configuration captures the two-dimensional in-plane stress state with high spatial resolution.

The strain components measured along the three directions (ε_a, ε_b, ε_c) correspond to angles of $0°, 60°$, and $120°$, respectively. Based on standard strain transformation relations, these measurements are used to reconstruct the normal strains (ε_x, ε_y) and the shear strain (γ_{xy}), as summarized in Eqs. (5)–(7). The full-field stress components (σ_x, σ_y, γ_{xy}) are then derived using Hooke's law for plane stress conditions, as shown in Eq. (8). The detailed derivation is as follows:

According to the strain transformation equation, the strain ε_θ along any direction θ can be expressed as:

$$\varepsilon_\theta = \varepsilon_x \cos^2 \theta + \varepsilon_y \sin^2 \theta + \gamma_{xy} \sin \theta \cos \theta \tag{3}$$

where ε_x and ε_y are the normal strains along the reference coordinate axes, and γ_{xy} is the engineering shear strain.

Applying this equation to the three known measurement directions yields:

$$\begin{cases} \varepsilon_a = \varepsilon_x \cos^2 \theta_a + \varepsilon_y \sin^2 \theta_a + \gamma_{xy} \sin \theta_a \cos \theta_a \\ \varepsilon_b = \varepsilon_x \cos^2 \theta_b + \varepsilon_y \sin^2 \theta_b + \gamma_{xy} \sin \theta_b \cos \theta_b \\ \varepsilon_c = \varepsilon_x \cos^2 \theta_c + \varepsilon_y \sin^2 \theta_c + \gamma_{xy} \sin \theta_c \cos \theta_c \end{cases} \tag{4}$$

Substituting the values of trigonometric functions and simplifying, we obtain:

$$\begin{cases} \varepsilon_a = \varepsilon_x \\ \varepsilon_b = \frac{1}{4}\varepsilon_x + \frac{3}{4}\varepsilon_y + \frac{\sqrt{3}}{4}\gamma_{xy} \\ \varepsilon_c = \frac{1}{4}\varepsilon_x + \frac{3}{4}\varepsilon_y - \frac{\sqrt{3}}{4}\gamma_{xy} \end{cases} \tag{5}$$

By solving the second and third equations simultaneously, the shear strain γ_{xy} can be expressed as:

$$\gamma_{xy} = \frac{2}{\sqrt{3}}(\varepsilon_b - \varepsilon_c) \tag{6}$$

Moreover, the sum of the normal strains satisfies:

$$\varepsilon_x + 3\varepsilon_y = 2(\varepsilon_b + \varepsilon_c) \tag{7}$$

Using the first equation $\varepsilon_x = \varepsilon_a$, we can solve for ε_y and γ_{xy}. After obtaining the strain components, the corresponding stresses can be derived based on the linear elasticity constitutive relations (assuming plane stress or plane strain conditions):

$$\begin{bmatrix} \sigma_x \\ \sigma_y \\ \tau_{xy} \end{bmatrix} = \frac{E}{1-\nu^2} \begin{bmatrix} 1 & \nu & 0 \\ \nu & 1 & 0 \\ 0 & 0 & \frac{1-\nu}{2} \end{bmatrix} \begin{bmatrix} \varepsilon_x \\ \varepsilon_y \\ \gamma_{xy} \end{bmatrix} \tag{8}$$

where E is the Young's modulus and ν is Poisson's ratio.

Further derivation yields that the value of the maximum principal stress is:

$$\sigma_{1,2} = \frac{\sigma_x + \sigma_y}{2} \pm \sqrt{\left(\frac{\sigma_x - \sigma_y}{2}\right)^2 + \tau_{xy}^2} \tag{9}$$

Finally, the maximum principal stress is computed using the standard transformation (Eq. 9), serving as the real-time feedback signal. This method allows compact and accurate 2D stress reconstruction within robotic fingers, facilitating both grasp stability and structural safety monitoring.

3.2 Finite Element Simulation

A numerical static structural analysis was performed using the finite element method in ABAQUS software to evaluate the strain distribution of the finger embedded with distributed optical fibers. A finite element model was established, including the optical fiber, silicone rubber, and rubber patch components on the robotic hand. The interaction between these parts was modeled using tied contact conditions. The simulation parameters are listed in Table 1. Since the

Table 1. Material Characteristics for Finite Element Simulation.

Name	Material	Young's Modulus (MPa)	Poisson's Ratio
Rigid skeleton	Al 6063	69000	0.33
Optical fiber	Silicone dioxide	72000	0.30
Silicone	Silicone-based polymer	7.0	0.45
Rubber pad	Sythnetic rubber	7.8	0.47

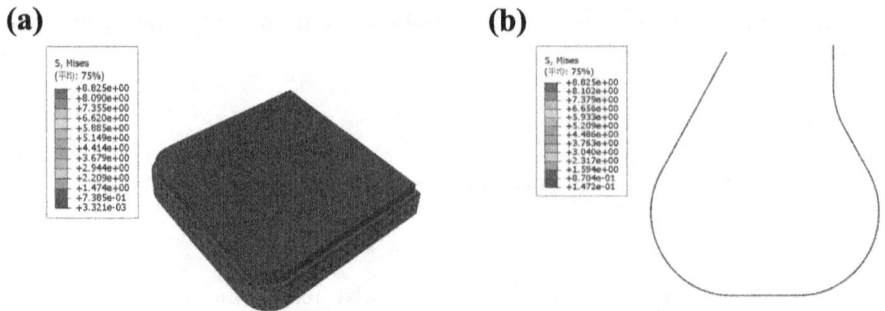

Fig. 3. (a) Stress contour of the overall structure of the robotic finger. (b) Stress contour of the optical fiber.

rubber patch and optical fiber structures are relatively regular and the primary focus of the simulation is on the stress/strain distribution within the optical fiber, hexahedral meshes were used for both the rubber patch and the optical fiber. The approximate global element size for the rubber patch was set to 0.5. Due to the small volume of the optical fiber, a finer global element size of 0.1 was applied to improve simulation accuracy, also using C3D8R elements. The mesh consisted of 8,955 nodes and 3,976 elements. The silicone rubber and robotic finger have irregular geometries and are not the main focus of the study, making structured meshing difficult; therefore, tetrahedral free meshing was adopted for these parts. A static general step was applied, with a load of 0.01 MPa imposed on the outer surface of the rubber patch (within the typical gripping force range) to simulate the force experienced by the robotic hand when grasping an object. The simulated stress distribution cloud map is shown in Fig. 3. The stresses on both the overall structure and the optical fiber remain within safe limits, validating the safety and rationality of our structural design.

3.3 Performance Characterization

We primarily characterized the thermo-sensitivity and force-sensitivity of the robotic finger embedded with distributed optical fibers. First, we investigated the temperature response by placing the finger in a temperature-controlled chamber and adjusting the temperature from 10°C to 60°C in 10°C increments, with each temperature held for 30 min. The sensitivity and real-time response of the FBGs to temperature variations were observed. As shown in Fig. 4(a), the Bragg wavelength shifts exhibited a linear relationship with temperature changes. The linearity coefficients for FBG 1 to FBG 3 were 0.988, 0.984, and 0.994, respectively, with corresponding temperature sensitivities of 16.777 pm/°C, 15.196 pm/°C, and 11.797 pm/°C. Figure 4(b) shows that the temperature-compensating fiber FBGc also demonstrated good linearity with a coefficient of 0.983 and a sensitivity of 17.099 pm/°C.

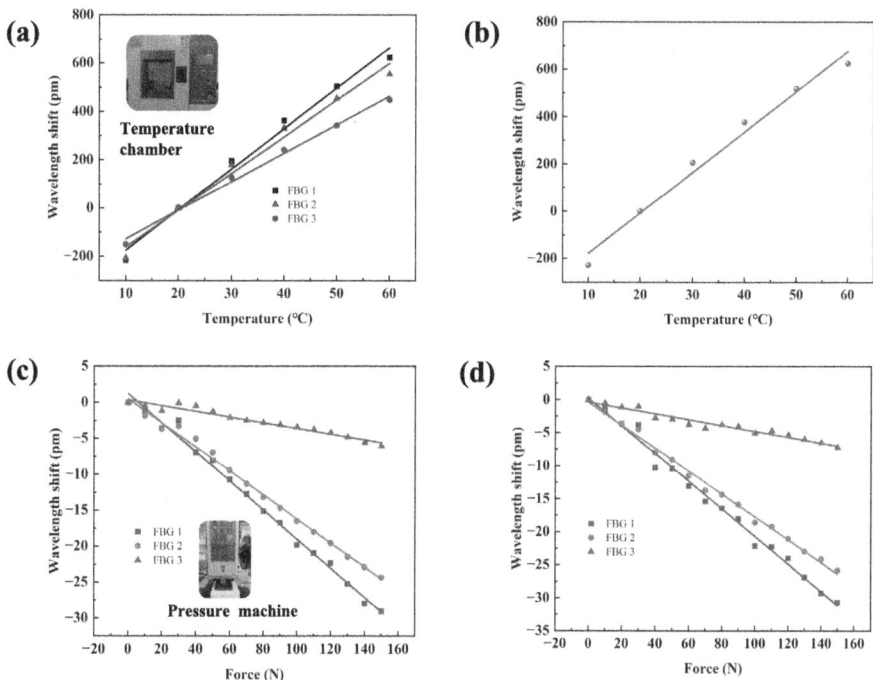

Fig. 4. (a) Relationship between wavelength shifts of FBG1–FBG3 and temperature variation. (b) Relationship between wavelength shift of temperature-compensation fiber and temperature variation. (c) Relationship between wavelength shifts of FBG1–FBG3 and pressure variation without temperature compensation. (d) Relationship between wavelength shifts of FBG1–FBG3 and pressure variation with temperature compensation.

Subsequently, we conducted force response testing by placing the center of the finger on a force testing machine. A normal force ranging from 0 N to 150 N was applied using a circular indenter with a diameter of 10 mm, in 10 N increments. Both force and temperature were recorded for 1 min. As shown in Fig. 4(c) and Fig. 4(d), there was little difference in response before and after temperature compensation, possibly because temperature remained relatively stable during the force testing. The FBG sensors embedded in the finger exhibited good linearity with respect to force. From FBG 1 to FBG 3, the linearity coefficients were 0.9898, 0.9948, and 0.9548, with sensitivities of -0.2091 pm/N, -0.1732 pm/N, and -0.0445 pm/N, respectively. Notably, FBG 3 showed significantly lower force sensitivit likely due to uneven embedding or fabrication defects.

Through the above temperature and force characterization experiments, it was confirmed that the FBGs exhibited both high sensitivity and good linearity to thermal and mechanical stimuli. After temperature compensation, the overall linearity of the force-induced wavelength shifts improved, validating the effectiveness of the compensation strategy.

4 Dexterous Manipulation

4.1 Fuzzy Logic-Based PID Control Strategy

In Sect. 3.1, a 2D stress field monitoring method based on the arrangement of FBG strain rosettes was derived. In this section, the feedback mechanism of principal stress from the FBG strain rosettes during the robotic gripper's grasping process is utilized to achieve dexterous manipulation. To simulate the intelligent perception strategy of human grasping, fuzzy logic control is integrated into the conventional PID grasping control scheme, aiming to enhance the system's adaptability and robustness under nonlinear and uncertain conditions.

In this control architecture, a fuzzy inference system dynamically adjusts the proportional, integral, and derivative gains of a traditional PID controller according to real-time error information. The inputs to the fuzzy system are the real-time control error $e(t)$ and its change rate $\Delta e(t)$, defined as:

$$\Delta e(t) = \frac{de(t)}{dt} \tag{10}$$

Based on these inputs, the fuzzy system outputs incremental modifications to the PID gains:

$$\begin{cases} K_p(t) = K_{p0} + \Delta K_p(t) \\ K_i(t) = K_{i0} + \Delta K_i(t) \\ K_d(t) = K_{d0} + \Delta K_d(t) \end{cases} \tag{11}$$

where K_{p0}, K_{i0}, and K_{d0} are the initial PID gains.

In the fuzzification stage, the crisp inputs $e(t)$ and $\Delta e(t)$ are mapped into linguistic variables using membership functions. Typical fuzzy linguistic sets include NB (Negative Big), NM (Negative Medium), NS (Negative Small), ZO (Zero), PS (Positive Small), PM (Positive Medium), and PB (Positive Big). Each fuzzy set is defined over a universe of discourse ($e(t) \in [-300, 300], \Delta e(t) \in [-100, 100]$). We choose triangular membership functions, denoted as $\mu_A(x)$.

The fuzzy inference system uses a set of heuristic rules in the form of: IF $e(t)$ is A_i AND $\Delta e(t)$ is B_j THEN $\Delta K_p = C_k, \Delta K_i = D_k, \Delta K_d = E_k$. The Table 2 is the fuzzy rule for ΔK_p, ΔK_i, and ΔK_d. The fuzzy outputs are defuzzified to crisp values using the center-of-gravity method:

$$\Delta K = \frac{\int_\Omega x \cdot \mu(x) \, dx}{\int_\Omega \mu(x) \, dx} \tag{12}$$

where $\mu(x)$ is the aggregated membership function and Ω is the output domain. The output control signal is calculated using the dynamically adjusted PID formula:

$$u(t) = K_p(t) \cdot e(t) + K_i(t) \cdot \int_0^t e(\tau) \, d\tau + K_d(t) \cdot \frac{de(t)}{dt} \tag{13}$$

This adaptive structure enables the fuzzy PID controller to cope with nonlinearities, parameter variations, and external disturbances, making it superior to traditional fixed-gain PID controllers.

Table 2. Fuzzy rule table for ΔK_p, ΔK_i, and ΔK_d

e/ec	NB	NM	NS	ZO	PS	PM	PB
NB	PB/NB/PB	PB/NB/PB	PM/NM/PM	PM/NM/PM	PM/NM/PM	PB/NB/PB	PB/NB/PB
NM	PB/NB/PB	PB/NB/PM	PM/NM/PS	PM/NM/PS	PM/NM/PS	PB/NB/PM	PB/NB/PB
NS	PM/NM/PM	PS/NM/PS	PS/NS/ZO	ZO/NS/ZO	PS/NS/ZO	PM/NM/PS	PM/NM/PS
ZO	PM/NM/PM	PS/NM/PS	PS/NS/ZO	ZO/NS/ZO	PS/NS/ZO	PS/NM/PS	PM/NM/PM
PS	PM/NM/PM	PM/NM/PS	PS/NS/ZO	PS/NS/ZO	PS/NS/ZO	PM/NM/PS	PM/NM/PM
PM	PB/NB/PB	PB/NB/PM	PM/NM/PS	PM/NM/PS	PM/NM/PM	PM/NB/PM	PB/NB/PB
PB	PB/NB/PB	PB/NB/PB	PM/NM/PM	PM/NM/PM	PM/NB/PM	PB/NB/PB	PB/NB/PB

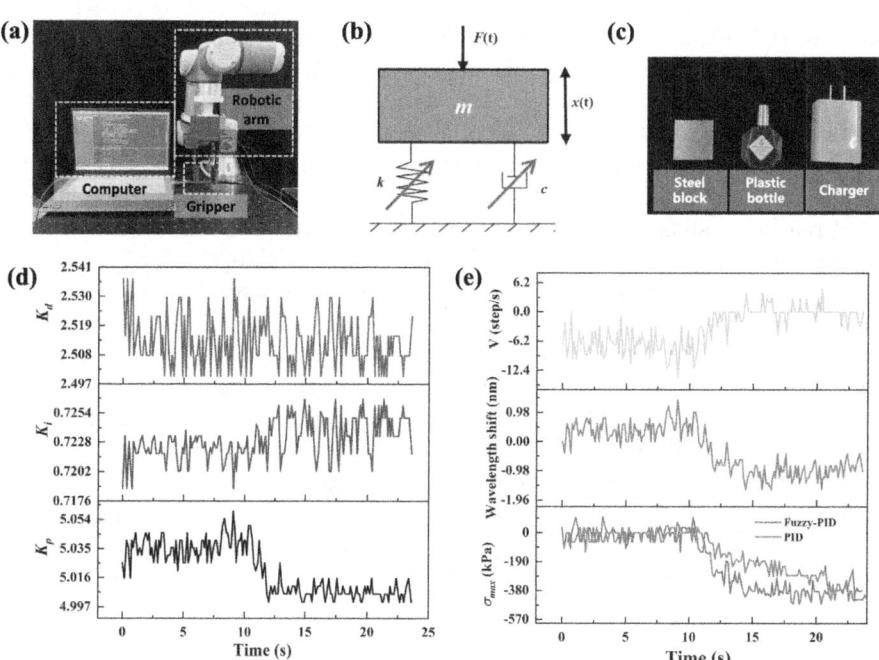

Fig. 5. (a) Robotic grasping system (b) Model of the robotic hand during object grasping (c) Object to be grasped (d) PID parameter tuning curves based on fuzzy PID control (e) Dynamic performance curves of the robotic hand based on fuzzy PID control (grasping speed, average wavelength shift, and variation of maximum principal stress)

4.2 Experiments and Discussion

To verify the dexterous manipulation capability of the robotic hand under the principal stress feedback mechanism based on FBG strain rosettes and the fuzzy logic control strategy, we constructed a grasping experimental platform, as shown in Fig. 5(a). The system mainly consists of an upper computer, a robotic arm, and a two-finger parallel gripper composed of robotic fingers. As illustrated in Fig. 5(b), when grasping different objects, the physical properties of the grasped items (such as mass, stiffness, and damping) are uncertain.

To simplify the analysis, the physical model of the grasping process is approximated as a typical second-order system:

$$G(s) = \frac{K}{s^2 + 2\zeta\omega_n s + \omega_n^2} \tag{14}$$

where ω_n denotes the natural angular frequency, reflecting the stiffness of the grasped object, ζ is the damping ratio, indicating the object's viscosity, and K is the gain coefficient, representing the response capacity of the grasping force.

As shown in Fig. 5(c), to comprehensively evaluate the real-time control performance of the robotic hand in various scenarios, we selected three objects with different stiffness and damping characteristics: a stainless steel block, a charger, and a plastic bottle (in order of decreasing stiffness). Taking the plastic bottle as an example, it exhibits the lowest stiffness and the highest viscosity, with a target principal stress setpoint of −400 kPa (compressive state, far below the yield strength). As depicted in Fig. 5(d), under the fuzzy logic control strategy, PID parameters can be autonomously adjusted in real time. In Fig. 5(e), the robotic hand reaches a steady grasping state at approximately 12 s, at that point, the motor speed drops to zero and the FBG wavelength shift stabilizes (-1nm). It is worth noting that compared with the stainless steel block and the charger, the dynamic response of grasping the plastic bottle is more significant, and the response time (from contact to secure grasp) is generally longer. This is likely due to the lower stiffness and higher elasticity of the plastic bottle.

As summarized in Table 3, we compared the performance of traditional PID control and fuzzy-PID control in grasping different objects. The results indicate that the fuzzy-PID controller consistently outperforms the traditional PID controller in terms of both response time (response speed increase of 18%) and steady-state error, demonstrating superior adaptability and robustness, particularly under uncertain and nonlinear conditions.

Table 3. Comparison of algorithm performance when grasping different objects.

-	Steel block (−500kPa)		Charger (−500kPa)		Plastic bottle (−400kPa)	
Algorithms	Response time	Error	Response time	Error	Response time	Error
PID	6.6 s	−64kPa	9.2 s	−38kPa	8.6 s	−41kPa
Fuzzy-PID	5.4 s	−45kPa	8.3 s	+6.5kPa	7.8 s	−23kPa

5 Conclusions

In this study, we propose a novel dexterous manipulation system that transcends traditional robotic force-tactile feedback mechanisms by enabling two-dimensional (2D) stress field monitoring and real-time feedback. Distributed optical fibers are embedded within the robotic fingers to achieve high-resolution 2D stress mapping, offering a force sensitivity of −0.2091 pm/N and a linearity of

0.99. Moreover, instead of conventional single-axis force, the system utilizes real-time maximum principal stress as the feedback signal, combined with a fuzzy logic-based adaptive control strategy. This enables structurally safe operation while facilitating stable and efficient grasping of objects with varying stiffness and viscoelastic properties. Compared to standard PID control, the proposed approach allows real-time gain tuning, reduces control error to within 6.5 kPa, and improves response speed by 18%.

Although fuzzy PID controllers are well-established, the key innovation of this work lies in leveraging maximum principal stress as the feedback foundation, thereby inherently integrating structural integrity assessment into the control loop. This novel feedback mechanism introduces a new paradigm for adaptive control in robotic grasping, particularly under uncertain and variable contact conditions.

In future work, we plan to integrate more advanced intelligent control algorithms to further enhance robustness and adaptability in dynamic and unstructured environments.

Acknowledgments. This work is supported by the Shenzhen "Pengcheng Peacock Program", the Beijing "Youth Talent Promotion Project", the Tsinghua SIGS Cross-disciplinary Research and Innovation Fund (Grant No. JC2022002), the Shenzhen Science and Technology Program (Grant No. WDZC20231128114452001), the Tsinghua SIGS Overseas Research Cooperation Fund (Grant No. HW2023001), the Tsinghua SIGS Scientific Research Startup Fund (Grant No. QD2022021C), the Dreams Foundation of Jianghuai Advance Technology Center (Grant No. 2023-ZM 01 Z006), the Shenzhen Key Laboratory of Advanced Technology for Marine Ecology (Grant No. ZDSYS20230626091459009), and the Ocean Decade International Cooperation Center (Grant No. GHZZ3702840002024020000026).

Disclosure of Interests. The authors have no competing interests to declare that are relevant to the content of this article.

References

1. Wang, J., Xu, C., Zhang, J., Zhong, R.: Big data analytics for intelligent manufacturing systems: a review. J. Manuf. Syst. **62**, 738–752 (2022)
2. Li, C., Chen, Y., Shang, Y.: A review of industrial big data for decision making in intelligent manufacturing. Eng. Sci. Technol. Int. J. **29**, 101021 (2022)
3. Goel, R., Gupta, P.: Robotics and Industry 4.0. A Roadmap to Industry 4.0: Smart Production, Sharp Business and Sustainable Development pp. 157–169 (2020)
4. Firoozi, R., et al.: Foundation models in robotics: applications, challenges, and the future. Int. J. Robot. Res. **44**(5), 701–739 (2025)
5. Kim, U., et al.: Integrated linkage-driven dexterous anthropomorphic robotic hand. Nat. Commun. **12**(1), 7177 (2021)
6. Kashef, S.R., Amini, S., Akbarzadeh, A.: Robotic hand: a review on linkage-driven finger mechanisms of prosthetic hands and evaluation of the performance criteria. Mech. Mach. Theory **145**, 103677 (2020)
7. Li, G., Liu, S., Wang, L., Zhu, R.: Skin-inspired quadruple tactile sensors integrated on a robot hand enable object recognition. Sci. Robot. **5**(49), eabc8134 (2020)

8. Yu, X., He, W., Li, Q., Li, Y., Li, B.: Human-robot co-carrying using visual and force sensing. IEEE Trans. Industr. Electron. **68**(9), 8657–8666 (2020)
9. Liu, X., Yang, W., Meng, F., Sun, T.: Material recognition using robotic hand with capacitive tactile sensor array and machine learning. IEEE Trans. Instrum. Meas. (2024)
10. Zhao, C., Yu, Y., Ye, Z., Tian, Z., Zhang, Y., Zeng, L.L.: Universal slip detection of robotic hand with tactile sensing. Front. Neurorobot. **19**, 1478758 (2025)
11. Rubagotti, M., Tusseyeva, I., Baltabayeva, S., Summers, D., Sandygulova, A.: Perceived safety in physical human-robot interaction–a survey. Robot. Auton. Syst. **151**, 104047 (2022)
12. Zhao, C., et al.: Ionic flexible sensors: mechanisms, materials, structures, and applications. Adv. Func. Mater. **32**(17), 2110417 (2022)
13. Luo, Y., et al.: Technology roadmap for flexible sensors. ACS Nano **17**(6), 5211–5295 (2023)
14. Sekhar, M.C., Veena, E., Kumar, N.S., Naidu, K.C.B., Mallikarjuna, A., Basha, D.B.: A review on piezoelectric materials and their applications. Cryst. Res. Technol. **58**(2), 2200130 (2023)
15. Habib, M., Lantgios, I., Hornbostel, K.: A review of ceramic, polymer and composite piezoelectric materials. J. Phys. D Appl. Phys. **55**(42), 423002 (2022)
16. Shin, S., Ko, B., So, H.: Structural effects of 3d printing resolution on the gauge factor of microcrack-based strain gauges for health care monitoring. Microsyst. Nanoeng. **8**(1), 12 (2022)
17. Sharma, K., Singh, T., Sehgal, S., Goyal, P.: Design and development of strain gauge for biomedical applications: state of the art review. Innov. Emerg. Technol. **11**, 2440013 (2024)
18. Butt, M.A., Kazanskiy, N.L., Khonina, S.N.: Advances in waveguide BRAGG grating structures, platforms, and applications: an up-to-date appraisal. Biosensors **12**(7), 497 (2022)
19. Tan, T., et al.: Cross section deformation correction of flexible tentacle shape based on fiber bragg grating. IEEE Trans. Instrum. Meas. (2024)
20. Mao, B., et al.: A bioinspired robotic finger for multimodal tactile sensing powered by fiber optic sensors. Adv. Intell. Syst. **6**(8), 2400175 (2024)

Radial Basis Function Neural Network-Based Adaptive Trajectory Tracking Control for Continuum Robots

Fuxin Du[1,2(✉)], Zhongtao Liu[1,2], Weikai He[3], Changwei Yin[1,2], Yang Zhang[1,2], and Rui Song[2,4]

[1] School of Mechanical Engineering, Shandong University, Jinan 250061, China
zhang-yang@mail.sdu.edu.cn
[2] Key Laboratory of High Efficiency and Clean Mechanical Manufacture of MOE, School of Mechanical Engineering, Shandong University, Jinan 250061, China
{dufuxin,rsong}@sdu.edu.cn
[3] School of Aeronautics, Shandong Jiaotong University, Jinan 250357, China
[4] School of Control Science and Engineering, Shandong University, Jinan 250061, China

Abstract. Continuum robots, as highly coupled nonlinear multivariable systems, suffer from significant model inaccuracies that limit precise motion control, especially in surgical and inspection tasks. To address this, we propose a neural network-based adaptive trajectory tracking framework. Radial basis function (RBF) neural networks are used to approximate dynamic uncertainties—gravity, elasticity, Coriolis forces, and external disturbances—while a norm lower bound for the inertia matrix is established. These are integrated into an adaptive backstepping controller that ensures globally uniformly ultimately bounded stability. Simulation results confirm the method's excellent tracking accuracy and strong robustness against unmodeled dynamics and disturbances.

Keywords: Radial Basis Function · Neural Networks · Continuum Robots · Adaptive Control · Trajectory Tracking Control

1 Introdction

Traditional rigid robots, actuated by joint-mounted motors and governed by precise kinematic models, perform well in structured environments but lack adaptability in complex or confined spaces due to limited degrees of freedom and rigidity [1]. In contrast, continuum robots, composed of flexible materials, offer large deformations and near-infinite degrees of freedom, enabling compliant motion and safe interaction in constrained environments [2]. These features make them ideal for minimally invasive surgery [3], wearable technologies [4], human-robot collaboration [5], and rehabilitation [6], particularly in assisting the elderly or disabled [7]. Bioinspired designs mimicking organisms like octopuses, trunks, and earthworms further expand their capabilities in underwater operations, adaptive grasping, and complex terrain interaction [8,10]. With high compliance and intrinsic safety, continuum robots are emerging as key enablers in medical robotics, intelligent manufacturing, and service industries.

Motion control for continuum robots has progressed rapidly, mainly through model-based and model-free methods. Model-based approaches simplify complex structures via mathematical approximations to relate configuration variables (e.g., cable length, chamber pressure) to task space. Key techniques include: Piecewise Constant Curvature (PCC) models for efficient inverse kinematics [11], Cosserat rod theory for capturing continuous deformation [12], and finite element methods (FEM) for modeling large deformations without geometric assumptions [13]. Control strategies built on these models—such as task-space feedback controllers [14], time-optimal trajectory planners [15], and integrated kinematics methods [16]—offer high precision, but often require simplification of nonlinear dynamics, reducing accuracy. Moreover, uncertainties in geometry, material properties, and external disturbances pose significant challenges to accurate modeling [17,19], limiting the practical use of model-based control.

To address these limitations, model-free methods rely on data rather than precise modeling to capture system behavior [20,21]. Examples include model-free feedback control [22], adaptive Kalman filtering for Jacobian estimation [23], and Zeroing Neural Networks (ZNN)-based control frameworks [24], which exhibit fast convergence [25] and broad applicability [26,31]. However, neural and fuzzy controllers remain sensitive to noise, lack interpretability, and offer only semi-global stability. Reinforcement learning (RL) methods enable control policy learning via environment interaction, with applications in soft manipulator positioning and grasping using DQN and DDPG [32,33], and genetic algorithms [34]. Yet, simulation-trained policies often fail in real robots due to model mismatches. Although real-world RL has seen some success [35,37], challenges such as data inefficiency, limited generalization, and constraints in biological environments hinder deployment.

To balance model accuracy and data efficiency, hybrid control frameworks have been proposed. These treat unmodeled dynamics—such as friction, elasticity, and disturbances—as unknowns estimated via neural networks, observers, or adaptive techniques. This approach mitigates model uncertainty while avoiding the high data demands of model-free methods. Representative works include extended state observer (ESO)-based anti-saturation schemes [38], function approximation-based adaptive control [39], sliding mode PID methods [40] visual servoing strategies [41], and time-delay compensation approaches [42].

Motivated by these findings, this work proposes a trajectory tracking control framework for cable-driven continuum robots with unmodeled dynamics, based on standard Lagrangian virtual dynamics and radial basis function (RBF) neural networks. The principal contributions of this work are outlined below.

1) An RBF neural network is employed to approximate unmodeled dynami components, including Coriolis forces, gravity, elasticity, and external distur bances.

2) Distinct from prior work [38], the rotational inertia is treated as an unknown. A norm lower bound of the inertia matrix is established and incorporated into the adaptive controller design, enhancing robustness.
3) Simulation results verify that the proposed RBF-based adaptive controller achieves superior tracking performance and strong robustness against nonlinear dynamics and external disturbances.

2 Problem Statement

2.1 System Description

The simplified Newton-Euler dynamic model of the continuum robot can be expressed by the following equation.

$$M(q)\ddot{q} + C(q,\dot{q})\dot{q} + N(q,\dot{q}) + D = \tau \tag{1}$$

where $q = [\theta, \phi]^T$, $\dot{q} = [\dot{\theta}, \dot{\phi}]^T$, $\ddot{q} = [\ddot{\theta}, \ddot{\phi}]^T$ represent the generalized angular position, angular velocity, and angular acceleration vectors of the continuum robot; $M(q) \in R^{3\times3}$ is the inertia matrix; $C(q,\dot{q}) \in R^{3\times3}$ denotes the Coriolis and centrifugal matrix; $N(q,\dot{q}) \in R^{3\times1}$ stands for the stiffness and gravity vector; $D \in R^{3\times1}$ is the vector of external disturbance; $\tau \in R^{3\times1}$ represents the control input torque vector. This paper assumes that the dynamics and external disturbances of the continuum robot are uncertain, that is, $M(q)$, $C(q,\dot{q})$, $N(q,\dot{q})$ and D are unknown.

To achieve the strict feedback form, the model 1 can be rewritten as 2 by letting $x1 = q$, $x2 = \dot{q}$, $u = \tau$.

$$\begin{cases} \dot{x}_1 = x_2 \\ \dot{x}_2 = g(x_1)u + f(\bar{x}) \\ y = x_1 \end{cases} \tag{2}$$

where $g(x_1) = M^{-1}(q)$, $f(\bar{x}) = -M^{-1}(q)[C(q,\dot{q})\dot{q} + N(q,\dot{q}) + D]$, and $\bar{x} = [x_1, x_2]^T$. In addition, two assumptions are required to provide the basis for the controller design and discussion that follow.

Assumption 1. There exists an unknown positive constant $\breve{g}$, $0 < \breve{g} < \|g(x_1)\|$.

Remark 1. Assumption 1 guarantees that the nonlinear system 2 is controllable for any x_1, which is commonly made in the literature.

Assumption 2. The reference signal y_d and its derivatives $\dot{y}_d^{(i)}$ are continuous and bounded for $i = 1, 2$.

2.2 RBF NNs

Neural networks (NNs) are well known for their powerful capability to approximate nonlinear functions, particularly when dealing with uncertain but bounded nonlinearities. In this context, radial basis function neural networks (RBF NNs) are employed to approximate an unknown smooth function $y(x) : R^q \to R$, where the input x belongs to a compact set $\Omega_x \subset R^q$.

The functional form of the RBF NN is given by

$$y(x) = W^T \Phi(x) \tag{3}$$

Here, $x \in R^q$ is the input vector, and q denotes the dimensionality of the input space. The weight vector is denoted by $W = [W_1, W_2, ..., W_l]^T \in R^l$, where l is the number of neurons in the hidden layer. The basis function vector is defined as $\Phi(x) = [\Phi_1(x), \Phi_2(x), ..., \Phi_l(x)]^T$, with each basis function $\Phi_i(x)$ modeled using a Gaussian kernel of the form

$$\Phi_i(x) = \exp\left(-\frac{(x-c_i)^T(x-c_i)}{w_i^2}\right), i = 1, 2, ..., l \tag{4}$$

where $c_i = [c_{i1}, c_{i2}, ..., c_{iq}]$ represents the center of the $i-th$ basis function, and w_i is its width parameter.

These RBF networks are then applied to approximate an unknown smooth nonlinear mapping $F(x) : R^n \to R$, which is represented as

$$F(x) = W^{*T}\Phi(x) + \varrho, \forall x \in \Omega_x \subset R^q \tag{5}$$

In this equation, ϱ stands for the approximation error, which is bounded such that $|\varrho| \leq \bar{\varrho}$, where $\bar{\varrho} > 0$ is a known constant. The ideal weight vector W^* is defined as the one that minimizes the worst-case approximation error over Ω_x, and is obtained by solving

$$W^* = \arg\min_{W \in R^l}\left\{\sup_{x \in \Omega_x} |f(x) - W^T\Phi(x)|\right\} \tag{6}$$

3 Controller Design

To design the adaptive NN controller, error variables are defined, which are as follows

$$\begin{aligned} z_1 &= x_1 - y_d \\ z_2 &= x_2 - \alpha_1 \\ \tilde{\theta} &= \theta - \hat{\theta} \end{aligned} \tag{7}$$

where y_d is the reference singnal, α_1 is the virtual controller, $\hat{\theta}$ is the estimation of θ.

Step 1: From 2 and 7, it can be obtained that

$$\dot{z}_1 = x_2 - \dot{y}_d \tag{8}$$

Select the Lyapunov function candidate as

$$V_1 = \frac{1}{2}z_1^T z_1 \tag{9}$$

V_1 can be expressed as

$$\dot{V}_1 = z_1^T \left(z_2 + \alpha_1 - \dot{y}_d\right) \tag{10}$$

Introduce the virtual controller α_1 as

$$\alpha_1 = \dot{y}_d - k_1 z_1 \tag{11}$$

where $k_1 = diag\{k_{11}, k_{12}\}$ with k_{11}, k_{12} are positive design parameters. Inserting 11 into 10 produces

$$\dot{V}_1 = z_1^T z_2 - z_1^T k_1 z_1 \tag{12}$$

Step 2:
The derivative of α_1 can be expressed as

$$\dot{\alpha}_1 = \frac{\partial \alpha_1}{\partial x_1}\dot{x}_1 + \frac{\partial \alpha_1}{\partial y_d}\dot{y}_d + \frac{\partial \alpha_1}{\partial \dot{y}_d}\ddot{y}_d \tag{13}$$

Then, the derivative of z_2 can be reformulated as

$$\dot{z}_2 = g(x_1)u + f(\bar{x}) - \frac{\partial \alpha_1}{\partial x_1}x_2 - \frac{\partial \alpha_1}{\partial y_d}\dot{y}_d - \frac{\partial \alpha_1}{\partial \dot{y}_d}\ddot{y}_d \tag{14}$$

Select the second Lyapunov function candidate as

$$V_2 = V_1 + \frac{1}{2\check{g}}z_2^T z_2 + \frac{1}{2}\tilde{\theta}^T \Gamma^{-1}\tilde{\theta} \tag{15}$$

where $\Gamma = diag\{\Gamma_1, \Gamma_2\}$ is a positive definite diagonal matrix. Then, the derivative of V_2 is deduced as

$$\dot{V}_2 = -z_1^T k_1 z_1 + \frac{1}{\check{g}}z_2^T g(x_1)u + \frac{1}{\check{g}}z_2^T \left(\lambda + f_k(\bar{\tau})\right) - \tilde{\theta}^T \Gamma^{-1}\dot{\hat{\theta}} \tag{16}$$

where $f_k(\bar{x}) = -\frac{\partial \alpha_1}{\partial x_1}x_2 - \frac{\partial \alpha_1}{\partial y_d}\dot{y}_d - \frac{\partial \alpha_1}{\partial \dot{y}_d}\ddot{y}_d$, $\lambda = f(\bar{x}) + \check{g}z_1$ is the unknown function. λ can be approximated by the FLS $W^T\Phi$ such that for any constant $\bar{\varrho} > 0$

$$\lambda = W^T \Phi(x) + \varrho, |\varrho| \leq \bar{\varrho} \tag{17}$$

With Young's inequality, it can be deduced that

$$\frac{1}{\check{g}}z_2^T f_k(\bar{x}) \leq \frac{3z_2^T z_2 f_k^T(\bar{x})f_k(\bar{x})}{4\check{g}\gamma} + \frac{\gamma}{3\check{g}} \tag{18}$$

$$\frac{1}{\check{g}}z_2^T \left(W^T\Phi(x)\right) \leq \frac{3z_2^T z_2 \|W\|^2 \|\Phi\|^2}{4\check{g}\gamma} + \frac{\gamma}{3\check{g}} \tag{19}$$

$$\frac{1}{\breve{g}}z_2^T \varrho \leq \frac{3z_2^T z_2 \varrho^T \varrho}{4\breve{g}\gamma} + \frac{\gamma}{3\breve{g}} \quad (20)$$

Therefore,

$$\frac{1}{\breve{g}}z_2^T\left(\lambda + f_k(\bar{x})\right) \leq \frac{\gamma}{\breve{g}} + z_2^T z_2 \Psi^T \theta \quad (21)$$

where

$$\Psi^T = \left[\frac{3f_k^T(\bar{x})f_k(\bar{x})}{4\gamma}, \frac{3\|\Phi\|^2}{4\gamma}, \frac{3}{4\gamma}\right]$$

$$\theta = \left[\frac{1}{\breve{g}}, \frac{\|W\|^2}{\breve{g}}, \frac{\varrho^T\varrho}{\breve{g}}\right]^T$$

Substituting 21 into 16 yields

$$\dot{V}_2 \leq -z_1^T k_1 z_1 + \frac{1}{\breve{g}} z_2^T g(x_1) u + \frac{\gamma}{\breve{g}} + z_2^T z_2 \Psi^T \hat{\theta} + \left(z_2^T z_2 \Psi^T - \dot{\hat{\theta}}^T \Gamma^{-1}\right)\tilde{\theta} \quad (22)$$

The actual controller u and adaptive law $\dot{\hat{\theta}}^T$ can be defined as

$$u = -k_2 z_2 - \Psi^T \hat{\theta} z_2 \quad (23)$$

$$\dot{\hat{\theta}}^T = z_2^T z_2 \Psi^T \Gamma - \hat{\theta}^T \sigma \quad (24)$$

where $k_2 = diag\{k_{21}, k_{22}\}$ and $\sigma = diag\{\sigma_1, \sigma_2, \sigma_3\}$ with $k_{21}, k_{22}, \sigma_1, \sigma_2, \sigma_3$ are positive design parameters.

Substituting 23 and 24 into 22, $\dot{V}_2$ is reformulated as

$$\dot{V}_2 \leq -z_1^T k_1 z_1 - \frac{1}{\breve{g}}z_2^T g(x_1)(k_2 z_2) - \frac{1}{\breve{g}}z_2^T g(x_1)\left(\Psi^T \hat{\theta} z_2\right) + \frac{\gamma}{\breve{g}} + z_2^T z_2 \Psi^T \hat{\theta}$$
$$+ \left(z_2^T z_2 \Psi^T - z_2^T z_2 \Psi^T \Gamma \Gamma^{-1} + \hat{\theta}^T \Gamma^{-1}\right)\tilde{\theta} \quad (25)$$

It is not difficult to show the following inequality, $\frac{g(x_1)}{\breve{g}} > 1$, that is $-\frac{g(x_1)}{\breve{g}} < -1$, which justifies

$$\dot{V}_2 \leq -\sum_{i=1}^{2} z_i^T k_i z_i + \frac{\gamma}{\breve{g}} + \tilde{\theta}^T \Gamma^{-1} \theta - \tilde{\theta}^T \Gamma^{-1}\tilde{\theta} \quad (26)$$

With Young's inequality, it can be deduced that

$$\tilde{\theta}^T \Gamma^{-1} \theta \leq \frac{1}{2}\tilde{\theta}^T \Gamma^{-1}\tilde{\theta} + \frac{1}{2}\theta^T \Gamma^{-1}\theta \quad (27)$$

Introducing 27 into 26 produces

$$\dot{V}_2 \leq -\sum_{i=1}^{2} z_i^T k_i z_i - \frac{1}{2}\tilde{\theta}^T \Gamma^{-1}\tilde{\theta} + \frac{1}{2}\theta^T \Gamma^{-1}\theta + \frac{\gamma}{\breve{g}}$$
$$\leq -CV_2 + B$$

where B is a positive constant, $C = \min\{2k_1, 2k_2\}$. All the signals in the closed loop system are bounded.

Table 1. Continuum model parameters

Parameter	Value
Length of the central elastic rod	0.1 m
Mass of the central elastic rod	1.5 g
Mass of the alloy wire	0.18 g
Mass of the disk	0.03 g
Diameter of the central elastic rod	0.002 m
Diameter of the disk	0.009 m
Diameter of the alloy wire	0.0003 m
Distance from alloy wires to central elastic rod	0.003 m

4 Simulation Results

To evaluate the proposed RBFNN-ATC scheme, simulations are conducted on a continuum robot and compared with the PID control method in [43] under both nominal and disturbance conditions. The robot parameters are detailed in Table 1, with dynamics formulated via Lagrangian mechanics [38]. The reference trajectory is defined as follows

$$\theta_d = 0.6 - 0.4\cos(0.5t) - 0.2e^{-0.5t}$$

$$\phi_d = 0.5\sin t$$

The initial positon of the continuum robot is set to $x_1(0) = [\theta_0, \phi_0]^T = [0.01 rad, 0 rad]^T$. RBFNN-ATC parameters are set as $k_1 = \begin{bmatrix} k_{11} \\ & k_{12} \end{bmatrix} = \begin{bmatrix} 300 \\ & 100 \end{bmatrix}$, $k_2 = \begin{bmatrix} k_{21} \\ & k_{22} \end{bmatrix} = \begin{bmatrix} 600 \\ & 600 \end{bmatrix}$, $\Gamma = \begin{bmatrix} \Gamma_1 \\ & \Gamma_2 \end{bmatrix} = \begin{bmatrix} 0.0001 \\ & 0.0001 \end{bmatrix}$, $\gamma = 1$, and $\sigma = 1$. The parameters of the radial basis function neural network (RBFNN) are configured as follows: the centers are given by $c = [-1.12, -0.75, 0, 0.75, 1.12]^T/(64(\pi/180))$, and the widths are defined as $w = [-0.2, 0.2, 0.2, 0.2, 0.2]^T/(64(\pi/180))$. To ensure the rigor and fairness of the experimental comparison, the PID control parameters are adopted from [43].

4.1 Experiment Without External Disturbances

In this section, we first evaluate the performance of the proposed RBFNN-ATC scheme for the continuum robot without external disturbances, and compare the performance with that of the PID method.

The performance of the proposed RBFNN-ATC scheme is first evaluated under disturbance-free conditions and compared with the PID method. The bending angle θ and rotation angle ϕ trajectories and their tracking errors are shown in Fig. 1. Both methods achieve tracking errors that converge to zero,

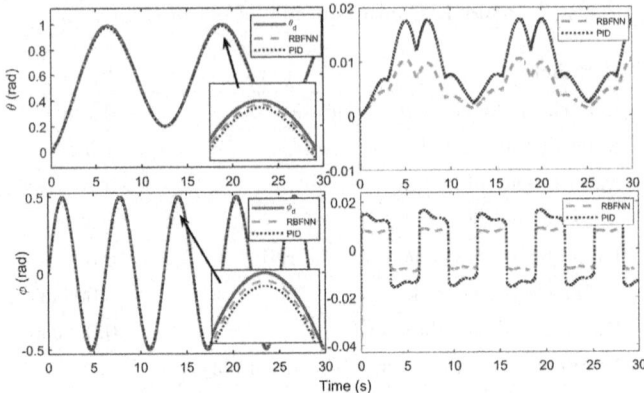

Fig. 1. Trajectory of θ and ϕ without external disturbances.

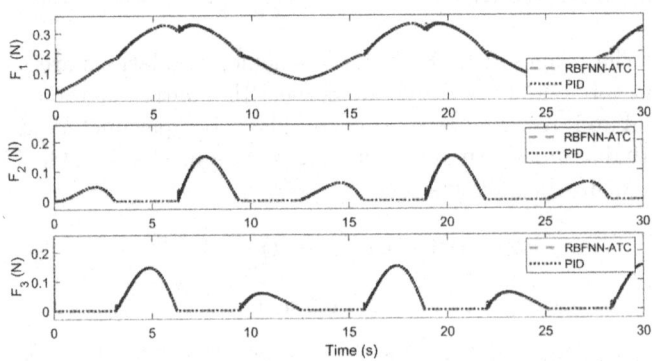

Fig. 2. Driving force without external disturbances.

with RBFNN-ATC demonstrating faster convergence. The trajectory tracking root-mean-square error (RMSE) of angle θ is 0.0048 rad under the RBFNN-ATC scheme and 0.0075 rad under the PID method. For ϕ, the RMSE is 0.0172 rad with RBFNN-ATC and 0.0199 rad with PID. Additionally, Fig. 2 shows the actuation forces without disturbances, where both methods yield stable and smooth force outputs.

4.2 Experiment With External Disturbances

In this section, to effectively demonstrate the performance of the proposed RBFNN-ATC scheme under unknown disturbances, external disturbances were applied to the continuum robot in the form $F_d = [F_{d1}, F_{d2}, F_{d3}]^T\ N$, where $F_{d1} = 0.8N(15\,s \leq t \leq 17\,s)$, $F_{d2} = 0.9N(15\,s \leq t \leq 17\,s)$, $F_{d3} = 0.7N(15\,s \leq t \leq 17\,s)$. A comparative analysis was then conducted between the RBFNN-ATC scheme and the PID method under the same disturbance conditions.

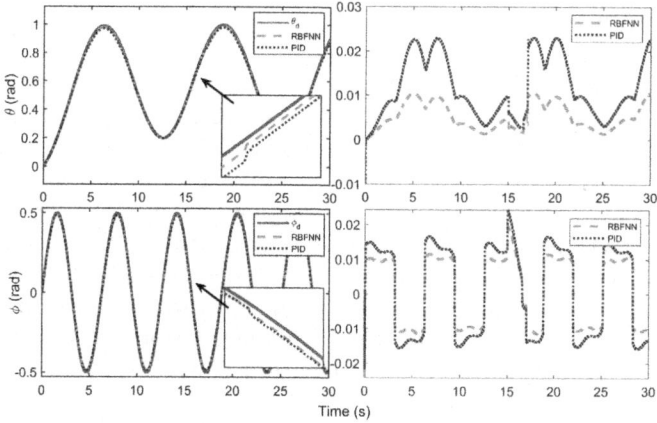

Fig. 3. Trajectory of θ and ϕ with external disturbances.

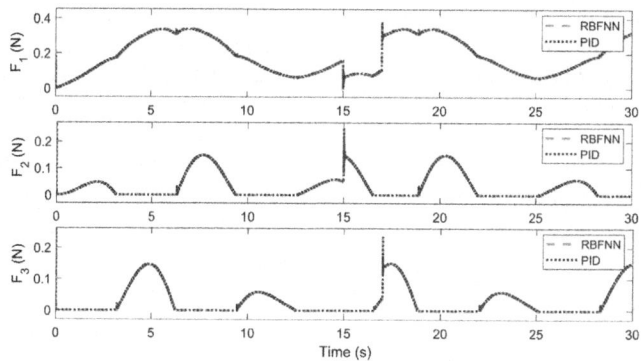

Fig. 4. Driving force with external disturbances.

The trajectories and tracking errors for the bending angle θ and rotation angle ϕ under external disturbances are shown in Fig. 3. Both the RBFNN-ATC and PID methods achieve error convergence, with RBFNN-ATC exhibiting faster convergence. The trajectory tracking root-mean-square error (RMSE) of angle θ is 0.0063 rad under the RBFNN-ATC scheme and 0.0091 rad under the PID method. For ϕ, the RMSE is 0.0201 rad with RBFNN-ATC and 0.0249 rad with PID. Compared to the RMSE under disturbance-free conditions, it is evident that external disturbances have a minimal impact on the RBFNN-ATC scheme, whereas the performance of the PID method deteriorates significantly. These results confirm that RBFNN-ATC offers better tracking accuracy and stronger robustness under disturbances. Figure 4 presents the actuation forces under disturbance conditions, showing similar trends for both methods as in the disturbance-free case. Although slight chattering increases are observed, both methods maintain reasonable and stable actuation forces.

5 Conclusion

This study addresses the long-standing challenge of model inaccuracies in continuum robots—highly coupled nonlinear systems that limit precision in surgical and complex environments. By integrating radial basis function neural networks with inertia matrix bounding, the proposed adaptive control framework compensates for unmodeled dynamics, including gravity, elasticity, Coriolis, and disturbances. The adaptive backstepping controller ensures globally uniformly ultimately bounded stability. Extensive simulations demonstrate superior trajectory tracking and strong disturbance rejection, establishing a new benchmark in continuum robot control. This work resolves the trade-off between model dependency and control performance, enhancing deployability in precision-critical applications.

Acknowledgments. This work was supported by the National Key Research and Development Program of China under Grant 2023YFB4705800, the National Natural Science Foundation of China under Grant 52375020, the National Key Research and Development Program of China under Grant 2022YFB4703000, the Key R&D Program of Shandong Province, China under Grant 2022CXGC010503, Shandong Provincial Postdoctoral Innovative Talents Funded Scheme under Grant 238226.

Disclosure of Interests. The authors declare that there is no competing financial interest or personal relationship that could have appeared to influence the work reported in this paper.

References

1. Yip, M.C., Camarillo, D.B.: Model-less hybrid position/force control: a minimalist approach for continuum manipulators in unknown, constrained environments. IEEE Robot. Autom. Lett. **1**(2), 844–851 (2016)
2. Rus, D., Tolley, M.T.: Design, fabrication and control of soft robots. Nature **521**(7553), 467–475 (2015)
3. Ranzani, T., Gerboni, G., Cianchetti, M., Menciassi, A.: A bioinspired soft manipulator for minimally invasive surgery. Bioinspir. Biomim. **10**(3), 035008 (2015)
4. Tolvanen, J., Hannu, J., Jantunen, H.: Stretchable and washable strain sensor based on cracking structure for human motion monitoring. Sci. Rep. **8**(1), 13241 (2018)
5. Ansari, Y., Manti, M., Falotico, E., Cianchetti, M., Laschi, C.: Multi objective optimization for stiffness and position control in a soft robot arm module. IEEE Robot. Autom. Lett. **3**(1), 108–115 (2018)
6. Tang, Z.Q., Heung, H.L., Shi, X.Q., Tong, K.Y., Li, Z.: Probabilistic model-based learning control of a soft pneumatic glove for hand rehabilitation. IEEE Trans. Biomed. Eng. **69**(2), 1016–1028 (2022)
7. Queiber, J.F., Neumann, K., Rolf, M., Reinhart, R.F., Steil, J.J.: An active compliant control mode for interaction with a pneumatic soft robot. In: IEEE/RSJ International Conference on Intelligent Robots and Systems, pp. 573–579 (2014)
8. Laschi, C., Cianchetti, M., Mazzolai, B., Margheri, L., Follador, M., Dario, P.: Soft robot arm inspired by the octopus. Adv. Robot. **26**(7), 709–727 (2012)

9. Joe, S., Totaro, M., Wang, H., Beccai, L.: Development of the ultra light hybrid pneumatic artificial muscle: modelling and optimization. PLoS ONE **16**(4), e0250325 (2021)
10. Menciassi, A., Gorini, S., Pernorio, G., Weiting, L., Valvo, F., Dario, P.: Design, fabrication and performances of a biomimetic robotic earthworm. In: IEEE International Conference on Robotics and Biomimetics, pp. 274–278 (2004)
11. Qiu, K., Zhang, J., Sun, D., Xiong, R., Lu, H., Wang, Y.: An effcient multi-solution solver for the inverse kinematics of 3-section constant-curvature robots. In: Proceedings of Robotics: Science and Systems (RSS). Daegu, Republic of Korea: RSS Foundation (2023)
12. Thamo, B., Dhaliwal, K., Khadem, M.: Rapid solution of cosserat rod equations via a nonlinear partial observer. In: Proceedings of 2021 IEEE International Conference on Robotics and Automation (ICRA), pp. 9433–9438. IEEE, Xian (2021)
13. Thieffry, M., Kruszewski, A., Duriez, C., Guerra, T.M.: Control design for soft robots based on reduced-order model. IEEE Robot. Autom. Lett. **4**(1), 25–32 (2019)
14. Peng, Z., Wang, J., Wang, D.: Distributed containment maneuvering of multiple marine vessels via neurodynamics-based output feedback. IEEE Trans. Industr. Electron. **64**(5), 3831–3839 (2017)
15. Falkenhahn, V., Bender, F.A., Hildebrandt, A., Neumann, R., Sawodny, O.: Online TCP trajectory planning for redundant continuum manipulators using quadratic programming. In: 2016 IEEE International Conference on Advanced Intelligent Mechatronics (AIM), pp. 1163–1168. IEEE, Banff (2016)
16. Cobos-Guzman, S., Palmer, D., Axinte, D.: Kinematic model to control the end-effector of a continuum robot for multi-axis processing. Robotica **35**(1), 224–240 (2017)
17. Wu, G., Shi, G.: Experimental statics calibration of a multi-constraint parallel continuum robot. Mech. Mach. Theory **136**, 72–85 (2019)
18. Felt, W.: An inductance-based sensing system for bellows-driven continuum joints in soft robots. Auton. Robot. **43**, 435–448 (2019)
19. Alambeigi, F.: SCADE: simultaneous sensor calibration and deformation estimation of FBG-equipped unmodeled continuum manipulators. IEEE Trans. Rob. **36**(11), 222–239 (2020)
20. Li, G., Song, D., Xu, S., Sun, L., Liu, J.: A hybrid model and model-free position control for a reconfigurable manipulator. IEEE/ASME Trans. Mechatron. **24**(2), 785–795 (2019)
21. Wang, Z.: Hybrid adaptive control strategy for continuum surgical robot under external load. IEEE Robot. Autom. Lett. **6**(2), 1407–1414 (2021)
22. Jin, Y.: Model-less feedback control for soft manipulators. In: 2017 IEEE/RSJ International Conference on Intelligent Robots and Systems(IROS), pp. 2916–2922. IEEE, Vancouver (2017)
23. Li, M., Kang, R., Branson, D.T., Dai, J.S.: Model-free control for continuum robots based on an adaptive Kalman filter. IEEE/ASME Trans. Mechatron. **23**(1), 286–297 (2018)
24. Tan, N., Yu, P., Zhang, X., Wang, T.: Model-free motion control of continuum robots based on a zeroing neuro dynamic approach. Neural Network **133**, 21–31 (2021)
25. Zhang, Y., Chen, K., Tan, H.Z.: Performance analysis of gradient neural network exploited for online time-varying matrix inversion. IEEE Trans. Autom. Control **54**(8), 1940–1945 (2009)

26. Jin, J., Qiu, L.: A robust fast convergence zeroing neural network and its applications to dynamic Sylvester equation solving and robot trajectory tracking. J. Franklin Inst. **359**(7), 3183–3209 (2022)
27. Zhang, Y., Yang, Y., Tan, N., Cai, B.: Zhang neural network solving for time-varying full-rank matrix Moore-Penrose inverse. Computing **92**(2), 97–121 (2011)
28. Zhang, Z., Yan, Z.: An adaptive fuzzy recurrent neural network for solving the non-repetitive motion problem of redundant robot manipulators. IEEE Trans. Fuzzy Syst. **28**(4), 684–691 (2020)
29. Jia, L., Xiao, L., Dai, J., Cao, Y.: A novel fuzzy-power zeroing neural network model for time-variant matrix Moore-Penrose inversion with guaranteed performance. IEEE Trans. Fuzzy Syst. **29**(9), 2603–2611 (2021)
30. Dai, J., Chen, Y., Xiao, L., Jia, L., He, Y.: Design and analysis of a hybrid GNN-ZNN model with a fuzzy adaptive factor for matrix inversion. IEEE Trans. Industr. Inf. **18**(4), 2434–2442 (2022)
31. Dai, J., Yang, X., Xiao, L., Jia, L., Li, Y.: ZNN with fuzzy adaptive activation functions and its application to time-varying linear matrix equation. IEEE Trans. Industr. Inf. **18**(4), 2560–2570 (2022)
32. Satheeshbabu, S., Uppalapati, N.K., Chowdhary, G., Krishnan, G.: Open loop position control of soft continuum arm using deep reinforcement learning. In: International Conference on Robotics and Automation (ICRA), pp. 5133–5139 (2019)
33. Lillicrap, T.P., et al.: Continuous control with deep reinforcement learning. In: 4th International Conference on Learning Representations (ICLR) (2016)
34. Goharimanesh, M., Mehrkish, A., Janabi-Sharifi, F.: A fuzzy reinforcement learning approach for continuum robot control. J. Intell. Robot. Syst. (2), 809–826 (2020). https://doi.org/10.1007/s10846-020-01237-6
35. Chattopadhyay, S., Bhattacherjee, S., Bandyopadhyay, S., Sengupta, A., Bhaumik, S.: Control of single-segment continuum robots: reinforcement learning vs. neural network based PID. In: International Conference on Control, Power, Communication and Computing Technologies (ICCPCCT), pp. 222–226 (2018)
36. Zhang, H., Cao, R., Zilberstein, S., Wu, F., Chen, X.: Toward effective soft robot control via reinforcement learning. Intell. Robot. Appl. 173–184 (2017)
37. You, X., et al.: Model-free control for soft manipulators based on reinforcement learning. In: IEEE/RSJ International Conference on Intelligent Robots and Systems (IROS), pp. 2909–2915 (2017)
38. Zhang, K., Liu, Y., Huo, B., Wu, Z., Yang, L., Yu, H.: ESO-based antisaturation motion control for cable-driven continuum robots. IEEE/ASME Trans. Mechatron. **30**(1), 517–529 (2025)
39. Xu, S., He, B.: Adaptive approximation tracking control of a continuum robot with uncertainty disturbances. IEEE Trans. Cybern. **54**(1), 230–240 (2024)
40. Wang, Y., Liu, L., Yuan, M., Di, Q., Chen, B., Wu, H.: A new model-free robust adaptive control of cable-driven robots. Int. J. Control Autom. Syst. **19**(9), 3209–3222 (2021)
41. Xu, F., Zhang, Y., Sun, J., Wang, H.: Adaptive visual servoing shape control of a soft robot manipulator using Bezier curve features. IEEE/ASME Trans. Mechatron. **28**(2), 945–955 (2023)
42. Wang, Y., Yan, F., Chen, J., Ju, F., Chen, B.: A new adaptive time-delay control scheme for cable-driven manipulators. IEEE Trans. Industr. Inf. **15**(6), 3469–3481 (2019)
43. Al-Mayyahi, A., Wang, W., Birch, P.: Design of Fractional-Order Controller for Trajectory Tracking Control of a Non-holonomic Autonomous Ground Vehicle. J. Control Autom. Electr. Syst. **27**, 29–42 (2016)

Author Index

A

Alam, Md.Mahbub II-581
An, Peiru I-397
An, Yi II-471
Azam, Hamza II-275

B

Bai, Ruiyu I-571
Bao, Chenyu II-459
Bao, Mengyi I-363
Besari, Adnan Rachmat Anom II-129

C

Cai, Hegao II-613
Cai, Huayi II-446
Cai, Huimin I-484, I-496
Cai, Jiahui III-150
Cai, Mengchen I-459
Cai, Mingxue III-49
Cai, Shibo III-298, III-310
Cai, Songtao III-650
Cao, Ruikai III-287
Cao, Wujing II-222, II-234, II-244, II-285, II-309
Cao, Zhongzhong I-201
Chen, Bowen III-473, III-534
Chen, Chen I-373
Chen, Chunjie III-323
Chen, Genliang I-559
Chen, Hao III-162
Chen, Haochu II-155
Chen, Huangchao I-423
Chen, Hui III-323
Chen, Junliang III-15
Chen, Junru II-421
Chen, Kaixuan II-698
Chen, Mingzhi I-153
Chen, Mu III-361
Chen, Peng III-298
Chen, Wenyu III-361
Chen, Xin III-310
Chen, Xingyu I-547
Chen, Yanhu I-227
Chen, Yanyun III-662
Chen, Yibin III-249
Chen, Yihan III-26
Chen, Yinhui II-650
Chen, Yujie II-244
Chen, Yun II-483
Chen, Zhiqiang III-49
Chen, Zhujin III-323
Cheng, Cheng III-447
Cheng, Hong III-631
Cheng, Xiangyu III-310
Cheng, Yun II-446
Cheng, Zhenyu II-297
Chu, Hui II-79, II-266
Chu, Shixuan III-235
Chu, Yao III-560
Cui, Jiatong II-322

D

Dai, Ruixuan III-124
Dai, Wenjie II-373
Deng, Linan III-447
Deng, Zongquan III-136
Ding, Cheng I-91
Ding, Han I-77, I-140, II-210
Ding, Liang III-136
Ding, Ning II-483
Ding, Shuchen III-587
Ding, Tao I-446, II-497
Ding, Ye II-337, II-349
Ding, Zhe II-545
Dong, Anqin III-348
Dong, Birong I-279
Dong, Kaijie III-174
Dong, Na III-398
Dong, Tenghui III-650
Dong, Wenhui I-215
Dong, Yan II-421
Dong, Yifei II-471

Dong, Yunlong   III-447
Du, Fuxin   I-595
Du, Mingyu   III-298, III-310
Du, Xinyang   I-350, II-285, II-557

F

Fan, Huijie   III-422
Fan, Shixun   I-496
Fan, Xuanhe   II-54
Fan, Yihui   II-210
Fan, Zuxin   II-567
Fang, Xing   III-662
Fang, Yinfeng   II-114
Fang, Yuelei   III-185
Fang, Zi   II-166, II-184
Fei, Xinyu   I-227
Feng, Luying   II-275
Feng, Shuo   III-573
Feng, Siyu   III-287
Feng, Zihe   III-611
Fu, Chenglong   II-67, II-197, II-255
Fu, Hang   III-162
Fu, Qiang   III-88
Fu, Zhijun   III-673
Fu, Zhuang   II-166, II-184

G

Gan, Yiming   II-37
Gao, Ang   II-361
Gao, Chao   III-275
Gao, Feng   III-112
Gao, Haibo   III-136
Gao, Liang   II-637
Gao, Naixing   I-385
Gao, Qingbin   II-650
Gao, Zhe   II-601
Ge, Ziyun   II-322
Gerževič, Mitja   II-275
Gong, Kening   II-175
Gou, Xuning   I-547
Gu, Guoying   I-65, I-547
Guan, Zimeng   III-650
Guo, Hongwei   I-525, I-536
Guo, Jiajie   III-249, III-484
Guo, Lei   I-239
Guo, Lina   II-3
Guo, Liucheng   II-545
Guo, Qixiang   III-197
Guo, Weichao   I-328

Guo, Weilun   II-409
Guo, Weizhong   III-162, III-235
Guo, Yikun   I-77
Guo, Yizhu   III-124, III-197
Guo, Ze-Sheng   I-509
Guo, Zhao   III-673
Guo, Zisui   I-201

H

Hai, Yong   III-611
Han, Bin   II-421
Han, Jianda   I-472
Han, Shiyu   III-348
Han, Tao   III-361
Han, Wei   I-166
He, Jiayuan   I-279
He, Shuangjiang   II-54
He, Weikai   I-595
Hirai, Takao   III-60
Hong, Lin   I-239
Hou, Haofei   I-459, II-567
Hou, Licheng   I-15
Hou, Siqi   II-509
Hou, Zeng-Guang   II-322
Hu, Hongbo   I-3, I-27, I-39
Hu, Junjie   II-459
Hu, Shibo   III-386
Hu, Wenyu   I-27
Hu, Yan   III-112
Hu, Yanbo   II-297
Hu, Zebin   I-446
Hua, Feng   III-447
Huai, Xiang   III-174
Huang, Chenyang   III-49
Huang, Chuwen   II-234
Huang, Hao   III-484
huang, Junfeng   III-197
Huang, Rui   III-631
Huang, Taoyuan   I-65
Huang, Wenze   III-473, III-534
Huang, Yedong   I-583
Huang, Yiren   III-611
Huang, Yongfeng   III-49
Huang, Yuxiang   II-545
Huo, Weiguang   I-472

I

Irshad, Ahmad   II-275

Author Index

J
Ji, Haoyu   III-473, III-534
Ji, Xiang   III-26
Ji, Yanyan   II-509
Jiang, Dongjie   I-103
Jiang, Gedong   II-397
Jiang, Jialin   III-26, III-38
Jiang, Li   II-175
Jiang, Ning   I-279
Jiang, Qin   II-210
Jiang, Ruoyuan   II-446
Jiang, Tianxiang   I-115
Jiang, Xugang   II-27
Jiang, Yao   I-316
Jiang, Zimo   III-473, III-534
Jin, Dongdong   III-15
Jin, Shuxiao   I-472
Jin, Taixian   II-662
Jin, Wei   II-567
Jin, Yaolun   II-114
Jing, Fei   II-166, II-184
Jing, Hongwei   II-91
Ju, Haotian   II-91, II-613

K
Kamegawa, Tetsushi   III-60
Ke, Shuai   I-77
Kuang, Qi   III-287
Kubota, Naoyuki   II-129, III-209

L
Lam, Tin Lun   II-459
Lang, Chenbo   III-112
Lei, Changjiang   II-197, II-255
Leng, Yuquan   II-67, II-197, II-255
Li, Bo   I-571
Li, Bocong   II-361
Li, Changle   II-601
Li, Chuanjiang   II-37
Li, Chunfeng   I-536
Li, Dachuan   II-433
Li, Di   II-509
Li, Duanjiao   II-483
Li, Duanling   III-101, III-124, III-150, III-174, III-197
Li, Feng   II-397
Li, Fengyi   III-162
Li, Guanglin   II-27
Li, Guangye   I-411

Li, Guo   II-397
Li, Guotao   III-611
Li, Haifeng   I-363
Li, Hongchen   II-349
Li, Hui   III-275, III-611
Li, Jianmin   I-434
Li, Jiayi   II-385
Li, Jinghang   II-155
Li, Jingyao   III-174
Li, Jinhua   I-434
Li, Jinke   I-350, II-143
Li, Kairu   II-3
Li, Ke   III-88
Li, Lele   II-91
Li, Li   II-54
Li, Liyi   II-637
Li, Qingdu   II-521
Li, Rankun   II-521
Li, Shunchong   I-91
Li, Tianming   I-423
Li, Tiemin   I-316
Li, Weimin   II-409
Li, Weipeng   III-249
Li, Xiangxin   II-27
Li, Xinchi   III-361
Li, Yanbiao   III-222
Li, Yazhou   II-3
Li, Ye   III-185
Li, Yinghui   III-235
Li, Youfu   II-675, II-686
Li, Yumeng   I-397
Li, Yuming   I-294
Li, Yuqi   I-525
Li, Yusen   III-560
Li, Zhe   III-631
Li, Zhiheng   III-662
Li, Zhipeng   II-397
Liang, Bin   II-385
Liang, Cheng   I-201
Liang, Dawei   II-91, II-613
Liang, Guangyu   II-322
Liang, Jian   II-662
Liang, Jiawei   III-599
Liang, Shengxiang   II-222
Liang, Shuai   II-37
Liang, Tian   II-534
Liang, Xu   III-611
Liang, Yunpeng   II-624
Liang, Zhenkun   I-559
Liang, Zibin   III-101

Liao, Da III-631
Liao, Zhaoyang I-294
Liao, Zhao-Yang I-509
Lin, Chengyu II-67
Lin, Junkai II-509
Lin, Sen III-422
Lin, Weixian I-52
Lin, Xubin I-294
Lin, Yichen I-350, II-285, II-297, II-309, II-557
Lin, Yuchen II-497
Ling, Shaobin II-459
Liu, Bang II-166, II-184
Liu, Changquan II-197
Liu, Chongfeng I-201
Liu, Dachuan II-650
Liu, Daming III-185
Liu, Donghan III-263
Liu, Gang I-472
Liu, Gangfeng II-601
Liu, Haitao I-166
Liu, Hong II-175
Liu, Honghai III-263, III-473, III-534
Liu, Houde II-385
Liu, Jian I-140
Liu, Jianming II-483
Liu, Lianfeng I-484
Liu, Lu I-177
Liu, Rongqiang I-536
Liu, Ruiheng I-227
Liu, Runze II-409
Liu, Shengbo II-483
Liu, Siyu III-673
Liu, Tao III-336
Liu, Xing III-447
Liu, Xingyu II-686
Liu, Yao III-323
Liu, Ying II-545
Liu, Yuanbo III-650
Liu, Yuchao III-249
Liu, Yuhan II-373
Liu, Zedong II-91
Liu, Zhongtao I-595
Liu, Zijie III-484
Liu, Zongying II-129
Liu, Zongyuan III-222
Long, Xiaojing II-297
Lou, Yunjiang III-88
Lu, Chunheng II-16
Lu, Hao II-244

Lu, Honglei II-497
Lu, Wenke I-350, II-309
Lu, Xingyu I-472
Lu, Yu III-599
Lu, Yuhan I-39
Lu, Zexin I-153
Lu, Zhe III-587
Lu, Zi-Wei I-509
Luo, Mingxiang II-222
Luo, Ruijie I-411
Luo, Xiang III-484
Luo, Xin I-52, I-127
Lv, Bo I-397

M
Ma, Guijun III-447
Ma, Guoyao III-49
Ma, Shentao I-252
Ma, Shiyu III-587
Ma, Tiancheng I-127
Ma, Wei I-166
Ma, Wen II-397
Ma, Xing III-15
Ma, Yue I-350, II-234, II-285, II-309, II-557
Mai, Xiaoming III-398
Mai, Ximing I-411
Mao, Baijin I-583
Matsui, Yusuke III-60
Matsuno, Takayuki II-103, III-60
Mei, Xuesong III-508, III-521
Melo, Kamilo III-249
Meng, Jianjun I-411
Meng, Tao III-336
Mi, Shuaibing III-398
Mu, Fengjun III-631
Mu, Xinxing II-409

N
Nie, Pingyun I-115

O
Obo, Takenori III-209

P
Pan, Jie I-77
Pan, Lizhi I-434
Pan, Mingxu III-434
Pang, Wen I-153
Pang, Xufang II-483

Pang, Yunfan   III-150
Peng, Xiaoke   III-348
Peng, Yan   II-521
Peng, Zhinan   III-631
Peng, Zhouhua   I-177
Piri, Saeid   III-3
Pradhan, Ashirbad   I-279

Q

Qi, Dexin   III-508, III-521
Qi, Jian   II-91
Qi, Zhanchuan   III-88
Qian, Huihuan   I-201
Qian, Letian   I-52
Qian, Shipang   I-227
Qiang, Junjie   I-52
Qiao, Zhehao   III-136
Qin, Pengjie   I-350, II-234, II-244
Qu, Juntian   I-583

R

Ren, Jieji   I-65
Ren, Weihong   III-473, III-534
Ren, Zengle   I-350, II-143, II-285
Ren, Zhouyi   III-174
Ruan, Lecheng   I-103, I-459, II-567
Ruan, Yizhang   III-548

S

Sakai, Nanako   III-60
Saputra, Azhar Aulia   III-209
Shan, Yihan   II-601
Shen, Xueyan   II-143, II-222
Shen, Yu   II-16
Sheng, Xinjun   I-306, I-328
Sheng, Yixuan   I-239, I-385, III-287
Shi, Changcheng   III-336
Shi, Jiaqi   III-494
Shi, Kecheng   III-631
Shi, Xiaoyu   II-581
Shi, Xin   II-244
Shi, Xulong   I-583
Shou, Zefeng   III-336
Si, Chuanyu   II-91
Siow, Chyan Zheng   II-129, III-209
Song, Ningning   II-409
Song, Qingwei   II-129, III-209
Song, Ran   III-662
Song, Rui   I-595

Song, Zhihong   II-16
Su, Chengyu   III-587
Su, Hang   II-361
Su, Tingting   III-611
Sun, Guangzhen   II-337
Sun, Jianquan   II-309, II-557
Sun, Kangkang   III-611
Sun, Peng   I-52, I-267, III-222
Sun, Shilong   II-650
Sun, Tairen   III-622
Sun, Wei   II-197
Sun, Yaowei   II-433
Sun, Zhe   I-267, III-222

T

Tan, Huachen   III-460
Tan, Wenhao   III-662
Tang, Lu   I-140
Tang, Qing   III-434
Tang, Xiaoran   II-175
Tao, Bo   I-15, I-423, II-497, III-386
Tao, Jianguo   I-536, III-136
Tao, Tao   III-508
Tian, Jiandong   III-411
Tian, Lan   II-27
Tian, Lingyan   I-373
Tian, Rui   III-587
Toda, Yuichiro   II-103, III-60
Tong, Yalong   II-3

W

Wang, Chen   II-322
Wang, Chengzhi   II-589, II-613
Wang, Chunbo   II-662
Wang, Chunfang   I-472
Wang, Chunlong   I-525
Wang, Conglin   II-37
Wang, Guofeng   I-166
Wang, Hai   I-279
Wang, Hao   I-559
Wang, Haoyu   II-275
Wang, Hongwei   III-49
Wang, Hongyu   III-494
Wang, Hui   I-91
Wang, Jiachen   II-534, III-3
Wang, Jiakang   II-534
Wang, Jiantao   I-252
Wang, Jiaole   III-573
Wang, Jingnan   II-234

Wang, Jun III-631
Wang, Junchen II-16
Wang, Junjie I-239
Wang, Keyi II-155
Wang, Lan II-155
Wang, Liming II-397
Wang, Lin II-27
Wang, Lu I-227
Wang, Meiling III-460
Wang, Mengdi II-497
Wang, Peixin II-675, II-686
Wang, Peiyao II-3
Wang, Peng II-79, II-266
Wang, Qiang III-422
Wang, Qining I-103, I-459, II-567
Wang, Shengli I-215
Wang, Shuhan I-52
Wang, Song III-101
Wang, Tao III-75
Wang, Weihao III-209
Wang, Wenjun III-521
Wang, Xiangyang II-557
Wang, Xiaoxin I-385
Wang, Xu II-79, II-266
Wang, Xuan II-373
Wang, Xuelian III-336
Wang, Yaling II-234
Wang, Yanzhuo II-155
Wang, Yi II-3
Wang, Yuan III-222
Wang, Yucheng III-460
Wang, Yueming I-340, I-363
Wang, Yunfei II-662
Wang, Zeyang III-373
Wang, Zhengbo I-472
Wang, Zhiyong II-197, III-473, III-534, III-573
Wang, Zhuoqun III-287
Wang, Zihao I-316
Wang, Ziqi III-185
Wang, Ziwei III-434
Wei, Wei III-298
Wei, Yuxuan I-411
Wei, Zhiao I-77
Wei, Zhongxing III-460
Wen, Huan I-340, I-363
Wen, Siqi II-37
Wen, Zhijie I-484, I-496
Weng, Yongjie III-298
Wu, Canhui II-166, II-184

Wu, Chaoqun II-446
Wu, Chenhao II-143
Wu, Chentao III-222
Wu, Dingze I-189
Wu, Han III-263
Wu, Hao I-446
Wu, Hongmin I-294
Wu, Hong-Min I-509
Wu, Jianhua I-252
Wu, Jingyu III-622
Wu, Longyan I-65
Wu, Peng III-422
Wu, Tianyu II-222
Wu, Xinhao III-422
Wu, Xinrui III-136
Wu, Xinyu II-143, II-222, II-234, II-309, III-323
Wu, Xiuyuan I-350, II-285, II-557
Wu, Xuan III-249
Wu, Zhigang II-210

X

Xia, Qingchao I-189
Xia, Tian II-497
Xia, Xin I-279
Xia, Yan I-536
Xia, Yu I-472
Xia, Yulong I-484
Xian, Haolan II-197, II-255
Xiang, Yang I-15
Xiang, Yuyaocen I-583
Xiao, Han I-267
Xiao, Hong I-525, I-536
Xiao, Juliang I-166
Xiao, Mubang I-484, I-496
Xie, Bangquan I-385
Xie, Erxuan I-115
Xie, Shiqin III-197
Xie, Wenkai III-650
Xie, Xing III-411
Xie, Yuhang II-521
Xing, Boyang II-698
Xing, Jianping I-215
Xiong, Zhenhua I-252
Xu, Enci II-421
Xu, Fengkun III-124
Xu, Guibin I-446
Xu, Guochao III-263
Xu, Jiajun II-675, II-686
Xu, Kedi I-340

Xu, Qingpo I-166
Xu, Ruoyu I-201
Xu, Shabei III-484
Xu, Sheng II-471
Xu, Tiantian II-471, III-49
Xu, Wenfu II-650
Xu, Wenzhu II-275
Xu, Xiaohu III-560
Xu, Yang I-397
Xu, Yanping I-177
Xu, Zhantao II-601
Xu, Zhihao I-294
Xu, Zhi-Hao I-509
Xu, Zhipeng II-698

Y

Yan, Jiejie III-548
Yan, Sijie I-140, III-434, III-560
Yan, Weixin II-624
Yan, Yushuai II-67
Yang, Canjun I-189, I-227, II-275, II-361
Yang, Chao II-483
Yang, Chen I-385
Yang, Dan III-373
Yang, En III-112
Yang, Fan III-650
Yang, Guang I-525, I-536
Yang, Hongkun II-37
Yang, Huaiguang III-136
Yang, Jiantao III-622
Yang, Jichao I-215
Yang, Kairui I-103
Yang, Lintao III-136
Yang, Mingchuan III-361
Yang, Minghui II-446
Yang, Siqin II-16
Yang, Wei II-275
Yang, Xiao III-673
Yang, Xinyu I-65
Yang, Yang III-49
Yang, Zeyuan I-140
Yang, Zhihao III-473, III-534
Yang, Zhiyuan II-613
Yang, Zixiang II-244
Yao, Chong II-601
Yao, Jia III-673
Yao, Jianfeng II-166, II-184
Yao, Lin I-340, I-363
Yao, Shutong III-398
Ye, Guoquan II-459

Ye, Huanpeng I-397
Ye, Linqi II-385, II-521, II-698
Ye, Xiaodong III-460
Yi, Shuowen III-673
Yin, Changwei I-595
Yin, Meng II-234, II-285, II-309
Yin, Yanqi I-571
Yu, Li II-54
Yu, Longjie III-310
Yu, Yang I-306, I-571
Yuan, Hao I-559
Yue, Zuogong III-447

Z

Zang, Xizhe II-79, II-266
Zeng, Qiming I-385
Zha, Pengxin I-3, I-39
Zhan, Xinrui I-496
Zhang, Bi III-599
Zhang, Bo I-115
Zhang, Dailin I-423, III-75, III-386
Zhang, Dinghuang II-545
Zhang, Fumin I-239
Zhang, Fuyong I-294
Zhang, Gan I-239
Zhang, Guilong III-361
Zhang, Hanqi III-222
Zhang, Haoran I-350, II-309, II-557
Zhang, Haoshi II-27
Zhang, Haoxiang II-91
Zhang, Haoyan II-662
Zhang, He II-662
Zhang, Hongwei I-385
Zhang, Huanghe II-534, III-3
Zhang, Jianguo II-483
Zhang, Jianhua III-275
Zhang, Jiaqi II-103, II-662
Zhang, Jiexin I-77, I-115
Zhang, Jinnuo I-65
Zhang, Junwei III-124, III-197
Zhang, Kewen III-310
Zhang, Li III-26, III-38
Zhang, Liang III-599
Zhang, Lunwei I-316
Zhang, Luobin III-298
Zhang, Ningbin I-65
Zhang, Qian III-662
Zhang, Shenglun III-386
Zhang, Shisheng II-143
Zhang, Shouyi II-91, III-185

Zhang, Tianze I-434
Zhang, Wei III-662
Zhang, Wenan III-336
Zhang, Xiaojian III-434
Zhang, Xinuo III-611
Zhang, Xuehe II-601
Zhang, Yang I-595
Zhang, Yi III-484
Zhang, Yijian III-185
Zhang, Ying I-472, II-483
Zhang, Yuan III-361
Zhang, Yuanwen II-255
Zhang, Yuhao I-15, II-497
Zhang, Yuqi II-129
Zhang, Zehui III-398
Zhang, Zhenwei I-15, II-497
Zhang, Zhihong III-508, III-521
Zhang, Zhiran III-75
Zhang, Zhonghai III-150
Zhang, Zhongkai I-3, I-27, I-39
Zhang, Zhuowen II-662
Zhao, Chuanlin I-127
Zhao, Feng III-373
Zhao, Guoshun III-348
Zhao, Huaici III-361
Zhao, Huan I-77
Zhao, Huijuan II-54
Zhao, Jie II-589, II-601, II-613, II-637, II-662, III-185
Zhao, Junhong III-460
Zhao, Mengcheng II-675, II-686
Zhao, Ranshuo I-215
Zhao, Runchao I-536
Zhao, Shize II-589, II-613
Zhao, Shunyi I-459, II-567
Zhao, Sikai II-589, II-613, III-185
Zhao, Tianren I-166
Zhao, Wensong III-587
Zhao, Xin II-210
Zhao, Xingang III-599
Zhao, Xingwei I-15, I-423, II-497, III-75, III-386
Zhao, Xu'an II-637
Zhao, Xu'ning II-637
Zhao, Yanwei I-472
Zhao, Yanzheng II-624
Zhao, Zeming I-328

Zheng, Han II-385
Zheng, Hao III-112
Zheng, Haoran III-263
Zheng, Lei III-75
Zheng, Tianjiao II-91, II-589, II-613, II-637
Zheng, Yue II-27
Zhengqing, Liu III-222
Zhong, Lei II-662
Zhong, Yucun I-363
Zhou, Dalin II-545
Zhou, Huilin III-336
Zhou, Jiaxing I-177
Zhou, Jinglin II-197, II-255
Zhou, Juanxia II-675, II-686
Zhou, Nanlin III-185
Zhou, Puzhe I-189
Zhou, Ruyi III-136
Zhou, Shijun III-411
Zhou, Xuefei I-340
Zhou, Xuefeng I-294
Zhou, Xue-Feng I-509
Zhou, Yan I-252
Zhou, Yangfan III-599
Zhou, Zeyu I-306, I-328
Zhu, Dahu I-446
Zhu, Daqi I-153
Zhu, Gaohen III-235
Zhu, Haifei I-294
Zhu, Jintao II-567
Zhu, Linqing II-521
Zhu, Liren III-587
Zhu, Qingmiao I-15
Zhu, Wenduo I-459
Zhu, Xiangye III-560
Zhu, Xingyue I-559
Zhu, Yanhe II-91, II-589, II-613, III-185
Zhu, Yanmei III-494
Zhu, Yanzheng I-215
Zhu, Yu I-350, II-557
Zhu, Yulan III-494
Zhuang, Chungang I-3, I-27, I-39
Zou, Huaiwu I-115
Zou, Jiang I-547
Zou, Kuansheng III-398
Zou, Rui II-322
Zuo, Guokun III-336

Made in the USA
Monee, IL
03 May 2026

49438527R00354